THE ENCYCLOPEDIA OF
WORLD RUGBY

THE ENCYCLOPEDIA OF
WORLD RUGBY

Keith Quinn

LOCHAR PUBLISHING • MOFFAT • SCOTLAND

© Keith Quinn 1991
Published by Lochar Publishing Limited
   MOFFAT DG10 9ED

British Library Cataloguing in Publication Data
Quinn, Keith
   The encyclopedia of world rugby
   I. Rugby Union football
   796.33303

ISBN 0–948403–61–6

A Shoal Bay Press book

Typeset in 8pt on 10pt New Century Schoolbook
Printed in Hong Kong through Bookprint Consultants Ltd,
Wellington, New Zealand.

AUTHOR'S NOTE

I have always been a rugby fan, first as a kid in the backblocks of the King Country region of New Zealand, then as a schoolboy in Wellington, and later as a young reporter on radio, before I became a touring TV rugby commentator with my employers, Television New Zealand. For years I have read and collected as many rugby books, programmes and memorabilia as I could find. My house and garage are full of them.

In 1985 it occurred to me that, with my local and international experience over a period of 20 years, and my collection of books and notes, I probably possessed as good a base as anyone for writing a book about the world rugby scene, possibly an encyclopedia.

I was inspired to pursue the idea further after reading and admiring Jack Pollard's excellent book *Australian Rugby Union– The Game and the Players*. This massive work, over 900 pages long, listed every state, club, and representative team, along with all the incidents and colourful stories associated with Australian rugby.

I was stunned by the magnitude of Pollard's work, and came to the conclusion that only a person deeply in love with the game, or touched by a little madness, could have attempted such a task. Was I mad enough, I asked myself, to undertake a similar work? I decided that I was, and late in 1985 I sat down at my word processor and tapped in the name 'Aarvold'. Six years later the work was completed.

My original concept had been to produce a book like Pollard's, albeit even more ambitious, as I would include everything from A to Z on rugby all around the world. But I soon realised that such a task would be impossible. Thousands upon thousands of players have played in rugby tests and tours, and there have been thousands of referees, administrators, states, provinces, unions, clubs, cups, and competitions. Nobody could write one book and mention them all, so I was forced to impose some restrictions, although I still wanted the book to be as comprehensive as possible.

I have included every individual player from the eight countries of the pre-1991 International Rugby Board who has played over 30 tests or internationals, up until the end of 1990, along with selected famous players from other countries, such as Hugo Porta of Argentina and Stefano Bettarello of Italy. Player and match statistics are up to date to the end of the Five Nations championship in the northern winter of 1991.

Of course many of the most famous players in the history of the game, such as George Nepia, Cliff Morgan, Jacques Fouroux, Naas Botha, Mark Ella, and many others, won fewer than 30 caps – but of course they had to be included. So the choice of players with fewer than 30 caps is my own, based on my personal views concerning their contribution to the broad history of the world game.

But I also wanted this to be a book that contained some of the rich, humorous and colourful stories that abound about rugby. So some of the entries feature comparatively unknown players who might have represented their country only once or twice, but whose stories are worth setting down.

When it came to clubs, provinces and states, it was relatively easy to include most of them from all over the world, apart from the hundreds of clubs in Great Britain– too many, alas, for all to be included. Once again I was forced to make my own decisions on British and Irish clubs. I hope those that have been omitted will forgive me.

Problems in terminology also presented themselves. Some countries say 'tests', while others say 'internationals' for the same type of game. You will notice that I sit firmly on the fence over this issue and use both terms; the same with standoffs, flyhalves, or first five-eighths, along with various other rugby descriptions.

Statistics are interesting too. There is a tendency for those who record such things and who live in the countries of the IRB to disregard other countries' records, and although I have tried my very best to include statistics for all those countries that play rugby union, there remain gaps in information from countries such as Romania, Japan, Argentina etc.

There are many people who have helped me to write this book. Foremost is Ray Cairns of Christchurch, who wrote, edited, read and re-read much of the text. His knowledge of South African rugby history, in particular, has helped immeasurably, while his detailed knowledge of rugby facts and feats, not to mention his experience as a rugby writer for a daily newspaper, make me deeply grateful to him for his professional and personal contribution.

The final editing, production and picture research for the book were done by Ros Henry and David Elworthy of Shoal Bay Press. Working from their base deep in the hills behind Whitianga, on the Pacific coast of New Zealand's Coromandel Peninsula, they gave commitment, encouragement and sometimes exerted gentle pressure to keep me going at all times. The presentation of my work here is the result of their endless hours of detailed and meticulous work.

I must also thank Ray Richards of Richards Publishing Agency in Auckland, who has been my literary agent since 1977, and my guide and mentor over the seven books I have written so far. His continuing assistance in the pursuit of further work is gratefully acknowledged and appreciated.

My family must also take great credit for the book. My wife, Anne, who has been my inspiration for 21 years, never stopped encouraging and cajoling me to keep going, even when pressure of internal and overseas tours resulted in gaps of weeks and sometimes months in continuity at the keyboard. Large areas of our home became cluttered with books, papers, letters, clippings, and notes, but there were never any complaints.

Our children Rowan, Bennett and Shelley also contributed. Shelley typed files onto disk, Rowan provided optimisim every day, while Bennett offered his inimitable advice. Now that the book is at last finished, I have moments of regret that the question 'what letter are you on now, Dad?' will no longer be asked in our house. I thank them and love them all.

I would also like to acknowledge Peter Bush and Ross Setford for photographs and assistance; Alan Honey, who taught me to use my word processor in 1985, and who was present when I typed in the first entry (for the next six years he called the book 'Aarvold'); Peter ('Tank') Rodger; Peter Sellers, my dear friend from Dunedin; Ron Palenski, Chris Thau, Grant Nisbett, Brendan Telfer, Grahame Thorne, Gavin Service, Garry Ward, Cyril Delaney, Peter Coates, Charles Ouko, Megumi Horokoshi; my mother Helen Andrews; long-suffering staff from Television New Zealand and Independent Radio Sports; and finally close friends Pauline and Andrew Cameron, Cheryl and Brian McGuinness, Alison and Brian Shennan, and all their beautiful children.

I am sure that each of the above, at some stage over the last six years, has doubted whether this work would ever be completed. Yet they never told me of their doubts: I received nothing but support from them all.

So to every one of them I say thanks, friends. It has been well worth it.

Keith Quinn
April 1991

A

AARVOLD, CARL

West Hartlepool, Headingley, Blackheath and England
16 internationals for England 1928–33
5 internationals for Great Britain 1930

This tall, elegant centre three-quarter
will always be found at the start of
any A to Z rugby book.

The brilliant Aarvold made his
international debut against the touring New South Wales 'Waratahs' of
1928, but made his biggest rugby impact in the 1930 Great Britain team in
New Zealand, where he scored three
tries in the second and third tests. On
that tour the British chose to not play
their tour captain, Doug Prentice, in
three of the tests and Carl Aarvold
captained in Prentice's absence.

He made a success of life after rugby,
becoming Sir Carl Aarvold, a judge at
the Old Bailey. He died in March 1991,
aged 83.

*Carl Aarvold, elegant English centre
of the 1930s.*

ABERAVON RFC

One of the more prominent Welsh clubs,
Aberavon was founded in 1876 and is
centred at Port Talbot, near Swansea.
After a particularly bright period of
play in the 1920s, the Aberavon team
became known as the 'Wizards'. The
name stuck and today a wizard is incorporated in the club's monogram.

With the tough industrial and em-
ployment conditions associated with
the coalfields and steelworks of South
Wales in recent years, so has Aberavon
undergone tough times. The club had
four famous three-quarters in the 1920s
– John Ring, Alun Edwards, Syd Williams and Arthur Bassett – but all
later switched to rugby league. The
club's 1984 top try-scorer, Kevin James,
also left the district to play league. In
1985 he played for Hull in rugby
league's top match of the year, the
Challenge Cup final.

Aberavon's leading cap-winner for
Wales is Allan Martin, who played 34
internationals for his country between
1973 and 1981. The big lock also toured
with the British Isles to New Zealand
(1977) and to South Africa (1980).

Other prominent Wizards from over
the years include John Bevan (Welsh
international 1975, British Isles tour
to New Zealand 1977 and Welsh
national team coach 1982–86); Ned
Jenkins (21 internationals for Wales
1927–32); Tony O'Connor (five internationals for Wales 1960–62, British
Isles tour to South Africa 1962); and
Clive Williams (Welsh international
prop 1977–83 who later played for
Swansea and toured New Zealand with
the British Isles 1977 and South Africa 1980).

The Aberavon team, which plays in
red and black hooped jerseys, used to
combine with neighbouring Neath to
play touring teams. Its closest results
as a combined team were a 3–5 loss to
the 1957 Wallabies and a 6–11 loss to
the 1963–64 All Blacks. Playing on its
own, Aberavon scored a win over Italy
by 13–4 in 1976, which was its first
victory over an international XV.

ABERTILLERY RFC

Founded in 1884, Abertillery is another of the strong scrummaging Welsh
club teams which always provide tough
opposition. The club has rarely dominated the Welsh club scene, but in combination with neighbouring Ebbw Vale
has provided many a touring team
with strenuous mid-week opposition.

Abertillery has a pretty home ground
at the foot of the mountains and it is
there that Haydn Morgan discovered
his love of rugby and a talent that was
to make him the club's most celebrated
Welsh cap. Morgan, a flanker, played
27 times for his country and toured
twice with British Isles touring teams
– to New Zealand and Australia in
1959 and to South Africa in 1962.

Other prominent Welsh internation-
als from Abertillery have been Alun
Pask (26 internationals for Wales be-
tween 1961–67 and two tours with the
British Isles – to South Africa in 1962
and to New Zealand in 1966); John
Webb (20 internationals for Wales
1907–12 and with the British Isles in
South Africa in 1910); and Allan Lewis
(six caps for Wales 1966–67, and a
New Zealand tour with the British
Isles in 1966).

Abertillery plays in green and white
hooped jerseys. It celebrated its centenary in 1984 with a match against a
touring Japanese team. After a close
encounter, Japan won 17–13.

ACKERMANN, DAWIE

Western Province and South Africa
8 internationals for Sth Africa 1955–58

A hard-nosed loose forward, Dawie Ackermann, described by one South African writer as 'symmetrically built', was at his very best as a flanker in the three tests he played against the 1955 British Lions team and in two tests against the All Blacks in 1956. After being part of the Springbok team which surprisingly lost to the French XV in 1958, he was no longer required by the South African selectors.

In his frustration Dawie Ackermann turned to the fledgling sport of rugby league and he is remembered as the captain of South Africa's first (and only) touring league team in 1963. The tour to Australia and New Zealand was not a success (even though the South Africans beat New Zealand) and Ackermann and league did not resurface in South Africa.

ADELAIDE

The home of rugby in South Australia. Adelaide qualifies for special mention as the city that has given the world the highest score in an international game involving an IRB country, and also the most points scored in one game by an international individual.

In 1974 the All Blacks fielded eight new caps against South Australia and ran up a relatively modest 39–6 lead by half-time. In the second half the All Blacks scored 78 points to wind up winning by 117–6! All Black fullback Joe Karam scored 41 of these points, then a record for any international player in one first-class match. Robbie Deans outscored Karam in Adelaide in 1984, with 43 points from three tries, 14 conversions and one penalty. On that day the All Blacks won 99–0.

AGEN RFC

A powerful and popular rugby club in the south of France. The club has had great success in the French club championship winning eight times: in 1930, 1945, 1962, 1965, 1966, 1976, 1982 and 1988.

The 1930 final was one of the most dramatic for the club. One of its players, 18-year-old wing Michel Pradie, was so badly injured in a qualifying match that he died that night in hospital. In the final in Bordeaux against the Quillan team, the score was 0–0 at

Frenchman Jean-Michel Aguirre, who was capable of kicking huge goals.

full-time. In extra time the Agen fullback Marius Guiral, who had replaced Pradie, seized the ball and drop-kicked a goal from 45 metres. Agen won 4–0 amid scenes of high emotion and relief. That night the president of the FFR said the dropped goal had the 'breath of poor Michel Pradie carrying it towards victory'.

In 1945 Agen won again with two of its strongest club personalities in the team: the indomitable Albert Ferrasse (later president of the FFR) and Guy Basquet.

The 1966 final was one to forget more than savour. Agen beat Dax by 9–8, but the game was so full of dirty play that the Minister of Youth and Sports was moved to ask officially what the FFR intended to do about it. The federation accordingly stepped in and suspended three participants in the game for life! (The suspensions were lifted after one year.)

In the 1976 final Agen won again by 13–10, but only after extra time. By this time the team had René Benesis, Daniel Dubroca, and Alain Plantefol, all current or future French internationals. Its opponent that year was the formidable Béziers club, which won so heavily in the championship in that decade.

In 1984 the club was not quite so lucky. Again the two teams in the final were Béziers and Agen. Again extra time was needed before Béziers won 3–1 on penalties after a 21–21 drawn scoreline.

Agen's most recent win was in 1988 when the prominent internationals Bérot, Lacombe, Sella, Montlaur, Berbizier, Erbani, Benetton, Gratton, Seigne and Dubroca made the Agen team a star-studded lineup. That year it beat Tarbes 9–3. The two rival hookers, Dubroca (Agen) and Dintrans (Tarbes) captained the two teams.

More than a rugby club, Agen has been the power centre of French rugby for a number of years. The elevation of Albert Ferrasse to the presidency of the FFR ensured that. The town hosted an International Rugby Board meeting in 1989. Several internationals have been held on Agen's home ground, the Stade Armandie, which was renovated to host a game for the 1991 Rugby World Cup.

AGUIRRE, JEAN-MICHEL
Bagnères and France
39 internationals for France 1971–80

A soccer player until he was 17, Aguirre gained his first international caps for France as a scrumhalf in 1971. A season later he changed to fullback and took to the role so readily that he was chosen to play for France in his new position against the All Blacks in early 1973. Injury kept him out of that game but shortly afterwards he coped so well at fullback against Wales that he became the replacement for Pierre Villepreux France had been seeking. He was rarely out of favour for the next six years.

A stylish attacker, Aguirre could also kick goals effectively. He landed six for France in the second test against Argentina in Buenos Aires in 1977, three of them from near halfway. His final tally of 18 points matched Hugo Porta's six penalties for the home team. The match was drawn 18–18.

Aguirre also landed a massive 65-metre kick on Wellington's Athletic Park in 1979. Yet it is as a brilliantly versatile runner that he is remembered. He played a major part in France's 24–19 win over New Zealand in 1979 – the famous 'Bastille Day' victory.

Originally a schoolteacher specialising in physical education in Bagnères, Aguirre later became a radio broadcaster on the game.

AITKEN, GEORGE
Buller, Wellington, and Scotland
2 internationals for New Zealand 1921
8 internationals for Scotland 1924–29

One of a number of players to have played for more than one country, Aitken came from Buller in New Zealand's South Island. He made his first-class debut as a teenager before the outbreak of World War I and resumed his career after the war.

Aitken's debut for New Zealand in 1921 was in the first test against South Africa – the first game between the two countries. After leading the All Blacks to a win in that game, he suffered badly from a bout of flu and was surprisingly dropped after the second test was lost.

Two years later Aitken, having been awarded a Rhodes Scholarship, was in England studying at Oxford University. After becoming an Oxford rugby blue he won his first cap for Scotland in 1924. (He had Scottish parents.)

George Aitken was a centre of considerable speed and talent. He is perhaps best remembered in the rugby world as part of a very fast and dangerous Oxford University three-quarter line, all of whom joined him in the Scottish international team at various times.

AITKEN, JIM
Gala and Scotland
24 internationals for Scotland 1977–84

A strong and fiery prop from the Scottish Borders area, who gained immortality in Scottish eyes for being Scotland's captain in the 1983–84 Five Nations championship series – its first outright win of the championship for 46 years. It was also Scotland's first Grand Slam (winning over each of the other four teams) since 1925.

Aitken was a sometimes controversial figure. The 1985 *Zimbabwe Rugby Yearbook* records an incident involving Zimbabwe's leading referee at a function after one of the Scotland v Zimbabwe matches. It is reported that Aitken 'felled him [the referee] unconscious with a head butt. It was inexcusable behaviour and soured the tour badly.'

ALBALADEJO, PIERRE
Dax and France
30 internationals for France 1954–64

Known universally as 'Monsieur Le Drop' because of his penchant for dropped goals, Albaladejo was also a very fine flyhalf.

Tall and stylish in the French style, Albaladejo made his debut as a fullback in 1954 against England. After just one game in the Five Nations championship, and another against Italy, he was passed over by the selectors for five seasons.

Re-appearing in 1960, Albaladejo soon won a reputation as an expert drop-kicker. In his second international of that year, against Ireland, he thumped over three dropped goals, a feat which has been equalled several times since, but never beaten in a full international.

After his retirement, Albaladejo won acclaim in France as a television commentator, providing expert insights on the game all over the world, working first with the famous French broadcaster Roger Couderc and later with his replacement, Pierre Salviac.

ALBERTYN, P. K.
Guy's Hospital, South-Western Districts and South Africa
4 internationals for South Africa 1924

One of the more unusual careers in international rugby belongs to Pieter Kuypers Albertyn, usually known as 'P.K.'. A product of the Stellenbosch high school and university, he never played for Western Province, nor did he play Springbok trials. Yet he captained the Springboks and was invited to play England trials.

When his father died in 1908, his mother forbade her 11-year-old only son to play rugby. His headmaster at Stellenbosch, the legendary Paul Roos, managed to overcome these objections three years later.

A severe knee injury in 1919 prevented Albertyn's debut for Western Province against the 1919 New Zealand Army side. But a nature cure specialist amazingly had Albertyn back on the field within six weeks.

Then, it seemed his career in South Africa was over. Albertyn headed for Guy's Hospital to study dentistry, having three outstanding seasons of rugby there, but declining the England trial to concentrate on his studies.

Albertyn returned home, nursing a smashed ankle from his last game for Guy's, and although he played for his club side, South African trials were far from his mind. Not from the sharp mind of that astute player-judge, A.F. Markotter, however. 'Mark' cabled Albertyn and told him to report in Durban before the first test with Great Britain.

Albertyn ran with the others when he arrived on the Thursday – having been told by Markotter to 'not make a bloody fool of yourself' – and when the team was posted that night, he was not only a centre but also captain.

Albertyn had a splendid series, in which the Springboks won three times and drew once. Twice he beat that excellent Scottish fullback, Dan Drysdale, and twice tries resulted, one of them to 'P.K.'.

The masterly Albertyn was also considered for the 1928 series against the All Blacks, but by then was past his best, and he retired finally in 1930.

He had a sharp turn of speed, unusually sharp for one with such an unsound limb and, perhaps even more surprisingly, he was a devastating sidestepper.

Although his career at the top only spanned those four matches, the 1921 Springbok captain, Theo Pienaar, was moved to comment at a 1955 reunion that Albertyn was 'the greatest back ever turned out by Stellenbosch, Western Province or South Africa'.

ALCOCK, ARNOLD

Guy's Hospital and England
1 international for England 1906

Arnold Alcock was a 'one cap wonder' who played just one game for his country, in rather unusual circumstances.

Alcock was a useful enough club player for Guy's Hospital who, it is insisted, never had pretensions at all of becoming an international. Imagine his surprise when he received in the mail an official invitation to play for his country against the touring 1906–07 Springbok team.

Alcock was initially shocked but then felt honoured and on the great day of the game he duly turned up at Twickenham all set to play. Upon seeing him, the secretary of the Rugby Union realised that the man before him was not the man the selectors had thought they were getting. Apparently they had chosen L.A.N. Slocock of Liver-

pool, and only by a typing error did Alcock receive his invitation to play. By then, of course, it was too late to summon Slocock from the north, so Alcock took the field for England. By all accounts he played sensibly and tolerably well. However, it was not a major surprise when Alcock was not invited to play for England again. Slocock was. In fact Slocock went on to play the next eight internationals.

Arnold Alcock later had a distinguished association with the Gloucester club, for which he was president for nearly 50 years.

ALL BLACKS

The name by which the international rugby union team of New Zealand is popularly known.

There are two schools of belief as to how the name arose. One has it that the players in the first New Zealand team in Britain in 1905–06 were so fast and elusive that a reporter dubbed them 'all backs' suggesting, no doubt, that even the slowest of the forwards could play as speedily as any of the backs if required. The report was apparently misprinted in newspapers and on placards as 'All Blacks.' The name soon gained popularity with the increasing exposure the team won in Britain.

It also fitted in with the other theory, which was that the nickname was simply the logical one to give, after having

seen the team in its playing colours. Since the turn of the century the New Zealand Rugby Football Union had adopted a kit for its national team that was all one colour – black (with the exception of the silver fern emblem on the left breast).

New Zealand continues to wear the all black uniform, except on occasions when visiting international teams take the field in New Zealand in colours too close to black to make for easy differentiation between the teams. Great Britain first caused this 'problem' in 1930. It wore dark blue, as did Scotland when it toured New Zealand in other years. For these games the All Blacks wear all white jerseys.

In modern times, to be named as an All Black is the pinnacle of many a young New Zealand footballer's career. But being an All Black is also a name-tag and responsibility that follows the recipient through all his days. When New Zealanders prominent in non-sporting endeavours pass away, their obituary notices tend to list academic qualifications or other achievements from general life. When a rugby player who has played for New Zealand dies, his achievements as an All Black, no matter how modest they might have been, will merit a paragraph of considerable size and will often stand as his major contribution to the community, no matter how successful he may have been in other fields.

The first New Zealand team to be named 'All Blacks'. The 'Originals' of 1905–06.

Trevor Allan (right) with Col Windon, posing with the Bledisloe Cup – won for the first time by Australia in 1949.

Fred Allen at a training session with members of the 1967 All Black team. At right, Grahame Thorne, Colin Meads and Ken Gray.

ALLAN, TREVOR
New South Wales and Australia
14 internationals for Australia 1946–49

A brilliant centre three-quarter, Trevor Allan was, in two seasons in particular, one of Australia's most successful test captains. He assumed the leadership of the Wallabies on the 1947–48 tour of Britain after the original skipper, Bill McLean, suffered a broken leg. At just 21, Allan was the youngest of all international touring captains. That Wallaby team may not have won the Grand Slam over the four home unions, but it maintained a record of not conceding a try in those games.

The injury to McLean meant the young man was put in charge of a team made up mainly of World War II veterans. Yet Allan was an enormous success with them and the team displayed tremendous loyalty to him.

In 1949 Allan led Australia to its first 'away' win in the Bledisloe Cup series against New Zealand, although New Zealanders will be quick to point out that the leading 30 All Blacks of

that year were involved in another series in South Africa at the same time.

Trevor Allan quit rugby for the professional game in 1951, playing rugby league in England for Leigh. After retiring from all football in 1954 he became a respected television rugby commentator.

ALLEN, 'ELLIE'
Derry, Liverpool and Ireland
21 internationals for Ireland 1900–07

One of Ireland's most distinguished early forwards. Allen captained Ireland in four of his seasons in international play and his leadership in the famous Ireland v Wales match in 1906 was described by the great rugby writer of the day, E.H.D. Sewell, as being a major factor in 'the greatest of all wins in international or any rugby'.

Apparently Allen implored his team with a powerful pre-match speech to tackle the Welsh star, Gwyn Nicholls, every time he touched the ball. This the team did and Ireland, the underdog, won one of its most famous victo-

ries by 11–6. For years, 'Ellie' Allen was the highest cap winner for his country.

ALLEN, FRED
Canterbury, Marlborough, Waikato,
  Auckland and New Zealand
6 internationals for New Zealand 1946–49

Fred Allen was one of the truly giant personalities of New Zealand rugby in the 30 years after the end of World War II. After being first recognised as a star of the famous New Zealand Army team (the Kiwis) which toured Britain in 1945–46, he gained selection and captaincy for his country in 1946. He was also made captain for two All Black tours, to Australia in 1947 and to South Africa in 1949, though he was dropped – at his own behest – for the final two tests in 1949.

After his playing days were over, Allen continued to make a remarkable contribution to New Zealand rugby.

He became coach of the Auckland team and took it through one of the province's greatest eras. Under Allen's guidance, Auckland defended the

Ranfurly Shield 25 times, then a record, between 1960–63.

Allen progressed through to selecting and coaching All Black teams. As coach he took the New Zealand team to a record 14 consecutive wins, a record which still stands. Allen and Charlie Saxton, his old captain from the Kiwis of 20 years before, formed a formidable managerial team behind the 1967 All Blacks in Great Britain. That side was also unbeaten.

After his retirement as the All Black coach in 1968, Allen continued to be a highly respected and recognisable personality in the game in New Zealand.

ALLIGADOO

A rugby term, sometimes spelt 'alickadoo' and rarely heard outside Britain, which means a club official or highly placed committee man.

Some say the spelling 'alickadoo' is derived from the words 'all he can do (is talk)'.

The other story comes from J.B.G. Thomas's *Great Rugger Players*, where it is said Ireland's 'Jammie' Clinch was asked by his team-mate, Ernie Crawford, about the subject matter of a story Clinch was reading on a train, while returning from an international in 1925. When Clinch replied 'I'm reading about a Spaniard called Alicardo, who thinks a lot of himself and is always blowing his load' (bragging), Crawford was highly amused and likened Alicardo to the rugby officials riding on the train with the team.

After that Crawford used the word frequently around Dublin. It became distorted by Irish accents to 'alligadoo' but it stuck as a term for an officious committee man. Crawford also took the word across to the Barbarians club, where he was a committee member, and it became familiar usage all over Britain.

ANDREW, ROB

Nottingham, Wasps and England
36 internationals for England 1985–91
2 internationals for British Isles 1989

A fine flyhalf in the modern style of maximum efficiency and a minimum of mistakes, Rob Andrew became England's most-capped player in that position in 1989, passing the record set in 1923 by W.J.A. ('Dave') Davies.

After appearing three times for Cambridge University in the annual Twickenham inter-varsity match, Andrew made his international debut against Romania in 1986 when he scored 16 points from six successful kicks. He has been a vital part of the England team ever since, and only on rare occasions has his form faltered. As he gained in confidence so has the performance of the English team. In one game in 1986 he scored 21 points against Wales, including six penalty goals.

Andrew spent some time in Australia playing club rugby and appeared there for England in the World Cup in 1987 and with England on tour in 1988.

His third visit to Australia was in 1989. He initially missed selection for the British Isles team for their tour but gained a lucky break when Paul Dean of Ireland was sidelined in the first game. Andrew was rushed in as a replacement.

He missed the first test but when added to the second test played a big part in the Lions' series win. His kicking was sure and his tackling an inspiration. The Lions won both the tests he played in.

In the second test, in place of the out-of-form goal-kicker, Gavin Hastings, Andrew landed three vital goals in the 19–12 win.

By 1991 Rob Andrew had reached 36 caps for his country as a flyhalf and was so well placed within the team that a tally close to 50 caps looked set to be seriously challenged.

He has a grand record as an England captain, leading the side once, against Romania in 1989, when England won by 58–3!

ANDURAN, JOE

Universitaire de France and France
1 international for France 1910

This player is another of rugby's unusual internationals from early in the twentieth century.

Joe Anduran, an art dealer, was in his shop in Paris one day when a taxi pulled up outside and several officials of the French Rugby Federation climbed out. Apparently they had just seen the French team depart from the railway station as they headed off to play Wales in Swansea on New Year's Day, 1910. But only 14 Frenchmen had gone on the train; the 15th was held up in Bordeaux while doing his military service.

So the officials were sent on an urgent errand around Paris to find another forward for the game to be played next day. Their search eventually took them to Joe Anduran's art shop.

Anduran was a useful club player in Paris but nothing more, and at first he thought it was a joke when the strangers asked him if he wanted to play for France the next day. He was persuaded to leave immediately, but he soon found his first obstacle in making the trip to Swansea was not so much the booking on the cross-channel ferry, but his wife!

Madame Anduran, it seems, did not share her husband's pride in being selected to play for France – she had made arrangements for Joe to do some family visiting with her the next day.

It is not recorded how it was achieved, but soon Joe Anduran was on the train for Swansea, where the next day he ran on to St Helen's field for his debut for France.

Wales won the game by the handsome margin of 49 points to 14. Not surprisingly, Joe Anduran was one of those who was axed by the French selectors in their reshuffle of the badly beaten team and he was never seen again in the French colours. However, he had his day under the sun and is listed in all the record books as a fully fledged French international. What is not noted is what his wife said on his return home!

ARGENTINA

Although the Argentines did not begin to assert themselves in world rugby until the mid-1960s, they have played the game longer than many of those countries that are considered to be rugby's traditional founders.

Rugby travelled to South America in the hearts, minds and kitbags of

APPEARANCE RECORDS

Most Appearances in All International Matches

Against any other nation's test team (i.e. not just International Rugby Board countries). Players are from the following countries: Australia, British Isles, England, France, Ireland, New Zealand, Scotland, South Africa and Wales. To March 1991:

Serge Blanco (France) 85	Tom Kiernan (Ireland and B.I.) 59	Moss Keane (Ireland and B.I.) 52
Mike Gibson (Ireland and B.I.) 81	Phil Orr (Ireland and B.I.) 59	Jackie Kyle (Ireland and B.I.) 52
Willie John McBride (Ire. and B.I.) 80	Jean-Pierre Rives (France) 59	Gerald Davies (Wales and B.I.) 51
Philippe Sella (France) 72	Laurent Rodriguez (France) 56	Jean-Luc Joinel (France) 51
Roland Bertranne (France) 69	Pierre Berbizier (France) 56	Roy Laidlaw (Scotland and B.I.) 51
Fergus Slattery (Ireland and B.I.) 65	Colin Meads (New Zealand) 55	Ian McLauchlan (Scot. and B.I.) 51
Michel Crauste (France) 63	Robert Paparemborde (France) 55	Simon Poidevin (Australia) 51
Benoit Dauga (France) 63	David Campese (Australia) 54	Jean Prat (France) 51
Gareth Edwards (Wales and B.I.) 63	Graham Price (Wales and B.I.) 53	Walter Spanghero (France) 51
J.P.R. Williams (Wales and B.I.) 63	Jim Renwick (Scotland and B.I.) 53	Sandy Carmichael (Scot. and B.I.) 50
Jean Condom (France) 61	Colin Deans (Scotland) 52	Michel Celaya (France) 50
Andy Irvine (Scotland and B.I.) 60	Amédée Domenech (France) 52	Philippe Dintrans (France) 50

Most Appearances for Individual Countries

Internationals played for country of residency only (i.e. British Isles games excluded).

Serge Blanco (France) 85	J.P.R. Williams (Wales) 55	Jim Renwick (Scotland) 52
Mike Gibson (Ireland) 69	David Campese (Australia) 54	Tony Neary (England) 43
Colin Meads (New Zealand) 55	Colin Deans (Scotland) 52	Rory Underwood (England) 43

British engineers pursuing lucrative Argentine railway contracts in the nineteenth century. In 1873 they formed two teams to play the first official rugby match in Argentina. This was only two years after England had first played Scotland, a mere 10 years after the formation of New Zealand's first club, Christchurch, and 16 years before the formation of the South African Rugby Board.

There are many colourful stories about the early days of rugby in Argentina. It is said that the first Argentine Rugby Union was formed primarily to control the roughs and toughs who played this crazy game on the worksites along the sprawling Argentine railway system. Police compared the game derisively with their beloved soccer and even banned it for nine years, so shocked were they at the high incidence of broken limbs and bones.

The game began to be played again in 1882, still largely ignored by the local population, but in 1899 the River Plate Rugby Union was formed (now the Union Argentina de Rugby). The links were all British, and the River Plate union remained directly affili-

ated to the Rugby Football Union until 1932. The first club for native-born Argentines was formed by engineering students at the University of Buenos Aires in 1904.

The following year Argentine rugby received a considerable boost when the former Springbok captain, 'Fairy' Heatlie, emigrated to Argentina. A versatile forward and sometime goal-kicker between 1891 and 1903, Heatlie continued playing in Argentina until an injury caused him to retire from the game in 1921 — at the age of 49!

The first overseas team to tour Argentina was sponsored by the RFU and arrived in 1910, managed by R.V. Stanley and captained by wing John Raphael. It was unbeaten in six vigorous games.

England returned under the managership of James ('Bim') Baxter in 1927. Though touring under the auspices of the RFU, this team was broad-based and captained by Cambridge and Scotland lock, David MacMyn. Britain returned in 1936, the strong team captained by England scrumhalf Bernard Gadney and including the famed Russian wing, Prince Alexander Obolensky.

No games were lost by the tourists during these first three British visits and they won 25. The 1927 and 1936 teams averaged nearly 40 points a game. Nevertheless, Argentines were now taking to the game more and more – the broadening interest being given impetus by the tour of the Junior Springboks in 1932. Joe Nykamp led his team home unbeaten; its manager was the first Springbok captain in Britain, Paul Roos.

Easier travel made rugby contact with Argentina simpler in the years after World War II. An Oxford-Cambridge universities team toured in 1948, but the most important breakthrough was the tour by France in 1949. Since then the rugby relationship between Argentina and France has been strong and very volatile. Some of Argentina's hardest matches have been against France, whose style of open, free-running back play appealed to the Spanish and Indian heritages of many of the new breed of Argentine rugby players.

The Pumas' coach, Enardo Poggi, said in September 1975: 'English-speaking players taught us the principles of the game, and for a long time, they were our models. But since 1949, when the Tricolours first toured in Argentina, it is the French style we have envied.'

South Africa proved to be another strong influence. The Junior Springboks toured again under the captaincy of Peter Allen in 1959.

In 1964–65 Natal coach Izaak van Heerden, who had written a coaching manual, *Tactical and Attacking Rugby*, which won him acclaim for its clarity and discipline, arrived in Argentina. He exercised considerable influence in a short time, especially on forward play, and it was he, along with Dr Danie Craven, who was instrumental in Argentina making its first overseas tour – to South Africa in 1965.

Reluctant to expose the fledgling internationals to the harsh realities of rugby, Craven worked out a cautious itinerary which avoided the big powers of South African provincial play. So off they went to mainly country areas where, to the delight of the Argentines, the dismay of the South Africans, the satisfaction of Van Heerden, and the chagrin of Craven, the touring team won 11 of 16 games, including the 'test' against the Junior Springboks, 11–6.

The Pumas of Argentina had arrived on the world rugby scene. Never again were they considered easy meat for international teams, and their new-found confidence resulted in some great victories over the next few years.

In 1968, during a Welsh tour of Argentina, the Pumas won the first test 9–5 and drew the second 9–9. To be fair, 10 of the top Welsh players were in South Africa with the Lions, but it was nevertheless a tasty test series win to Argentina.

In 1969 they shared a series with Scotland at home after winning the first test 20–3; and in 1970, when Ireland toured, captained by its great fullback Tom Kiernan, Argentina won the first test 8–3 and the second 6–3.

Argentina made its first trip to Europe in 1973 – an often fiery tour of Ireland and Scotland. Outbreaks of fighting in the Munster match were followed by leading player and future coach Luis Gradin being sent off against Ulster. And Gordon Brown of Scotland was laid low by an Argentine prop's punch at Murrayfield – the unusual difference in this sadly all-too-common occurrence was that the punch was thrown under the grandstand after the game!

The Argentines lost to the Scottish XV 11–12. Three years later, they went down to a Wales XV, 19–20. That year, 1976, was a watershed for Argentina: it finally made contact with New Zealand, and although the All Blacks who toured South Africa were not considered for the trend-setting visit to South America, it was still a very good team led by Graham Mourie, then embarking on a distinguished international career, and guided by celebrated coach Jack Gleeson. More than half the team had played or would later play in 'full' All Black sides, including Stu Wilson and Andy Haden. The tourists won all eight matches including the two internationals (not considered test matches by New Zealand), 21–9 and 26–6.

Argentina played host to France in 1977 – one of the most aggressive of a long line of fiery series between the two nations. In a game that was described as 'very dirty', more than 20 kicks for goal were taken from penalties dished out for fighting and dirty play.

Jean-Michel Aguirre landed six goals for France and Hugo Porta six for Argentina. The drawn match – all penalties – was headlined by one newspaper as 'Porta 18, Aguirre 18 – Rugby nil'!

UNION ARGENTINA DE RUGBY

UNION DE RUGBY DE INGLATERRA

**PARTIDOS CON EL
SELECCIONADO DE INGLATERRA
TEMPORADA INTERNACIONAL 1990**

Left: Argentina at the 1987 World Cup. Juan Lanza (centre), Jorge Allen in support. The Fijian player is Rusiate Namoro. Fiji won the match 28–9.

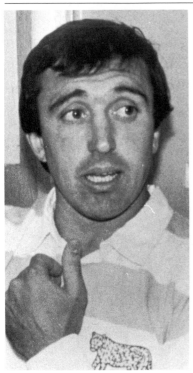

Hugo Porta, the captain, mastermind and dictator of Argentine rugby.

Putting aside their Latin temperament, the Pumas' rugby continued to prosper in the 1970s. They drew with England, 13–13, in 1978; beat Australia the next year in the first test in Argentina, 24–13; and in 1982 won the first test against Australia at Brisbane, 18–3.

Argentina toured New Zealand for the first time in 1979, but was still refused full test match status by the New Zealand Rugby Football Union. The Pumas lost three of their nine matches, including both to New Zealand, 9–18 and 6–15.

New Zealand referee Bob Francis commented, after the 1985 Argentina v France series, that it was his most demanding and difficult assignment, so fired up were the two teams. The 1988 tied series between the two nations was no less volatile, with French lock Alain Lorieux becoming the tenth man sent off in a full international.

The captain, mastermind and dictator of Argentine rugby for virtually all the 1970s and 80s was Hugo Porta, whose rare absences made the Pumas look a leaderless bunch, devoid of ideas of their own. The great flyhalf, with a deceptively bulky-looking build, could run at great pace, throw defence-splitting passes, and kick with great judgment from all distances and angles. Single-handedly, he secured perhaps Argentina's finest result, a 21–21 draw with the 1985 All Blacks.

Porta's decline coincided with the first World Cup in 1987. The side was seeded to reach the quarter-finals but instead finished last (on a countback) in its pool. The Pumas lost to Fiji 9–28, and New Zealand 15–46, and beat lowly Italy by only 25–16. On a return visit to New Zealand in 1989, they slipped to huge defeats (9–60 and 12–49) to the All Blacks in the tests and it was clear a major slump had hit their game.

The slump was underlined in 1990 when Argentina toured Britain for the first time since the Falklands War. The 39-year-old Porta was recalled to lead the team, but the losses were heavy: only 18–20 to Ireland, but 0–51 to England and 3–49 to Scotland.

Yet internally the game remains healthy. Although it is mostly played by adults, with children being grounded in soccer, Argentina is reckoned to have about 60,000 playing the game and it is now the second sport, after soccer. It is mostly played in very large athletic clubs catering also for other sports.

The headquarters and the main centre of interest is naturally the capital, Buenos Aires, with its huge population; other leading rugby centres include Cordoba, Mendoza, Tucuman and Rosario. Crowds at big club matches reach about 30,000. The demand for tickets for test matches has grown so large that officials have had to move internationals from the Ferrocaril Oeste Stadium to the 50,000-capacity Velez Sarsfield Stadium across the city.

ARMIT, 'BARNEY'

Otago and New Zealand
New Zealand rep. in 9 matches, 1897

The Scottish-born Armit's career and life were over before New Zealand played its first match, and his end was directly the result of a rugby accident.

A feature of the fleet wing's play was his penchant for hurdling a prospective tackler – a spectacular feat which brought many tries, six on his tour of Australia.

On August 26 1899, playing for Otago against Taranaki, Armit tried to hurdle the renowned Alf Bayly who, crouching low, rose as Armit sailed over and tipped his heel. Armit crashed on his neck and broke it. Paralysed, he died 11 weeks later in Dunedin Hospital. A distraught Bayly gave up serious rugby soon afterwards. Happily, no-one has made a serious effort to emulate Alexander Armit's hurdling feats in subsequent years.

ASHWORTH, JOHN

Canterbury, Hawke's Bay and New
  Zealand
24 internationals for N. Zealand 1978–85

A strong, feisty prop of the 1970s and 80s, who formed part of the long-serving New Zealand front row which was dubbed the 'Geriatrics' by the news media. Along with fellow prop Gary Knight and hooker Andy Dalton, the three played together in 20 internationals. At the end of their sequence of test matches together, their combined ages added up to over 100 years!

Ashworth gained some notoriety in his career for two well-publicised incidents involving rough play. He was heavily criticised for his role in a face injury suffered by J.P.R. Williams, the great Welsh fullback, in a match against Bridgend in 1978. Ashworth was also involved in a controversial high tackle on Hugo Porta, in the Argentina v New Zealand game in Dunedin in 1979.

Nevertheless, he is remembered as an excellent loosehead prop and a consistent footballer. He ended his career as New Zealand's second oldest test player (after Ned Hughes). Ashworth was 35 years 287 days old when he

John Ashworth

played his last test match against Australia at Auckland in 1985.

ASIAN CHAMPIONSHIP

This tournament began in 1969 in Tokyo and has been a biennial event since.

The first seven events were won by Japan, obviously a reflection of the strength that country has been able to build up with regular and continuing contacts with International Rugby Board countries. The main opposition in those early years came from the expatriates of Hong Kong, but in the 1980s Korea (South Korea) made a rapid rise in standard to win the championship in Singapore in 1982. The final against Japan was 9–9 at full-time, then Korea's flyhalf Moon Yung Chan wrote himself a page in Asian sporting history by drop-kicking a goal 16 minutes into extra time to deny Japan another victory.

Japan was back in the winner's circle in 1984 beating Korea. In 1986, 1988 and 1990 Korea was again the winner, continuing the rivalry between the two countries. Japan lost the 1986 final after a controversial dropped goal by Chang-Kyu Sin in injury time: the awarding of the kick was disputed by All Japan as many on the field and watching felt that the kick fell well short of the goal-posts.

ATHLETIC PARK, WELLINGTON

A sign facing the crowd at Wellington's famous Athletic Park says 'Home of Rugby in New Zealand'.

RESULTS OF THE ASIAN CHAMPIONSHIP

	Winner	Runner-Up	Score	Venue
1969	Japan	Korea	23-5	Tokyo
1970	Japan	Thailand	42-11	Bangkok
1972	Japan	Hong Kong	16-0	Hong Kong
1974	Japan	Sri Lanka	44-6	Colombo
1976*	Japan	Korea		Tokyo
1978	Japan	Korea	16-4	Kuala Lumpur
1980	Japan	Korea	21-12	Taiwan
1982	Korea	Japan	12-9	Singapore
1984	Japan	Korea	20-13	Tokyo
1986	Korea	Japan	24-22	Bangkok
1988	Korea	Japan	17-13	Hong Kong
1990	Korea	Japan	13-9	Colombo

*No final played. A round robin league series was played instead.

Situated in the centre of a high-sided valley running down to Cook Strait, Athletic Park is in an exposed position, and has been battered many times by ferocious Wellington winds.

The most infamous day was in 1961 when the Wellington Rugby Union's new pride and joy – the Millard Stand – was being officially opened on the day of the France v New Zealand match. The southerly storm that weekend brought in winds gusting up to 80 mph (140 km/h) – one of the worst days of Wellington's history. A large luxury liner, the *Canberra*, was so buffeted in Cook Strait that the ship could not enter the harbour, just miles away. Yet in this tempest a test match was played!

New Zealand won by 5–3, with Don Clarke, the All Black fullback, kicking a sideline conversion that travelled across the wind in a crazy curving arc.

Athletic Park has also had its moments in the mud, no more so than in 1977 when the British Lions played the New Zealand Juniors. Not a single player from either side could be recognised at the end of the game.

But Athletic Park can be as pretty a ground as anywhere in the world and it has, for many of its top days, presented a flat true ground with an excellent playing surface and seating for the fans that is close to the action.

The capacity of the ground has been reduced in modern times to about 40,000, which is considerably less than the record attendance of 57,000 which crammed in to watch the second test between New Zealand and the British Isles in 1959.

New Zealand played its first home test match at Athletic Park, against Great Britain in 1904. In the 1980s the All Blacks scored what was then their highest test score against a major country. The All Blacks won 42–15 against England in the second test of 1985. Later in 1987 Argentina was beaten 46–15 in a World Cup game and was beaten again in 1989 by 49–12. The latter remains the highest score posted by New Zealand on Athletic Park.

ATTENDANCE RECORDS

For many years the record for the largest crowd to watch a rugby international has been the 95,000 that

The crowd invades the pitch at Athletic Park, with the imposing Millard Stand in the background.

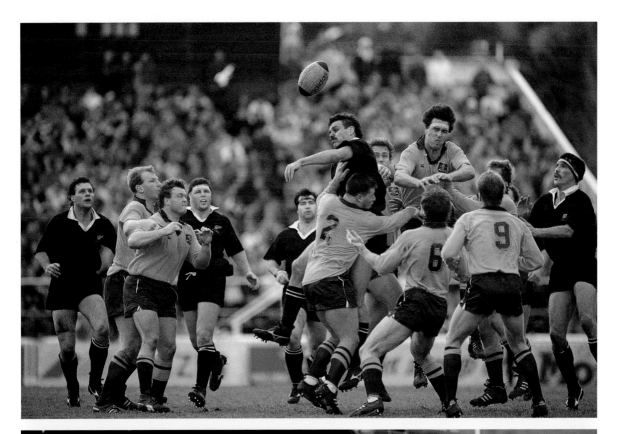

Top: Gary Whetton disputes lineout possession with Steve Cutler.
Below: David Campese, a superstar of Australian rugby. Peter Bush

Australia v New Zealand, first test, 1990. Top: Nick Farr-Jones sets his backline alight.
Below: Australian players await a conversion attempt. From left, Viliami 'Ofahengaue, Rod McCall, Steve Tuynman, Nick Farr-Jones, Peter FitzSimons, Greg Martin, Ewen McKenzie, Tony Daly. Fotopacific

packed into the old Ellis Park ground in Johannesburg in 1955 to watch the first test between South Africa and the British Isles. There were also 95,000 present in Bucharest in May 1957 to see France play Romania, although it should be mentioned that the game was actually played as a curtain-raiser to a major soccer match!

A new record was thought to have been set at Murrayfield in Edinburgh in 1975, when it was reported that a crowd of 104,000 watched the Wales v Scotland international. However, in the end the official attendance figures were listed as 80,000, which stands only as a record for a British rugby crowd.

The biggest crowd to watch a test match in Australia was the 48,898 who came to see New Zealand play Australia at the Sydney Cricket Ground in the third test of 1980; while the New Zealand best is the 61,240 who attended Eden Park in Auckland for the fourth test between New Zealand and South Africa in 1956.

At the other end of the scale, there have been many times when officials have been disappointed with the size of crowds that have turned out to see major rugby matches.

Easily the tiniest crowd to watch a significant rugby match would have been the several dozen people who stood about on the sidelines of a polo field in Glenville, in upstate New York, for the match between USA and South Africa in 1981.

To avoid anti-apartheid protesters and prying news media, the two teams travelled in secret to a destination which only a few officials knew about. They also had quietly scheduled the match to begin 24 hours ahead of its planned playing time, and goal-posts were only erected five minutes before kick-off. When the teams ran on to the field, 60 state police leapt from unmarked cars to guard the event, but they cannot be claimed as boosters to the total attendance figure of 25!

Had there been a scoreboard at the ground it would have shown a final score of South Africa 38, USA 7. Perhaps this was the only international where there were more points scored than people attending.

AUCKLAND RFU
Founded in 1883 and one of the original members of the New Zealand Rugby Football Union, the Auckland union is today, in terms of assets and playing numbers, one of the richest of its type in the world.

In a city that now boasts a population of around a million, Auckland's rugby has always been strong. In the early days the boundaries of the union stretched to the far parts of the Auckland province, but in the years since several smaller unions have broken away as independent unions: South Auckland Counties (now known as Counties) in 1955 and North Harbour in 1984.

The Auckland rugby team, in its blue and white hooped jerseys, has always been formidable opposition for any other New Zealand provincial team, as well as those overseas touring teams that choose to arrive at Eden Park.

Auckland could claim that its unbroken tenure with the Ranfurly Shield from 1985–90, when it defended the shield 40 times, was its greatest era. Under the challenge system the much-revered trophy can change hands on the vagaries of one game. Week after week at Eden Park, the Auckland team withstood assaults from the best provincial teams from elsewhere in the country, not only keeping the rugby population in a high state of excitement but helping engender a very real togetherness among the people of Auckland. Earlier, between 1960–63, it had another magnificent sequence with the Ranfurly Shield, defending it 25 times.

Auckland has had notable success against international teams, beating various British teams from around the turn of the twentieth century (winning in 1888 and 1904, and in 1908 against the Anglo-Welsh tourists). Auckland also beat Great Britain in 1930 (with a team described by the British manager, 'Bim' Baxter as the 'finest in the Dominion') and the British Isles team of 1983 and the England team of 1985.

Auckland has beaten Australia four times, and in 1965 it beat the Springboks in a close match, 15–14.

Naturally Auckland has provided a high percentage of New Zealand's star rugby players – men such as Fred Allen, Des Connor, Andy Haden, Mac Herewini, Waka Nathan, George Nicholson, Bob Scott, Wilson Whineray, Hallard ('Snow') White, Bryan Williams, John Kirwan, Gary Whetton, Michael Jones and Grant Fox.

Coach Maurice Trapp reminds Auckland that 6–3 at half-time is not good enough!

The club competition trophy each winter in Auckland honours one of the city's most famous rugby sons. The clubs vie for the Gallaher Shield, named in honour of Dave Gallaher, who captained the first All Blacks to tour Britain.

AUSTRALIA
It is a tribute to the varied and considerable talents of the rugby players of Australia that they have been able to compete successfully and set new standards of brilliance and flair while being able to draw on only two major playing centres, Sydney and Brisbane, which have provided 95 per cent of Australian test and touring teams for much of Australia's rugby history.

Moreover, world class standards have been upheld while the Australian Rugby Union has faced pressures from two other games that are played with

The Australian team which played New Zealand in Sydney in 1903: ten players from New South Wales, and five from Queensland. The gentlemen in black, at the back, were the selectors of the team.

fanatical fervour – rugby league and Australian rules. Indeed, much of the history of the game in Australia is touched by its struggle to stay afloat as a public drawcard in the face of the popularity of these two codes. Somehow the crisis of repeatedly losing players (to league especially), and large crowds (to both league and rules) has been survived by rugby union in Australia. Today the game thrives in its own right with a considerable following in places other than just Brisbane and Sydney.

The first governing body for rugby in Australia was formed in 1874, well before the game had reached that stage in Ireland, Wales, South Africa or New Zealand. From that date it faced many inroads into its organisation and confidence. In the early years it was the game of Victorian rules (later known as Australian rules) that attracted young footballing talent and, in Melbourne, Adelaide and Perth particularly, a fanatical following.

When the New Zealanders of the first touring rugby league team headed to Britain in 1907, with the sniff of money in their nostrils, to play the breakaway Northern Union game, something about playing rugby for money 'clicked' with a good percentage of sports-mad Australians. They

watched that New Zealand team play en route to the UK, and the game of rugby league, which was eventually to gain a firm hold on Australians, began to provide further opposition to rugby.

The effect of World War I should also not be underestimated. Rugby union in Brisbane did not survive after it. It is said the Queensland Rugby Union decided to close down because of lack of manpower and in deference to those who claimed that all able-bodied young men should be away at the war anyway. The game, on an organised basis, disappeared in Queensland for 10 years and talented rugby men from the north wanting to play had to live in or near Sydney.

In the nineteenth and early twentieth centuries, distance and travel difficulties meant that games between the Northern and Southern Rugby Unions (later to become Queensland and New South Wales) were haphazard. Tours to New Zealand were encouraged. The first took place in 1882 when 16 players from the Southern Union toured, playing seven games in four weeks, winning four and losing three. Today they are entered in the record books as New South Wales.

That team effectively touched off a rugby rivalry between New Zealand and Australia that today extends not

just through international and provincial level but right through from schoolboys to 'Golden Oldies'. Any rugby player on either side of the Tasman wants to test himself and beat those from the other side who dare to challenge.

The first New Zealand national team (not yet known as All Blacks) to tour Australia went there in 1884. Its first match in Australia – and the first played in that country by any overseas side – was at the Parramatta Ground in Sydney where New Zealand beat Cumberland County 33–0.

Four years later a British team made a rather longer journey and toured Australia playing the game that they (the British) had invented. Like the New Zealanders of 1884 they too were unbeaten.

The English struck the first of the diversions with which Australian rugby has always had to cope. They were invited to play Australian rules in Melbourne and, having enjoyed the game thoroughly, they enquired about other games on tour under these rules. They ended their tour having played 19 games under Australian rules laws, and only 16 under rugby rules!

Australia first played as a unified team in internationals against the British in 1899, when a second Great

Britain team toured for a four-test series. With nine players from New South Wales and six from Queensland, Australia won its first test match 11–0. Thereafter the selectors had to pay some heed to the costs of travelling players and sometimes Queenslanders were included only to make sure it was a 'mixed' team. Australia was slightly weakened as a result, and Great Britain won the last three tests.

The first Australian team to tour outside the country was the 1905 team to New Zealand.

When rugby revived in Queensland in 1929, after the decline of the war years, the fruits of success did much to enhance the popularity and standing of the code. Five Queenslanders were included in the first unified Australian team to play for 15 years when the touring All Blacks arrived that year. The fact that Australia won all three tests in the series (the only time it has ever achieved this feat) and the fact that several of the team's stars were Queenslanders lifted the game's profile in Brisbane. Thereafter it has never again looked like fading.

Rugby also received a boost in Victoria. It too had been in recess since World War I and after reformation in 1926 gained its first test player in 1929. Gordon Sturtidge played in front of a crowd of 18,000 at the Exhibition Ground in Brisbane in the Australian team which won the second test.

While rugby was slowly taking hold in other parts of Australia (notably the country areas of New South Wales, Adelaide and Perth) the strength of the Australian game was being consolidated in Sydney.

In the years after the war New South Wales continued to involve its top players in tours and 'test' series. New South Wales held high the banner of Australian rugby in this time, touring to New Zealand and hosting the All Blacks in return.

Then there was the famous 'Waratahs' tour in 1927–28, when New South Wales embarked on an ambitious and highly successful tour of Britain, France and Canada. Five full internationals were played for three wins and two losses.

Beyond the dry facts of the record books was the excitement engendered at the style of play the team produced. The Waratahs threw the ball about with brilliant back play and their name

is still fondly recalled by British rugby historians. Nearly 60 years later the Australian RU retrospectively granted full Australian test status to the Waratahs' internationals.

Australia has had its dark moments when its national team has not always been a consistent winner. But the investment in an attractive style of play, continuing on the spirit of the Waratahs, soon made the Australian Wallabies a vital part of the world rugby scene.

They have had many famous and dramatic moments on the rugby stage and many of the game's most famous players have come from the land 'down under'. Tommy Lawton, Aub Hodgson, 'Wild Bill' Cerutti, Trevor Allan, Ken Catchpole, John Thornett, Mark Loane, Paul McLean, Mark Ella, David Campese and Michael Lynagh are just some who have graced the game of rugby union and whose feats will live on forever in the game.

So too will the memories of some of Australia's teams, like the 1933 Wallabies in South Africa who played a

rare five-test series and stunned South Africa with brilliant attacking play to win two tests.

Then there was the 1947–48 team in Britain. Although hit hard by the early loss of the tour captain, Bill McLean, with a broken leg, the team failed to have its line crossed in its internationals. Only penalty goals by Wales cost Australia a Grand Slam of wins over the home nations.

The 1949 Wallabies in New Zealand are remembered fondly as well. They beat the All Blacks to take home, for the first time, the Bledisloe Cup, the symbol of trans-Tasman rugby supremacy.

John Thornett's team in South Africa in 1963 carried on the tradition of the 1933 side by bringing brave rugby to the huge Springboks, and went home afterwards with a drawn series.

In 1984 the Wallabies reached the status of one of the world's great rugby powers with a tour to Britain under the leadership of Andrew Slack. This was a team which simply stunned the British and Irish with its tactics and individual flair. Playing brilliantly, it

Always able to make a pass, the superbly balanced Mark Ella in action for Australia v France, Sydney 1981.

won for Australian rugby an achievement that was previously only the property of the mighty All Blacks and South Africans. The Wallabies of 1984 won a Grand Slam of wins over all four home countries.

That success continued in 1986 when Australia won the Bledisloe Cup again in New Zealand. In the Rugby World Cup in 1987, Australia lost a thrilling semi-final match to France and then, disappointingly, lost the third place match against Wales in Rotorua. There were losses in other years, but before the 1991 Rugby World Cup there were many tipping Australia to win that event.

Not coincidentally, many of the problems which had earlier faced Australian rugby have diminished in the swell of success. No longer do players swap to rugby league in the masses they once did. The flush of being successful has no doubt helped Australian fans to decide which game is worthy of their attention. After years of pain and distress Australian rugby, in the 1980s, came into its own at last.

AUST. CAPITAL TERRITORY

Known familiarly as A.C.T., the union has its headquarters in the federal capital, Canberra, and is a fully fledged member of the Australian Rugby Union. In recent years ACT has enjoyed considerable success in opposition to overseas teams. Its first win over a touring team was in 1973 when Tonga

Captain Nick Farr-Jones and coach Bob Dwyer—jubilant about Australia's victory over the All Blacks in the third test, 1990.

was turned back by 17–6. The cheers really rose up in 1978 when the mighty Welsh were beaten on Canberra's Manuka Oval by 21–20. Admittedly the Welsh did score four tries to ACT's one, and the referee was a local, but still, a victory it was!

Rugby's strength in Canberra was originally tied in with the presence of servicemen posted to the country's capital or to the Royal Military College at Duntroon. This dependence has waned somewhat and these days it is

young men native to the region who are coming through and staying with the game. Its most famous son, David Campese, is one of the top backs in the history of the game in Australia and though he played in Sydney in his later career, he still calls himself a local lad! It was Campese who led the way for ACT's most resounding international win, in 1983. He scored 19 points as the home team thrashed Argentina by 35–9.

B

'B' INTERNATIONALS

Played mostly among the countries of Britain and France. Some of the hardest games of the European season come in the 'B' matches, especially the Wales v France match, which has perhaps the strongest tradition and rivalry. It was played annually, alternating between each country, from 1970–89. Difficulties over dates for the match meant it was suspended in 1990.

Internationals involving 'B' teams have not been so popular in South Africa, Australia or New Zealand, though each has dabbled with the concept of fielding a 'second' team at some stage. From time to time New Zealand has fielded All Black teams that have been 'second' selections, but they have never been called a 'B' team. South Africans used to call their 'second' selection the 'Junior' Springboks. Australia fielded a 'B' team for the first time in 1988 when it met New Zealand.

For many years the biggest problem for any country having a second team has been how to decide who is eligible to play. Some countries have rules where any player who has been a full international at some stage is not then permitted to play in a 'B' match. Other countries are more liberal. Arrangements for eligibility are generally worked out between the two countries when they arrange to play each other.

BABY ALL BLACKS

After the unauthorised tour to South Africa in 1986 by senior All Blacks (the 'Cavaliers'), players who toured were banned for two test matches. The selectors had to cast further afield for a team to play a test against France in Christchurch and the first test against Australia at Wellington, choosing from younger or second-string players.

The relative youth and inexperience of the new team soon earned it the nickname 'Baby All Blacks'. The team's popularity was ensured when it beat France, 18–9 and lost narrowly, 12–13, to Australia.

The Baby Blacks included a number of players who were to become sea-soned All Blacks: David Kirk was their captain, while Joe Stanley, Sean Fitzpatrick, John Kirwan, Frano Botica, Terry Wright, Mike Brewer and Andy Earl all represented New Zealand for years.

BADELEY, CES

Auckland, North Auckland, and New Zealand

2 internationals for New Zealand 1921

Although he played first-class rugby between 1916 and 1928, and in 15 matches for New Zealand 1920–24, Ces Badeley is better known as the man who was briefly captain of the 1924 All Blacks.

Twenty-three of the players who later were to become the 'Invincibles' on their tour of Britain, France and Canada, first made a four-match visit to Sydney.

Badeley was the captain, but played only the first match because of a knee injury. Returning to New Zealand, the team, and Badeley, played two further matches, and the captain's play received wide praise.

Before the team had left for Sydney, the New Zealand union stated the captaincy would be reviewed before the British tour. Nevertheless, it was a surprise when, no sooner had Badeley made a speech on behalf of the team at a parliamentary farewell, than Cliff Porter was announced as captain.

In later years, Badeley supposed his knee injury was a reason, but it is possible that a clique of senior players privately decided on Porter during the voyage back from Sydney. Mark Nicholls was said to be a key factor in these deliberations as – like Badeley – he was a five-eighths, and a confident one at that: he was in no doubt he should play all the major matches.

The offhand treatment of Badeley didn't finish there. He played only the eighth and tenth games on the 32-match tour, despite being clearly fit to play, and his major activity for the rest of the tour was to act sometimes as back coach.

Once the team was well on track for its unbeaten record, Badeley had no chance of playing. The under-utilised young wing, Alan Robilliard, who himself had only four games in Britain and France, has said that the unbeaten record became paramount to the team and it was inevitable the top players would be fielded for most games.

BAHRAIN

Rugby is primarily played in Bahrain by expatriate workers from New Zealand, Australia and the United Kingdom. The Bahrain union was formed in 1972 and affiliated to the Gulf Rugby Union.

Enthusiasm for the game is high and results have been generally very good in their annual 15-a-side games against neighbouring states (Qatar, Abu Dhabi, Dubai, Sharjah, Muscat etc).

Bahrain has an excellent record in the annual Dubai Sevens tournament. Encouraged by this, the territory extended its horizons as far as the Hong Kong Sevens, in which it was first invited to play in 1978. The team is now a regular participant in this prestigious rugby occasion and the Bahrain players and spectators, with their colourful Arabic headwear, are an integral part of that tournament.

BAIRD, ROGER

Kelso and Scotland

27 internationals for Scotland 1981–88

4 internationals for British Isles 1983

A seemingly ageless wing who claimed a high number of caps. In the end, though, he might be remembered by the statisticians as the man who played on the wing for Scotland in 27 tests but who never managed to score a try.

The baby-faced Baird, a former schools' scrumhalf and an expert in the sevens game, was blessed with many talents. He was fast and elusive, and although slightly built, he had courage beyond his size. His speed was real: he once cleaned up three Scottish Borders track and field titles in one afternoon.

As a try-scorer, Baird had impressive credentials at every other level than for Scotland in test matches. His

Roger Baird

total of tries for the South of Scotland was a record, and he scored many in sevens rugby, including at the Melrose Sevens and on trips to the Hong Kong tournament. Whereas Baird did score one test try for the British Isles in New Zealand in 1983, in the third test in Dunedin, the honour of a test try for Scotland always eluded him.

Baird made his debut for Scotland as a 21-year-old against Australia at Murrayfield in 1981. He toured to New Zealand in 1981 and to Australia in 1982, and went back to New Zealand in Scotland's World Cup team in 1987, though he didn't play a game. His last international was against Ireland in Dublin in 1988.

The tactics employed by Scotland in the years Roger Baird played must have frustrated him enormously. He must have felt even more chagrined when one of the wings who followed him into the team, Tony Stanger – with arguably no more talent – had scored 10 tries in his first 13 tests.

BAJADA

A term given to the rugby world by Argentina. Bajada (also known as bajadita) was the name given to the style of pushing in a scrum where the hooker kept his feet back and the scrum pushed forward using the thrust of all eight men. While that in itself was not a new technique, Argentine teams, at both club and national level, shocked the rugby world with secret variations

of the eight-man shove in the early 1970s.

The results were often astounding. South African players and officials were perhaps the first outsiders to feel the power of bajada when the Buenos Aires club, San Isidro, took the technique to South Africa in 1973. The locals there were shocked to find their teams, with all of South Africa's history of powerful scrummaging, frequently pushed into a backslide.

Law changes have tended to deflate the power of the scrum in more recent years but the legacy of powerful scrummaging is still left with Argentine rugby today. The term 'bajada' (meaning 'downhill') deserves to be remembered.

BAKER, 'SNOWY'
New South Wales and Australia
2 internationals for Australia, 1904

Though Reg Baker's international career of playing halfback in both losses against the 1904 British side reads unglamorously, he is listed here as one of the sport's earliest all-rounders. He became the first man to represent Australia in five sports: rugby, boxing, polo, swimming and diving. He actually competed in 24 other different games! Among his greatest achievements was to represent Australia at boxing in the 1908 Olympic Games, where he lost the middleweight final to J.W.H.T. ('Johnny Won't Hit Today') Douglas, later an England cricket captain. For the record, the bout was refereed by Douglas's father!

After his brief rugby career, Baker settled in Hollywood where he taught film stars to ride, swim, fence and fight. He also starred on screen himself several times. By that time his younger brother Harald had also represented Australia in rugby and had won Australian titles in boxing, swimming, water polo, and wrestling. Harald Baker was a lock in three tests against New Zealand in 1914.

It goes without saying that 'Snowy' Baker won his nickname for having distinctive blond hair.

BALL BOYS

A vital part of the rugby game in New Zealand and Australia, but not always used in other parts of the rugby world. The ball boy's role is to field balls that fly across the touchline and return

them to the players so the game can be restarted without delay.

It is a duty much vied for by young rugby players who relish the opportunity to take part in a big occasion, and to watch their heroes close up.

BALLS

You cannot have a rugby match without a ball. The ball that William Webb Ellis picked up and ran with at Rugby School in 1823 was almost certainly similar in shape to the oval ball of today. Why Rugby School played with an oval football before running with it in one's hand was allowed is something of a mystery, but the evidence is that balls of that shape were used for many years before Webb Ellis attended the school.

It could be that different forms of football were traditionally played with a pig's bladder as the ball. Any good pig-hunter will tell you that a pig's bladder, when inflated, is basically oval in shape. When, by 1840, leather covers were made for the bladders, they were fitted to that shape.Thus today's rugby ball is a direct throwback to the pig's bladder balls that were kicked around the playing fields of Rugby School early in the nineteenth century. The 'feet only' game of association football adopted the round ball on its own.

The first rubber bladders were made in 1870. The last significant change to the rugby ball came in 1931 when the rather squat shape of the early ball, which made for easier place-kicking and drop-kicking, was replaced by a narrower, more torpedo-like shape that is able to be passed more easily. The length was shortened by one and a half inches (35mm).

For years South Africa favoured using an eight-panelled leather ball, as distinct from the standard four panels used elsewhere. In 1961 it joined the rest of the world in adopting the four panel ball. The only differences that now exist are the various brand names, synthetic leathers and the use of a ball that does not have the lace that used to hold the inner bladder in place.

BALLYMORE, BRISBANE

The headquarters of rugby in Brisbane, the Ballymore ground gives perhaps the closest and best view of the game from a major ground in Australia.

Before the building of Ballymore, the QRU hosted its test matches at either the Woollongabba Ground, the Brisbane Exhibition Ground or the Brisbane Cricket Ground. Ballymore's big advantage over the other venues is that it is essentially a rugby field, not a cricket ground as well. It is continually being improved, and in the 1980s grandstands were built along both touchlines which not only provided excellent close-up views, but made provision for the offices of the Queensland Rugby Union. There is a fine sports training and exercise facility situated behind the main grandstand.

The first major international match to be played on the ground was on June 18 1968, when the touring All Blacks beat Queensland by 34–3. Four days later the ground hosted its first test match when the All Blacks met the Wallabies in the last match of that tour. The All Blacks changed into their playing gear in a brown army tent and had their team-talk in an area of open ground behind the only grandstand.

It was a game tinged with controversy. Late in the game referee Kevin Crowe, a local identity, awarded a penalty try against Australia. When the try was converted from in front of the goalposts, the points gave the All Blacks a slender 19–18 winning margin.

Ballymore has had some great moments in its short history, none better, perhaps, than in 1971 when Queensland beat the British Isles – a team which went on to New Zealand where it beat every provincial team it faced.

The first rugby test on a Sunday was played at Ballymore on June 25 1972 when France beat Australia 16–15.

Ballymore has become a very hard ground for visiting teams to win on as, coupled with the rise in rugby standards in Queensland, is the fanatical support for their team from the local fans. A trip to Ballymore has become a character-testing experience for most of the world's top teams and players.

BANCROFT, BILLY
Swansea and Wales
33 internationals for Wales 1890–1901

One of Wales's first rugby heroes, W.J. ('Billy') Bancroft was a brilliant fullback. He was a master at punting and scoring points from place- or drop-kicks, and he was an elusive runner.

He played all his club football for Swansea, where he was idolised as one of its most famous sons.

In a statistical sense he is remembered as the first player to drop-kick a penalty goal in an international, v England at Cardiff in 1893, Wales's first home win over England.

Bancroft played his 33 internationals consecutively – a feat made even more impressive when it is remembered that he did not play against France or teams from New Zealand, Australia or South Africa and had the possibility of only three internationals per year.

Billy Bancroft was small in stature – only 5ft 5in (1.65 m) tall. His brother Jack was also a Welsh international fullback, playing 18 internationals between 1909 and 1914.

BANNERMAN, JOHN
Glasgow High School FP and Scotland
37 internationals for Scotland 1921–29

A robust lock, Bannerman is remembered as one of Scotland's great early players. Bannerman played his internationals consecutively and was also a Scottish captain. His 37 caps stood as a Scottish record until it was beaten in 1962 by Hugh McLeod. Interestingly, he never played in an international involving Australia, New Zealand or South Africa.

Bannerman was a Gaelic speaker, and later a prominent Scottish RU administrator (president in 1954–55), though one of the conservatives partly responsible for Scotland's bleak international record in the early 1950s. A Liberal politician, he became Lord Bannerman, a Life Peer, less than two years before his death.

BARBARIANS CLUB
It is said that the honour of playing for the Barbarians club in Britain is second only to playing for one's country, such is the prestige and tradition that has built up around this club since its inception in 1890.

The Barbarians club was formed in Bradford, in northern England, at a late night supper following a London invitation team's end of season tour. One of the players, W.P. ('Tottie') Carpmael, was enjoying himself so hugely that he became the driving force in a discussion and decision to form a club that could play end of season games, such as they had just

enjoyed, on a regular basis. Thus the Barbarians club was formed.

Several rules were set up that have become, a century later, quaint traditions. For instance, there are no meetings of the Barbarians in Britain: they conduct virtually all their business by telephone or post. Team selection is the same. A player is invited to play for the Barbarians – one cannot ask to join. There are no entry fees or subscriptions and the funding of the club is done from guarantees received from the host clubs for their traditional matches.

The honour and pleasure of playing for the Barbarians has arisen out of the club's mix of dignity, tradition and good old-fashioned rugby fun. The games the club plays are always exciting to watch, for it is the unwritten law of the Barbarians always to attack with the ball – even when attacking looks the craziest option to take. There are no recriminations afterwards for risks taken which do not come off.

The Barbarians' fixture list is built around an ongoing series of games, the first of which occurs over the Christmas holiday period at the Welford Road ground in Leicester against the local club team. Many a player has impressed the international selectors of his country by playing well in this game. Then on the first Thursday in March comes their match with the East Midlands county side at Northampton. This is the Mobbs' Memorial match, named in memory of

Edgar Mobbs, a Northampton club player, an England international and an outstanding Barbarian, who organised fund-raising matches for worthy war-time causes. (*See* MOBBS)

Easter completes the regular fixtures on the Barbarians' calendar. Two matches are played in South Wales, both of long-standing tradition. There is always a golf match between the players on the Sunday where tradition has it that new golfers must play with those who play regularly. Only one set of golf clubs is permitted for every four players on the course.

The Barbarians do undertake other games and tours. They have been overseas several times, notably to Canada and South Africa, with occasional visits to France. They sometimes play the home international countries, such as in 1915 when they played Wales in a British Red Cross fundraiser, when they played Scotland in 1970 and 1982, or when the club celebrated its centenary in 1990. There was even a rare game celebrating the Queen's Silver Jubilee in 1977, which was played against the Lions team recently returned from New Zealand.

The Barbarians are perhaps best known for the game they play against major touring teams who have been on full scale visits to Britain that season.

The tradition of this game began in 1947–48, when the Australian Wallabies were touring. More money was needed to boost the coffers and cope with the tour expenses, and scheduled games were running out. The Four Home Unions Committee, the body which organises major tours, felt that a Barbarians game would be a crowd-puller and a money-raiser.

It was by no means a foregone conclusion that the Barbarians committee would accept the invitation as it had been trying to cut down on its fixtures. There was also a certain reluctance to accept the match, as many rugby folk in Britain and Ireland were starting to see a Barbarians match as being the only occasion that a truly 'British' team would play at home. The Barbarians wanted to stay with their club traditions and not play as a representative team of the British Isles.

In the end the conditions of the game were acceptable to the club, and in the years since many millions of rugby fans have been grateful they were.

Phil Bennett playing for the Barbarians against the 1973 All Blacks. Mike Gibson is the player on the ground.

The traditional end-of-tour fixture has always been a thrilling spectacle and in almost every case the adventuresome rugby ideal has been adhered to.

Several of these games are amongst the most famous of all rugby history. Britons generally regard the match against the 1972–73 All Blacks as a classic. Gareth Edwards scored what has become known by some as 'the greatest try of all time' and the Barbarians went on to win 23–11.

New Zealanders might more readily recall the game early in 1964 when Wilson Whineray's All Blacks thrashed a powerful Barbarians team by 36–3. Whineray himself scored the last try and the sight of a prop selling a dummy to the last of the Barbarians defenders and then running on to score like a back delighted the huge Cardiff crowd, not to mention the thousands listening at home in New Zealand.

The 1961 game against South Africa was interesting as it was played in not quite the usual Barbarian spirit. The Springboks were unbeaten after 29 games, and great was the desire in Britain for at least one team to topple them. So the Barbarians played a tighter game for the first time in their

association with touring teams. The Springboks, on the other hand, although badly hit by injury, tried to play a bright game. The irony is that most of their winning rugby on that tour was dull to watch. So the match against the Barbarians brought about a juxtaposition – the Barbarians playing a conservative game, the Springboks with a carefree style. The Barbarians won, but there were those who questioned whether they had maintained the traditional spirit of the game.

There are several nice touches about the way some of the games against touring teams have been played. First, the Barbarians always try to include at least one uncapped player, which has led to several club players having their day in the spotlight. Some have gone on to become internationals.

On special occasions the Barbarians invite members of the touring team to play for the Barbarians against their own team-mates. This is done to downplay the image that has sometimes been promoted by the media – that Barbarians teams are almost Lions-like in appearance. So Wallaby Nick Shehadie played for the Barbarians against Australia in 1958, and Ian

Clarke of New Zealand did the same in 1964 (and actually scored the Barbarians' only points – with the now defunct goal from a mark). In more recent times leading French players have appeared in the end-of-tour game (Jean-Claude Skrela and Jean-Pierre Rives v New Zealand 1978 and Serge Blanco and Jérôme Gallion against Australia in 1984). Australian Nick Farr-Jones played for the club against the All Blacks in 1989.

The club celebrated its first 100 years in 1990 with special matches against England and Wales, for which Wales awarded full test caps. (England won 18–16 and the Barbarians beat Wales 34–21.) There was also a match against Bradford, in commemoration of the location of the club's founding. A match against the Pumas of Argentina was also played (won by 34–22).

This is arguably the most famous club in the world. It has no ground of its own, no clubhouse and virtually no money. Yet the 'Baa-Baas' (their monogram with gambolling lambs ensures the nickname) have done the game of rugby union a unique service by establishing traditions of great worth to the game everywhere.

Other Barbarians Clubs

The Barbarians idea was bound to be copied around the world and so far four of the major rugby-playing nations have Barbarians clubs. All operate on similar principles and concepts to the 'mother' club in Britain. Each club quotes the British Barbarians' motto: 'Rugby is a game for gentlemen of all classes, but never for a bad sportsman of any class.'

The New Zealand Barbarians were formed by two former All Blacks, Hugh McLean and Ron Bush, in 1937. Australia's equivalent club was established in 1956, South Africa's in 1960 and France's in 1980. (The French Barbarians' first game was on May 1 1980 in Agen, when Scotland was beaten 26–22.)

The South African club, which is based in the Natal coastal area, played its first overseas team in partnership with the Quaggas club, which was Transvaal-based. The Quaggas had played the Lions in 1974 (losing 16–20) before combining with the Barbarians to meet the All Blacks in 1976. If any old Barbarians in Britain were worried about the proper traditions of

the club being continued, they should have been at Ellis Park on this day! The Quagga-Barbarians stunned the All Blacks to lead 31–9 with 20 minutes to play. The outcome seemed obvious. But the All Blacks, under captain Andy Leslie, had other ideas. They threw attack upon attack at the opposition (which included two Irish internationals, Fergus Slattery and Tom Grace). Eventually the score reached 31–28, and the crowd was calling for the referee to blow his whistle for full-time and a famous victory. But there was time for just one more play.

The All Blacks bustled the home team backwards, won the ball and it went spinning to wing Terry Mitchell, who so far had had a modest tour and had seldom been in the spotlight. But in this moment his hands were secure and he flew in to score in the corner for one of the great comeback wins by any team – and one of the greatest games ever seen in South Africa. The Barbarians may have been in combination with the Quaggas, but the spirit of 'Tottie' Carpmael and the other forefathers of the club was intact!

The South African Barbarians had their first solo game against a touring team in 1980, when they lost 14–25 to the British Isles.

The New Zealand and Australian clubs have a reasonably regular exchange of tours, the highlight being a Barbarian's 'test match' (not that the Barbarians club would ever countenance such a title!).

New Zealand Barbarians have played the Barbarians club in Britain once, in 1987, with the New Zealand side winning 68–16!

BASQUET, GUY
Agen and France
33 internationals for France 1945–52

One of the most influential players in France's rugby history, Guy Basquet was the man many claim led France out of the wilderness and into respectability as a rugby power.

At the time of Basquet's debut, France tended to allow its opponents to win rather easily, but from his position of No. 8, Basquet developed discipline and drills. His greatest day as a player came in 1951 when he led France to its first win against England on Twickenham. On a day when the French back row trio could claim the

triumph virtually as theirs alone, Basquet scored one of the tries.

He ended his playing career in 1952, still as captain, and was hailed as the one player who had shown France's leading players how to approach and succeed in international fixtures. While Basquet was captain there were no thrashings for the French XV.

He later had a further influence on French rugby when he became chairman of the national selectors. He was the coach of the French team to New Zealand in 1961. In 1990 he was still involved in the administration of the game in France.

BASTIAT, JEAN-PIERRE
Dax and France
32 internationals for France 1969–78

Jean-Pierre Bastiat was first capped as a lock against Romania in 1969. Although he played his first 10 internationals as a second-rower, it was as a No. 8 that he made his reputation.

The 2 metres (6ft 6in) tall Bastiat was part of a thrilling French loose forward trio, with Jean-Pierre Rives and Jean-Claude Skrela. He could run as well, and was also the French goal-kicker in several games. Although injuries and unavailability disrupted his career, Bastiat became one of the most feared forwards of his day.

He was appointed the French captain in 1977–78, his last season. Under his leadership France won its first three championship games; in the same season so did Wales. The two teams met at Cardiff Arms Park, with the Grand Slam at stake. Sadly for Bastiat and France, Wales was too good and won 16–7.

In later years Bastiat became a French selector.

BATH RFC
The spa town in south-west England was once famous for its Roman baths. In sporting terms, the Bath Rugby Club emerged in the 1980s as one of the most powerful English clubs. Formed in 1865, the club's blue, white and black colours have been seen on its two main grounds (the Recreation Ground and Horse Show Ground) ever since.

Ronald Gerrard held the club record for most appearances for England (14 internationals from 1932–36) for 50 years. Gerrard, winner of the DSO, was killed in action in World War II. His widow, Molly, later became club president, making Bath one of the first clubs in England to have a woman president. She is also reputed to be the first, if not the only woman to have provided a radio commentary of a rugby match.

John Hall, the loose forward, set a new club record for appearances for England in the 1986–87 season. By the end of 1990 he had reached 20 caps.

In Bath's champion team of the 1980s there were many past or present international players, including Richard Hill, John Hall, Stuart Barnes, Jeremy Guscott, John Palmer and Gareth Chilcott, all of whom had represented England. The club's senior prop in those years was David Sole, who played for Scotland in the Five Nations championship as well as the 1987 World Cup. Other well-known players to play for the club include John Horton, David Trick and John Kendall-Carpenter.

In its very successful sequence of John Player Cup wins in the 1980s, Bath was brilliantly coached by Jack Rowell. After its win in the 1990 Pilkington Cup, Bath had won six of the last seven finals.

BATTY, GRANT

Wellington, New Zealand
15 internationals for N. Zealand 1972–77

The Scottish TV commentator Bill McLaren best described this busy and talented All Black. He said that Batty went at his game like a 'little buzz-saw', and indeed he did.

Grant Batty was a rarity in All Black rugby of the early 1970s. He was a back (a wing mostly) who had genuine speed, aggression and inventiveness. Although small in stature, he was never one to step back from a physical confrontation, no matter how imposing his 'opponent' might have been. Not everyone in New Zealand could cope with a player of his brilliance and physical approach, and although New Zealanders were more than grateful on several occasions for his feisty presence on the field, he was always regarded as 'controversial'.

Batty was received in a similar light wherever he played in the rugby world. Cardiff crowds booed him when he

Grant Batty bursting through against Cambridge University, 1972.

played there with the All Blacks in 1972–73. He replied by playing brilliantly. South African crowds treated him the same way. Batty responded by showing immense courage and playing on even after sustaining a near-crippling knee injury. Such was his value to the All Blacks that they insisted on playing him in the tests even though he had to run about with a metal cast hidden under his knee bandages.

In 1977 Batty played for the All Blacks in what was to be his last test match, at Athletic Park in Wellington, for the first test against Phil Bennett's British Isles team. The Lions, leading by 12 points to 10, were on attack in the first half. Halfback Brynmor Williams made a break and in a flash he had four men outside him and only Batty ahead. A try for the Lions was a certainty.

This was the kind of situation little Batty relished and he dashed forward among the Lions attackers. Perhaps aware of his approaching presence and the possibility of being in receipt of a typically hard Batty tackle, one of the Lions flung a pass too high. Batty nipped in for the interception and headed off for the try-line 50 metres away. Though his knee had slowed

him down considerably there was no holding him back. He ran on to score a try that was later dubbed a '12-pointer' by the Lions coach John Dawes.

Expecting a score of 18–10 and a fairly safe bet for a victory, the Lions instead were suddenly down 12–16. And that's how the score stayed to the end. Batty with his 'buzz-saw' approach became the match-winner.

Sadly, Batty's knee problems became so bad he was forced out of rugby at the age of 25.

Controversial he might have been, but the crowds in New Zealand and elsewhere always flocked in to watch Grant Batty. Love him or hate him, they had to see him play.

BAXTER, JAMES

Birkenhead Park, and England
3 internationals for England 1900

Respected as a diligent and determined administrator in England, but reviled in New Zealand as the man who stole the All Blacks' birthright, 'Bim' Baxter holds a key place in rugby history.

Already a member of the IRB, and England team manager to Argentina in 1927, Baxter was appointed manager of the 1930 British touring team to New Zealand and Australia.

There he was outspoken, to say the least, in his denunciation of the New Zealand wing forward position. (A wing forward was a marauder who stood off the 2-3-2 scrum and usually fed it for the halfback. He also hounded opposition inside backs.) Manager Baxter stated the wing forward was 'nothing more than a cheat', and his influence on the world scene led to the framing of laws which effectively stamped out the two-man front row, and with it the wing forward position.

Baxter was also highly critical of the game of rugby league. When being shown the sights of Auckland, Carlaw Park, the local rugby league ground, was pointed out to him. Baxter offered a quip that has always been quoted by Kiwi league followers when their rivalry with rugby union is discussed. Baxter said of the park, 'Every town must have its sewers.'

Baxter was an international referee on nine occasions and was on the IRB from 1926–39. A silver medal-winning yachtsman at the 1908 Olympics, Baxter was also deeply involved in golf and rowing.

BAY OF PLENTY RFU

Founded in 1911 and headquartered in Rotorua, this rugby province has one of the widest areas in New Zealand from which to pick its talent for its one first class representative team. It is broken up into five sub-unions and within these sub-unions there are nearly 50 clubs.

The Bay had a great moment in 1976 when it won the first national provincial first division championship. Considering the province had never won the Ranfurly Shield, this was an outstanding accomplishment. The coach of the team in that season was the 1960 All Black prop, Eric Anderson.

The Bay's best known international player is perhaps Hika Reid, who made his debut for New Zealand in 1980 as a hooker. He served the All Blacks for six years, though for some of them he was understudy to Andy Dalton.

Victories over touring teams have been hard to come by for Bay of Plenty. It managed a win over Fiji in 1970, but it was in 1982 that it had its first great win. Bay of Plenty met the Wallabies at Rotorua's Stadium and, though Australia was fresh from a test win over the All Blacks, the Bay crushed the tourists 40–16! Hika Reid, enormously popular with the big crowd, scored two tries. The Bay also beat Australia in 1990.

In 1981 Bay of Plenty had played a thriller against South Africa, only to lose 24–29. For that game it was helped by another member of the 1976 All Blacks in South Africa, Kevin Eveleigh. Formerly with Manawatu and for a time in Zimbabwe, the flanker played outstandingly, scoring one of the tries for the home team.

Rotorua also provided the venue for the most exciting game of the 1959 British Isles tour of New Zealand. Bay of Plenty combined with players from neighbouring Thames Valley to play an open, dashing game which thoroughly appealed to the huge crowd. There was a high state of excitement in Rugby Park when wing Ray Wells of Thames Valley scored a try to take the lead late in the game by 24–21. The noise of the crowd was so loud that it could be heard all over Rotorua !

But these Lions had style and character. They came back and scored a last minute try (by Ken Scotland) which Malcolm Thomas converted, to win the game 26–24.

BEAUMONT, BILL

Fylde and England
34 internationals for England 1975–82
7 internationals for British Isles 1977–80

William Blackledge Beaumont was just a lad of 11 when England won the Five Nations championship in 1963. When England next won the championship in March 1980, Beaumont was six days past his 28th birthday and was captain of the team. It was England's first championship win for 16 years, and its first Grand Slam for 23 years, and it ensured Beaumont a prominent niche in that country's rugby history.

In the 1970s a depression hung over English rugby – five times in that decade it had finished last in the Five Nations championship. The first signs of resurgence came when Beaumont, who had been a lower grade fullback at his club eight years before and an England lock for four years, led the Northern Division of England to victory over the 1979 All Blacks. His quiet style and unassuming manner belied a determination to succeed on the field. These qualities were somehow transferred to the England team of 1980 and, with Bill Beaumont's example to follow, its season of glory was won.

Beaumont led the British Isles to South Africa in 1980, a controversial tour accompanied by anti-apartheid protests in many parts of the world.

Bill Beaumont played well on the field and off it behaved with quiet dignity and respect. Sadly, his Lions team was not able to win for him another notable victory, going down 1–3 in the series.

Bill Beaumont (with the ball) with Derek Quinnell (left) and Brynmor Williams, on tour with the British Isles, 1977.

Beaumont was a lock who had deceptive pace around the field and excellent ball skills. He was a front-of-the-lineout jumper and his strength at scrum time was a grand help to many an English international effort.

Beaumont's playing career came to an abrupt end. In the 1982 English county final he complained about a head injury, which had affected him in several previous games, and he left the field. Beaumont took medical advice and quit the game, right at the peak of his powers.

There was great sadness in English rugby circles but the ever-cheerful Beaumont carried on, making a name for himself as a TV commentator and TV sports quiz panellist.

BEBB, DEWI
Carmarthen Trinity College, Swansea and Wales
34 internationals for Wales 1959–67
8 internationals for British Isles 1962–66

Dewi Bebb was a fast and elusive wing who made a spectacular start to his international rugby career by scoring

Dewi Bebb in a typical bursting run.

the winning try for Wales against England at Cardiff, surely a feat that will hold him dear to Welsh fans for life!

In 1962 Bebb toured South Africa with the British Isles and four years later toured to Australia and New Zealand, again with the Lions. He played in eight tests for the Lions, and this, coupled with 34 caps for Wales, makes him one of that country's most capped players.

Bebb had real speed on the wing and is remembered as a stylish and inventive player. After his retirement from active rugby in 1967 he pursued a career in sports reporting and became a familiar television performer for Harlech TV in Cardiff.

BEDELL-SIVRIGHT, 'DARKIE'
Cambridge University, Edinburgh University and Scotland
22 internationals for Scotland 1900–08
1 international for Great Britain 1904

One of the first men in rugby to gain a reputation for being a tough, hard-nosed footballer, D.R. Bedell-Sivright (spelled Bedell-Sievewright by some historians) was a vigorous forward (and a Scottish heavyweight boxing champion), perhaps a forerunner of the tough men of later generations.

There were some who disapproved of Bedell-Sivright's uncompromising methods, considering them 'ungentlemanly'. Nevertheless he built an excellent record in the Scottish forward pack.

He was chosen as captain of the Great Britain team that toured Australia and New Zealand in 1904. Winning that position ahead of an Englishman was perhaps the greatest tribute paid to 'Darkie', as the team was chosen by the (English) Rugby Football Union.

Bedell-Sivright, whose brother John also played for Scotland, was for a time a stock-rearer in Australia. He died of blood-poisoning at Gallipoli during World War I.

BEDFORD RFC
Bedford, whose players turn out in light blue and dark blue wide-hooped jerseys, was founded in 1886. Its headquarters are at Goldington Road Ground in Bedford.

Surprisingly, its percentage of England caps is not high but it has had several very prominent players.

D.P. ('Budge') Rogers played 34 internationals for his country, a record at the time, and after his retirement from an outstanding career as a loose forward, he was prominent as an England selector.

A character from Bedford was G.T. ('Beef') Dancer. He was one of the toughest forwards in England in the years before World War II but he did not, it seems, impress the England selectors sufficiently. However, in 1938 Dancer caught the attention of the British Isles selectors, who sent him in their team to South Africa where he played in all three tests.

Also from Bedford and well-known, perhaps for other reasons, is Danny Hearn. He was a solid and dependable centre three-quarter and an England international. His career was tragically cut short when he was crippled by a massive neck injury in a game against the 1967 All Blacks (when playing for Midlands, London and Home Counties).

BEDFORD, TOMMY
Natal and South Africa
25 internationals for Sth Africa 1963–71

A brilliant flanker and No. 8 for the Springboks in the 1960s, 'Tearaway' Tommy Bedford was a first choice for South Africa for nine seasons, apart from the time he spent in Britain studying at Oxford University.

Bedford's baby face belied his ferocious desire to be successful as a rugby player and captain. He was a speedster from loose play who could be a dynamic and dominating presence on the field, especially in combination with Piet Greyling and Jan Ellis – together they formed one of South Africa's most potent loose forward trios.

He made his debut for the Springboks against Australia in 1963. He played as a flanker, but it was at No. 8 that he was to make his biggest impression on the rugby scene.

While studying architecture at Oxford University on a Rhodes Scholarship, he made three appearances against Cambridge University at Twickenham. He led Oxford to victory in 1967, a win he regards as one of the most satisfying of his career.

Bedford's knowledge of British players and conditions was of considerable value on the tour there by the 1969–70 Springboks, and he provided vital tactical assistance to the team's

'Tearaway' Tommy Bedford

captain, Dawie de Villiers. That tour was marked by extensive anti-apartheid demonstrations in the United Kingdom and Ireland, and the 1971 South African tour to Australia was also an unhappy affair because of anti-tour protests. It was also a disappointment to Bedford, who suffered a serious facial injury and had to return home after playing only three matches.

Tommy Bedford never played a test against the All Blacks. He toured New Zealand in 1965 and was certain to be a first choice player, but he broke an arm in the third tour match against Wellington. By the time of the next clash between these two countries in 1970, Bedford was out of favour as a player and potential captain and was not picked.

Bedford captained his country in three of his 25 test match appearances. Later in his career he was to become outspoken, both in his opinions on rugby in South Africa and life in general in that country.

BEHOTEGUY, ANDRE
Bayonne, Cognac and France
19 internationals for France 1923–29

A French centre three-quarter of the 1920s who played in 19 internationals (including five with his brother Henri).

André Behoteguy was unique in rugby, as he played every match wearing a black beret!

BEKKER FAMILY
An outstanding Northern Transvaal sporting family which deserves its place in a rugby encyclopedia, even though some members of the family represented their country in other sports.

The best known member was H.P.J. (Jaap) Bekker, a tough prop who made his debut for the Springboks in the 1951–52 tour of Britain. In 1953 his brother Dolf played with Jaap in the Springbok team in two of the tests against the visiting Australians. Dolf had the same strong build as his brother, but had speed as well, and played for his country on the wing.

Jaap Bekker played a vital role in the Springboks' plans on their tour of New Zealand in 1956 and was known as one of the toughest props ever to visit that country. He had a massive chest measurement and only the famous New Zealand strong man of the time, Kevin Skinner, was able to contain him.

The family involvement in rugby continued after the retirement of Jaap and Dolf Bekker. In 1960, a younger brother, Martiens, also made his way into the Springbok rugby team as a prop. Martiens played against Scotland but later missed selection for the Springboks for the 1960–61 tour of Britain.

Another member of the family, Daan, went to the 1956 Melbourne Olympics as a heavyweight boxer in the South African team. He performed well in the tough competition and won a bronze medal. Four years later, in Rome, Daan went one better and won the silver medal.

A sister, Corrie, made it through to South African representation in track and field. Thus the Bekker family, in rugby, boxing, and track and field, is remembered as one of the most accomplished families of South African sport.

BELGIUM
Belgian rugby has come under the influence of both its powerful rugby-playing neighbours. British expatriates started the game in Antwerp by forming a club in 1920. Five or so years later, Frenchmen living in Brussels formed a second club.

The Belgium RFU was founded in 1931 although the country's first international was a match with Holland in 1930. Belgium became affiliated to FIRA in 1934, just two months after it had been formed. Official FIRA championships did not start until 1973–74 and Belgium played in its first European competition as an entry in Division III in 1979. Though the team has had a number of victories it has never made it to the élite of FIRA competitions, the Group A series.

Rugby is well established in Belgium and in 1981 the union celebrated its 50 years of existence with a special tournament.

Belgium's entry to the second Rugby World Cup featured games in a qualifying group in Madrid in 1989. Sadly for the development of their game, the Belgians sustained only losses: to Poland (23–25), Netherlands (12–32) and Spain (6–58).

BENESIS, RENE
Narbonne, Agen and France
30 internationals for France 1969–74

A tough forward who made a successful international career as a hooker, especially when playing between his two Basque props, Jean Iraçabal and Jean-Louis Azarete. Together they powered their way through most of the scrums they opposed. Their total of 14 tests as a unit was just two short of the French record of the time, which was set in the early 1960s by Domenech, de Gregorio and Roques.

Benesis was a product of Narbonne, where he began playing first as a No. 8, then a prop, before settling as a hooker. As a junior he was an international in all three positions. He switched to the powerful Agen club and was a member of the team which won the club championship in 1976.

Benesis made his international debut in 1969 in an 8–8 draw with Wales at Stade Colombes. It was the first time in 10 matches that the French had not lost. The tide seemed to turn for the team, for it lost only once in the next 10 matches.

Benesis once said about rugby, 'I am heavily indebted to the game. It has opened many doors for me and widened my horizons. I pay my debt to it in 80-minute instalments, by playing with all my heart and hoping that I will never betray the game's true spirit.'

BENNETT, PHIL
Llanelli and Wales
29 internationals for Wales 1969–78
8 internationals for British Isles 1974–77

A brilliant flyhalf, Phil Bennett was capable of breaking open a game with his dazzling footwork and sheer darting speed off the mark. There was no better example of this than in the New Zealand v Barbarians match at Cardiff in 1973. Three sidesteps of prodigious width by Bennett, who was deep in his own half, led to an attack from which the Barbarians halfback, Gareth Edwards, scored one of rugby's greatest tries.

Bennett's early rugby was played in the shadow of the great Barry John, and it was not until John's retirement that he came to be a permanent member of the Welsh team. He played some exciting rugby in South Africa in 1974 when a member of the British Isles team. His jinking, weaving try from 50 metres in the second test is still considered a classic.

Three years later he was a surprise choice as the Lions' captain on their tour to New Zealand and Fiji – a surprise inasmuch as it was feared that the natural modesty of the man might affect his ability to lead the mixed-nations Lions group. History might judge that to have been true, but Bennett played extremely well on that

The distinctive, slightly hunched running style of Phil Bennett.

tour and some of his tries and attacking plays to set up others will always be remembered in New Zealand. He was only the second Welshman to captain a Lions team.

After his retirement from international play, Bennett continued to give loyal service to his club, Llanelli. He played an excellent game for the Barbarians against the 1978 All Blacks and he was still around in 1980 to play for Llanelli against Graham Mourie's All Blacks.

BERBIZIER, PIERRE
Agen and France
56 internationals for France 1981–91

A brilliant and long-serving French halfback who scored his country's only try in the Rugby World Cup final of 1987. He lost – but regained – his place in the French team after one of the confusing and bitter political rows that have periodically marked France's rugby history.

A former centre and fullback, Berbizier played his first international in 1981 against Scotland. He immediately proved a vital acquisition to the French team for, in his first season, France won the Grand Slam in the Five Nations competition.

But Berbizier was by no means guaranteed a regular place in the seasons that followed. He shared the scrumhalf position with Gérard Martinez, Jean-Pierre Elissalde and Jérôme Gallion until 1985.

On the French tour of Argentina he cemented his place in the team, and played 30 out of the next 32 internationals. In that time the cheeky style of Berbizier won him world-wide respect. He was speedy and sharp, a good runner with excellent tactical instincts.

Berbizier was the top French halfback in the Rugby World Cup squad of 1987. He played in five of France's six games, including the final where his try, late in the game, gave his country some consolation for defeat at the hands of New Zealand. By that time, although Daniel Dubroca was the French captain, Berbizier was being called 'the director of play' and was being tipped not only to be the next captain, but the next coach as well.

The first of those predictions came true. Berbizier was an excellent captain, but slowly found himself at odds

Pierre Berbizier

with his coach, Jacques Fouroux. The story of the spat between the two 'big' men of French rugby became big rugby news in France. Though Berbizier had been his captain and confidante and had greatly influenced the French team through six championship wins, Fouroux dropped him from his squad in 1990.

Fouroux himself quickly followed, so Berbizier had the last laugh when he was brought back for the Five Nations series of 1990–91 by the new coach, Daniel Dubroca.

BERMUDA
Bermuda has 365 islands in its group but only 22 square miles of land mass. However, that is sufficient for a number of enthusiastic rugby clubs and the game has been played in the islands for well over 100 years.

Bermudan rugby struggled for some years until British clubs realised that, in the jet age, the islands were close enough to be the perfect place for end-of-season tours.

The Bermuda Rugby Football Union was formed in 1964 and when the Caribbean championship was started in 1977, Bermuda won the first three.

In recent years Bermuda has hosted several highly successful World Classic tournaments for former international players aged over 35. New Zealand teams won the first two tournaments in 1989 and 1990.

BERTRANNE, ROLAND
Bagnères and France
69 internationals for France 1971–81

He was France's most-capped player for nine years. Roland Bertranne was a centre three-quarter who survived the traditional vagaries of French selection panels for a decade to become one of the most dependable players in his position in the world. He hailed from Bagnères, a small village on the lower slopes of the French Pyrenees which also gave Jean-Michel Aguirre to the French teams of the 1970s.

He was a sharp three-quarter, often brilliant on the dashing run. There was no shortage of this ability in French back lines, but he was probably a survivor because he was a solid player – which could not always be counted on to the same extent in some others.

Bertranne began his international career at Twickenham in the Five Nations series of 1971. Within months he was in South Africa with the French team which drew one test and lost one on a short tour. He remained in international football for 10 years and completed his career with two tests against Graham Mourie's All Blacks in 1981.

BETTARELLO, STEFANO
Rovigo, Benetton Treviso, Mogliano and
   Italy
51 internationals for Italy 1979–87

One of Italy's greatest players, Bettarello was a brilliant flyhalf and a prodigious points-scorer – the first player in world rugby to score more than 400 points in full internationals. But in no way could Bettarello be called just a kicker. He was first an attacker and could, and did, score test match tries. He was a sharp runner, dummied well and his sidestep was legendary. He was a pupil of the great Welshman Carwyn James, when he coached at Rovigo.

Stefano Bettarello was the third in his family to play rugby union for his country. His father, Romano, was capped twice in the 1950s and his uncle, Ottorino, three times, 1958–61.

Stefano made his debut for Italy against Poland in 1979. In 1983 on the Italian tour of Canada, he scored 29 points against Canada, which was then a world's best for one player in an international between any two countries.

Sadly for Bettarello and Italy, he had to miss the 1987 Rugby World Cup when he was unable to take time off from his salesman's job. At that time he was the second highest capped Italian player of all time; he had scored more than 450 points for his country and more than 2000 points in the Italian league.

He had also played for the Barbarians in England and attempts were made for a while to lure him to play for Toulouse, then the champion club in France.

BEZIERS
The most powerful club in France in the 1970s, Béziers won seven French championships in that decade and 10 in the 15 years before 1985. The club also provided the French national team with some of the top players of the era.

But the Béziers story is more than just about winning. The club's distinctive style was based on tough, hard forward play. Such a style had been unheard of before in France's club rugby history and the team soon built up the reputation of nurturing rugby supermen. Not all the public reaction to Béziers was one of admiration: in many parts of France the hard-nosed methods of this great French club were regarded with disfavour, sometimes hostility.

Béziers is a Mediterranean city with a population of less than 100,000. It is more than 800 kilometres (500 miles) from Paris but in many championship finals in the 1970s the capital thrilled to the awesome power of Béziers rugby.

It first made it to the final in 1960, losing to Lourdes which had dominated the championship in the 1950s. In the Béziers team that year was a young man named Raoul Barrière, a prop. A year later he was with Béziers when it won the title for the first time. Barrière played for his country in South Africa in 1958, where he had come to admire the uncompromising attitudes of South African forwards.

When Barrière became coach of Béziers in 1968–69, the club's fortunes swiftly began to improve. By 1970 his influence had caused Béziers rugby to become an expression of toughness and brute force in the forwards, assisted by backs only when the hard work had been done up front.

With this new formula, the number of wins for the club soon increased. So too did honours for the Béziers players. Against Ireland in 1972, seven of the French XV were Béziers men. There were 12 and 10 internationals respectively in their teams which won the championship finals of 1977 and 1978. Some of those names were among the most famous French rugby men of the

*Italy's most famous rugby player, Stefano Bettarello (left), with his father, Romano,
also an international player.*

day: Richard Astre, Jack Cantoni, Henri Cabrol, Alain Estève, Olivier Saisset (later a Béziers coach as well), Michel Palmie, Alain Paco, Armand Vaquerin, and Pierre Lacans are just some of those who played for France during the golden era of Béziers.

By 1984 and the 11th championship win, Claude Saurel was the coach and Pierre Lacans the captain. Tragedy struck the club in 1985 when Lacans lost his life in a car accident.

The club was founded in 1911.

BLACKHEATH FC

The world's oldest independent rugby club, founded in 1858. Rugby was introduced to Blackheath Proprietary School by an old boy of Rugby who had taken up a teaching post at Blackheath. The club was formed when boys wanted to play the new game after leaving school. Soon there was an annual match between 'School' and 'The Club' with rules similar to those played at Rugby.

Once the Blackheath Football Club was formed other 'football' clubs, notably Richmond, took to playing rugby as well as playing that other game where you use only your feet! Blackheath drew up some laws for the game of rugby in 1862 and the next year delegates from the club were present, with several other interested bodies, when the Football Association (today the parent body of soccer in Britain) was formed. There were some enormous problems to surmount in the framing of laws to the satisfaction of all the clubs involved. That this proved impossible led to Blackheath breaking away from the FA, and the eventual formation of an official 'carrying game' in 1871, when Blackheath and 20 other clubs formed the Rugby Football Union.

Later the same year the club supplied the first England captain, Fred Stokes, who led his team in the game's first international, England v Scotland.

In 1883 the club moved to its present ground, Rectory Field, and many of England's international matches were played there until the time Twickenham was purchased. The first overseas touring team to play there was the 'Natives' of New Zealand in 1889. It beat Blackheath but lost to England on the same ground.

It was Blackheath which introduced many of the first subtleties in the art of playing rugby. For instance it made best use of the 1877 law change which required players to release the ball in a tackle. The red-and-blacks of Blackheath would use their forwards to clear the ball back quickly, rather than have them struggle into yet another long and pointless wrestling maul.

But its position as one of England's leading clubs was slowly eroded by accusations from some quarters that Blackheath was a place for the snobs of rugby's society. These took many years to shrug off, and for several decades Blackheath's top team was not of the highest quality.

Nevertheless Blackheath supplied scores of England internationals. Harry 'Jumbo' Vassall, a forward who scored four tries in his debut international (against Wales in 1881), was deemed the greatest player of the Victorian era, a tribute to the manner in which he influenced both Oxford University and Blackheath to pass the ball in planned moves that revolutionised the game.

Blackheath's most-capped player was the brilliant England wing Cyril Lowe who played 25 times for England between 1913 and 1923. Another top player was the scrumhalf Arthur Young, who had 18 caps, as did 'Cherry' Pillman and Leonard Brown. Carl Aarvold, a member of the 1930 Great Britain team's back line in New Zealand, was a Blackheath man.

The number of international players from Blackheath had all but dried up by 1990. Mike Bulpitt, the 1970 England player, was the club's only England international of the past 20 years.

BLACKROCK COLLEGE

One of the most famous clubs in Ireland, Blackrock College has provided some of the top players for the Irish international team, as well as for the British Isles. The club was founded in 1882.

Well-known Blackrock College players include Fergus Slattery (the club's most-capped individual with 61 tests for Ireland), Ray McLoughlin, Hugo MacNeill, Mick Doyle, Willie Duggan and Niall Brophy – all members of various Lions teams.

BLANCO, SERGE
Biarritz Olympique and France
85 internationals for France 1980–91

Capable of being the most brilliant running fullback in the world, Serge Blanco could sometimes play indifferent rugby, gaining him a reputation, especially in Australia and New Zealand, for inconsistency. His goal-

The world's highest-capped player, Serge Blanco (right) with Didier Codorniou.

Top: Argentina plays New Zealand at Ferrocaril Oeste Stadium in Buenos Aires, 1985.
Below: Serge Blanco prepares for a kick at goal. Peter Bush

Top: Serge Blanco shows his form as he evades Scotland's Peter Dods in their 1989 Five Nations championship game.
Fotopacific
Below: Blanco kicks, watched by Denis Charvet (centre) and Patrice Lagisquet. Peter Bush

kicking was the same: he could land the most sensational goal one day but miss an easy one the next.

Born in Caracas, Venezuela in 1958, Blanco has lived most of his life in the south of France. In his early career he was equally at home as fullback or wing but later he was to specialise as a fullback.

He first came to the notice of the rugby world when he played a brilliant game against the 1977 All Blacks for a French selection in Agen. After playing nine matches for France 'B' he joined the French touring team in New Zealand in 1979, though he did not play in either of the internationals.

His debut in a test match came in 1980 in Pretoria against South Africa, and after 1981 he rarely missed a game for France.

In 1983 Blanco scored 36 points in Five Nations championship matches, beating the record Guy Camberabero had set in 1967.

At the first World Cup in 1987 his play was hampered by a thigh injury, but he still managed to score the match-winning try against Australia in the thrilling semi-final in Sydney. He played in the World Cup final against New Zealand but was not at his absolute best, again because of injury.

He became France's captain for the tour of Australia in 1990. There, at the age of 31, he showed he could still outsprint most opposing players. His 90-metre try in the second test at Brisbane was immediately recognised as one of the best ever seen in a test. Blanco retained the captaincy – and was assistant coach for the home series with New Zealand in 1990.

In 1991 he became the world's most-capped player and, but for his announced pending retirement, could have become the first rugby player to approach 100 test appearances.

BLAZEY, CES

A long-serving New Zealand rugby administrator who won prominence on the world scene when he became a member of the International Board (1964–86) and the International Laws Committee (1972–85).

Blazey took over from Jack Sullivan as the chairman of the New Zealand Rugby Football Union in 1977 and held that position through the stormy years of 1981 and 1985 when controversy raged throughout New Zealand

New Zealand administrator, Ces Blazey, who gave 50 years of service to New Zealand and world rugby.

about whether rugby contacts should be continued with South Africa.

The New Zealand union, under Blazey, invited South Africa to tour in 1981. When the tour took place, massive and highly organised anti-apartheid protests brought civil disorder the likes of which New Zealand had never seen before. In 1985 the NZRFU accepted an invitation to tour South Africa, against the wishes of the New Zealand Government. Only a High Court injunction taken out by two lawyers stopped the tour going ahead. Blazey was forced to announce the cancellation of the tour because of disruption to the schedule caused by the court case.

Ces Blazey became a household name and an instantly recognisable figure in New Zealand because of his many appearances on television and in newspapers defending the NZRFU's decision to continue to associate with South Africa. He operated with a high degree of control and dignity and won respect, from friend and foe, as a person of resolution and determination.

He retired from his role in rugby in 1986 after 50 years as a New Zealand and world rugby administrator.

BLEDISLOE CUP

The Bledisloe Cup was presented in 1931 by Lord Bledisloe, then Governor-General of New Zealand, as a trophy to be played between the test teams of Australia and New Zealand. Lord Bledisloe's gesture has led to some fierce competition for the cup over the years.

Matches are played either in a test series, with the trophy going to the series winner or, as adopted in the 1970s, to the winner of a single match between the two nations when there is just one match played in a season.

The first game for the trophy was played at Eden Park in Auckland in 1931, New Zealand winning by 20–13. The game, played in front of Lord Bledisloe, was notable for the small crowd that turned out (only 15,000) and for the scoring of 14 points by the New Zealand fullback, Ron Bush of Otago. It was then the New Zealand record for the greatest number of points scored in a test match, let alone a debut, though Bush did not get to play for his country again.

In the history of Bledisloe Cup matches since, New Zealand has had a distinct edge. In the 60 years until 1991, Australia won only 17 games while New Zealand won 52. There were four draws. .

A measure of the delight Australians have in winning the cup could be gauged by their players' reaction when they beat the All Blacks 12–6 in Sydney in 1979. They picked up the huge trophy and running at top speed, they and their coach Dave Brockhoff took it on a victory lap which had the big crowd roaring with delight.

New Zealanders in the crowd could only gape. Had the All Blacks won the trophy so often they had forgotten the significance of it? Since then there has been an increased intensity by All Black teams when they play the vastly improved Wallabies with the Bledisloe Cup at stake.

Australia has only won a series in New Zealand twice, in 1949 and 1986.

BOLAND RU

Based at Wellington, 50 kilometres (30 miles) from Cape Town, this provincial union has been in action only since 1939. Players from the Cape Province region were affiliated to Western Province until transport difficulties, plus rapid population growth, led to the formation of the new union.

Boland played its first major touring team in 1949 when its hard forwards pushed the New Zealand All Blacks to a narrow 8–5 win. Playing for the Boland team was a young prop, Chris Koch, who played his way into the South African team for three tests against those All Blacks and then went on to become one of South Africa's greatest Springboks and its greatest cap-winner for a time, with 22.

Boland had to wait until 1969 before it scored a victory over a touring team, when it beat the Wallabies 12–3 at Wellington in a tough game. Boland was captained by Mike Jennings, the son of a former Springbok forward, Cecil Jennings. The victorious young skipper also went on to become a Springbok, touring to Great Britain in 1969–70.

Other leading Boland players include F.P. ('Buks') Marais, the Springbok wing of 1949–53, along with both the hookers on the tour to New Zealand by the 1956 Springboks, Bertus van der Merwe and Melt Hanekom.

One of the great rugby influences in the region was Dawie de Villiers, the Springbok captain and halfback who

Wallabies Peter Horton, Chris Handy (behind) and Phil Crowe parade in triumph with the Bledisloe Cup, won from New Zealand in 1979.

lived in Wellington for a time. He was a minister of the Dutch Reformed Church and left the area shortly before the famous win over Australia. It was an irony that his absence gave the opportunity for a new scrumhalf, Thys Doubell, to play and score nine of the Boland team's winning points.

BONIFACE, ANDRE
Mont-de-Marsan and France
48 internationals for France 1954–66

BONIFACE, GUY
Mont-de-Marsan and France
35 internationals for France 1960–66

These brilliant French brothers were the stars of many French internationals either when playing together in the centres, or apart. André, the elder, began in 1954 as a 19-year-old. Guy, arriving on the international scene six years later, complemented his brother's brilliance. The two frequently staggered opponents and critics with their ball skills and an unnerving rapport.

Guy was killed in a car crash in 1967 while returning home from a match. André has continued to take a close interest in rugby and has had published several excellent articles on back play.

BORDER RFU
The Border Rugby Union was founded in 1891, the year the Currie Cup competition was inaugurated, and remained in the forefront of South Africa's provincial competition for over 80 years. Border shared the Currie Cup with Western Province in 1932 and 1934. When the Currie Cup system was changed in 1974, Border's modest playing record resulted in its

Guy Boniface

relegation to the second division, playing for the Sport Pienaar Trophy. Since then it has been unable to rise again into the top ranks.

Based in East London, Border has had its share of the spotlight, none more so than in 1949 when the team played the touring All Blacks twice. In the first match it inflicted the first loss for the All Blacks on tour, winning by 9–0. One of the Springbok selectors said afterwards that he would be 'inclined to play the whole of the Border team in the first test'.

Led by Basil Kenyon, who was to become the Springbok captain in the fourth test, Border had a return match between the third and fourth tests, and again provided some stiff opposition. This time the score was a 6–6 draw and thus Border came very close to the rare feat of scoring two wins over a touring team on the same tour. Border also stunned the 1955 Lions, beating them by 14–12.

Basil Kenyon is perhaps the best known player to have come out of the Border union, but the area has had a number of top personalities over the years, including Jimmy White, the hard-tackling centre of the 1930s, and Bennett 'Peewee' Howe, who played during the Springbok tour of New Zealand in 1956.

BORDERS

That area of southern Scotland where there is an intense interest, love and history of the game. Officially called the Scottish Rugby Union South District, the area is built around the clubs Gala, Hawick, Jedforest, Kelso, Langholm, Melrose and Selkirk. In its early years of development, Scottish rugby relied on the 'old school tie' associations of former pupils of the leading schools of Glasgow and Edinburgh; but in the Borders areas rugby was always the game of the everyday people. There they play a hard remorseless game which has concerned many a touring team and has delivered countless Scottish inter-district championships.

So while it is true that none of the Borders clubs was in the original group that formed the Scottish Rugby Union in 1873, there is no doubt that in modern times the strength of Scottish rugby has rested securely among them.

Scottish Borders gave to the game the concept of seven-a-side rugby.

Sevens rugby, first played in 1883, still exists very strongly in the area.

The Borderers' most famous moments in matches against touring teams have been:

1931–32 drew with South Africa 0–0
1966–67 beat Australia 13–0
1969 drew with South Africa 3–3
1973 drew with Argentina 13–13
1982 beat Fiji 23–17
1984 beat Australia 9–6
1986 beat Japan 45–12

BOSCH, GERALD
Transvaal and South Africa
9 internationals for South Africa 1974–76

Although he played only nine internationals over three years, Gerald Bosch had a considerable influence on world and South African rugby. He was a flyhalf who specialised in the kicking game. As a place-kicker and drop-kicker he was regarded as South Africa's most deadly ever. His record even stands up when compared with that of the great Naas Botha, who followed him four years later into the Springboks. In his nine internationals Bosch scored 89 points, as against Botha's 86 points in his first nine, but four of those tests were against South America, generally regarded as weaker test opposition.

Bosch made his debut for South Africa in the second test against Willie John McBride's Lions in 1974. Though he scored all nine points for the Springboks, he was dropped, much to

the Lions' relief, and did not reappear for his country until the tour later that year to France. He played two tests on that tour and then two more against France in 1975. In the second test in Pretoria in 1975 Bosch scored 22 points, a South African record for an official test. His total included six penalties, equalling the IRB test record. Earlier in his career he had scored 36 points in a Currie Cup match and 17 points in a cup final.

In 1976 Bosch made his most significant contribution to the history books. Playing in all four tests against the All Blacks, he scored 33 of the Springboks' 55 points. His accurate goal-kicking was the difference between two even teams.

Bosch was a round-the-corner kicker who came in to the ball at such an acute angle that he resembled a Fosbury-flopping high-jumper approaching the bar. He struck the ball from a crouched position with the instep of his right foot. When Bosch played, wings and centres knew they would not see much ball from set play, but they also knew they were playing with a match-winner whose temperament for the big occasion was impeccable.

BOTHA, NAAS
Northern Transvaal and South Africa
23 internationals for Sth Africa 1980–89

When the All Blacks of 1976 were in South Africa they could not help but notice a brilliant youngster playing at

Gerald Bosch and his distinctive kicking style. Ken Stewart attempts a charge-down. South Africa v New Zealand, fourth test, 1976.

Naas Botha

stand-off for the Northern Transvaal under-19 team in a number of the tour's curtain-raiser games. This was the young Naas Botha who already had the stamp of a future Springbok star.

The inevitable happened: Botha became a Springbok in 1980 and within months was a vital man in the South African team that played the British Isles. As a tidy and efficient player his skills were augmented by a brilliant goal-kicking talent. He kicked a number of important goals to help the Springboks win the series against the Lions, three tests to one.

A year later Botha was a vital player in the Springbok team on its controversial tour of New Zealand. Botha never seemed put off by the vehement anti-apartheid protests taking place around him, and he kicked goals in a machine-like manner all over New Zealand, including 20 points in the second test (a record for any player against the All Blacks in a test match).

Just to prove he was human, Botha missed a chance to win the test series for South Africa in the third test at Auckland. In a dramatic match, with barbed-wire, a high police presence and a low-circling protest plane overhead, the two teams arrived at 22–22 with just minutes to play. Botha had a

moderately easy conversion attempt which would have put the Springboks out to a 24–22 lead. To that point in the game he had not missed one kick and had been successful with four. With the whole rugby world either watching or listening – protesters had cut the TV picture to South Africa – Botha stepped up and kicked. The ball sliced away and New Zealand went on to win.

Botha was back in the headlines several seasons later when American football scouts, attracted by his prodigious goal-kicking, invited Botha to try out for the Dallas Cowboys. Botha was away from home for a time attempting to crack the big time (and the big money) but the move was not deemed a success. In the end he was reinstated as an amateur and went back to South Africa to play rugby again.

In his 23 tests for South Africa Botha scored 268 points, a South African record. This included twice kicking three dropped goals in a test match: the first against South America in 1980 and the second against Ireland in the second test of 1981.

Domestically, Botha was always a scoring machine. There was no better example of his prowess under pressure when he kicked all 24 points for Northern Transvaal in the Currie Cup final against Transvaal in 1987. In all he landed eight kicks: four were penalties and four were dropped goals.

BOUQUET, JACQUES
Bourgoin, Vienne and France
34 internationals for France 1954–62

A brilliant individualist as a centre three-quarter in the French teams of the late 1950s, 'Jackie' Bouquet was an elegant player with sharp speed and good attacking instincts. With his distinctive blond hair, he was easily recognisable among the French players of his era. But like all players who choose to run on their own, he had his ups and downs with the selectors.

He was slow to capture a regular test spot, starting against Scotland in 1954 as a 20-year-old, but playing only once that season and once in the 1955 season. After that he sealed his place, playing some explosive football, always with touches of initiative and flair.

He was part of the famous team of 1958–59, the first French side to win

the Five Nations championship outright. About that time he was voted France's top centre. One critic wrote, 'He charmed even his detractors.'

Bouquet missed France's tour of South Africa in 1958 because of loss of form and he also suffered on the 1961 French tour of New Zealand and Australia. He was vice-captain of that team but did not play in any of the tests on tour. He returned to the French team for the next season before finishing, at 34 caps, in 1962.

BOURGAREL, ROGER
Toulouse and France
9 internationals for France 1969–73

Roger Bourgarel created history in 1971 by becoming the first black player to tour South Africa, although previously New Zealand had sent four coloured (Polynesian) players with the All Blacks of 1970. Bourgarel had to overcome suggestions that his was a political selection, for he was not originally in the French touring party. However, after his late inclusion he played well enough to be placed in the test teams against the Springboks.

He was very popular with the South African crowds, earning their respect with speedy running from the wing and great courage on the tackle. In the first test, only the black Frenchman lay between the charging Springbok veteran Frik du Preez and a try which would have celebrated du Preez's record number of tests for South Africa. Somehow the much smaller Bourgarel bundled du Preez across the touchline. Many other internationals had found du Preez an unstoppable force in similar situations, so perhaps it was that act that finally convinced the sceptics in South Africa that Bourgarel was not just a political plant and could actually play the game.

Bourgarel, nicknamed the 'Black Arrow', played only one more time for France after that tour, against Scotland in 1973.

BRAND, GERRY
Western Province and South Africa
16 internationals for Sth Africa 1928–38

One of the all-time great fullbacks, Gerry Brand played for his country over a decade. Counting tours, he played 46 games and scored 293 points, a record which stood until beaten by

Naas Botha in 1982. Although he scored only two tries for South Africa in his 46 games, Brand was a prodigious left-footed kicker, a fine positional player, a good runner and a deadly tackler.

He was chosen for two great Springbok touring teams: in Great Britain in 1931–32 and in New Zealand and Australia in 1937. On the latter tour he amassed 209 points.

Against England in 1932, Brand pulled off one of the greatest kicks of all time. He fielded a missed clearance at half-way and let fly with a dropped goal attempt that drew gasps of admiration from the Twickenham crowd of 70,000. His kick into a strong wind went on and on, finally clearing the cross-bar and then carrying on well into the crowd. The kick was later measured at over 85 yards (77 metres) from impact to landing.

Brand was to play his last test match in 1938 at Ellis Park in Johannesburg

against the British Isles. There, he landed several brilliant kicks, including a long left-footed drop-kicked penalty which was taken from his own side of half-way. By then the crowds in South Africa had come to love the man some British writers called 'Fire' Brand. They were not to know then that days later he would be injured and would not play for his country again.

BRIDGEND RFC

Bridgend has never been considered one of the 'big four' clubs of Wales, yet in recent years it has built up its strengths to the point where it could reasonably make a claim to be right up among the very best in Welsh rugby.

Founded in 1879, Bridgend plays at the Brewery Field, though it has not always done so: twice the rugby club has lost it to other interested groups in the town, the first time in the 1928–29 season when a greyhound racing syn-

dicate moved in. In 1935 the club moved back but in 1948–49 it was again forced to vacate the Brewery Field, this time for a rugby league club. But the union lads didn't leave until they had spirited away, in the dead of the night, their precious goal-posts!

Bridgend RFC won a 21-year lease on the ground in 1956 and has been there ever since, building it into a complex that reflects its increasing stature as a top rugby club.

Bridgend waited patiently for a match against a major touring team – games which usually went to the 'big four' clubs (or combined teams) while Bridgend and similar clubs had to make do with touring teams such as Fiji and Canada. In 1978, in its centenary season, Bridgend was at last awarded a match against the All Blacks. What a shame this will only be remembered for sour reasons.

Bridgend's captain that day was the master fullback J.P.R. Williams –

Gerry Brand and his famous left boot, feared by teams playing against the Springboks for 10 years.

The notorious 'Bridgend v New Zealand' incident, 1978. J.P.R. Williams, on the ground, right, has his face scraped.

arguably the most famous player in Wales at that time.

The All Blacks, led by their own great player, Graham Mourie, came on to the field determined to retain their unbeaten record (for that tour) in Wales. Bridgend was equally determined to secure a victory to top its centenary celebrations.

Sadly, the game began in explosive fashion with physical and unsightly clashes between the players of both teams. Soon Williams had been badly scraped in a ruck by an easily identified All Black forward. The reaction to the sight of Williams leaving the field with a deeply gashed face was not good, and ill-will continued right to the end.

It was a game that had echoes right around the rugby world, and many were the charges and counter-charges made about the actions of players from both teams. The main point is, of course, that such a game was not at all worthy of the fine traditions that Bridgend had built up in its previous 99 years.

Other top players who have worn the royal blue and white hoops include Vivian Jenkins, the Welsh and British Isles fullback (and later one of the game's finest writers); Bobby Delahay, capped 18 times and a Welsh international at halfback, flyhalf and centre; Roddy Evans, the Welsh and Lions lock; Gary Prothero, also a Lion; Steve Fenwick, a Welsh captain and a Lion; and John Lloyd, a Welsh international and also Welsh coach.

Bridgend had one great sequence in the Welsh Rugby Union's Schweppes Challenge Cup. It was in four consecutive finals 1979–82, winning in its first two appearances and losing the other two. In 1990 the club beat the Welsh XV in the national side's build-up to its match with New Zealand. That year Bridgend made the Schweppes final for the fifth time, losing 10–16 to Neath.

BRISTOL FC

One of the strongest clubs in England's West Country, Bristol was formed in 1888. The club's first outing was against Cardiff and a 0–24 loss resulted, probably the equivalent of about 0–100 today! Bristol's first major match was against the 1905 All Blacks where it received a 41–0 thrashing.

Bristol came back from that misfortune to host an international a few seasons later (England v Wales in 1907–08), and had developed into a powerful club by World War I.

After the war a memorial fund was established to commemorate the large number of Bristol members who had lost their lives. This eventually enabled the club to buy a local ground called Buffalo Bill's Field, where it had played occasionally before the war. Appropriately, the new venue was re-named Memorial Ground and it is there that Bristol hosts its visitors today.

Bristol has always favoured an open style of rugby (in recent times called 'Bristol fashion') and over the years some of England's finest players have worn the club's blue and white colours.

The most-capped international from Bristol was the hooker John Pullin, who played 42 tests for his country.

Also from Bristol came J.S. (Sam) Tucker, who played 27 internationals between 1922 and 1931. *See* TUCKER.

Other topline players include Len Corbett, John Currie, Richard Sharp, Alistair Hignell, and Mike Rafter. The England international wing Alan Morley scored 479 tries in senior rugby. In the club's first 100 years, 67 of its members represented their country.

Mike Rafter's Bristol team gave the club a proud moment in 1983 when it won the knock-out John Player Cup, the symbol of club supremacy in England. It was Bristol's first win and achieved in front of a record finals crowd at Twickenham. It also made the finals in 1983 and in its centenary year, 1988.

BRITISH COLUMBIA

Rugby's original Canadian home was in Quebec where the Montreal Football Club was formed in 1868 by students returning from Britain. In the 1880s the game spread west to British Columbia, whose more temperate winters provided a better climate for playing rugby. A large number of New Zealand immigrants also helped boost interest in the game around this time.

The British Columbia Rugby Union was formed in 1889. The first overseas tour to Canada was by Ireland in 1899.

Most of the touring All Black and Wallaby rugby teams played British Columbia on their way home from long tours of Great Britain. The 1905 New Zealand team was the first.

Its manager, George Dixon, had apparently been told the weather would be too bad in Canada when his team was returning home, so he cabled the BCRU to ask if his All Blacks could play BC in San Francisco instead. (Dixon must have been under the impression that those two cities were very close together!) Undaunted, the British Columbians sent a team by train down to San Francisco – some 700 miles away! New Zealand won the two games 43–6 and 65–6.

The 1913 New Zealand team that toured the United States and Canada won all its games comfortably, but it was involved in a tragic occurrence in British Columbia.

In its second game against the Vancouver Island team of Victoria, the local fullback Peter Ogden left the field with severe head injuries. Sadly, he died on the way to hospital, the only instance this writer can find of a death occurring directly from a major international rugby union match.

The 1924 New Zealanders drew 9000 people to their game against Vancouver, the crowd being described by one writer at the time as 'the largest ever to witness an outdoor sporting event in Vancouver'.

There was a rugby rarity in Vancouver that year, when the All Blacks played a North Island v South Island match there – a game that used to provoke an intense rivalry in New Zealand. Eight local players were roped in to take the place of injured All Blacks, and the game created great interest. For the record, the exhibition was won by the North Island 25–14.

After that team departed for home it donated a trophy, the New Zealand Shield, which is still played for annually by schools in the Vancouver and district inter-high schools competition. Rugby is a major sport in the schools system of British Columbia.

British Columbia's best wins against New Zealand teams came in 1962, when Vancouver beat the New Zealand Universities team 3–0 and British Columbia beat it 9–6. Universities had a strong lineup and, though injury-hit, it included players who were then or later to become All Blacks.

British Columbia has had rather better results against Australian teams. In 1912, Vancouver, Victoria and British Columbia each beat Australia. BC defeated the 1958 Wallabies by 11–8 and the combined Oxford-Cambridge touring team in 1955 by the same score.

British Isles teams returning from tours of New Zealand and Australia also used to stop in Canada. In 1959, Ronnie Dawson's Lions could only beat British Columbia by 16–11, but in 1966 came the local team's greatest day.

Mike Campbell-Lamerton's team of Lions had not had a happy time in New Zealand but they were still thought to be way ahead of the Canadians. But British Columbia played extremely well and Peter Grantham scored the winning try for a famous 8–3 win. Fourteen of the BC team played for Canada against the Lions several days later, losing 8–19.

There have been several players-turned-administrators who have exerted powerful influence over British Columbian rugby, but three in particular deserve mention.

D.L. 'Buzz' Moore first played for the province in 1938 and he was the captain of Canada on its tour to Britain in 1962 – 24 years after his debut! In an amazing display of endurance, Moore played in all 16 games on the trip. He had captained BC against Australia in 1948 and then again in 1958 when BC had scored its famous victory. A prop, Moore was an outstanding figure in Canadian rugby.

So too was Grahame Budge. This former Scottish and British Isles international was Canadian-born but lived most of his life in Scotland. He toured with the Lions of 1950, before returning to his native Canada to live, where he played for British Columbia against the All Blacks in 1954.

Budge became one of Canada's best known players and was sadly missed when he died suddenly in 1979. His death was entirely in character, after a life devoted to the game of rugby. He collapsed during a training session at Vancouver's Brockton Oval with a team for players over the age of 40, and literally died with his boots on.

Later, a plaque was placed on a nearby tree and the ashes of Budge's body and his rugby boots were scattered on the ground nearby. British Columbian rugby people knew there could be no more fitting memorial to him.

Donn Spence was another whose commitment to rugby in Canada and British Columbia was immense. After a fine career as an international player

he became rugby coach at the University of British Columbia. Spence had a very powerful influence on the game at both provincial and national level for 20 years. He too was lost to the game at a young age, dying of hepatitis in 1985.

BC celebrated its centenary in 1989, hosting international teams from Australia, Ireland, Japan, New Zealand and Wales B. The programme was a resounding success, even though some of the visiting teams scored some largish scores against their hosts!

BRITISH ISLES

The rugby team that represents the four nations of Great Britain and Ireland is officially called the British Isles Rugby Union Team, but its nickname is the 'Lions'. It is formed almost exclusively for tours outside of the United Kingdom and Ireland, mostly to New Zealand, Australia and South Africa, and has played only a few times inside Britain.

Although there was a number of Great Britain touring teams before 1910, it is generally agreed that that the one that went to South Africa in that year was the first fully representative of a complete selection from the four home unions. Some of the early teams were called Great Britain, even though only two countries contributed players.

The first Great Britain team to be called the 'Lions' (after the Lion logo on the team tie) was the team in South Africa in 1924, while the first team to tour under the name British Isles did so in 1938, also to South Africa.

On tour, Lions teams have their share of successes and some of the rugby played by them in their various test series have been among the best in the history of the game.

The first Great Britain team, in 1888, was the brainchild of three English cricketers who toured Australia the previous year. They felt a similar tour of Australia, but playing rugby, would be popular as well.

The tour proved them right and deserves credit as the first major journey any rugby team had attempted: previous international tours were confined to the exchange of visits between neighbouring countries.

There was tragedy on the tour: the captain R.L. Seddon was drowned during an outing to the Hunter River in New South Wales. One of the cricketing organisers, A.E. Stoddart, took Seddon's place as skipper.

The 1891 team in South Africa (made up only of Englishmen and Scots) remains the only representative rugby team from Britain to win all its games on tour, anywhere. The British beat South Africa in three test matches (South Africa's first test matches against any country) and from their 19 tour games they conceded only one point! (Tries were worth one point in those days.) Randolph Aston, the Blackheath centre, scored 30 tries.

The 1896 team in South Africa also enjoyed great success. After an early drawn match with Western Province the team (made up this time of Irish and English players) won the first three of the internationals against South Africa. South Africa won the fourth test by 5–0 – its first test win.

The Great Britain team of 1899 went only to Australia (most tours there since have included New Zealand). The team included players from all four home unions but most of the 21 in the team had never won an international cap for their individual countries. Great Britain won the test series 3–1.

The 1903 British team in South Africa was the first touring team to experience the rapid improvement in the game in the colonies – they had, after all, only learnt the game from the British a few decades before! This British team, containing only one Welshman, could not win a test: it

drew two and lost one, winning only 11 of the 22 games on tour.

The 1904 team in Australia and New Zealand (with no Irish players) won every game comfortably in Australia but faced a tougher time in New Zealand, winning only two of its five games there. The strengths and weaknesses of the British team in New Zealand were to form a familiar pattern over the years: it was weaker in the forwards than in the backs, while New Zealand was the opposite. New Zealand won the only international, 9–3.

The 1908 team on the same tour was officially an Anglo-Welsh team because of Scottish opposition at the time to New Zealand (see SCOTLAND) but it was not a success. New Zealand won two tests by 32–5 and 29–0. The second test was drawn 3–3 after the New Zealand selectors rested six players.

The 1910 team in South Africa was a fully representative British team but many of the players' names have been long forgotten. But one who will always be remembered in South Africa is C.H. ('Cherry') Pillman. A very loose forward, virtually playing as a 'rover' or 'wing forward', Pillman staggered South Africans with his brilliant play. It was no fault of his that the British lost the series 2–1.

The 1924 team was also disappointing in South Africa, winning only nine tour matches out of 21.

The first British team to make an extensive tour – the 1888 team to Australia and New Zealand.

'Bim' Baxter, manager of the 1930 team, who outraged New Zealanders with his opinions!

The 1930 Great Britain team in New Zealand caused controversy when its manager, James ('Bim') Baxter, spoke out forcefully on the way the New Zealand teams favoured playing the 'rover' or 'wing forward' game. Baxter did not endear himself to the locals when he called the wing forward a 'cheat'. The All Blacks were unaffected by the storm of public outrage and won the tests 3–1.

The 1938 Lions team, captained by Sam Walker of Ireland, was the last to tour for 12 years; World War II saw to that. The fullback and vice-captain, Vivian Jenkins, was later to become one of rugby's most significant journalists.

After the war, the first three tours undertaken by the British Isles were perhaps their most popular, yet all concluded without a series win. In 1950 in New Zealand and Australia, Karl Mullen of Ireland was the skipper, but the team could not turn its immense popularity into test victories, drawing one and losing three.

This was the team that showed the world for the first time the now familiar British Isles playing colours. They turned out in red shirts, white shorts and blue socks with green tops – colours representative of each of the four home unions.

The 1955 team in South Africa, under captain Robin Thompson of Ireland, was rated then as the strongest team to visit that country. Though it won the first test in a thriller, 23–22, the series could not be clinched. The Springboks won the second and fourth tests, and the Lions' win at Pretoria in the third meant that the four matches were shared.

There were men who became renowned in the rugby media in this team too: Clem Thomas and Cliff Morgan are both still prominent in television and newspapers in Britain.

The 1959 Lions in New Zealand continued where the team in South Africa had left off. This was the period of British rugby when brilliant running backs abounded. In New Zealand in the 1950s a running back who could sidestep was an absolute rarity, so the 1959 Lions raised eyebrows wherever they went. Again, though, their backs alone could not ensure winning rugby. The All Blacks, with forward power and efficiency, won the series 3–1.

In the next three tours the Lions tried, in vain, to match what New Zealand and South Africa were doing. And again they failed. Trying to turn the emphasis from twinkling backs to hard-driving forwards, to match a world trend, was at least a 10-year task. In the tours to South Africa in 1962 (under captain Arthur Smith of Scotland), in 1966 to New Zealand (captain, Mike Campbell-Lamerton of Scotland), and to South Africa in 1968 (with captain Tom Kiernan of Ireland), there were no test wins at all, only two draws and 10 losses. This was the watershed of British rugby.

By 1971 the British had become committed to a philosophy of efficiency and safety first. The speedy backs of 1955 and 1959 were just a memory as the Lions turned into a combination of powerhouse forwards with backs who moved the ball only when dominance had been won up-front. The coach in 1971 was the deep-thinking Welshman Carwyn James and the captain was John Dawes (the first Welshman to lead the Lions). Dawes's style as a sturdy, steady centre embodied what that team demanded from the backs under the new approach to the game.

All New Zealand was stunned by a Lions win in the test series that year. Although New Zealanders still claim their team contained one of its weakest backlines, the home forwards were as good as ever, so when they lost their first-ever series to the Lions there was much soul-searching in New Zealand.

John Dawes (centre), Gerald Davies (partially obscured) and manager Dr Doug Smith acknowledge the applause of the Eden Park crowd, after the Lions had won the fourth test against New Zealand, and the series, in 1971.

The British Isles team returned home to a rapturous welcome and the scenes were repeated in 1974 when their next touring team went even one better – it beat the Springboks in South Africa!

Captained by Irish veteran Willie John McBride, the team played as it had in New Zealand. This time the Springboks could not win a test and the 1974 Lions became the first team since the 1891 and 1896 British teams to beat the Springboks in a four-test series in South Africa. Neither New Zealand nor Australia has ever achieved a similar feat.

Confidence was high for the 1977 Lions tour of New Zealand. But Phil Bennett's team was weakened when a high number of leading players declared their unavailability, with the result that the team was unbalanced.

The forwards were every bit as good as those of the 1971 and 1974 Lions, but the backs proved disappointing. While British rugby had been turning to the forwards in recent years, the All Blacks were changing to a more expressive game through their back division, so, although beaten in the forwards, the All Blacks played the games at a greater pace and with much more invention, moving the ball through the backs to score.

The Lions who went to South Africa under Bill Beaumont in 1980 and Ciaran Fitzgerald's 1983 team to New Zealand were also devoid of much initiative in the backs. South Africa won the series 3–1 in 1980, though the results could just as easily have been reversed, so close were the teams.

The same could not be said in 1983 when the Lions were soundly thumped by an All Black team that was rebuilding after the Graham Mourie era. The 38–6 thrashing of the Lions in the fourth test was the saddest day British rugby had had to that point.

Many were the questions asked as to the on-going value of the forward-style game and whether it should be encouraged to continue. Many were the calls to go back to that original mode of Lions play, (running through the backs) that had thrilled crowds all over the world and which had been so successful.

In 1989 the Lions made their first modern tour exclusively of Australia. Captained by Scotsman Finlay Calder, the Lions won the tests 2–1.

This writer knows of only three significant occasions when a British Isles team has played at home.

In 1951 a team made up of members of the Lions team that had toured Australia and New Zealand in 1950 played a match at Cardiff Arms Park to celebrate the 75th anniversary of the founding of the Cardiff Rugby Football Club.

In 1977 the British Isles team of that year played a special match against the Barbarians at Twickenham to celebrate the Queen's Silver Jubilee. The Barbarians team was effectively composed of the best of the players who had missed out on the tour, supplemented by three French players. The Lions won the game by 23–14 in front of a capacity crowd which included the Queen and the Prince of Wales.

The third occasion was in 1986 when a British Isles team played a Rest of the World XV in Cardiff as part of the IRB's centenary celebrations.

No international caps were awarded for those three games.

BROCKHOFF, DAVE
New South Wales and Australia
8 internationals for Australia 1949–51

A hard-nosed flanker who later became an Australian coach. Brockhoff made his debut for the Wallabies in 1949, at a time when Australia awarded full international status to matches against the New Zealand Maoris. Later that season he was part of the Australian team which beat the All Blacks in New Zealand, the first time in 15 years the Bledisloe Cup had been won by the Wallabies, and the first time they had ever won a series in New Zealand.

He played tests against the British Lions in 1950 and the All Blacks in 1951 before touring South Africa in 1953. There he was passed over by the selectors for the tests and he retired from international football afterwards.

'Brock' was coach of Australia for several years in the 1970s and faced, at times, severe criticism for the vigorous methods used by the Wallabies during his term.

Perhaps Brockhoff's greatest moment as a coach was in 1979 when his Australians beat the All Blacks 12–6 at Sydney. It was a tight match in which little attractive rugby was dis-

played and no tries were scored. The Australians took the Bledisloe Cup on a victory lap of the Sydney Cricket Ground and coach Dave Brockhoff joined in – a gratifying moment for a survivor of the 1949 team which had been the last Australian team to hold the cup.

BROTHERS CLUB
The oldest rugby club in Queensland and one of the most powerful in Australia, with more than 50 international players.

The club was founded in 1905 but played rugby league for the years after World War I, when rugby union was not played in Queensland.

Many of Australia's top players came through the Brothers club on their way to international careers. These included the modern players Tony Shaw, Jeff McLean, Paul McLean, Dick Cocks, David L'Estrange, Chris Handy, Brendan Moon, Tony D'Arcy, Des Connor and Mark McBain.

Since 1970 the club has dominated the Brisbane first grade premiership, and for a number of years must have been close to being the strongest club team in the world. In the 45 years since World War II, the Brothers club won Brisbane's premiership 20 times.

BROWN, GORDON
West of Scotland and Scotland
30 internationals for Scotland 1969–76
8 internationals for British Isles 1971–77

BROWN, PETER
West of Scotland, Gala and Scotland
27 internationals for Scotland 1964–73

A grand pair of Scottish tight forwards of the 1960s and 70s. One of the best locks produced by Scotland, Gordon Brown was the more prominent. He made his debut against South Africa in 1969. With an impressive build and excellent ball skills, he quickly established himself as a two-handed lineout taker of the highest class and one of the leading players in his position in Britain.

Although he was only 23, which is young for an international tight forward, Brown made the 1971 Lions tour of New Zealand where he played two of the four test matches. Injury curtailed his play for two seasons after that tour, but he was back to his best for the Lions' visit to South Africa in

BROTHERS IN RUGBY

There are literally hundreds of examples of brothers who have played international rugby, either in the same teams or in different teams years apart. But some were 'firsts' and others were particularly notable.

First brothers to play internationals:
In 1882 Arthur Evanson and Arthur Taylor both played for England against Wales. Their brothers, Wyndham Evanson and Henry Taylor, had earlier played for their country.

Greatest number from one family to play international rugby:
The Neilson brothers of Scotland. Four of them played internationals in the nineteenth century, though never more than two in a team at one time.

First international game to have brothers in each side:
Scotland v Wales 1885. George and Richard Maitland played for Scotland and Arthur and Bob Gould for Wales.

First international to have three sets of brothers playing:
Wales v Scotland 1982. Evan and David James for Wales; C.E. and J.E. Orr, and William and George Neilson for Scotland.

First international to have three brothers playing:
South Africa v Scotland 1912. The Luyt brothers, Richard, John, and Fred, played for South Africa, as they did in two other internationals on the tour.

First brother to replace his brother in an international:
Gordon Brown came onto the field as a replacement for his injured brother, Peter, for Scotland v Wales in 1970.

Teenaged brothers who both scored on their international debut (in the same game):
A record that is unlikely to have more than one claimant – but it did happen. In the Ireland v Wales match at Cardiff in 1924, Frank Hewitt played at flyhalf and his older brother Tom on the wing. Frank was Ireland's youngest ever international (17 years, 5 months, 5 days) and Tom was five days short of turning 19. Both scored tries in Ireland's 13–10 win. Another Hewitt brother, Victor, became an Irish international for six games in 1935–36. Tom's son, David, was an international for Ireland and the British Isles 1958–65.

Other famous brothers who have played international rugby:
Argentina: Alejandro and Marcos Iachetti; Juan and Pedro Lanza; Alejandro and Gabriel Travaglini.
Australia: Jim and Stuart Boyce.
England: John and Francis Luscombe; Graham and Stephen Meikle; Adrian and Frederick Stoop; Rory and Tony Underwood.
Ireland: Ellie and Glyn Allen; George and Charles Beamish; Dick and William Collopy; Harry and Des McKibbon; Alistair and Christopher McKibbon (the sons of Harry).
Italy: Rino, Nello, Bruno and Ivan Francescato.
Netherlands: Hans, André, Mats and Peter Marcker.
New Zealand: Jack and Maurie Goddard; Robbie and Bruce Deans.
Scotland: David and Robin Chisholm.
South Africa: Eben and Joggie Jansen; Dawie and Jackie Snyman; Arthur and Peter Marsburg, Hennie and Hugo van Zyl.
Wales: Richard and Paul Moriarty; 'Ponty', Jack and Tuan Jones.

(*See also* BANCROFT, BEHOTEGUY, BONIFACE, BOTHA, BROWN, BROWNLIE, CALDER, CAMBERABERO, CLARKE, ELLA, GOING, GOULD, HASTINGS, JAUREGUY, JOHNSON, KAVANAGH, KRIGE, LACAZE, LOUW, MCLEAN, MACLEOD, MEADS, MILNE, MORKEL, OSLER, PILLMAN, PRAT, ROOS, SPANGHERO, STEPHENSON, THORNETT, WHETTON, WILLIAMS)

1974, when he scored eight tries and became a vital part of the great Lions' series win.

In 1977 Brown was sent off during a televised game for a much publicised retaliation after he had been kicked by an opposition player. He was suspended for the international season.

But the selectors kept their faith in him by picking him for his second tour to New Zealand in 1977. In that series, which was to be his last in international rugby, Brown eventually found England's Billy Beaumont as his locking partner and the two formed an excellent platform for the Lions forward performance. They were far from blameworthy for the Lions' defeat in three of the four tests.

Peter Brown was also a top Scottish player in his day. As well as being an excellent forward, he is also remembered for his curious goal-kicking style. He would place the ball for the attempt, look at the posts and then turn his back completely on the target. Only when at the back of his run would he turn again to face the ball for the kick at goal. Generally he was successful!

Gordon and Peter (and a third rugby-playing brother) were the sons of Jock Brown, a former Scottish soccer international goalkeeper.

Gordon Brown

Maurice Brownlie leads the 1928 All Blacks on to the field before the fourth test at Newlands, Capetown.

BROWNLIE, CYRIL
Hawke's Bay and New Zealand
3 internationals for New Zealand 1924–25

BROWNLIE, LAURIE
Hawke's Bay and New Zealand
New Zealand rep. 1921

BROWNLIE, MAURICE
Hawke's Bay and New Zealand
8 internationals for New Zealand 1924–28

The Brownlie brothers were all big raw-boned lads off the farm, and rugby was a game tailor-made made for them. All three played for their country and two are remembered well by rugby historians to this day.

The first to play for New Zealand was the youngest, Lawrence, who did not play a full international but appeared in the New Zealand 'second' team against New South Wales in 1921. Later in that season a knee injury ended his career for good.

Maurice came into the New Zealand team the next year and did not lose his place until he retired after the 1928 tour of South Africa, during which he captained the All Blacks.

In his time one of the greatest players the game had seen, he was a loose forward and a fearless exponent of hard forward play.

He had two major tours, to Britain and France in 1924–25, and to South Africa in 1928 when his team shared the series 2–2, the best result for an All Black team there.

Cyril was the oldest of the three and the biggest, standing 6ft 3in (1.90m) tall and weighing more than 15 stone (96 kg). He was also in the two major touring teams that New Zealand sent away in the 1920s. Like Maurice, he played his three internationals as a flanker in the three-man second row that New Zealand favoured in the scrums in those days.

Cyril Brownlie has a place in rugby history as the first man sent off in an international, receiving his marching orders from referee Albert Freethy in the match against England in 1925. In a fiery match, Freethy had issued a general warning that the next man to offend would be sent off, whoever it was. In the next lineout Cyril Brownlie was adjudged to be involved in another unsavoury incident, and so he made the first of rugby's 'longest walks'.

BRUCE, NORMAN
Gala, Blackheath, London Scottish and
  Scotland
31 internationals for Scotland 1958–64

One of the many rugby internationals to have come from an army background, Norman Bruce was a captain in the Royal Army Ordnance Corps during much of his rugby career. Originally from the Borders, he played most of his rugby in the south. He was prominent in loose play as well as being an effective striker for the ball in scrums.

Bruce made his debut against France in 1958 and became one of the Scottish hookers who went on to play a long sequence of games for his country – 29 internationals in a row. He toured South Africa with the Barbarians club in 1958 and with Scotland in 1960.

BULLER RFU

Buller is one of the minor unions of New Zealand, but nevertheless a loyal one. It is centred on a small mining and timber community in the northern half of the west coast of the South Island. It was founded in 1894 and has struggled on without having much of a population base to draw on, ever since.

Buller is not to be confused with West Coast, its neighbouring union to the south. The two have played together in many 'combined' teams to meet overseas sides (and together they have beaten Australia twice) but, separately, they like nothing better than to beat the living daylights out of each other in their Rundle Cup matches.

The typical Buller rugby man or woman has developed a keen sense of wry humour, essential, one supposes, to cope with all the disappointments that come with being a small union.

The story is often told of Buller challenging North Auckland for the Ranfurly Shield in 1972 – at a time when North Auckland was very strong and had in its team the All Black star, Sid Going. The game went as predicted. North Auckland played well on the slippery ground and was, in the end, 35 points too good for Buller.

But Buller had the last laugh. In one of the game's moves Going lost one of his boots in a tackle. Following through behind the play was the Buller lock, Orlando Nahr, a veteran of 123 games in the cardinal and blue hoops of his province. Seeing 'Super Sid's' boot lying in the mud, Nahr scooped it up and tucked it into his shorts out of sight. None of the North Auckland team saw where it went, but the crowd who had seen the 'snatch' all hugely enjoyed the joke. Going played on with just one boot: the other was destined to head south as at least one trophy to show for Buller's long journey.

BUTTERFIELD, JEFF

Northampton and England
28 internationals for England 1953–59
4 internationals for British Isles 1955

Jeff Butterfield formed a formidable partnership with strong-tackling Phil Davies in the mid-1950s, which proved very effective on the successful 1955 tour of South Africa.

Butterfield won a reputation as one of the world's most thrustful and constructive centres, but in the twilight of his career he received few chances – due both to injury and strong competition for his position – especially in New Zealand in 1959 when he again toured with the Lions.

Butterfield's 32 consecutive caps for England and the Lions were won in a series of games that included only nine losses. His total of 28 caps for England was, at the time, a record number of international appearances for any English back.

Originally a schoolteacher, Butterfield played a significant role in setting up and managing the 'Rugby Club' in London, which has become one of the game's most celebrated social spots.

C

CAD

Cad, a possible forerunner of rugby, is a game said to have been played by all branches of the Celtic race in Britain and Ireland for over 1000 years, before being eased out by the big public schools of England in the eighteenth century where they preferred the solely kicking game.

Named cad, after the bull's scrotum that was inflated and used as the ball, this game of carrying, kicking and rushing was played in two variations: cross-country cad was inter-parish, played all day between two teams of unlimited number, the object being to take the ball back home; and field cad, which was played on a restricted field with set numbers.

Cad met an untimely death in its last bulwark, Ireland, when Gaelic football was started in 1884 as a handling variation of soccer. Purists insist cad is the traditional game of Ireland, not the upstart Gaelic football.

CAKABAU, GEORGE

A distinguished player and official with Fijian rugby, George Cakabau began his playing career in the years prior to World War II. He toured New Zealand as captain and an outstanding five-eighths with the famous unbeaten Fiji team of 1939. (Another member of that team was Penaia Ganilau, later Ratu

Ratu Sir George Cakabau, as a young footballer in the 1930s.

The Calcutta Cup

Sir Penaia Ganilau, who became Governor-General of his country and who played a major part in the negotiations following the military coup in 1987.)

Ratu Sir George Cakabau's prominence in the administration of Fijian rugby marks him as one of the fathers of the game in that country. He was Fiji's coach in 1954 and became manager of various Fijian touring teams from 1951 until 1969.

A grandson of the last king of Fiji, he was a long-serving politician, rising to the rank of cabinet minister. In 1972 he was appointed Governor-General of his country.

Cakabau (pronounced Thakambow) was also a Fijian cricketer.

CALCUTTA CUP

The only trophy for competition between two of the Five Nation championship teams each season, the Calcutta Cup is played for between England and Scotland.

The trophy originated in India where the Calcutta Football Club, started by some former pupils of Rugby School in England, found itself facing recession after only four years of existence. It had only modest resources, but as a closing-down gesture the members withdrew its remaining rupees from the bank and had them melted down and worked into a handsome trophy with three distinctive handles shaped like snakes and an elephant mounted on its lid. The Calcutta Cup was presented to the Rugby Football Union in 1878 for competition between England and Scotland, and since then (with the exception of the war years) has been a much-prized trophy in an annual competition.

Scotland has twice held the trophy for four consecutive years, but England's longest winning sequence was from 1951 to 1963.

CALDER, FINLAY

Melrose, Stewart's-Melville and Scotland
28 internationals for Scotland 1986–90
3 internationals for British Isles 1989

CALDER, JIM

Stewart's Melville and Scotland
27 internationals for Scotland 1981–85
1 international for British Isles 1983

Twins from a family of four rugby-playing brothers from Edinburgh, Jim and Finlay Calder held a unique place in world rugby: between them they virtually occupied one position in the Scottish team for 10 seasons.

Jim Calder was first into the Scottish team, playing as flanker against France in 1981. From then until 1985 he was a first choice in 27 Scottish test sides, missing only one international right through until the disastrous Scottish season of 1984–85. He scored the vital try against France that clinched the Grand Slam win for Scotland in 1983–84.

Finlay Calder took over his brother's position as flanker in the Scottish team. His internationals were played consecutively as well, apart from missing one test, because of injury, in 1988 and another in 1989. His career ended in New Zealand after the Scottish tour there in 1990.

By then the brothers had played on the side of the scrum in 55 of the 59 internationals Scotland played from 1981–90. Both had taken part in a Scottish Grand Slam; Jim in 1984 and Finlay in 1990.

Jim Calder held firmly by Dave Loveridge. British Isles v New Zealand, 1983.

Finlay Calder was a Scottish captain in 1988–89 and a British Isles skipper as well. In 1989 he led the Lions to Australia in his usual rollicking good-humoured way – off the field, that is. On the field he was grim and vigorous. The 2–1 test series win was the first the Lions had had on any tour for 16 years.

Although the Calder twins did not actually play a test match together they, along with their brother John, were all together in the Scotland party which toured Australia in 1982. John Calder, also a loose forward, was equal top try-scorer on that tour.

CAMBERABERO, GUY
La Voulte and France
14 internationals for France 1961–68

CAMBERABERO, LILIAN
La Voulte and France
13 internationals for France 1964–68

CAMBERABERO, DIDIER
La Voulte, Beziers and France
26 internationals for France 1982–91

Uncapped brothers Guy and Lilian surfaced in international rugby when both toured New Zealand with France in 1961. Poor Lilian, one of the victims of the heavy early-tour loss to Waikato, was one of the three halfbacks for the 13-match tour and, though he was never injured, that was his only match.

He went on to play 13 internationals between 1964 and 1968, only once on a losing side.

Flyhalf Guy played one test on the 1961 tour, the first of his 14 interna-

tionals, of which France won 10 and drew one. He scored 113 international points, including the France Five Nations championship's record of 32 in 1967. He dropped a record five goals (in three matches) that season.

Guy's son, Didier, also reached international level as a flyhalf, in 1982, 14 years after his father's career had finished. Didier was a brilliant goalkicker, setting a world record of 30 points in one game, in France's World Cup match with Zimbabwe at Auckland in 1987. He was something of a curiosity – he played most of his internationals wearing a hair-piece.

CAMBRIDGE UNIVERSITY RFC
Rugby union was introduced to Cambridge University in 1839 by an old boy of Rugby School, Arthur Pell. Around that time, players keen to play football used to gather at Parker's Piece, a playing field in the centre of Cambridge. However, before a game could be played a long discussion had to take place between the captains of the various old schools, each of whom wanted to play the rules of their alma mater. Rugby's rules eventually held sway, although the university club was not formed until 1872 – the year of the first match against Oxford University.

One of the significant figures in Cambridge rugby in the 1920s was also one of the great rugby personalities of the times, the Cambridge and England captain, Wavell Wakefield. One of his priorities as a forward and leader was to work on defensive patterns and organisation of the forward pack, strategies which he took into the very successful England team of that era.

Cambridge is still a highly respected club, and has contributed many world class players to British teams; among them Cliff Jones, Carl Aarvold, Wilf Wooller, 'Darkie' Bedell-Sivright, Ronald Cove-Smith, Mike Gibson, Ken Scotland and Clem Thomas.

CAMPBELL, OLLIE
Old Belvedere and Ireland
22 internationals for Ireland 1976–84
7 internationals for British Isles 1980–83

A high-scoring and brilliantly creative Irish flyhalf who only late in his career received the credit he deserved. He first played for his country against the touring Australians in 1976 but after a modest performance was passed over by the selectors for the next three and a half seasons. In that time Tony Ward rose to prominence in the No. 10 jersey for Ireland and kept out any other flyhalf contenders.

On the 1979 Ireland tour of Australia, Campbell received another opportunity to play international football. He arrived on the tour very much still in the shadow of Ward, but this time he took the chances offered and after

Lilian Camberabero scores against Australia, Paris 1967 – brother Guy is on the left. The two brothers scored all the points in France's 20–14 win.

Ollie Campbell, supported by Peter Winterbottom, in action for the British Isles in New Zealand, 1983.

124 points and played all four internationals.

In the next home season for Ireland, Campbell appeared only twice in the Five Nations championship. Typically in those two matches he landed seven penalty goals, making up all his side's points. His total of points for Ireland in internationals rose to 217, a record which stood until 1988 when it was surpassed by Michael Kiernan.

Illness, then injury, prevented Campbell being chosen for his country after the 1983–84 season. He retired in 1987 after spending his last three seasons playing only for his club, Old Belvedere.

Seamus Oliver Campbell at all times exhibited the delightful modesty of a true sporting champion. He was one of Ireland's most popular players as well as being one of its best.

CAMPBELL-LAMERTON, MIKE
Halifax, Army, London Scottish and
    Scotland
23 internationals for Scotland 1961–66
8 internationals for British Isles 1962–66

A Scottish lock who went on two tours with the British Isles team. Mike Campbell-Lamerton played 19 of 24 matches on the Lions tour of South Africa in 1962, and went as captain to Australia and New Zealand in 1966.

Campbell-Lamerton leaving the field after a game played in shocking conditions v New Zealand Juniors 1966.

landing six penalty goals against Queensland he made the Irish test team.

In the first test at Ballymore Campbell was superb. He landed six place kicks from six attempts (including two from half-way and three from the sideline) in a goal-kicking display that some rueful Australians said was the best ever seen on the ground. A dropped goal gave him a final tally of 19 points, an Irish record for an international, and one which secured for Ireland a shock 27–12 win.

On the basis of that game and others which followed, Campbell shut out the brilliant Ward from the Irish team. He played all the internationals but one over the next four seasons, including all four in 1981–82 when Ireland won the Triple Crown for the first time in 33 years.

He was a consistent match-winner, scoring all 21 points v Scotland in 1982 and 21 points v England in 1983 (new Irish records which were still standing in 1990).

In 1980 he toured South Africa with the British Isles, playing in three of the internationals, but he was hampered by hamstring injuries.

In 1983 Campbell made his finest contribution on the rugby field. As a member of the Lions touring team in New Zealand, he was one shining light in an otherwise mediocre back division. Time and again he sparkled while others around him struggled. His play as a flyhalf expanded to even higher dimensions. He controlled the planning in the Lions backline; he passed creatively (always a facet of the game he enjoyed); he ran with judgment and speed; he tackled like no other flyhalf ever seen in New Zealand; and he totalled points in big numbers from his simple and highly consistent goal-kicking technique.

Sadly, the team could not give Campbell top class support and the Lions were shut down 0–4 in the test series. It was a measure of the New Zealander's respect for Campbell that they planned much of their test match strategy to keep him in check, and tried to avoid conceding penalties within Campbell's goal-kicking range. Campbell top-scored on this tour with

David Campese, playing as fullback against New Zealand, 1990.

ball from behind his own goal-line in a test against the British Isles. He was caught in possession and the resulting loose ball was seized by the Lions who scored.

But Campese's fans were a loyal band who overlooked supposed indiscretions, claiming that he scored and assisted far more tries than he ever conceded. Such debates made him one of the most discussed players in modern rugby.

Rugby league clubs made a number of lucrative offers to David Campese, but he remained loyal to Australian rugby union. He also made a big impact on the game in Italy, where he played club rugby for a number of seasons.

In 1990 he became the first Australian back to play 50 tests and became Australia's highest-capped player when he passed Simon Poidevin's previous record of 51.

CANADA

Though much of the credit for the introduction of rugby to Canada must go to British immigrants in the nineteenth century, a number of young Canadians also brought the game back after studying in schools and universities in England.

The first Canadian rugby club was formed in Montreal in 1868 by students of McGill University, along with soldiers stationed in that city. By 1882 rugby had spread to Ontario and British Columbia.

By 1889 the British Columbia Rugby Union had been formed. In 1899 Canada played host to its first major overseas team (an Irish selection). Club teams from the United States had been welcome visitors for many years before that.

Canada undertook an ambitious tour of the British Isles in 1902–03 – many

Here he had the misfortune to lead the Lions at a time when New Zealand rugby was at a peak: the All Blacks won a clean sweep in the four test series.

An injury and non-selection kept Campbell-Lamerton out of two of the tests, but he would probably point to the two test series with Australia on that tour as the highlight of his career. His team won both tests, the second by 31–0 – one of the biggest defeats inflicted on the Wallabies.

A regular officer with the Duke of Wellington's regiment, Campbell-Lamerton did not receive his first cap until he was 27.

His son Jeremy, also a forward, played for Scotland in the 1987 World Cup in New Zealand.

CAMPESE, DAVID
Australian Capital Territory, New South
   Wales and Australia
54 internationals for Australia 1982–90

A brilliant member of Australian test teams in the 1980s and 90s, Campese was one of the quickest and most elusive runners in the modern game. He became famous for his 'goose-step' or 'stutter-step', which was achieved by running hard at an opponent then taking an exaggerated step which

suggested he was slowing, but which in fact propelled him forward at an even faster rate.

Campese played his early rugby in Canberra where, in the early 1980s, rugby was not of a particularly high standard. Yet Campese was quickly recognised as a unique prospect for Australian rugby.

At the age of 19 he made the Wallabies team as a wing for the New Zealand tour in 1982 and by the end of that trip had clearly outplayed Stuart Wilson, by then a player rated as one of New Zealand's all-time best.

By 1986 Campese had shifted to Sydney where he joined the leading club, Randwick. He continued to make test teams as either a wing or a fullback, and his brilliant running soon saw his tally of test tries build up.

During the World Cup semi-final against France at Sydney in 1987, 'Campo' became the highest scorer of tries in tests. The previous best was 24 tries scored by Ian Smith between 1924 and 1933. His total of test tries at the end of 1990 was 37 and he was still top of the record list.

Campese's brilliant and unorthodox play earned him many critics, and his sometimes impetuous and individualistic displays made huge headlines. In 1989, for instance, he tried to run a

A 1907 illustration of 'the Canadian rugby game'.

years before a national governing body for Canadian rugby had been formed. There was a full schedule of 21 games against major clubs and universities. Although they did not play internationals, the Canadians were there years before any of the so-called major tourists, New Zealand, Australia and South Africa, although the New Zealand 'Natives' had toured 14 years earlier. For the record, the Canadian team scored seven wins (including defeats of Ulster, Bristol and London Scottish), 12 losses and a draw.

In the early years of the twentieth century Canadian rugby wrestled with the twin problems of weather, with severe winters breaking each season into two parts, and vast travelling distances. In 1939 a meeting was called to discuss the formation of a Canadian Rugby Football Union, but it was abandoned with the outbreak of World War II.

After the war domestic rugby, still without a unifying force, carried on. Teams from Australia and New Zealand provided some opposition, mainly in British Columbia, for many years. The Australian Wallabies were the first post-war visitors to pass through after a successful tour of the United Kingdom. So keen were they to play in Canada, they had asked that a special match be played at the end of their British tour to raise funds for that very purpose. The game, against the Barbarians in Cardiff, began a famous tradition that has continued on major

tours since. Perhaps it helped lead to an association between Canada and the Barbarians club, which has toured Canada twice, in 1958 and 1976.

By 1962 Canada's confidence as a rugby nation was beginning to expand once more. That year it attempted again a full tour of Britain, but the results were shattering. Only one win was recorded out of 17 games. The best result was a 3–3 draw with the Barbarians. The fact that the team was captained by a 41-year-old prop ('Buzz' Moore) might, in hindsight, be a comment on the lack of depth in the game at that time in Canada. Moore himself should not be criticised. He played outstandingly and appeared in every game.

It was not until 1965 that the Canadian Rugby Union was finally formed. Immediately the new body began chasing greater opportunities for Canada's leading players to play international football and to gain the experience and expertise that was so obviously lacking on their tour three years earlier.

September 17, 1966 was the historic day of Canada's first full international game. (The previous time Canada had lined up against a national team was against Japan in 1932.) Its opponent was the British Isles touring team, returning home after a 0–4 thrashing by the All Blacks in New Zealand, but a pleasing win against the Wallabies.

British Columbia's provincial team had done the decent thing for Canadian

rugby and rocked the tourists with a win in the first tour game. As a result 14 players from BC were picked in the first international team to play in Toronto a few days later. Geoff Robinson of Quebec was the sole eastern Canada representative. Under a sunny sky and in a temperature of 70 degrees, the Lions defeated Canada 19–8, but not without some stern opposition. For the record, Canada's two tries came from Mike Chambers and Jim Ryan.

A year later England toured, followed by Fiji in 1971. Canada then embarked on a tour of Wales where it had two wins out of five games, losing 10–56 to a Welsh XV in the tour's climax.

Since then Canada has hosted and returned tours to most of the major rugby nations and rugby is well-established in all 10 provinces, with the problems of the long distances between rival provinces now alleviated by both air mail and air flight. The weather still creates difficulties. In most of the country the game is played between May and October to avoid frozen, rock-hard grounds; only in parts of British Columbia is rugby a genuine winter game.

In 1977 the union formalised its contact with the United States and the Can-Am series was begun – one game played each year between the two countries on a home and away basis. (*See* CAN-AM SERIES)

Canada has never played with or in South Africa – traditionally Canadian governments have had strong opposition to any contact with South Africa.

Canadian rugby has been blessed with some very able and willing administrators as well as talented players. Graham Budge, 'Buzz' Moore and Donn Spence have been mentioned (*see* BRITISH COLUMBIA). Others of note are Bob Spray, Mike Luke, Ro Hindson, Hans de Goede, Bob Elder and Peter Clarke.

Luke is perhaps Canada's best-known player of recent vintage. He was Canada's captain for several years and like Graham Budge, 'Buzz' Moore and Ken Wilke is a member of the Barbarians club of Britain.

Canada played in the first World Cup in New Zealand in 1987. It won its opening game against Tonga 37–4, but lost to Ireland 19–46 and to Wales 9–40, thus being eliminated. The team was captained by veteran lock Hans de Goede who became one of the World Cup personalities. The Canadians had no objection to TV cameramen and microphones approaching their half-time huddles and de Goede's rousing speeches to his men were heard in every home as a result.

Progress continues in Canadian rugby. In 1989 British Columbia celebrated its centenary; and Canada qualified top of the American group in preparation for the World Cup in 1991.

CANTERBURY RFU

Founded in 1879, Canterbury is the oldest provincial union outside Britain. Some historians claim New South Wales is older, having started as the Southern Rugby Union five years earlier, but that was an association of various unions, whereas Canterbury represented one province.

The union was actually formed in the southern city of Timaru but Christchurch, the largest city in the South Island, has always been the union's headquarters. Over the years the 'red and blacks' of Canterbury have developed into one of New Zealand's most powerful rugby teams, supported by some of the country's staunchest rugby devotees.

At one time or another, Canterbury teams have beaten all the major international rugby countries they have played.

Perhaps the most famous wins were over the South African touring teams of 1921 and 1956. The 1921 game was played on a rainy day and, because of injuries, the home team was reduced to 14 men for the last, gripping moments. The locals held on to win 6–4, even though they had been hopelessly outweighed by the Springboks. Not for the first time, local rugby supporters were incensed when none of their team made the All Black team for the test matches that series.

In 1956 Canterbury again beat the Springboks, 9–6, thanks to a late penalty awarded to the home team and kicked by 'Buddy' Henderson. Afterwards the Springbok manager, Dr Danie Craven, had some words of criticism for the match's referee, but Dr Craven also praised the sell-out Lancaster Park crowd for being 'one of the most sporting' they had struck in New Zealand. Such sentiments have not always been applied to Canterbury's noisy embankment crowds.

Against British teams, Canterbury won in 1908 (v Anglo-Welsh), 1930 (v Great Britain), and 1959 and 1983 (v British Isles). Canterbury also won against England in 1973, Scotland in 1975, Ireland in 1976 and the All Blacks in 1957. Victories over Australian teams came in 1931, 1936, 1946, 1962 and 1986.

Canterbury has had several magnificent runs of success while defending

---

CAN-AM SERIES

A home-and-away series, begun in 1977, between Canada and the United States. Results have been:

1977 at Vancouver: Canada 17 USA 6
1978 at Baltimore: USA 12 Canada 7
1979 at Toronto: Canada 19 USA 12
1980 at Saranac Lake: Canada 16 USA 0
1981 at Calgary: Canada 6 USA 3
1982 at Albany: Canada 3 USA 3
1983 at Vancouver: Canada 15 USA 9
1984 at Chicago: USA 21 Canada 13
1985 at Vancouver: Canada 21 USA 10
1986 at Tucson: Canada 27 USA 16
1987 at Vancouver: Canada 33 USA 9
1987 at Victoria: Canada 20 USA 12
1988 at Saranac Lake: USA 28 Canada 16
1989 at Toronto: Canada 21 USA 3
1990 at Seattle: USA 14 Canada 12

Note there were two matches in 1987. After 15 matches Canada leads by 10 wins, USA has had four wins and there has been one drawn match.

Canada's scrumhalf Chris Tynan takes on Eagles Jeff Peter, Mike Saunders and Pat Johnston. A Can-Am series game at Victoria, 1987.

the Ranfurly Shield. It held the trophy from 1931 to 1934, defending on 15 occasions and also had it from 1953 until late in 1956, defending it 23 times. Most recently it beat Wellington for the shield in 1982 and didn't lose it until late 1985, after equalling the record for 24 defences in one era.

Canterbury added a new dimension to Ranfurly Shield rugby when, under New Zealand domestic rules, it declined to have scrums when its hooker, former All Black John Buchan, was ordered off in the 1990 challenge against Auckland. Canterbury failed in that challenge, a bizarre but frenetically-paced exhibition of a mixture of rugby league and touch football, only by 30–33.

Canterbury has had many famous players in its ranks: All Blacks Bob Deans, Duncan McGregor, Read Masters, Bill Dalley, Charlie Oliver, Kevin and Bob Stuart, Maurie Dixon, Bob Duff, Stan 'Tiny' Hill, Fergie McCormick, Dennis Young, Lyn Davis, Alex Wyllie, Tane Norton, and more recently the Deans brothers, Robbie and Bruce. When those men appeared the Lancaster Park crowds bayed with approval. To them, there were no finer players in the world, anywhere.

CAPS

Read or listen to any announcement of an international rugby team and you will hear the term 'caps'. A new player is said to have 'won his first cap' while a player who has appeared a dozen times is said to have been 'capped 12 times'.

The term is one which can be traced back to Rugby School in England and the very origins of the game. Apparently players who were good enough to play the new form of football were given a special cap to wear. The headwear distinguished them from the others who were allowed to stand behind the posts. The cap entitled the wearer to 'follow up' the ball rather than act as one of the many goalkeepers. The tradition was carried on into international rugby. In the early days a velvet cap was presented to each player for each match played – today the term is mostly symbolic, although some countries still present actual caps to international players on their debut.

There have been a few instances of players being capped without ever

having taken the field for their countries. Harry Eagles and Percy Robertshaw were both selected for the England team which did not play any matches in 1888 because of the dispute over the formation of the International Rugby Board. Although they were not chosen again they were both awarded caps.

Bruce Deans was the first New Zealander to be capped as an All Black without taking the field, because the New Zealand Rugby Union ruled that all members of the 1987 World Cup squad had All Black status.

Two fully capped internationals were on the field of play for only a matter of seconds: the game between Wales and Australia in 1973 was in injury time when Clive Shell replaced Gareth Edwards in his only appearance for Wales; and New Zealander Marty Berry had 38 seconds on the field against Australia in 1986.

CAPTAINCY

Opinions vary on the qualities and attributes of a great captain. Some former captains rate communication to team-mates as the prime requisite; others say planning and ensuring efficiency from the team, both on and off the field, rate highly. Still others say firmness and control are vital factors. Indeed, all these elements make captaincy an additional responsibility to a player's role on the field. Whatever his ability, the captain becomes every team's most important player.

One of rugby's longest debates is over which playing position on the field best suits a captain. Many authorities say that a forward position is essential, if only because this is the area where every game is primarily won or lost. Others claim a back – either a halfback, flyhalf or even a centre – is best placed to lead a team because he has the widest overall view of the game.

Least favoured positions are fullback or wing: communication is difficult – especially if a large vocal crowd is in attendance. It was originally thought that having a hooker as captain was also disadvantageous, but the modern game of running, open football has meant that the hooker, in years gone by buried in the darkness of rucks and mauls, has come out into the clear spaces and is now seen by many as an ideal person for team control.

Listing 'great' international captains is fraught with danger, since such a list is bound to be subjective. But the following names stand out:

Fullbacks

J.P.R. Williams and Andy Irvine captained Wales and Scotland well from fullback. Tom Kiernan of Ireland had a most successful sequence as an international captain, including on the 1968 British Isles in South Africa.

'Basie' Viviers led the Springboks in New Zealand in 1956 from fullback and Roy Dryburgh led the South Africans in two tests from fullback in 1960. The All Blacks were led by Mike O'Leary, then a fullback, in 1913 in two tests against Australia, which was led in one of those games also by a fullback, Larry Dwyer. Serge Blanco captained France from this position in 1990–91.

Wings

From this unlikely position the best known captain was probably Arthur Smith of Scotland, who led the British Isles to South Africa in 1962. New Zealand's Stuart Wilson led the All Blacks on the tour of England and Scotland in 1983 from the wing, but later admitted it was not a satisfactory position for a captain. Christian Darrouy of France and Tom Grace of Ireland were two others who captained from the wing.

Centres

The best and most successful captain from centre would probably be John Dawes of the highly successful 1971 British Isles tour to New Zealand. Trevor Allan of Australia had two successful seasons as captain, while still playing well himself, from 1947 to 1949. Andrew Slack and Geoff Shaw also captained Australia from the centres. Bleddyn Williams of Wales led both Wales and the British Lions from that position, while Ron Elvidge led New Zealand five times. By 1991 Will Carling had become England's most successful captain. All of his wins were at centre.

Flyhalves or Five-Eighths

Australia offers Mark Ella and Tommy Lawton; Ireland, Jackie Kyle; South Africa, Bennie Osler and Naas Botha; and Argentina, Hugo Porta. Phil Bennett led the 1977 British Lions from

Two great captains: Bill Beaumont (left) and Graham Mourie, after Beaumont had led Northern Division to victory over the All Blacks in 1979.

flyhalf, and New Zealand's first two test captains were Jimmy Duncan and Billy Stead, both five-eighths.

Halfbacks

Wales has produced many fine captains from close to the scrum: Haydn Tanner, Rex Willis, Clive Rowlands spring to mind first, and Gareth Edwards, despite his own misgivings, was near to the best. Ken Catchpole was outstanding for Australia, as was Nick Farr-Jones, while Dawie de Villiers of South Africa played 22 internationals as 'skipper', a world's best for a halfback.

Danie Craven captained the Springboks only four times, but was an outstanding leader on the rugby field. Des Connor captained Australia and led New Zealand in non-internationals.

In 1975 France could not decide which of two halfbacks should lead its touring team to South Africa, so they appointed Richard Astre and Jacques Fouroux as 'co-captains'. The idea was not rated a success.

The first World Cup-winning team in 1987 was captained by a halfback, David Kirk of New Zealand.

No. 8s

Mark Loane of Australia, Mervyn Davies of Wales, Morne du Plessis and Hennie Muller of South Africa were all successful captains from this posi-

tion. New Zealand has had three outstanding No. 8 captains: Brian Lochore; the 1953–54 New Zealand captain Bob Stuart; and 'Buck' Shelford, who led the All Blacks 32 times – including 14 internationals – without defeat, but was then dropped!

Flankers

Jean-Pierre Rives of France was a hugely successful leader from the side of the scrum, as was Graham Mourie of New Zealand. Rives led France 34 times. At the end of 1990 this was the world's highest total for a test captain.

Greg Davis of Australia led his country 16 times from the side of the scrum, one less than Fergus Slattery of Ireland. Cliff Porter of New Zealand led the unbeaten 1924–25 All Blacks as a loose forward, and the All Black captain in 1905 was also a loose (or wing) forward, Dave Gallaher.

Other fine leaders from this position were the Frenchmen Michel Crauste, François Moncla and Jean Prat. The captain of the series-winning British Isles in Australia in 1989 was the Scottish flanker, Finlay Calder.

Locks

Bill Beaumont of England and Willie John McBride of Ireland lead a strong list from this position. Australia had John Thornett, while South Africa produced Avril Malan and Johan Claassen. The French had Lucien Mias, not originally chosen as captain, who led his team to its famous series victory in South Africa in 1958.

Three great leaders from the past were Mark Morrison of Scotland, Wavell Wakefield of England and Philip Nel of South Africa. Colin Meads was New Zealand's captain against the Lions from the lock position in 1971 and Bob Duff was ultimately the triumphant captain in the dramatic 1956 series against South Africa.

Props

Best known in this position was New Zealand's Wilson Whineray, an outstanding leader who captained the All Blacks in 30 of his 32 tests, which included only five losses. Hannes Marais of South Africa led his country 11 times. Scotland had Ian McLauchlan as a fine captain in the 1970s, while for both of Scotland's modern Grand Slams in 1984 and 1990, the captains were Jim Aitken and David Sole, both props.

Hooker

The British Isles led the way in making hookers the team leaders. Karl Mullen led their tour to New Zealand in 1950 and Ronnie Dawson in 1959. Ciaran Fitzgerald led the Lions to New Zealand in 1983. France enjoyed success under Philippe Dintrans and Daniel Dubroca; New Zealand under Andy Dalton.

Although he did not lead his country in many internationals, John Pullin fashioned one of the most enviable records as captain and hooker. Under him, England beat teams from South Africa, Australia, New Zealand, Fiji, France, Scotland and Wales. Other English hooker-captains included Eric Evans and Peter Wheeler. Colin Deans was a fine Scottish leader.

The captains listed above had the opportunity to lead their sides for some time so that they could imprint their own style on the team pattern. It is not always the case.

Wales, for instance, used four captains in the 1953–54 season (Bleddyn Williams, Rees Stephens, Rex Willis and Ken Jones). The situation has been far worse in recent years. In the four years from January 1987, Wales used nine different captains: David Pickering, Billy James, Richard Moriarty, Jonathan Davies, Bleddyn Bowen, Rob Norster, Paul Thorburn, Kevin Phillips and Robert Jones.

New Zealand had different captains for three consecutive test matches in 1968 (Chris Laidlaw, Kel Tremain, and Brian Lochore). In the space of eight internationals 1952–54, Scotland had five different captains.

South Africa couldn't settle on a captain for its first test series against the 1891 British side. Herbert Castens made his only appearance for South Africa in the first test (though by the time of the third international he was both the referee and a national selector!); Robert Sneddon made *his* only appearance, as captain in the second test; and Alf Richards was the third captain in as many tests.

Captaincy is not generally regarded as a young man's job, but England's first captain, Frederick Stokes, was still four months short of his 20th birthday when he played against Scotland in 1871.

Trevor Allan had just turned 21 when he succeeded to the captaincy of the Australian team touring Britain in 1947–48; so had New Zealand's youngest captain Herb Lilburne, when he led the All Blacks against Australia in 1929; and Ken Catchpole led Australia at 21. Claude Dourthe led France in tour matches in New Zealand in 1968 when only 19; and a countryman, René Crabos, was a test match captain at 21.

At the other end of the age-scale, the oldest of international captains was 'Buzz' Moore, who was 41 when he led Canada on its British tour in 1962. And Harry Watkins, who was on the wrong side of 30 when he played the first of his six tests for Wales, captained Victoria (British Colombia) against the 1913 All Blacks at the age of 42.

Some men, it seems, are born only to lead, and New Zealand, in particular, seems to have a policy of thrusting a new man into the captaincy and leaving him there.

Among those who were captain in all their internationals were Cliff Porter, Andy Leslie and Fred Allen. There were also those who only had one or two matches, like Pat Vincent, George Aitken and James Duncan. Whineray and Mourie were both captains in all but their first two internationals.

South Africans to enjoy a brief moment of glory, in addition to the 1891 men, were Basil Kenyon, Wynand Claassen, Felix du Plessis, and P.K Albertyn, as well as a one cap wonder, Des van Jaarsveldt.

Arch Winning captained Australia in his only test, but could not live up to his name; Jim Mitchie had a singularly unsuccessful two games as Ireland's captain, his only two tests; and when Wales fielded 13 new caps against England in 1934, one of them, hooker John Evans, was given the captaincy. That loss finished his career, too!

CARDIFF ARMS PARK

Arguably the world's most famous rugby arena, the Arms Park in Cardiff is easily the most accessible for the rugby public anywhere in the world. It is situated only a matter of metres from the busiest mid-city shopping and business streets of Cardiff, and teams preparing for internationals have often changed into their playing gear in hotels across the street and walked to the park.

Inside the stadium, it is the unique atmosphere created by the crowds, whose knowledge and devotion to the game is obvious, that makes Cardiff Arms Park such a special place. Locals say the singing of the crowds is not as good as it was in the past, but even today many a visiting player has been unnerved by the power and volume of the Welsh crowd singing traditional rugby hymns and songs. And few can remain unmoved at the distinctive feel of being in a Cardiff Arms Park throng.

The first international on the ground was in 1884, when Wales beat Ireland by a dropped goal and two tries to nil. The advantage Wales has had on its home ground ever since is no better exemplified than by its matches with England. When England won at the Arms Park in 1963 it was to be its last win there until 1991.

It is often asked – why the name 'Arms' Park? The site was near a coaching inn called the 'Cardiff Arms', so the recreation ground that grew out of wasteland across the street became known as the 'Arms Park'.

CARDIFF RFC

One of the most famous of all rugby clubs in the world. One of the 'big four' in Wales – along with Newport, Swansea and Llanelli – it is a powerful club in terms of playing strength as well as influence.

Cardiff was formed in 1876 from an amalgamation of the Glamorgan and the Wanderers Football Clubs, which came together to combat rising standards in rival clubs from Llanelli, Swansea and near neighbours Newport.

To this day Cardiff's annual matches with its great Welsh rivals attract big crowds. In 1951, 48,500 went to the Arms Park to see Cardiff play Newport, a record for a club match anywhere in the world.

After playing one season in black jerseys with a skull and cross-bones as symbol, the club introduced its famous light blue and dark blue colours.

Cardiff's influence on the game in its early years was considerable. Under the leadership of Frank Hancock, it was the first team in the world to play successfully four three-quarters. Introduced in 1883–84, this style is played by almost all British teams today.

Cardiff has always had strong teams and has produced literally hundreds of international players. The best known are names that are synonymous

Members of the 1953 Cardiff team that beat New Zealand celebrate the win every year with a grand dinner.

with Welsh, and therefore world rugby: F.E. Hancock, Percy Bush, Gwyn Nicholls, Rhys Gabe, H.B. Winfield, Wilfred Wooller, Cliff Jones, Haydn Tanner, Bleddyn Williams, Cliff Morgan, Rex Willis, Jack Matthews, Sid Judd, Barry John, Gareth Edwards and Gerald Davies.

Cardiff has had considerable success against visiting touring teams. Its most significant achievement is never having lost to any Australian international team – in six games from 1908–09 right through to 1984.

Cardiff was the only team in Britain, except Scotland, to beat the Springboks of 1906–07. Cardiff won 17–0, a famous victory, and in 1953–54 also beat the All Blacks, a victory that has been celebrated with an annual dinner ever since.

Cardiff now plays on its club ground which is immediately behind the Cardiff Arms Park.

CARISBROOK, DUNEDIN

The home of rugby in Otago, New Zealand, and venue for many rugby test matches. Carisbrook has seen many famous days, especially when it played host for the Otago team's golden era with the Ranfurly Shield between 1936 and 1949 and for Otago's famous victories over various British teams.

The first international match played at Carisbrook was in 1908, when New Zealand beat the Anglo-Welsh 32–6.

The game was refereed by an Otago man, Jimmy Duncan, who had been the captain of New Zealand's first official test team, in 1903.

New Zealand suffered its first defeat at Carisbrook in 1930, losing 3–6 to Great Britain. Thereafter the All Blacks didn't lose there until 1971, though this includes a 9–9 draw with the Lions in 1950 and the 'infamous' six-penalties-to-four-tries win over the Lions in 1959. The All Blacks have not lost a test at Carisbrook since 1971, although they were beaten there in 1973 by the New Zealand Juniors.

CARLETON, JOHN
Orrell and England
26 internationals for England 1979–84
6 internationals for British Isles 1980–83

A strong-running English wing who went on two British Isles tours. Carleton's international debut was against New Zealand at Twickenham in 1979. In his second season for England he scored three tries in one game of the Five Nations championship, against Scotland at Murrayfield – the first time in 56 years the feat had been accomplished by an Englishman in a test match.

Carleton had one win over South Africa, in the fourth test on the 1980 Lions tour, on which he travelled only after resigning his job as a physical education teacher. He had a good Li-

ons tour of New Zealand in 1983, appearing in three tests and scoring four tries in one tour match, against West Coast at Greymouth. His form in New Zealand was good, although he tended to suffer because of the indifferent form shown by the centres inside him. On that trip he·never repeated the excellent combination he had shown for England with Clive Woodward. In all John Carleton played five test matches against New Zealand. Only in his last appearance against the All Blacks was he on the winning side, for England in its 1983 game at Twickenham.

Work commitments prevented Carleton returning to South Africa with the England team in 1984.

CARMICHAEL, 'SANDY'
West of Scotland and Scotland
50 internationals for Scotland 1967–78

A prop who achieved the honour of 50 full internationals for his country. He also toured twice with the British Isles, to New Zealand in 1971 and to South Africa in 1974.

Carmichael's tour to New Zealand ended in controversial circumstances. Amid the fighting which marred the Lions match against Canterbury, Carmichael received facial injuries, presumably caused by punching, which were so severe that he had to leave the tour and head home.

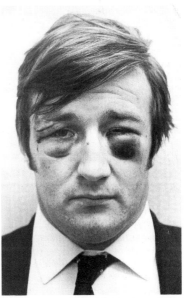

Sandy Carmichael with injuries suffered in a game against Canterbury in 1971.

In 1974 in South Africa he did not play any test matches, but he was a valuable back-up, both as a tighthead and loosehead prop, for the incumbent test players of that fine team.

At the time of his retirement in 1978 Carmichael held several records. He was the first Scottish international player to play 50 times for his country, and he was the first prop from any IRB country to achieve that feat. He played his career at a time when Scotland had little success in the game; indeed in his 50 internationals 'Sandy' Carmichael was only on the winning side 19 times.

CASSAYET, AIME
Tarbes, Narbonne and France
31 internationals for France 1920–27

A lock and No. 8 who had only five wins in his eight seasons as a French international, and only two wins in 26 games in the Five Nations championship.

Nor did Cassayet enjoy any other international success. France won a place, with Aimé Cassayet in its ranks, in the rugby finals at both the 1920 and 1924 Olympics. The United States triumphed on both occasions.

Cassayet captained his country eight times and his total of caps, 31 in all, was a French record at the time. He was a superb lock, excellent in the lineouts and one of the most famous French players of his day.

Tragically, within months of playing for France against Wales in March 1927, Aimé Cassayet contracted a fatal illness. He died in May 1927.

CATCHPOLE, KEN
New South Wales and Australia
27 internationals for Australia 1961–68

A brilliant halfback who is widely remembered for his ability to deliver the ball at optimum efficiency and speed to his outer backs. Catchpole's talent was recognised very early on and as a 21-year-old was not only in the Australian test team but he was captain on his debut (v Fiji 1961).

Catchpole continued as the number one halfback for the Wallabies until his premature retirement in 1968. He never fully recovered from a mauling at the hands of the All Blacks in the first test in Sydney that year. Playing in combination with fly-half Phil Hawthorne, he was largely responsible for

three famous Wallaby wins in the 1960s: at Wellington against the All Blacks in 1964; against Wales at Cardiff in 1966; and against England on the same tour.

He later commentated for the Australian Broadcasting Commission.

CATLEY, HAS
Waikato and New Zealand
7 internationals for New Zealand 1946–49

Evelyn Haswell Catley had a remarkable career as a hooker which stretched from 1935 to 1956. He was a triallist for the All Black tour of Britain 1935–36 but, largely because of World War II, did not play for New Zealand until nine days short of his 31st birthday. After playing against Australia at home and away in 1946–47, Catley toured South Africa in 1949, where he and props Kevin Skinner and Johnny Simpson formed a formidable front row.

Six days short of his 34th birthday, Catley played his final match for New Zealand – selectors thereafter decided he was too old, though his form remained superior to those who succeeded him. He stretched his career over 21 seasons for Waikato and played his final first class match, at the age of 41, for the Harlequins (NZ) club v Waikato in 1956.

A strong six-footer with an excellent technique, Catley hated yielding a scrum. In his first test in 1946, his side was under pressure; commonsense dictated it should yield the scrum to

the Wallabies. Catley's successful strike for the ball caused problems for his team, and when asked afterwards why he had gone for the ball, Catley pointed out he had to – his wife was keeping count of the scrums!

He won the scrums in that match 23 to 2 (some say 23–6), but those conceded scrums must have weighed heavily on the selectors: they dropped him for the second test!

CAVALIERS
This word had little or no significance in the sport of rugby until 1986, when the name 'Cavaliers' was adopted by a rebel team of New Zealand players which toured South Africa in 1986. Those against the tour commented that the actual meaning of the word was highly appropriate ('offhand, showing haughty disregard' – says the *Collins Dictionary*). Those, mostly from South Africa, who believed the Cavaliers tour was a good thing for rugby, rarely used the name at all – they called them 'All Blacks' instead!

The tour, its significance and aftermath, made headline news all over the rugby world. The players who went to South Africa in defiance of their own union's wishes stated it was a compensation for having the 1985 All Black tour of South Africa stopped by legal action in Auckland.

The team of 30 left New Zealand in separate groups to avoid protest action. The players assembled in South Africa and undertook a 12-match tour from April to June 1986. Their captain was

Australian Ken Catchpole in action. A superb passer and a speedy halfback.

Andy Dalton, who had been captain of the All Blacks until the previous year, and the manager and coach were the well-known former All Blacks Ian Kirkpatrick and Colin Meads. When Dalton was put out of the tour by a broken jaw, suffered in a punch from Northern Transvaal flanker Burger Geldenhuys, the captaincy was assumed first by Andy Haden, then by Jock Hobbs.

At the completion of the tour, the players in the Cavaliers were placed under suspension by the New Zealand Rugby Football Union, pending an investigation into playing in South Africa without approval, and also into allegations that the players had been paid while on tour. The players were suspended for two international matches before becoming eligible for selection for the All Blacks again.

In May 1987, Russell Thomas, chairman of the NZRFU, announced that due to insufficient evidence, all charges concerning the Cavaliers' payment were dropped. Nevertheless, there are many people in New Zealand who believe that the players involved never adequately explained the 'expenses' set-up of a rebel tour.

For the record, the Cavaliers played 12 matches on tour, winning eight and losing four. The four 'test' series was won by the Springboks by three matches to one. The South African Rugby Board, which originally denied all knowledge of the tour, awarded full test caps for the Springboks involved in the series.

CAVANAGH, VIC

A coach who had a profound influence on New Zealand rugby, yet never actually coached the All Blacks. Indeed, that Vic Cavanagh was denied the chance to coach at an international level is one of the long-standing mysteries of New Zealand sport.

Cavanagh is credited with inventing the 'Otago style' of rugby which, put simply, had a hallmark of vigorous rucking with players staying on their feet, and the backs only spinning the ball when the forwards had cleared enough space for them to move openly.

He coached Otago in the years immediately after World War II when that province enjoyed its rugby heyday. Cavanagh's Otago team completely dominated New Zealand rugby in that era, so much so that in 1949 11 members of his team were selected to tour South Africa. In one of New Zealand rugby's inexplicable decisions, Vic Cavanagh was passed over as coach. Instead Alex McDonald, a former All Black (from 1905), took the team and it lost all four test matches. Cavanagh stayed home to rebuild his decimated Otago team which went on to hold the Ranfurly Shield all season, a great tribute to Cavanagh's style and discipline.

Soured by his treatment, Cavanagh retired from coaching in 1950, but any Otago player or supporter of the time will still speak long and loud in praise of the Cavanagh method.

His father, also Vic Cavanagh, also coached and played for Otago.

CELAYA, MICHEL

Biarritz Olympique, Stade Bordelais, and France
50 internationals for France 1953–61

After being in the French international team for five seasons from 1953, and captain from 1956, Michel Celaya was appointed captain for the tour of South Africa in 1958. But on that tour bad luck played a major role. Injuries meant he played only three games, and because of injury in the first match, he had to hand over the leadership in the two test matches to Lucien Mias. That Mias was able to lead France to a famous series win guaranteed his place in French rugby history, while Celaya is remembered as the man who could have had the glory but instead missed out.

Celaya nevertheless had a distinguished playing career and reached the milestone of 50 internationals as a loose forward for his country, against Romania in 1961. He was a prominent coach of the French XV after his playing days were over.

CENTRE THREE-QUARTERS

A backline position where speed, unselfishness and inventiveness are very necessary qualities. In most rugby countries the two centres occupy the midfield backline positions after the scrumhalves and between the two outer wing positions. The player nearer the scrum is called the 'inside centre' – the other, obviously, is the 'outside centre'. New Zealand has different terminology calling the inside centre a 'second five-eighths' and the outside centre, 'centre three-quarter'.

Centres need to be capable of creating play for the speedy wings waiting beyond. They should be expert passers of the ball and explosively fast runners, though not necessarily the fastest players in a team. On defence, centres must be solid tacklers – to stop opposite numbers putting into practice the qualities listed above !

CENTURIONS

In rugby parlance, a man who has played 100 games at a particular level.

In Wellington, New Zealand, there is a Centurions club which was originally formed to provide social and charity rugby for former Wellington players and personalities.

Very few players have become centurions for their country, and with the reduction in modern times of the number of games played on overseas tours, it is not expected that record totals will be easily improved upon.

Probably the first man to play 100 games for his country, in either test matches or first-class tour games, was Nicholas Shehadie, who passed the total for Australia while on tour in Great Britain in 1957–58. In 1966, John Thornett repeated the feat for Australia in a game against the South of Scotland at Hawick; Greg Davis achieved the milestone at Rugby Park in Gisborne for Australia v Poverty Bay-East Coast in 1972.

The first New Zealander to pass 100 games was Colin Meads for New Zea-

Michel Celaya

land v Sydney in 1968. He went on to play 133 first-class games for New Zealand including 55 internationals. Other New Zealanders to become centurions were Ian Kirkpatrick v Western Province in 1976; Bryan Williams v Cardiff 1978; Bruce Robertson v Wales 1980; and Andy Haden v French Selection at La Rochelle in 1981.

No South African has played 100 games for his country.

Because it is not always established which tours had full first-class games, the keeping of the records of match centurions is not widely followed in the Britain or Europe. There, international caps are more closely accounted for. Mike Gibson played 155 matches for Ireland and the British Isles, which must surely be the world record for matches for international sides against first-class opponents. Serge Blanco of France, still playing in 1991, got closest to threatening this record.

CESTER, ELIE
Toulouse OEC, Valence and France
35 internationals for France 1966–74

For 12 years Elie Cester was France's most-capped lock. He appeared 30 times as a lock, and gained a reputation as a tough hard and consistent forward.

From the beginning of his test career in 1966, Cester never played in a losing French team until he played against the All Blacks in 1968. After that he played 10 internationals without winning.

The restaurateur ended his career after the Five Nations championship in 1974. His record as France's most-capped lock was broken by Jean Condom in 1987.

CHAMP, ERIC
Toulon and France
36 internationals for France 1985–90

A fiery and controversial French loose forward, whose style of play won both acclaim and criticism. In his early days as a top player, Champ was hard-working and energetic; later, there were some who thought his methods bordered and sometimes crossed that invisible barrier between 'energetic' and dirty play.

At his best Eric Champ was a classic rugby animal – tall, lean and mean in attitude. His climb to rugby stardom was mercurial. By the time he reached

New Zealand in 1987, he had a reputation as one of the world's best. Yet only two and a half years earlier he had not been rated in the top 10 of France's loosemen. New Zealanders regarded him as a force to be countered if their beloved All Blacks were going to become world champions. That New Zealand achieved its goal and won was not due to Champ slipping in form. He maintained it to the end.

But in the years that followed the World Cup, Champ's progress first faltered, then declined. He was dropped from the French team several times, only to recapture the selector's eye and return. His total of caps climbed to 36 after adding one more, against New Zealand, in late 1990.

Champ captained the Côte D'Azur against New Zealand in 1990, in a game that seemed to encapsulate the footballing enigma that was Eric Champ, the player.

In the first half he made a number of glaringly late tackles which were penalised and converted into points by the All Blacks. He was also involved in several disagreements with the touring team. Yet, in the second half, his attitude changed and he concentrated solely on rugby. He pulled off several spectacular plays which unsettled the All Blacks and from the front he led his team to a superb win. As a result he returned to the French team for the first test against the same team.

CHILE
The Chilean union was formed in 1948. Chile plays few games of international status other than those with neighbouring countries. It regularly beats Uruguay, Paraguay and Brazil in the South American championships, but has never beaten Argentina.

The Springboks played two matches in Chile in 1980 when they were on a tour of South America, in which South Africa awarded full caps for the two internationals played.

In the second 'test', played at the Prince of Wales club ground in Santiago, South Africa won by 30–16. However, the home team was 'South America' and not Chile, and the players who made up the team were all from Argentina. Earlier a Chilean invitation team lost by 12–78.

When South America toured South Africa in 1980 and 1982, several Chilean players were included in the tour-

ing party but none played in the 'tests' v South Africa.

CHOLLEY, GERARD
Castres and France
31 internationals for France 1975–79

Another of the long list of French forwards to become an international after changing positions. Gérard Cholley had played as a lock for 10 seasons before it was suggested he might prop the scrum. This he did, taking to it like to the manner born. He was probably one of the tallest props to make the big time, at 1.90 metres (6ft 3in) tall.

He was five months off 30 years old when he made his international debut against England at Twickenham in 1975. Only four years later he was finished with big rugby and had racked up a total of 31 internationals.

Cholley was notorious for becoming the first Frenchman sent off in a representative match. Referee Ian Gourlay ordered him off for punching and head-butting during the France v Eastern Transvaal game in 1975.

Years later Cholley was a French selector.

CHRISTCHURCH
One of New Zealand's biggest cities and the headquarters of Canterbury rugby, Christchurch is also the name of the oldest club in New Zealand and one of the oldest in the world.

Christchurch Football Club was formed in 1863, before the Canterbury provincial union. Later the union adopted the Christchurch colours – red and black hooped jerseys, black shorts, black socks with red tops, though true Cantabrians refer to the red as scarlet.

The Christchurch club provided the first New Zealand captain, William Millton, in 1884; his brother Edward was also in that side. Over 100 years later Christchurch had produced 28 All Blacks, the third greatest total by a club in New Zealand, with Morrie Wood, Bob Duff, Jack Manchester and 'Jock' Hobbs joining Millton as captains of New Zealand sides.

CLAASSEN, JOHANNES
Western Province and South Africa
28 internationals for South Africa 1955–62

Johannes Claassen was a lock with excellent lineout skills who became

Springbok captain, then coach, and later still manager of a South African touring team.

Claassen made his debut for the Springboks in 1955 and a year later was a vital member of the Springbok pack on the tour of Australia and New Zealand. He had the dubious distinction of captaining South Africa during the first test series the Springboks lost at home in the twentieth century – against France in 1958. He captained South Africa in seven other internationals in 1961 and 1962 without defeat. On his retirement Claassen had played 28 internationals, a Springbok record.

By 1968 Johan Claassen was the coach of the Springbok team. He guided it on three tours, to France in 1968 and 1974 and to Australia in 1971. In 1981, by then a Professor of Education at the University of Potchefstroom, he was the manager of the Springbok team on its protest-ridden tour of New Zealand.

Johan Claassen (left) as manager of the 1981 Springboks in New Zealand. On his left are Abe Williams, the assistant manager, and the captain, Wynand Claassen.

CLARKE, DON
Waikato and New Zealand
31 internationals for N. Zealand 1956–64

CLARKE, IAN
Waikato, and New Zealand
24 internationals for N. Zealand 1953–63

Don Clarke was a big man who became one of the best-known sporting personalities of New Zealand.

It was surprising that a lad so big would opt for the position of fullback, but this he did, and soon became recognised as a player of great potential in this position.

He might have made the New Zealand team sooner but for some serious knee injury problems, so it was not until 1956 that he joined the All Blacks.

South Africa toured New Zealand that year and the series was drawn at one win apiece when the All Black selectors drafted in the new young fullback. He was an immediate success, scoring eight points in each of the third and fourth tests, and he was largely responsible for the Springboks going home beaten in an away test series for the first time in the twentieth century.

His massive kicking soon earned Clarke the nickname 'The Boot', but his field skills also belied his 16–17 stone size. He especially thrived on the hard fields of Australia and South

Africa, where he stunned the locals with the length of his punting and goal-kicking. One of his touch-finding kicks on the All Black tour of South Africa in 1960 was said to have travelled nearly the length of the field.

Don Clarke scored 207 points for the All Blacks in test matches – a world record until it was passed by Andy Irvine of Scotland nearly 20 years later, and surpassed as the New Zealand record only in 1988, by Grant Fox.

Don Clarke, New Zealand's rugby hero.

Soon after his retirement from rugby he went to live in South Africa.

Don's older brother, Ian, was also a fine All Black, playing for his country from 1953 until 1964. Primarily a prop, he played as No. 8 when he captained New Zealand against Australia in 1955. He had a sweet moment in Cardiff in 1964. As a non-test player during the All Black tour, he was invited to play for the Barbarians against his team-mates. During the game he shocked everyone by drop-kicking a goal from a mark!

Three other brothers (Doug, Brian and Graeme) all had careers in first-class rugby. On one celebrated day in 1961 all five played together for Waikato against Thames Valley.

CLINCH, JAMES
Wanderers, Dublin University and
  Ireland
30 internationals for Ireland 1923–31

Known throughout the rugby world as 'Jammie' Clinch, this fine Irish flanker was a famous player of the 1920s. His father had been an Irish international between 1892 and 1897.

Clinch was known as a defensive forward with the innate ability to hang back and predict where the opposition would kick or pass the ball. Many times he saved Ireland with his presence in defence to clear or tackle.

He was known as an excellent kicker of the ball which, in those days, was an art not widely practised by forwards, but he never scored a try in an international, so committed was he to his defensive role.

He was a man of lively humour. Before his death in 1981 he told how an Irish-Welsh international was yet to get underway when he heard a voice from the crowd bellow, 'Send the bastard off now, ref!' With a twinkle in his eye, Clinch rated that the finest compliment ever paid to his vigorous style.

Clinch lived for 29 years in Wales, where he practised as a doctor.

COACHES

There are said to be two types of rugby coach. One is the 'rip, snort and bust' merchant who thunders exhortations on the practice field, in the dressing shed and from the sideline. The other takes a more psychological approach: he finds the key to motivating players and quietly turns that understanding into confidence on the field.

No doubt this distinction is apocryphal and the best of coaches blend elements from both extremes. Certainly a coach requires a thorough understanding of his game, the ability to teach and motivate his side and to devise winning tactics.

Strict adherence to the amateur principles of rugby, which did not allow a team's captain to be given help in preparing for a game, slowed the development of coaching in British countries. Indeed, until relatively recently British coaches, especially in England and Scotland, were called 'advisers to the captain'. Elsewhere, as in New Zealand, coaches were often known as 'assistant managers'.

Nevertheless, from Britain and Ireland have come world-renowned coaches like Carwyn James, Sid Millar, John Burges, Clive Rowlands, Noel Murphy, Don Rutherford, Ray Williams, Jim Telfer, Bill Dickinson, John Dawes and Ian McGeechan.

France has had the coaching talents of Jacques Fouroux in recent years. Before that came Michel Celaya, Guy Basquet, André Garrigues and Jean Pique.

New Zealand has enjoyed the excellent coaching of Fred Allen, J.J. Stewart, Jack Gleeson, Brian Lochore, Norman McKenzie, and Alex Wyllie.

Australia has given the rugby world Des Connor, Bob Templeton, Dave Brockhoff, Bob Dwyer and Alan Jones, among many others.

South Africa's most prominent coaches include Danie Craven, of course, Johann Claassen, A.F. Markotter and Hennie Muller. Another South African, Izaak van Heerden, played a large part in introducing the art of coaching rugby in Argentina.

A most prominent Argentine coach is Hector Silva, who directed his country's efforts at the first World Cup.

John Dawes, coach for the Lions and for Wales during its glittering era of the 1970s.

Alan Jones, a successful, colourful and controversial coach of Australia in the 1980s.

Several other notable coaches never made it to an international level. These include Burmann van Zyl of South Africa, Vic Cavanagh of New Zealand and Brother Henry Gaffney of Australia, while Carwyn James never coached Wales.

One of New Zealand's greatest coaches, Fred Allen, once said 'Coaching is the resolving of the complexities of the game into simplicities.' There is another adage which rings true: 'Coaches are seldom satisfied, seldom happy and seldom home.'

CODORNIOU, DIDIER
Narbonne, Toulouse and France
31 internationals for France 1979–85

A question often asked in the early 1980s was – why does Didier Codorniou not get more games for France? It seemed a fair question to be directed at the French national selectors, for Codorniou was, to any outsider, one of the most brilliant attacking players in the world. From his position as a centre, he could scream through a gap with blinding speed; he could outrun defenders; he had brilliant ball skills; and for his diminutive build seemed to be more than adequate as a tackler.

Yet this marvellous Narbonne player could not make the French team after his 27th year. It seemed the French selectors just did not want too much flair in the centres. So Didier Codorniou, who had startled New Zealanders with his brilliance in the 'Bastille Day' victory at Auckland in 1979, stopped adding to his total of caps. Frenchmen still puzzle over the question – why?

Codorniou was twice a member of a team which won the French championship: with Narbonne in 1979 and with Toulouse in 1989.

COFFEY, JOHN
Lansdowne and Ireland
19 internationals for Ireland, 1900–10

A regular forward selection for Ireland, including playing against the original touring sides from both New Zealand and South Africa, 'Jack' Coffey retired after playing in 1907–08 against Wales.

Two years later, he returned briefly and unusually, against France. Poking his head into the Irish dressing-room to wish his old team-mates luck, the 32-year-old Coffey was drafted into the team on the spot: one of the players had taken ill at the last moment. By the luck of the Irish, Coffey's inclusion in the team proved fortuitous. Ireland won the match 8–3.

Two years later, Coffey returned to international rugby, this time as referee for Scotland v France. In 1924, he began a 21-year term as IRU president, a position he held until his death.

COLCLOUGH, MAURICE
Wasps, Angoulême, Swansea and
England
25 internationals for England 1978–86
8 internationals for British Isles 1980–83

A big tousle-haired lock, Colclough lived for a time in France, commuting back for both club and international rugby.

He was a powerful player at both scrum and lineout, who first played for England against Scotland in 1978. He went on the first of his two British Isles tours in 1980, appearing in all four tests against the Springboks. It was originally thought Colclough would not make the test side, but solid early tour form in the midweek games brought him promotion to play as the second-row partner to fellow Englishman Bill Beaumont. Earlier that year they had been a powerful force in England's Grand Slam-winning combination.

Colclough played all four tests in New Zealand in 1983, gaining selection for the tour even though he had missed most of the build-up British season because of injury.

His last year at the top was in 1986, when he appeared in all four Five Nations matches, before retiring to Swansea to run a popular restaurant on a sailing ship in the docklands area.

COLLAR
An obsolete rugby term meaning to tackle a player. In accounts of rugby matches from the game's early days and into the twentieth century, the word appears many times. Presumably when a player was 'collared' he was grasped by the shirt. Tackling around the legs came later.

COLOMBES STADIUM
The home of French international rugby from 1920 until 1972, and the home of the Racing Club de France.

The first international match was actually played there in 1914, when England beat France 39–13 – the last championship match before the outbreak of World War I.

When internationals resumed, several were played on Parc des Princes before the FFR finally opted for the Colombes Stadium, 8km north-west of Paris. After the complex was expanded and modernised for track and field events at the 1924 Olympic Games, it was used regularly for soccer and athletics as well as rugby, and became a familiar venue for sports fans in Paris all year round.

Although the stadium was a multi-purpose venue, it was a rugby player for whom it is officially named. Yves du Manoir was a popular and brilliant French international who lost his life in a plane crash in 1928 at the age of 24. Such was the measure of his loss that the authorities officially named the ground the Stade Yves du Manoir.

In later years Colombes Stadium came under criticism, and eventually Parisian city authorities had to choose between a difficult expansion programme or moving to a new ground. Thus, when the old Parc des Princes ground was rebuilt with a seating capacity of 100,000, Colombes Stadium was dropped as a venue for international rugby.

In the last international game there, on 26 February 1972, the French team beat England 37–12, a record score for France in an international.

CONCORD OVAL
Developed as Sydney's new rugby home, Concord Oval (named after the inner western suburb where it is located) was the result of the local rugby union's desire that the game in Sydney should establish its own identity.

With 20,000 fewer seats than the Sydney Cricket Ground's 40,000, it was a controversial choice for the staging of the 1987 World Cup games in Sydney. However, only smallish crowds turned out in Australia for the cup, so Concord proved a satisfactory venue.

There were long-term development plans to bring the ground and its facilities up to international standard, but massive financial difficulties hit the New South Wales Rugby Union and the ground had to be abandoned. Seating was sold and future internationals in Sydney were located at the new Sydney Football Stadium.

CONDOM, JEAN
Boucau, Biarritz Olympique and France
61 internationals for France 1982–90

A tireless player, Condom racked up a huge total of caps as a lock for his country. Noted for his consistency of effort over many seasons, he was also a strong mauler and scrummager. In many respects he was an 'old-fashioned' type of forward, preferring to work solidly in the tight play rather than be flashy in the loose.

Condom made his debut against Romania in 1982, when he was member of the Boucau club. In 1986 he shifted to nearby Biarritz.

He was such a permanent figure in French sides of the 1980s, it became a statistician's delight to count the number of locking partners he played with in the national XV. When he made his 61st appearance for France, as a replacement in the third test v Australia in Sydney in 1990, he locked with Olivier Roumat, who became his eleventh partner in the second row.

Condom was a member of the French team that played in the first Rugby World Cup final in Auckland, 1987.

His 61 internationals to the end of 1990 made him France's most capped lock – but in all those games he never scored a try!

Jean Condom

CONNACHT RFU
There are four provincial rugby unions in Ireland. Ulster covers the north, including Belfast; Leinster the east coast, including Dublin; Munster, the south and south-west and Connacht, the north-west coast. Connacht is the smallest of the four Irish rugby unions and has had the least success in the Irish provincial championship.

Connaught joined the Irish championship in 1947 although it had been playing 'friendlies' for some years before. With the arrival of Connacht, the championship became an all-Ireland event for the first time. Connacht's year of consolidation came in 1956 when it shared the championship with Ulster. That season it also won in Cork to record its first win on Munster soil, then beat Ulster at Ravenhill by 6–3 to make it consecutive away wins over Ulster. But for 17 long seasons between 1963 and 1979, it could not win a match in the inter-provincial series. There was a declining population in the area and a number of clubs had difficulty in maintaining their playing numbers.

Connacht rugby is centred around the city of Galway, with the club teams Galwegians and Corinthians the two traditional leading teams of the province.

Perhaps the father of Connacht rugby was Henry Anderson. In 1904 he became the first Connacht man to be capped for Ireland (even though he played at the time for Old Wesley in Dublin). Anderson later became the province's first representative on the Irish Rugby Union's committee and in 1946 was the first Connacht man to be elected president of the union.

CONNOR, DES
Auckland and New Zealand; Queensland and Australia
12 internationals for Australia 1957–59
12 internationals for N. Zealand 1961–64

One of a string of fine Australian halfbacks, Des Connor first played for Australia on the disastrous 1957–58 tour of Britain, in which the team lost all its international matches. Connor was one of the few success stories of the tour: his scrumhalf play was always strong and sure, his passing was long and accurate, and he exhibited deftly controlled variations in his tactical kicking.

Connor quickly chalked up 12 internationals for the Wallabies and was a consistent star for Queensland, his home state. He later took up a teaching post in Auckland, New Zealand and before long became a leading contender for the All Blacks.

His debut for New Zealand was against France in 1961, on his adopted 'home' ground, Eden Park in Auckland. The first minute of play brought New Zealand a try with three players involved who had never touched a ball in All Black test rugby before. Connor passed from a scrum he had just fed to new five-eighths Neil Wolfe who sent it on to the new wing, Don McKay, who sped over in the corner for a try.

From this auspicious beginning Connor rarely looked back. In his 12 tests he was always vice-captain for New Zealand, but when he went back to Australia with the 1962 All Blacks he was given the honour of leading New Zealand against his former home team, Queensland.

Surprisingly dropped from the All Blacks for their tour of Britain in 1963–64, Connor was back in the team a year later for his last international.

After his retirement from playing, and back living in Brisbane, Connor turned to coaching. By 1968 he was the coach of the Wallabies. He did not have great success, but he is remembered as the man who introduced to the game the short lineout as a legitimate tactic for countering opposition teams with much bigger jumpers.

COOK ISLANDS RUGBY
Rugby is pursued enthusiastically in this Pacific island group. Standards are not high, but Cook Island's rugby administrators are always on the lookout for new opponents.

The national team undertook its first major tour in 1976, to New Zealand. The team played six games and though all were losses the crowds were generally big and the standard of play was good enough for the Cooks' officials to hope for continuing contact with New Zealand.

The biggest moment for the Cook Islands came in 1980 when the national team beat the Italian team which had just toured New Zealand. Cooks won by 15–6 at Rarotonga, the largest island in the group.

In 1985, at the mini South Pacific Games, Cook Islands won the gold

Des Connor (left) and Greg Davis – an Australian who played for New Zealand, and a New Zealander who played for Australia.

medal, beating New Caledonia in the final. (Fiji, Western Samoa and Tonga did not attend the tournament.)

Rugby in the Cook Islands still struggles from lack of contact with outside countries. Indeed the Cooks' nearest rugby-playing .neighbours – Samoa, Tonga, Fiji and New Zealand – did little in the early days to encourage an association on the rugby field. A more unified rugby scene in the Pacific is an ideal that Cook Islands officials still hope to gain.

COOKE, BERT
Auckland, Hawke's Bay, Wairarapa,
  Wellington and New Zealand
8 internationals for New Zealand 1924–30

Although he played so few internationals, Bert Cooke is remembered as one of New Zealand's speediest and most talented backs and a famous figure in New Zealand rugby. He was the team's top try scorer (23) with the 1924–25 'Invincibles' All Black team in Britain.

On that tour, one writer, R.A. Byers-Barr, described Cooke as 'the most brilliant back in the New Zealand team'. He was also 'as swift as a hare', 'as elusive as a shadow'. He 'strikes like lightning', 'flashes with brilliance'. 'Cooke is the shining star of the side.' 'He is meteoric in method; penetrates like a bayonet-point and thrusts like steel.' 'Cooke is Eclipse. . . !'

Bert Cooke played for New Zealand over five more seasons, but after being selected for the 1928 tour of South Africa withdrew for business reasons. He later turned to rugby league in which he also represented New Zealand. Cooke was the first New Zealander to score 100 tries in first-class matches, tallying 121 from only 131 matches.

CO-OPTIMISTS RFC
Perhaps the rugby club with the oddest name, the Co-Optimists of Scotland are very definitely a force in rugby. It is the friendly invitation club of Scotland. George Murray and Jock Wemyss

formed the club, naming it, for reasons unknown, after a theatrical company that toured Scotland in the 1920s.

The club is joined by invitation only and has only one set fixture – against East Lothian, which was its first opponent in 1924. Co-Optimists include a high number of Scotsmen, but have others from all over the rugby-playing world. In recent years they have travelled overseas on a number of occasions; Hong Kong's Sevens tournament is one that has been graced by the open running style of the Co-Optimists.

CORK CONSTITUTION RFC
An Irish club formed in 1892. Early members came from the staff of a now defunct newspaper from the town of Cork, in the province of Munster.

The club's best-known players are the famous Irish captains, Tom Kiernan and Noel A.A. Murphy.

Kiernan played 54 times for Ireland, during his career captaining his club, the province of Munster, Ireland and the British Isles. Murphy played 41 caps for Ireland and was also an Irish captain. His father, Noel F. Murphy, also an international, played for Constitution, as did Donal Lenihan, the Irish captain at the first Rugby World Cup in 1987.

The club plays home games at Temple Hill Ground in Cork and has flourished in the strong rugby environment of south-west Ireland. It has won the Munster Cup 21 times in its first 100 years – at least once in every decade. In the Munster league in recent times it enjoyed a remarkable run, winning 15 times in 25 years.

COTTON, FRAN
Loughborough College, Sale, Coventry
  and England
31 internationals for England 1971–81
7 internationals for British Isles 1974–77

An international prop who forged a reputation as a tough hard customer, Fran Cotton had one historic day in the game at Workington. He was captain of the North-Western Counties team which beat the All Blacks in 1972, thus making him the leader of the first non-international English team to beat an All Black team. Later he was to pass Ron Jacobs's record as England's most-capped prop.

Fran (actual name Francis) came from a rugby league background, his

Fran Cotton

father having played for Britain before and after World War II. His brother David was also a notable rugby league player.

Cotton made three tours with the British Lions. In South Africa in 1974 he was one of the test front row which never lost to the Springboks. He was also a vital part of the Lions' power scrum in New Zealand in 1977 but by 1980, when he made his second tour to South Africa, he ran into serious health problems. He left the field against the South African Proteas with what was originally thought to have been a heart attack. He did not take any further part in that tour but made it back into the England team for one further match in 1981.

COUGARS RFC
The Cougars RFC is the Barbarians-type rugby club of the United States, principally known for its tour of South Africa in 1978, where it won one match out of the seven played. The main match was against the South African Under-25s and the Cougars impressed by holding the Gazelles to 16–20. Their only tour win was an 18–15 result over a Northern Transvaal XV. Their captain was the United States captain of the time, Clarence Culpepper.

COUNTIES RFU
From 1926 until 1955 players from the area immediately south of Auckland were members of the South Auckland sub-union but played for Auckland. Approval was given for full first-class status in 1955, and the team played its first games as South Auckland Counties that year. The next year the name was shortened to just Counties.

The province soon built a reputation for playing bright, running rugby, possibly because it knew it would have to play attractively to draw crowds away from nearby Auckland.

In their early years Counties were fortunate to have two coaches, Barry Bracewell and Hiwi Tauroa, who set the team running from all points of the field. Soon this became known as the 'Counties' style.

Counties had their biggest year in 1979 when they won the national Division One championship and just missed beating Auckland to win the Ranfurly Shield. It remains one of the biggest unions in New Zealand never to have won the coveted shield. Counties' best efforts were thrilling drawn challenges against Waikato in 1981 and with Canterbury in 1982.

Counties have produced many famous players, probably the best known of whom is All Black captain and hooker Andy Dalton, who played all his rugby in the province and was an All Black 1977–87. The 1972–81 All Black centre, Bruce Robertson, who played 102 games for his country, was another Counties hero.

The union's first All Black was Pat Walsh in 1955 and others included Kevin Skinner, Bruce McLeod, Rod Ketels, John Spiers and Nicky Allen. The Scottish international Sean Lineen had 64 games for Counties before leaving to play in Edinburgh and later becoming a member of the Grand Slam-winning team of 1990.

Counties beat Argentina in 1979, Australia in 1982 and Canada in 1990. They had a successful tour to South America in 1989.

COUNTY CHAMPIONSHIP
The annual competition between the counties of England which dates back to 1889 when the Rugby Football Union declared the winner to be the county with the best record of wins that season. Yorkshire was declared the first county champion.

Over the years the competition has undergone various formats and changes but has rarely been popular with the fans. The most recent of these changes occurred in 1982–83, when sponsorship money was used to prop up sagging interest in the traditional event, now played in divisional county groupings. Whatever its drawbacks, the championship provides top class exposure for playing talent from those areas without strong club teams.

In recent years one of the most successful counties has been Gloucestershire, which won five times between 1972 and 1984, and Lancashire which won seven times between 1969 and 1990. Warwickshire won seven times in eight years in the late 1950s.

COVENTRY RFC
One of the leading clubs of the Midlands, Coventry was formed in 1874. The club has had several 'golden' eras, the first being in the 1950s and 60s when the club sometimes supplied up to 12 players in the Warwickshire county side which won the county championship seven times in eight years. The second came in 1973 and 1974 when the club won the Rugby Football Union's club knock-out competition, playing a record 14 games without defeat.

Leading players include the famous England wings David Duckham and Peter Jackson. Duckham is the club's record cap-winner with 36 for England. The regular England prop of the 1960s, Phil Judd, was also a Coventry man, as were Marcus Rose, Huw Davies, and Alan Rotherham. Fran Cotton was a Coventry man for a time.

Since 1921 the club's headquarters have been Coundon Road in Coventry.

COVE-SMITH, RONALD
Old Merchant Taylors and England
29 internationals for England 1921–29
4 internationals for Great Britain 1924

Easily distinguished on the field of play with his thick, black eyebrows and black moustache, Ron Cove-Smith of England was part of a fine English era of forward play. In his 27 internationals in the Five Nations championship, he was in the winning team 21 times. He captained his country in 1928, beating the New South Wales 'Waratahs' at Twickenham and leading his team to a Grand Slam win in

Ronald Cove-Smith, in England's victory over the Waratahs in 1928.

the Five Nations championship. He also led the Great Britain team in South Africa in 1924. His 22 wins in the English jersey remained a record for 60 years and his total of caps was second only to the great Wavell Wakefield, who was his team-mate many times for England.

Cove-Smith was an outstanding tight forward. Wakefield once said of him, 'He was a player of great moral value to the side, for the sense of security he infused.' How modern reporters would love to hear quotes like that!

CRABOS, RENE
Racing Club, Saint-Sever and France
17 internationals for France 1920–24

One of France's earliest star players who became a powerful administrator and selector for the national team.

A dashing centre three-quarter and captain for France before he had turned 22, Crabos had his playing days cut short when he broke a leg in two places when playing against Ireland in 1924. During his short sporting career he also played athletics, soccer, lawn tennis and pelota with distinction.

He later became a national selector and was president of the Fédération Francaise de Rugby from 1952–62. He won acclaim as president by insisting on recalling Lucien Mias from semi-retirement in 1957; what followed in 1959 was France's first outright win in the Five Nations championship under Mias's leadership.

Crabos managed French teams on three tours to Argentina.

CRAUSTE, MICHEL
Racing Club, Lourdes and France
63 internationals for France 1957–66

One of the greatest of French players, Michel Crauste was a driving, tireless loose forward who eventually set a record for appearances in the French international jersey.

He first came into the French XV in 1957 for two matches against Romania. The following year he was unavailable for the famous 1958 French team which beat the Springboks in South Africa, but by 1960 Crauste had been voted France's top player. The former captain, Jean Prat, said he had 'never seen a better, more complete forward' than Crauste.

Nicknamed 'Attila' or 'Mongol', Crauste remained in the French team until 1966. He led France on its second tour of South Africa in 1964, when his team won the only test match by 8–6, at Springs. His record of most appearances for France stood until Benoit Dauga equalled it in 1972.

Crauste achieved notoriety on the French tour of New Zealand in 1961, when his rough play so incensed a woman spectator at Timaru that she strode onto the field and punched him in the back with her clenched fist. No penalty was awarded!

CRAVEN, DANIE
Western Province and South Africa
16 internationals for Sth Africa 1931–38

Undoubtedly one of rugby's greatest and at the same time most controversial figures, Danie Craven rightfully earned the nickname 'Mr Rugby', such was his contribution to the game both in South Africa and on the world scene.

In the 1960s and later, when the storm and scorn of world opinion rained down on South Africa's apartheid policies, Dr Craven was seen by some as being an apologist for South African Government ideals. Such charges were without real foundation. The cause Danie Craven stood for in his life was the game of rugby, and South African rugby in particular. It was no more and no less than that.

Craven's devotion to the game and his desperate hope that international rugby might return to his country, saw him placed in an invidious position at the time of the 1986 rebel New Zealand tour of South Africa.

When the details of the tour broke publicly, Danie Craven called it news that was 'too good to be true', a remark that could be interpreted as his true feeling on the matter. Within days he had to wear his International Rugby Board hat and call for the total cancellation and denunciation of the tour. The scandal of whether he knew, or did not know, of the plans of the Cavaliers' tour rather marred his later years in the game, but there can nevertheless be no denying he was one of rugby's most famous and significant figures whose career deserves its place on the game's Roll of Honour.

Danie Craven was an outstanding player who made the dive-pass seem like his own (actually he was improving on the invention of another Springbok, Dauncey Devine). In the dressing room and on the field of play, he was a brilliant schemer and tactician.

Born in 1910, Craven was first picked for his country for the 1931–32 tour of Britain. He quickly established himself as a test match regular and in all played 16 internationals for his country until what was seen by his supporters as a premature retirement in 1938. He played for the Springboks in four test positions: halfback, flyhalf, centre three-quarter and No. 8. He also played at fullback against Queensland in 1937.

Craven soon rose in eminence as a coach and administrator of rugby. He was the mastermind behind the highly successful 1951–52 Springboks' tour to Great Britain and the driving force behind the powerful South African team which gave New Zealand the 'Battle for the Rugby Crown' in 1956. Craven's utterance – 'It's all yours, New Zealand', after the All Blacks had won the test series – is one of the

Danie Craven's famous dive pass, v New Zealand at Auckland, 1937.

Dr Danie Craven, 'Mr Rugby'.

cherished quotes of New Zealand rugby.

Craven rose to be president of the South African Rugby Board in 1956. He was still president in 1990, holding the position far longer than any other national rugby executive. He was also a long-serving member of the International Rugby Board.

At times he was cast as a rather bitter figure in his later years, due to disappointed comments from a frustrated, often grumpy face to the various news media, but it was through none of his endeavours that South Africa was set adrift from the rugby world. Craven campaigned tirelessly to destroy rugby's racial barriers. If others imposed boycotts and protests against Springbok rugby, that did not deter him from his hope of seeing a multi-racial team accepted in world rugby.

When he turned 80 in 1990, several celebratory dinners and functions were held, including a game at his beloved Stellenbosch between Northern Transvaal and a team of current and former Stellenbosch players.

Danie Craven could look back on a life of achievement, having earned himself three doctorates – in anthropology, psychology and physical education (the history of major games). Apart from his academic life he has been a star player, coach, selector, manager, author and administrator of the game with which his name became synonymous. As one writer said in 1990, 'Say Craven and you say rugby.'

CRAVEN WEEK

Established in 1964 Craven Week, named after Dr Danie Craven, is a week of competition between the best of South Africa's provincial schools' teams. Current and former Springboks help with arrangements and coaching, and the event, multi-racial since 1980, has been the nursery for many prominent adult players.

CRAWFORD, ERNIE

Lansdowne and Ireland
30 internationals for Ireland 1920–27

Ernie Crawford was a courageous and innovative Irish fullback in the 1920s who possibly missed playing his best rugby because of World War I. He made his debut for Ireland in 1920 as a 29-year-old, but had played for Ulster against South Africa in 1912. He played his final international match as a 36-year-old in 1927.

The famous New Zealand fullback George Nepia was one who was particularly impressed by Ernie Crawford, describing him as 'one of my heroes . . . and, until Bob Scott came along, the greatest fullback I ever saw.'

Crawford could kick well, was fearless on the tackle and possessed a powerful personality respected by all who played alongside him. One writer said that Crawford as a player 'mixed subtlety of movement with sarcasm of tongue, and was never afraid to use both attributes'.

He was an Irish captain, and president of the Irish Rugby Union 1957–

58. He is also alleged to be the first to use the word 'alligadoos' to describe the rugby game's officials and administrators.

CRAWSHAY'S CLUB

A private rugby club founded in 1922 by a radical Welsh Liberal, Captain Geoffrey Crawshay. In its early days the club fielded teams that played for Captain Crawshay at his expense, but today it is like the Barbarians, i.e., it provides exhibition and invitation games for prominent players away

Ernie Crawford

from the usual rivalries of their Welsh clubs. Most of Wales's leading players have played in Crawshay's colours at some time.

Outside Wales, Crawshay's is perhaps best known for its several appearances in the Hong Kong Sevens tournament.

The club toured to South Africa in 1985, causing considerable upset, with some prominent members who opposed such visits resigning. The team, captained by Chris Williams, contained five players who had played for the Lions – Elgan Rees, Graham Price, Ian Stephens, Alan Phillips and Allan Martin. It played provincial teams and won two games out of six.

CROSSAN, KEITH
Instonians and Ulster
36 internationals for Ireland 1982–91

Being a trifle small as a wing never bothered this effervescent Irish player. Keith Crossan was a solid and consistent performer for his country for 36 internationals to the end of 1990–91.

A slow starter in his international career, he toured South Africa in 1981 without playing a test match. After his test debut, against Scotland in 1982, he was missing from the Irish team for the best part of two seasons. But after a recall for the 1983–84 season he became a fixture in the side, generally losing his place only because of injury. At the World Cup in 1987 he appeared in all of Ireland's games and crossed for two tries against Canada in Dunedin.

By the end of the 1991 season Crossan had scored 12 tries in tests, placing him third on the all-time Irish test list.

CULLEN, ROSS
An Australian touring team member in 1966–67 who had a very short stay in international football, but a place in rugby history nevertheless.

Ross Cullen was a New Zealand-born hooker who became involved in an incident when playing only his second match in Australia's colours, against Oxford University.

The local prop, Ollie Waldron, an Irish international, was taken from the field late in the game with a torn ear. Later it was alleged that Waldron had had his ear bitten in a scrum by one of the Australians. The Wallabies'

manager, Bill McLaughlin, took it on himself to identify the offender, and Cullen admitted that it was he who had bitten Waldron's ear. McLaughlin then took the unprecedented action of dismissing Cullen from the tour.

The incident and its unhappy aftermath made news headlines throughout Australia. Cullen was flown home and has rarely, if ever, been seen at a rugby match of any description since.

Some Australian records, obtusely, make no mention of Cullen ever having been a touring Wallaby.

CURLEY, TERRY
New South Wales and Australia
11 internationals for Australia 1957–58

Hailed as potentially Australia's finest fullback, Curley crammed his 11 test match appearances into a one-year period, then disappeared from the sport at the age of 20. A fledgling solicitor, he entered the priesthood and his rugby days were over.

The Wallabies won only twice in Curley's career – a so-called 'test' against New Zealand Maoris and the second test of the 1958 tour of New Zealand.

CURRIE CUP
The premier trophy for inter-union rugby in South Africa, presented in 1891 by Donald Currie, head of the Castle Shipping Line, to William Maclagan, captain of the British touring team which travelled on the *Cunard Castle*.

Currie charged Maclagan with giving the handsome gold cup to the team which performed best against these original tourists to the colonies. The British went unbeaten, and Griqualand West was chosen as the best loser. They were a sporting lot the Griquas, for they gave the trophy back to the South African Rugby Board for inter-provincial competition.

Inter-area competition was then irregular and disorganised in South Africa. In 1884, a group from the diamond fields travelled to Cape Town to try its luck against Western Province clubs.

The following year, the first inter-town tournament was played at Grahamstown, but only teams from the Cape Colony took part and no records were kept, other that that the winner was Cape Town. Other competing

teams were Grahamstown, Kimberley, Port Elizabeth and King William's Town.

The next tournament, in 1889, organised by the South Africa Rugby Board at Kimberley, was for the South African Rugby Football Trophy – a challenge trophy.

The tournament in 1892 was for both the board's trophy and the Currie Cup, an arrangement that continued up to and including 1956.

Again Western Province, Griqualand West and Transvaal took part, this time joined by Border (the 'banana colony') and Natal (the 'fighting port'). Western Province again won the final, though it conceded its first points of the tournament to Griqualand West.

The Orange Free State joined the band in 1894, when the Western Province successes continued, as they did in 1895, 1897, and 1898 (for the tournament was not played every year). But there was considerable sympathy for Transvaal, beaten by only three points in 1898, because on the way to the tournament the team lost its fullback, David Cope, a youthful international, and a centre, 'Boy' Tait, both killed in a railway accident.

Rhodesia took part in this tournament.

With war imminent, Transvaal and the Free State could not take part in the 1899 tournament, but against the protests of Western Province and Natal, a tournament was played at Kimberley. In this lightweight contest, Griqualand West finally succeeded, winning over Eastern Province, Rhodesia and Border.

When the competition resumed in 1904, Western Province won yet again, as it did in 1906 and 1908. Griqualand West won in 1911, and Western Province again in 1914 and 1920.

The system then changed to a series of home and away matches, and from 1939 was played in sections – northern and southern that year, followed by A and B divisions.

There were two more changes of format. In 1956 there were three sectional winners, Natal beating Western Province in the final – the last year in which two trophies were presented. The board trophy was contested in 1957 and 1959, while the Currie Cup competition was held as a round-robin, the first leg in 1957 and the second leg in 1959.

To that time, Western Province had been beaten only eight times and while it has continued to feature strongly, Transvaal and Northern Transvaal especially have ensured no such dominance continues.

Further changes took place in 1974, after South Africa was swept aside by the all-conquering Lions. In an attempt to bring the top provinces together the SARB arranged for the top 10 teams to play off in an élite group for the Currie Cup – causing problems with the provinces that did not make the top group.

Indeed the format of this competition has become a perennial hot potato of South African rugby, but whatever format is used, however, there is no doubt that while South Africa's isolation from world rugby continues, the Currie Cup, with all its tradition and its magnificent final, is a vital part of rugby in that country.

It should be noted that the Currie Cup is far and away the oldest of inter-union competitions in the world. France has had a club championship since 1892, but while so-called 'friendly' matches were played in New Zealand from 1870, and Ranfurly Shield challenge matches from 1904, the New Zealand national competition did not start until 1976. Australia had its years when only New South Wales was active, while 'league' competitions, whether between clubs or county groupings, are a relatively recent phenomenon in Britain and Ireland.

CURTAIN-RAISERS

Part of the rugby tradition in New Zealand, Australia and South Africa, the curtain-raiser is the match that precedes the main match of the day. Playing in the curtain-raiser of, say, a test match is a special honour, giving players of lesser light the chance to play in front of a big crowd and experience something of the 'big match' atmosphere.

The practice is frowned on in many parts of Britain, where the view is held that such matches can disturb the quality of the playing surface for the match which follows. The first curtain-raiser to an international was played in Britain in 1988, when a New Zealand under-21 combination played its Scottish counterpart before the match between Australia and Scotland at Murrayfield.

It simply seems to be a difference in attitude. In the United Kingdom, for the price of a ticket, crowds see one match which must stand on its own as the afternoon's rugby entertainment; in other countries there are often several curtain-raisers featuring promising players, 'B' teams, or even children. There have been many occasions when disgruntled fans have left the ground proclaiming that the main game wasn't as good as the curtain-raiser.

CUTLER, STEVE
New South Wales and Australia
39 internationals for Australia 1982–89

They called him 'Sky-lab' because he stood more than 2 metres (6ft 6in) in height, weighed 110kg (17 stone), and towered over virtually every other leading lineout forward in the world.

After playing as a replacement in one test on Australia's 1982 tour of New Zealand, Cutler became a first-choice test pick in the 1984 home series against the All Blacks, and a long run of consecutive matches was broken only by his unavailability to play against Argentina in 1986.

But he was back for the triumphant tour to New Zealand later the same year, then played all but one of Australia's six World Cup matches. Unavailable for the 1990 tour to New Zealand, Cutler was accordingly overlooked for the home internationals, but he again became available in 1991, the Rugby World Cup the lure.

CZECHOSLOVAKIA
Rugby was first played in Czechoslovakia in 1926, when several clubs were formed in the provincial areas. Development was swift and it was only five years before an international match was played – Germany beat the first Czech team by 31–0 in Leipzig in 1931.

When France was expelled from the IRB in 1934, and called for a meeting to discuss setting up an alternative international grouping, Czechoslovakia was one of the first to respond. From this meeting the FIRA was born.

Steve Cutler jumping against his great rival, New Zealand's Murray Pierce.

Rugby has not always had an easy time in Czechoslovakia. It virtually ceased during World War II, and by the 1950s was far surpassed by soccer as a leading contender for public popularity. Even as recently as 1978, financial difficulties forced the Czechs to withdraw from the FIRA championships. Four years later it rejoined, with apparently little or no loss of playing standards.

By far the most significant clubs in the country are T.J. Prague, Slavia Prague and Skol Vyskov, and from these three, players come to make up the bulk of the Czech national squad.

D

DALTON, ANDY
Counties and New Zealand
35 internationals for N. Zealand 1977–85

New Zealand's most-capped hooker, Dalton was also the son of an All Black vice-captain (Ray Dalton in 1947).

Andy Dalton did not make his debut for New Zealand until he was 26, but thereafter maintained his place until the World Cup in 1987, when bad luck hit his cup aspirations.

After being named as New Zealand's captain for the series, he was struck down by a hamstring muscle injury and did not play. Instead, he watched as his replacement, Sean Fitzpatrick, took over and established himself as one of the top players of the series. Even after he had recovered, Dalton could not win back his place in the New Zealand team.

Dalton became New Zealand's hooker in 1977, taking over from Tane Norton, who had previously played 27 consecutive internationals in that position. Dalton played 35 tests, so only a handful of players played test matches in the No. 2 jersey for the All Blacks over a period of 20 years.

In the absence of Graham Mourie in 1981, Andy Dalton became New Zealand's test captain for the controversial series against the Springboks. He soon built a reputation as an excellent leader on the field and a diplomatic and sincere one off it. There were many in New Zealand who felt that when Mourie returned later in 1981 Dalton should have continued as captain.

Dalton again took over the leadership after Mourie retired, and captained the team for the test series against the 1983 British Isles, the All Blacks beating the Lions comfortably by four tests to nil. Apart from the times he declared himself unavailable, Dalton maintained the captaincy until the end of his playing days, leading his country in 17 tests for 15 wins.

He was named captain of the New Zealand team to tour South Africa in 1985 but, when that tour was cancelled following court action, he was denied the chance to follow in his father's footsteps and play in an All Black team in South Africa.

In 1986 Dalton joined the rebel Cavaliers tour of South Africa as the tour captain and it would be true to say that his involvement in the secrecy surrounding the setting up of the tour, and his association with it, cost him something in terms of public acceptance and popularity.

On their return home, Dalton and the other Cavaliers were banned by the NZRFU for two test matches, a decision which arguably did not affect Dalton as he was out with injury anyway – a badly broken jaw received on the tour.

Andy Dalton played a significant role in New Zealand rugby, as a forerunner in embracing the style of a busy loose forward, without neglecting the tight forward play of a hooker. He was an expert striker for the ball in scrums and an accurate thrower to the lineouts. He was the first New Zealand hooker to become the lineout thrower. Before Dalton, that job was done by wings.

Dalton was one of the All Black front row trio – together with props John Ashworth and Gary Knight – to be nicknamed the 'Geriatrics'. They played their first test match together in 1978 and their last in 1985 – 20 tests in all.

DANOS, PIERRE
Toulon, Béziers and France
17 internationals for France 1954–60

A café proprietor from Béziers, Danos was a key member of the French team which beat the Springboks in South Africa in 1958. He was the darting, diving scrumhalf of the team, committed to sharp running and passing, as well as being a dropped-goal specialist. It was his goal at Newlands which drew the first test for a French XV which had looked in danger of defeat. Indeed, it was said that Danos had such a sharp eye that he only ever drop-kicked for goal when he was certain it would go over. On that tour he made three attempts for three goals.

A last minute try by Andy Dalton helps New Zealand beat Ireland in 1978. Referee Clive Norling, in his international debut, is about to blow his whistle.

Danos is remembered for coining one of rugby's classic quotes. Describing the differences between the various physical types who could play rugby, Danos simplified them to being just two types – 'Those who play pianos and those who shift them.'

DARROUY, CHRISTIAN
Mont-de-Marsan and France
40 internationals for France 1957–67

A Mont-de-Marsan wing who scored 23 tries in internationals for his country and who stayed in the French team for 10 years. Captain of his country in 1967, taking over from fellow club man Michel Crauste, Darrouy led the team to a Five Nations championship win and was so pleased he sent a famous telegram to President de Gaulle containing just two words – 'Mission accomplished.'

He was once described as a 'greyhound' wing in the style of Adolphe Jaureguy, a star French player in the 1920s.

Darrouy was captain on his last tour, to South Africa in 1967, one of the few wings to lead an international team on a tour. This was France's only four-test series: his team lost the first two games but surprised with a win in the third and a draw in the fourth.

At the time of his retirement he was France's highest try-scorer in internationals and had also beaten Jean Dupuy's record as France's most-capped wing.

His best performance in an international came when he scored three tries against Ireland at Lansdowne Road in 1964. He also had the satisfaction of sprinting nearly 50 metres to score the winning try against South Africa in Springs in the only test of France's 1964 tour.

DAUGA, BENOIT
Mont-de-Marsan and France
63 internationals for France 1964–72

Benoit Dauga was a versatile forward who played for his country in three positions – lock, No. 8 and flanker. A lineout specialist, he was an expert leaper and despatcher of the ball to his halfback. Some of the media called him the 'control tower' of French lineout play, and others the 'Eiffel Tower'. He was also a strong runner and a highly competitive forward.

Benoit Dauga

Dauga's debut in international rugby was not auspicious. He had to wait until his fifth test before he was in a winning team (v Italy 1964). He maintained his place in French test teams until he reached 63 caps, which equalled the record set by Michel Crauste in 1966.

A big man, Dauga stood 1.94 metres tall (6 feet $4\frac{1}{2}$in) and weighed 110 kilograms (17 stone). His frame was such that he stretched rugby shirts to their limit and socks could not pass over his calf muscles!

Dauga was highly regarded and played in most countries in the rugby world, including New Zealand and Australia in 1968, and South Africa in 1971. He was a French captain as well.

His rugby playing days ended in 1975 when he was injured in a club match for his beloved Mont-de-Marsan, suffering temporary paralysis of the arms and legs, and requiring a long spell in hospital before recovering his fitness and resuming his interest in the game.

DAVIES, GARETH
Cardiff and Wales
21 internationals for Wales 1978–85
1 international for British Isles 1980

A stylish and efficient Welsh flyhalf and an excellent tactical kicker, Davies played his first game for his country while on tour with Wales in Australia in 1978. That game and his next two,

another against Australia and one against New Zealand, were all losses. Davies overrode those disappointments to become a vital part of Wales's effort over the next four seasons. He formed a strong halfback combination with Terry Holmes, the two playing together in tests 17 times. He went on to captain Wales in the 1981–82 season, when it scored two wins and three losses. Davies was also a Lion in South Africa in 1980.

A graduate of Oxford University, he was manager of a building society for a while before becoming the head of sports broadcasts for the BBC in Wales.

DAVIES, GERALD
Cardiff, London Welsh and Wales
46 internationals for Wales 1966–78
5 internationals for British Isles 1968–71

One of the most brilliant wings the game has known, Gerald Davies was the prince of sidesteppers, a master of speed and a crowd-pleaser in the extreme. Had he not missed several tours for personal reasons, his talent would have been more widely acclaimed.

Davies finished his schooling and education at Loughborough College and Cambridge University. Imbued with their spirit of playing enjoyable rugby, he soon made his way into the Welsh team. His first international was against Australia in 1966, as a centre.

He played 12 full internationals in that position before making the change to the wing. If he was a success as a centre (good enough to be chosen as a British Lion to South Africa in 1968) he became a wing of exceptional class. His size (only 73kg – $11\frac{1}{2}$ stone) meant that he was rapidly becoming outmoded as a centre at a time when crash-ball specialists were being used more and more. It was as a wing that he could display more expressively his talents for speed and balance.

Davies was considered one of the best sidesteppers the game has seen, especially off his right foot. Many of his markers and opponents could attest to this, none more so than the Hawke's Bay team in New Zealand in 1971, which played the British Isles at Napier. Davies sidestepped repeatedly at high speed and ran in four brilliant tries.

Davies played all four test matches for the Lions on that tour, having earlier played in the third test at Cape Town in South Africa in 1968. He declined to tour twice with the Lions, to South Africa in 1974 and to New Zealand in 1977, but continued as an international until June 1978, when he quit at the age of 33. His last test match was Wales v Australia at the Sydney Cricket Ground.

His 46 appearances on the wing and at centre makes him Wales's most-capped three-quarter. He and Gareth Edwards shared the record (20) as the highest try-scorers in Welsh internationals.

Gerald Davies joined the list of former players who now write and broadcast about the game. He had a number of books published and covered the 1987 World Cup for *The Times* of London. He is also an expert television presenter and commentator.

DAVIES, JONATHAN
Neath, Llanelli and Wales
27 internationals for Wales 1985–88

One of the long line of Welsh flyhalves to delight the rugby world with the sheer expanse of their playing gifts, Jonathan Davies could make the cynical gasp in admiration, hush rival fans down to a whisper of approval and make the noisiest crowds cheer even louder. That made it doubly, trebly, sad for rugby union when he switched to rugby league in early 1989.

Davies was a star who sparkled in test rugby for a little over three years. He first came into the Welsh team for its 1985 game against England at Cardiff. Of course Wales won. Six months later there was another victory over Fiji (40–3) and then a full Five Nations championship season.

By then Davies was recognised as a top flyhalf. He could run and jink and swerve, kick adroitly and pass well. He was everything that Barry John, Dai Watkins, Cliff Morgan, and Phil Bennett had been in the past. There were some who said it was because he had been educated at Gwendraeth Grammar School, where the skills of flyhalf play had been handed down through other old boys of the school, men like Barry John, Carwyn James and Gareth Davies.

Davies toured to the Pacific in 1986 and then went out to the 1987 Rugby World Cup in New Zealand. There he appeared in all six games Wales played in the tournament, as a replacement v Tonga and as captain against Canada.

In 1988 Wales won the Triple Crown and headed for New Zealand. After injuries had laid low the earlier tour captains, Bleddyn Bowen and Rob Norster, Davies led the team in the last four tour games, including the second test at Auckland. Though Wales took a thumping, 9–54, for many in the ground the highlight was Davies' brilliant 90-metre runaway try. Even hardened New Zealand fans, awash in the glory of their team winning so well, had to admit that the Davies try was something special.

But for rugby fans the sight of Jonathan Davies in action was to be all too short. After playing two early season home internationals in the 1988–89 season, against Western Samoa and Romania, when he had again been captain, Davies shocked everyone by announcing he was 'going north'.

His signing for the Widnes rugby league club was thought to be for a then world record sum (reportedly £225,000).

Davies gave early hints that once he fully understood the differences in the two games, he could go on to become a great league player as well. By 1990 he had represented Great Britain in his new sporting code.

DAVIES, MERVYN
London Welsh, Swansea and Wales
38 internationals for Wales 1969–76
8 internationals for British Isles 1971–74

Mervyn Davies played his 38 internationals consecutively for Wales. With his caps for the Lions he was, at his retirement from the game, the world's most-capped No. 8.

His best features as a player were his consistency of performance and his total reliability. He was an excellent lineout forward and whether he was captain of his club or Wales he led by example in a most disciplined and uncompromising way.

He was known in rugby as 'Merv the Swerve', and his trademark was a wide white headband which made him easily identifiable on the field.

Davies played a vital role for three of the most famous teams in rugby's history – the Welsh team from 1969 to 1976 with its five Five Nations championship wins; and the victorious British Lions touring teams of 1971

Mervyn Davies

(in New Zealand) and 1974 (in South Africa).

In 1976, during a televised semi-final of the Welsh Challenge Cup between Swansea and Pontypool at Cardiff Arms Park, Davies fell to the ground unconscious. It was diagnosed that he had suffered a brain haemorrhage. In his subsequent retirement Davies took to writing about the game for a London newspaper.

DAVIES, W.J.A. 'DAVE'
United Services, Royal Navy and
    England
22 internationals for England 1913–23

Whether due to England's fluctuating selection policies or his own ability, W.J.A. ('Dave') Davies was listed in all the record books as England's most-capped international flyhalf until 1989 when his record was passed by Rob Andrew.

Davies began his career in 1913, when he played for his country against the touring South Africans. The loss to the Springboks in that game was to be the last he would have in an international match.

Davies played eight times before World War I and resumed his rugby career after it, when the Five Nations championship resumed in 1920. During the war he was a lieutenant-commander in the naval constructor corps and served on the staff of the commander of the fleet at Jutland. He was awarded the OBE.

In his post-war rugby he teamed up with the halfback Cyril Kershaw and played his last 14 internationals in partnership with his Royal Navy team-mate. They were known as 'Dave and K.' In the four seasons they played together England once shared the championship and twice won it outright.

Davies was a player noted for his understanding of midfield tactics, his long-striding running style and his left-footed drop-kick. He played a major part in one of the 'golden eras' of English rugby. When he retired in 1923 at the age of 32, he had never played in a losing England team in the Five Nations series.

DAVIS, GREG
Thames Valley, Auckland, Bay of Plenty,
    New South Wales and Australia
39 internationals for Australia 1963–72

Born a New Zealander, Greg Davis is remembered as one of the all-time great Australian players. A fierce tackling flanker with a strong sense of commitment and competitiveness, he and Queenslander Jules Guerassimoff were a potent pair of flankers in many Wallaby test matches.

Davis was raised in New Zealand club and provincial rugby as a back, but on moving to Australia in 1963 he became a flanker for the Sydney club Drummoyne. He so quickly attuned to

A 1920 caricature from The Tatler *of 'Dave' Davies*

A testimonial match was held for Greg Davis by his old club, Drummoyne, featuring a number of internationals.

that position that before the end of 1963 he had won selection and was on tour with the Wallabies in South Africa, where he played brilliantly and helped Australia share the test series with the Springboks. He also took part in the Wallabies' thrashing of the All Blacks, 20–5, in the third test of 1964. Generally, though, Greg Davis played for Australia in a time when it experienced defeat regularly and he shared in only 10 wins in 39 tests.

After numerous tours Davis was made captain of Australia in 1969 against Wales at Sydney. He held on to the leadership through 16 consecutive internationals until his retirement in 1972. He was one of Australia's highest-capped internationals – his total of 39 tests was just three behind the then record held by the hooker Peter Johnson.

He played test matches against his fellow New Zealanders in 1964, 1967,

1968 and 1972 and returned to live in his country of birth at the end of his playing days.

Greg Davis died in 1979 – three days short of his 40th birthday. The respect in which he was held by his old club Drummoyne was such that it initiated a very successful benefit fund throughout Australia and New Zealand for his dependents.

DAVY, EUGENE
University College of Dublin,
    Lansdowne and Ireland
34 internationals for Ireland 1925–34

A very tidy and complete Irish flyhalf and centre who enjoyed a long career at the top level, Davy began his international career with Ireland in 1925 and continued for a decade. He later became president of the Irish Rugby Union (1967), and toured to Australia as Ireland's manager that year.

He was part of the Lansdowne club's three-quarter line which played together in the Irish team in three successive internationals in 1931 and against South Africa in 1932.

Against Scotland at Murrayfield in 1930, Davy scored three tries in the first half, which equalled the Irish record for tries in an international. The record still stood 60 years later.

Davy's tally of 34 caps for Ireland stood as a Lansdowne club record until Moss Keane beat it in 1980.

DAWES, JOHN
London Welsh and Wales
22 internationals for Wales 1964–71
4 internationals for British Isles 1971

When John Dawes was picked as captain of the British Isles in 1971, he was the first Welshman to be given that honour. Dawes had exceptional playing qualities as a selfless centre serving only good ball to his wings. He also had a shrewd ability to read the game, and became an established and successful captain.

Dawes first played for his country in 1964 against Ireland, scoring a try. Later that year he was part of the Welsh team which toured South Africa. In the years that followed, Dawes became a regular in Welsh teams, except when he was dropped entirely for the

John Dawes

season of 1966. He continued to play solidly and when he returned to the Welsh team he was made captain. Once back, Dawes soon became one of the safest centres and best leaders in Britain.

In 1969 he was vice-captain of the Welsh team which toured New Zealand where he gained a real understanding of All Black rugby. This knowledge was to serve him well two years later, when he returned as captain of the Lions. His team won the test series, the first time a full New Zealand team had lost at home since 1937. Dawes played in all four tests and, as well as being an outstanding leader, proved to be one of the team's steadiest and sturdiest players. That success came after his leading Wales to a Grand Slam win in 1971.

After the 1971 tour Dawes retired from international play, though he was still good enough to lead the Barbarians to victory over the All Blacks at Cardiff in 1973.

Dawes then became the Welsh national coach and in 1977 returned to New Zealand, this time as coach to the Lions. But this time they were not as strong as the 1971 team (or the 1974 team that had beaten South Africa). When the Lions lost, it was Dawes who naturally took plenty of criticism. As Wales's coach it was a different story. By the time he stepped down in 1979 Wales had won four successive Triple Crowns and two Grand Slams.

In 1980 he took up a post as the WRU's national coaching director, a position he held until 1990. He was made an OBE in 1972 for his services to British rugby.

DAWSON, RONNIE
Wanderers, Ireland and British Isles
27 internationals for Ireland 1958–64
6 internationals for British Isles 1959

Ronnie Dawson began his career as hooker in Ireland's first victory over a touring side, against Australia early in 1958. His leadership qualities were quickly recognised and for the 1958–59 season which followed he was made captain.

A hooker who had a fine tactical sense of play, he was immensely popular later in 1959 as the charming leader of the Lions tour party to Australia and New Zealand. On that trip Dawson was under considerable pres-

sure to keep his test team place from the Welshman Bryn Meredith, who had been the number one hooker with the British team of 1955 in South Africa. Dawson in the end played all six internationals on the tour. He was the fourth Irishman – on successive tours – to captain a Lions tour party.

He also captained the first Irish touring team to visit a major rugby country (South Africa) in 1961. Perhaps his most significant victory as a captain came when he led the Barbarians club to its famous win over the Springboks of 1960–61.

A broken leg marred some of Dawson's later rugby, although he played for Ireland until 1964, earning 33 international caps in all.

Later he spent a period as the Ireland coach, and coach for the British Isles in South Africa in 1968. In 1974 he was elected to the IRB, beginning a long spell as one of the game's most significant administrators.

DEAN, PAUL
St Mary's College and Ireland
32 internationals for Ireland 1981–89

It took a while for the Irish selectors to make up their mind about Paul Dean, their neat flyhalf of the 1980s. He was first picked for the tour of South Africa in 1981, where he played one test as a centre and one as a flyhalf. The next season he was a centre for all the Irish programme. Then he was unsighted for two seasons, coming back again as a flyhalf in 1984–85.

After that he totalled an impressive number of appearances, and was a regular selection until 1989. His form was so good that year he was picked to tour Australia with the British Isles touring team. But he struck bad luck when he was severely injured in the first tour match at Perth and replaced by England's Rob Andrew. To the end of 1990 he had not reappeared in top rugby.

DEANS, BOB
Canterbury and New Zealand
5 internationals for New Zealand 1905–08

Although he played so few test matches, the name of Bob Deans is one of the most famous in rugby history. As a 21-year-old, Deans, from Christchurch, took part in the 1905–06 All Blacks tour of Britain and was involved in one of the most controversial decisions ever made by a referee.

In the international against Wales at Cardiff Arms Park, All Black centre Deans appeared, to New Zealand eyes, to have crossed the line for the try that would have drawn New Zealand level with the Welsh. The match referee, John Dallas of Scotland, ruled that Deans had not made it to the goal-line and the try was disallowed. Amid great protest the game ended with the All Black team suffering its first and only defeat on the tour.

In the years that followed every Welshman, it seemed, claimed to have been there and to have seen entirely accurately that Deans had NOT scored. At the same time every New Zealander, even 12,000 miles away, claimed to know someone who was in Cardiff that day and who DID believe Deans had scored!

Of course the controversy raged around Bob Deans who, when asked, would always say that he believed he had grounded the ball fairly. Those who knew Deans well – and he was a very devout and high-principled young man – believed that his word was sacrosanct. Those people, of course, were New Zealanders!

For many years visitors to Cardiff Arms Park were taken to the spot on the playing field to see where the Deans controversy took place.

Deans was a brilliant centre three-quarter and one of the stars of New Zealand rugby at that time. His life ended in tragic circumstances. He last played a test match for New Zealand in 1908 against the Anglo-Welsh touring team, and a little over two months later died from complications after an appendicitis operation. Two All Blacks of the 1980s, Robert ('Robbie') and Bruce Deans are the grandsons of his brother, Max.

DEANS, COLIN
Hawick and Scotland
52 internationals for Scotland 1978–87

At the first Rugby World Cup in 1987, Colin Deans became the most-capped hooker in rugby test history, having passed 50 internationals for Scotland in a game against Zimbabwe at Athletic Park in Wellington. On his retirement, his total of 52 internationals equalled the Scottish record set by his Hawick team-mate, Jim Renwick.

A rugged player with an accurate lineout throw, Deans played his first

Colin Deans

10 internationals, from 1978 to 1980, without a win. Indeed he had more than his fair share of defeats in his career, having begun his international play at a time when Scottish rugby was not strong. It was due to his con-

Deans sent a telegram to the Daily Mail *with his version of the controversial try against Wales in 1905.*

siderable influence that Scotland rose to be such a formidable opponent for teams in the World Cup.

Deans was also a member of the Scotland Grand Slam-winning team of 1984. After his first cap in 1978 he missed only two internationals, due to injury.

He was elated when he was chosen for the British Isles touring team to New Zealand in 1983, but he was in the difficult situation of being the touring captain's understudy. Most observers of that tour felt Deans was hard done by, as he was clearly a better hooker and forward than the team's captain, Ciaran Fitzgerald. Deans took his situation cheerfully and stoically and had his reward in 1986 when he was chosen to captain the Lions in their match against the Rest of the World at Cardiff.

DE VILLIERS, DAWIE
Western Province, Boland, Transvaal
  and South Africa
25 internationals for Sth Africa 1962–70

A halfback with a baby face and a charming smile, Dawie de Villiers won thousands of hearts when he captained the Springboks on their tour of New Zealand in 1965. The disappointment he must have suffered on that tour may well have been somewhat compensated for when he led his country to victory over the All Blacks in South Africa in 1970. But between those two emotions must have been feelings born of frustration and disappointment when his team of South Africans, on the tour of Britain in 1969–70, became the first team to face demonstrations and protests at their presence.

De Villiers made his debut for the Springboks in 1962 in the very close test series against Arthur Smith's British Isles tourists. He became a Springbok from that very fine South African rugby nursery, Stellenbosch University. Serious knee injuries threatened his sporting career for a time, but he rose above those setbacks to lead South Africa on three tours.

After the satisfaction of beating New Zealand in 1970, de Villiers retired, as he said, 'a contented man'. He had captained his country in 22 test matches, a record for a South African player.

In his career away from rugby, de Villiers was originally a lecturer of

Clearly they won! Springbok captain Dawie De Villiers (left) with Jannie Engelbrecht and Sakkie van Zyl.

philosophy at Rand Afrikaans University and a church minister, but he soon branched into politics. After seven years as a Member of Parliament he was appointed South Africa's ambassador to London in 1979. Later he returned to Parliament, serving for a time as a cabinet minister and the Cape Province's leader of the ruling National Party.

DEVINE, DAUNCEY
Transvaal and South Africa
2 internationals for South Africa 1924–28

Dauncey Devine was not one of the great figures of world rugby, playing only two tests for South Africa in the 1920s. Nevertheless he played a significant role in the game, as the player who perfected the dive pass technique for halfbacks.

Devine, from Johannesburg, played the third test against the Great Britain team in 1924 and the second test against New Zealand in 1928. When making a pass off the ground Devine took to falling down as he made the dispatch, a technique that was later passed on to others. One player, Danie Craven, perfected the style and was soon exhibiting the dive pass worldwide.

Dauncey Devine's career was notable in one other aspect. Thirteen years

after first playing for the Springboks, Devine was a triallist for the 1937 South African team's tour to Australasia – an unusually long career for a halfback, then and now.

DINTRANS, PHILIPPE
Tarbes and France
50 internationals for France 1979–90

A hooker, Philippe Dintrans was well established as the French captain until injury forced him out of play in the 1985–86 season. Thereafter he could not make it back into the top XV, and instead of being in the heat of battle for his country, as he had been every season since 1979, Dintrans began a new career as a reserve, watching his replacement Daniel Dubroca as both hooker and captain. Dubroca played in 16 of the next 17 internationals including the World Cup final. (The French selectors allowed Dintrans to play only the minor World Cup match against Romania.)

Dintrans began his rugby days as a flanker with a reputation for being somewhat bad tempered, but he toned his act down after becoming a regular in the French team. He made his international debut in Christchurch against New Zealand in 1979.

For the next tour of New Zealand in 1984, he had the daunting task of

Philippe Dintrans

Amédée Domenech (with the ball), Colin Meads and Jean-Pierre Saux. France v New Zealand, 1961.

taking over from Jean-Pierre Rives as the French captain. To outsiders it appeared Dintrans made a good job of being team leader, even if France did not win too often under his command. The decision by the selectors, after his shoulder injury had healed, to prefer Dubroca was one that made for much discussion in France.

Dintrans became France's most-capped hooker in 1982–83 when he passed Alain Paco's previous record of 25 caps. For his 50th test match, in 1990 against Romania in Auch, he was presented again with the honour of the captaincy. Unfortunately the occasion was not what it might have been for Dintrans: France lost to the Romanians for the first time on French soil.

DOBSON, DENYS
Newton Abbot and England
6 internationals for England 1902–03

Denys Douglas Dobson rates inclusion, not because of his outstanding rugby prowess, but for two unusual events that marked his life both on and away from the rugby pitch.

Dobson was a useful forward who made the England team in 1902 and 1903 and who also toured to New Zealand and Australia with the British team in 1904. On that tour he achieved a 'record' of sorts when he became the

first man ever to be sent from the field in a major match for 'obscene language' directed at the referee. It is not reported anywhere what Dobson said, but he was suspended for eight months for the offence.

Dobson played his club rugby at Newton Abbot, which had been the host village for many touring teams on their arrival in Great Britain.

When he moved out to Ngama in Nyasaland to start a new life as a farmer, things went well for a time, but in 1916 the former rugby player died after being trampled underfoot by a charging rhinoceros. On hearing the news, his former headmaster is reputed to have observed drily that Dobson's fend always was a bit weak!

DODGE, PAUL
Leicester and England
32 internationals for England 1978–85
2 internationals for British Isles 1980

A steady centre who, it was once said, was more appreciated by his team-mates than spectators. In his long career, Dodge was never a spectacular player who could thrill crowds, but at the same time he rarely made mistakes.

Paul Dodge played all his rugby for the Leicester club and first won England selection in 1978. After two seasons and eight internationals he was

apparently only fourth choice for centre during the 1980 season, and it was only because of injuries to others that he made the England team for two of the games of its Grand Slam series win.

In 1980 he was again called into the Lions tour of South Africa as a replacement, playing in two tests. He missed the 1983–84 season because of a broken leg, but by 1985 he was the senior back in the England team and was asked to take over the captaincy from Peter Wheeler, his Leicester team-mate.

After beginning with a draw and a win, Dodge's team then lost its remaining two matches in the Five Nations series, followed by two test losses in New Zealand. The second defeat of that tour, 15–42 at Wellington, was a record loss by England in an international. Next season Dodge was not asked back into the England team.

He continued to play club rugby for Leicester after his international days were over, appearing in the three John Player Cup finals which Leicester won in 1979–80–81.

DOMENECH, AMEDEE
Vichy, Brive and France
52 internationals for France 1954–63

Known far and wide in French rugby as 'Le Duc', Amédée Domenech was a strong but controversial French prop selection over a period of nine years. In his time he was so criticised for his individual, free-ranging approach that he was dropped from the top French XV for 23 months between March 1958 and February 1960.

On his return to the French team, Domenech played more in the traditional role as a prop rather than as a rover, and he enjoyed a continuation of his international career until 1963. In 1961 he toured to New Zealand and Australia, playing in all four internationals.

Like many figures embroiled in controversy with officialdom, Domenech enjoyed a great following with French fans. And once he surprised the staid English fans of Twickenham.

During a match against England in 1961 the French wing, Jean Dupuy, left the field for a time, injured. In those days, when there were no replacements, it was usually expected that a lean flanker or loose forward would move out to the wing to substitute. But François Moncla, the French captain, remembered Domenech's old roving, running style and posted the prop on the wing!

Domenech marked the former Empire Games sprinter, John Young, and by all accounts was a very speedy handful for the Englishman. No doubt afterwards he might have said to his detractors – 'touché!'

DON WAUCHOPE, ANDREW
Fettesian-Lorettonians and Scotland
12 internationals for Scotland 1881–88

The first of the great Scottish halfbacks, and once rated the best of them all. Scottish rugby's first historian, R.J. Phillips, considered Don Wauchope 'a completely equipped all round player. Heavily built around the haunches, he ran with a comparatively short stride, and had the power to abruptly change his course.'

Don Wauchope was a great running halfback, a brilliant sidestepping run bringing him a memorable try against Ireland in 1885, when Andrew and his younger brother Patrick formed the first halfback brothers' combination in international rugby.

Don Wauchope later refereed and umpired international rugby and was Scotland Rugby Union president in 1889–90.

DOOLEY, WADE
Preston Grasshoppers, Fylde and
    England
41 internationals for England 1985–91
2 internationals for British Isles 1989

At 6ft 8in (2.03m) one of the biggest men in world rugby, Wade Dooley was a policeman who played rugby league until his late teens. When he switched to rugby union his size at lineouts and in scrums quickly made an impression. He became an England international in 1985, gaining a place in the sweeping changes that took place that year (20 new caps chosen in 10 months).

His debut was against Romania in its first game with England. He then became a regular in England teams and played in three matches in the Rugby World Cup in 1987.

Dooley was an excellent forward who improved steadily, even in the later years of his career. He and his locking partner, Paul Ackford, won many plaudits in England packs in the late 1980s. The two also locked the scrum together in two tests for the British Isles in their successful test series with Australia in 1989.

DOURTHE, CLAUDE
Dax and France
33 internationals for France 1966–75

An aggressive centre three-quarter in French teams for nine years, Dourthe gained a reputation as a player who niggled away at opposition teams, sometimes incurring their wrath, as well as the referee's. Nevertheless he was a talented player with speed and a fine touch. He was part of expressive French backlines in South Africa in 1967 and in New Zealand and Australia in 1968.

He captained France in two tour matches in New Zealand when aged only 19, and also captained France in two Five Nations matches in 1975.

At the time of his first game for France (v Romania in November of 1966) he was only 18 years and one week old – France's youngest international.

DU MANOIR, YVES
Racing Club and France
8 internationals for France 1925–27

As far as it is known, the first statue in the world of a rugby player was erected

outside the gates of Colombes Stadium in Paris. The player depicted in the sculpture is Yves du Manoir, a brilliant flyhalf who had just three seasons in international football. He was killed when flying a military plane over the Colombes Stadium in 1928 – a pre-match event for the Scotland v France match that day.

Du Manoir was a charismatic, flamboyant figure who was also well-known as an airman, motor-cyclist, tennis player, swimmer, gymnast and canoeist. One rugby writer described him as a totally 'chivalrous' flyhalf. He had such a following in Paris at the Racing Club, which was the part-owner of Colombes, that there was great sadness at his death at only 23. As a

The statue, erected in memory of Yves Du Manoir, which stands outside Colombes Stadium in Paris.

tribute to his memory, the club renamed the stadium the Stade Yves du Manoir and erected the statue.

Later the club founded a rugby tournament in du Manoir's name, which aimed to promote 'chivalrous' rugby. To that end, teams that played brutal rugby or had bad reputations did not secure an invitation to play. The tournament continues to this day and invitations are much sought after.

A quote about du Manoir used to be directed at young boys playing rugby in France. 'Model your play and personality on those of du Manoir and you'll be a man,' the young French players were told.

DU PLESSIS, MORNE

Western Province and South Africa
22 internationals for Sth Africa 1971–80

Born in 1949, only a few months after his father, Felix, had captained the Springboks to three test wins over the All Blacks, Morne du Plessis rose to achieve the same position from 1975 to 1980. They were the first Springbok father and son captains.

Du Plessis was a No. 8 of great height and skill who had to rise above enormous criticism directed at his playing style from many sections of South Africa's rugby public. In the end he retired a hero, but only after some harrowing years when his talents were constantly called into question. Despite calls that he was either 'too rough', 'too loose' or 'too soft', du Plessis became one of the most powerful personalities of South African rugby in the 1970s.

He is one of the scores of successful players to have emerged from Stellenbosch University to take Springbok honours. And it was Stellenbosch's most famous rugby man, Danie Craven, who made the suggestion that du Plessis change from being a tight forward to being a loose man.

He first played for his country in 1971, on the protest-disrupted tour of Australia. In 1974, in the home tests against the British Isles, he suffered the ignominy of being dropped by the Springbok selectors after the disastrous loss of the second test match, 9–28. He was not alone in this fate – the selectors used 33 players in all during the four tests of that series.

Du Plessis was captain of South Africa when it beat the All Blacks three tests to one in 1976. He played a pow-

erful part in the Springbok team, leading from the front when his home team, Western Province, also beat the tourists.

He was captain in 1977 against the World XV, for which South Africa awarded caps.

By 1980 du Plessis had over-ridden much of the public scorn that had followed him in the early years and was the first choice to continue as Springbok leader against the British touring team. In a series that du Plessis admitted could have gone the other way, the Springboks won 3–1 – his greatest triumph. At 31 years of age du Plessis retired to become a successful businessman.

DU PREEZ, FRIK

Northern Transvaal and South Africa
38 internationals for Sth Africa 1961–71

Frederik Christoffel Hendrik du Preez, known far and wide in rugby as 'Frik' du Preez, was a great lineout jumper and all-purpose forward, and was to South African rugby in the 1960s what Colin Meads was to New Zealand. In his first 17 internationals from 1961 to 1965 he appeared eight times on the flank and nine as lock. The South Africans seemed unsure where they should place him, but du Preez excelled in both positions.

He locked horns in rugby battle with some great players, including Meads and Willie John McBride of Ireland and the Lions. Both were bigger physically than du Preez, who was not especially tall as modern forwards go. But as a forward he played far beyond his mere physical size.

He was also, for a time, a prodigious if inconsistent goal-kicker. He once drop-kicked a 77-metre penalty on Loftus Versfeld Stadium in Pretoria.

He was also surprisingly fast. In one tour match in New Zealand in 1965, du Preez was the only Springbok to chase fleet wing Bill Birtwhistle when he ran 85 metres to score Canterbury's try. Du Preez did not lose a metre to the flying future All Black.

The Springboks went through some lean times in the 1960s but they were always delighted when Frik du Preez was in form and in their playing ranks.

DUBLIN UNIVERSITY RFC

The oldest senior rugby club in Ireland, formed in 1854 by students at

the university. Also known as Trinity College, Dublin, it is accepted worldwide as the second oldest rugby club in the world.

Scores of players who have appeared in the all-white playing strip of the club have gone on to play for Ireland, among them the legendary forward J.D. ('Jammie') Clinch, who holds the club record for most caps for Ireland (30); the flyhalf Dick Lloyd; James Cecil Parke, the world-famous tennis player; and Mark Sugden, the scrumhalf. Sugden only embarked on a career in that position when his club could not find anyone else to play there one day, and he went on to play 28 internationals in that position. (A number of these appearances came after he had joined the Wanderers Club, also in Dublin.)

Trinity College has its headquarters at College Park in Dublin.

DUBROCA, DANIEL

Agen and France
33 internationals for France 1979–88

The captain of the French team that played in the final of the first World Cup at Eden Park in Auckland, Dubroca made his debut for his country on the same ground in 1979, playing as a prop. The French won that Bastille Day battle by 24–19.

Daniel Dubroca, captain in the 1980s and coach of France in the 1990s.

Frik du Preez (left) closing in on his great rival, Colin Meads. 1970.

David Duckham

In his early days with the Agen club Dubroca was a utility forward and played anywhere he could in the scrum. After serving for a time as an international prop, it was as a hooker that he eventually gained a permanent place in the French pack. Following injury to Philippe Dintrans in 1986, he also became captain when he was drafted into the top French XV. Later that year he led France to a win over New Zealand at Nantes and in the new 1987 season captained France to a win in the Five Nations championship.

Even though the World Cup final ended in disappointment for French rugby, Dubroca remained one of only five Frenchmen to have beaten New Zealand twice in a test match.

His international career ended after the 1988 Five Nations series. But by then he had been well groomed as the successor to Jacques Fouroux and took over as national coach for the 1990 series with the All Blacks.

DUCKHAM, DAVID
Coventry and England
36 internationals for England 1969–76
3 internationals for British Isles 1971

David Duckham was a big wing or centre three-quarter who was a strong and vital member of England teams for seven years. He was a member of the champion 1971 British team in New Zealand, playing in three of the internationals on that tour. In one match at Greymouth he scored six tries, then a Lions record for one match (later equalled by 'J.J.' Williams).

Duckham (nicknamed 'Quackers') was a fast and determined runner who could sidestep adroitly, specialising in scoring tries from broken play. The sight of Duckham, at 1.85m and 90 kg (6ft 1in and 14 stone), securing the ball in midfield and setting off towards the opposition's line was one of the few high points of English rugby at the time, for he suffered from playing for England at a time when it won a low percentage of its matches. Duckham was in the winning team only 10 times in 36 test matches.

DUFAU, GERARD
Racing Club de France and France
38 internationals for France 1948–57

Known as 'Zeze', this physical culture instructor first played for his country against the famous Irish Grand Slam-winning team of 1948.

Dufau was described by the 1951–52 Springboks as the 'best scrumhalf in Europe'. His bearing around the field was in the essential spirit of French rugby – vivacious, bright, perhaps inconsistent, but never dull.

Apart from numerous wins in Five Nations matches, he was probably most proud of being a member of French XVs that beat Australia in 1948 and New Zealand in 1954.

DUGGAN, WILLIE
Blackrock College and Ireland
41 internationals for Ireland 1975–84
4 internationals for British Isles 1977

A steady and sturdy No. 8 from Blackrock College and Leinster, who made his debut against England in 1975. Duggan toured to New Zealand with Ireland in 1976 and with the British Isles in 1977, playing in five test matches on those tours.

He played for Ireland during the time the side won the Five Nations championship (in 1982) and shared it (in 1983). At the end of his career he was Ireland's most-capped No. 8.

He gained notoriety by being sent off in the Ireland v Wales match in 1977: he and Geoff Wheel of Wales were dispatched by Scottish referee Norman Sanson in the same incident.

DUNCAN, JAMES
Otago and New Zealand
1 international for New Zealand 1903

James Duncan is remembered as one of the greatest of rugby thinkers, players and tacticians around the turn of the century, and is famous in the story of rugby development as the man who invented the five-eighths position.

Originally a wing forward, Duncan also played in the new position he created. He played for Otago between 1889 until 1903, when he was nearly 34, in the then extraordinarily high number of 50 matches.

He was a leader in many areas. He captained Otago for six seasons, then, after first playing for New Zealand in 1897 in Australia, he captained his country against both Wellington and the touring New South Wales side in 1901. He returned to Australia in 1903, again as the captain, and had the distinction of leading New Zealand in its first official test match.

In later years he invariably wore a cap to hide his total baldness. On one celebrated occasion he 'sold a dummy' by tossing his headgear to an opponent who lunged for it, leaving a gap for Duncan to race through and score. No doubt these days, that try would have been disallowed!

Retired, he was appointed coach of the 1905 'Original' All Blacks to tour Britain, France and North America – long before such an idea was officially sanctioned.

But the appointment was not without controversy, and there is evidence of some strain between the southern group of players, who held to Duncan's coaching methods, and the northerners, who stuck firmly to the captain, Dave Gallaher.

It seems Gallaher and his vice-captain, Billy Stead – ironically from the deep south – had a greater influence on the game plans and preparation than did the coach.

But Duncan went on to new heights, refereeing a test between the All Blacks and the touring Anglo-Welsh in 1908 – not in itself unique, but an unusual achievement for one man to captain, coach and then referee his country's team, all in the space of five years.

His legacies are the five-eighths system – and the more ready acceptance of coaches at an international level, even if Duncan had such a rough time from his so-called subordinates.

DUPUY, JEAN
Tarbes and France
40 internationals for France 1956–64

Jean Dupuy served France well on the wing, so much so that he set a record of 39 internationals in that position – a total beaten by Christian Darrouy in 1967. Dupuy scored 19 tries in internationals and had one cap as a centre.

Nicknamed either 'Le Pipiou' or 'The Railway Engine', Dupuy was part of the pioneering French touring teams to South Africa in 1958 and to New Zealand and Australia in 1961. He is well remembered in New Zealand for his thrilling run to score into a 140 km/h (85 mph) wind in the second test at Athletic Park in 1961.

He played all his rugby for Tarbes.

Bright young stars of English rugby in the 1990s: Simon Hodgkinson, top, and brothers Rory and Tony Underwood, left (Fotopacific); Jeremy Guscott, in the Barbarians' colours, right (Peter Bush).

Top: Will Carling in action. By the end of 1990–91 he was England's most successful captain.
Below: England's Neil Back is well caught by a trio of Italian players. England B beat Italy 33–15 at Rovigo in 1990.

Fotopacific

E

EAST COAST RFU

One of the smallest rugby unions in New Zealand, covering the easternmost tip of the North Island. East Coast might not have won many matches since its formation in 1921, but every season it wins more friends. The spartan, outback nature of the East Coast region and its warmhearted, inventive people have combined to give this union real character.

East Coast has sometimes found it difficult to field a representative team and there are stories about recruiting prospective players from the local pub just moments before a game. Once, the team was on tour in the North Island when a combination of injuries and late nights took its toll on the players available for the next match. With typical East Coast resourcefulness, the management invited the team's bus driver to play! So a rather portly chap of middle-aged years was surprised to make his first-class debut many years after retiring from the game.

East Coast players often arrive at their games on horseback. Perhaps it was one of these horses that wandered on to the field to graze near the opposition 22-metre line during a game against the Junior All Blacks. In true East Coast style, nobody tried too hard to chase it away, and all the while heavy smoke drifted across the field from the Maori 'hangi' (food cooked in the ground) which was being prepared for the after-match party.

Two East Coast players have become All Blacks. The area's most famous rugby son was the great George Nepia. Although he played most of his early rugby in neighbouring Hawke's Bay, Nepia was born on 'the Coast' and played all four tests against the Great Britain team of 1930 from the province. He lived his last years back on the Coast and the high percentage of Maoris in the populace deeply mourned his death in 1986.

Centre Andy Jefferd was an East Coast All Black in 1980 and again in 1981.

East Coast has contributed several 'records' to New Zealand rugby. One was being beaten 7–101 by Counties in 1972, a New Zealand record for most points conceded in one first-class match.

EASTERN PROVINCE RFU

Based in the friendly city of Port Elizabeth, the Eastern Province Rugby Union was formed in 1888. Port Elizabeth has always been a very powerful centre in the South African rugby world. First the Crusader Ground at St George's Park, and then the Boet Erasmus Stadium have been regular venues for Springbok tests.

Eastern Province players have built themselves a reputation for being tough and hard. They beat the 1924 British team, 28–14, and the Lions of 1955 by 20–0. Local writers called the latter a 'great day for Oostelike Provinsie', while British historians claim their team was 'severely depleted by injury and illness'

The Eastern Province match with the All Blacks of 1960 was called the 'Battle of Boet Erasmus', so stern was the scrummaging and the general play, with a number of outbreaks of fighting. And when the 1974 Lions came to the same ground, some uncalled-for violence left that match a rather sour memory as well. Local rugby supporters may wince, but an Eastern Province player was quoted after one of those two games as saying 'that's the way we always play it here in P.E.!'

Eastern Province has never won the Currie Cup, South Africa's symbol of provincial rugby supremacy, though in recent years it has climbed back up through to the A section of the cup competition.

There have been numerous famous players from the area, such as the shrewd front ranker Amos du Plooy, who led the province to victory over the Lions in 1955 and won a Springbok blazer the same season; J.G. Hirsch, who toured with the first Springboks to Britain in 1906; John Luyt of the 1912–13 Springboks, who toured in that team with his two brothers from Western Province; Fred Turner, the fullback who became a successful wing in the 1930s; Willem Delport, the hooker who played in one of South Africa's strongest front rows in 1951–52; Gabriel Carelse, the huge lock of the 1960s; the Springbok prop and captain Hannes Marais; and the recent superstar centre Danie Gerber, who is the most-capped player in Eastern Province's history.

EASTERN RFU

One of the four territorial rugby unions that make up the United States Rugby Union. The Eastern Rugby Union was formed in 1934 by eight clubs, four of which bore the illustrious names of Harvard, Yale, Princeton and New York. Growth was gradual until World War II suspended activity. The ERU was not reactivated until 1954, but from then its borders expanded, as did its responsibility. Since the formation of the United States rugby union in 1975, Eastern encompasses all rugby in the eastern seaboard states, as well as Pennsylvania, Kentucky, Alabama, Tennessee, West Virginia, Mississippi and Louisiana.

Financial and logistical problems prevent ERU representative teams getting together very often. A high point was a tour to South Africa in 1976, where the team won only one of seven tour games but learned much about top class rugby.

In 1981 the union's leading administrator of the time, Tom Selfridge, invited the Springboks to come to the East Coast on their way home from their troubled tour of New Zealand. Their arrival put rugby on to the front pages of major US dailies and TV bulletins. Protests were directed at Selfridge and his union and a bomb went off at the ERU headquarters, causing damage to the office and nearby buildings.

The Eastern Union team played a game against South Africa, losing 0–41, while 2500 protesters jeered outside Bleeker Stadium in Albany, New York. Then the famous (or infamous) match between the United States and South Africa was staged, under the organisation of Selfridge and the ERU.

It took place on a farmland polo ground in upstate Glenville, New York, one day before it was scheduled. A few protesters turned up, only to be thwarted by a strong police presence. About 25 spectators watched the game, the smallest ever for an international, which South Africa won by 38–7.

EASTERN TRANSVAAL RFU

Founded in 1948, this South African provincial union has its headquarters in Springs, about an hour's drive from Johannesburg. The union was formed in 1948 to provide more first-class rugby for local players, who were being denied that opportunity by being affiliated to the large and powerful Transvaal union.

The Easts began as a provincial force by winning their first international match, against the 1949 New Zealand team. On that day, 32,000 crammed into the union main ground, the P.A.M. Brink Stadium, on its official opening. Eastern Transvaal won by 6–5.

Eastern Transvaal drew with the 1955 British Isles team and beat the 1962 team by 19–16.

Springs became notorious to New Zealand rugby fans in 1970 when an Eastern Transvaal forward kicked the famous New Zealander Colin Meads in the arm. The broken bone kept Meads out of action for five weeks and there were many who said that the injury cost New Zealand a fair chance of beating the Springboks in that test series.

A test match was played in Springs in 1964 when France toured. In a match marred by outbreaks of fighting and rated as one of the worst seen for many a year, the French XV beat South Africa by 8–6. Springs was never again asked to host a test.

In its first 40 years Eastern Transvaal supplied only five Springbok players and of those only Norman Riley was a test cap, playing as a flyhalf in the third test against Australia in 1963.

EDEN PARK, AUCKLAND

Headquarters for rugby in Auckland, New Zealand, and venue for the first

Rugby World Cup final in 1987. Eden Park has also seen other great sporting moments (such as cricket tests and one-day games, and the 1950 Empire Games) but it is primarily a rugby venue, for which it has an excellent playing surface.

Before World War I Eden Park was a lake crossed by a causeway, but following reclamation the ground became a rugby test venue only 11 years later. At the ground's first test, in 1921, 40,000 highly excited but ultimately disappointed spectators watched New Zealand lose to South Africa 5–9 in the second test of that series.

A paucity of tests during the 1920s meant it was nine years before Eden Park again hosted an international. In 1930 the All Blacks beat Britain 15–10 on the ground and since then it has been used regularly in every major international series played in New Zealand.

Eden Park held a record crowd of 61,240 on September 1 1956 when the

Not a typical Eden Park day, but one of the ground's more memorable occasions. The 'water polo' test of 1975, New Zealand v Scotland.

All Blacks won the fourth test – and the series – against South Africa. Such scenes of excitement have rarely been repeated anywhere in the rugby world.

Two of the best games of rugby in the park's history resulted in defeats for the All Blacks: the 16–30 loss to Australia in 1978 and the 19–24 loss to France on Bastille Day 1979. It is to the credit of the Eden Park fans that on both occasions their compliments to the winners were loud and long.

Two rugby test days at Eden Park are remembered for different reasons. In 1975, when Scotland played its first test in New Zealand, Auckland turned on such a violent storm that the field soon became flooded like the lake it once was. In hindsight, the game should have been cancelled – it was suggested seriously afterwards that players could have been in danger from drowning, such was the depth of some of the ponds on the field – but being rugby men they carried on! It was near to qualifying as history's first underwater rugby test match.

It was New Zealand that turned the 'tide' to come home on a 'wave' of success and win by 24–0.

The second day was not so much famous as infamous: the third and final test between the All Blacks and the Springboks in 1981, which was under severe pressure from anti-apartheid and anti-tour protests. *See* PROTESTS.

Eden Park has enjoyed two long strings of Ranfurly Shield defences, in the 1960s and in the 1980s. The consistent strength of Auckland's representative teams on Eden Park has made the ground a very difficult place over the years for visitors to earn victories.

EDINBURGH

The heart of Scottish rugby, with the city's ground at Murrayfield the venue for all Scotland's home internationals.

Edinburgh rugby clubs continue the traditional rivalries born at the great schools of the city: the Academy, Watson's, Heriot's and Stewart's-Melville. Old boys from these schools form the basis of the adult clubs in the city. Academicals ('Accies') is the oldest, but in recent years Heriot's has been the strongest.

Edinburgh has been part of the Scottish inter-district championship since its inauguration.

Gareth Edwards gets his pass away, with his close rival, Sid Going, in pursuit.

EDINBURGH ACADEMICALS

Founded in 1857–58 by former pupils of Edinburgh Academy, the Edinburgh Academicals is the oldest rugby club in Scotland and after Guy's Hospital and Dublin University, one of the oldest in the world. Among its most famous players was William Maclagan, who captained the first British team to South Africa in 1891. Its highest-capped player, from among its 100 or so internationals, was the Scottish flanker and captain Douglas Elliot, with 29 caps. Other leading players were the 1971 British Isles player, Rodger Arneil, and the 1989 Lion and Scottish Grand Slam captain in 1990, David Sole.

It was on the club's ground at Raeburn Place that the first rugby international was played, in 1871, and internationals were played there regularly until 1895.

EDWARDS, GARETH
Cardiff and Wales
53 internationals for Wales 1967–78
10 internationals for British Isles 1968–74

Gareth Edwards was one of the most widely acclaimed rugby players of all time – a brilliantly versatile halfback and a strong physical competitor who captured the imagination and admiration of players and followers all over the world.

Edwards first came to prominence outside Wales as a teenager on the Cardiff club's tour of South Africa in 1967, where he played in a number of positions in the backline. Once back in Wales his enormous talents were soon focused on scrumhalf play. He was chosen for his country three months before his 20th birthday and was never dropped until his retirement. Ten years later, with 53 caps, he had set a record for most internationals for Wales, which stood until passed by J.P.R. Williams in 1981. Edwards's tests were consecutive – both a world record and a monumental feat.

In all his internationals, he was in the losing side on no more than 15 occasions. He scored 20 tries in internationals, at the time a Welsh record, although later equalled by Gerald Davies. His total of 63 internationals remains the world's highest for a scrumhalf. He was Wales's youngest ever international captain (20 years, seven months in the match against Scotland in February 1968).

At the time of his debut for Wales, in the Five Nations match v France in 1967, Edwards was a physical education student at Cardiff Training College. Later, he switched clubs to Cardiff and became a successful businessman. Later still, at the end of his playing days, he was a media commentator and reporter on the game.

A master of the spin-pass, Edwards had all the other attributes of the complete scrumhalf. His kicking was skilful, his running devastating to any of the opposition that could stay near his electric bursts, and his competitiveness was relentless. He dominated many matches simply because of his presence on the field. He was a brilliant opportunist and scorer of tries.

Perhaps the only aspect of his game that did not reach the highest level was as a captain. Many people felt he was inhibited slightly as a leader, with the result that other Welshmen came past him to lead the national XV. He did not resent this, rather it allowed him to return his full concentration to the scrumhalf role. In all, he was captain of his country in 13 tests.

Edwards played superbly in partnership with that other great Welsh personality, Barry John. The two were together as a scrum-outside half combination on 23 occasions, then the world record.

Edwards was part of the great era in Welsh rugby that followed almost exactly the dates of his career. He also played superbly for the British Isles in New Zealand in 1971 and in South Africa in 1974. Both those series were won during what were some of British rugby's greatest days.

He took part in and, indeed, scored the try that is often hailed as one of the greatest ever seen in the game. It was for the Barbarians club against the All Blacks of 1972–73 at Cardiff. The capacity home crowd of 60,000 roared so loudly they distorted forever the television recordings of Edwards diving in at the end of a 90-metre movement.

Edwards possessed a most charming and modest personality, and became in his time one of the most revered characters in Wales – and the rest of the rugby world. Stories abound about his prowess at the game. On the day of an England-Wales game at Twickenham, one Welsh supporter could not get a ticket so he waited forlornly outside the ground hoping at least to soak up some of the atmosphere and to hear the result. Eventually he became frustrated at not knowing what was

happening in the game, so he called up to some people in the ground and asked them what was happening. They happened to be English, so they called back ungraciously that all the Welsh team except Gareth Edwards had been carried off injured.

This disturbed the already sad Welsh supporter, but he remained typically optimistic. When a huge roar erupted from the ground a few minutes later, he again called up to the crowd. 'What's happened, what's happened? Gareth scored, has he?'

Such a story is typical of the admiration and affection that existed for the great man.

ELLA, MARK
New South Wales and Australia
25 internationals for Australia 1980–84

ELLA, GARY
New South Wales and Australia
6 internationals for Australia 1982–88

ELLA, GLEN
New South Wales and Australia
4 internationals for Australia 1982–85

Three brilliant Australian aboriginal brothers who, in combination at either school, club, state or international level, dazzled and delighted rugby crowds with their backline interplay.

The Ella brothers came from a modest family of 12 children in La Perouse, Sydney. Glen and Mark were twins and Gary was 13 months younger.

Mark was a flyhalf possessed of brilliant balance, speed and intuition; Glen, a fullback who sometimes played as a centre, and Gary, a long-striding runner, who was used mostly as centre and occasionally on the wing.

The brothers first made headlines as schoolboys. Their uncanny understanding of each other's play brought suggestions of telepathic aboriginal powers – when viewing some of their tries and plays it was hard to argue otherwise. From Matraville High in suburban Sydney, all three made the 1977–78 Australian Secondary Schools touring team which went on a nine-week tour of the United Kingdom, France, Japan and the Netherlands.

The team went unbeaten in 16 games. Australian writers were quick to point out that only the 1924–25 All Black 'Invincible' team had done as well on tour in Britain. The team also scored 110 tries on the tour (averaging nearly eight a game), and between them the Ella brothers scored a quarter of all the points.

Everywhere the team went the Ella brothers were high in curiosity value for the media. Nor did they let the reporters down. They became stars of the Australian rugby scene before they had even left school. It was inevitable that in time their talents would be utilised in the Wallabies.

Mark was the first to make the grade. After having shone for his club Randwick, Sydney and New South Wales, he toured to Argentina with the Wal-

The Ella brothers – Glen, Gary and Mark.

labies in 1979 and thereafter became a regular and vital member of Australian test sides. He was made captain for the Wallabies tour to New Zealand in 1982, when aged only 23, and led the team until 1984 when a new coach, Alan Jones, preferred Andrew Slack. That did not deter Ella from playing brilliant rugby and on the 1984 tour of Britain, though seemingly at odds on a personal level with Jones, he was one of the team's brightest stars. He became the first touring player in Britain to score a try in each of the home internationals, a feat he had also achieved on the schoolboys' tour seven years earlier (though that team did not play Scotland).

Mark Ella retired at the age of 25, having played 25 internationals, amid rumours that he could no longer tolerate playing in teams coached by Alan Jones. He resisted many lucrative offers to play rugby league and settled into a life as a businessman, TV commentator and newspaper columnist. He returned to Sydney club rugby in 1989 and also played and coached in Italy.

Twin brother Glen and younger brother Gary also played for Randwick in Sydney and both joined Mark in the Wallabies for the 1981–82 tour of Britain. Injuries damaged both their chances of playing consistently on that tour and neither joined Mark in the international matches.

The trio's best tour for their country was to New Zealand in 1982. Mark was captain and, along with David Campese, he was the team's star player. Glen was an excellent fullback but could not force his way into the test team ahead of Roger Gould. Gary's form was such that he made the first two tests at centre. Once again the brothers' consummate passing and mutual understanding surprised opposition backlines and astonished the hard-to-please New Zealand crowds.

Surprisingly the three Ella brothers never played together in a test match. Gary retired with a knee injury in 1986 and Glen bowed out after being part of yet another Randwick championship winning team in 1987. Gary returned to play one test against the All Blacks in 1988.

Former Wallaby coach Bob Dwyer, who had coached the trio for Randwick and Australia, said 'the influence of the Ella brothers on Australian rugby

has been absolutely immeasurable. They were best summed up by the word that was coined by Australian journalists to describe their play – 'Ellamagic!'

ELLIS, JAN
South-West Africa and South Africa
38 internationals for Sth Africa 1965–76

Along with the tight-loose forward Frik du Preez, flanker Jan Ellis shares the record for most test matches played by a South African.

Ellis came from far-flung South-West Africa (now independent Namibia) where the nearest rugby club was 60 miles (100 km) away. His keenness and determination to play the game soon built into a talent that was recognised in Johannesburg, Pretoria and Cape Town, the main centres of South African rugby.

Ellis made the first of his 38 test appearances for the Springboks in New Zealand in 1965. He played modestly for the first six or seven games, but then he discovered his own strength and speed and by tour's end he was one of the most improved players in the team. Thereafter his powerful running from loose play and strong tackling made him a regular in Springbok sides.

He played many of his tests in the politically-charged atmosphere of anti-apartheid protests, but if such demonstrations worried Ellis it was never seen. His play was always of a consistently high standard.

In 1976 Ellis equalled Frik du Preez's total of 38 internationals, but was denied the chance to beat the record when he was dropped from the Springboks team after the first test against the All Blacks.

ELLIS PARK, JOHANNESBURG
The brick field and rubbish dump that became the most ambitious rugby stadium in the world.

At the turn of the century Ellis Park was just a place that produced bricks for the construction of the fine houses that adorned the suburbs of the new city of gold. Johannesburg rugby was played at the Wanderers ground, but when that was taken for Johannesburg's new railway station a new stadium for Transvaal rugby was needed.

Ellis Park, named after a prominent local body official of the time, who had battled hard to secure it as a rugby

stadium, was opened in 1928, in time to host the match between the first New Zealand tourists and Transvaal, which the home team won by 6–0.

Later in the same year, with the wooden grandstand from Wanderers set up temporarily on the touchline, Ellis Park hosted the first international on the ground – the second test, a gruelling match which the All Blacks won by 7–6. The big rough-hewn prop and captain Phil Mostert shocked by kicking a goal from a mark. The crowd of 38,000 was then a South African record for any sport. The most expensive seats cost £2 2s and the total gate of £14,500 went a long way towards establishing Transvaal's union as one of the richest in the world.

The soft kikuyu grass on the new ground was a vast improvement on the rock-hard Wanderers surface. However, the new Ellis Park was not admired for its contribution to spectator comfort and viewing ease. Rather it was an antiquated-looking ground with low sloping terraces and rickety, climbing scaffolds. It was often the lot of spectators to be sitting nearly 100 metres from the centre of the field.

Its turf eventually became one of the best surfaces in South Africa, although visiting teams had to counter curiously high bounces of the ball. Conversely, a ball kicked flat across the dry, even surface would spin end over end for much longer distances than on the lushly grassed fields of Britain or New Zealand.

In 1955 the Springboks and the British Isles played one of rugby's classic games on Ellis Park. The ground was jammed to the doors with 95,000 spectators – a world record for a rugby crowd. The Lions won the first test of that series in a thriller by 23–22. A missed late conversion lost the game for the Springboks.

By 1972 the deficiencies of Ellis Park's facilities could no longer be denied and Jannie le Roux, the president of the Transvaal RU, began to plan bold developments. The old Ellis Park was demolished and rebuilt as the last word in spectator luxury. Capacity was cut back to 71,000, but the seating was much closer to the playing area, in a sharply rising two-tiered stand stretching right around the playing field.

Today a huge video screen provides instant replays of tries and controversial incidents. Restaurants, bars, private viewing boxes and conference halls make the stadium a facility second to none in the rugby world.

Unfortunately, in its first years of operation it was not easy to generate the kind of financial return required to turn the project into a profit-making venture. There were some who described the ground's early financial situation as 'nightmarish'. Nevertheless, Ellis Park is a wonderful addition to rugby's facilities in South Africa.

ELLIS, W. W, *See* WEBB ELLIS, W.

ENGELBRECHT, JAN

Western Province and South Africa
33 internationals for Sth Africa 1960–69

Jan Engelbrecht was a tall, fast and elusive wing three-quarter who built a reputation as a try-scorer in his years in the Springboks team. He came into rugby from Stellenbosch University and after only three games for Western Province was chosen in the Springboks team to play Scotland on its tour of 1960. The year before he had toured South America with the Junior Springboks.

He missed the tests against the All Blacks later that year, although he was called into the fourth test, only to miss the game because of tonsilitis. Thereafter he played 32 more tests, all on the right wing.

In his last game for South Africa, in the second test in Australia in 1969, he equalled John Gainsford's South African test record of 33 internationals. With his impressive speed and swerve, he also scored two tries that day. In all he scored eight tries in tests and 44 in all matches for his country.

Jannie Engelbrecht evades Australia's John O'Gorman to score in the second test against Australia, 1965.

ENGLAND

Whether you subscribe to the theory that William Webb Ellis's 'illegal' run at Rugby School was the beginning of rugby, or whether you believe it evolved naturally from other ball games, there is little doubt that today's game of rugby owes its origins to the English.

That 'rugby' game started in England; the English formulated the break away from the Football Association; the English formed rugby's first governing body in 1871 (the Rugby Football Union); the English shaped the first widely accepted code of laws; and many of the early changes in the playing structure of the game came from English ideas.

To this day, the English influence in rugby union is considerable, although it has to be said (even though Englishmen might grind their teeth in frustration) that the English influence in the actual playing of the game has diminished. The authority of the English in rugby these days comes from their direction to others in matters of law-making, administration and control of the game.

The English 'style' of presenting the social side of the game still extends far

beyond their main ground at Twickenham (or 'Headquarters' as its known). In Canada, Hong Kong, Japan, Zimbabwe and even Australia, recognisable features from English rugby's social life are incorporated to a high degree. After-match dinners and clubhouse activities in those countries are direct 'replicas' of the way the English have been doing it for years.

Twenty-one clubs met in the Pall Mall restaurant in Cockspur St, London, in January 1871, to form the Rugby Football Union. Eight of those clubs are still operating, including Blackheath, Richmond, and Harlequins. Later that year an England team met Scotland in Edinburgh in the first international rugby match, played with 20 men a side. The first international on English soil was played at Kennington Oval in 1872.

So much of England's rugby history is tied in with the history of the game itself that it is difficult to separate the two. For instance, the distinctive amateur ethos of rugby stems totally from English attitudes. In the very early days rugby was primarily for boys of the public schools of England. Those who wanted to make money from football and augment their working-class salaries followed the route of soccer. Public school and university players from wealthier families stayed with rugby.

When moves were made, in the late 19th century, for 'broken time' from work to be compensated for with monetary payments, the public school types had no need to trifle with such problems. Thus many of the clubs from the industrial and mining north of England were lost to a professional version of the game, later called rugby league. The type of player left in rugby wanted to keep the game purely amateur and this attitude remains much the same in England today. (The advent of rebel tours in modern times suggests that other attitudes hold considerable sway in countries such as South Africa, New Zealand and Australia.)

England has enjoyed two great periods of success on the field of play. The first was from 1910–14 when it won the Five Nations championship three times and shared a fourth. The second came during the 1920s, when England won three championships in four years. Although there have been many other golden moments, like winning against the All Blacks in 1935, 1973 and 1983, and winning against South Africa in 1969 and 1972, it has to be said that English rugby was in decline in the

Members of the England team of 1905, before their match with New Zealand.

1970s and 80s. England was the Grand Slam-winner in the championship in 1980, but finished wooden spoon holder five times in the previous decade.

Although England beat Wales at Cardiff on the way to a championship win in 1963, 28 years passed without another win at Cardiff. The 25–6 win in 1991, aided by seven penalty goals, brought great relief to English supporters. The side went on to win a Triple Crown and Grand Slam in 1990–91 and gave hope to its supporters that

it would be a strong force in the 1991 World Cup competition.

A consistent lack of organisation of club leagues had counted against England at international level in the past. A very disappointing effort by England at the 1987 World Cup was the spur for a major reformation of club competition, improving England's chances to raise its standards. The leading players may have had lots of games each season, but too many were social ones and did not provide the tough preparation needed to win consistently at test level.

But it could never be said that England has contributed few top playing personalities since the days it started the game. Some of them are men like Wavell Wakefield, the great utility forward and captain of the 1920s; 'Dave' Davies and 'K' Kershaw, the superb halfback combination of the 1920s whose names went together like pepper and salt; Prince Alex Obolensky, who scored the winning tries against New Zealand in 1935; Dickie Jeeps, the superb halfback of the 1950s; Jeff Butterfield, the stately centre of the same time; Peter Jackson the wing with the twinkling feet; Bev Risman and Richard Sharp, the authoritative flyhalves; David Duckham, the sturdy centre and wing of the 1960s–70s; and Bill Beaumont, the courageous and honest lock of modern times. There were many other fine exponents of the game who wore with honour the white jersey with the red rose emblem.

The first international on English soil – England v Scotland at the Oval, 1872.

Twickenham, the home of English rugby since 1910 has proved a successful ground for England. Scotland could not win there until 1926, Ireland not until 1929, Wales first in 1933 and France not until 1951. It is such a fine venue that it was entirely appropriate that it should be chosen as the setting for the 1991 Rugby World Cup final.

ERBANI, DOMINIQUE
Agen and France
46 internationals for France 1981–90

One of a number of versatile French forwards in the 1980s who totalled high numbers of internationals without ever qualifying for any all-time great player lists.

Erbani was first capped in 1981 in Brisbane, in the same match in which his long-time touring companion, Laurent Rodriguez, also made his debut. Like Rodriguez and others, his place in any French team was uncertain until he played as part of the magnificent French team against New Zealand at Nantes in the first test of 1986. Erbani was one of the heroes, and his storming form there saw him play on a regular basis after that. He played on the side of the scrum in the Rugby World Cup final in 1987.

A tall man, Erbani was more than useful at the end of the lineout. He was also an aggressive runner with the ball, and tough in close-quarter forward exchanges. Erbani also played as a test lock and a No. 8.

EVANS, ERIC
Sale and England
30 internationals for England 1948–58

An England hooker and captain who won 30 caps for his country between 1948 and 1958, Evans first played a test against Australia in 1948 as a prop. He did not play internationally again until 1950, when he was picked as a hooker, in a team with nine newcomers. Most of the others were

discarded promptly by the selectors, but Evans played on through seven of the next eight seasons and rose to be England's captain through two unbeaten seasons.

When he retired Evans was one short of Wavell Wakefield's England record of 31 caps. He was captain of England 13 times and in 1957 led it to its first Grand Slam since 1928.

EXETER RFC
Exeter Club was formed in 1872, the second oldest in south-west England (the oldest being Tiverton).

The 1905 All Blacks played their first game on British soil in Exeter, at the club's County Ground headquarters. But their match against Devon was only the curtain-raiser to a club game involving Exeter against 'the Next XVIII'. New Zealand beat Devon by 55–4, stunning the rugby world.

The Exeter players watching from the grandstand were so impressed they promptly adopted both the New Zealanders' 2–3–2 scrum formation and their uniform. To this day Exeter players wear black jerseys (though they changed their mind about the scrummaging style within a few years).

In the club's first 100 years, 12 Exeter men played international rugby, 11 for England and one for Scotland. J.C.R. Buchanan was Exeter's highest capped international, with 16 caps.

EXILES CLUBS
Formed in London to allow exiled nationals to play with fellow countrymen while living in London, these clubs have added colour to London rugby.

London Scottish (formed 1878)
London Scottish has played an important part in the history of Scottish rugby – more than 100 of its players have played internationals, among them 10 players who helped the Scottish team beat the 1906–07 Springboks as well as win the Grand Slam. Famous players include William

Maclagan (captain of the 1891 British team in South Africa); 'Darkie' Bedell-Sivright (the captain of the 1904 British team in New Zealand); the 1921 New Zealand captain George Aitken, who later played for Scotland; and Iain Laughland, who was the most-capped Scotland international until Alistair McHarg (44 caps) came along. The modern Scottish fullback Gavin Hastings is also a club player.

London Welsh (formed 1885)
London Welsh, which has had its headquarters at Old Deer Park in south-west London since 1957, celebrated its centenary in 1985 with a special match at Twickenham against the Barbarians. Its greatest year in terms of international selection was 1971, when it contributed the captain (John Dawes) and six other players in the victorious British Isles team which toured Australia and New Zealand. Five of the seven players – Dawes, J.P.R. Williams, Gerald Davies, Mervyn Davies, and John Taylor – appeared in all four tests against New Zealand, a club record that is unlikely to be surpassed. The other two players were Mike Roberts and Geoff Evans.

Other exiles who played for London Welsh include Willie Llewellyn and Teddy Morgan, famous players of the turn of the century; Rhys Gabe, Wilfred Wooller, Claude Davey and Haydn Tanner; Vivian Jenkins, the 1938 Lions vice-captain and rugby writer; and Clive Rees of the 1974 Lions.

London Irish (formed 1898)
Though, traditionally, not as strong as the other two, several leading personalities have played for the club over the years, including the Lions Andy Mulligan, Tony O'Reilly, John O'Driscoll and Ken Kennedy, all Irish internationals; and the Irish flanker and 1966 Lions manager, Des O'Brien. The club provided four backline players for the Irish team of 1990–91, including captain Rob Saunders.

F

FARR-JONES, NICK
New South Wales and Australia
44 internationals for Australia 1984–90

Two significant records tumbled for this outstanding Australian player in 1990. First, in his seventh season as the Wallabies' halfback, Nick Farr-Jones took over from the great John Hipwell as Australia's most-capped test player in that vital position. He also became Australia's most-capped captain, appearing as skipper in his 21st test as the 1990 season ended (beating Andrew Slack's record of 18 tests). And he and his partner, Michael Lynagh, looked set to beat John Rutherford and Roy Laidlaw's record for most tests together for any country as a scrumhalf-flyhalf combination.

Nick Farr-Jones made his first tour to Fiji in 1984 and played his first test on Twickenham against England. He was an immediate success, and in combination with Mark Ella played a vital role in the Wallaby team that went on to win a Grand Slam over British countries. Two years later he helped Australia win the Bledisloe Cup in New Zealand.

Since then the elegant yet aggressive style of Farr-Jones has marked him as one of the world's most significant modern players. He passes slickly (in the Australian scrumhalf tradition of Cyril Burke, Des Connor, Ken Catchpole and John Hipwell), he is a fast and explosive runner, has a wide tactical knowledge of the game (including the best ways to exploit the blindside), while his strength and fitness, enthusiasm and popularity among his fellow players have aided his from-the-front style of captaincy. Many critics considered him the world's best halfback as the new decade began.

Injury around Rugby World Cup time in 1987 restricted his appearances and performances in that series.

Farr-Jones took over the captaincy of Australia in 1988 and although Wallaby teams under his leadership have lost a number of series and games, his own form has not diminished. He can count several successes as captain,

Nick Farr-Jones

including beating England in Australia in two tests in 1988, and beating Scotland, France and New Zealand at least once on their home soil in a little over 18 months.

With Nick Farr-Jones at the helm, Australia remains a strong force in world rugby. He has also made a tremendous contribution to Australian rugby by his personal example. He is a learned rugby thinker and an eloquent speaker. In the face of the enormous popularity of rugby league in Australia he has always represented his game with true style.

FARRELL, JAMES
Bective Rangers and Ireland
29 internationals for Ireland 1926–32
5 internationals for British Isles 1930

Jimmy Farrell played consistently as a lock, flanker, and even prop on one occasion, in the very good Irish teams of the 1920s and 30s. He was part of the first Irish teams to win at Murrayfield and Twickenham and for his efforts made the 1930 Great Britain team which toured New Zealand and Australia. He played all four tests in New Zealand and one in Australia and was a zestful and hard-working forward throughout. Farrell's last game for his country was against Wales in 1932.

FENWICK, STEVE
Bridgend and Wales
30 internationals for Wales 1975–81
4 internationals for British Isles 1977

A hard-running midfield back whose consistency of play and continuity in the Welsh team led to his breaking an 83-year-old Welsh record: his 30 caps

Steve Fenwick

overtook the previous record of 25 as a centre set by the great Arthur Gould in 1897.

Fenwick made his debut for Wales v France in 1975. In 1978–79 he scored 38 points in the Five Nations series, which equalled the best scored by any player from any country. He toured New Zealand with the 1977 British Isles, playing in all four test matches. After captaining Wales in its centenary fixture with New Zealand in 1980, Fenwick was dropped in the 1980–81 season. He later went over to rugby league, in which he also represented Wales.

FERGUSON, CRAIG

A leading Australian international referee from 1963 to 1971. Perhaps the most significant of the six full tests matches Craig Ferguson controlled were two of the three tests played by the Springboks against Australia in the protest-troubled tour of 1971, games riddled with tension and pressure, played on fields surrounded by police.

The South Africans had already seen Ferguson six years before when he handled the first test between the same two nations at Sydney. The Springboks winced at his penalty count of 17–5 against them in the match, which Australia won by 18–12, including four penalty goals. The South African press was very critical of Ferguson's refereeing, pointing out that the Wallabies had 17 shots at goal in the game to the Springboks' three.

During his career, Craig Ferguson controlled 165 Sydney first grade games.

FERRASSE, ALBERT

Elected president of the French Rugby Federation in 1968, Albert Ferrasse of Agen built for himself the formidable reputation of being the most powerful administrator in French rugby.

Born in 1917, Ferrasse played at lock in the Agen team which won the national club championship of France in 1945. Later he made the reserves for the French XV. After his playing days were over, he took to refereeing with considerable success, refereeing the French club final of 1959.

Under his guidance France was admitted to the International Rugby Board in 1978. Ferrasse, very pro-British in his outlook, also fought

sternly to allow South Africa to maintain its place in world rugby. Through France's association with FIRA, he kept a weather eye on the emerging countries of European rugby.

Well known for taking a strong stance on rough play in rugby, Ferrasse also introduced the rigid club transfer rules in France. Outsiders asked about the apparent 'liberal' attitude in France towards the amateur spirit of the game, but Ferrasse repeatedly claimed he investigated any complaints of the amateur spirit and could find few, if any, breaches. Talk is one thing, proof is another, he has said, when questioned about reported professionalism in French club rugby. He was also once quoted as saying that 'it is quite an achievement that rugby still resists the aggression of money'.

Albert Ferrasse was chairman of the International Rugby Board in 1987 during the first Rugby World Cup in Australia and New Zealand.

FERROCARIL OESTE STADIUM

The main rugby stadium in Argentina in the years up to 1986, when the matches against the touring French team were moved to the bigger Valez Sarsfield soccer stadium which could cope with 50,000 fans.

Ferrocaril Oeste Stadium (translation: West Railway Stadium) was the venue for many of Argentina's great rugby moments during that country's rise to prominence as a rugby world force.

Many overseas players and referees commented on the acoustics of the ground and the noise created was often a great weapon of advantage for Pumas teams in action against visitors: 30,000 screaming Argentines sounded like three times that number. Australian referee Kerry Fitzgerald said when the fans at the Ferrocaril Oeste Stadium whistled in anger the noise seemed 'louder than a jumbo jet'.

FIELD GOAL

A method of scoring which was outlawed in 1905. A field goal was scored by kicking a ball rolling loose in the field of play, rather like a lofted soccer goal. If the ball sailed over the crossbar then four points were awarded. It was not permissible under the laws to handle the ball in any way, or to kick a field goal from a punt or from a ball that had just been kicked off.

It was a scoring method which was probably directly related to the game of Association Football, but a rugby ball was harder to kick on the bounce or volley than a round soccer ball, and there were very few field goals successfully taken.

When the field goal was abolished in 1905 the value of a goal from a mark was reduced at the same time from four points to three. These were the last changes to the rugby scoring system for 42 years.

In modern times the term 'field goal' is sometimes used by writers and commentators to describe a dropped goal. Technically this is an erroneous use, though it has gained quite common usage, especially in Australia. In rugby league it is the official terminology for a dropped goal.

FIJI

Fijian players, with their courage, friendliness and winning smiles (whether in defeat or victory), have been, down the years, great ambassadors for their country and for the game.

In early years Fijian rugby was so surprisingly inventive, exciting and visual, that it took many top overseas sides by surprise. In those years Fiji chalked up some marvellous victories. Only in recent times have the more established countries realised that Fijian forward play sometimes lacks the vigour and commitment of its back play. Thus there were some heavy scores posted against Fiji in the 1970s and 1980s by teams playing hard in the forwards and not allowing the still dangerous Fiji backs to run with the ball.

At one time there were two rugby unions in Fiji. The Fiji Rugby Union was formed in 1913, comprised mostly of players from European backgrounds, while the Native Rugby Union, for Fiji-born players, was formed in 1915. The two unions amalgamated in 1945 to become the Fiji Rugby Football Union. The word 'Football' was deleted in 1963 and 'FRU' are now the letters that appear under the palm tree emblem on the Fijian players' jerseys.

There is evidence that the first rugby game was played in a town called Ba in 1884. Some of the players involved were police and military men from a British background – the almost traditional way for the game to be spread around the world.

A club competition began in Suva in 1904, but early newspaper reports suggest that the teams were almost totally expatriates. Indeed, in the early days, soccer and cricket seemed to appeal more as games of this country. It was only later that the running nature of rugby, combined with the courage that was needed to play well, caught on with the big raw-boned Fijians. Once it did the rugby world sat up and took notice, because no team in the world played as spectacularly as did some of the early Fijian national teams.

Fiji's introduction to teams from overseas came with games against visiting warships in the early years of the twentieth century. The 1913 All Blacks were said to have played a match against the Pacific club, which was led by another New Zealander, the former Otago player Paddy Sheehan, on its way home from a tour of Canada and California. Played at Albert Park in Suva and won 67–3 by New Zealand, the game is largely lost in New Zealand historical records.

Fiji's first overseas match was in Apia, Samoa, in August 1925 – a game that is remembered for its unique venue and timing. The playing area for the game was a large marked field, its singular feature a large tree, positioned well inside the field of play! Kick-off time was 7.30 in the morning, to allow the local players time to get to work following the game. Fiji played in all black uniforms and won by 6–0.

In 1926 Auckland University was the first overseas team to tour Fiji officially, playing four matches. Tonga also toured that year, beginning a long rugby association on the rugby field

with its neighbour. Fiji took the field for 'tests' that year in the colours that they have used ever since: white jerseys, black shorts and palm tree emblem badge.

The Fiji team which toured New Zealand in 1939 became the first – and last – overseas team to finish undefeated on a full tour of New Zealand.

The 1939 Fijians were amazing: only the season before they had taken to wearing boots for all their games and had to contend with heavy pitches for much of their tour. Their itinerary included Auckland and New Zealand Maoris, and in addition there were the stresses of the approaching World War II. (The last five matches were played after the declaration of war.) But they played outstanding rugby, surprising the New Zealanders with their opportunism and counter-attacking play, something not emphasised in the New Zealand game of the time, and their superb fitness.

The years after World War II showed the real strength of Fiji rugby. Their tours to New Zealand (1951 and 1957) and to Australia (1952 and 1954) were enormously successful and popular.

The carefree abandon with which the Fijians played the game drew massive crowds, especially in Australia where the successful tours by Fiji did much to bring the game back from the brink of being swamped by rugby league and Australian rules football. A record 42,000 watched a Fiji v Australia match in Sydney in 1952, and the 1954 tour was extended to 17 games so that even more Australians could witness the brilliance of the Fijian running play.

FIJI R.U.

By the 1960s Fijian rugby was looking beyond the Pacific. The opportunity to tour Britain came in 1964, when the Welsh Rugby Union invited the Fijians to visit, a tour not approved by the International Board. The Welsh were keen that another union should also host the Fijians, because they feared a financial loss. France stepped in and a tour was arranged of five games in each country.

Within days of their arrival the Fijians, with their modesty and smiling courtesy, had won their way into Welsh hearts. Their rugby proved an eye-opener to Welsh fans and the tour was a huge financial success. In the last game at Cardiff, 14 Fijian players came storming back in the last 10 minutes to score 13 points against a Welsh XV, only to be pipped by 22–28; 50,000 Welshmen cheered them to the echo.

In France the rugby was harder for the tourists. Coping with the cuisine and the language created problems for the Pacific Islanders, but the Fijians competed vigorously and they were grateful that the French became only

The Fijian rugby team issues a challenge with the performance of the cibi, or war dance.

Orisi Dawai (left) and Joe Levula – Fijian rugby stars in the 1950s.

Senivalati Laulau outsprints Roger Baird at the Hong Kong Sevens.

the second country, after Australia, to grant them a match against an official top team. At half-time in their match with France in Paris, the score stood at 3–3, but although it slipped to 3–21, the performance was still rated a marvellous effort against a full international French team.

Further games of significance followed, such as the 1968 All Blacks visit to the islands. Sadly, administrative conservatism meant that the New Zealand team had to take the field billed as only a 'New Zealand XV'. The first official game between New Zealand and Fiji took place in 1980. In the tours before that, Fiji had met New Zealand Maori teams in their New Zealand 'test' matches.

Another great day for Fijian rugby came in 1977 when the British Isles team was repulsed by 25–21 at Buckhurst Park in Suva, Fiji's best-known rugby ground.

The 1980s bought a change in Fiji's performances. Many reasons have been offered for this change in fortunes: social difficulties in the country, brought about by an economic downturn, meant that many leading players preferred to work rather than to be

unemployed rugby players; other players left the country to work and play in places like New Zealand and Australia, so that Fiji teams chosen from players still at home were not necessarily the best.

Some severe defeats followed as a result. The 1982 touring team to England played 10 matches and lost them all, while in the South Pacific championship, Fiji suffered several humiliatingly heavy defeats including 9–72 to Auckland in 1989.

Some of these losses occurred because opposition teams had worked out how best to counter their running open rugby by playing Fiji through the forwards. When Fiji tried to counter such tactics by working hard to improve its forward play the traditional, exciting qualities of Fijian back play became neglected.

Still another theory is that Fijian rugby only flourishes when the national team is coached by a European. When a native coaches, tribal differences and rivalry influence some of the play.

There were signs of an improvement during the World Cup of 1987. Fiji was the one team at the competi-

tion that caused a major surprise when it beat Argentina by 28–9. Thereafter it was delightfully inconsistent, losing to New Zealand 13–74, losing to Italy 15–18, but qualifying for the quarter finals on the number of tries it scored in all matches.

In the quarter-final Fiji played France at Eden Park. The effervescent, running rugby that followed will be remembered as one of the best games in the whole series. France won by 31–16, but only after a thrilling display of rugby from both teams.

The manner in which Fiji played hinted that it might soon return to the best form of the 1950s and 60s, although the loss of a number of players to the rebel South Pacific Barbarians tour to South Africa later in 1987 was a setback, as was the military coup d'état at home.

The Fijians find one form of rugby irresistible. At the seven-a-side version, they are surely the world's best. The open field running of the game suits them admirably, and their win over New Zealand at the 1990 Hong Kong Sevens was one of the most spectacular games ever seen at that tournament.

Many Fijian players have made their presence felt on the rugby fields of the world. Perhaps the first player to be widely known outside his own country was Josaia Vorege, the star wing of the 1939 team in New Zealand. Knowledgeable writers in New Zealand claimed he was better than anything the All Blacks had at the time.

Josefa (Joe) Levula was the brilliant star of Fiji teams in the 1950s and 60s. His high-stepping running action at great speed earned him the reputation in some quarters of being the best wing in the world.

Accompanying Levula in most of the teams of that time was the strong centre, Orisi Dawai, also fast and elusive and an excellent captain. Both these players attracted the attention of rugby league scouts and ended their careers playing professionally in the north of England. Later Epi Bolawaqatabu was a sturdy and courageous No. 8 who played successfully for Fiji and in Queensland. He later became a coach of Fiji.

Other stars of Fijian teams were Pio Bosco Tikoisuva in the 1970s, who played some of his club rugby as a twinkling flyhalf for Harlequins in London; Senivalati Laulau, a speedy centre of the 1970s and 80s who would have graced many an international team in other countries; and Severo Koroduadua, a latter day Fiji hero with his huge kicking from fullback, and a big hit with the crowds in New Zealand during the World Cup in 1987. Many writers consider Waisake Serevi to be the best exponent currently playing the sevens version of the game.

Fiji rugby is unique. One writer has said it is fast, funny and furious, none more so than when played against Pacific neighbours. It is to be hoped the discipline of earlier years can return to Fijian rugby once again.

FINLAND

One of the more modest rugby-playing countries of Europe. In the 1980s it was reported there were five clubs in the country and that Finland had played several internationals with Switzerland and made several tours to Sweden.

This is not a country that has strong associations with rugby but nevertheless the sport is gaining in popularity all the time. Headquarters are in Helsinki.

FIRA

The Fédération Internationale de Rugby Amateur is the world's largest rugby organisation, with considerable influence, especially in Europe.

Usually referred to by its abbreviation, FIRA was formed in 1934 on the initiative of the French and German rugby federations. When France was dismissed from the Five Nations championship in 1931 it sought alternative methods of arranging international fixtures.

Germany, which had provided France with its strongest opposition since then, joined France as the co-hosts of a meeting in Paris in January 1934, to which seven other countries sent representatives – Holland, Italy, Catalonia (the Barcelona region of Spain), Romania, Czechoslovakia, Portugal and Sweden. The last named later withdrew, to be replaced by Belgium.

The meeting set up the organisation of FIRA and pledged to help and encourage each other, especially with international fixtures.

After World War II, FIRA expanded its authenticity when France was re-admitted to the Five Nations tournament in 1947.

Many of FIRA's ideas were innovative and a direct challenge to those propounded by the conservative London-based IRB.

One such idea was the short-lived European club championship which was proposed at the eighteenth annual FIRA congress in Casablanca in 1960. This was won by the powerful French club Béziers in 1962 and by the Romanian team Grivita Rosie in 1964, before difficulties with travel, visas and costs caused the competition to lapse.

Later FIRA turned its attention to restoring rugby to the Olympic Games or creating its own international tournament. It was the second option that won favour and in 1973–74 the FIRA European championship was established.

France has dominated the competitions, regularly fielding its top international XV against Romania, but for other games selecting what is called an 'A' team, made up of those close to the top XV.

FIRA continues to expand. A number of Eastern European countries have joined to make FIRA competitions

genuine European events: only the absence of British and Irish teams prevent it being complete. A significant entry to its ranks was the Soviet Union, admitted in 1976 and developing quickly to achieve division one status just two years later.

FIRA has also increased its influence outside Europe. A group of African countries has taken associate membership of FIRA, and a further seven countries – Western Samoa, Hong Kong, Solomon Islands, Chile, Paraguay, Barbados and Taiwan – signed up in 1987 as full members. At various other times Argentina, Japan, Canada and the United States have expressed interest in joining.

Politically those new members and affiliates give FIRA six times as many members as the IRB, yet it is the IRB that still controls the world game of rugby. France is the only member of both bodies.

The men in authority in the FIRA are Frenchmen. Marcel Batigne, elected in 1967 to the presidency, exerted huge influence during his long term in office. Another powerful man during the formative years of the FIRA championship was the General-Secretary, Jean-Claude Bourrier.

WINNERS OF FIRA CUP (Division One)		
	Winner	Runner Up
1974	France	Romania
1975	Romania	France
1976	France	Italy
1977	Romania	France
1978	France	Romania
1979	France	Romania
1980	France	Romania
1981	Romania	France
1982	France	Italy
1983	Romania	Italy
1984	France	Romania
1985	France	Romania
1986	France	Soviet Union
1987	France	Soviet Union
1988	France	Soviet Union
1989	France	Soviet Union
1990	France, Romania, Soviet Union – a three-way tie	

FITZGERALD, CIARAN

St Mary's College and Ireland
25 internationals for Ireland 1979–86
4 internationals for British Isles 1983

A hooker who captained Ireland and the British Isles, Ciaran Fitzgerald enjoyed a successful rugby career, but also came to know the other side of the coin: controversy, disappointment and defeat.

From an army background, Fitzgerald first played for Ireland on the tour to Australia in 1979. Injuries disrupted some of his early seasons and when he was appointed as captain of Ireland in 1981–82, he had missed the whole of the previous season because of a shoulder injury.

At the time Ireland was going through a bad patch (only one loss away from its worst losing streak in the twentieth century), but Fitzgerald led it back superbly. His team was called 'Dad's Army' such was the high number of older players in the team. Ireland won the Triple Crown for the first time in 33 years – its first championship win in eight seasons. Remarkably it used only 15 players in the four matches of the championship.

Although it was the defending champion the following season, Ireland was not the favourite. But thanks to solid team-work, outstanding play from its star Ollie Campbell, and Ciaran Fitzgerald's decisive leadership, it shared the title with France.

On the basis of those two seasons Fitzgerald was appointed captain of the 1983 British Isles team to New Zealand. Alas Fitzgerald's Lions did not have the playing depth to match a rampant All Black team and the tourists crashed to a 4–0 test series defeat. Much of the blame fell on Fitzgerald, not so much for his captaincy as for his general play and hooking role. It was widely felt and expressed that Fitzgerald was not the better hooker in the team; many preferred Colin Deans of Scotland, who because Fitzgerald had been named tour captain, seemed destined to be always cast as number two.

Controversy flared after a less than perfect performance by Fitzgerald in the first test against the All Blacks at Christchurch. A number of times in that game Fitzgerald's lineout throwins were not straight and critical possession was lost to his team. When the closely fought match was lost 12–16, the critics looked to Fitzgerald. In the remaining games his form often suffered in comparison with Deans but Fitzgerald was always preferred in the tests.

Fitzgerald remained a member of the Ireland team during its next three topsy-turvey seasons. In 1984 it failed to win a game, but by 1985 was back as winners. In 1986, it was last again. Fitzgerald led Ireland through all those seasons, missing only two games because of injury in 1983–84.

In 1987 he announced his unavailability for the World Cup, which signalled the end of his distinguished playing career. He was Ireland's most successful captain since World War II. He was appointed Ireland's coach for the 1990–91 season, a period which will encompass the 1991 World Cup.

FITZGERALD, KERRY

The Australian referee who controlled the first Rugby World Cup final at Eden Park in Auckland in June 1987.

Fitzgerald took up refereeing at the end of his playing days in 1977. He rose swiftly and by 1981 was controlling tour games in Australia and inter-provincial matches with New Zealand teams.

His first game between two countries was New Zealand v Fiji at Suva in 1984. His first full international game was the Ireland v France match at Lansdowne Road in Dublin in 1985, followed a fortnight later by the Wales v Ireland match in Cardiff. His rise to prominence was confirmed early in 1987 when, along with Bob Fordham, he was chosen as one of Australia's two referees for the World Cup.

Fitzgerald impressed with his control in the early matches England v United States in Sydney, and Wales v Ireland at Wellington. It was after his decisive control of the semi-final between New Zealand and Wales at Brisbane that he was awarded the final between France and New Zealand.

Most critics from New Zealand, France and Australia seemed satisfied with Fitzgerald's display in the final but, being a referee, he could not please everyone. Sportswriters from Britain poured scorn upon him. One writer called the game 'the snore of the century' and a number of others wrote critically of the little Australian's refereeing role. It must be assumed it was not a coincidence that they had all, in earlier reports, expressed the hope that a British referee would control the final.

Perhaps the final word on the subject should come from the winning

Rival captains Ciaran Fitzgerald and Andy Dalton on the Eden Park balcony, 1983. It was an unhappy moment for Fitzgerald: his Lions team had just lost the fourth test 6–38 and the series 0–4.

captain, David Kirk of New Zealand. After the match Kirk told rugby's assembled news media that Fitzgerald was 'one of the best, if not the best referee in world rugby'.

In 1989 Fitzgerald became the first overseas referee to take up a second series of appointments in the Five Nations championship. In 1990 he controlled World Cup preliminaries in North America, and seemed destined to play a prominent role in the cup games in Britain and France in 1991.

FITZPATRICK, SEAN
Auckland and New Zealand
30 internationals for N. Zealand 1986–90

When the Cavaliers made their unauthorised tour to South Africa in 1986, and were subsequently suspended for two games, New Zealand had to re-cast a rookie team – labelled the 'Baby Blacks' – to play France in a one-off test at home. The hooker chosen was Bruce Hemara, and when he was injured the reserve who stepped in was also the Auckland provincial reserve. But Sean Fitzpatrick had a rich rugby pedigree, for his father Brian was a sturdy centre with the 1953–54 All Blacks on their British tour, who all but scored a match-saving try against Wales.

The feats of Fitzpatrick junior soon surpassed those of his father. He had to give way to long-serving hooker Hika Reid briefly in 1986, but regained the position in France later that year. When designated World Cup skipper Andy Dalton was forced to miss the pool matches, Fitzpatrick took his place – so emphatically that a fit-again Dalton could not regain his position.

Fitzpatrick was then unchallenged as New Zealand's hooker, and by the end of the 1980s few disputed his claim to being the world's best in that position. He also established a penchant for scoring test match tries, lurking often on the blindside wing and crashing over from quickly-won ball. His two tries in the Bledisloe Cup match of 1987 equalled the record for a hooker in an international.

FIVE-EIGHTHS
A positional term used almost exclusively in New Zealand; other countries use 'stand-off', 'flyhalf' or 'outside half'. It originated with the 1903 New Zealand captain, Jimmy Duncan.

In those days players who stood up closest to the opposition were called, as they are today, forwards. Those who were furthest behind were fullbacks (sometimes 'wholebacks'), and those who were halfway between the two were, of course, halfbacks. It was logical for any player standing between halfback and fullback to become known as three-quarters.

Duncan, a shrewd tactical judge of the game, devised a plan to pull one of his forwards out of the scrums and mauls and place him standing off a little way from the halfback. It proved a valuable ploy as the player in the new position could either send the ball out to the three-quarters or run forward and link with the forwards.

As the new place was positioned at the mid-way point between halfback and threequarter, it was logical that it become known as the 'five-eighths'.

New Zealanders further adapted the term to have 'first five-eighths' and 'second five-eighths'. The second man stood further out again – but not quite as a three-quarter. *See also* FLYHALF.

FIVE NATIONS CHAMPIONSHIP
See INTERNATIONAL CHAMPIONSHIP

FLANKERS
The men who add weight to each side of the second row at scrum time, but who then break away to roam the field. A flanker in modern rugby needs to be the fittest man in the team, and he has to have three attributes: speed, endurance and courage. He must be built to move explosively but yet be still sufficiently sturdy and strong to take on the tough physical exchanges of forward play. Ideally, flankers need to be tall, yet some of the best in the game have been quite short, by forward standards.

The openside flanker packs on the open side of the scrum where the opposition have lined out their backs. This player is a fetcher, capable of chasing an opposition inside back with the ball. He must be fast, a destroyer on the tackle and tough in the forearms and shoulders.

The blindside flanker always packs down on the narrow side. With his slightly slower pace he might be the one who is second to the tackle, but he is the one who will receive the ball from the fetcher to carry on the rush with push, strength and leg-drive.

Some countries have not fully embraced the openside-blindside flank forward game. South Africa is one which has played much of its rugby with the flankers being left and right players (they always pack on that side of the scrum). Springbok flankers tend to be very big and powerful but not necessarily super-quick.

Many coaches and analysts of the modern game feel that the one way to beat the Springboks in their own country would be to employ a speedy flyer on the side of the scrum to chase down flyhalves who are not used to playing under that kind of pressure on the hard grounds. Sadly, for political or personal reasons, the All Black players Graham Williams, Graham Mourie and Michael Jones, all chasers, never got to test that theory in South Africa. Jean-Pierre Rives, a Frenchman who played a similar game, also played rarely in South Africa.

Other fast-breaking flankers include John Taylor and Dai Morris of Wales, Tony Neary of England, Fergus Slattery of Ireland, Rodger Arneil and Jim Calder of Scotland, Greg Davis and Jeff Miller of Australia, and Ken Stewart and Leicester Rutledge of New Zealand.

Flankers from the 'bigger' mould include men such as Ian Kirkpatrick and Kel Tremain of New Zealand, Noel Murphy of Ireland, Michel Crauste of France, Piet Greyling and Jan Ellis of South Africa, and Simon Poidevin of Australia.

FLOODLIT RUGBY
The first game of rugby under lights took place as far back as 1878 when Broughton met Swinton at Broughton in England. The lighting was from two 'Gramme's Lights' fixed to 30ft poles. In London in the same season games there were played under the illumination of two Siemans 'electri-dynamo' machines, each with four lamps.

There was one classic story from the early days of rugby under lights. In 1879 Hawick met Melrose in a game which attracted great local interest. Over 5000 fans came to the night fixture and many of them used the dark corners of the field to slip into the ground without paying. Officials were angry, but they kept the lights on and the game was played in falling snow.

After Hawick had won by a goal to nil, the officials at Buccleuch Park got their revenge. As soon as the game ended they switched off the lights (perhaps to cut their losses from the modest 'gate') and thousands of fans were left slithering, sliding and falling over each other in the snowy slush underfoot.

Games have been played in many parts of the world under lights since World War II, and most modern clubs try to retain lights at their grounds, even if only for training purposes. But some conservative rugby unions still have reservations about playing the game at night. Scotland in particular, and also England do not readily embrace floodlit rugby. To them it is 'not in the best interests of the game'.

In 1987 there was major consideration given by World Cup organisers to having night matches in the competition in New Zealand and Australia. The idea was finally shelved because New Zealand had no floodlit grounds up to an international standard, but planning for the 1991 World Cup indicated that such games would take place.

FLYHALF

This position is known in some countries as 'flyhalf', 'outhalf' or 'stand-off', and in other places, particularly New Zealand, as 'first five-eighths'. Perhaps 'the wearer of the No. 10 jersey' might be a better name! Whatever it is called, the position is vital on the rugby field.

The flyhalf is often the dictator of a team's tactics. Standing where he does, one player wider than the halfback and forwards, with good vision of both forwards and backs, he is in the best place on the field to make tactical decisions.

A flyhalf needs to have a good footballing brain. He should be a runner, a passer and a kicker all rolled into one. He must be strong defensively, able to gain ground through touchline kicks or make corner-flagging runs to assist in tackling.

Flyhalves have a history of being little, nippy players, full of confidence and brashness. Cliff Morgan of Wales is an excellent example; so too are others of Welsh extraction – David Watkins, Barry John, Phil Bennett, Gareth Davies and Jonathan Davies. The Welsh song tells of a mould at a 'flyhalf factory' where players are churned out in the same style.

Tony Ward was an Irishman who fitted the flyhalf formula, though the other great Irishman in that position, Jack Kyle, was a more upright and orthodox player. Still, Kyle was a master of the No. 10 jersey. A subtle player and kicker, when he chose to run he could be devastating as well.

There have been flyhalves heavier in build, and the greatest of these must be Hugo Porta of Argentina. Sturdily built around the thighs, making him hard to stop when he ran at speed, his greatest asset was his ability and repertoire as a kicker. He could either thump a punt upfield or chip a short kick behind oncoming players; and he could kick goals from huge distances or the widest of angles.

A modern version of flyhalf has now emerged – a cross between the nimbleness of a Morgan and the heaviness of a Porta. The best examples of the new type are men like Michael Lynagh of Australia, Grant Fox of New Zealand, Naas Botha of South Africa, Rob Andrew of England and Didier Camberabero of France. All are solid and, it has to be said, slightly unspectacular, preferring to win their matches with sensible play and enormous goal-kicking talents. Their collective attitude sums up what is required in the high-pressure tests of today: steadiness first, brilliance later and the ability to kick goals by the dozen!

FOUROUX, JACQUES
La Voulte, Auch and France
27 internationals for France 1972–77

One of the smallest players to play international rugby, Jacques Fouroux rose to be one of the biggest personalities of the game in France. He was a tiny halfback who barked and yelped at his much bigger forwards in matches for France in the 1970s, his size and bullying leadership style soon earning him at least two nicknames –'Le Petit General' or 'Napoleon'.

As a captain, Fouroux was courageous and inspirational. The fierce commitment of one so small seemed to draw out the best in his team-mates. In his 21 matches as leader, France lost only seven times.

Fouroux took part in one tour where he and another player, Richard Astre, acted as joint captains – to South Africa in 1975. The experiment was not rated a success.

After retiring from active rugby Fouroux soon accepted a selecting and coaching role for France and under his guidance French teams enjoyed great success.

In the 1980s his teams won or shared the Five Nations championship six times, including two Grand Slams. In the World Cup France, under Fouroux, made the final before losing to New Zealand.

Grant Fox gives everything in an attempt to charge down a Michael Lynagh kick. Lynagh and Fox were two of the most influential flyhalves in the 1980s. Their match-winning performances typified the modern flyhalf game.

Faces of French rugby. Top: Albert Ferrasse of the FFR, chairman of the International Rugby Board in 1987.
Below, left: Daniel Dubroca, former captain of France and coach in 1990–91. Right: Loose forward Eric Champ. Peter Bush

Top: French scrumhalf Aubin Hueber gives instructions to his front row – to no avail on this occasion, the third test against Australia, 1990, for Australia won the match, and the series.
Below: French players Didier Camberabero, with the ball,   Philippe Sella,   Henri Sanz and Patrice Lagisquet.   Fotopacific

'Le Petit General' – Jacques Fouroux

Fouroux was great fodder for sportswriters: he was always good for a colourful quote or thoughtful opinion on the game and the apparent incongruity between his physical stature and the rugby power he wielded was grist to the media mill. He frequently hit the headlines with the Gallic logic of his selection policies. Many were the controversies – whether Gallion or Berbizier should be France's halfback, or whether Dintrans or Dubroca should lead the side. Whatever logic was offered up in counter arguments, Fouroux stuck resolutely to his own views.

There was also controversy when his style of coaching changed from a traditional emphasis on back play to one of forward supremacy. In his later years, Fouroux picked huge forward packs to play for France and encouraged them to smash repeatedly at the opposition. This brought wide criticism, even though victories still far outnumbered losses. In 1989, in a radical departure from usual practice, he was total boss on France's tour to New Zealand, both manager and coach.

After a bad run in 1990 after which his national XV had lost nine of its last 13 tests, including an embarrassing home defeat by Romania, Fouroux resigned as coach, carrying on instead as chairman of the panel of selectors.

FOX, GRANT
Auckland and New Zealand
27 internationals for N. Zealand 1985–90

New Zealand's finest goal-kicking exponent, Grant Fox was the highest

points-scorer in the first Rugby World Cup in 1987, totalling 126 points in the six games New Zealand played and won in the tournament – a phenomenal average of 21 points per game. He scored 26 points against Fiji, his best total in a test.

Fox toured to Fiji with the All Blacks of 1984 and made his international debut in 1985 in the first test match against Argentina in Buenos Aires. A member of the rebel Cavaliers team on the tour of South Africa in 1986, Fox was not a regular member of All Black international teams until the World Cup series of 1987.

His kicking style became known as one of the most efficient and accurate anywhere in the world. Other kickers might have been more successful from longer distances, but none was more accurate from a distance of up to 40 metres (45 yards). In 1988 he scored with 10 out of 10 successful goals in the second test against Wales, a total of 22 points. Later that year he passed Don Clarke's record of test points for New Zealand. Clarke had taken 32 tests to reach 207 points; Fox passed that total in his 12th test. He had earlier passed 100 test points in only his sixth test, the fastest by any player in world rugby.

In 1988 he also became the highest scorer in New Zealand provincial rugby as well as the highest scorer in all Ranfurly Shield matches. In 1989 and 1990 there were more high totals for Fox in just about every outing he made for New Zealand. Twenty-two seemed to be a favourite total of his. He scored 22 points in tests five times. At the end of 1990 he had scored 430 points in his 27 tests at a truly remarkable average per test of nearly 16 points. Only Michael Lynagh and Hugo Porta had scored more.

As a player Fox initially gained a reputation for being just a safety-first kind of first five-eighth. Later his general play improved noticeably, no doubt buoyed by the confidence gained from playing in highly successful teams such as New Zealand and his home province of Auckland. He looked destined to be in both those teams, and therefore scoring heavily, for many years to come.

FRANCE
The Fédération Francaise de Rugby was formed in 1920. It played a key

role in the formation of FIRA in 1934 and was given full admission to the IRB in 1978.

It is said that 'the best of French rugby is the best of world rugby', typified by swift, lithe athletes, adept at passing and catching, kickers who control the oval ball to travel and bounce where they want it, and strong forwards doing the things strong forwards are expected to do well. The bubble and fizz of French rugby at its best makes the term 'champagne rugby' appropriate.

Yet throughout the history of their game, the French have often been their own worst enemies. Their domestic rugby often erupts into fierce fighting and dirty play. Thankfully, this has been kept in check at an international level so that the 'brutal' rugby, as the FFR once called it, is not often a problem for outsiders.

Then there are the politics of French rugby. Observers often scratch their heads in bewilderment at what appears to be the French selectors' complete inability to pick the best players for the best French sides. It seems the large group of national selectors has to engage in various manoeuvres and parochial machinations (what some other countries might call 'horse trading') before arriving at a test team. This has often meant highly gifted players have been left out of French test teams, sometimes forever.

These political struggles have not just existed internally. France's attitude towards the amateur ethos of the rugby game has often been called into question. In 1931 the four home unions decided to expel France from the international championship because they were not satisfied that 'the control and conduct of the game' in France were in keeping with the strictly amateur rules

of the International Rugby Board. To put it another way, the acrid whiff of professionalism was in the air.

So France was thrown out of the British-based rugby world, and stayed out until the 1939–40 season when the home unions decided that it could return if certain assurances were given about the amateur structure of French clubs – and there was a suggestion that the offer was made only because of the impending war. It was officially reinstated in the 1946–47 season.

One French historian has written, 'Whatever our differences with the British, they gave us rugby and that was a precious gift.'

France was relatively slow in developing its rugby. It first entered the Five Nations championship in 1909–10, 10 years before the formation of the national federation, but never truly made its mark on the world scene until the 1950s. Along the way there were times when the French must have wondered whether the game was worth pursuing.

In France's first official international, the 'Original' All Blacks scored 10 tries and thrashed it 38–8. Two months later, England scored nine tries and won 35–8. Other nightmares followed: South Africa beat it 55–6 in 1906–07 and Wales by 47–5 in 1909 and 49–14 in 1910. France was the easy-beat of European rugby. Between 1911–20 it lost 17 consecutive Five Nations games.

Some of the early French players had records which reflected this dismal trend: Emile Lesieur played 12 tests, all of them losses; Paul Mauriat had 19 tests and only one win; Marcel Communeau had 20 tests for just one win, although he was captain for that one! Dreams that one day France might beat the Springboks or the All Blacks must have been very distant in those times.

But slowly France's rugby gained credibility and success followed. It is said it was the Bayonne club that first decided that fast bouts of short, swift passes could move the ball away from sluggish opponents. Later the validity of that free-flowing style was endorsed by the New Zealand Maoris who played 15 matches throughout France in 1926, the first time a foreign team had toured extensively. Everyone interested in rugby in France got a look at these tourists. The Maoris' natural style then was a fast, slick-passing game, full of 'joie de vivre', and the style appealed.

After World War II other nations recognised the 'new' French strengths. By 1954 France had scored three wins in the championship for the first time, sharing the title and beating the All Blacks in the same season. This was regarded as a turning point for French rugby, and was in no small measure due to the formidable leadership skills of Jean Prat. The team did much the same in the next season for another share of the title.

France really hit the headlines in world rugby in 1958. After losing its first two internationals of the season, it bounced back with a 19–0 victory over Australia in Paris. Then followed France's first win on Cardiff Arms Park over Wales, and two more wins over Italy and Ireland.

The French left for their first tour of South Africa with a strong side, yet with no real high hopes of winning.

Victory at last! After 16 defeats, this was the first French team to beat England. The game was at Colombes Stadium on April 2, 1927; the score, 3–0.

The All Blacks, the Lions, and the Wallabies could not win a series over the Springboks, so how could France, who had never won anything, hope to achieve the impossible?

That France did win in South Africa remains one of rugby's greatest stories. The Tricolours, plagued by withdrawals and injuries, drew the first test with the Springboks and, in highly dramatic circumstances, won the second test 9–5. The tour captain, Michel Celaya, was one of those hurt and so Lucien Mias took over, inspiring his colleagues to a famous win. Two penalties and one dropped goal to a converted try, and France had arrived as a world rugby force!

A win in the Five Nations championship followed in the next home season, with France led again by Lucien Mias. François Moncla took over the captaincy and the upswing continued with Grand Slam wins in 1959–60 and 1960–61. These were the golden years of French rugby. At the end of 1960–61, the unbeaten sequence by France extended to 18 games. The run of misery in the early years must have seemed a long time ago.

But France's bubble burst on its 1961 tour of New Zealand. The trip was billed as the 'world championship', but New Zealand won all three tests over the French team, captained by Moncla. Prominent French writers Alex Potter and Georges Duthen had earlier that year published a book called *The Rise of French Rugby*, which documented the glories of the 1950s; but after losing so heavily to the All Blacks it was suggested that the same two writers might care to publish a sequel – with the obvious title!

In the 1960s another change came over French rugby. The so-called 'champagne rugby' of the 1940s and 50s disappeared. New terms such as 'complete rugby' and '15-man rugby' were used. But what it amounted to was a slow erosion of the earlier flair with which the Tricolours had played the game. Winning became the prime objective of the new rugby and the 1960s and 70s saw France play some tough rugby with big 'donkeys' in the second row winning ball for efficient and tactical flyhalves who only rarely let the ball out to the previously flashing three-quarters. Only on occasions were there glimpses of brilliant back play.

Walter Spanghero, Christian Carrère and Elie Cester celebrate France's first Grand Slam win in 1968.

By the 1980s Jacques Fouroux had been appointed coach of France. He had had a glittering playing career which included captaining France when it won the Grand Slam for the second time, in 1976–77. Fouroux endorsed the change in France's style of play. He used heavy scrummaging packs, tall loosemen and big, mauling locks to smash aside opposing teams. The backs still had the skills – players like Serge Blanco and Philippe Sella had arrived on the international stage by then – but too often they were under-used.

There were many who lamented the way French rugby had gone, but Fouroux stuck to his guns. His followers argued that every other country in the world pursued victory as a first priority, so why not the French?

France made the final of the World Cup in New Zealand in 1987. It was a great day for French sport; never before had any team from its country made a world cup final, in any sport. Under Daniel Dubroca's leadership, the team had beaten Australia by 30–24 in the semi-final in one of the most thrilling games of rugby seen anywhere. The already sizable contingent of French reporters in New Zealand was swelled by over 50 in the last week.

The All Blacks might have won the final by 29–9, but public interest in French rugby soared again just by seeing the team doing so well.

In the late 1980s France's topsy-turvey status as a rugby nation continued. From the highs of winning or sharing the Five Nations championship for four seasons in a row, it plunged to a home test loss to the Wallabies (in 1989), then a three-test series loss to Australia in Australia (in 1990). France also lost four times to the All Blacks (including 3–24 and 12–30 losses at home in 1990) and suffered the ignominy of losing at home for the first time to Romania (6–12 at Auch).

The rough play was still about (two men were sent off in internationals in 1990); the rumblings about the style of play were still evident; and so was the politicking – Fouroux was ousted in 1990 as coach and replaced by Daniel Dubroca.

All over the world big crowds still push to get into the games *l'équipe de France* plays. But while winning has such a high significance, it seems a return to the sparkle and effervescence of the old days can not be assured, though Dubroca's team of 1990–91 was more entertaining than those of Fouroux.

FRENCH CLUB CHAMPIONSHIP

An often maligned, often changed, but always eagerly awaited event right across the country is the major rugby

The 1961 championship semi-final between Agen and La Voulte – an ill-disciplined outbreak sadly typical of many French club games.

tournament of any French season, the *Championnat de France* – the competition that excites and promotes French club loyalties like no other. The final is one of the most boisterous, noisy and colourful occasions in all French sport, and live television takes the game into every home in France.

Explaining to an Englishman how the French championship works is rather like explaining to a Frenchman how the English play cricket. It has taken many different forms since 1892: in the first 35 years after World War II the system of finding the two finalists was changed no fewer than seven times. Even these days it is not a simple process.

Hundreds of clubs from all across the country, large and small, enter the event at the appropriate level. Top clubs play together in leagues (or *poules*). Over the years the number of clubs in these has varied considerably. There are home and away games with each of the other teams in the league, then the top teams in each league qualify for the exciting knock-out series which follows.

After the quarter-finals and semi-finals of the knockout, the top two teams are found. The final used to be spread among the cities of the rugby-mad south-west of France, but now is always held at the Parc des Princes in Paris. A new tradition in the game in France is the exodus from the south at

finals weekend – a triumphal march to Paris with all the supporters, noise, banners, banter and bunting that is part of the grand final.

Even though it is a hugely popular contest, there have been many serious critics of the *championnat* over the years. The sudden-death system of knock-out brings to the surface all the passion of the French character, and many of the critics feel that the pressure to win is so great that the rugby is encouraged to be brutal and rough. Others claim that the rugby is often over-safe and cautious, even dull.

But on the other side of the coin is the enormous excitement that championship games engender, with crowd fervour at its noisiest and most colourful. A game that produces a close score with time running out, albeit through dull play, sees the most agonizing and soul-stirring tension, for players and supporters. That is the magic of the *championnat*.

It is doubtful whether any club trumpets louder about the championship than Béziers, whose famous sequence of successes began in 1960 when it qualified for the final, which it lost to Lourdes. In the 1961 final, Béziers beat Dax 6–3 and in the 25 years that followed the mighty men of Béziers won 10 finals and played as runners-up in four others, easily the best record of any club in the history of this most prestigious rugby event.

FRONT ROW FORWARDS

The front row forwards are the three players who make up the first line in a scrum – two props and one hooker.

Two front rows in international rugby stand out for their consistency and the character they developed as a unit. In Wales in the 1970s the Pontypool front row of 'Charlie' Faulkner, Bobby Windsor and Graham Price performed in many matches for their club and country. They were immortalised in song by Welshman Max Boyce.

New Zealand's 'geriatric' front row of John Ashworth, Andy Dalton and Gary Knight was so-named because some rugby writers felt, with affection, that the players had been in the game too long!

The front row is a hard, bruising place to be. Scrums are not much fun, so you need special physical and mental qualities to specialise in playing there.

As a result of the fun that is often poked at them by team-mates, front-row players often build up a special rapport and camaraderie among themselves and with their opponents.

It is said that forwards can be easily recognised as the ones who push a door labelled 'pull', or vice-versa. Not so front row forwards: they go straight through without even opening the door! That is all part of the myth that front rowers are blockheads, but increasingly in the 1970s and 1980s international sides had men at the heart of the scrums as their captains.

John Pullin and Peter Wheeler of England, Colin Deans of Scotland, Philippe Dintrans and Daniel Dubroca of France, and Andy Dalton of New Zealand were notable leaders, while Karl Mullen, Ron Dawson and Ciaran Fitzgerald were all Irish hookers who led Lions teams to New Zealand. The last two were held to have retained their places in the face of fierce opposition from Bryn Meredith and Colin Deans respectively only because of leadership qualities.

Increased mobility has also become a requirement of front row men who were previously expected to perform unwaveringly at one scrum and manage to be there for the next. A South African later living in New Zealand, Graeme Barrow, wrote an entertaining and discerning book, *Up Front*. It traversed the many changes in attitudes to front row play, from the days when the scrum was seen – as in rugby league – as nothing more than a means to restart play, and as quickly as possible, to the obsession of some teams to make it the cornerstone of a game.

The successful All Black front row of the late 1980s and into the 1990s – Steve McDowell, Sean Fitzpatrick and Richard Loe – is perhaps the best example of the new requirements and also highlights the fact that a team could possess a front row not bettered by any other in the world, yet not be a slave to it.

FRY, CHARLES

Charles ('C.B.') Fry was one of the English-speaking world's top sporting heroes at the turn of the century. He played cricket for England, captaining it in 1912 and heading the batting averages for six years. He shared the world long jump record in 1893 and represented England at soccer in 1901. He was also a brilliant scholar, gaining first class honours in Classics at Oxford University. He was, for a time, a delegate to the League of Nations and was reputed to have been once invited to be King of Albania, an honour he refused.

He was also a rugby player of considerable standing. He used his speed on the right wing and only by a cruel injury did he miss being capped by Oxford. He toured successfully for the Barbarians club and was generally felt to be one of the best players never to win an international cap. Many judges of the time felt he was near to England selection. What might have counted against him was the fact that he often simply did not have enough time to play all the games and sports at which he excelled.

C.B.Fry played for the Blackheath club in London. He once said 'I liked rugger better than I liked soccer and found it a finer game.'

FULLBACK

Some of the game's greatest personalities have been fullbacks. In the past they were always the greatest kickers and point-scorers, but this position has changed enormously in the modern game. When rugby was a 20-a-side game there were three fullbacks, but on the reduction to 15 men a side one man assumed the role of the 'custodian'.

Fullback was always known as the last line of defence on the field and defence was its original priority. Rugby people always talked about 'safe' fullbacks – until 1968 when the laws of the game were changed to prevent kicking the ball out of the field of play on the full.

The role of fullback expanded overnight and in the modern game it is now seen often as the first point for counter-attacking play to begin.

A fullback's skills used to be catching, tackling, kicking and goal-kicking. Now, in the manner of players like Andy Irvine of Scotland and Serge Blanco of France, the fullback is better known as a runner, feeder and scorer of tries. Of course, to achieve those things he must still be able to catch and tackle securely, but he also needs speed, acceleration and a good intuition for when to attack from the back.

The old and the new style of fullback play: Don Clarke of New Zealand, the solid and steady kicker of the 1950s and 1960s, and Andy Irvine, Scotland, the play-making runner of the 1970s.

The epitome of the fullback under the old kick-out-on-the-full days was New Zealand's massive Don Clarke. He was a large, bulky man who had excellent positional and catching skills and he would often kick the ball prodigious distances to save his team on defence. Clarke was capable of coming into a backline, but he was not a speedy runner like Blanco, Irvine or New Zealand's World Cup success of 1987, John Gallagher. Those three had the speed to play for their countries in the three-quarters as well. Still, for the game of his time, Don Clarke was a superb match-winner.

A modern fullback who combined attacking brilliance with defensive play was Wales's John (J.P.R.) Williams, who played both before and after the law changes and set the early standards for running play from fullback. Whereas Irvine and Blanco sometimes missed tackles, Williams was one of the best ever seen in defence, anywhere.

There have been some brilliant and powerful personalties in the fullback position. New Zealand contributed many great ones: Billy Wallace (also a wing), George Nepia, Bob Scott and Fergie McCormick all deserve to be compared with Don Clarke. South Africa gave the game Gerhard Morkel, Gerry Brand, Lionel Wilson, Johnny Buchler and Johan Heunis; Australia, Jim Lenehan, Terry Curley, David Campese and Roger Gould; France, Serge Blanco, Claude Lacaze, Michel Vannier and Jean-Michel Aguirre; Wales, J.P.R. Williams, Billy Bancroft, Arthur Gould, Terry Davies, Vivian Jenkins and Herbert Winfield; Scotland, Andy Irvine, Ken Scotland, Gavin Hastings and Dan Drysdale; Ireland, Ernie Crawford, Tom Kiernan and Hugo MacNeill; England, 'Tuppy' Owen-Smith, 'Dusty' Hare and the precision kicker Bob Hiller.

These were just some of the great exponents of a most noble rugby playing position.

G

GABE, RHYS
Cardiff, Llanelli and Wales
24 internationals for Wales 1901–08

At the age of 12, in 1893, Rhys Gabe walked from his home near Llanelli to watch Wales play Ireland at Stradey Park, a distance of five miles. He and his friends played with a rugby ball all the way there and back, and the game had a profound influence on young Gabe. Thereafter he only wanted to be a centre and based his play on his hero who had played that day, Sam Lee of Ireland.

Gabe made his debut for Wales in 1901 against Ireland at Swansea in a match that marked the last appearance of the great Billy Bancroft for Wales.

Gabe, as a centre capable of beating his opposites with deception and speed, was a brilliant player in the Welsh teams which won the Triple Crown in 1902, 1905 and 1908, and which enjoyed a period of success called Wales's first 'golden era'. He also toured New Zealand with the Great Britain team of 1904.

It was Rhys Gabe who made the run that led to Teddy Morgan's try which enabled Wales to beat the 1905 All Blacks. He also took part in the famous 'foggy' game of 1908 when Wales beat England by 28–18. Gabe scored twice that day – one of the tries was not seen by the England defence because of the murky weather.

There is another story that Gabe was kicked so hard in the backside in the Wales v Scotland game in 1905 that he could not sit down for six months! Being a schoolmaster it meant he had to conduct his lessons standing on his feet. However, the records also show that he was fit enough to play in Wales's next match just three weeks later.

Gabe lived until 1967.

GACHASSIN, JEAN
Lourdes and France
32 internationals for France 1961–69

Physically one of the smallest players to appear regularly in international rugby, Gachassin was also a brilliant exponent of the best running skills of back play. He appeared for his country in four backline positions: first as a wing in 1961 and later as a fullback, centre and flyhalf.

Gachassin was only 1.62 metres tall (5 ft 4 ins), and weighed 63 kilograms (9 stone 12lbs). One journalist listed the following nicknames for Gachassin at one or another time in his career: the 'Pocket Wing', 'Peter Pan', the 'Mighty Atom', or the 'Bagnères Flea'. Nevertheless, he was one of the most popular figures in French rugby in the 1960s.

GADNEY, CYRIL
The most accomplished referee of the 1930s who later became a powerful administrator of the game at an international level.

Gadney took charge of 15 internationals and six Oxford-Cambridge matches between 1936 and 1948. Among the major games he refereed were the New Zealand touring team of 1935–36 against Scotland and against Wales; France v Australia in 1948, and no fewer than 10 Five Nations games.

He later became a president of the Rugby Football Union and one of England's representatives on the International Rugby Board (1965–71).

Gadney was a specialist in rugby law and played a major part in the rewriting of the rugby law book to change the wording from out-moded English to a concise, more modern version. He also wrote the updated version of *The History of the Laws of Rugby Football* in 1972.

Cyril's brother Bernard was also an accomplished player, who appeared 14 times (nine as captain) for England as a scrumhalf between 1932 and 1938.

GAGE, DAVEY
Wellington and New Zealand

A tough New Zealand utility back in the years before international matches were played, Davey Gage performed an astonishing feat of endurance on the 1888–89 New Zealand Natives world tour when he played in 68 of 74 matches in Britain – twice as many as some of his fellow team members. He was nicknamed 'Pony' because of his small size but enormous work-rate on that tour. (*See* NATIVES)

Gage toured Australia with the New Zealand team of 1893 and was captain of his country against Queensland at Wellington in 1896. None of the matches played was considered a 'test' match.

Gage is remembered for another role during the Natives tour. The team adopted 'On The Ball' as its team song and he gained a reputation all over Britain as being the player who would stand up, climb on a table and lead its singing. The song, written in New Zealand, became a hit all across the country and is a rugby song that has endured ever since.

GAINSFORD, JOHN
Western Province and South Africa
33 internationals for Sth Africa 1960–67

One of South Africa's greatest players, John Gainsford played a record number of internationals for a centre in the Springbok colours.

A big, strong-running centre with positive instincts for attack, he made his first-class debut as a 19-year-old, before joining the Junior Springboks for their 1959 tour of Argentina. He came into the South African test team in 1960, when he appeared in the only test against the Scotland touring team and in all four games the same season against the All Blacks. Thereafter, until 1967, only injury kept him out of test teams.

In his seven seasons as a Springbok, Gainsford earned world-wide respect. After only five years he became the highest-capped South African player, beating the old mark of 28 tests, held by Johan Claassen, in the third test at Christchurch on the 1965 New Zealand tour. This was a feat which he celebrated by scoring two brilliant tries as the Springboks came back from 5–16 at half-time to score a notable victory.

At the time of his retirement, after the 1967 tour by France, Gainsford was South Africa's top test try-scorer, with eight tries. Both his appearances and try tally records were broken in subsequent years, but 23 years after his retirement he was still South Africa's highest-capped centre.

Perhaps the greatest tribute to Gainsford's style of play came with the emergence of Danie Gerber in the Springboks of the 1980s. The new man, who turned out to be a brilliant runner and consistent performer, was, the experts said, 'just like John Gainsford'.

GALA RFC

Great rivals of the Hawick club, Gala, formed in 1875, is one of the fine traditional clubs of the Borders area of Scotland, that has contributed dozens of prominent Scottish players and internationals. Peter Brown, the Scottish lock, is its most-capped player, having played 27 times for his country as either a lock or No. 8.

Although towards the end of the 1960s its backs played stylish and attractive rugby, Gala produced a powerful and talented forward pack that dominated the club's tactics for the next few years. Many members of that pack went on to play for Scotland, including Jim Aitken (who captained Scotland to win the Grand Slam in 1984), Ken Lawrie, Rob Cunningham, David Leslie, Gordon Dickson, David White and Tom Smith.

Among the other famous names from Gala are Peter Dods, Nairn McEwan, Jock Turner, Tom Elliot and Duncan Paterson. One of the most famous sons of the club was the great rugby writer and broadcaster, Jock Wemyss.

GALLAGHER, JOHN

Wellington and New Zealand
18 internationals for N. Zealand 1987–89

One of the most brilliant attacking fullbacks of his time who, at the peak of his powers, was lost to rugby league.

John Gallagher was a young fullback living in London who decided to accept an offer of a rugby-playing holiday in New Zealand in 1984. By 1986 his life had changed. He had decided to stay in New Zealand, he had embarked on a career with the police force, and late in the year he was included with the New Zealand All Blacks for their tour to France. He was very much a second-stringer on that tour, playing twice at centre.

John Gainsford rubs Colin Meads's face in it, after the third test at Christchurch in 1965. This was the match where New Zealand led 16–5 at half-time, but South Africa won 19–16, after a last-minute penalty by 'Tiny' Naude. Gainsford and Meads were mates, hence the amusement in the incident.

It was a different matter in 1987. Given the confidence of being chosen as the number one fullback for the World Cup, Gallagher's speed and brilliant intrusions from fullback became a powerful weapon in the All Black armoury.

In his second test match, against Fiji at Christchurch, Gallagher scorched in for four tries (equalling the New Zealand record for one test match) and helped make many more as the All Blacks raced out to a 74–13 win. Wing Craig Green also benefited, scoring four times as well.

Gallagher played five of the All Blacks' games at the World Cup, including the final, and was seen as one of the tournament's most brilliant players. That kind of form followed him through 1988 and 1989, on four other All Black tours.

In May 1990, Gallagher, by then firmly ensconced as one of the country's most popular sporting heroes, suddenly announced that he was heading for rugby league. The news sent shock waves through New Zealand rugby circles. There was at first disbelief and a little scorn, although soon emotions quietened and sensible Kiwis wished him luck in his new career.

The departure of Gallagher to rugby league, along with fellow All Blacks Frano Botica, John Schuster and Matthew Ridge, awakened New Zealanders to the realisation that their national game was not the only one on the sporting horizon. The departure of 'Kipper' Gallagher also left an extremely hard-to-fill gap in the All Black backline. No player would be quite like the flying redhead from Wellington.

Gallagher signed with the Leeds rugby league club after 18 tests for the All Blacks. He scored 13 tries in tests, and in one game, in Japan in 1987, he scored 30 points. His signing fee was reported to be $NZ1.3 million (at the time about £420,000), well in excess of the previous reported world record fee.

GALLAHER, DAVE

Auckland and New Zealand
6 internationals for New Zealand 1903–06

The captain of the first All Blacks team in 1905–06 and a controversial player in the eyes of some British writers of the time. Gallaher (originally spelled Gallagher) was born in Belfast, Northern Ireland, and brought to New Zealand by his parents as a young boy.

He served in the Boer War for the Sixth Contingent from New Zealand.

Because of the absence of international fixtures and Gallaher's period of military service, he did not play his first test match until he was 28. Originally a hooker, he later became a 'rover' or wing forward, the position New Zealand created by packing down only seven men in each scrum.

Gallaher's play in the wing forward position earned him enormous criticism while on tour in Britain in 1905–06. There were those who labelled him unsporting, and even a cheat. His wing forward style of waiting off scrums, mauls and rucks, either to defend attacks on his own halfback or disrupt the opposition's man, was not at all appreciated by opposition teams, who had no apparent counter. Several referees penalised him heavily.

As a leader Gallaher was brilliant, though he was not originally a popular choice. A story has recently emerged that on the ship on the way to Britain in 1905, Gallaher offered to resign as captain and only a vote among the players saw him happy to continue (although it is said the vote was only 17 to 9 in his favour).

Gallaher was the first rugby captain to 'psyche' his team up. On match days he would ask each man to spend an hour on his own to 'rest and contemplate the game ahead'. He insisted his team be totally disciplined and pay attention to detail, both on and off the

Dave Gallaher, captain of the 1905 All Blacks.

field, much in the manner of professional teams of today.

The 1905 New Zealand team was the first team to use liniment as a playing aid, and to chew gum (not at all advisable these days). It had code names for team moves, and used extra men in back moves, skip passes, decoys and other ruses not before seen in Britain.

All of these innovations were devised and encouraged by Gallaher. His team, growing to believe totally in his leadership style, soon built up a formidable record. Only the controversial loss to Wales prevented the All Blacks from having an unbeaten tour record from 35 games.

Gallaher retired at the conclusion of the tour and became a provincial and, later, All Black selector. Tragically he lost his life in Belgium in 1917, during World War I.

Since 1922 the senior club championship in Auckland has been played for the Gallaher Shield, in commemoration of one of its greatest rugby sons.

GARNETT, HARRY
Bradford and England
1 international for England 1877

Another of rugby's unique characters, Harry Garnett was a rugged forward who wore no boots when he played. This did not appear to hinder his play as he was selected and played for England against Scotland in 1877.

The Bradford skipper took the field at Raeburn Place in Edinburgh for the match against Scotland and by all accounts he played tolerably well in bare feet, although Scotland won by a dropped goal to nil.

In 1877 rugby was essentially a forward game with long mauls and scrums twisting and turning across the field, and although there are no reports of the condition of Garnett's feet after the game, it is easy to speculate that playing without sturdy boots must have been extremely hazardous.

Garnett was later to become a president of the Rugby Football Union in 1889–90.

GARRYOWEN RFC
Garryowen's name has passed into rugby vocabulary. The 'up-and-under' kick, where the ball is lofted high and the defenders have to quake underneath as thundering forwards ap-

proach, became a specialist tactical ploy of the Garryowen club in the 1890s. The crowds at Market's Field in Limerick, the club's original home ground, used to bray for Garryowen's tactical kickers to put the ball high into the air. When such a kick was delivered, enormous encouragement was shouted at the home team players to rush forward and pressurise the catchers. The poor visiting player waiting to catch the ball had plenty of time to consider what would, and often did, happen when the ball and Garryowen players arrived at the same time!

Many famous Irish players have come from this club. Tom Reid, his brother Paddy, Seamus Deering snr and Seamus Deering jnr, Jimmy Kelly, Mick Doyle, Tony Ward and Noel Murphy were all Garryowen men at one time in their careers.

The highest-capped Garryowen man was prop Gordon Wood, who won 29 caps for Ireland and travelled to New Zealand with the 1959 British Isles team.

The club was formed in 1884 and after the first 100 years of the Munster Cup competition, the main competition of each Munster season, it had won more cup titles than any other of its rivals – 32 to Cork Constitution's 21. However, in the 1980s Garryowen fell on lean times, failing to win the Munster Cup with any regularity.

Garryowen's emblem on its sky blue jerseys is a five-pointed star, said to represent the five parishes of Limerick.

GARUET, JEAN-PIERRE
Lourdes and France
42 internationals for France 1983–90

He may sometimes have cut a comic figure on the field, for he was built with short legs and a wide girth, but Jean-Pierre Garuet was a proud and powerful prop who served France admirably in the good years they had in the 1980s.

Garuet was a late starter in international rugby, not getting a test match until he was past 30 (v Australia at Clermont-Ferrand in November, 1983) but his powerful scrummaging quickly won him a world-class standing.

Garuet was a potato farmer and secured increased business with some unlikely promotion in 1984. In his first Five Nations game, against Ireland at the Parc des Princes, Garuet was sent off by the Welsh referee Clive Norling – the first Frenchman sent off in an international. Garuet later reported that sales of his potatoes went up 25 per cent in the weeks after his much publicised dismissal!

Garuet played in the Rugby World Cup final in Auckland in 1987, the oldest man on the field. His last international was in 1990, against England at Paris, when he was aged 36 years and 6 months.

GAZELLES

Before the Gazelles team was started, promising young South African players of any age could be chosen to play for the Junior Springboks, which was virtually a South African 'B' team. In 1966 a new team was formed, the Gazelles, and the criterion for selection was changed to include only those players under 24 years of age.

The first Gazelles toured Argentina in 1966, returning with an unbeaten record. Because of the vast improvement Argentine rugby had shown, a number of internationals from the 1965 South African tour of Australia and New Zealand were members of this team, including the captain, Dawie de Villiers.

In 1969 the Gazelles played their first game at home against a major touring team, losing 17–27 to Australia

at Springs in what was a thrilling match. The 1970 Gazelles narrowly lost to the All Blacks 25–29 at Potchefstrom. Eight of that team went on to become full Springbok players. The All Blacks of 1976 also beat the Gazelles, but only after another close game, 21–15.

The Gazelles continued the strong relationship they (and previous Junior Springboks teams) had with Argentina, touring there in 1972 under captain Jannie van Aswegen. The team returned home with 13 wins from 15 games.

The Gazelles' first win at home over a major touring team came in 1981 when they edged out Ireland by 18–15 in that tour's opener.

GEFFIN, AARON ('OKEY')

Transvaal and South Africa
7 internationals for South Africa 1949–51

A player who made the headlines in 1949 when his prodigious goal-kicking for the Springboks helped them to beat the touring All Blacks 4–0 in the test series.

In the first test New Zealand led South Africa by 11 to 3 at one stage. Goal-kicking duties had been allotted to the Griquas fullback, Jack van der Schyff, for the match, but after he missed the first two shots, the captain

Felix du Plessis gave the ball to Geffin – a prop on his test debut.

Geffin put over five penalty attempts, virtually beating New Zealand, 15–11, on his own. It was a record number of penalties for any player in a test match up to that time.

He did the same in the third test, scoring all of South Africa's points in its 9–3 win, and in the other two tests he kicked three further goals.

Hailed as a hero that year, Geffin made the Springbok team for the 1951–52 tour of Britain where he also scored impressively with seven conversions – a test record – against Scotland. South Africa won 44–0.

By then Geffin was 31 years old and he eventually lost his place in the Springboks' scrum. But he will always be remembered as a match-winner by fans of the Springboks – and by disappointed New Zealanders!

A note on Geffin's names. A given name was not bestowed on Geffin at birth and he subsequently adopted Aaron as his name – perhaps not a wise choice, given that he was to be interned in Nazi prisoner-of-war camps! There he helped organise 'test' matches between South Africa and New Zealand. His nickname of Okey came from his habit of responding 'Okay' when called to take a shot at goal.

GERBER, DANIE

Eastern Province and South Africa
19 internationals for Sth Africa 1980–86

One of the great modern South African centre three-quarters who, because of political boycotts and protests, was not seen by a wider international rugby audience.

Danie Gerber first played for the Springboks on their tour of South America in 1980. Always a tough centre, capable of making strong breaks and linking swiftly with his outsides, he scored a try in each of his first two internationals. In 1981 against Ireland he added two further tries in the first test, making four from his first three tests. During the troubled tour in New Zealand later in 1981, Gerber continued to play superbly and proved an enormous worry to the All Blacks in all three tests.

His try-scoring continued with three scored against South America in Pretoria in 1982 and three further tries

Danie Gerber, South Africa's explosive mid-field back of the 1980s.

(within the first 18 minutes of the game) against England in the second test of 1984. His tally soon surpassed the Springbok test record of 12 tries held by Gerrie Germishuys. Gerber finished with 15 test tries from 19 internationals.

In spite of his limited exposure to the world rugby scene, Gerber scored four tries for the Barbarians against Cardiff in 1983. He also appeared for the Overseas XV against the Five Nations XV at Twickenham in 1986, to celebrate the centenary of the IRB.

Later that same year he played in all four tests against the New Zealand rebel team, the Cavaliers, and maintained his impressive form. Though he continued in provincial rugby, they were to be his last caps for his country.

GERMANY

Germany's rugby federation was founded in 1900, although there is evidence to suggest that at least one club had been formed in Heidelberg as early as 1846, which, if true, would mean it would have been one of the earliest clubs in the world.

Rugby has had its moments of glory in Germany. In the 1920s and 30s the country had a close rugby association with France, especially after France had been expelled from the International Rugby Board in 1931, and the two countries met regularly. In 1927 France won the first match between the two in Paris by 30–5, but a month later in Frankfurt the Germans reversed the result, winning by 17–16.

In the 1930s the two countries met on 10 occasions, with Germany winning just once, 3–0, in Frankfurt in 1938. There is no doubt that to that point Germany was shaping up to be one of most powerful rugby forces in Europe, but the momentum was lost during World War II.

After 1945 the story of German rugby is essentially about West German rugby. When fixtures with France began again in 1955, they were usually with French selections or France 'A' teams. Playing standards in Germany dropped quite dramatically and by the 1970s rugby was quite weak. In recent years it has played in the FIRA leagues, but without spectacular success.

West Germany entered the 1991 Rugby World Cup series and was given a preliminary match with Netherlands in Heidelberg, which remains its strongest rugby city. One report called it 'the most important game in the history of the game in West Germany'.

The Germans put up a brave showing but lost 12–6 in the dying seconds. The Netherlands went on to play in the European zone final qualifying series, so it is to be hoped that the Germans will take encouragement from the closeness of the score and with the possible advantages of reunification with East Germany rebuild again to be the rugby force it once was.

GIBSON, MICHAEL

North of Ireland and Ireland
69 internationals for Ireland 1964–79
12 internationals for British Isles 1966–71

The most-capped rugby international of his time and one of the game's greatest players.

For one who stayed in the game for so long and amassed such a high total of test match caps, Mike Gibson was a relatively late starter. He was 22 when he played for Ireland against England at Twickenham in February 1964. His presence at flyhalf helped Ireland score a brilliant win, its first over England for 16 years. The new man was hailed in his first international season as 'a player for the future' and he soon soon built a consistency of performance that made him first choice for Irish and Lions teams until his career ended in 1979.

Gibson was blessed with cool but super-quick thought processes which enabled him always to take the right option. He was an elusive but direct runner, very quick over the first 20 metres, with a sharp sidestep. He was an excellent tactical kicker, a strong tackler (even though he was not especially big) and a superb passer of the ball. His unselfishness was another hallmark, but when necessary he was capable of making a decisive individual break. When he did pass the ball his job was never over for he always supported the outer backs.

Mike Gibson was an excellent example to young people, always presenting himself perfectly for a game, no matter how modest it might be. His unassuming personality made him a great favourite off the field as well as on.

A product of Belfast but a graduate of Cambridge University, Gibson was a blue winner in 1963–64–65. The All

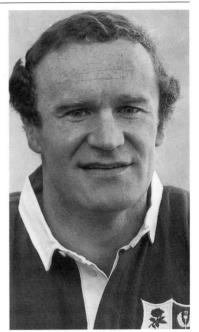

Mike Gibson

Blacks of 1963–64 were the first overseas team to see him in action and were hugely impressed by him when they played against Cambridge on their tour. He became a permanent fixture in the Irish team from 1964, as a flyhalf until 1969, and then specialising as a centre. Near the end of his career he became a wing for Ireland for a short time.

Forty of his Irish appearances were at centre, 25 at flyhalf and four on the wing. His total of caps eventually passed the 63 won by Willie John McBride when he played on the wing for Ireland against Wales at Lansdowne Road in March, 1978. The crowd cheered him roundly but later they booed the Welsh fullback, J.P.R. Williams, for a heavy late tackle on their hero.

Gibson's last two internationals for Ireland, to make his final tally 69, were played in Australia in 1979, when Ireland shocked the Wallabies by winning both test matches.

As a British Isles representative on four tours, Gibson played 69 matches as well, 12 of them full internationals – four as a flyhalf and eight as a centre. In 1971 he was a decisive and commanding figure in New Zealand when his play earned him the highest plaudits of local critics. The Lions beat New Zealand in the test series, under the captaincy of John Dawes and the coaching of Carwyn James, and Gibson was a key man in the British success.

His dominance in the Lions test teams of 1974 in South Africa and in 1977 in New Zealand was less noticeable, possibly because these sides preferred to play the game through their forwards, thus limiting opportunities for brilliance from backs like Gibson. He travelled to South Africa as a replacement (not originally being available) but was not picked for the three tests. That Lions team, on a winning roll, preferred Dick Milliken and Ian McGeechan as the centres.

In 1977 in New Zealand McGeechan and Steve Fenwick were preferred as test centres by the Lions, but Gibson was the only member of the touring party to play in each winning game on tour.

When he retired from international play, after the Irish tour of Australia in 1979, Cameron Michael Henderson Gibson was hailed as having been one of the greatest of all backline players.

GLOUCESTER RFC

This powerful English club, formed in 1873, has played a major part in West Country rugby.

From 1873 until 1891 Gloucester played its rugby at The Spa, better known as a cricket ground. Later the club moved to Kingsholm, where its headquarters are today.

Gloucester built up a big forward pack in the 1970s, when it became one of the most powerful clubs in the country. It was the first winner of the English county knock-out, later to become the John Player Cup series. Gloucester also won in 1978 and 1982.

Gloucester has provided over 30 international players for English teams, among them some of England's finest, including Tom Voyce, Don Rutherford, Dai Gent, Phil Blakeway and Mike Burton. Voyce, Gloucester's most-capped international with 27 caps, was a classic English player who enjoyed huge success, though he annoyed every opposition side with his obstructive offside tactics from the rover position. He later represented Gloucester on the RFU from 1931 to 1970, as president 1960–61.

The club had a unique honour in 1984. For England's first test against South Africa in Port Elizabeth, there was an all-Gloucester front row – Phil Blakeway, Stephen Mills and Malcolm Preedy.

GOAL

A rugby term for a try that has been converted, making six points under modern scoring values. The term had its birth when a try and the successful kick which followed were termed a 'goal' – so the kick was an attempt to convert a try into a goal.

The term is mostly obsolete now, used only by some newspapers and publications in Britain. It is never used in New Zealand, Australia or South Africa where a 'goal' is called a 'converted try'.

GOING, SID

North Auckland and New Zealand
29 internationals for N. Zealand 1967–77

A brilliant New Zealand halfback who dazzled and mystified crowds and opposition teams all over the world. A Maori player, Sid Going played his rugby with all the skill and flair of his race, so it was entirely appropriate that he became known to fans worldwide as 'Super Sid'.

He first played for the All Blacks in 1967 in the 75th jubilee match against Australia and the following year joined the All Black party to travel to Britain and France, where he began his rivalry for the All Black test halfback position with Chris Laidlaw.

Both were brilliant players but very different from each other. Laidlaw was a superb passer of the ball from scrums or rucks, thus setting backlines moving. Going ran with a very low centre of gravity and could break from scrums and rucks to devastating effect, setting up massive forward rushes. One of New Zealand rugby's most vigorous debates was waged over which player should be the number one choice for the halfback spot.

Sid Going replaced the injured Laidlaw in the All Black team for the third test against France at Eden Park in 1968, and promptly shot across the line for two tries. However, earlier in the series Laidlaw had tactically guided New Zealand to two test wins, and he continued to be the selectors' first choice in South Africa in 1970, although on those occasions when Going was included he proved to be a matchwinner.

Following Laidlaw's retirement from the game after 1970, Going became New Zealand's highest-capped scrumhalf, continuing to be selected until the third test against the British Isles

'Super Sid' Going, Greg Davis (Australia) and Jeff Matheson, in the third test between Australia and New Zealand at Auckland in 1972.

A tense match between the Glenfield Grizzlies and Wak Sun of Japan, at the Golden Oldies tournament in London, 1985.

in 1977, and expanding his reputation as a world star player.

He had rivalries with other halfbacks. Gareth Edwards of the British Isles and Wales was one in particular who always was kept busy when playing against the little New Zealander.

Going's tactical kicking was of a very high standard. When he toured South Africa with the 1976 All Blacks, he was called on to kick for goals in the test matches. He promoted exciting games whenever he played, but to some purists there was continued debate whether he should attend more to his passing technique and accuracy.

But discussion about his style of play was of little consequence to Sid Going, who continued to play and draw a huge following, especially in Whangarei, in his home province of North Auckland.

His brothers Ken and Brian were also top players. Ken, a fullback, joined Sid in the All Blacks for the tour to Ireland and Wales in 1974. Brian, a first five-eighths, was an All Black triallist and a New Zealand Maori tourist a number of times.

When the three brothers played together their understanding of one another's positions on the field was uncanny, much as with Australia's Ella brothers. Some called it 'Maori magic' as the Goings unleashed intricately planned moves involving scissor-passing and sleights of hand that had never before been seen in New Zealand.

One of the Going brothers' moves was called the 'Maramaku Special', named after their home town. It could only be described as a blindside triple passing and dummying interplay that usually had defenders grasping air.

Naturally such inventive rugby produced an enormous following for the brothers, but Sid Going in particular was the superstar. At the end of his playing days a book, *Super Sid*, was written about his career by journalist Bob Howitt.

Sid Going, a quiet man and deeply Christian in his beliefs, continued to serve the game as a coaching adviser after his retirement.

GOLDEN OLDIES RUGBY

International tournament rugby for players over 35 was first organised in 1979 by Tom Johnson, a prominent New Zealand provincial player and New Zealand Rugby Union councillor, who expanded an idea for 'middle-aged rugby' after hearing and seeing the success of similar schemes in the United States, Canada and Japan.

The first Festival of Golden Oldies was held under the sponsorship of Air New Zealand in Auckland in 1979, and attracted 500 players. Only two years later in Long Beach, California, 1900 players took part from 11 countries. By 1983 more than 5000 players from 16 countries converged on Sydney, Australia, consuming more than 28,000 beer cans on the first day alone – tribute to the social success of the venture!

The festivals of 1985 in London and 1987 in Auckland were even bigger. Auckland claimed the 1987 Golden Oldies was the biggest sporting festival New Zealand had ever hosted.

The success of Golden Oldies rugby is due to the social nature of the tournament. 'Fun, Friendship and Fraternity' is the motto under which they are run.

The rugby is played at a pace which is considerably less demanding than the socialising. Many players who were stars in their younger days have turned to Golden Oldies football as an opportunity to stay in touch with the game and maintain their fitness. The financial security of the older age groups also allows players to take their wives, girlfriends and families along if they wish.

The age of players taking part varies considerably. Some are just days over 35, while others are over 70, 80 or even 90! The ages of all players are displayed by the colour of their shorts. A man in a gold pair is over 80 years of age, and should be handled gently.

The names of the teams taking part reflect the fun of the idea. Some examples: The Gangreens, The Crippled Crows, The Horny Derelicts, The Prisoners of Mother England, The Toothless Wonders, The Unquenchables, and a reflective Australian team called Coodabinawallabi (say it slowly)! There are hundreds of imaginative nomenclatures, all appropriate to the age, physical condition and libido of the team members.

Rugby officials were originally sceptical of the Golden Oldies idea and it was reported that the more staid members of the Rugby Football Union were slightly shocked at the antics on their beloved Twickenham turf during the festival in London in 1985.

But Golden Oldies rugby flourishes. It is financially sound and its organisation is self-contained requiring only the blessing of any existing rugby union. The big cities welcome the festivals for obvious reasons ($A7 million was injected into Sydney's economy in 1983). The players and supporters generally set an excellent example in behaviour, so as a result the organisers are looking to staging even more spectacular festivals in the future.

GORDON, THOMAS
North of Ireland and Ireland
3 internationals for Ireland 1877–78

An old boy of Rugby, who played just three internationals for Ireland as a halfback, Thomas Gordon played rugby without the use of his right hand, which he lost in a firearms accident.

There are very few instances of rugby players reaching the top without full use of all their limbs. Gordon is one example, as was Denny Veitch of Canada who played international games as a flanker for British Columbia (in the years before the formation of the Canada RFU).

New Zealand had Bob Forsyth of Taranaki, who refereed to an international level in the 1950s with only one arm. There are numerous instances of players playing test rugby with only one eye, most notable being the Springboks Martin Pelser (1958–61) and Johan de Bruyn (1974). There are reports that in the France v England game of 1920 no fewer than three players, possibly war veterans, had only one eye. Wallabies prop Keith Besomo (1979) was deaf from birth.

GOSFORTH FC
Gosforth Football Club was formed in 1877 and celebrated its centenary with a win in the John Player Cup at Twickenham, having also won the cup there the previous year.

Gosforth went through lean times in the years before World War II, living what at least one club historian has called a 'nomadic' existence, shifting from one ground to another.

With the security of a permanent new home ground in the 1960s, the club grew steadily over the next decade, its forward power and disciplined play making it one of the best of the English clubs and resulting in the John Player Cup wins of 1976 and 1977 and runner-up position in 1981.

In the more local north-east county competition for the Northumberland Cup, Gosforth had a sequence of 19 consecutive appearances in the final with victories from 1971 to 1984.

The club's most-capped international is Irish and British Lions prop Ray McLoughlin, with 40 caps. Other Lions, Peter Dixon, Roger Uttley and Steve Bainbridge, were all with Gosforth at one stage of their careers, as was the well-capped Scottish hooker Duncan Madsen.

Uttley was a loyal club man, representing England only from Gosforth and coming back from a broken leg in 1976 to lead it in its 1977 John Player Cup win.

GOULD, ARTHUR
Newport and Wales
27 internationals for Wales 1885–97

One of the early rugby heroes of Wales, Arthur Gould's final tally of 27 caps was a Welsh record for his time. An elusive running fullback and centre, he had a profound influence on the game in Wales, moving them from a concentration on the forward struggle to make more use of fleet-footed backs.

In his time Wales scored its first Triple Crown win, in 1893.

Gould was enormously popular in Wales and it was decided, late in his career, to present him with a testimonial. Fans and supporters raised £600, a sum big enough to allow the deeds of a house to be presented to Gould. All hell broke loose when the International Rugby Board discovered what had happened. Gould was labelled a 'professional' and as a result neither Scotland or Ireland would play Wales in the 1896–97 season. The incident was one of the first scandals of world rugby, making headlines and cartoons all over Britain and leading eventually to a tightening of the rules concerning professionalism.

Gould was widely known by his nickname 'Monkey', because of his ability, displayed more than once, to be able to climb trees and goal-posts!

Two of his brothers, Bert and Bob, also played for Wales, all before the turn of the century. Three other brothers also played for Newport club.

Gould's 18 games as captain of Wales was a record that still stood 90 years later.

GOULD, ROGER
Queensland and Australia
25 internationals for Australia 1980–87

A big-kicking Australian fullback who built a commanding reputation for his aggressive running, and who, but for injury, might have acquired a greater reputation as a top international.

Gould first played for Queensland in 1978 and in the same year joined the Australian team for its tour of New Zealand. Due to niggling injuries he only appeared on the field for 17 minutes of play (spread over two games!) during a six-week tour.

Undaunted, Gould recovered and made the Australian team for the tour to Argentina in 1979. After two matches he was injured again. He played in three tour matches, but the Wallabies preferred Paul McLean as fullback in the tests.

Gould's first international came against the All Blacks in Australia in 1980. His form was so good he became Australia's first pick in the fullback position in the years that followed. In addition to his ability to kick the ball prodigious distances, he had the build of a forward and often used his pres-

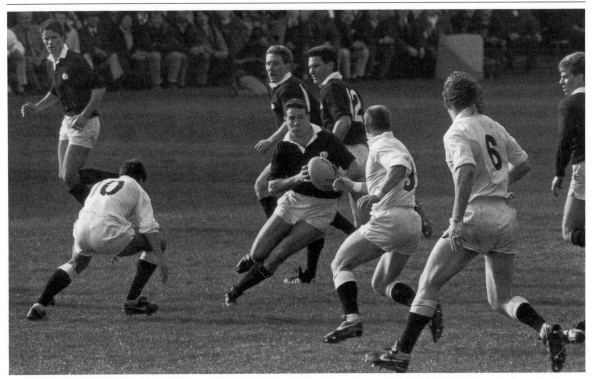

Scott Hastings attempts to shake off the attention of English players Rob Andrew, Richard Hill and Mickey Skinner (6), 1990.
Scotland's 13–7 win over England gave it the Grand Slam, the Triple Crown, and the Calcutta Cup!

ence in an abrasive manner about the field.

Perhaps his best form was in New Zealand in 1982, when he played superbly, without the distractions of the leg and back injuries that had disrupted his career in 1981 against France and in 1983 against New Zealand. He scored 35 points in the three tests, including a try in the first seconds of the third test at Eden Park in Auckland which he converted to give Australia a six point advantage with only a minute gone. It was not Gould's fault that New Zealand came back later to win the game.

Gould was also a leading performer in the Grand Slam-winning Australian team in Britain in 1984, kicking five goals in the game against Wales and setting up three of the tries in the last victory of the 'slam' against Scotland.

Gould's strong presence at fullback was expected to be a powerful force for Australia in the World Cup in 1987, but he played only part of the team's first match against England, cut down once again by injury.

At the end of his career in 1987, his 25 international caps was a record for an Australian fullback.

GRAND SLAM

Terminology for any rugby side winning all its games on tour or in one season, but more particularly referring to the wins of one team in the Five Nations championship against each of the other four. Although there is no trophy involved, the Grand Slam is a much valued prize.

Winning a Five Nations Grand Slam is not easy. For a start it means four straight international wins, home and away, with no losses. In the years that five teams have competed (1910–31 and 1947 onwards) there were only 21 instances. England has had most Grand Slams (9 up to 1991), followed by Wales (6), France (4), Scotland (3) and Ireland (1).

Welshmen will claim eight 'slams' in that time because their team also beat France in 1908 and 1909, before France was included in the championship proper.

England had a marvellous sequence in the 1920s, winning in 1921, '23, '24 and '28. Wales had three Grand Slams in 1971, '76 and '78. Scotland, on the other hand, experienced 59 barren years between 1925 and 1984. Ireland's only win was in 1948, while

France failed to win a Grand Slam until 1968.

Incidentally, the England team of 1928 neither kicked nor conceded any penalty goals in its five internationals that season.

Three Englishmen, Ronald Cove-Smith, 'Dave' Davies and Cyril Lowe hold the record for having played in four Grand Slam-winning seasons.

Perhaps the most famous Grand Slam games were in 1925 and 1990, when England met Scotland at Murrayfield. On each occasion both teams were unbeaten so the Triple Crown was also at stake, as well as the Calcutta Cup. The 1925 game, Scotland's first at Murrayfield, was immensely exciting. The lead changed three times but a dropped goal by Scotland's Herbert Waddell gave the home team a 14–11 win.

In 1990 Scotland was again the victor, shocking a confident English side 13–7. It was such an upset that a number of clothing manufacturers lost money after they had made souvenir shirts and jerseys depicting England as Grand Slam winners.

The Scotland team of 1990 set another record. It could claim six wins in its Grand Slam season, as it also beat Fiji and Romania at home.

Although the term 'Grand Slam' applies specifically to the international championship, some touring teams to Britain and France which have gone through their internationals unbeaten also claim to have won the accolade. South Africa achieved the impressive feat of beating all five teams on its tours of 1912–13 and 1951–52. In 1960–61 it beat the four United Kingdom teams but drew with France, and in 1931–32 it beat the four UK teams and might have done better still had it played France.

New Zealand has had less success. The All Blacks won their only Grand Slam against British Isles countries in 1978, but did not play France on that trip. The 'Invincible' All Blacks of 1924–25 won four internationals, including against France, but did not play Scotland. The 1967 New Zealanders won four internationals on their tour but did not play against Ireland. Australia won its only Grand Slam against all four countries in 1984.

While all Grand Slams attract much praise from the critics, perhaps the England effort of 1928 deserves to called the greatest, when it beat all the other teams in the Five Nations championship as well as the 1928 season's touring team, New South Wales. (New South Wales was the famous 'Waratahs' team which toured and played full international matches in the absence of an Australian team.)

GRAVELL, RAY
Llanelli and Wales
23 internationals for Wales 1975–82
4 internationals for British Isles 1980

A talented footballer who was as passionate about his Welsh nationality as he was about his rugby, Gravell was a tireless centre with an urgent playing style. His aggression swung him a place in the Welsh team in 1975, and until he ended his career in 1982 he was a regular and highly popular member of the team.

Gravell made the tour to South Africa with Bill Beaumont's Lions team in 1980, playing with typical courage and resolution in all four tests.

He later became a prominent radio and television personality in Wales, specialising in speaking and commentating in the Welsh tongue. He was also a rock band leader for a time, singing in Welsh with all the intensity he put into his rugby.

GRAY, KEN
Wellington and New Zealand
24 internationals for N. Zealand 1963–69

One of New Zealand's strongest and most versatile props who played in one of the most impressive forward eras in New Zealand's rugby history.

Ken Gray's time in the All Blacks came in the 1960s when the All Black forward pack included men such as the Meads brothers (Colin and Stan), Kel Tremain, Waka Nathan, Wilson Whineray, Ian Kirkpatrick, Brian Lochore and Bruce McLeod. Forward packs dominated by these men were dynamic units for New Zealand. Individually Gray was one of the stars of his time: a strong scrummager, a good lineout man at the front and a powerful runner in the open.

He played all his rugby in New Zealand for Wellington and was a stalwart of the famous Petone club. He played 24 tests for the All Blacks and was only in the losing side twice, one of the highest percentages of success by any long-serving player in the history of the game, from any country.

Ken Gray ended his international career in 1969 at the comparatively young age of 30. It was revealed several years later that he chose to retire in that year so that he would not be considered for the tour of South Africa in 1970. His continued opposition to apartheid was again in prominence in 1981, when he was an outspoken critic and active protester against the troublesome tour of New Zealand by the Springboks.

He had a keen interest in politics and to many Labour Party supporters his failure to win selection as a parliamentary candidate was a disappointment, as he was regarded as prime ministerial material.

GREYLING, PIET
Orange Free State, Transvaal and South Africa
25 internationals for Sth Africa 1967–72

A dynamic and thrusting flanker who gained world fame as a partner in foraging for the loose ball with Jan Ellis. The two played together in 24 test matches.

Greyling began his representative rugby in Rhodesia but later played for Orange Free State and Transvaal. He had a memorable international debut, scoring two tries in the first test against France at Durban in 1967.

Greyling's greatest attributes, apart from his combination with Ellis (and to a lesser extent with Tommy Bedford) were his commanding presence

Ray Gravell, playing for Wales against Australia at Brisbane in 1978, leaves Paul McLean sprawling. J.P.R. Williams is in the background.

Ken Gray, with ball, Wellington 1975. Also, from left: Andy MacDonald (SA), Bruce McLeod (NZ) and Abe Malan (SA).

Chris Laidlaw (New Zealand) and Piet Greyling leave the field after the third test at Port Elizabeth, 1970. The Springboks won the test, 14–3, and the series, 3–1.

and imposing power about the field. He was a crushing assaulter of half-backs and a grabber and feeder of the ball after Ellis had made the initial tackles. He was also an excellent lineout man at the back.

On the 'demo tour' of Britain in 1969–70, Greyling was a most consistent player who, it is reported, was not distracted by the anti-apartheid displays that interrupted almost every day of that tour. He played superbly, scoring tries against England and Ireland. He was also a major contributor to South Africa's test series win over New Zealand in 1970.

Greyling was made captain of South Africa in 1972 against England at Johannesburg, but the Springboks' loss by 9–18 would not have been one of his happier moments in rugby.

Business pressures caused his early retirement in 1973.

GRIQUALAND WEST RFU

The rugby union that serves the northern part of the Cape province of South Africa, north of the Orange River, which is called Griqualand after the people of mixed ancestry,

mainly European and Hottentot, who settled there after 1803. Annexed by the British in 1871 – the year diamonds were discovered in the region – after a dispute with the Orange Free State, Griqualand became part of the Cape in 1880.

Several significant moments in South African rugby history involve Kimberley, the main town of Griqualand West. In the early 1880s Kimberley club players became the first rugby touring team in South Africa when they travelled to Bloemfontein for a series of games. In 1889 the South African Rugby Board was formed and to celebrate that event the first major provincial rugby tournament in South Africa was staged in Kimberley. Western Province won the SARB Cup.

In 1886 the Griquas union was formed. In 1891 the British team under the captaincy of the famous Scottish international William Maclagan toured South Africa and played four matches in Kimberley against club teams. The shipping businessman Donald Currie had given a gold cup to Maclagan to present to the team that put up the best performance against

the British team. As no team could beat it on tour, and Griquas had gone closest, they were awarded the cup.

Griquas then generously presented the cup to the South African Rugby Board for competition among its major teams. It was named, of course, the Currie Cup and became the major rugby trophy in South Africa.

Griquas beat the Australian touring teams of 1933, 1953 and 1969 and the French team, by 20–14, in 1967. They twice beat the 1903 British team, 11–0 and 8–6, as well as beating the 1910 British team and holding the 1962 British Isles team to an 8–8 draw.

Some of Griqualand's players have been famous Springboks.

Arthur Marsberg was a speedy wing and fullback known as the 'Lion of the Plains'. His brother Peter was also a Springbok.

Frederick ('Uncle') Dobbin, who rose to captain South Africa against Scotland in 1912, was from Griquas, as was Herbert Kipling (1931–33), Jack van der Schyff, the fullback (1949 and 1955), Dick Lockyear, the halfback (1960–61), and Piet Visagie, the big-kicking flyhalf (1967–71). Many others have contributed to rugby in Griquas and South Africa, making it one of the most solid unions in South African rugby.

The union has its headquarters at the De Beers Ground in Kimberley, appropriate because the area is rich in diamond mines and this has led to many fine players being drawn to the area to work for the De Beers Company.

GRIZZLIES, THE

The strongest rugby union in the United States, the Pacific Coast Rugby Football Union is the collective union for teams representing Northern and Southern California Rugby Unions, along with clubs from Arizona, Oregon, Washington, Idaho and Alaska. It was one of the four regional unions that made up the USARFU when it was formed in June 1975. The grizzly bear, widely found in the west of the North American continent, was deemed an appropriate symbol for rugby in California and on the Pacific Coast.

The Grizzlies proved a big hit when they toured New Zealand in 1972. Their team beat their hosts, a full strength New Zealand Universities team by 13–6 in the tour's last match. The Americans played their rugby with considerable influence from the American football game, sometimes hurling strong lateral passes across the field and wearing jerseys with the very high numbers that are common in American professional sport.

As part of a seven-year plan adopted by the USARFU board of directors in 1982, tours for one of the four regional territories teams were set for every second year. The Grizzlies returned to New Zealand in 1984 under this scheme and were paid the tribute of a tough itinerary. They scored wins over the division one team Hawke's Bay, and Mid-Canterbury, and lost narrowly to Manawatu, Taranaki and Counties. A loss, by 0–41, to Otago, underlined that rugby on the Pacific Coast still had a way to go.

Rugby has a long and illustrious history on the west coast of the United States. The area first hosted a national team in 1906, when the New Zealand All Blacks played two matches, one in Berkeley and one in San Francisco (against British Columbia!). Australia toured California for a full 13-match tour in 1912 and the All Blacks visited for 13 matches in 1913. In those days rugby was flourishing in the west, although it later lost its popularity to the American football game.

In modern times rugby is again popular there. Clubs abound, overseas players populate the area, and tours and tournaments are very popular. Since the formation of the United States inter-territorial tournament in 1977 the Pacific Coast team has easily built up the most impressive record in matches against the other three regions: the Eastern RFU, the Western RFU, and the Midwest RFU.

GUY'S HOSPITAL RFC

Guy's Hospital club, established in 1843, became a founder member of the Rugby Football Union when it was formed in 1871. Winning the Hospitals' Cup series when it was first played for in 1875, the club had a magnificent spell in this traditional competition, winning 27 times between 1898 and 1933. By 1975, 100 years after its introduction, Guy's had won the cup twice as many times as any other hospital.

There is evidence that young men played a version of running and passing football in 1839 at Cambridge University, but a club was not formed there until 1872. Blackheath claims to be the oldest independent rugby club, Liverpool claims to be the oldest 'open' club, but Guy's Hospital still sticks vigorously to its claim of being the oldest 'closed' club in the history of the game.

Until the 1950s, Guy's symbolised the strength that old boys and hospital clubs offered to English rugby. When the emphasis shifted to the major clubs, Guy's continued to exist, but the club did not have the strength on its fixtures list it once had. Like all the hospital clubs of London, it draws its membership from staff, students and graduates. One of the strongest influences came from the many South African students who came to that hospital to complete their medical studies.

In 1905 Guy's was the first club in the world to allot specific places to players at each scrum. Previously forwards took their places in each scrum haphazardly, in the order they arrived at the new scrum mark.

The club celebrated its centenary in 1943 with two matches and a celebratory dinner. Among the hundreds who attended was Dr Teddy Morgan, the Welsh international of 1902–08, who was perhaps the most famous player to appear for Guy's Hospital.

H

HACKING

Once allowed in rugby, hacking was the practice of bringing a running player down by kicking him in the shins. After several players were severely injured, and one was even killed, measures were taken to have the practice banned in 1871. Many were the protests in Letters to the Editor columns of London newspapers at the time, centred mostly on a 'softening' of the game! A number of clubs wanted to maintain hacking as it endorsed the 'manliness' of the sport.

In fact hacking played a significant part in the formation of the sport of rugby. When the Football Association (soccer) was formed in 1863, its rules banned handling, running with the ball and hacking. The Blackheath club refused to accept that type of game and helped to confirm the new game based on the running, handling rules of Rugby School, which allowed hacking and tripping of a ball-carrying player. Ironically, Blackheath and Richmond later led the drive to have hacking banned after the toll of injuries became too high. The practice was even banned at Rugby School.

Since then hacking has (thankfully) been lost to the game of rugby.

HADEN, ANDY
Auckland and New Zealand
41 internationals for N. Zealand 1977–85

At 2 metres (6ft 6ins) the tallest man to play internationals for his country, Andy Haden became a giant in the sport in other ways. He rose above early arguments that he was not aggressive enough to make a career as a top-class international forward, and by the end of his time in top rugby he was one of New Zealand's great locks.

Haden had excellent lineout skills, was a solid scrummager, and around the field he often surprised with his mobility. As a captain and touring All Black he became one of the craftiest competitors in the game. Every Welshman will tell you how Haden 'cheated' to make referee Roger Quittenton award a last-minute penalty to New Zealand against Wales at Cardiff

in 1978. The big New Zealander tilted and dived out of a lineout, giving the impression that he had been pushed. When the penalty – awarded for an offence by Geoff Wheel, not for Haden's dive – was converted into points by Brian McKechnie, the All Blacks won the game by 13 points to 12. One suspects Haden will have to live with Welsh criticism of his dive at Cardiff that day far longer than he will have to live with the fame the game brought him.

He first made the New Zealand team for the 1972–73 tour of Britain and France, but did not make the international games on that tour, and after being dropped the following year, he disappeared off the New Zealand domestic scene for a time. He continued to play rugby, but combined it with seeing the world, becoming a truly global footballer, playing for clubs in France, England and Italy.

Back in New Zealand in 1976, Haden was chosen for the All Black team for the tour to Argentina where, under

Andy Haden

captain Graham Mourie and coach Jack Gleeson, he blossomed, playing in both the unofficial tests. By 1977 he was drafted into the All Black test team for his first official caps.

Thereafter Haden was a regular choice for his country and he went on every tour on offer, except when business interests interrupted his rugby in 1983 and 1984. In domestic rugby he rose with the Auckland team that dominated provincial rugby in New Zealand in the early 1980s, finally captaining it when the side won the Ranfurly Shield from Canterbury in 1985.

Haden became one of the champions of players' rights and he took on the rugby establishment in New Zealand. His attempts to better the lot of New Zealand's international players led to misunderstanding and suspicion of him, resulting in charges of professionalism being laid on him by the New Zealand Rugby Football Union in 1984. He defended these successfully, though there were many who were not as convinced of his innocence in 1986 when he was part of the Cavaliers' tour to South Africa. Charges were levelled that the team took payment to play its tour and Haden, as one of the principal organisers, faced many questions on his return.

Haden played his last game for New Zealand in 1985 in Buenos Aires on the All Black tour that replaced the cancelled official tour to South Africa. He had accumulated 41 test caps and 117 tour matches for his country, feats only bettered by Colin Meads (55 tests and 133 games).

At the end of his career he wrote *Boots 'n' All*, a book about his life in rugby.

HAGET, FRANCIS
Agen, Biarritz Olympique and France
40 internationals for France 1974–87

A no-nonsense French lock whose international career was spread over 14 seasons. At 37, he had the distinction of being the oldest player to appear in the first Rugby World Cup series in New Zealand in 1987.

A clean take for Haget. At left is Jean Condom.

Haget was a big man, standing 2 metres tall (6ft 6in), and he was a strong lineout jumper. His debut for France was on the tour of Argentina in 1974 and his last games for France were at the World Cup 13 years later. During his rugby days he was croupier at a casino in Biarritz.

HAKA

A Maori challenge, or war dance, which is traditionally performed by New Zealand rugby teams before their test matches. Vigorous, aggressive and intimidating, the haka was a ritual dance performed as much to fire up its proponents as to strike terror into the hearts of the enemy. In the rugby context, the haka issues to the opposition the challenge to play hard and well.

The first New Zealand team to perform the haka was the 1905–06 team in Britain. The 1928 All Black team in South Africa did the haka and the South Africans replied with a war chant of their own, made up on the morning of the game!

New Zealanders know that when All Black teams are made up only of Pakehas (Europeans), the haka is never performed with the vigour and feeling exhibited by Maori players, or when it is performed by teams representing the New Zealand Maoris, such as those touring overseas in 1982 and 1988.

Originally the haka was only performed by New Zealand teams when they were playing away from home, but when Scotland toured New Zealand in 1975 and during the World Cup games in 1987, the haka was seen in New Zealand too. It is enormously popular in all the countries visited by New Zealand teams.

(*See also* MAORI RUGBY)

HALFBACKS

A key man as the link between forwards and backs, the halfback either distributes the ball by passing to the backs or runs from his position to link up with the forwards. He is the putter of the ball into all scrums and in some countries is required to throw into lineouts as well. Without doubt, the position is one of the most difficult places on the field in which to play, and one of the most satisfying in which to play well.

A halfback must have a strong tactical presence; quick thinking and alertness is a vital part of his makeup. Ability to pass the ball off either hand is essential, but he must be able to kick adroitly too. He should also be sharp in pace, if only over the first 25 metres.

Some countries refer to the halfback as a scrumhalf, a term from the early days of rugby when there were two halfbacks who stood behind the heaving, tussling packs of forwards. The halfback who played closer to the scrum was called the scrumhalf, while the one who stood off wider was the 'stand-off half'. Those terms have largely stuck in Britain, but in New Zealand and Australia the term 'halfback' is used more frequently.

In recent years New Zealand has consistently fielded the best halfbacks in world rugby. Is it a coincidence that the All Blacks results have been so

George Nepia leads the 1924–25 'Invincibles' in the haka.

British Isles and Scotland halfback, Roy Laidlaw, clears. Behind is All Black Mark Donaldson, playing for Manawatu.

good in that time? Men like David Loveridge, Mark Donaldson, Sid Going, Chris Laidlaw and David Kirk, have helped give New Zealand teams the edge over their opponents. Each of those players was regularly challenged for his test place and the depth of talent in the halfback position goes right through to New Zealand provincial rugby.

Australia has also produced some brilliant halfbacks. Was there ever a quicker, slicker passer than Ken Catchpole? Was there a more resilient player than Nick Farr-Jones? Who could beat Cyril Burke for steadiness, unless it was Des Connor? One writer described Syd Malcolm of the 1930s as 'strong, mercurial, gutsy and persistently ebullient'. John Hipwell was another great Australian halfback.

From South Africa came men like Danie Craven, who perfected (but did not invent) the dive pass, and who displaced another champion in little Pierre de Villiers. Dawie de Villiers was a shrewd captain and tactician; as were Divan Serfontein of modern times; and 'Uncle' Dobbin was a champion at the turn of the century.

France's highest capped halfback was Pierre Berbizier, who beat the record set by 'Zeze' Dufau in the 1950s. Dufau was a player cast in the mould of many of the world's top halfbacks. He was nippy, sharp and elusive. Jérôme Gallion was another Frenchman who delighted crowds all over the world. Strangely, his style did not always impress the French selectors and Berbizier, a more solid player, but like most French backs capable of touches of brilliance, was preferred.

Gareth Edwards was the greatest halfback produced in Britain – fast, strong and tactically very aware. He would be high on any list of all-time great halves. Wales also produced Dicky Owen, Rex Willis and Robert Jones.

England had men like Dickie Jeeps. of the 1950s, a cheeky and highly skilled player. Steve Smith of the 1970s was England's highest-capped scrum-half and a very robust and strong player.

Roy Laidlaw of Scotland built a powerful combination as one of the 'halfbacks' with John Rutherford. Laidlaw finished in 1988 with 47 caps: the feat of 50 has been achieved in rugby's first 100 years only by Gareth Edwards.

Ireland's highest-capped halfback to the end of 1990 was Mark Sugden with 28 caps, followed by John Moloney with 27 international appearances.

Any discussion about which halfbacks merit being rated as 'best' in any facet of play must be subjective, but this writer would nominate Chris Laidlaw as the best passer of the ball (followed closely by Ken Catchpole); Sid Going as the best runner; Gareth Edwards as the best all-round halfback; and Danie Craven as the most influential.

HAMLET, GEORGE
Old Wesley and Ireland
30 internationals for Ireland 1902–11

One of Ireland's earliest rugby heroes. A tough forward from one of Dublin's most respected clubs, Old Wesley, George Hamlet rose to be a highly respected captain of his country. When he retired from international rugby, his total of 30 caps was a record for an Irish player.

In 1926 Hamlet was president of the Irish Rugby Football Union.

HARE, 'DUSTY'
Leicester and England
25 internationals for England 1974–84

A man who was capped 25 times by his country over a span of 10 years, but who was also dropped five times by the selectors during the same period. In 1981, William Henry Hare (always known as 'Dusty') became the highest scorer of points at a first-class level in the history of the game, passing the previous best tally of 3651 set by Sam Doble, another England fullback.

A great stalwart of the Leicester club, Hare made his international debut in 1974 in England's winning match against Wales at Twickenham. He was promptly dropped and did not reappear until January 1978. After his second appearance for England, Hare was dropped again. He returned to the England team the next season, but again, after one match, he was dropped.

Hare's first season of full international play was in 1980, when he scored 34 points in England's Grand Slam-winning performance. His off-again, on-again relationship with the selectors continued in the 1980–81 season, when again he was stood down, this time after scoring 30 points in the two internationals he played.

'Dusty' Hare

He was passed over in 1981–82 but returned for the France game after an injury put out the original choice, Nick Stringer. Hare hit top form in Paris and landed seven out of eight kicks, a contribution of 19 points towards England's 27–15 win.

Dusty Hare retired before the 1984–85 season, after he had earned 25 caps. His final total of 240 points in test matches was an England record which still stood at the end of 1990.

Hare was known as a running fullback in his early days, although his reputation rested on his relaxed and effective kicking.

He toured New Zealand with the 1983 British Isles team but did not play in the international matches. He scored 88 points in six appearances on tour, including 24 v West Coast and 21 v Wanganui.

HARLEQUINS FC

A fashionable London rugby club, the Harlequins club has had a strong influence on the game since its formation in 1866. It was one of the founder members of the Rugby Football Union five years later.

The club was named in an unusual way. Known in its early days as the Hampstead Football Club, members decided to choose a less parochial name, without losing the attractive HFC letters and logo on their playing shirts. So club stalwarts thumbed through a dictionary until the word 'Harlequin' caught their attention, and the club's distinctive name was born.

The Harlequins play their early-season games at Twickenham, and have their headquarters at the nearby Stoop Memorial Ground.

Adrian Stoop is one of the great names in the history of the Harlequins club. He first played for it in 1902 and by 1905–06 was made captain of the top team. The years he led the first XV have become known as the 'Stoop era' of the club – and in histories and articles the word 'autocrat' is often used to describe him. He drove his players relentlessly in pursuit of an attacking formula for rugby. The enjoyment and success the club had in those years led to many players being chosen to play for England.

Stoop himself was an international player, making his debut as a flyhalf in 1905. One of his most satisfying days must have been in 1911, when the England backline picked to play against Wales included Stoop and his brother Frederick, a centre, plus three other Harlequins in the backs – John Birkett, Ronald Poulton and Douglas ('Daniel') Lambert.

Another great influence on the Harlequins was Wavell Wakefield, who played every international for England between 1920 and 1926 and was one of rugby's greatest forwards. His organisation of the Harlequins XV ensured it stayed a top club through that time. Wakefield was a powerful force in the club for the rest of his life, rising to be the president for many years.

Another star player of the period was Leslie Gracie, an unorthodox wing capable of brilliant speed. He had 13 caps for Scotland and scored one of the game's most famous tries when Scotland beat Wales 11–8 in 1923. That international is now remembered widely as 'Gracie's Game'.

In Harlequins' first century, more than 100 of its players became internationals. Nigel Starmer-Smith, later to become well-known as a television commentator on the game, was an international from the club, as were David Marques, John Young, John Currie, Bob Hiller, Mike Davis, Peter Winterbottom and Will Carling.

In the 1960s and 1970s, the Harlequins club's reputation for being somewhat exclusive cost it strength for its top playing teams, as players with serious intent and ambition often preferred to play elsewhere. Later in the 70s, there was a change of attitude at the club: better organisation and recruitment meant that Harlequins flourishes today.

The Harlequins' traditional colours are harlequined squares of light blue, magenta, chocolate, and French grey with sleeves of light green and black.

HARRIS, STANLEY

Blackheath and England
2 internationals for England 1920
2 internationals for Great Britain 1924

Stanley Harris is remembered as one of the most versatile sportsmen of his time. He lived most of his life in South Africa, but represented England in 1920 in two rugby internationals as a wing. In 1924, while playing rugby for the Pirates club in South Africa, he was included in the Great Britain team that was to tour South Africa.

His other achievements make fine reading: he was a finalist in the world ballroom dancing championships, a skill he had taken up to recuperate from serious injuries received in World War I; it is said he turned down the chance to represent Britain in the modern pentathlon in the 1920 Olympic Games; he won the South African amateur light-heavyweight boxing championship in 1921; he was a brilliant tennis player winning at Wimbledon in the mixed doubles championship; he played Davis Cup tennis for South Africa; and he played for England at polo.

In World War II, as a colonel, he was captured by the Japanese and served three and a half years in a prisoner-of-war camp. He was awarded the CBE. He died in 1973 at 80 years of age.

HASTINGS, GAVIN

Watsonians, London Scottish and Scotland
31 internationals for Scotland 1986–91
3 internationals for British Isles 1989

HASTINGS, SCOTT

Watsonians and Scotland
30 internationals for Scotland 1986–91
2 internationals for British Isles 1989

Gavin is the older of these two brilliant Scottish brothers by nearly three years, yet they are the same 'age' in terms of international experience.

They made their debuts for Scotland in the same game, against France at Murrayfield in 1986 – the first brothers to do so since William and George Neilson in 1891.

Gavin, the fullback, made an inauspicious beginning to his test career by putting the kick-off to that match out on the full. However, both he and his centre three-quarter brother, Scott, became vital members of Scotland's team. Gavin had built a reputation as one of the game's finest fullbacks: a bursting runner, a thunderous punter and a heavy scorer of points. Scott was a sharp midfielder with good running skills, as well as being as punishing on a tackle as anyone in the world.

Both were members of the 1989 British Isles team in Australia, Gavin appearing in all three tests and Scott in two. In the home season which followed, both were part of the Grand Slam win by Scotland in the 1989–90 Five Nations championship.

Gavin Hastings, a strong, driving runner, in action for Scotland v New Zealand, 1990.

Gavin Hastings created a number of significant points-scoring records. In his first game, against France, he kicked six penalties, equalling All Black Kieran Crowley's record for a player on his test debut. He scored 52 points in the Five Nations championship that season, a Scottish record.

In the Rugby World Cup in 1987, he scored 27 points in Scotland's match against Romania at Dunedin, a new world record for one player in an IRB-sanctioned test, but one which lasted for just two hours: Didier Camberabero scored 30 points for France against Zimbabwe later in the same afternoon in Auckland.

Hastings also kicked five penalties for the British Isles in Sydney in the third test of 1989, effectively winning the game for the Lions and sinking Australia's hopes of winning the series.

Scott Hastings had injury worries in the World Cup series and played for only a few seconds against Romania, but he reached great form on the Lions tour of Australia in 1989, playing in nine of the 12 tour games, including the second and third tests. By the end of 1990, with the game against Argentina at Murrayfield, his test try tally stood at six.

At the end of the 1990–91 season, Gavin Hastings had clocked up 301 points for Scotland in international matches, passing Andy Irvine's previous record of 273. Added to that total were 28 points gained from his three Lions tests in 1989, his 329 points in tests the best total by a Scotsman. (Irvine's total, together with Lions tests was 301.)

HAWAII RFU

The rugby union of the Hawaiian Islands group. It has never joined with the mainland rugby body that represents the rest of the United States.

The first major club formed in the islands was the Hawaii Harlequins in 1964. Other clubs began soon after. The Hawaii Rugby Football Union was formed in 1966 to co-ordinate all rugby in the islands.

Hawaii hosts several significant tournaments. The Pan American world club series, begun in 1979, is the most prestigious and secures large numbers of competing clubs, including strong representation from Australia and New Zealand.

Hawaii competed twice in the Hong Kong Sevens tournament, in 1978 and 1979.

HAWICK RFC

This famous Scottish Borders club, with headquarters at Mansfield Park in Hawick, was formed in 1873. Then and now the club has been one of the strongest and most loyal to the game in Scotland.

Keenness for rugby certainly prevailed in the district in its early days. A floodlit match was played in Hawick in 1879, the action being viewed with the help of lighting from two dynamos powered by a steam engine. Hawick hosted the first touring side in Scotland: in 1888 the New Zealand Natives went to Mansfield Park and won by 3–1 (a goal to a try). The club won the first unofficial Scottish championship in 1895–96.

Hawick has always played its rugby in the best Borders traditions: consistent effort based around stern forward play. Hawick rugby has never been complicated but has always been based on a solid 15-man game of support play and commitment.

The club has had many famous players. In the early days William Kyle was a hard-nosed forward (21 caps for Scotland, 1902–10), as was Jock Beattie (23 caps, 1929–36). In more modern times, hooker Colin Deans was a club stalwart, but his retirement with 52 international appearances for his country only equalled a Hawick club member's best previous effort, that of the brilliant Scottish and Lions centre, Jim Renwick. Hugh Mcleod is another successful Hawick player who won 40 caps for his country, as a prop between 1954 and 1962.

Other well-known names from the club include Alistair Cranston, Colin Telfer, Derek Grant and Alan Tomes.

The Hawick 'Greens' continue to be one of the most powerful forces in Scottish rugby. At the end of 1990 the club had won 10 Scottish club championships since 1973.

HAWKE'S BAY RFU

A province on the east coast of the North Island of New Zealand which has had two glorious rugby eras, producing two of the most powerful provincial teams in that country's history.

Hawke's Bay RFU was founded in 1884. Its first period of dominance in New Zealand rugby was in the 1920s, when its powerful team was based on the skills of the famous Brownlie brothers, Maurice, Cyril and Laurie.

New Zealand provincial rugby was very strong at the time and many All Blacks either emerged from or were attracted to play in the famous Hawke's Bay team. The great George Nepia became an All Black from Hawke's Bay, while Bert Cooke, Lui Paewai, Bert Grenside, Jimmy Mill, Lance Johnson and the Brownlies all displayed the prominence that was to lead them into the All Blacks team.

The prized Ranfurly Shield was won from Wellington in 1922 and was defended by Hawke's Bay until the early part of the 1927 season – a string of 24 defences, then unparalleled in Ranfurly Shield play. In 1926 the black-and-whites beat their neighbours Wairarapa 77–14, Wanganui 36–3, Wellington 58–8, and Auckland 41–11, playing glorious, running rugby throughout. The coach during this era was Norman McKenzie, who coached from 1916–46.

It was not until 1963 that Hawke's Bay's record for Ranfurly Shield defences was challenged. Auckland's 25th defence was against, coincidentally, Hawke's Bay. The game is remembered as an Eden Park classic as the two sides fought out a 3–3 draw. In Ranfurly Shield matches a draw is as good as a win, so Auckland beat Hawke's Bay's 37-year-old record.

Hawke's Bay's second golden era began late in 1966 when, captained by Kelvin Tremain, the great All Black flanker, the Bay lifted the Ranfurly Shield from Waikato. Over the next three seasons, Hawke's Bay defended against all challengers at Napier's McLean Park. Twenty-one determined teams were turned away in week after week of rugby that had the Hawke's Bay province as unified and excited as they had been 40 years earlier.

Tremain was one of New Zealand's great players, but the team also starred Bill Davis, Neil Thimbleby, Ian MacRae and fullback Ian Bishop, who was a record-breaking goal-kicker.

Since Canterbury lifted the Shield in late 1969, Hawke's Bay rugby has been sadly in decline. Young men became drawn to working in the bigger cities, leading to a loss of rugby strength in the province. Though there is vigorous work being done under the recent chairmanship of Kel Tremain, Hawke's Bay has shown few on-field signs of gaining the strength that marked its two famous golden eras.

HAWTHORNE, PHIL
New South Wales and Australia
21 internationals for Australia 1962–67

A tidy and talented Australian flyhalf who specialised in drop-kicking goals, Phil Hawthorne was one of the first (and few) players to land three dropped goals in a test match, a feat which he achieved in 1967 at Twickenham against England.

Hawthorne first played for his country in 1962 against New Zealand, when he was just 18 years old. He played 21 internationals in his career and perhaps his best rugby was played as a member of the 1966–67 Wallaby team in Britain and France. His combination with halfback Ken Catchpole was quick, clean and sharp, and their play together helped Australia to wins over both Wales and England. Hawthorne scored 28 points in the internationals on that tour, then an Australian record.

His last international was against the All Blacks in the NZRFU's jubilee test in 1967. Hawthorne then took an Australian record fee when he signed for rugby league. He played for his country at that sport too, in 1970.

HEARN, DANNY
Bedford and England
6 internationals for England 1966–67

A hard-running and strong-tackling defender who tragically became one of rugby's casualties in 1967, when a broken neck halted his promising career as an international centre three-quarter.

His severe injury was sustained in a game for Midlands, London and Home Counties against the All Black touring

Phil Hawthorne escapes the clutches of Colin Meads in the 1967 jubilee test at Wellington.

team. He was just 27 years old. It was a sad irony that the injury and Hearn's struggle with its aftermath made him a well-known figure in the rugby world. Though he became restricted to walking on sticks or using a wheelchair, Hearn travelled widely, his courage earning the total admiration of the sporting world. His recovery from total paralysis enabled him to resume teaching economics at Haileybury.

HEATLIE, 'FAIRY'
Western Province and South Africa
6 internationals for Sth Africa 1891–1903

Barry Heatlie played against each of the first three British teams to tour South Africa, in 1891, 1896 and 1903, but the 12-year time span brought him a paltry tally of six tests. Contrast the international careers, only marginally longer, of two modern players: Willie John McBride and Colin Meads played 63 and 55 test matches respectively.

'Fairy' Heatlie was a determined, hard working, solid forward, usually at lock, so his nickname sat strangely on him. A Western Province man throughout his career, he featured in three milestone series.

Though not chosen for the first of all South African internationals, Heatlie played the remaining two tests against Great Britain in 1891. Dropped for the second and third tests of 1896 against the second British tourists, Heatlie returned for the final match as captain and led his team to its first victory in an international.

In 1903 'Fairy' (or sometimes 'Ox') Heatlie was 31 and a South African selector, not that his position got him a full series: he kicked two conversions in the drawn first test against Mark Morrison's tourists, but did not play in the scoreless second international. Returning himself to the third test side, Heatlie took the interesting step of choosing the forwards according to their build, not their positions, so that it was a fairly uniformly-built scrum. The 8–0 win made him South Africa's first captain of a series-winning side.

In 1905 Heatlie went to Argentina and became an important coach and rugby leader, playing until he was 49. Four years later he returned to South Africa. He was on his way to a rugby event – the annual dinner of Diocesan Old Boys – when he was killed in a car accident. He was 79.

HENDERSON, NOEL
Queens University, Belfast, North of
Ireland FC and Ireland
40 internationals for Ireland 1949–59
1 international for the British Isles 1950

A highly popular Irish centre three-quarter who played for his country over a decade. A strong runner and excellent tackler, Henderson was never dropped from an Irish team. Only injury cost him a consecutive sequence of caps.

Henderson scored the winning try for Ireland over Australia in Dublin in 1958, an historic score as it marked the first occasion that Ireland had ever beaten an international touring team.

In addition to his caps as a centre, Noel Henderson had one appearance on the wing (for the British Isles in the third test against New Zealand in 1950) and five as a fullback (his last five internationals in 1958–59). He captained his country 10 times.

Henderson was also a top-line badminton player who represented his country at that sport. He and the great Jack Kyle were brothers-in-law.

HERIOT'S FP
The club of former pupils of George Heriot's school in Edinburgh. Formed in 1890, it became well known to the wider rugby world for its sequence of fullbacks who played for Scotland.

Heriot's great player Andy Irvine played for Scotland 47 times as a fullback (and four times as a wing). Before him, from the same club, Daniel Drysdale, James Kerr, Tommy Gray, Ian Thomson, Kenneth Scotland, Colin Blaikie and Ian Smith totalled 135 appearances for Scotland.

The versatile Ken Scotland won 27 caps between 1957–65. Dan Drysdale, who had 26 caps between 1923 and 1929, was president of the Scottish Rugby Union 1951–52.

Other internationals include Iain Milne (a big front rower who played in the Scottish team that won the Grand Slam in 1984, as well as in the 1987 World Cup team) and David Kerr (also a prop) who became the Scottish Rugby Union's president in 1960–61.

The club has its headquarters at Goldenacre, Inverleith, Edinburgh.

HEWSON, ALLAN
Wellington and New Zealand
19 internationals for N. Zealand 1981–84

A remarkable, controversial, brilliant, yet sometimes erratic fullback, Allan Hewson came into the All Blacks for the tour of England and Scotland in 1979, but was not called on to be a test

Allan Hewson in action for the All Blacks in the second test v France in 1984.

player until, not an original selection, he played for New Zealand against Scotland in 1981.

The 20 points he scored in his second test began a remarkable series of individual performances by Hewson on Eden Park in Auckland. Later in 1981, on the same ground, he kicked the last-minute penalty goal that won for New Zealand the deciding third test against South Africa. In 1982, in the third test match against the Wallabies, Hewson scored 26 points, which stood until 1987 as the world record for points in a recognised rugby test match. In 1983, in the fourth test against the British Isles, he scored a further 18 points in the All Blacks' 38–6 win. In his feats on Eden Park, Hewson scored 73 points in four tests, an average of more than 18 per test.

Hewson was essentially a product of Wellington rugby. For that, and his often erratic play in defence, he was not widely admired on the terraces of grounds like Lancaster Park in Christchurch. Canterbury fans gave him a tough time, for they favoured their player, Robbie Deans, as an All Black fullback and resented Hewson being repeatedly picked. Yet even the man's harshest critics could not deny his often uncanny ability to win games. His outstanding qualities, apart from his excellent left-footed goal-kicking technique, were sharp speed, good handling and superb ball skills.

Hewson was of such a frail build that he had a reputation for sometimes not being able to finish games. Several times during matches played on cold winter's days he had to leave the field suffering from exposure.

HIPWELL, JOHN
New South Wales and Australia
36 internationals for Australia 1968–82

John Hipwell had a harsh introduction to rugby when, as an 18-year-old playing for the New South Wales Country team against the 1966 Lions, he had his front teeth kicked out in a cowardly act by one of the British team. A lesser person might have cried 'enough', but Hipwell recovered quickly and was included as the tour 'baby' in the Australian team that travelled later that year to Britain and France.

Hipwell went on to become one of Australia's great halfbacks, with excellent speed, handling and durabil-

John Hipwell, playing for New South Wales v Waikato.

ity. He could burst strongly from ruck or maul and his tackling suggested the power of a man with a much bigger frame.

Hipwell learnt the finer arts of halfback play from the former international Cyril Burke at the Waratah club in Newcastle. On the 1966–67 tour of Britain, he observed the multiple talents of Ken Catchpole, who was then the number one player in the halfback position for Australia. Hipwell combined facets of both of those excellent players into his own style of play.

He seemed to have more injury problems than most, and actually played a full game on the 1966–67 tour with a broken fibula. When he damaged cruciate ligaments in his leg on a later tour to Britain in 1975–76, his strength and determination came through again, and although he missed two seasons, by 1978 he played his part in the Wallabies' stunning 30–16 win over the All Blacks at Eden Park.

More injury problems followed on the 1981–82 tour of Britain, but he returned to fitness in time to play solidly in the last international against England at Twickenham.

That game was his last for Australia. His 36 internationals for his country was then a record for a Wallaby halfback. He was captain of his country nine times.

HODGSON, AUB
New South Wales and Australia
11 internationals for Australia 1933–38

A colourful and powerful figure in the 1930s, Aub Hodgson would have played many more games for Australia but for the outbreak of World War II.

He was as tough a footballer as Australia has ever put on the field and soon gained a reputation as a fervent patriot, probably because of his willingness to slug it out with the tough guys of opposition teams. The most notorious day in his career came in Sydney in 1937, when he took part in the game that became known as the 'dirtiest test' – the second test match against the touring South African team. In front of a crowd of 30,000, Hodgson and the Springbok Harry Martin slugged it out in just one incident of the rough-house game.

But Hodgson should not be dismissed as just a fighter. He was a grand loose forward who played great football from the No. 8 position on the 1933 Australian tour of South Africa and the 1936 tour to New Zealand.

It was sad for Hodgson that he was never able to extend his reputation into Britain. He was in the 1939 Australian team which arrived to tour Britain but was forced to return home without playing a game after the outbreak of war.

Long after his active rugby days ended, Aub Hodgson remained well known to Australian and world rugby. He was a hugely popular man who was very visible at rugby occasions as a boisterous host or guest. He was a man who loved nothing more than to watch a match then have a drink with his mates and discuss the great game that had made him famous all those years before.

HOLMES, TERRY
Cardiff and Wales
25 internationals for Wales 1978–85
1 international for British Isles 1983

The player who had the difficult burden of taking over from the great Gareth Edwards as scrumhalf behind the Welsh forward pack.

Terry Holmes went on to fashion a reputation as a tough, strong player in his own right and one of Wales's best modern players. Later in his career, injuries to shoulder and knee some-

Terry Holmes passing for the British Isles v New Zealand at Christchurch in 1983. Behind him are Iain Paxton, Murray Mexted and Dave Loveridge.

times restricted the display of his talents.

As a scrumhalf, Holmes was blessed with a confidence that had one writer at the time saying, 'He never once took a backward glance as he assumed the No. 9 shirt of Wales from Gareth Edwards.' Indeed, to win his Welsh cap after Edwards, Holmes had to rise through the Cardiff club ranks, where the two men ahead of him had both been Lions (Edwards and Brynmor Williams). Holmes played so well in his first international season that some wits in the crowds used to call out 'Gareth who?'.

He became a very popular player, on whom the country pinned its hopes of rugby success. In a country where there are so many rugby opinions, Holmes eventually attracted some that said that he was an even better player than Edwards himself.

Holmes had a long pass but he was also a devastating runner, almost impossible to stop near the goal-line. He was imbued with the strength and commitment usually associated with a hard-nosed loose man, especially at those times of the game when tough tackling was required.

Holmes toured twice with the British Isles, to South Africa in 1980 and to New Zealand in 1983. After sustaining serious shoulder injuries, he was invalided home from both tours.

After his last international, against the touring Fijian team at Cardiff in 1985, Holmes could not resist a record breaking £80,000 offer to transfer to rugby league. He joined the Bradford Northern club, but after only 40 games in the new game he suffered a knee injury that ended his active days on a football field.

HONG KONG

Rugby in some form or other has been played in Hong Kong since the British arrived there in 1841. There were always plenty of players to choose from among the army, navy and trading occupiers of Hong Kong and later, as the city expanded and the banking business boomed, still more potential rugby players arrived. Many of the early records were destroyed in World War II but there are records of rugby clubs as early as 1886.

The Hong Kong Rugby Football Union was formed in 1953, and later the colony pushed hard for the formation of the Asian Rugby Football Union, a natural consequence of which was the playing of the first Asian championship in 1969. Hong Kong's best performance in this annual event was in 1972, when it hosted the tournament and finished runner-up to Japan, losing the final 0–16.

In terms of administration strength, if not in playing ability, the Hong Kong Rugby Football Union is probably the leading force in Asian rugby. The rugby community in the city and surrounds is still mainly made up of 'ex-pats', but the HKRFU is instigating strong programmes designed to bring the game to the ethnic Chinese population. Such plans have to be firmly in place before the colony is handed back to the People's Republic of China in 1997.

The major annual rugby date in Hong Kong is the weekend when the prestigious Cathay Pacific Hong Kong Sevens is played. This has wide participation, attracting 24 teams from all over the world. It also serves to keep Hong Kong rugby well publicised. Hong Kong teams won the plate final in 1976 and the bowl final in 1985 and 1987.

Hong Kong has hosted full 15-a-side internationals as well, most notably the England team of 1971 (which beat Hong Kong 26–0), the Welsh team of 1975 (it beat Hong Kong 57–3), Scotland in 1977 (winner by 42–6) and France in 1978 (winner as well, 26–6). Neither the All Blacks nor the Wallabies have ever played in Hong Kong, though the New Zealand Juniors of 1958, who played there, had eight All Blacks and another five of the future. This very powerful young side won 47–0.

HONG KONG SEVENS

One of the most exciting and colourful rugby tournaments in the world. Since its inception in 1976, the Hong Kong Sevens has risen in size and status so that it is established as the 'world championship' of the seven-a-side game.

Changes were forced on the tournament when the New South Wales Sevens started in 1987 and the word 'international' was forced out of the Hong Kong title. But even as an invitation event the lustre of the Hong Kong Sevens has not dimmed. Those who have attended any of its tournaments have no doubt which is the more enjoyable event.

The tournament's first winner in 1976 (from 12 starting teams) was the Cantabrians club of Christchurch, New Zealand, neither New Zealand nor Australia sending national teams in those days. Australia sent one in 1977, but New Zealand persisted with its provincial sevens champions until 1982 when the Hong Kong organisers, who felt that the New Zealand Rugby Union had been off-hand, did not invite a New Zealand side back. Quick to take the hint, New Zealand sent its 'All Black' sevens team in 1983.

Since that year the pressure was on the four home unions and France to send national squads. Wales did in 1990 and France in 1991, but there are sound reasons for the reluctance of the others. The rugby season is still in full swing in Europe at the traditional March date of the Hong Kong Sevens, so national squads have been difficult to form. Instead, Britain has been represented by some of the great traditional clubs: Barbarians, Crawshay's, Irish Wolfhounds, Scottish Borderers, Penguins, Public School Wanderers,

Co-Optimists etc. The French were originally represented by their Barbarians club.

Essentially, though, the Hong Kong Sevens is an Asian rugby event and many have been the colourful characters that have emerged from the teams of the region. Success has been slim for Asian teams – their size is still a hindrance when facing top players – but some of the most enterprising rugby has come Korea, Japan, Kwang Hua Taipei and, of course, Hong Kong itself.

The tournament attracts huge local interest, with 30,000 people filling the Hong Kong Stadium. It is played over two days with three main groupings: the bowl event for teams eliminated on the first day; the plate for losing quarter-finalists; and the cup for those teams that make it through the last pressurised knock-out rounds.

WINNERS OF THE CATHAY PACIFIC HONG KONG SEVENS

1976 Cantabrians (NZ)
1977 Fiji
1978 Fiji
1979 Australia
1980 Fiji
1981 Barbarians (England)
1982 Australia
1983 Australia
1984 Fiji
1985 Australia
1986 New Zealand
1987 New Zealand
1988 Australia
1989 New Zealand
1990 Fiji
1991 Fiji

Australia wins the Hong Kong Sevens, 1983.

HOOKERS

The player in the centre of the front row who specialises in hooking the ball back to his team-mates from a scrum. The ball is put in by his own team on the loosehead side (the easier side as the hooker's head is closer to that side of the scrummage); conversely, a ball put in by the other team, is said to be on the tighthead side – thus 'winning a tighthead' is hooking from the opposition's put-in.

Hookers are a special breed. They need to be strong, supple and able to bend low from the waist. When a scrum is set low a hooker's face may be only centimetres from the ground, yet still he must be able to hook the ball cleanly. No other player is pitted so directly with his opposite. Good hookers also need to be cunning and shrewd. It is sometimes said that in a losing team's dressing room the only team member who might be smiling is the hooker – but only if he won tightheads off his opposite!

In modern times, the role of the hooker has expanded. He is now widely used for the throwing-in to lineouts and as the fourth loose forward, moving swiftly, strongly and efficiently, in both attack and defence, about the field. Most leading rugby countries have a number of top hookers capable of playing brilliantly from the position that used to be one of the least glamorous on the field.

Hookers seem blessed with longevity and some of the highest capped international players in the world have worn the No. 2 jersey. Scotland in particular has had a modern history of hookers who have served their country honourably at international level. Colin Deans retired in 1987 after earning 52 caps, the first international hooker to pass 50 caps. Before Deans, Duncan Madsen (14 caps), Robert Clark (9 caps), Frank Laidlaw (32 caps) and Norman Bruce (31 caps) ensured that Scotland used virtually only five hookers in nearly 30 years of internationals. When Deans retired, he was immediately – though briefly – replaced as captain by the reserve hooker Gary Callander.

By 1990, England's second highest capped player was a hooker – John Pullin, with 42 caps, followed by Peter Wheeler, one cap behind him. Eric Evans played in 30 internationals. All three captained England successfully.

The happy hooker? Peter Wheeler leaves the field after the Lions' defeat of the All Blacks in the second test in 1977.

Ken Kennedy was Ireland's leading hooker (45 caps), while 1983 Lions captain Ciaran Fitzgerald was a hooker, as were Ronnie Dawson, captain of the 1959 Lions, and Karl Mullen, Lions captain in 1950.

Wales had Bryn Meredith as its leading hooker (34 caps); while Norman Gale, whose career partly coincided, had 26. Bobby Windsor later had 30 games and Jeff Young 23.

New Zealand's successful captain Andy Dalton was a hooker, with 30 wins from 35 test matches, while Tane Norton played 27 All Black test matches in a row from 1971 to 1977 when he captained the team. To the end of 1990, Sean Fitzpatrick had played 30 tests, 28 of them in succession.

Australia's all-time cap record-holder from 1971–87 was a hooker, Peter Johnson, who played in 42 internationals.

Inexplicably, South Africa has had a high turn-over in hookers. Its most-capped player in this position is G.F. ('Abe') Malan, who appeared 18 times in tests, the last in 1965.

For hookers, there is a lifetime of stories about how and when and where hooking was successfully or unsuccessfully achieved. They say that only they can talk with authority on the 'art' of hooking!

HOPWOOD, DOUG
Western Province and South Africa
22 internationals for Sth Africa 1960–65

Doug Hopwood, one of South Africa's most accomplished forwards, first played for his country against the touring Scotland team in 1960, gaining 22 caps over six seasons as a fast-running, hard-working No. 8, a player in the tradition of the great Hennie Muller.

Hopwood toured to Britain and France with the 1960–61 Springbok team, to Scotland and Ireland with the 1965 team and to New Zealand, also in 1965.

Despite a recurring back injury, Hopwood fashioned a rugby career that has him rated among the best loosemen South Africa has produced. Some maintain he should have been a Springbok captain, as he possessed a keen tactical brain, but controversially he was always passed over. The selectors named him as their choice to Britain in 1965, but the South African Rugby Board vetoed the appointment and instead chose Avril Malan.

HOROWHENUA RFU
One of the smaller unions of New Zealand, from the coastal area of the North Island, north-west of Wellington.

Horowhenua joined its eastern neighbour, Manawatu to form Manawhenua, which won the Ranfurly Shield in 1927. Today, Horowhenua supports teams from three main areas – the rural towns of Levin and Foxton, and the southern resort area of the Kapiti Coast.

Horowhenua has produced only two All Blacks: Hohepa (Harry) Jacob who toured to Australia with the All Blacks in 1920 and who played for the union for 16 years; and Joe Karam, the former Wellington fullback who played for the resort town club of Paraparaumu when he played for New Zealand in 1975.

HOSPITALS' CUP
A traditional competition among the big teaching hospitals of London, which began in 1875. It is the oldest competition in the game, starting only four years after rugby's formal beginnings in England.

The series is a happy ritual, with crazy, zany support for each of the hospital teams coming from their staff.

A traditional ritual of the Hospitals' Cup final – a spirited flour-bomb battle.

There is much hilarity at the cup final with 'ragging', bands, singing and dancing, and flour and soot being thrown at spectators dressed in outrageous costumes. Outsiders have sometimes frowned at the antics of the crowds, but the event goes on in its traditional manner, popular not only with current nurses and doctors but also with former staff and students.

Twelve teams take part in the knockout competition and the final series, traditionally held at the Richmond Athletic Ground in Surrey, is always a hugely popular event. Hospitals that take part are Guy's, St Bartholomew's, St Thomas's, London Hospital, St Mary's, Middlesex, King's, Royal Free, University College, Charing Cross, Westminster and St George's.

The Hospitals' Cup has not just been a chance for ragging and hilarity over the years. The competition, apart from being the oldest in the game, also devised the modern points-scoring system. Touch judges and umpires were used for the first time in any rugby match in a Hospitals' Cup series.

HUNTER, JIMMY

Taranaki and New Zealand
11 internationals for N. Zealand 1905–08

Remembered for the scoring feat he achieved while a member of the 1905–06 All Blacks on tour in Britain, France and the United States. Hunter, a second five-eighths, scored 44 tries in 24 games on the tour, a total that has never been approached by any other touring player, from any country.

The change of touring styles, cutting modern tours down to a maximum of only 13 or 14 games, means that Hunter's record will probably stand for all time.

Hunter was a brilliant and elusive runner whom most British players could not read – apart from the Welsh, who detached a single player from the scrum solely for the purpose of containing him. Their system worked: Hunter did not score a try in Wales.

Jimmy Hunter was an All Black captain (once in 1905, later on a tour to Australia in 1907, and once in 1908) but later his life was touched by tragedy. Twin sons died at birth and later an infant daughter from a second set of twins died during a poliomyelitis epidemic. Another son, named Robert Deans Hunter (after his father's famous team-mate of 1905), gave his life for his country during World War II.

I

INDIA

Formed in 1980, the India Rugby Federation has approximately 7000 players and 150 clubs.

The British presence in India meant early establishment of the game. Affiliation to the Rugby Football Union (of England) came as early as 1874 – India is claimed to be the first overseas union to be thus associated with the mother country. India's main contribution to the game might well have been the presentation in 1878 of the Calcutta Cup, for annual competition between England and Scotland (*see* CALCUTTA CUP). At the time, the Calcutta Football Club was dying, but later it reformed and today is the strongest club in India. In 1926 the Rugby Football Union presented a trophy, the All India Cup, which is presented each year to the country's annual tournament winner.

INDONESIA

The Indonesia RFU was formed in 1977 from five clubs, made up mainly of expatriate Australians and Europeans working in Jakarta, and French oil workers from Kalimantan (Borneo).

Rugby has only a precarious hold in this country of vast distances and more than 12,000 islands. The two main clubs, ISCI (International Sports Club of Indonesia) and Balikpapan have to travel some 1300 km just to have a game with each other!

Strong efforts have been made to persuade Indonesians to play the game but, as in some other Asian nations, soccer is preferred.

Indonesia has played a number of times in the Hong Kong Sevens tournament. It was admitted to the Asian Rugby Football Union in 1978.

INTER-ISLAND MATCH

A game begun in 1897 which became an annual one (with the exception of 1930 and the war years) until 1986, between teams representing the two main islands of New Zealand.

The inter-island series, North Island against South Island, was, through the 1920s right up to the early 1970s, consistently up to international standard. In its heyday, the game was eagerly looked forward to by everyone in New Zealand as it featured a match that often had the look of New Zealand 'A' against New Zealand 'B' (the 'A' team being the side which won!). Sometimes the game did officially double as an All Black trial.

In the 1970s lack of promotion of the game led to loss of interest. The New Zealand Rugby Union, after years of playing the inter-island game at major grounds, started moving it to lesser towns. Public support fell away and towards the end the game was marked by the number of top players who declared their unavailability rather than by those who did turn out. It was sad for New Zealand traditionalists when the match was abolished in 1987 and replaced by a three-way regional trial series featuring teams from three new zones, Northern, Central and Southern.

The last game in 1986 was typical of the decline of the North v South game. Played in little Oamaru in the South Island, the game had a local college match as curtain-raiser. When the college game finished, most of the crowds of local schoolchildren drifted away, leaving the inter-island match to go ahead in front of a much smaller audience. The North Island won the game 22–10, ending the series with 49 wins. South had won 26 times and there were three drawn games.

Ironically the inter-zone series which followed lasted only three seasons before it, too, folded through lack of interest.

INTERNATIONAL CHAMPIONSHIP

The annual matches played between England, Ireland, Scotland, Wales and France have become known as the Five Nations championship, or the international rugby championship.

In fact there is no such official tournament. The matches played are the annual fixtures between the countries and it is only the media and fans who award a 'championship' at the end of the season. There is no official trophy or title at stake, yet the international rugby championship is probably rugby's most watched annual series of games.

Terry Godwin, who wrote a book in 1984 on the international championship's first 100 years, can find no definite date when public reference to a 'championship' was first made. Godwin believes it was near 1893 or 1894, some 10 years after annual matches had begun involving all four British and Irish teams. In the years that followed, only random mention was made to the 'championship' winners or 'wooden spoon' winners each year. And even when France was added to the list of annual fixtures for the four 'home' teams, it was left off published championship tables until after World War I.

Matches in the international championship these days are all played in the new year on a revolving roster of paired home and away games. One team rests each weekend on which there are championship games involving the other four teams.

The tournament has encouraged its own terminology, also unofficial. A 'Grand Slam' is the winning against all four other teams in the same season. A 'Triple Crown' refers to British teams winning against the other three home country teams. France cannot win a Triple Crown.

In the first 108 years of the championship, Wales won the title outright more times than any other country – 21 in all. England followed with 19

CHAMPIONSHIP RECORDS

Highest score
Wales 49, France 14 in 1910

Most tries in a match: 12
Scotland v Wales 1887
Wales v France 1910
England v France 1914

Most titles in sequence: 4
France 1959–62

Longest spell without a title win: 27 years
Scotland 1939–73

wins, Scotland 13, Ireland 10 and France 9.

England has been a Grand Slam-winner on nine occasions, and Wales and England have each won 16 Triple Crowns.

INTERNATIONAL RUGBY BOARD

The controlling body of world rugby, based in London with, since 1990, 12 members. The IRB makes and interprets the laws of the game, deals with questions of an international character, including tours, and sees that members abide by the rules, especially those pertaining to the protection of the amateur principles of the game.

The board celebrated its centenary in 1986. Regarded by many in the game as being slow-moving and conservative, it has, nevertheless, played a major role in the development of rugby.

The board's origins go back to a dispute that arose after an international match between England and Scotland in 1884. A referee's interpretation of a point of law decided the match in England's favour but Scotland's players objected.

The argument that followed was long and acrimonious, and as a result the two countries did not meet each other in the next year. This gap disrupted the full international schedule of games which was into its second season, so the secretary of the Irish Rugby Union suggested that a neutral board be set up to settle all future problems with the laws.

A meeting took place in Dublin in 1886 where Scotland agreed to accept the English victory in the 1884 game if, in turn, England agreed to join an international board in which all four countries of Britain would have an equal number of representatives.

Later in 1886 a meeting was held in Manchester at which, in spite of England's absence, a constitution was drawn up. When England's officials saw the wording of the proposed constitution they refused to accept the idea, mainly because, as the largest country, they felt England should have proportionately more representatives.

In the next season, 1887–88, what amounted to an ultimatum from Scotland, Ireland and Wales informed England that they would not play against it, unless it joined the board. So there were no matches with England that season.

The following season the board went part of the way to meeting England's original request by offering three seats to two each for the other countries – but still no matches were played in 1888–89.

In the next year the Rugby Football Union (of England) and the board agreed to submit the disagreement over delegate numbers to independent arbitration. The arbitrators were the Lord Justice Clark (Lord Kingsburgh) and the president of the Football Association (Major F.A. Marindin) who awarded England six seats to two each for Scotland, Ireland and Wales. All parties agreed to this and a new constitution was drawn up. England joined.

It was only at this point that the IRB had its first chance to control and reform the laws of the game. Before 1890 any decision on law changes lay entirely with England as, of course, it had codified and formalised the game.

In 1909 Scotland again requested that each country should have an equal number of representatives and in 1911 England voluntarily gave up two seats. This configuration of delegates lasted until 1948, when England gave up two more representatives to accommodate the admission of one from each of the three Dominion unions – Australia, New Zealand and South Africa.

This step was taken cautiously by the board members, who had always resisted pressure from the Dominions for full membership, and there remained a feeling that they had been reluctant to open up their ranks. For a considerable period an attitude of 'us' and 'them' had irked overseas rugby officials. One writer has said that respect for the Dominions only consolidated when it was seen how supportive the countries had been to Britain in two world wars.

In 1958 the composition changed again to allow two members each from all countries. This was the major breakthrough that the 'colonial' members so keenly desired. The board celebrated this new status of equality by meeting overseas for the first time, in New Zealand in 1959, not for an annual meeting but for one deemed a 'special' meeting. A second meeting overseas was held during the jubilee celebrations of the South African Rugby Board in 1964. Since then other meetings have been held in various world loca-

LONG-SERVING MEMBERS OF THE IRB

The RFU
W. Cail, 1890–1925
E. Temple Gurdon, 1890–1928
Sir George Rowland Hill, 1890–1928
Sir Percy Royds, 1927–49

Scottish RU
J. Aikman Smith, 1888–1930
J.D. Dallas, 1912–39

Irish RFU
R.G. Warren, 1887–1938
J.B. Moore, 1892–1937
H. Thrift, 1931–56
G.P.S. Hogan, 1947–71

Welsh RU
H.S. Lyne, 1887–1938

New Zealand RFU
C.A. Blazey 1964–86

South African RB
Dr D.H. Craven, 1957–87

tions, though generally they are held in London.

The question of France in the International Rugby Board was a vexed issue for many years. As far back as 1920 representations were made for France to attend meetings with a view to possible membership. These were shelved in 1930 when the board imposed an eight-year ban on matches with that country. There were suspicions that professionalism was rife in French club teams and no reasonable explanations by the French could shake the board from a determination that 'home' nations should only play those countries steeped in the concept of amateurism.

Matches between France and IRB countries resumed in 1947, but through the 1950s and 60s further suspicion existed about the state of the game in France By 1978 all public fears by board members about the amateur status in French clubs appeared to have been allayed, and France was allowed full membership.

In 1986 the board celebrated its centenary with a series of games in Cardiff and Twickenham and an International Board Congress to which *all*

Above: Brendan Mullin with the ball in the Ireland v Wales match in Pool Two at the 1987 World Cup. Wales won 13–6.
Left: One of Ireland's modern day greats – Donal Lenihan, who has won 47 caps for his country since 1981. Peter Bush

Top: Michael Kiernan with the ball against France, 1990. Below: Scotland's Finlay Calder races past Fergus Aherne in Ireland's Five Nations game against Scotland. 1990 was not a happy year for Irish rugby and Ireland lost both games: 12–31 to France, and 10–13 to Scotland, the eventual winners of the championship. Fotopacific

rugby playing countries were invited. By now the main issue confronting the board was further pressure to extend membership to some of the more than 120 countries that had embraced the game. Many of these countries have since been granted associate membership of the IRB, but the incomplete infrastructure of the rugby world is seen by many as a major cause of concern for the game's future.

So too is the continuing question of the game's amateur structure. While board members still adhere rigidly to the principle that rugby is an amateur game, there is confirmed evidence that modern players have sought some relief from that concept.

In 1990 Sir Ewart Bell of Ireland made a report, passed by the board's traditional two-thirds majority, which proposed sweeping changes to the strict amateur code of the game. Players could be paid for speaking engagements, writing books, etc, but could not accept any direct financial reward for playing the game. The new concept was readily accepted in New Zealand and Australia, but the more conservative officials of the Rugby Football Union sought to have contentious parts overturned. Thus began a debate which may continue well into the 1990s.

Of further significance was the decision taken in 1990 to allow four new countries on to a new executive committee, bringing the total to 20 votes. One representative from Argentina, Canada, Italy and Japan would join the two members each from England, Ireland, Scotland, Wales, France, Australia, South Africa and New Zealand. In addition, 38 other countries were to be given board status without representation on the executive.

INVERLEITH

The home ground for Scotland's international matches between 1899 and 1925, Inverleith was the first headquarters ground to be acquired by any of the home unions.

The first game there was a defeat for Scotland, 9–3 to Ireland (Ireland's first win on Scottish soil) and the second international was the most postponed ever: four times bad weather prevented the game being played. Eventually Scotland posted its first win on Inverleith, beating Wales 21–10.

By 1925 the ground, which could take no more than 30,000 spectators, had become too small, so Murrayfield was constructed to cater for crowds twice as large.

IRAÇABAL, JEAN
Bayonne and France
34 internationals for France 1968–74

He had a baptism of fire in test rugby, making his debut for France in New Zealand in 1968, playing in two of the three tests, with a game against South Africa later in the same year.

Jean Iraçabal was a powerful scrummager who, after his initial tests, formed a formidable front row in combination with his fellow Basque, Jean-Louis Azarete, also a prop, and René Benesis, the hooker. The three were enormously powerful as a front row unit, as they battled their way through 14 internationals together. Included in their successes was a win over New Zealand at Parc des Princes in 1973.

IRELAND
Rugby is probably the only international sport in which the term 'Ireland' can be used to describe that island's team: not Northern Ireland or Ulster; not Eire or the Republic of Ireland. For the rugby team of Ireland is truly a representative side, knowing no political or religious boundaries, and it has largely been that way since the formation of the forerunner of the Ireland Rugby Football Union in 1874.

Trinity College at Dublin University formed the country's first rugby club in 1854, and claims to be older than any other rugby club in the world, save Guy's Hospital. The first game was on December 1 1855, between new and original members of the club. For five years, the only 'rugby' matches at Trinity were internal: English educated v Irish educated, Rugby and Cheltenham scholars v The Rest, 'alphabet' games and so on.

External competition came in 1860 when a team styled Wanderers (not the later club, but old boys of Trinity) met the club team. Trinity was reorganised in 1867, and the second XV played St Columba's College, Hume Street School and Dungannon School, thus establishing the game in Ulster.

A rugby section of the North of Ireland Cricket Club was formed in 1868, and it had a momentous match when Queen's University club was formed in 1869. The two played a three-day match, starting on January 16, 1870, with the 18-strong Queen's team beating 13-man Norths as it kicked the only two goals of the game.

The first 'unification' of Irish rugby came in 1871, when North and Trinity played for the first time, in a 15-a-side match, with Trinity the winner. Irish rugby went international with North playing in Scotland the same season, and it was in that year that England and Scotland met in the world's first international, setting new targets for rugby in Ireland, which was developing quickly. Wanderers (1869), Lansdowne (1872), Dungannon (1873) and Queen's College, Cork (formed in 1874, though it had played in 1872) were new clubs.

What could be called the founding meeting of the now Ireland RFU was held in the Trinity College rooms, No. 27, of George Stack, on December 7 1874, where it was agreed an executive should be formed at a meeting a week later. Stack, the Trinity captain, became chairman; Richard Peter of Wanderers the treasurer; and H.D. Walsh from Engineers the secretary. A committee was set up to organise the team for the projected international with England.

The next step was to liaise with the newly-formed Northern Football Union, and after delicate negotiations, it was decided both unions should have seven 'automatic' selections and could nominate up to a further 11 players from whom would be chosen (by a panel of six, evenly decided) the balance of the 20 players. In the event, the team, appropriately captained by Stack, included nine Trinity players, six from North, three from Wanderers and one each from Windsor and Methodist College.

The 1898 Ireland and England international, played at Richmond.

Stack was to die less than two years later from an accidental overdose of chloral. His pioneering team took the field at the Oval in Kennington in green and white hooped jerseys and stockings and white knickerbockers – not too different from Ireland's eventual colours. The white jerseys used the next year carried the now familiar shamrock.

With such a democratic but haphazard method of selection, the Irish were well beaten on February 15 1875 by the organised English; and they did no better against England in the first home game on December 13 1875 at the Leinster Cricket Ground, Rathmines.

By 1877 Ireland had capitulated to England's request for their matches to be 15-a-side, the Irish preferring a more cluttered pitch of 40 bodies to hide their lesser skills. In the same season they had played Scotland for the first time. The Irish must have wished their Celtic cousins had never travelled to Ormeau in Belfast, for the visitors scored two tries and six goals to deliver a dreadful hiding.

But 1877 was still a momentous year, for the spread of the game brought Leinster and Munster into opposition for the first time; and the Dublin-based administration made the first formal attempts to bring about amalgamation with the north. As Belfast hedged, the selection of two Limerick players in the team to play England at Lansdowne Road must have given it the message that a true national side was emerging.

The amalgamation eventually came about in February 1880, just six days before another big event in Irish rugby history: in its eighth international, against England at Lansdowne Road, Ireland scored its very first points, a doctor named John Cuppaidge getting a try under the posts. Never having faced a conversion attempt before, fullback R.B. Walkington 'trembled from top to toe' and fudged the kick. By the time Walkington played his last international in 1882, he was also president of the Irish union.

It was not unusual for the Irish to thrust responsibility on young men. A.J. Forrest, a 21-year-old forward,

captained the side in 1881, and so had charge on a great occasion: when three-quarter John Bagot kicked a last-ditch dropped goal, in answer to a Scotland try, and Ireland won an international for the first time.

Wales became Ireland's third opponent in 1882.

Many tend to regard the late 1890s as one of the golden eras of Welsh rugby, but it's worth noting that Ireland won the prized Triple Crown in 1894 and again in 1899. A half century was to pass before Karl Mullen's sides of 1948 and 1949 again won this mythical prize. Ireland had subsequent successes in 1982 and 1985 – the wins, when they come, come in double doses.

Consistency has not been a trait of Ireland sides, though that charge should not be laid against the selectors. Once they settle on a player they tend to stick with him, to the extent that durable lock Willie John McBride and outstanding back Mike Gibson had records of international longevity bettered only by Frenchman Serge Blanco. And the Irish rugby story is replete with many other names of men who played internationally well into their 30s.

Ireland first toured in 1899 to Canada and won 10 of its 11 matches. At the same time a British team including three Irishmen was touring Australia. The next Ireland tour was not until 1952, and again it was to an area outside the mainstream of rugby strength – Des O'Brien's team visiting Argentina and Chile. While Ireland was not at full strength for this tour, it was a surprise it should win only six of the nine matches, one of the two draws being in one of the two internationals. The other was won.

Ireland's first major overseas excursion was to Australia in 1967. Noel Murphy was originally chosen as captain but Tom Kiernan took over when the veteran flanker was forced to withdraw. Prospects for the sole international did not look bright when Ireland lost 9–21 to New South Wales, but it beat Australia for the third consecutive time, 11–5, and won four of the six tour matches.

Argentina again played host to Irishmen in 1970. Kiernan was still captain and former skipper Ron Dawson the coach. It was something of a fractious tour, the Irish losing two of the three internationals 3–8 and 3–6, and also losing to Argentina C, 0–17. An Irish player, Ron O'Callaghan, was sent off in the first of the tests, along with Argentine Ron Foster; there were many injuries; the refereeing proved a worry to the tourists; and when the hosts struck an airline problem at Rio de Janiero, the touring party was grounded for a few days on the pretext of some misconduct!

Ireland celebrated its centennial in 1974 with matches against an Overseas XV and the All Blacks, the latter making their first tour principally to Ireland. This was reciprocated in 1976, when Ireland lost the only international, 3–11. Australia was visited again in 1979, and Ireland maintained a distinctly useful record against that nation by winning both internationals, 27–12 and 9–3. Ollie Campbell was a surprise choice for only his second international, in place of Tony Ward, but he scored a record 19 points in the first match.

But Campbell suffered from injuries on the next tour, to South Africa in 1981, when Fergus Slattery was again captain. Many of the Irish players had

to resign their jobs to tour, and the visit was not well received by many at home. The results did nothing to assuage the pain, for the tourists lost four of their seven matches, including the internationals, 15–23 and 10–12.

Irish players did not feature in the early British (later Lions) sides. There were none in the 'Shaw and Shrewsbury' team to New Zealand and Australia in 1888, nor to South Africa in 1891, and the 1908 tourists to New Zealand were accurately labelled the 'Anglo-Welsh'. But the nine in the 1896 side to South Africa is the best Irish representation in a 'Lions' side to this day.

Another record held by Ireland is in the matter of providing Lions' captains. Tom Smyth set the pattern in South Africa in 1910, and a great run was started by lock Sam Walker in South Africa in 1938. The next Lions team, to New Zealand and Australia in 1950, was led by hooker Karl Mullen; in South Africa in 1955 the captain was young lock Robin Thompson; back to Australia and New Zealand in 1959 it was another hooker, Ron Dawson. The pattern was broken, inevitably, but more often than not the home unions selection panels turned to an Irishman as leader: Tom Kiernan to South Africa in 1968; Willie John McBride, also to South Africa, in 1974, his record fifth tour as a Lion; and Ciaran Fitzgerald to New Zealand in 1983.

Irishmen have also had a considerable influence on the management of Lions sides, especially since World War II. Jack Siggins managed the 1955 team, and former international referee, Ossie Glasgow, was the 2IC in 1959. Former Ireland captain Des O'Brien managed the 1966 side, but raised some eyebrows when he took off for a holiday in Fiji in mid-tour.

Dawson (1968) and Millar (1974) were both Lions coaches in South Africa, the latter team losing an unblemished record only with a draw in the final test; while McBride, after attempting to win the coach's position with the 1983 Lions, then had to settle for manager. He was markedly less of a success in that role than as a player.

Ireland has beaten all the world's major rugby-playing nations, with the exception of New Zealand. The two first met in 1905, and the only time the Irish have avoided a defeat was the 10–10 draw in 1973 – but that result

prevented the New Zealanders from achieving a Grand Slam.

Ireland's first win over a major touring side was in 1958, against Australia, and it went on to win again in 1967 and in late 1968, and twice in 1979.

After being drubbed 38–0 by South Africa in 1912, Ireland must have taken special pleasure in finally beating the Springboks in 1965, and also in securing a draw in 1970.

The Irish first played France in 1909, not losing to the Tricolours until 1920, and a heavy loss that was: five tries to one, with Ireland fortunate that France could kick no conversions.

Mention has been made of rugby being the one activity which brings Irishmen together peacefully. But having two nations involved posed the problem of flying a flag at internationals. The IRFU thought it had resolved the problem by designing its own flag in 1925, but it had to yield to pressure in 1932 and fly the Irish (Eire) flag at Lansdowne Road internationals.

It has made a rich contribution to rugby, this united Ireland, and many touring teams observe that the reception they receive in Ireland is warmer than anywhere else on their tours. Thus it was a pity Scotland and Wales refused to play their Dublin matches in 1971–72 because of the political unrest; while the 1967 All Blacks had to cancel their Ireland match because of a foot-and-mouth epidemic.

Ireland has had a true provincial championship since 1947, when Connacht started playing Ulster, Leinster and Munster on a regular basis.

IRVINE, ANDY
Heriots FP and Scotland
51 internationals for Scotland 1972–82
9 internationals for British Isles 1974–80

After his last international in 1982, Andy Irvine was the world's highest scorer in test rugby, as well as being Scotland's most-capped player and the first back from that country to play 50 internationals.

Irvine was one of the great players of the modern game. A devastating runner of the ball from the fullback position, he was a marvellous support runner of his team-mates. He could goal-kick with great distance and accuracy, and commanded respect as a player who could turn the course of a

Andy Irvine outsprints three defenders as he crosses the line for a try.

game with his attacking brilliance. His natural speed was such that in his early days he often played on the wing.

He was a product of Edinburgh's famous rugby nursery, George Heriot's School, and became the eighth of that school's former pupils to play fullback for Scotland.

Irvine played superbly in his international debut against New Zealand at Murrayfield in 1972 and thereafter remained a first choice for Scotland. He was also vitally important for the touring British Isles teams of 1974 (to South Africa), 1977 (to New Zealand), and 1980 (to South Africa again).

He challenged traditional thinking on fullback play, for before he rose to prominence it was rare for fullbacks to score tries. In his total of 301 points in internationals, he scored 10 tries for Scotland and one for the Lions. He scored five tries in all matches on the 1974 British Isles tour of South Africa and 11 in New Zealand in 1977 (the team's top try-scorer). He touched down for a further four in South Africa in 1980.

Irvine had his critics who felt he should have concentrated more on his defence, perhaps in the manner of J.P.R. Williams of Wales. Perhaps

there was validity in these arguments, as Irvine was not one of the game's great tacklers and sometimes he was creaky under the high ball. But at his peak there was no more charismatic player of rugby anywhere in the world. His instinct was to run and score tries. and he tried to do that in every game.

One of his best moments came at little Taumarunui in New Zealand in 1977 when he set a world record of five tries by a fullback in one game. He also scored a scorcher of a try for Scotland against Wales at Murrayfield in 1979. In 1980 he scored 16 points, including two tries, in the last 15 minutes to help Scotland to come back from 4–14 and defeat France 22–14.

Irvine showed his goal-kicking prowess on many occasions, not the least being for the Lions against New Zealand at Wellington in 1977 when he thumped a great 50-metre kick over the crossbar after a first minute penalty.

Andy Irvine, an Autobiography was published in 1985.

ISRAEL

Formed in January 1971 by South African students and immigrants, the Israel RFU was affiliated to the Rugby

Football Union (of England) and in 1980 was admitted to FIRA.

A national league began in 1971 which continues, albeit with fewer than 10 clubs and only about 500 players. In 1981 Israel toured for the first time, drawing 9–9 with Switzerland.

In 1989 Israel took part in an early World Cup qualifying round but, even though it was heavily fortified by expatriate South Africans, it lost to Switzerland, Denmark and Sweden and did not progress to the next round.

ITALY

Italy had modest beginnings as a rugby nation. A student returning from France, Piero Mariani, organised a game in 1910, but it did not catch on and rugby barely existed until 1927. Thereafter the pace of Italian rugby picked up. The 16 clubs that did exist were so keen that they felt the need for a central body to control the national rugby destiny. Thus the Italian Rugby Federation was born in 1929.

The first national championship was played in 1929 with the winners Ambrosiana Milano (from Milan). The same year Italy played its first international, losing to Spain by 0–9. The attendance in Barcelona for the game was said to be 80,000. The King of Spain, Alfonso XIII, attended and presented the players with a commemorative medal afterwards. In 1934 Italy became one of the foundation members of FIRA.

Italy's official rugby history (marking 50 years in 1979) records several internationals as having been played during World War II. In April 1940 Romania beat Italy 3–0; in May of the same year Italy beat Germany 4–0; and in May 1942 Italy beat Romania 22–3. Clearly rugby flourished during the Mussolini era.

After the war Italy embarked on a golden era of success at an international level. The FIR (Federazione Italiana Rugby) embraced a policy of playing regular internationals against its rugby-playing neighbours and was almost always the winner. The French XVs, however, were always just too hard to beat. After first playing France at the Parc des Princes in Paris in 1937 and playing a regular game almost every year since (war years excepted), Italy has *never* won. The closest contest was a 3–6 loss in 1962. After three resounding wins in the later 1960s, France thereafter sent a XV rather weaker than its top side. At the time of writing Italy has still never beaten its neighbour, though in 1983 a 6–6 draw in Rovigo gave Italy hope for the future.

Italy scored 18 wins for only two losses against the other countries played in the period 1950–66.

Italy embarked on tours beyond Europe in 1973 when it visited South Africa. Sadly the tour was a disaster: the team won only one of nine games. Tours to Britain were also unsuccessful, but Italian rugby surged again after a brave 29–13 defeat of the England under-23s.

In the years that followed, Japan was beaten 25–3 in 1976; Romania 13–12 in 1976 and Argentina 19–6 in 1978. There were at least three significant drawn games in that time and narrow losses to Australia by 15–16 in 1976 and New Zealand by 12–18 in 1979.

When the FIRA Cup Nations competition was introduced in 1965, Italy was one of the first teams to be involved. Despite strong opposition from the likes of the Soviet Union, Romania and France, Italy claimed second spot in 1976, 1982 and 1983, and in the other years usually battled for third place.

The game has some problems in Italy, most notably narrow club politics, a neglect of the disciplined parts of the game (especially in forward play) and poor refereeing. On the other hand the Italian club scene is soundly based with good sponsorships and the annual nationwide league championship title is keenly pursued.

The strength of the club scene lies in the north around the towns of Padua, Petracha, Treviso, Rovigo etc, but the game is also soundly based in big cities like Milan, Genoa, Parma and Rome. The influx of overseas coaches and players has helped the game enormously. The talents of New Zealand, Australian and South African players in particular have influenced the clubs and, while the IRB frowned on the idea of easy swapping of players between countries, it could be argued that players like Andy Haden, Roger Gould, Craig Green, Wayne Smith, Theuns Stofberg, David Campese, Rob Louw, John Kirwan and many others assisted the game immeasurably.

Italy has also maintained its policy of touring. Its players are among the highest 'capped' in the world. When Italy's team reached New Zealand to play in the Rugby World Cup in 1987, players like Serafino Ghizzoni, an international for 10 years, had won more than 60 caps – the highest-capped international of the 16 competing teams.

In the World Cup Italy proved to be one of the most popular teams. Certainly it crumbled 6–70 to New Zealand, but the Italians took it as a great honour to be chosen to play the first game in the cup against the host nation. Italy then played soundly against Argentina but lost 16–25.

The third match in its qualifying group was against Fiji, which had earlier beaten Argentina. Italy took the field for the game in Dunedin and played bravely for an 18–15 win. Only a count-back of tries prevented Italy from qualifying for the quarter-finals and the team and officials returned home well satisfied.

New Zealand fans immediately picked two favourite players in the Italian team – the captain and brave flanker, Marzio Innocenti, who spoke so passionately on television for the cause of his team (in halting English), and the wing Marcello Cuttita, who dazzled everyone with his brilliant speed and skill. His try against Argentina was one of the finest seen on Lancaster Park in Christchurch.

Italy was coached by Marco Bollesan, himself one of the great Italian players who earned 47 caps, was captain 30 times and played 29 tests in a row. It was sad for Bollesan that in his World Cup team he did not have another of Italy's all-time greats, the flyhalf Stefano Bettarello. A pupil of Carwyn James, when the Welshman spent time coaching in Rovigo, Bettarello had to cry off the tour because of work commitments.

Italy also had the Francescato brothers, Rino, Nello and Bruno, dashing backs in the 1970s. Rino was invited to tour with the 'World XV' to South Africa, under New Zealand coach Brian Lochore in 1979. A fourth brother, Ivan, made a brilliant debut for Italy in its final 1990 World Cup qualifying round.

The Italian front row at the 1987 World Cup (from left): Emilio Lupini, Stefano Romagnoli, Giancarlo Cucchiella.

Stefano Bellandi is remembered as the man instrumental in starting the game properly in 1929. Ambrosia Bona was another name in Italian rugby. From a South African background, he played for Italy for 10 years and led the team on its first tour of New Zealand in 1980.

The Italians have imported some good coaches over the years. The brilliant former French fullback, Pierre Villepreux, left his mark on the game in Italy when he worked as technical administrator. His training methods and coaching framework, based on French methods, produced some thrilling advances, especially in back play, and under his guidance Italy had some excellent results. Other well-known coaching names like Roy Bish, Gwyn Evans and Isadoro Quaglio have all assisted with the national team over the years.

Italians, like most athletes from their region of Europe, are emotional characters on the rugby field. They can play brilliantly and their backs can 'frighten' anyone in the world on a good day. It is when they can harness an attitude of committed hard work in the tight forward play that further improvement will come, and the promise that they have shown over the years – never better exemplified than at the 1987 World Cup – may well make Italy one of the new true forces in world rugby, just as it is with soccer. Indeed, in the 1991 World Cup qualifying rounds it hosted and won the final European group, beating Spain 30–6, Netherlands 24–11 and, in the final, Romania 29–21.

From the trivia file: the Italian rugby team of 1980 is the only team ever to have played two internationals on the same day – in separate countries. On July 5 1980 Italy played New Zealand Juniors in Auckland at the end of its New Zealand tour before flying that night to the Cook Islands where, on July 5, it played and lost to the home team, thus completing two matches on the same day in different countries. The catch is, of course, the team had crossed the international dateline on its flight out of Auckland!

IVORY COAST

An emerging force in African rugby, the Ivory Coast team made a solid effort to qualify for the 1991 Rugby World Cup. It may have lost all games in the quadrangular series with Zimbabwe, Morocco and Tunisia, but there are signs that in the future of African rugby Ivory Coast will play a bigger role.

The rugby federation in the Ivory Coast was formed as recently as 1970, after the game was first taken there by expatriate Frenchmen. In 1984 the team played its first international against Senegal. The first of the qualification series for the 1991 Rugby World Cup was only the second international game played by Ivory Coast.

The appearance of a number of Ivory Coast players in French club teams is seen as a further sign that the country's team will only improve.

Djakaria Sanojo played a significant role in the Côte de Basque team which beat New Zealand in 1990. Sanojo was a tall and powerful lock. If there are others like him, then the Ivory Coast's rugby is in for some exciting and competitive years ahead as it joins the list of fast developing African rugby outposts.

J

JACKSON, PETER
Coventry and England
20 internationals for England 1956–63
5 internationals for British Isles 1959

Jackson was a nimble and quick-footed wing, one of England's finest, who made a speciality of outwitting defenders with the magic of his feet. He was a runner who turned many unlikely situations into try-scoring chances for his teams.

In his debut match Wales was the winner, 8–3, but Jackson showed the Twickenham crowd the first glimpses of his talents, making a twinkling run up to the Welsh line just before half-time. Jackson believed he had scored a try, even if the referee didn't, but the dazzling Jackson runs were soon to become regular features of England's play.

Jackson's form was such that he was a first choice for the Lions touring team of 1959, when he played both tests in Australia and three of the four against New Zealand, scoring 19 tries in 18 games – only Tony O'Reilly, with 21 tries from 21 games, scored more. New Zealanders scoffed initially at his pallid face and body colour (the legacy of a childhood kidney complaint) but his jinking runs from unpromising positions on the field soon confirmed that he was something special.

In 1960 Jackson was surprisingly replaced by John Young and it was not until early in 1963, after missing the best part of three seasons, that Jackson was back in the England team for all four championship games. That was the last season, both for Jackson and for the seasoned backs Jim Roberts and Richard Sharp. Without these three England's back play declined, and it won only twice in the next 19 internationals.

Jackson scored many memorable tries for England, but none ranked better than the one in injury time at Twickenham in 1958 against Australia. With the scores level, he began a 50-metre run along the touchline, eluding tacklers all the way. His try in the corner won the game for England by 9–6.

Peter Jackson's running style was described as 'a cross between Nijinsky and Stanley Matthews'. Another writer called him the 'old dancing master'.

JAGUARS, THE
Combined teams made up of South American nations. They consisted principally of Argentines, but included players from Paraguay, Uruguay and Chile.

The Jaguars came about as a counter to the policies of the then government of Argentina, which allowed no contact between the Pumas and the Springboks. The top players responded by leaving the country and forming a combined team with the best from their neighbouring countries.

The first Jaguars team, which toured South Africa in early 1980, was, with one exception, the entire Argentine team from its home series which had played four months before against Australia. It played superbly against the Springboks, who were gearing up for a full tour by Bill Beaumont's British Lions. South Africa won the two tests 24–9 and 18–9, but the victories came mainly because of the kicking of Naas Botha, who scored 26 points in two games, including three dropped goals in the second game at Durban. South Africa gave the Jaguars full international status on this tour.

Later in 1980 South Africa toured to South America. Politically, the same rules applied, so no contact could be made directly with a team bearing the name of Argentina. So the Pumas players went to Chile and Uruguay for two tests. Again South Africa was successful, winning 22–13 and 30–16.

The third test series involving South America and South Africa took place in 1982. Again leading Argentinian players mixed in with other nationalities (42 players in all were in the touring party) and two tests were played. The Jaguars actually fielded two teams each match day. The 'second' team went through its seven matches undefeated.

After South Africa won the first test in Pretoria by 50–18, many cynics in the republic felt that the Jaguars' tours

were proving little about South Africa's current rugby strength. But a week later the Springboks were rocked by one of the biggest upsets in rugby. The Jaguars, again all Argentine players, devised a second test game plan built around their captain Hugo Porta's kicking. They stunned South Africa at Bloemfontein, winning by 21–12. Porta scored all 21 points.

The fourth and final series involving the Jaguars against the Springboks took place in 1984. Again the South Americans toured South Africa, the Springboks winning the two tests 32–15 and 22–13.

Since then the Jaguars have not had any further contact with South Africa – nor with any other teams for that matter. Their days are over, perhaps, but their players could look back on their one win over South Africa with satisfaction.

Hugo Porta captained the Jaguars in all eight of their 'tests' against South Africa.

JAMES, CARWYN
Llanelli and Wales
2 internationals for Wales 1958

A brilliant rugby man whether as a player, coach, lecturer, broadcaster or writer.

Carwyn James had the misfortune to play in the same era as the great Cliff Morgan, and it was not until 1958 that he played flyhalf for Wales, when it beat Australia by 9–3 at Cardiff. James kicked a dropped goal. Later that season he played centre against France, outside Morgan.

It was as a coach that the quietly-spoken James made his mark on world rugby. Without ever having coached Wales, he was elected to guide the 1971 British Isles team in New Zealand. Under his quiet tutelage the Lions played winning rugby against the All Blacks, and James's innate tactical judgments and expert reading of opposition strengths shot him into world prominence.

His reputation was enhanced in 1972–73, when he coached Llanelli to its famous win over the All Blacks. He was also the guiding hand behind the Barbarians club's fortunes against the All Blacks in the final game of that same tour — a game said by many to be the greatest game ever played. James later coached with considerable success in Italy, where his influence on the players at the Rovigo club was said to be enormous.

Personal differences between James and some members of the Welsh Rugby Union meant that he never coached the national team, although at the time he was clearly the best candidate for the job.

After his spell of coaching he turned to writing and broadcasting, where he proved to be very successful, with a turn of phrase that said much for his intellect and rugby wisdom. He wrote several coaching and historical manuals on the game and was an expert interpreter of rugby on television and radio.

James was an ardent Welsh nationalist who turned down an OBE after the Lions tour of New Zealand. He spoke Welsh fluently and encouraged others to do the same.

Carwyn James collapsed and died in the Netherlands in 1983, and was deeply mourned by his friends and colleagues. Many called him a genius of rugby, though it was also said he was a prophet of the game who was never honoured in his own country. The prominent English writer, John Reason, called Carwyn James 'the best coach the world has yet seen'.

JAPAN

The game's strongest ally in the far east, where rugby lies third behind baseball and sumo wrestling in popularity. Nearly 100,000 adults play rugby on winter weekends in Japan, thrashing the few grounds they possess until many of them become devoid of grass.

The Japanese Rugby Union was formed in 1926, but rugby had been played in the country since 1899. Development of the game was slow in the first half of the twentieth century and it was not until the 1950s that Japan made real progress, largely because of Shigeru Konno, a remarkable man who used his impeccable English to close the gap between the rest of the world and the mystical east. *See* KONNO.

Rugby, like everything else in Japan, had been devastated by World War II

and out of the ruins American sports like baseball were encouraged by the American military still living there. Visiting teams came only slowly: Cambridge University in 1952, followed by French, New Zealand and Canadian club or colts teams. None were of test strength.

But the Japanese learned quickly and by the 1960s they were extremely competitive: a number of teams they played could not work out how they had lost to teams of Japanese, who were many kilograms lighter, man for man. At Wellington in 1968 the New Zealand Juniors were trounced 23–19 by All Japan on its first tour of New Zealand; nine of the juniors went on to become senior All Blacks.

In fact the Japanese turned their lack of height and darting speed to their advantage. Bigger men found they could not readily cope with players who were super-quick off the mark and able to slip under their tackles. At lineout time, for instance, rather than throw the ball high to lineout jumpers they threw the ball low to kneecap height. They had other tricks as well, such as short lineouts or fast put-ins.

Of course trickery can only last so long, and soon the world worked out the Japanese ways. Since the 1970s they have struggled to keep up with the big, faster, modern forward packs.

At the World Cup in 1987, Japan played its traditional game of fast hands and fast movement, but lost all

of its games. In the end it had no counter for consistent battering from bigger men who could control the ball. The 1987 All Blacks beat All Japan 106–4 in a game in Tokyo which 'Shiggy' Konno, by then chairman and 'Mr Rugby' of Japan, called a 'disgrace' to their rugby honour. It was, in fact, a superb performance by the New Zealand team, one which would have comfortably beaten most teams in the world.

On May 28 1989 Japan scored its first win over a major rugby-playing nation. It beat Scotland 28–24 amid great celebrations. The Japanese win was described by a Tokyo news agency as a 'fast and furious display of open rugby', yet the same game was reported by one Scottish newsman as 'negative rugby that cannot have helped to benefit the game in Japan'. The local team was jubilant, and maybe the Scots

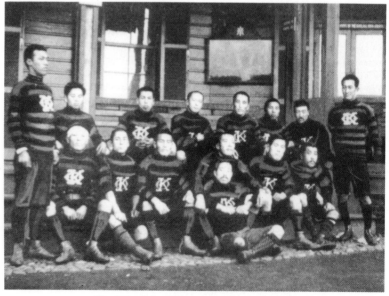

The Keiogijuku University rugby team, 1903.

were a trifle bitter at having to play the 'test' without nine players who were on duty in Australia with the British Isles.

The Japanese have been the regular giants at the biennial Asian rugby championship and have won it eight out of the 12 times it has been contested. It is true that Korea has won four of the last five championships, but Japan has never been worse than second in any of the tournaments.

In the build-up to the 1991 Rugby World Cup, Japan showed the benefit of its years of association with the best of world rugby. The team that had done so well against Scotland was retained for the Asian-Pacific qualifying series and went into serious training. The benefits were well worthwhile: Japan beat Tonga, which had performed so well at the 1987 cup, and Korea, which had lately been its nemesis. Despite a loss to Western Samoa the two victories gave Japan a passage into the 1991 finals group with Scotland, Ireland and Zimbabwe.

Seiji Hirao, Japan's captain in 1990, is a recognised and acclaimed figure. He is a gifted and sharp midfield player who made his national debut at 19; eight years later had accumulated 22 caps.

'Demi' Sakata was the star wing of the 1960s. He was sharp and elusive and his four tries in the famous rout of the New Zealand Juniors in 1968 gained him great respect in New Zealand. He later returned to live there for a time and played for the top provincial side, Canterbury.

Tadayuki Ito was another star wing. He was strong and reliable and is best remembered in Britain for two dynamic tries scored at Cardiff against the Welsh XV in 1973. He gained 19 Japanese caps.

In the forwards, Hiroshi Ogasawara was a powerful and gutsy lock in the late 1960s and early 1970s. He won 24 caps and made a number of overseas tours, including two to New Zealand. More recently, Atsushi Oyagi and Toshi Hayashi have both benefited from the trend for players to spend time in other countries playing the game: Oyagi played in New Zealand for a time, and Hayashi studied and played in England.

Tetsunosuke Ohnishi was a highly successful and charismatic coach. He was with the All Japan team in New

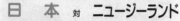

Zealand, and the team which nearly toppled England, losing only 3–6, in 1971 in Tokyo.

Footnote: Is Japan the only country in world rugby which has scored 100 points in a game and conceded 100 points in another game? In 1974, while on tour in Sri Lanka, Japan battered a Country XV by 122–0, but, as earlier mentioned, the New Zealand All Blacks turned the tables and beat All Japan by 106–4 in 1987.

JARDEN, RON
Wellington and New Zealand
16 internationals for N. Zealand 1951–56

In his time Jarden was one of New Zealand's best-known players. A speedy wing and a prolific points-scorer, he made his debut for New Zealand on the tour of Australia in 1951 and also toured with Bob Stuart's All Blacks to Britain and France in 1953–54. By 1956 he was respected world-wide as a left wing who was just about unstoppable in full flight. He specialised in a high centering kick for which several of his team-mates would surge down the centre of the field in anticipation. His left-footed goal-kicking was generally dependable.

In 1956 Jarden was a key figure in the dramatic All Blacks-Springboks test series. He scored a runaway try in the first test at Dunedin and a try in the third test at Christchurch. In the fourth and final test at Auckland, with the series at stake, Jarden left the field suffering from a serious arm in-

jury, but returned as an extra full-back, and played on bravely to assist his team to its first series victory over South Africa.

Jarden ended the series a hero, but apart from one or two club games and one first-class match in 1957, he never played at any level again. He retired at 26, an age many said was too young, but a move which he himself never regretted.

His career total of 145 tries remained a New Zealand record for nearly 30 years. In one game in Australia in 1951 he scored 38 points, then a record for one player for the All Blacks. He is still regarded by many as the best left wing New Zealand ever had.

Later in life he represented New Zealand at yachting in the Admiral's Cup at Cowes in 1975. He also built a successful business career in invest-

Ron Jarden

ments and broadcasting. He died suddenly, aged 47, in 1977.

JARRETT, KEITH
Newport and Wales
10 internationals for Wales 1967–69

Keith Jarrett gained fame throughout the rugby world when he scored 19 points on his international debut before he had even turned 19.

One month before his 19th birthday and only four months out of school, Jarrett played at fullback for Wales against England at Cardiff in April 1967. His selection was seen as a desperate gamble by the Welsh selectors, as their team had lost all four previous internationals that season.

Jarrett's debut game was a thrilling affair in which all sorts of records were set. Wales won by 34–21 and Jarrett's total of points was made up of five conversions, two penalties and a try (for which he ran 50 metres to score under the posts).

His total was then a world record for a player in his first international. It also equalled the record for points in an international by a Welsh player. Jack Bancroft had scored 19 points for Wales against France in 1910; Phil Bennett scored 19 in 1976, but Paul Thorburn set a new mark of 21 points when Wales awarded caps against the Barbarians in 1990.

Jarrett became an instant star. He told the delightful story of the end of his great day. Wanting to return to his home town of Newport later on that night, he went to the Cardiff bus station, only to find that the last bus had already departed. A bus inspector, heading for home at the end of his shift, recognised that afternoon's star player. So a double-decker bus was taken out of the yard and Jarrett rode home on his own in style!

In 1968 Jarrett made the Lions team that toured South Africa, but because of a shoulder injury he played only five games. He toured to New Zealand with Wales in 1969.

Jarrett made just the one famous appearance for his country at fullback. In September 1969, when he had established himself as a permanent centre three-quarter and had played 10 times for Wales, he shocked the Welsh rugby world by 'going north', signing for the rugby league club, Barrow, for a record fee of £14,000. The officials of

Keith Jarrett, wearing the colours of Newport.

his new game obviously had confidence in his talents: they picked him to play for Wales even before he had played one match of rugby league.

Jarrett had only a short career in rugby union, but in that time made a memorable mark on the game. Sadly for him, his career in rugby league was also not a long one. He retired at an early age after suffering from an internal haemorrhage which threatened his life.

JAUREGUY, ADOLPHE
Racing Club, Toulouse and France
31 internationals for France 1920–1929

A dashing wing who was one of France's outstanding backs in the 1920s, Jaureguy played in France's first international after World War I, against Scotland in Paris. He played in the 1924 Olympic Games final, winning a silver medal.

He formed a powerful three-quarter combination with René Crabos, a clubmate from the Racing Club de France. Crabos later became the president of the French Rugby Federation, and Jaureguy a deputy president. Jaureguy was also the assistant manager of the French team which toured Argentina in 1949.

His older brother, Pierre, was also a French international.

JEEPS, DICKIE
Northampton and England
24 internationals for England 1956–62
13 internationals for British Isles 1955–62

Dickie Jeeps was a resilient and powerful halfback who hailed from Cambridge but played most of his senior rugby at Northampton. He made his international debut, not for England but for the British Isles, in one of rugby's outstanding test matches – the first test between the Lions and the Springboks in 1955. Jeeps emerged from the game, played at Ellis Park in Johannesburg and won 23–22 by the Lions, as a true international, and he retained his place as halfback throughout the series. The other two halfbacks on the tour, Johnnie Williams (England) and Trevor Lloyd (Wales), were internationals but had only seven caps between them.

On his return home from South Africa, the England selectors were keen to try Jeeps for their own team and he made his debut for England against Wales at Twickenham early in 1956. However, he was one of three players dropped after the game was lost.

It was not until the next season, in 1957, that Jeeps established himself as an England regular. That year England won its first Grand Slam in 29 years and he was a vital part of the unit, always willing to take on the opposition loose forwards yet never willing to distribute 'bad ball' to his backs.

He was a first choice for the 1959 Lions tour of New Zealand and Australia, where he played the first five tests on tour (two against Australia, three against New Zealand) before a hip injury put him out of the fourth test at Auckland.

Jeeps's strength and toughness earned him considerable praise in New Zealand. Prominent writer Terry McLean called his 'reckless courage [a combination of] Horatius, Wild Bill Hickok and the boy who stood on the burning deck whence all around had fled'.

Jeeps took over the England captaincy in 1960 and kept it until 1962. He toured to South Africa with the 1962 Lions team, again playing in all four test matches. At the end of the tour, Jeeps announced his retirement and resumed working full time at his fruit farm business near Cambridge.

Dicky Jeeps, a skilful and totally committed England halfback.

His commitment to rugby and sport was confirmed when he quickly became an England selector, holding that position for the years 1965–71. Later he had a successful, if controversial, sojourn as chairman of England's Sports Council. He was president of the Rugby Football Union in 1976–77.

JEFFREY, JOHN
Newport and Wales
1 international for Wales 1967

A player who throughout his playing career bore the stigma of a single mistake made in one game.

John Jeffrey was a 22-year-old student who, in 1967, was selected for the first time to play for Wales in an important game against New Zealand.

Sadly for Jeffrey he made a mistake. Early in the second half of a tension-filled game the All Blacks took a shot at goal into a howling Cardiff wind. As the kick came down short of the posts, young Jeffrey kept his appointment with destiny. He caught the ball but then flung an erratic pass over his head as the All Black tacklers stormed down on him. The ball flew to open ground and a New Zealander, Bill Davis, following up quickly, dived on it to score.

Wales lost the game 6–13 and the Welsh selectors knew who to make their scapegoat. They dropped Jeffrey from their team and he was never asked to play for Wales in an international again.

Years later there were claims that Jeffrey's play as a No. 8 was never realistically assessed; many lesser players were given much better chances to prove themselves in the international arena. But it is not widely remembered that Jeffrey toured Argentina with the Welsh team in 1968. He also played for the Barbarians on tour in South Africa in 1969 and for them against South Africa at Cardiff in January 1970.

Jeffrey's inclusion here is, perhaps, a reminder that the vagaries of selectorial whim and hasty judgments both on and off the field can make or break a rugby player, no matter how good he might be.

JEFFREY, JOHN
Kelso and Scotland
35 internationals for Scotland 1984–91

A distinctive nickname, the 'White Shark', sums up this aggressive and stalwart Scottish and British Isles flanker. His play on the side of the scrum in Scottish teams of the 1980s earned him high regard all over the rugby world.

He first came into the national side for the game against the Grand Slam-winning Australian touring team in 1984. It took two years for him to become a regular in the Scottish pack, but by 1987 and the first World Cup he was a vital member of it.

In 1989 Jeffrey toured Australia with the British Isles, but did not play any of the test matches. In 1990 he played superbly in all the matches of Scotland's Grand Slam and he also toured New Zealand.

JOHN, BARRY
Llanelli, Cardiff and Wales
25 internationals for Wales 1966–72
5 internationals for British Isles 1968–71

One of the great players of world rugby, Barry John was an elusive and stylish

John Jeffrey (Scotland) fends off a Canterbury player, 1990.

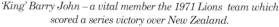

'King' Barry John – a vital member the 1971 Lions team which scored a series victory over New Zealand.

Jean-Luc Joinel

flyhalf who always had time to achieve in an instant what lesser lights would get caught doing. He was a exciting player to watch, as his laconic exterior belied an explosive and slippery running technique. As a tactical kicker he was capable of ruining the playing careers of many hapless opponents, such was the accuracy of his placement. He was also an expert at drop-kicking.

At the peak of Barry John's career, television took him into every living room in Britain. His matchless performances, especially for the British Isles in New Zealand in 1971, made him one of rugby's first TV superstars. He was nicknamed 'King' John.

Barry John came from Gwendraeth Grammar School and Cefneithin, two great nurseries of Welsh rugby. He made his first-class debut for the Llanelli club, but later made a timely move to Cardiff. There he teamed up with Gareth Edwards and, with only a few hitches, the two went on to dominate Welsh tactical planning for years.

Their partnership is widely regarded as one of rugby's great combinations.

John made his international debut against Australia in 1966, in combination with scrumhalf Allan Lewis. Wales lost. Two months later, with John playing in combination with Billy Hullin, there was another loss for Wales. The selectors were obviously not impressed and dropped John for the rest of the season. Meantime, Gareth Edwards was introduced to partner Dai Watkins in the last two internationals of that season.

It was not until 1967 that John and Edwards, the Cardiff club pair, played together for Wales. Their first outing was against New Zealand, but again it was another loss for the scarlets. In all that season Wales won only one game, but Barry John and Gareth Edwards impressed the Lions selectors enough for them both to be included in the 1968 British Isles team to tour South Africa. Sadly injury prevented John from being a success; he was invalided

out of the tour after breaking a shoulder in the first test.

Still, the year had seen the consolidation of the John–Edwards partnership as one worth sticking with. They went on to play 28 internationals together (23 for Wales and five for the Lions).

After winning the Five Nations championship in 1968–69, Wales went to Australia and New Zealand where the team was able to win only one test match, in Sydney. New Zealand beat Wales comprehensively in two tests.

While he played soundly on that tour, Barry John's greatest days in rugby were from late in 1970 through to early 1972, when his consummate skills helped the Lions and Welsh teams he played in to lose only one test match out of 10.

Those were the days when extensive television coverage of a tour was just becoming a reality. In New Zealand in 1971, as John whipped his way through New Zealand defenders, drop-kicked goals from all over the field, and place-kicked marvellously, the highlights of his and the Lions team's winning action were seen by a much wider audience. John and the team that beat New Zealand in 1971 came home famous men.

In New Zealand John scored 180 points on tour, more than 100 better than any British tourist had ever done before. His coach, Carwyn James, allowed full rein to his talents – and the whole team covered for the deficiencies that did exist in his game (John was not a great tackler or faller on the ball). As a result Barry John eluded just about every defender New Zealand could field, scoring some sensational tries.

His cross-field kicking also spelt the end of the long career of New Zealand's tough fullback, Fergie McCormick. At Dunedin in the first test, John angled so many kicks away from the grasp of the veteran McCormick that the Lions won the test and McCormick was dropped forever by the All Black selectors.

Barry John retired at the end of the 1971–72 season, having again assisted Wales to an unbeaten record. In his last Five Nations series, his tally of points was 35, a new Welsh record (from only three games). His final to-tal of 90 points in his test career was also a Welsh record, though it has since been passed.

John was only 27 when he retired. Many said that he should have carried on, but he could not be persuaded. He gave the game away when he was at his best, and for Barry John that was setting a standard that has rarely been approached, before or since.

JOHN PLAYER SPECIAL CUP
The long-standing, annual club knock-out in England. The sudden-death nature of this series has made it England's most exciting club event. In essence it is the FA Cup of English rugby.

The competition was begun in 1971–72, and first won by Gloucester. The John Player sponsorship began in 1975–76 and the cash injection enabled promotional lustre to be added to the event.

In the early years crowds were small and Twickenham seemed not quite the place to hold the final. But in 1987 a record crowd of 35,000 turned up at Twickenham to see Bath beat Wasps 19–12. By then the event had confirmed its status as the major club final in England.

The deal involving John Player as sponsor expired after the 1988 final and, in the years that followed, Pilkington Glass took over as sponsor of the (renamed) RFU Club Knock-out series.

JOHNSON, PETER
New South Wales and Australia
42 internationals for Australia 1959–72

Peter Johnson held the record for 15 years as Australia's most-capped player. A hooker, he came into the Australian team in 1958 on the tour of New Zealand, for which he was understudy to Ron Meadows. Johnson made his test debut in 1959, when he played in two tests against Ronnie Dawson's Lions team. From then, he made the Australian hooker's jersey his own, until the end of the tour of France in 1971–72. He was captain of Australia on the short tour of Ireland and Scotland in 1968.

Johnson's total of 42 caps went unchallenged until 1987, when it was surpassed by flanker Simon Poidevin. At one point Johnson played a record 37 consecutive internationals for the Wallabies.

Peter Johnson, whose brother Brian was an Australian international before him, was a rugged forward and strong scrummager, who played loyally for the Australians in the years when winning games were not easy for them, the Wallabies winning only 13 internationals during this period. Several of those victories were significant: the two test wins over South Africa in 1963 and 1965; a shock victory over New Zealand in the third test in Wellington in 1964; wins over both Wales and England on tour in 1966–67; and an 11–10 win over France in Sydney in 1968, when Johnson was captain.

After his retirement, Johnson gained a reputation as a witty writer, after-dinner speaker and commentator about the game.

JOINEL, JEAN-LUC
Brive and France
51 internationals for France 1977–87

A brilliant French flanker or No. 8 from the Brive club, Joinel was first called into the French XV for its test series against New Zealand in 1977. He became a polished loose forward in the powerful French team of the late 1970s and early 80s. He was a solid worker in tight play and could shine in the open, relishing running with the ball in hand.

It was bad luck for Joinel, after being a solid force in the French team for so many years, that his international career seemed to be almost over when the 1987 Rugby World Cup was staged in New Zealand. He made the squad to tour, but out of the six games the Tricolours played in the series, he appeared in only one, against Zimbabwe. Younger men were preferred by coach Jacques Fouroux.

Joinel made many tours, including four to New Zealand, where his reputation as a fine forward became as well established as it was in Europe.

JONES, ALAN
He was always in the news, either as a top rugby union coach, rugby league coach or as a businessman and radio broadcaster. He was one of Australia's most controversial sporting figures of the 1980s and always commanded headlines. One writer called him 'one of Australia's flashiest achievers'.

Alan Jones was a product of Darling Downs in Queensland. In a matter of

RFU club competition		
1972	Gloucester 17	Moseley 6
1973	Coventry 27	Bristol 15
1974	Coventry 26	London Scottish 6
1975	Bedford 28	Rosslyn Park 12

John Player Special Cup		
1976	Gosforth 23	Rosslyn Park 14
1977	Gosforth 27	Waterloo 11
1978	Gloucester 6	Leicester 3
1979	Leicester 15	Moseley 12
1980	Leicester 21	London Irish 9
1981	Leicester 22	Gosforth 15
1982	Gloucester 12	Moseley 12
1983	Bristol 28	Leicester 22
1984	Bath 10	Bristol 9
1985	Bath 24	London Welsh 15
1986	Bath 25	Wasps 17
1987	Bath 19	Wasps 12
1988	Harlequins 28	Bristol 22

Pilkington Cup		
1989	Bath 10	Leicester 6
1990	Bath 48	Gloucester 6

years he rose from being a schoolmaster at a private boys' school, to become a household name in his country. On the way to sporting fame he had been, for a time, an Oxford University student, a Liberal party candidate in a state election, a speechwriter to Australian Prime Minister Malcolm Fraser, the executive director of the New South Wales Employers' Federation and a radio talk show host.

He became Australia's rugby coach in 1984 and quickly established himself as a master motivater. His Wallaby team in Britain that year became known and admired world-wide when it won the Grand Slam against the four home unions. His team also won a three-test series to take the Bledisloe Cup from New Zealand in 1986. In all, he coached his country in 30 tests for 21 wins.

While he was successful, he was also controversial and outspoken. When his team suffered the disappointment of being only fourth at the 1987 World Cup, the long knives came out from the Australian Rugby Union and before the 1988 season he was axed as team coach.

After his demise, Jones continued to have strong public views on the game. In 1990 he rocked the rugby world when he switched codes and became the coach of the Balmain rugby league club in Sydney. Such a decision was typical of Alan Jones: somehow, whatever he did made the news.

JONES, CLIFF
Cardiff and Wales
13 internationals for Wales 1934–38

Cliff Jones rose to become one of the brightest stars of Welsh rugby in the 1930s. Not originally enamoured of the game, his early love of soccer gave him the necessary skills to be both a powerful and deft kicker of the ball. As a flyhalf he was a dazzling runner.

Jones was slightly built and had troubles with injuries, but he rose to captain Wales in 1938. Earlier he had played superbly for Wales in its 13–12 win over the 1935–36 All Blacks.

Playing in the three-quarters that day was Wilfred Wooller, with whom he was often in superb combination for Cardiff, Cambridge University and Wales. Together, the two presented problems to opposition teams for the best part of a decade.

After his playing days were over, Cliff Jones became a Welsh selector and served on the 'Big Five' for 21 years. Then he became a coaching coordinator and in his time greatly assisted Wales in setting up its highly successful squad system for training the national team.

Cliff Jones was a superb president of the Welsh Rugby Union in its centenary season of 1980–81.

JONES, IVOR
Llanelli and Wales
16 internationals for Wales 1924–30
5 internationals for Britain 1930

A working class man from the steelworks of South Wales, Ivor Jones's versatile rugby talent enabled him to see the world at a time when only the wealthy were able to travel.

Jones made his debut for Wales against England in 1924. When that

Ivor Jones

game was lost, as was the next one (Wales conceding eight tries to Scotland), Jones was lost to the Welsh team until 1927. In 1924 he was invited to tour South Africa with the Great Britain team, but he turned the honour down because, as he said, he was 'not ready for it'.

When he returned as a more mature player, Wales quickly made full use of his astute rugby brain. A big man, he was a strong tackler and an excellent and artistic runner. He could also kick goals, totalling more than 1200 points for the Llanelli club, for whom he played from 1922 to 1939. He captained the club for nine years, including in the games against the Maoris (1926), Waratahs (1927), South Africa (1931) and New Zealand (1935).

The 1930 Great Britain team used him to excellent effect while in New Zealand and Australia. On that trip Jones played in five different positions: scrumhalf, fullback, centre three-quarter and wing, as well as his customary role as a loose forward. In one match in Brisbane against an Australian XV he scored 22 points.

Many regarded the quiet Welsh speaker as the star of that team. Long before Barry John, New Zealanders called Ivor Jones the 'King'.

Jones captained his country three times. He was later a Welsh selector, the WRU president in 1968–69, a life member of that union, and a delegate to the International Rugby Board. He was awarded the CBE for his services to the game.

JONES, KEN
Newport and Wales
44 internationals for Wales 1947–57
3 internationals for British Isles 1950

Kenneth J. Jones played for Wales from 1947 to 1957 and was one of the greatest of post-war wings, playing 43 internationals in succession for his country, beating the previous Welsh record of 35 held by Dicky Owen. In all, his final total of 47 caps (including three for the British Isles) was at the time a world record for a rugby individual.

Jones was a superb runner, blessed with speed that took him to the Olympic Games and the Empire Games. (He was a silver medallist for Britain in the 4 x 100 metre relay at the 1948 London Olympics.) Possessing all the good rugby wing's attributes, he soon became noted as the scorer of match-winning tries.

Two of his most famous tries for Wales were scored against New Zealand. At Auckland, on tour with the Lions in 1950, he sprinted 70 metres for a try in the fourth test, chased all the way by New Zealand's sprint champion Peter Henderson – and Jones won the race!

In 1953, in front of a live television audience (the first for a home Welsh game), he picked up a fortuitous bounce from an unorthodox cross-kick taken by Clem Thomas. The bounce put Jones past his famous marker, New Zealand's Ron Jarden, and Jones scored under the posts. The conversion sent the All Blacks tumbling to defeat.

JONES, MICHAEL
Auckland and New Zealand
15 internationals for N. Zealand 1987–90

An unassuming superstar of New Zealand rugby, whose dashing openside flanker's play had much to do with that country's World Cup success. That he was still available for the 1991 World Cup was a tribute to expert surgeons and his own courage and tenacity.

After first playing for Western Samoa against Wales in 1986, Jones made his debut for New Zealand against Italy on the World Cup's opening day. It was a portent of things to come when he scored the first individual try of the series. Four weeks later he scored the first try in the final against France.

In between, the shy Samoan made an extraordinary impact on the hard-nosed rugby world of New Zealand where, traditionally, the fans like their heroes tough and hard – Meads-like in fact. But the studious, quietly-spoken Jones, with his modest expression of his faith in God, won over thousands of hearts. The fact that he preferred not to play on Sundays was understood by the public, for once.

In 1988 Jones's top form continued and he played scorching games against Wales and Australia. However, in 1989, playing in his 13th test at Wellington against Argentina, he twisted a knee so severely that the surgeons' first opinions were that he would never play again.

Jones exercised his amazing calm and determination over a long period

of recuperation, and in 1990 he took his first tentative steps back into rugby saying, 'I don't care if I don't make the All Blacks again, I just thank God I can play.'

Jones returned to the All Blacks, as everybody in New Zealand knew he would, for their tour of France in 1990. There, he showed his form was *almost* as good as it had been in his earlier years. His 15 tests so far – all on the winning side – look set to be added to in the years to come.

JONES, PETER
North Auckland and New Zealand
11 internationals for N. Zealand 1954–60

One of the most popular figures of New Zealand rugby in the 1950s, Peter Jones is also remembered as the man who made a post-victory speech that will never be forgotten in New Zealand.

To opposition sides, Peter Jones was always a problem, whether as a flanker or a No. 8. His strength was enormous and his speed, for so big a man, was formidable. His nickname was 'Tiger'

In spite of injury problems during his career, Jones was selected consistently for the All Blacks from 1953 until 1960. He toured Britain with the 1953–54 New Zealand side and scored 10 tries on the trip. He also toured South Africa in 1960, more regularly playing at lock.

In 1956, injuries at first prevented his playing for New Zealand in its home test series with the Springboks, but he appeared in the third test, which New Zealand won by 17–10 to give it a 2–1 lead in the series before the final test in Auckland.

New Zealand was in a state of feverish excitement in anticipation of a series win over South Africa. In the second spell of the game, in front of a record crowd at Eden Park, a bouncing ball popped into the hands of 'Tiger' Jones and he raced 20 yards for a try which was then, and still is, hailed as 'one of the greatest ever scored by an All Black'. In truth, newsreel films show it as a straight passage to the goal-line for Jones, but it was the effect on the score that endowed it with greatness for the crowd of 61,000 spectators.

When the game ended and the All Blacks had triumphed by 11–5, the crowd began a chant for Jones to speak to them on the public address system.

Not the famous occasion, but someone was brave enough to let Peter Jones at the microphone one more time – this time after his last game for North Auckland.

He made his way into the grandstand, and national radio (there was no television) stayed with the link to hear what he had to say. Jones grabbed the microphone and said 'Ladies and gentlemen, I hope I don't ever have to play in such a tough game again. I'm absolutely buggered!'

In the conservative 1950s, such language on radio was unheard of. Gales of laughter resounded through the nation. The candid expression endeared Peter Jones to the New Zealand public for life – as well as the fact that he had scored the try that clinched the series against the mighty Springboks!

JONES, ROBERT
Swansea and Wales
34 internationals for Wales 1986–91
3 internationals for British Isles 1989

In late 1990 there was a pause in the momentum built up by the Welsh scrumhalf Robert Jones in his rugby career He had set a cracking pace in his early rugby, totalling 32 test caps for Wales in a little over four years. Then in 1990, along came Ron Waldron of Neath as the new Welsh coach and, for the moment at least, there seemed

Robert Jones of Wales

no place in the top Welsh team for the little Swansea scrumhalf.

To observers of the game in Wales, the decision to drop Robert Jones seemed surely to be only a temporary halt to his progress. He was too good a player to leave out, especially as he seemed to be moving inexorably towards the Welsh scrumhalf record of 53 caps, set by the Gareth Edwards.

Jones first made the Welsh team in 1986 and missed only one international match until 1990. He and Jonathan Davies impressed as the shining lights in an otherwise drab Welsh backline scene. The two played 22 internationals together as a halfback pairing.

Jones toured with the 1989 British Isles team to Australia, where he severely tested Nick Farr-Jones in each of the three tests.

Jones, the son-in-law of another great Welsh rugby figure, Clive Rowlands, played superbly for the Barbarians club against Argentina in 1990 at Cardiff Arms Park. It seemed just a matter of time before this grand little scrumhalf would again grace a Welsh XV.

JUNIOR ALL BLACKS

'Junior All Blacks' is a nickname, first used in 1959 in a match against the touring British Isles team in Wellington, for the under-23 national team of New Zealand. Although officially called 'New Zealand Juniors' the public quickly dubbed the team the 'Junior All Blacks.'

The Junior All Blacks became the vehicle for 'senior' All Black players of the future to have their first taste of international play, although it must be said that in their 25-year history the team never beat a major touring side. But there were victories over teams like Tonga, Fiji, Japan and Italy.

By far the greatest day for New Zealand Juniors came in 1973, when they beat the full All Black team 14–10 at Dunedin. Eleven of that side later became All Blacks themselves, including Graham Mourie, who became a New Zealand captain.

In 1984 the NZRFU decided that the category of 'under 23' was too restrictive for the selectors, who had come see the Juniors team as a second XV for New Zealand. So the Juniors were replaced by the 'Emerging Players' team. That was not successful either, lasting only two seasons.

JUNIOR SPRINGBOKS

The Junior Springboks were a team without age restriction, open to those players who had not previously represented a full Springbok team, and so virtually became a second XV of South African rugby.

The Junior Springboks were on the rugby scene much earlier than their New Zealand and Australian counterparts, touring to Argentina in 1932 and 1959 and to Rhodesia in 1950. They struck up a special rapport with Argentine rugby, where on both their tours they played full national XVs. In 1932 the Junior Springboks won by 42–0 and 34–3, and in 1959 by the lesser margins of 14–6 and 20–6, an indication of the steady improvement in Argentine rugby over that time.

The first home match for the Junior Springboks was against the 1955 British Isles touring team. The Lions won by 15–12 at Bloemfontein.

Perhaps the most significant day for the Junior Springboks came in 1958 when they beat France 9–5 at Port Elizabeth. Unfortunately it cannot be remembered as a marvellous occasion for rugby, as rough play spoilt the game and two Junior Springboks, including the captain, Peter Taylor, were carried off the field injured.

In 1965 the Junior Springboks repaid some of the hospitality they had received on the two tours of Argentina, but the 'Pumas' (first called that on this tour) beat the Juniors on Ellis Park on June 19, the same day as the full Springboks were being beaten by Australia in Sydney. South African rugby writers called it the 'black day' of Springbok rugby!

In 1966 the 'Junior Springboks' were replaced by a national under-24 team called the Gazelles. But old habits die hard, and many people still call the team the 'Junior Springboks.'

JUNIOR WALLABIES

The Australian Rugby Football Union fielded 'Junior Wallabies' teams against only two major touring teams: the 1968 All Blacks and the 1971 Springboks.

Their first match was in 1968 at Norwood Oval in Adelaide, when they lost to New Zealand by 3–43. That Junior Wallaby team was not restricted in any way by age and was simply the best 15 uncapped players of the time. Thirteen members of the team went on to play at international level.

The Junior Wallabies played South Africa, also without age restriction, in Brisbane in 1971. The star of the team was future international Russell Fairfax, but he could not stop the Springboks going to a 31–12 win. Since then Junior Wallabies have virtually disappeared from Australian rugby.

The first Rugby World Cup – from beginning to end.
Top: A pose before the first game, New Zealand v Italy,
kicks off in Auckland. Left to right: New Zealand
captain David Kirk; Scottish touch judge, Jim Fleming;
referee, Bob Fordham of Australia; touch judge, Kerry
Fitzgerald, Australia; and Italian captain, Marzio
Innocenti.
Left: Victorious captain, David Kirk of New Zealand,
holds the prized Webb Ellis trophy and, above, Zinzan
Brooke and John Kirwan take part in rather less formal
celebrations below the grandstand! Peter Bush

A Fijian team huddle before a 1987 World Cup game.
Right: Bearded Fijian winger Tomasi Cama clears out from the Welsh defence to cross the line for a try. Peter Bush

K

KAVANAGH, RONNIE
University College Dublin, Wanderers
and Ireland
35 internationals for Ireland 1953–62

An Irish loose forward who, a former
captain once said, was 'the toughest
man pound for pound' he had ever
seen in rugby. Ronnie Kavanagh was
in the Irish team over 10 seasons and,
when he ended his international days,
the most-capped Irish forward ever.
His tally of 35 caps bettered the 30
appearances made by both George
Hamlet and 'Jammie' Clinch.

Kavanagh was always a superbly fit
and dedicated player and his supporters were very unhappy when he was
passed over for selection for both the
1955 and 1959 British Isles teams.

His brother Paddy was also an Irish
international (two matches 1952, 1955)
and both played water polo for Ireland
as well.

KEANE, MOSS
Lansdowne and Ireland
51 internationals for Ireland 1974–84
1 international for the British Isles 1977

A dedicated player who became the
third forward from Ireland to reach 50
international appearances. Keane was
never a great lineout leaper or scrummager or runner in the open. Rather
he played the game in the dark depths
of rucks and mauls, where he was as
good a grafter as the game has seen.
For heart and pride, and the desire to
do his utmost for Ireland, he could not
be bettered.

Maurice Ignatius Keane first played
for Ireland in 1974 in a 6–9 loss to
France, but wins in two other matches
that season gave Ireland the Five Nations title. In Keane's fourth international season for Ireland, he made
the British Isles team to tour New
Zealand, after one of the team's originals, Geoff Wheel, had to withdraw on
medical advice.

Keane was in the Irish team that
won the Five Nations championship in
1982 and in the one that shared the
title with France in 1983. The other
years of his international career were

lean: in 52 internationals Keane was
only in the winning team 17 times.

Keane had a delightful personality
and a wicked sense of humour and
many stories, true, exaggerated or
otherwise, are still told about him.

In the 1978 New Zealand v Ireland
match at Dublin, the Irish were being
well beaten in the lineouts, where
Keane was marking the All Black giant Andy Haden. The only chance
Ireland had to win lineout ball was
with their complicated lineout calls,
which none of the New Zealanders
could decipher. The All Blacks were
helped on one occasion when the
lineout call went out from the Irish
halfback and they heard Keane cry,
'Oh God no, not to me again'!

Moss Keane was the first Gaelic
footballer to play rugby union for Ireland after eligibility rules were
changed. He remained an enormously
popular figure in Ireland after his retirement.

KELLEHER, KEVIN
An Irishman and one of rugby's best
performed referees, in charge of 23
internationals from 1960 to 1971.
Kelleher had a very successful career
as a referee, but he is largely remembered for being the man who sent Colin
Meads off at Murrayfield during the
Scotland v New Zealand match in 1967.

Kelleher ruled that Meads's lung-
ing kick at a loose bouncing ball near
the Scottish flyhalf, David Chisholm,

Moss Keane, backed up by Mick Quinn.

was dangerous and, having previously issued a warning in the vigorous encounter, he dismissed Meads. As the New Zealander was arguably the world's most famous player at the time, the sending-off created a storm.

Ironically, Meads and Kelleher became friends and for many years exchanged Christmas cards. Kelleher was flown to New Zealand in 1988 to appear on the TV show 'This is Your Life – Colin Meads.'

Although New Zealanders poured scorn on Kelleher as a referee, they tended to overlook his exceptional record with the whistle. Kelleher's first international was Wales v Scotland in 1960, and his last was France v Scotland in 1971.

At the end of 1990 his total of 23 appearances as a test referee had been equalled by two others, Gwynne Walters and Clive Norling.

KENNEDY, KEN

Queen's University, Belfast, London
  Irish and Ireland
45 internationals for Ireland 1965–75
4 internationals for British Isles 1966

A doctor who became the world's highest-capped hooker, Ken Kennedy had 11 seasons in the Irish scrum. He became a member of two Lions teams, in 1966 and 1974 – missing selection in the two tours between those dates.

In 1968 he was injured and therefore unavailable for the Lions tour of South Africa. John Pullin of England was one of those who went in his place. Pullin was again selected to tour with the Lions in 1971, but in a surprise move Kennedy was recalled for the 1974 tour.

Kennedy was an enthusiastic player who was a great talker on the field. He also tended to the medical needs of any injured player in the game, no matter which side he was on.

When he played for Ireland against New Zealand in 1974, he passed Australian Peter Johnson's total of 42 as the most-capped hooker in world rugby. His final tally of 49 caps was equalled by John Pullin in 1976, a total that was not beaten until Scotland's Colin Deans reached 50 during the World Cup in 1987.

KENYA

The first recorded game of rugby in Kenya was in 1909, when the Settlers played the Officials. The union was formed in 1921, although the first game under its auspices was not until 1923.

Nairobi has always been the main rugby centre in Kenya. The Nairobi District championship, begun in 1925, is the country's oldest competition.

In 1953 the Rugby Union of East Africa was formed, which took in the districts of Uganda and Tanganyika and the coastal regions as well as Kenyan provinces. Teams from the RUEA were called the 'Tuskers', almost all of whom were Kenyan players. The union hosted several touring teams such as the British Isles in 1955, the Springboks in 1960, and Wales in 1964. One of its best wins was in 1979 when it beat Zambia.

Eventually the East African union broke up into Uganda and Tanzania. In Uganda, progress in rugby, as in every other sphere of that country's development, was seriously impeded as a result of the atrocities of Idi Amin. So Kenya pushed forward on its own, helped of course by rugby's popularity with the British colonial community.

Contact with the many British clubs (Barbarians, Blackheath, Wasps and Harlequins, to name a few) was suspended in 1974 for five years because of British rugby's support for sporting contact with South Africa.

Kenyan rugby is based on a solid administration and facilities are generally excellent. The game was originally dominated by expatriate white players, but the situation has changed in modern times. Black Kenyans made the national team for the first time in 1980 and now 70 to 80 per cent of the players in Nairobi are black. All the Kenyan squad invited to the 1986 Hong Kong sevens were black Kenyans, including the country's most famous rugby man, Jackson Omaido.

This was Kenya's first introduction to the world rugby scene, and the tries the Kenyans scored against mighty Australia in the Hong Kong event brought the watching crowds to their feet. Sadly, after being invited to the same event in 1987, Kenya withdrew in protest at members of the unauthorised 'Cavaliers' team playing for New Zealand. Four years later it had not been reinvited to participate at the Hong Kong tournament.

Jackson Omaido, a centre, played consistently for Kenya for nearly 15 years, captaining every representative or national team that played inside Kenya or beyond. He was the country's first rugby hero: a pacy runner with a devastating tackle and a sure boot.

The main clubs in Nairobi are the Nondescripts ('Nondies'), Impala, and the Kenya Harlequins. Several teams have fearsome nicknames like the 'Mean Machine' (Nairobi Uni.) and 'Black Blood' (Kenyatta Uni.).

These days, Kenya's main rivals are Zimbabwe and Zambia.

KERSHAW, CYRIL

Blackheath and England
16 internationals for England 1920–23

Cyril Kershaw was a brilliant halfback for England, who is especially remembered for his combination with his regular flyhalf W.J.A. ('Dave') Davies. The two played together in 14 internationals and never lost.

Kershaw (nicknamed 'K') was, like Davies, a superb all-round sportsman. He represented his country at fencing at the 1920 Olympic Games and also played hockey and cricket. Both were naval officers and saw distinguished service in two world wars.

An attacking halfback in the brilliant England team of that era, Kershaw specialised in running to link with his loose forwards Voyce, Conway and Wakefield. His partner Davies once said that he doubted if he ever saw Kershaw kick the ball more than a dozen times in the four seasons they played for England together. Kershaw's passing was also swift and sure. He often asked Davies to stand over 20 yards away and the two spent hours together every week practising their combination. There is little doubt that England's record of international success in that time was due in no small part to the efficiency and brilliance of Davies and 'K'.

KIERNAN, TOM

University College, Cork, Cork Constitution and Ireland
54 internationals for Ireland 1960–73
5 internationals for British Isles 1962–68

A rock steady fullback for Ireland and the Lions, who was also a fine leader and later a coach of his country, Kiernan was picked to play for Ireland in 1960 before he had played in the fullback position at a senior level – before that he had been a centre.

'The best pair of halfbacks England ever had.' Kershaw passes to 'Dave' Davies, 1921.

When the Irish selectors took a gamble and put him in the national team they never regretted their decision, for he went on to establish himself as a solid, dependable player, who kicked well, tackled strongly and frequently added plenty of thrust to counter-attacks.

In Kiernan's first season Ireland did not win one game in the Five Nations championship of 1960. In 1961 there were more lean times, Ireland winning only once (against England) and losing its only test in South Africa. However, Kiernan played strongly, scoring 38 of the team's 59 points. It was that form that won him a place in the Lions team for South Africa in 1962.

Kiernan returned to South Africa in 1968, this time as captain of the Lions. His team did not win a test in the series, but Kiernan was a popular leader and scored well himself on the tour, landing 17 points in the first test and 35 in the four test series, then a British record. The only other points in the series came from a try by Willie John McBride in the first test.

He continued to represent Ireland until 1973, earning 54 caps, making him Ireland's most-capped fullback. He also captained the team 24 times, an Irish record. In his last match he finished with a flourish, scoring a try in the corner at Murrayfield against Scotland. His 158 career points was also an Irish record.

Kiernan continued a strong relationship with the game after his playing days were over. He became the Munster branch president and scored a magnificent coup for Irish rugby by coaching Munster to victory over the 1978 All Blacks.

When he became Ireland's coach in 1980–81, he took it to South Africa in 1981, and his teams later won the Five Nations championship in 1982 and shared it with France in 1983.

Kiernan is from a family that has built a significant record in international rugby. The various branches (uncles, cousins and nephews) have between them totalled over 150 international appearances for Ireland. Relations who have regularly represented the emerald greens are Michael Lane, Gerry Reidy, Noel Murphy (snr), Noel Murphy (jnr), and Michael Kiernan.

KIERNAN, MICHAEL
Dolphin, Lansdowne and Ireland
43 internationals for Ireland 1982–91
3 internationals for British Isles 1983

A member of the famous Munster rugby family, an intelligent centre and wing, and a superb goal-kicker, Michael Kiernan became Ireland's record test match points-scorer. By the end of 1990 his total of points was heading towards double the previous record his team-mate Ollie Campbell had set and nearly twice as many as his famous uncle, Tom Kiernan, had set in his games for Ireland.

Kiernan's first appearance for Ireland was on the 1981 tour of South Africa, but he did not play in a test match there. His first cap came in 1982, and he was chosen only one season later for the 1983 Lions in New Zealand. He appeared in three of the test matches as a centre.

By 1988–89 the Irish selectors were experimenting with him as a wing. Kiernan was never a speedster but his timing and solidity were a vital part of the Irish team.

Having Ollie Campbell as a team-mate meant Kiernan did not kick his first goal in an international until his 11th test match. Thereafter he regularly kicked for his country and at the end of the 1990–91 season he had reached 308 points, a total which had been passed only by Hugo Porta, Michael Lynagh, Grant Fox, Andy Irvine and Gavin Hastings.

KING COUNTRY RFU
The rugby union from the central North Island of New Zealand, founded in 1922, which gave the world Colin Meads, one of the great figures of the game. Its headquarters are in Taumarunui, a small town that serves the timber and farming communities in the area.

King Country's first All Black was Bill Phillips, who was a wing in the second test of the 1937 series with South Africa. King Country scored its first win over a full overseas touring team in 1957, when it beat Fiji 26–14.

But it was the Meads brothers, Colin and Stanley, who gave King Country a high profile in the 1960s. Together they raised the standard of performance of King Country's representative team to point where, in 1965, it was the only representative team in New Zealand with an unbeaten record.

King Country rugby had its greatest day in 1966 when it supplied 12 of the combined Wanganui-King Country team to play the British Isles team at Spriggens Park in Wanganui. The Meads brothers completely outplayed the midweek Lions XV and the game was won for the home team 12–6. The 1977 Lions had their revenge on the same combined team by beating it by 60–9 – a game that is remembered for Andy Irvine scoring five tries from fullback, a world record.

When King Country hosted Auckland in 1988 for the first 'away' Ranfurly Shield defence for 62 years, a small pig wandered on to the field. The animal grazed on one side of the field for most of the second half and has gone down in local history as an entirely appropriate rural supporter of King Country rugby.

KING'S CUP

Arguably the most famous tournament ever played by servicemen was for the King's Cup. In 1919, after the Armistice, many troops from the then British Empire were waiting to be transported home. While they waited in camps and bases throughout Britain, a rugby tournament was organised. King George V presented a trophy which bore his name, for the winning team.

The entrants were Royal Air Force, Mother Country, Australian Imperial Forces, Canadian Expeditionary Force, South African Forces and New Zealand Army. The New Zealanders beat Mother Country 9–3 in the final in front of the King at Twickenham.

KIRK, DAVID

Otago, Auckland and New Zealand
17 internationals for N. Zealand 1983–87

The first man to hold aloft the Rugby World Cup as its winning captain, David Kirk had a short but distinguished career for New Zealand before retiring from international rugby when he took up a Rhodes Scholarship at Oxford.

A halfback, Kirk first played for New Zealand in 1983 on the short tour of England and Scotland. He also toured to Australia and later to Fiji in 1984. On all those tours he was the second string halfback behind Andy Donald of Wanganui. In 1985 Kirk made his international debut against England at Christchurch. He was later in the New Zealand team chosen to tour to South Africa: when an injunction was taken out against the tour, the team went to Argentina instead.

When the 1986 rebel tour of South Africa was mooted by some of the disgruntled All Blacks of 1985, David Kirk won equal amounts of praise and scorn for electing to stay out of the team. The Cavaliers toured South Africa without permission and were banned for two tests on their return to New Zealand. Kirk was made captain of the All Black team chosen from the remainder of players who had stayed at home. Known as the 'Baby All

Blacks', they gained instant acclaim by beating France by 18–9 at Lancaster Park. Kirk was later captain against Australia but New Zealand lost the test series by 1–2. Kirk was then displaced by the Canterbury flanker, Jock Hobbs, as captain for the 1986 tour of France.

By 1987 there was much conjecture as to who would lead New Zealand in the World Cup series. Hobbs was available, as were Kirk and Andy Dalton, the hooker, who had missed most of the previous year with a broken jaw. In the end, injuries gave David Kirk a lucky break. Hobbs was forced into early retirement because of recurring concussion and Dalton pulled a hamstring muscle just before the first game of the cup series.

Even though many New Zealanders saw Kirk as third choice, he was superb as captain, silencing those critics who had called for his permanent replacement after the 1986 series loss to Australia. Kirk's play as a halfback rose too. He was never one of the great passers of the ball but his running became courageous and his leadership positive and alert. Dalton's leg injury and the form of Sean Fitzpatrick prevented his return as hooker or captain, so in the World Cup final against France, David Kirk had the honour of leading New Zealand.

It was his greatest day in rugby. He scored a try himself in the second half and moments later he sprinted from a maul to set up another for his right wing, John Kirwan. When New Zealand won by 29–9, Kirk was mobbed by the crowds as he climbed into the grandstand to be presented with the cup. The picture of him holding the World Cup high became one of the most familiar images of the game that year.

David Kirk was much more than just a rugby player. He looked absurdly young to be a doctor of medicine and conveyed at all times a boyish enthusiasm, with a grin that endeared him to millions and helped in no small way to rebuild the image of the game in New Zealand, which had become tarnished after the Cavaliers' opportunistic trip to South Africa. In the language of 1987, he was the perfect role model for rugby.

Kirk was also a most articulate young man, able to handle the media perhaps better than any other New

Zealand captain, and a man of great presence. As he held aloft the World Cup for the whole world to see, he called forward the original and popular All Black captain Andy Dalton to hold the cup as well. The gesture was greatly appreciated by the public of New Zealand.

David Kirk took up a Rhodes Scholarship at Worcester College in Oxford 1987. He appeared for Oxford University against Cambridge at Twickenham in 1987 and 1988.

KIRKPATRICK, IAN

Poverty Bay and New Zealand
39 internationals for N. Zealand 1967–77

Ian Kirkpatrick was a brilliant New Zealand player who became his country's most capped international flanker, playing 113 games for his country in all matches. Known to all as 'Kirky', he played first for New Zealand on their 1967 tour of Britain and France. At the beginning of his career he was competing for a place in test teams with great men like Waka Nathan and Kel Tremain, and played in major games only when injuries allowed him a place. His test debut was against France at Paris, when neither Nathan nor Tremain could play.

Kirkpatrick first marked himself as a regular test player when he replaced his captain, Brian Lochore, in the first test of 1968 against Australia at Sydney. Kirkpatrick, unaccustomed to the No. 8 position, got straight into the action and scored three tries before the game had ended. Thereafter he was included in every All Black test team for the next nine seasons – a remarkable run of 38 tests in a row. He also picked up tries in internationals at a steady rate. His final tally was 16, at the time the best by a New Zealand test player.

His most famous try was against the British Isles at Christchurch in the second test in 1971, when he pushed off defender after defender in a bursting 50-metre run to the goal-line.

Kirkpatrick was All Black test captain for nine tests between 1972 and 1973, including the ill-fated tour of Britain and France. When he was displaced as leader by Wellington's Andy Leslie in 1974 it was a measure of the man that he upped his work rate on the field in support of the new

Ian Kirkpatrick is chaired off Cardiff Arms Park after captaining the All Blacks in the famous 1973 Barbarians match.

The aggression and power of John Kirwan, playing for his Auckland club, Marist.

skipper. He was eventually dropped from the New Zealand team for the tour to France in 1977. Kirkpatrick's replacement as the All Blacks' standout flanker had to be a good one – and so it proved: he was Graham Mourie.

When he retired Ian Kirkpatrick did not seek a place in the national administration of the game, but surfaced in 1986 as manager of the rebel Cavaliers in South Africa.

KIRWAN, JOHN
Auckland and New Zealand
37 internationals for N. Zealand 1984–90

Plucked from third grade rugby in 1983 to play for Auckland against the British Isles, John Kirwan was rated unlucky to miss selection for New Zealand's tour to England and Scotland later that year. But, at barely 19, Kirwan became an All Black in 1984 and over the next six years won acclaim as a regular All Black and one of modern rugby's most outstanding wings.

A big man for an outside back (1.90m tall and about 90kg), Kirwan was brilliantly sharp, fast and strong. There was no better example of his bursting talent than the try he scored against Italy in the opening game of the Rugby World Cup in 1987. Crashing through and around defenders 70 metres out from the goal-line, he gathered speed and proved unstoppable.

In 1988, Kirwan passed Stu Wilson's record of 19 tries for the All Blacks in internationals, and only persistent back and achilles tendon problems seemed likely to prevent him doubling that total.

There were those who said that Kirwan's form fell away after being severely injured at Pontypool in 1989, but he was back in 1990 and played in all seven tests, to become New Zealand's most-capped wing.

At the end of 1990 his tally of test tries had climbed to 28, placing him third on the all-time list behind David Campese (37) and Serge Blanco (33).

'KIWIS', THE
As soon as hostilities ceased in Europe in 1945, Lieutenant-General Sir Bernard Freyberg, the Commander-in-Chief of the 2nd NZEF, put into motion plans for a rugby tour by a team chosen from the New Zealand soldiers serving in Europe. The team, known officially as the Second New Zealand Expeditionary Force team of 1945–46, became universally known as the 'Kiwis'.

It is doubtful if there has ever been a more popular international side. The reason is twofold: the people of Britain (and also France and Germany, where the team played four and two matches respectively) had spent six years of hardship and deprivation and a sporting tour was a welcome relief; the other reason was that Major Charles Saxton's side played marvellous open rugby.

The Kiwis never claimed to be a full All Black team, but it was a hugely talented side, with giants such as full-

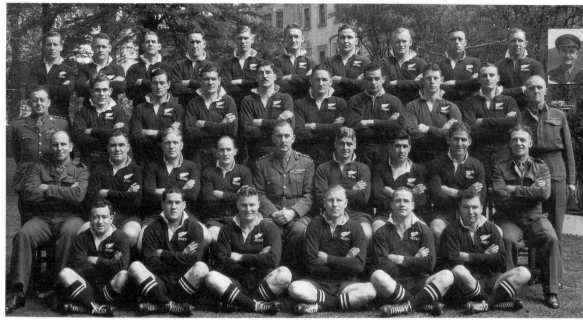

The 'Kiwis', 1945–46

back Bob Scott, three-quarters Wally Argus and Johnny Smith, five-eighths Fred Allen and prop Johnny Simpson, plus halfback Saxton himself, among the 17 who played at some stage for full New Zealand sides.

They were captained brilliantly by Charlie Saxton, an All Black halfback from before the war, who carried out to the letter the aims of the tour, which were to re-establish the game in Britain and to play enjoyable and entertaining rugby, winning not being the most important factor.

The Kiwis did just that. They tried at all times to play to Saxton's adage of the 'three Ps' of rugby: position, possession and pace, and in the end they won 32 matches of the 38 they played, including victories over England, Wales and France (twice). Scotland beat the Kiwis 11–6.

The Kiwis are fondly remembered in Britain, where their carefree rugby reminded people who had lived through the dark war years that life was worth living again and that rugby was worth playing again.

KNIGHT, GARY
Manawatu and New Zealand
36 internationals for N. Zealand 1977–86

A powerful prop, Gary 'Axle' Knight was a regular in New Zealand forward

packs for 10 seasons. He was a popular figure, usually because the fans recognised that he was a player who gave his all to any team he was in.

Originally a wrestler, Knight reached international status in this sport as well, winning a bronze medal at the 1974 Commonwealth Games in Christchurch.

When he joined the New Zealand rugby team for the tour of France in 1977, his test debut was a baptism of fire, marking the tough Frenchman Gérard Cholley in the scrums. Allegations of eye-gouging followed the first test at Toulouse, when Knight left the field with a torn left eye.

In the seasons and tours that followed, Knight went from strength to strength as a prop and a test footballer. Never a fast runner, he made up for his lack of mobility with a powerful scrummaging technique.

From 1978 he became associated with John Ashworth and Andy Dalton in a regular front row trio for New Zealand. Together they played 20 tests for the All Blacks between 1978 and 1985, 17 of which were wins for New Zealand. The three were all also members of the 1986 Cavaliers team which toured to South Africa.

Knight was involved in one of the more unusual incidents in a test match. In 1981, during the controversial

Springbok tour of New Zealand, an aeroplane circled Eden Park dropping various protest items during the third test match. A flour bomb hit Knight on the head and he was temporarily knocked out. Typical of this popular New Zealander, he recovered quickly and played on until the end, scoring a try in New Zealand's 25–22 win.

KONNO, SHIGGY
Shigeru Konno is the most powerful man behind rugby in Japan. He was a prominent club player for Doshisha University in the years after World War II then took to administering the game, first as honorary secretary to the Japanese Rugby Union and then as chairman for the JRFU's tours committee. Later he became chairman of the Japan union.

Konno's perfect English, gained from the years he spent at school in England while his father worked in London as a banker, stood him in good stead when it came to negotiating for tours to and from Japan.

Shiggy Konno was made an OBE by Queen Elizabeth II in 1985 for his services to Anglo-Japanese sporting relations – a singular and deserved honour for one of the most popoular figures in world rugby.

During the 1987 New Zealand rugby tour of Japan, Konno spoke about his training as a kamikaze pilot during World War II. Fortunately he was never called to fly in combat, which Konno says was because he was not a good enough pilot. This has saved for Japanese rugby a remarkable and powerful servant of their game.

KOREA

Formed in 1945 after the game had been played unofficially in the country for years, Korea (South Korea) is now one of the strongest powers of Asian rugby. Its rivalry with Japan has been the feature of recent play at the biennial Asian championship.

Rugby was brought to Korea by students returning from Japanese universities, who took the game to the schools where they had been sent to teach. As the same people were required to do a spell of military service, the game of rugby in Korea is centred on schools, universities and the army.

In recent years Koreans have undertaken a programme of tours to places beyond their traditional horizons, such as Australia and England, and their record in recent Asian championships has been excellent. Runner-up in four of the first seven tournaments between 1969 and 1980, Korea won in 1982, 1986, 1988 and 1990, each time beating their great rivals, Japan. (*See* ASIAN CHAMPIONSHIP.)

Korea has always performed strongly at the Hong Kong Sevens tournament, causing a major upset in 1979 when it beat the hitherto unbeaten and highly favoured Fiji team. Korea has twice won the Plate series at Hong Kong.

In 1990 Korea attempted to qualify for the World Cup finals, but in the Asian-Pacific qualifying group it lost to Tonga and Western Samoa and surprisingly also lost to Japan, 10–26.

KRIGE, JAPIE
Western Province and South Africa
5 internationals 1903–06

The legendary A.F. Markotter reckoned 'Witkoppie' Krige the finest of all South African centres, if not the greatest back of all, and the little 'Artful Dodger' won a huge reputation in an all too brief international career. In later years it would have been more extensive, for the precocious Krige, also nicknamed 'Hasie' (Rabbit) for the speed and style of his running, was

at the great rugby university, Stellenbosch University, at the tender age of 15.

One of eight sons of a Dutch Reformed minister, Japie Krige, like five of his brothers, was a centre. One, Willie, toured Britain with the Springboks in 1912–13 without playing a test; a much younger brother, 'Tinie', played for Western Province after the Great War; and Jannie, 19 years younger than Japie, played for England against Wales in 1920 when studying at Guy's Hospital.

But Japie was far and away the greatest. He made his debut for the Stellenbosch first team in the Grand Challenge Cup final against Hamiltons in 1897, then only 17 and looking even younger. In 1897, still not 18, Krige first represented Western Province, in the fifth Currie Cup centralised tournament. By the time he played his last match for the famous union, it had never been beaten with Krige on the field.

The Boer War played its part in the long period (1896–1903) when South Africa was without international rugby, so he was 23 before playing for the Springboks.

His first appearance, against Mark Morrison's British side, was a draw, and Krige was a frustrated young man. The halves, 'Uncle' Dobbin and Jackie Powell, hogged possession, and Krige refused to play the second test (also drawn) because, he told friends, he 'would never see the ball'. Krige had a record for not suffering fools gladly, and he once walked off the field in a trial match at Stellenbosch because his fellow-centre gave him bad ball! The South African selectors must have thought more of Krige than of the long–serving halves who were dropped and replaced by Paddy Carolin and Tommy Hobson. South Africa won the test and the rubber.

The great domestic reputation of Japie Krige spread overseas when he toured Britain with the first Springboks of 1906–07. He disliked the wet conditions, but his speed, both off the mark and on the run, dodging ability and an ability to create an opening for a team-mate, placed Krige in a special category.

He teamed well with his cousin, 'Boy' de Villiers, in the centres, and even better with the great right wing, Bob Loubser. A small man of only 5ft 8in

(1.72m) and 10st 10lb (68kg), Krige could perhaps be best compared with Bert Cooke, the great All Black centre of the 1920s.

Krige was bothered by illness on his only international tour, but he played the Irish, Scottish and Welsh internationals and eight other games, before having an appendectomy and not playing again on tour. In the Welsh international Krige made an impression on demanding home spectators by outplaying Rhys Gabe and Gwyn Nicholls.

The illness made for a quieter Krige than usual, and in one of the non-international matches an English official remarked to one of the non-playing Springboks, Pietie le Roux, that he didn't think much of Krige. Le Roux promptly struck a bet for £1 with the man that Krige would score three tries in the game. When the ball went into touch, the crafty le Roux was able to pass on news of the bet to Krige – and a large stake it was. Krige promptly came alight, and carved through for the required three tries. Then, just to make sure, he checked with le Roux, with 15 minutes to play, whether it was three or four tries he was expected to score!

Krige joined the government service, becoming a magistrate. That, and his operation for appendicitis, conspired to finish his rugby career. He competed in the Civil Service sports in 1909 and won the cricket ball throw, hurdles, high jump and long jump. It was said he could clear 21 feet (about 6.4m) in the long jump in street clothes. The Krige sporting career finished in 1909 with his playing soccer at Griquatown, because they couldn't raise 30 players for a game of rugby!

KYLE, JACK
Queen's University Belfast, North of
   Ireland Football Club and Ireland
46 internationals for Ireland 1947–58
6 internationals for British Isles 1950

One of the most honoured sons of Irish rugby, who rose to prominence in the rugby world in the post-World War II years.

A beautifully balanced flyhalf and every inch an athlete, Kyle made his debut for Ireland when the Five Nations championship resumed after the war, in 1947. Those were to become the golden years of Irish rugby, when the team lost only twice in two years. Ireland won a Grand Slam in 1947–48 and a Triple Crown in 1948–49. In both those seasons Ireland's inspiration came from Karl Mullen in the forwards and 'Jackie' Kyle in the backs.

These two players were also instrumental in making the 1950 British Isles team, which Mullen captained, one of the most popular touring teams ever to travel 'down under'. In New Zealand and Australia Kyle was rated a master; from his platform at flyhalf the Lions attacked strongly through their backs in all tour matches. Kyle, brilliant in his own right, was the pivot who served the cause of his team nobly.

He was a player with a distinctive pitter-patter style of running, which was very difficult for defenders to counter. He was sturdy in defence and tactically an excellent kicker, though it has to be said he never really mastered the dropped goal as a scoring method. Only once in all his tests did he try one (v Wales 1956). Mind you, it went over!

Kyle steadily built up an impressive record for Ireland. He was part of the national team which scored the first win over a touring team (9–6 v Australia in 1958). In particular he was a bogey for Scottish teams. He played against them 11 times, including his last international in 1958, and was always in the winning team. He ended his career as the world's most-capped player.

Kyle left Ireland to live in Malaya (Malaysia). Then, after a spell in Belfast, he emigrated to Zambia to carry on his work in medicine. In Ireland John Wilson Kyle, always known as Jack or Jackie, is still recalled fondly. One Irish writer wrote that he was 'a genius, surely among the greatest of all rugby players'.

L

LACAZE, CLAUDE
Lourdes, Angoulême and France
33 internationals for France 1961–69

Pierre Lacaze, nicknamed 'Papillon' (the 'Butterfly'), was a brilliant star of French rugby for just two years, scoring a dropped goal and a penalty in France's famous 9–5 win over South Africa in Johannesburg in 1958. He switched to rugby league soon after, where he also won world-wide acclaim.

His brother, Claude Lacaze, was six years younger then Pierre, only 21 when he toured New Zealand in 1961. He made his debut in Wellington on one of the worst days a game of rugby has ever been played. He tried to clear a ball from behind his own goal-line into winds that had gusted up to 140 km/h! The kick was charged down, New Zealander Kelvin Tremain scored, and the game was lost. It is reported that Lacaze burst into tears !

However, on that tour his talent was recognised as the equal of his brother; he also took over the 'Papillon' nickname.

At test level Lacaze was equally adept as a flyhalf or a fullback. One of his finest moments was when, as a fullback, he kicked a huge dropped goal (from a penalty) to help France beat South Africa at Ellis Park, Johannesburg (as his brother had done nine years earlier).

Lacaze was the first Frenchman to make two tours of New Zealand, returning in 1968 and captaining his country in the first test at Christchurch. His last test was against England in 1969, when he was a flyhalf. He went out on a losing note, but true to the family tradition he drop-kicked a goal.

Rival captains Claude Lacaze (France) and Kel Tremain (New Zealand) lead their teams on to Lancaster Park for the first test, 1968.

LAGISQUET, PATRICE
Bayonne and France
44 internationals for France 1983–91

At the end of the 1990–91 season, Patrice Lagisquet, the speedster from the deep south, had become the highest-capped French test wing of all time, comfortably passing the record of 40 caps held by Christian Darrouy.

Lagisquet began his tests in 1983 against Australia at Clermont-Ferrand. At the World Cup in 1987 he played in five of the games, including the final against New Zealand. At the end of the tournament he was widely rated as one of the top men in the world in his position, though he had some defensive horrors in the cup final.

He had been a prominent track sprinter, who once clocked 10.8 seconds for 100 metres and he used his speed to great effect on the rugby field.

In his 44 tests (24 of them in succession) he had scored 19 tries, making him fifth on the all-time French test try-scoring list (behind Blanco, Darrouy, Sella and Dupuy).

LAIDLAW, CHRIS
Otago and New Zealand
20 internationals for N. Zealand 1964–70

Chris Laidlaw, a brilliant passing and tactical halfback, first came into the

Patrice Lagisquet, France's most-capped wing.

153

New Zealand rugby team as a 19-year-old, in the touring party that travelled to Britain in 1963–64. There, he played well and established a reputation as a superb passing halfback. He could deliver strong, swift passes off both hands to five-eighths who could afford to stand 20–25 metres from him if they pleased. Laidlaw went on that first tour as number two halfback to Kevin Briscoe of Taranaki, but became the test halfback against France in Paris.

Later in the 1960s, after a highly successful run as first-choice test halfback (especially against the Springboks of 1965 and the Lions of 1966), Laidlaw was to come up against a formidable rival in Sid Going, whose skills as a halfback almost exactly complemented Laidlaw's. Going was a runner, Laidlaw a passer. Which halfback the selectors would choose for an upcoming test match was the subject of much debate.

In 1968, after an injury to the New Zealand captain Brian Lochore, Chris Laidlaw was appointed captain for the second test against Australia.

Laidlaw left New Zealand after that season to take up a Rhodes Scholarship at Oxford University, where he led the university to a memorable win over the 1969–70 Springbok touring team. Laidlaw returned to New Zealand in time to make the All Black tour of South Africa in 1970 where both he and Going were given a tough time by the South African loose forwards. Laidlaw was struck down by appendicitis and missed the last part of the tour. He did not play international football again.

At the completion of his active playing days Laidlaw wrote a bestselling book, *Mud in Your Eye,* which was autobiographical but also strongly critical of the administration of rugby. His comments on sporting contacts with South Africa riled many supporters of continued contact with that country. For some years it seemed Laidlaw was not welcome in rugby circles in New Zealand. However, most of his views on South Africa eventually became the policy of the NZRFU.

Chris Laidlaw became a career diplomat, becoming New Zealand's first High Commissioner to Zimbabwe, before being appointed New Zealand's Race Relations Conciliator in 1989.

Frank Laidlaw

LAIDLAW, FRANK
Melrose and Scotland
32 internationals for Scotland 1965–71
2 internationals for British Isles 1966

One of a succession of highly durable hookers to have played for Scotland since the 1960s, Frank Laidlaw also made two tours with the British Isles, both to New Zealand, in 1966 and 1971. He was unavailable for the Lions tour to South Africa 1968, but he did tour that country with the Barbarians in 1969. He toured to Argentina (1969) and Australia (1970) with Scotland.

His lively and at times brilliant displays as a hooker eventually brought him captaincy of Scotland in 1970, taking over from his Melrose clubmate, Jim Telfer.

LAIDLAW, ROY
Jedforest and Scotland
47 internationals for Scotland 1980–88
4 internationals for British Isles 1983

Scotland's sturdy halfback of the 1980s, who became totally dominant in that position for his country. From his debut in the first match in 1980 (against Ireland in Dublin) Laidlaw played 31 internationals in a row in the Scottish No. 9 jersey. An injury against France in 1985 meant he was replaced for two games by Gordon Hunter of Selkirk. Laidlaw returned and missed only one other test match, when he stood down (as against being

Chris Laidlaw scores for New Zealand in the second test against South Africa at Newlands, 1970.

dropped) for Scotland's World Cup game against Zimbabwe in Wellington, New Zealand in 1987. (Greig Oliver of Hawick played instead.)

Laidlaw's consistency came wth strength and courage. As a halfback he rated as one of the best Scotland has ever produced, yet in any one of the specialist parts of the halfback's game he would not rate as Scotland's best. He was not the greatest passer or kicker of the ball. The most constant part of his game was his strength and his ability to conduct the halfback's business behind a beaten pack. He played in all four test matches for the 1983 British Isles in New Zealand.

He is also well remembered as one half of a remarkable combination with his close friend and flyhalf John Rutherford. Together they played 35 times as an international scrumhalf pairing, a world record. Only a severe knee injury to Rutherford prevented them playing on together for more years.

At the end of 1990 their partnership record was still intact, though under threat from the Australians Nick Farr-Jones and Michael Lynagh.

Laidlaw was captain of Scotland a number of times and travelled with it six times on major tours. His total of 47 caps for Scotland left him as the second highest-capped halfback in world rugby (behind Gareth Edwards's 53 caps for Wales).

Roy Laidlaw created this impressive record while playing most of his club rugby for the second division club Jedforest.

LANCASTER PARK
The international rugby and cricket ground of Christchurch in the South Island of New Zealand. The ground has served the city in many different ways since its opening in 1882: it was the venue for a Davis Cup tennis final, the place where Peter Snell set world athletics records, the location for national swimming and cycling championships and, in World War I, a massive potato patch! It has also been used for religious rallies and pop concerts, harness racing, speedway, rugby league, hockey and soccer internationals, and marching.

The first rugby international played on the ground was in 1913, when Australia beat New Zealand 16–5 in the third test. A gap of 17 years followed

until the next official test match on the ground, when the All Blacks beat Britain by 13–10 in the second test.

In recent times Lancaster Park has become a happy hunting ground for the All Blacks. Losses there to Australia in 1958, the Springboks in 1965 and the Lions in 1977 meant that, on average, the All Blacks only lost once every decade on the Oval. In terms of New Zealand wins, the margins over Wales, 19–0 in 1969 and 52–3 in 1988, are impressive.

Over the years there have been many classic rugby clashes on the ground. Perhaps none was more exciting, and more disappointing in the view of the locals, than when South Africa won the third test of 1965. The Springboks were behind 16–5 at half-time but with resolution and determination they clawed their way to a famous win by a penalty goal, 19–16.

Lancaster Park is also the winter home for the Canterbury rugby team and many a scarlet and black forward rush or backline sprint has been applauded vigorously from the stands and the open embankment.

The ground has had its rugby favourites, none more so than the legendary Fergie McCormick, who played half of his 222 games for the province on that ground.

LANSDOWNE ROAD
The stadium in Dublin where Ireland has played internationals since 1878. Before 1954, home games were shared with Belfast's Ravenhill, but increased capacity at Lansdowne Road meant it then took over as the permanent place for Ireland at home.

Although the stadium has been greatly updated, expanded and modernised in recent times, it remains one of the best grounds from which to view a rugby international.

Its lush turf, one of the best in the world to play on, has often inspired the Irish team to play superbly. In 1947 it trounced England 22–0 in Ireland's first win since the war, and in 1956 scored a dramatic victory over Wales in front of 50,573 exultant fans, the record crowd for the ground. Even so it is still the smallest of the major grounds in the United Kingdom.

Ireland also scored a victory over the 1965 Springboks and drew with the 1969–70 team on Lansdowne Road, as well as having a sequence of three

wins over Australia from 1958 to 1967. Sadly for the Irish they have never beaten New Zealand there – although they have come very close. Only a late try by Andy Dalton for the All Blacks prevented a draw in 1978. The 1972 match with New Zealand was drawn, 10–10.

Three times in recent years Ireland has won the Five Nations championship on Lansdowne Road – in 1974, 1982 and 1985. In 1986 Ireland beat Romania there by 60–0, a world record score, for a time, for an international between two major nations.

To be sure the Irish spirit might slump a little when the home team loses on the ground, but the cheering throngs are always back, with typical Irish goodwill and optimism, for the next time that Ireland plays on Lansdowne Road.

LANSDOWNE RFC
The fourth oldest club in Ireland and one of its best known, the club is based on the same plot of ground (but just behind) the international pitch of Lansdowne Road.

Founded in Dublin in 1872, the young club lured Trinity players away

Irish Rugby Football Union

IRELAND

v

SOUTH AFRICA

Lansdowne Road
Saturday 10th January 1970

Because of anti-apartheid demonstrations, only a flimsy programme was produced for the Ireland-Springbok match in 1970, the most recent occasion the two teams have met. The game was drawn 8–8.

to play casual games, and because of this was known as the 'second Trinity'. Difficulties arose when Trinity had its own games and the 'borrowed' players rejoined their own club. Lansdowne struggled for a time to find its own identity, but eventually flourished and became a powerful entity in Irish rugby.

Lansdowne was a founder member of the IRFU in 1874, and took part with Trinity, Wanderers and the now defunct Kingstown in the first Leinster Senior Cup in 1882. In that competition Lansdowne has had considerable success.

The club supplied the complete Irish three-quarter line – Ned Lightfoot, Eugene Davy, Morgan Crowe and Jack Arigho – for three internationals of the 1931 season. Between them, these four won 74 Irish caps and 22 senior cup medals. Of the Lansdowne team of 1931, nine were then or later to become Irish international players.

The great Ernie Crawford was a Lansdowne man, and so was Ronnie Dawson, the famous Irish and British Isles captain of 1959. Mickey English, the flyhalf, was also a Lion in 1959. Other prominent Irish internationals were Alan Duggan, the Rev. Robin Roe and Michael Kiernan.

Eugene Davy's club record of 34 international caps stood from 1934 until 1980 when it was passed by Moss Keane, who finished with 51 caps for his country.

The Lansdowne team plays in jerseys of red, yellow and black hoops.

LAUGHLAND, IAIN
London Scottish and Scotland
31 internationals for Scotland 1959–67

One of Scotland's most reliable backs, Iain Laughland began as a centre against France in 1959. Most of his internationals were played in that position but he filled the flyhalf berth a number of times as well, becoming a permanent flyhalf late in his club career.

Laughland's tally of 31 caps was a record for international appearances by a player from the London Scottish club, which stood until Alistair McHarg broke it in 1975–76. Laughland, who was considered unlucky not to be chosen as a Lion, became a specialist sevens player and was acknowledged as the architect of much of his club's

Tom Lawton clears to Michael Lynagh for Australia, at Wellington, 1986.

success in sevens tournaments in the early 1960s. He was also a talented cricketer and soccer player.

LAWS OF RUGBY
The first rules and regulations for the game of rugby were not set down until after the formation of the Rugby Union in London in 1871. Before that there had been many departures and variations from what William Webb Ellis had unwittingly started when he ran with the ball at Rugby School in 1823.

In modern times the laws are set out in a handbook *The Laws of the Game of Rugby Football*. This is a small book of 130 pages containing language in dire need of simplification to make for easier reading.

LAWTON, TOMMY
Queensland, New South Wales and
  Australia
12 internationals for Australia 1925–32

Tommy Lawton was a stand-off half, or five-eighths, noted for the smoothness of his play, his ability to pass well and his excellent goal-kicking. A Queenslander, he moved to Sydney

when rugby went into recession in Brisbane during and after the First World War.

Lawton was a Rhodes Scholar at Oxford University, winning three blues. He later toured Britain and France with the famous 'Waratahs' team – New South Wales – in 1927–28. He was a vital man in that team and scored 127 points, a record for an Australian on such a tour.

In 1929 he returned to Queensland and led the re-formed Australian team against the All Blacks. Lawton was a brilliant tactician and guided Australia to a clean sweep of the three-test series. He was also captain of Australia in one test in 1930 (against Britain) and in 1932 for two tests against the All Blacks. He captained a losing test team only once.

His tally of 44 points – including points scored in the subsequently recognised 'tests' of the Waratahs tour – was not beaten as an Australian record until the 1960s.

Tommy Lawton died in 1978 and did not see his name carried on in Australian rugby by his grandsons, Tommy jnr (*see below*) and Robbie, who came into international rugby in 1988.

LAWTON, TOMMY
Queensland, Natal and Australia
41 internationals for Australia 1983–89

A grandson of the father of Queensland rugby (see above), the Tommy Lawton of the 1980s was a big bustling hooker who became a powerful figure in Australian rugby. With his aggressive play and imposing presence on the field, Tommy Lawton was a first-choice hooker for Australia every year after his international debut against France in Paris in 1982. However, such was the competition for places in his home area he actually played for his country before he played for his state team.

As a hooker Lawton was perhaps the biggest of all time. He weighed in at 110 kilograms (17 stone) in his best playing years.

Like all hookers, he delighted in scoring tries, scoring one in 1983 on Cardiff Arms Park in the international against Wales, thus emulating the feat achieved by his grandfather in 1927. In 1988 Lawton had a great game against Scotland at Murrayfield, scoring two tries.

Earlier, in 1986 he played for the Rest of the World XV against the British Isles in the International Rugby Board's centenary series.

On the tour of Canada and France in 1989 Lawson captained the Australians in three midweek matches.

In 1990 Lawton shifted to Durban in South Africa, where he played hooker for Natal in its first Currie Cup win.

LEICESTER FC
One of the most famous of English clubs, Leicester men are known far and wide as the 'Tigers'. Many of England's best players have played for the club.

Leicester first appeared as an amalgamation of three smaller clubs in 1880. Twelve years later the club settled at its Welford Road ground, which is still its headquarters. It is the largest ground in England, apart from Twickenham, and several internationals were played there early in the twentieth century. It was chosen as a venue for one of the 1991 World Cup games.

Leicester has some notable traditions, one of which is its annual game against the Barbarians. The fixture began in 1909 and apart from the war years has continued ever since, the match being played immediately after Christmas.

Leicester originally played touring teams on its own, but later combined with Leicestershire and East Midlands to host visitors. That combination was the only team to beat the 1931–32 Springboks, and all the backs that day were Leicester players. The 30–21 score was the highest points total posted by any team in history against the Springboks. Sixty years later that record still stood.

In modern times, games against touring teams held at Welford Road usually feature the Midlands Division. On its own, Leicester narrowly lost, 15–18, to Australia in 1981–82.

One of the club's proudest days was in 1924–25 when the entire Leicestershire county team was made up of 'Tigers' and won the county championship.

Many successful players have appeared in the scarlet, green and white colours of Leicester. In recent years, Peter Wheeler and 'Dusty' Hare set all manner of appearance and points-scoring records. Paul Dodge, Les Cusworth and Clive Woodward were contemporaries of those fine players.

In earlier times Doug Prentice, the 1930 British captain and later RFU secretary, Harold Day, 'Kicking Ginger' Kewney, Phil Horrocks-Taylor, Bernard Gadney, and Tom Berry (an England selector 1951–66) were all Leicester players. George Beamish, Tony O'Reilly and Ken Scotland were others who played for this English club, though they won their international caps for other countries.

Although he was also a famous Harlequins player, Wavell Wakefield's name was listed for many years as Leicester's most-capped English international.

Perhaps the club's proudest period was in 1979, 1980, and 1981, when it won the John Player Cup series for the RFU club championship. On the way it set a competition record of 18 winning cup games in a row, won mostly with stylish back play and solid scrummaging. In those years the 'Tigers' were coached by 'Chalky' White.

Leicester's win in the final in 1981 was particularly sweet, as it was the club's centenary year. In keeping with the competition's rules the third con-secutive win gave the original John Player Trophy a permanent place at the Leicester clubhouse.

The proximity of the Leicester Football club's ground at Welford Road to Filbert Street, the home of the Leicester City soccer club, has caused much merriment and confusion over the years. Many a soccer supporter has arrived at Welford Road to be stunned by seeing rugby goal-posts in place! There is even one famous story of a soccer referee changing into his strip under the Welford road grandstand and only realising he was in the wrong ground when he emerged to check the pitch and saw the unfamiliar goal-posts!

The club had the distinction of winning Division One in the first season of league rugby in 1987–88.

LENIHAN, DONAL
UC Cork, Cork Constitution and Ireland
47 internationals for Ireland 1981–90

Donal Lenihan did everything right in his climb through the ranks of Irish rugby. When he became a full Irish international, v Australia in 1981, he was one of only seven Irishmen to have played for his country at schools level, under-23, Ireland 'B' and Ireland.

Lenihan was a hard grafting lock from Munster who built up a fine reputation as a quality forward and a leader of men. He captained his country in the 1987 World Cup and then through two seasons of the Five Nations championship. When success was hard to come by, the Irish selectors decided to experiment with others as captain – Phil Matthews and Willie Anderson – but by 1990 they were back with Lenihan as leader. He missed the 1991 international season because of injury.

Lenihan twice toured with the British Isles, to New Zealand in 1983 and to Australia in 1989, but played no test matches. In 1983 he was chosen for the New Zealand tour, but cried off with a shoulder injury; later he received a call to fly out and replace Rob Norster of Wales. He did so and appeared in two games.

In 1989 on the Australian tour he became the popular captain of the midweek team – 'Donal's Donuts' they were called. It was typical of Lenihan that, under his cheery influence, the midweekers contributed much to the high spirits of the touring party.

Donal Lenihan (right) and Graham Price competing in a lineout.

Going into the 1990s, Lenihan was set to become the third Irish lock, after Willie John McBride and Moss Keane, to pass the milestone of playing in 50 internationals.

LESLIE, DAVID

Dundee HSFP, West of Scotland, Gala and Scotland

32 internationals for Scotland 1975–85

A solid and reliable Scottish loose forward who, but for injuries, might have played in more internationals than his final total. David Leslie came into the Scottish team in 1975 for the first international of the season against Ireland. Later that year he went on the tour of Australia and New Zealand.

After two seasons as a regular in the Scottish team, in which he won 10 caps, Leslie suffered severe leg injuries, which kept him out of the Five Nations championship for three seasons (1977–78–79, with only one match in 1980). At one stage during a span of 50 Scottish internationals, Leslie had played 27 and missed 23, mainly through injury, although on each occasion he recovered.

Leslie was not a big player but he was a fast-moving loose forward with excellent ball skills and courage. He played his international rugby at flanker or No. 8, specialising in an almost suicidal technique of falling on the loose ball. His best season was 1984, when he was a vital part of the Scottish team which won the Grand Slam. *Rugby World* named him 'Player of the Year' after that season.

One curiosity about Leslie's career was that even though he was always close to the ball in all his 32 test matches, he scored only two tries. A tribute, perhaps, to the unselfish way he played the game.

LIDDELL, ERIC

Edinburgh University and Scotland

7 Internationals for Scotland 1922–23

When Eric Liddell won the dramatic Olympic Games 400 metres final in Paris in 1924, a story told in the award-winning film *Chariots of Fire*, he must have found his surroundings at Colombes Stadium familiar. For it was on that ground that he had made his international debut in rugby for Scotland against France two years earlier.

Liddell played only two years as a rugby international, but only once was he on the losing side (in the highly charged Calcutta Cup match of 1923). After that that he gave the game away to concentrate on his build-up to the 1924 Olympic Games.

After the Games, Liddell, a deeply religious man, returned to Tientsin, Northern China, where he was born in 1902, the son of a Scottish missionary. It is said that he played rugby in China in matches involving army staff.

Liddell died in an Japanese internment camp in early 1945.

LINEOUTS

The two lines of up to eight forwards that stretch out at right angles from the touchline at the point where the ball has gone out of play. The opposing forwards attempt to regain possession of the ball when it is thrown in between the two ranks of players.

Lineouts have become one of the most controversial areas of the world game. The technicalities of rugby's laws have meant that a referee can blow his whistle at any lineout for literally dozens of offences, and it is widely held that only sympathetic refereeing allows many lineouts to proceed.

Arguments and accusations fly, about mythical advantage lines, gaps between players front, back and sideways, obstruction, compression, lifting by team-mates, blocking of the opposing team's jumpers, the length of the lines, the numbers of players allowed in or out of the line, and arriving and leaving the lineout properly.

Many critics regard the lineout as the principal 'shambles' of the modern game, and the law of advantage needs to be freely applied at lineout time.

Nevertheless there have been many great lineout exponents, with Frik du Preez of South Africa being arguably the best the game has ever seen. He was not as tall as perhaps a lock should be, but he had an amazing ability to grasp lineout throw-ins with two hands. It was du Preez's clean ball in the lineout that was a major reason why South Africa was so strong during his years at the top (1961–71).

The biggest change in lineout play came in 1968 when the Australian test team, under coach Des Connor, called for shortened lineouts in its test series against New Zealand. This tactic meant that up to six forwards stood out in mid-field taking no part in the lineout, thus reducing the numbers remaining in the line to two each side.

The move was initially scorned as negative rugby, but it has become recognised as a reasonable tactic for use by a weak lineout team against a strong one. Shortened lineouts can also be used as the platform for attacks, with more players available in midfield for variations of strategy.

Throwing in to lineouts used to be solely the domain of wings, but the task has now been taken over mainly by hookers, although French international teams of the 1980s regularly used their halfbacks for the job. Wings who previously threw in on their touchline now roam the midfield so they can be used as extra attacking players in back moves.

LIONS, THE

The nickname for teams representing the British Isles. According to historian Wallace Reyburn, in his book *The Lions*, the term was first applied to the Great Britain team which toured South Africa in 1924, because of the lion symbol on the 1924 team's ties. How-ever, other books of the time make no reference to that team being called 'Lions' and the 1930 Great Britain team was never known by that name in New Zealand. 'Lions' was a recognised name by 1950 when the British Isles toured New Zealand. (*See also* BRITISH ISLES)

LIVERPOOL RFC

The oldest open rugby club in the world, founded in 1857, one year before Blackheath.

Liverpool's greatest year was perhaps in 1911 when the club had three international captains playing for it — Richard Lloyd (Ireland), Ronald Poulton Palmer (England) and the club's captain Frederic Turner (Scotland).

The club's most-capped player for more than 70 years was the great Irish forward, 'Ellie' Allen. His 21 caps between 1900 and 1907, were not beaten until Mike Slemen, the England and Lions wing, totalled 31 caps for England between 1976 and 1984.

Other internationals from the Liverpool club include Reg Higgins, Mike Beese, Thomas Brophy and Martin Regan.

In 1986 the club merged with neighbouring St Helens, which had been formed in 1919 by old boys of Cowley School, to create a stronger rugby presence in the north of England. Following the amalgamation the former Liverpool club's headquarters moved from St Michael's in Liverpool to Moss Lane in St Helen's.

LLANELLI RFC

Founded in 1872, with headquarters at Stradey Park in the west Wales town of Llanelli, the club (the 'Scarlets') was quickly recognised as one of the leading clubs in Wales. It has, for many years, been considered one of the 'big four' clubs of the principality, along with Cardiff, Newport and Swansea. All four clubs are regular hosts to the major touring teams to Wales.

Llanelli is known widely for its fanatical passion and parochial feeling for the game, though this was not always the case. In the years immediately after it was formed, the club had to endure criticism from the pulpit as well as from some sections of the town. But these days, Llanelli is the archetypal Welsh rugby town.

Because its main industry was tin-plating, the tune 'Sospan Fach' ('The little saucepans') became the club's anthem and theme song. A parody, with changed lyrics, to celebrate the club's first victory over a major touring team (Australia in 1908) had a last line asking, repetitively,'who beat the Wallabies?' Sixty-four years later, in 1972, Llanelli scored its most famous win, beating the New Zealand All Blacks by 9 to 3. The last line in the lilting Llanelli song was accordingly changed to 'Who beat the All Blacks?' and is still sung on many a winter's afternoon at Stradey Park.

Lineouts: a referee's nightmare. Spot the infringements here!

LLANELLI

GOALS	TRIES	POINTS
2	1	9

SELAND NEWYDD

1		3

Llanelli's most famous scoreboard – from the club's 1972 victory over the All Blacks. The score was left up for some years, but by 1980, when this shot was taken, it was only displayed for the benefit of touring teams.

International players are regularly chosen from Llanelli – in the club's first 100 years, 106 players pulled on the scarlet jersey of Wales, and in only one year – 1900 – was there no representative in the Welsh team from Llanelli.

Famous players included the great Rhys Gabe, the brilliant centre three-quarter, who played in three Welsh Grand Slam-winning teams in the early years of the twentieth century; Albert Jenkins, and Ivor Jones. Of Jenkins it was said the old men of the town could 'die happy' if they had 'seen Albert play'. He was an extraordinarily talented centre.

Ivor Jones was a steadfast and unwavering Llanelli forward, who, after a splendid playing career for his club, Wales and Britain, gave further devotion to Llanelli as an administrator. He captained the club in its victory over the 1926–27 New Zealand Maoris.

The list of Llanelli internationals includes: Rhys Williams, also a Lions forward; Archie Skym, the utility forward of the 1930s; the post-war fullbacks, Lewis Jones and Terry Davies; the highly inventive scrumhalf of the 1950s, Onllwyn Brace; the great Barry John (until he went to Cardiff); and other players of the modern era such as Phil Bennett, Ray Gravell, Derek Quinnell, J.J. Williams, Jonathan Davies and Delme Thomas.

Thomas became a local hero when he captained Llanelli to its first win over New Zealand in 1972. Having already enjoyed a long career with Wales and the British Isles, he told his Llanelli team that day that he would gladly give up all the honours he had already won from rugby if his team of 'Scarlets' could give him victory. It is said players in the dressing room wept when they heard him and ran on to Stradey totally committed to die for the cause. Another story says that 15 coffins were brought to the ground because the Llanelli players would rather die than lose!

The team arrived on the field to a crescendo of cheering and singing from a crowd that demanded victory, and only victory. The All Blacks, with hindsight, really had no chance that day. They were playing against supermen!

There was only one try scored, by Roy Bergiers, the centre. Phil Bennett, later to captain the British Lions in New Zealand, landed the conversion and later a dramatic, long-distance penalty by the wing Andy Hill sealed the victory. The All Blacks scored only a Joe Karam penalty goal.

That game, the perfect celebration of Llanelli's centenary, was also immortalised in song. The ballad '9–3', by Max Boyce, quickly became a modern Welsh folk song.

It was about this time that Llanelli won the Welsh Cup four times in succession. The club had earlier shown great innovation when it toured to the Soviet Union, playing there in 1957.

The club owed much to the great Carwyn James, who coached and plotted the defeat of the All Blacks on that famous day in 1972, and contributed on a myriad of other occasions. He was a star performer as a flyhalf in his playing days and later, as a coach, he helped Llanelli to confirm a reputation as one of the toughest teams anywhere in Britain. Thanks to Carwyn James's influence, Llanelli at Stradey Park was always one of the hardest teams to beat.

LLEWELLYN, WILLIE
Llwynypia and Wales
20 internationals for Wales 1899–1905

An early Welsh rugby star who lived to a great age, eventually becoming the last living Welsh authority on the famous 1905 game against New Zealand, in which he played on the wing.

Willie Llewellyn had been in the Welsh team since 1899 and was known as a great try-scorer. He scored four against England at Swansea in his first test, a record for a debut, and the tally of four tries in one game still stands as a Welsh record, though it has been equalled several times since. His final total in internationals was 16 tries.

Willie always believed that Bob Deans did not score the disputed try. He confirmed that belief, loud and long, right through until his death in 1973 at the age of 94. Near the end, however, he was quoted as saying that he had no opinion on whether Deans had scored or not as he was 'flat on his back' at the time, having just tackled Billy Wallace, his New Zealand marker.

Llewellyn toured New Zealand and Australia with the Great Britain team in 1904.

LOANE, MARK
Queensland and Australia
28 internationals for Australia 1973–82

Mark Loane was three weeks short of his 19th birthday when he first played for Australia in 1973, against Tonga at Sydney (an official cap for Australian players). Australia won by 30–12. Loane was the youngest Wallaby for-

FACES OF WORLD RUGBY: HONG KONG SEVENS

HONG KONG

CANADA

JAPAN

TONGA

WEST GERMANY

MALAYSIA

PAPUA NEW GUINEA

KOREA

NETHERLANDS

Top: Hong Kong Rugby Stadium, venue for the annual Hong Kong Sevens tournament.
Below: Spectators add to the colour of the event. Contingents from Papua New Guinea (left) and Bahrain.   Peter Bush

ward of all and the second youngest in any position, including the backs. (Brian Ford, the Queensland wing, was 18 years 3 months old when he played against New Zealand in 1957.)

Loane's debut as a No. 8 forward, at such a young age, had been a gamble by the then Wallaby coach, Bob Templeton. But when Australia was tipped over in the second test against Tonga, losing by 11–16, it was obvious that heads would roll. Loane was dropped for the short tour of England and Wales that followed, as was Templeton.

Steeled by such treatment, Loane came back as an aggressive and determined No. 8 who, for the rest of his playing days, was one of the stars of the game both in Queensland and throughout Australia.

He was a dynamic forward, capable of storming through hapless defenders, and his bullocking runs won the hearts of the loyal fans at Ballymore. His tackling was ferocious and his determination legendary around the rugby world. He epitomised the 'hard man' of Australian rugby.

From 1974 only injuries (on the tour to New Zealand in 1978) and absence from Australia (1980) hindered Mark Loane from stacking up an impressive number of test match appearances. He became a Wallaby captain for a time (v New Zealand in 1979, and on tour to Argentina in 1979) but was replaced as leader when he took a year off in 1980.

In his time away from Australia, Loane visited South Africa, where he quickly became recognised in Natal and throughout the republic as a loose forward of true quality. The South Africans seemed keen to make Loane a Springbok, but he returned home in the 1981 season to try to qualify for the Wallaby tour to Britain.

On that tour he resumed the captaincy at the end, leading the team against England, and was also captain when Scotland toured Australia in 1982.

After leading Australia to an impressive win in the second test at Sydney, Loane joined with nine others in declaring himself unavailable for the following tour to New Zealand. He retired from the game and resumed his previously interrupted medical career.

In his time in rugby he contributed mightily to Queensland's successful interstate record. To all followers of the game around Brisbane and the Sunshine State, there was no other forward worth talking about. Mark Loane was their man!

LOCHORE, BRIAN
Wairarapa-Bush and New Zealand
25 internationals for N. Zealand 1964–71

Not only was Brian Lochore one of the most successful All Black captains of all time, leading his country in 18 test matches for 15 wins, he also was a class player who later went on to become an All Black selector. His career was topped in magnificent style when the New Zealand team, under his guidance as coach, won the first Rugby World Cup in 1987.

Lochore entered major rugby in 1963 as a shy young farmer from the Wairarapa, a small farming and coastal region in New Zealand's lower North Island. After some outstanding form in the trials he was included in Wilson Whineray's New Zealand team for the 1963–64 tour of Britain and France, where he quickly proved himself the equal of some of the most famous rugby names of that time.

He played two of the internationals so well (against England and Scotland) that he was in the test team permanently from then on.

In 1966, only two years after making the New Zealand team, Lochore was elevated to the captaincy, ahead of people like Colin Meads, who might perhaps have won more favour with the All Black fans of that time. However, Lochore's quiet but determined approach soon won over players, officials, and supporters, and he became one of New Zealand's most popular and successful skippers.

Lochore was an unflagging No. 8 who was tough and determined. He would have comfortably made the team from that famous era of New Zealand rugby on ability alone, even without the obvious and outstanding leadership qualities he possessed.

His major success as a captain came in 1967, when he led the All Blacks on an unbeaten tour of Britain and France. Under coach Fred Allen and manager Charlie Saxton, the All Blacks team thrilled Britain with the speed and style of its game. It is re-

Mark Loane (Australia). Behind him is his team-mate, Tony Shaw.

Brian Lochore

membered as one of the great touring teams by British fans.

Lochore led New Zealand teams on two other tours, to Australia in 1968 and to South Africa in 1970. In Australia he broke his thumb in the first test and took no further part in the series, which New Zealand lost. In South Africa in 1970 he did not play until the sixth tour game, because of a cracked bone in his hand, sustained in Perth in a practice match on the way. That test series was also lost.

Lochore retired at the end of the 1970 tour, but was soon back in action as the captain of the President's XV, a selection of the world's leading players who travelled to England to celebrate the centenary of the Rugby Football Union by playing an international for which England awarded caps. The President's XV won by 28–11.

In 1971 Brian Lochore was called out unexpectedly to play lock in the third test against the British Isles at Wellington. The experiment was not a success for New Zealand (the Lions won) and afterwards Lochore was happy to stay in retirement, as a player, although he did not stay idle from rugby. After a spell as the coach of his home union of Wairarapa-Bush, Lochore was put in charge of the All Blacks in 1985, beginning his national coaching career with an emphatic series win over the England touring

team, including a then record 42–15 test win at Wellington.

Disappointment was to follow, with the much anticipated 1985 tour of South Africa being cancelled on a legal technicality. In its place Lochore took the All Blacks to Argentina, where his team remained unbeaten.

There was a setback to Lochore's coaching career in 1986, when the unauthorised Cavaliers tour of South Africa disrupted his plans for that season. His depleted team, called the 'Baby All Blacks', won a test match against France in Christchurch, but then lost a test series at home to Australia. The All Blacks then toured to France, where they won one out two tests. In all, New Zealand scored only four tries in its six tests of 1986, so things were not looking good for the inaugural Rugby World Cup, then only eight months away.

But 1987 became one of the great years of New Zealand rugby, with some people hailing Lochore's World Cup winning squad as the best team New Zealand had ever fielded.

After the victory in the World Cup, Brian Lochore took the All Blacks back to Australia and won back the Bledisloe Cup by 30–16, after which he retired from all involvement in the game.

Starting from his junior playing days, through his All Black years, the provincial coaching years and culminating with the World Cup, he had spent

nearly 30 years in the public eye being associated with rugby. Hearing it put that way, and buoyed by the success he had given the All Blacks in 1987, Brian Lochore's thousands of fans did not begrudge him some time to himself, at last!

LOCKS

Only the strong, tall and hard men need apply to be a lock! A rugby team's two locks are the men who sweat out their sporting existence in the second row of the scrums – definitely no place for the faint-hearted or timid. Or they graft for the ball in lineouts, rucks and mauls – again no place for the craven.

Yet this total devotion to hard work seems insufficient for modern locks who have expanded their repertoire to include leaping, jumping and running, providing back-up to the attacks of others. In other words, let no man tell you a lock these days is just a plodder, a blockhead used for the brawny work in scrum or lineout. A top, modern international lock needs to be a lean, tall, immensely strong, powerful athlete to survive modern rugby's explosive forward action.

The evolution of locks from stolidity to mobility probably stems from the arrival on the international scene of Colin Meads of New Zealand. During his long international playing career, Meads expanded the horizons of the

Two of the greatest locks of all time. Willie John McBride and Colin Meads exchange jerseys.

lock's position so that they were soon allowed by coaches and match planners to do things that were previously the domain of the much speedier flankers or No. 8s. It was not an evolution that met with universal approval, as many rugby watchers felt he was 'too loose'. Nevertheless it was the Meads style of play that became the yardstick for the locks who followed him.

In the old 2-3-2 scrum days there was only one lock, who would go down in each scrum with one arm around each of the flankers, much as hookers do today. It was in that scrum, and in the 3-4-1 formation that followed, that men like Wavell Wakefield (England), Philip Nel (South Africa), George Hamlet (Ireland), and John Bannerman (Scotland) built their reputations.

In the post-war years Meads dominated as a lock, but Willie John McBride (Ireland), Johan Claassen (South Africa), 'Tiny' White (New Zealand), Rhys Williams (Wales), Benoit Dauga (France), Bill Beaumont (England), Moaner van Heerden (South Africa), Alistair McHarg (Scotland), Rod Heming (Australia), Moss Keane (Ireland), Andy Haden (New Zealand), Steve Cutler (Australia) and Gary Whetton (New Zealand) were all powerful locks in the world game.

LOFTUS VERSFELD

The main rugby stadium of Pretoria. Playing fields were first developed there in 1908 and the original wooden grandstand went up four years later. Upgrading of the ground was undertaken in the 1930s, and Loftus Versfeld Stadium, named after of one of the early great players of the city, R.L.O. (Loftus) Versfeld, was opened in 1938.

There had always been grand plans for stadium development at Loftus Versfeld, but for many years the ground was lined by trees and Pretoria was not considered a suitable venue for tests. Today's modern, magnificent stadium in Pretoria has a capacity of 65,000 and is the home of the famous and powerful 'Blue Bulls'. Many a thrilling Currie Cup match has taken place on the ground.

Loftus Versfeld was first used for a test match in 1955, when the Springboks lost to the British Isles in the third test by 6–9. The weather was so hot that September that many rugby followers blamed the Pretoria heat for

the sluggishness of the Springboks. Perhaps that was why the next international at Loftus was not played until 1963, when Australia was beaten 14–3. Since then the ground has been on South Africa's regular roster of test venues.

Major improvements to the facilities in 1976 cemented the ground's reputation as one of the first picks for any major touring team.

LORIEUX, ALAIN
Grenoble, Aix-les-Bains and France
30 internationals for France 1981–89

A tall and athletic lock who was always in the thick of the game, Lorieux made his debut for France (against Australia in 1981) from Grenoble, then transferred to Aix-les-Bains, a much smaller club. The transfer signalled a rise in his work rate around the field, and by 1987 he was a regular as a lock, and in the French team which travelled to the World Cup. He played in the final against New Zealand at Eden Park.

In 1988 Lorieux joined the small band of players to have been sent off in a test match: he was dismissed from the second test against Argentina in Buenos Aires in 1988 by Irish referee Owen Doyle.

LOTZ, JAN
Transvaal and South Africa
8 internationals for Sth Africa 1937–38

The paucity of international play when he was at his peak, and the advent of World War II, cut heavily into Jan Lotz's international career. But by common consent, the nephew of Phil Mostert and the possessor of much of his great dribbling skill, was regarded as the finest of South Africa's hookers.

Sometimes labelled the 'Cat', because of the speed of his striking in the scrum, Lotz carried a heavy responsibility on the 1937 trip to Australia and New Zealand. In the trials he had annihilated hooker after hooker and, faced with this shortage of back-up skills, the selectors named him as the only hooker. He was rested by 'Boy' Louw in two of the 11 games in Australia, but played all but two of the 17 matches in New Zealand.

It had been a calculated risk by the selectors, who must have been grateful that this strong, well-proportioned

man suffered no injury. As it was, after the third New Zealand test when, under the laws of the time, South Africa took scrums instead of lineouts, he could not move his neck.

Lotz was a forerunner of the modern mobile front-ranker: a splendid all-round forward and a champion snarer of scrum ball.

He played all the home tests against the 1938 British side, before the outbreak of war put an abrupt end to his career. Even so, in 1949, Lotz was the one pre-war Springbok still playing when South Africa turned its attention to the upcoming tour by New Zealand, but by the time the All Blacks arrived Lotz was 38, and his day was done.

LOUBSER, BOB
Western Province, Transvaal, Orange
Free State and South Africa
7 internationals for South Africa 1903–10

Old-timers consider Johannes Albertus Loubser to be the greatest Springbok wing of all. Called 'Bob' by an English governess who couldn't manage his given names, Loubser played no rugby at all until he was 18. His father regarded it as a dangerous game and the boy could only watch games at the old Noorder Paarl School, afraid to defy his father. He went to Stellenbosch High School in 1902 to matriculate, and tentatively offered his name for the third team, as a forward. The speed he revealed in practice games persuaded the first team captain, F.P. Hoogenhout, to send him to the backs – and almost immediately to a place in the first team.

A broken arm cut his season short in June, but by the next year Loubser had started a long and fruitful association with Japie Krige – the two, together with their partners in the Stellenbosch three-quarters line, 'Boy Bekkies' de Villiers and Anton Stegman, made up one of the greatest backlines in world rugby.

Just past his 19th birthday, Loubser was called up to play the first international against Mark Morrison's British team, but he turned down the opportunity on the advice of his future father-in-law, Dr J.H. Neethling, who thought he was too young and the Wanderers' ground too hard.

He was chosen for – and accepted – a place for the third test, and the white-booted young Loubser, already sporting a flowing moustache, joined the select group to play for his country before his union (Western Province).

The products of Stellenbosch – 'Maties' – dominated the original Springbok touring side of 1906–07 and Loubser, already the youngest Springbok of all, set another record with 24 tries in his 21 appearances in the British Isles.

He was exceptionally fast, an 'evens' man over 100 yards, and extraordinarily strong for someone only 1.7m and 72kg (5ft 7in and 11st 2lbs). He did the legendary Sandow's bodybuilding course and could pick up nearly 50kg in one hand. He was also a strong bumping runner who could batter away all but the most determined of tacklers with his pumping knees.

When running with the ball seemed to offer few scoring options, Loubser could kick just as effectively, whether the short kick ahead for himself, or the centre-kick – the 'tally-ho' as it was then known.

He was a storming tackler too, and he and Krige developed an unusual but effective policy. Loubser would cut in from his right wing and down the centre, usually with the ball, leaving the incisive Krige available to snatch up the loose ball or to scrag the wing on the few occasions the opponent managed to pass the ball.

Another of Loubser's tactics was to catch the ball with just his left arm. His first season's break had left him with a permanently damaged right arm, which he could not straighten for the rest of his life. But he also felt that taking the ball in both hands meant slackening pace slightly and once Loubser had steam up, he wanted to maintain it. It was not an unusual sight to see Loubser crossing the goalline with the ball tucked on his left hip – he hadn't had time to transfer it to a more conventional grip.

Loubser played all four internationals in the British Isles in 1906, and also against France, not then considered a full test opponent. The only back to play all the internationals, he scored two tries in the 15–12 win over Ireland and a vital storming try in the 11–10 win over Wales.

Though always regarded as a Western Province man, Loubser left the Cape late in 1908 and worked in mines. Eventually he captained Transvaal

and also played for Orange Free State, returning to his beloved Stellenbosch in 1915, his final season.

His last internationals were the first and third tests against Tom Smyth's touring British team of 1910, both of which the Springboks won. Loubser was not available for the second test, which the Springboks lost.

A surveyor by trade, Loubser entered Parliament in 1948, the year South Africa's apartheid policies were laid down.

LOUW, 'BOY'
Western Province and South Africa
18 internationals for Sth Africa 1928–38

Kicking around an old rugby ball stuffed with cabbage leaves and corn stalks with his eight brothers marked the beginning of rugby interest for Matthys Michael ('Boy') Louw, one of the greatest forwards produced by South Africa.

One of his brothers, Fanie, played alongside him in the Springboks and Boy's twin, Japie, might have too, but was tragically killed at a young age. All nine boys reached at least senior club status.

A great favourite with the crowds, mostly because of his versatility as a forward, Boy Louw was strong and hard. The people liked him because he was always 'up to something' in the pack. He could, and did, play successfully in every position up front. Although not physically imposing, Louw was tough enough to take part in any rough and tumble. He was also a forward who could pass or dummy effectively.

By the time he was 18 he had made sufficient mark in rugby to be included in the Western Province team which played Cove-Smith's 1924 British touring team. Louw made his debut for South Africa in 1928 in two of the tests against the All Blacks. That series was drawn, but after that the Springboks won each series that Louw was involved in. It was appropriate that he was a member of one of South Africa's greatest teams, the 1937 team that proved so successful in New Zealand.

It was indicative of the times that Louw, nicknamed the 'Master', actually took part in only five test series spread over ten years. However, his total of 18 international appearances

stood as the South African record until 'Salty' du Rand beat it in 1956.

When Louw died in 1988, aged 82, his former Springbok team-mate, Danie Craven, described him as 'probably the greatest player in his era'.

LOVERIDGE, DAVE
Auckland, Taranaki, Harlequins and New Zealand
24 internationals for N. Zealand 1978–85

After the All Blacks had secured a hard-fought win against the British Isles at Wellington in 1983, the home coach, Bryce Rope, was asked, 'What about Dave Loveridge?' The articulate Rope turned his eyes skyward (or rather to the bare rafters of the dungeon under the old stand at Athletic Park): 'I said to Dave, "That is the finest display I have seen from any halfback in any game, anywhere in the world."'

Rich praise indeed for 'Trapper' Loveridge, and justified after that masterly display, the best of many outstanding appearances by one of the best of New Zealand's halfbacks.

First a reserve, and then chosen for New Zealand in 1978 when he was already 26, Loveridge became the regular test halfback in 1979 and remained there until forced, by a serious leg injury, to miss the 1984 season. He fought back to win a place in the 1985 All Blacks picked to tour South Africa – a team which ended up in Argentina instead – but retired from international rugby after playing the second test there. He then played a short while in England. He was captain of New Zealand in 1979 and 1980.

LOWE, CYRIL
Blackheath and England
25 internationals for England 1913–23

It is a remarkable commentary on Cyril Lowe's try-scoring ability that his record of 18 tries in 25 internationals for England was not broken until Rory Underwood passed it in 1990! A snappy right wing, Lowe stood only 5ft 6 ins (1.67 m) tall and weighed 9 stone (59 kg). But he had great athletic ability in a number of different sports.

Lowe came into the England team before World War I. During the war he was a crack fighter pilot, who won the MC and the DFC, and rose to the rank of Group Captain. After the war he

Dave Loveridge, one of New Zealand's finest halfbacks.

The Michael Lynagh kicking style.

became part of the most successful rugby era England ever had.

During the 13 years Cyril Lowe played for England it won four Grand Slams and four championships in the Five Nations series. For a short time he was England's most-capped player (later beaten by Wavell Wakefield). Allowing for the war years, all his caps were won consecutively.

Lowe was much more than a try-scoring wing. He was a hero on the field because he gave so much more than one would have thought possible for a man his size. He was a ferocious tackler, an expert kicker, and there were many who called Cyril Lowe 'England's greatest wing'.

LUX, JEAN-PIERRE
Tyrosse, Dax and France
47 internationals for France 1967–75

With his great friend Claude Dourthe, Jean-Pierre Lux was one of a pair of dentists, both from Dax, who played together many times for France.

Unlike many of the brilliant players of his era, Lux was a steady and consistent player, but he still exhibited a high degree of skill and efficiency. He won some caps on the wing during his long career, but centre was the position he much preferred. His total of 38 caps as a centre was the French record for a time.

Lux played first for France in 1967 and later that year toured to South Africa. He also visited New Zealand in 1968 and Australia in 1972.

LYNAGH, MICHAEL
Queensland and Australia
43 internationals for Australia 1984–90

The joint holder of the world record for points in international rugby – he passed the then record of Argentine Hugo Porta in 1990, with 564 points, only to be matched again by Porta, following the latter's tour of Britain with the Argentine team. Lynagh also held a much over-looked record, having scored in every one of his internationals, including a try against Wales in the Australian Grand Slam tour of 1984, when he was temporarily relieved of kicking duties.

Lynagh has often been compared with the other 'down under' kicking machine, Grant Fox, and their records are indeed comparable. Critics claim that Lynagh has scored many points against 'inferior' opposition, but an analysis indicates his record is in no way embellished by these matches. In fact he has had hefty points tallies against France (24 [the record], 23, 17 and 16); Scotland (21); Wales (18); New Zealand (17); England (18); Ireland (17), as well as 20 or more against Canada, Italy, Argentina and the United States.

Born in October 1963, Lynagh's first sporting love was cricket, and as a boy he played soccer and rugby league. He also played gridiron during the year he spent in the United States at the age of 15. It was not until he shifted to Brisbane as a teenager that he started playing rugby and, because his kicking prowess with a soccer ball was already known, he was given the kicking duties as well.

Lynagh made his Queensland debut at 18, in 1982, and he toured Italy and France with the Wallabies late in 1983, when he had just turned 20. The magical Mark Ella was then the man in charge of the flyhalf position for Aus-tralia, but Lynagh had his first taste of test rugby as inside centre against Fiji in 1984. He missed the home series against New Zealand, but played out-side Ella in all the Grand Slam tests in Britain.

There was no stopping Lynagh, who had seven conversions and three pen-alties against Canada in 1985, and six conversions against Italy, a prelude to his scoring 17 points in the four home internationals of 1986. In 1990, he took his own Australian test record to 24 points against France, then equalled it against the United States.

Lynagh was something more than just a goal-kicking flyhalf, however, and for most of the 1980s he remained a strong challenger for recognition as the world's finest all-round player in this position. He had all the other skills: he was an accurate tactical kicker and a coverer and defender, as well as possessing much more than adequate attacking flair and ball skills.

He had occasional failures and some poor games – but not many. The Wal-labies would have performed less successfully in the 1980s without 'Noddy' Lynagh.

M

McBRIDE, WILLIE JOHN
Ballymena and Ireland
63 internationals for Ireland 1962–75
17 internationals for British Isles 1962–74

One of the outstanding figures of world rugby who set a record for most international caps by an individual in his time, and who gained great respect as a leader.

During the latter days of his playing career, William James McBride became known as 'Willie John'. He was an imposing lock, immensely powerful in all aspects of forward play, who specialised in giving only good ball to his halfback whether from lineout, maul or scrum. He had enormous determination and his rivalries with other top players of his day, such as Colin Meads of New Zealand and Frik du Preez of South Africa, were worth travelling miles to see. Perhaps his greatest attribute was his ability to inspire others to play with equal dedication.

In his time McBride knew success: as pack leader for the 1971 Lions in New Zealand, as captain of the 1974

Willie John McBride, 1983

Lions in South Africa and as captain of Ireland in its first championship win in 23 years, in 1974. But he also knew defeat: 26 of his games for Ireland were losses. From those varying results McBride emerged as a player of true character and greatness. He never gave in. He was idolised at home and deeply respected abroad.

McBride, then known as 'Bill', began his international rugby as a lock for Ulster in 1960–61, marking the great South African, Johann Claassen, in a Springbok tour game. The young McBride was one of nine new caps brought in by the Irish selectors for the match against England in 1962. Even though he was not in the winning team that day, or indeed that season, he was chosen soon after, as a 21-year-old, for the British Isles tour of South Africa. His courage was epitomised that season when he played the last part of the game against France with his left tibia bone broken.

South Africa in 1962 was a baptism of fire. The young Ballymena man played in two tests: both were losses. He also suffered the pain of defeat in New Zealand in 1966 when the All Blacks wiped aside the Lions by four tests to nil. Two wins against Australia were small consolation.

In 1968, on the Lions tour to South Africa, McBride was again in the losing team, and it was not until 1971 in New Zealand that he smelt the sweetness of victory.

His ultimate performance was with the British team of 1974, which won its test series with the Springboks so dramatically. On that tour McBride, the captain, exhorted his men to 'take no prisoners'. They reacted superbly to his leadership demands and did not lose a game on tour. Their three test victories, with a draw in the fourth test, represented the biggest humiliation for a major 'home' team in rugby history.

On that tour the cry '99' was also used. It was said that McBride had previously suffered at the hands of All Blacks and Springboks in the physical side of the game. He was determined that there should be no more. Thus '99'

called for all his players to get alongside their team-mates and fight the opposition together. It was a controversial tactic but one which McBride and his team felt was necessary.

Between his Lions tours he added to his tally of Irish caps, building towards the massive total of 63. His five Lions tours, three in all to South Africa and two to Australia and New Zealand, added another 17 caps, bringing his total to 80 caps. Thus he became the world's greatest cap-winner, an honour he kept until his fellow Ulsterman Mike Gibson passed it by one in 1979.

In all his test matches McBride scored only one try, against France in his second to last game for Ireland.

After his retirement in 1975 he was, for a time, the Irish coach. In 1983 he was manager of the British Isles team in New Zealand.

McCORMICK, FERGIE
Canterbury and New Zealand
16 internationals for N. Zealand 1965–71

New Zealand has had a long line of outstanding fullbacks – Wallace, Nepia, Scott and Clarke were four of the best – but to them can be added the name of Fergie McCormick. And while the rag-tag McCormick was not a stylist like the others, his great attribute was his strength: physical, mental and psychological. He had a total commitment to the cause of his team, a pride which refused to allow him to bend the knee to anyone – and he was an extremely good rugby player. He was an unflinching and crunching defender, an outstandingly strong runner into the backline, deceptively fast (known to outsprint scorching wings the length of the field), and an accurate if untidy-looking goal-kicker.

After just one test against South Africa in 1965, McCormick returned to the New Zealand side in 1967 and remained first choice fullback until kicked off the field by Barry John in the opening test of the 1971 series against the British Isles.

His selection for the tour of Britain in late 1967 came in surprising circumstances. The incumbent in the fullback berth since the retirement of Don Clarke had been Mick Williment, who played the jubilee test against Australia. But when the side to tour was announced, McCormick was the only fullback named. There were two theories bandied around. One was that Williment had concealed an injury to play the jubilee test, a prestige occasion, and that angered coach Fred Allen. Another has it that the All Black selectors in fact named 31 players when they handed their list to NZRFU chairman Tom Morrison, and it was he who deleted Williment's name.

A sometimes abrasive character, McCormick gained notoriety in South Africa in 1970, when a stiff-arm tackle laid out Springbok wing Syd Nomis, and his long career for Canterbury came to an end after 17 seasons when he kicked an opposition player on the ground.

Though not a regular kicker for his club side, nor for Canterbury early in his career, McCormick scored 443 points in 43 matches for New Zealand. He scored a then world record 24 points in the second test against the 1969 Welsh tourists, and his New Zealand record of 2065 points was broken only in 1988 by Grant Fox.

McDOWELL, STEVE,

Bay of Plenty, Auckland and New
 Zealand
31 internationals for N. Zealand 1985–90

As the 'Geriatrics' – props Gary Knight and John Ashworth and hooker Andy Dalton – wound down their test careers in the mid-80s, a relative lightweight emerged as a prospective replacement. Steve McDowell had already had his prospects of representing New Zealand, at judo, dashed by New Zealand joining the boycott of the 1980 Moscow Olympic Games. So he single-mindedly chased rugby representation instead and was rewarded with selection for the (cancelled) South African tour in 1985. Actual representation came on the replacement tour to Argentina, McDowell propping in both internationals on the unfamiliar tighthead side; and once he and the other 'rebel' Cavaliers had served a two-match penance for their unauthorised tour in 1986, he was back in the New Zealand test side as the loosehead prop.

Only Gary Whetton was to join him as an ever-present player in All Black teams for the balance of the 1980s and into the 1990s, and McDowell became recognised as the finest prop in world rugby, perhaps the finest forward. Though relatively light for a prop, he was never bested in the scrums and his very quick acceleration and low centre of gravity made him a damaging runner with the loose ball.

This technically correct and very strong man also had firm ambitions. Long before the second World Cup was to be played he admitted to harbouring a desire to play in the third World Cup as well, and to captain New Zealand in it!

In 1989 McDowell was one of three New Zealanders to play for the historic 'Anzac' XV against the touring Lions in Australia. The others were fullback Kieran Crowley and inside centre Frano Botica.

McGEECHAN, IAN

Headingley and Scotland
32 internationals for Scotland 1972–79
8 internationals for British Isles 1974–77

A tidy centre or flyhalf who, after captaining his country nine times over two seasons – 1976–77 and 1978–79 – went on to become its coach. Later still he became coach to the 1989 British Isles team for its tour of Australia.

Ian McGeechan was a Scottish international with a slight Yorkshire accent, having moved from north of the border to Headingley in Leeds as a 16-year-old. He first played for Scotland against the All Blacks in November 1972. Another newcomer in the backline was fullback Andy Irvine. Between the two of them they scored Scotland's points, McGeechan with a dropped goal and Irvine with two penalties. Still the game was lost, 9–14.

From that season, McGeechan became a first choice for his country, though his preferred position was never truly resolved by his selectors. Of his 32 caps, 12 were as a flyhalf and 20 as a centre. In 1973 he played the whole of the Five Nations championship as a flyhalf, yet in 1975 he played the same matches as a centre. Although McGeechan might own up to a preference for the outer position, he was stylish, efficient and authoritative in either place.

In one of his matches as captain, against New Zealand in 1978, McGeechan very nearly secured a draw for Scotland. The weather had closed in to create surely the darkest conditions in which any game has been played in Edinburgh. In the gloom the All Blacks were leading 12–9, with only minutes remaining, when McGeechan secured the ball and attempted a dropped goal from a handy position. Given his talent at such a kick, a drawn match could have resulted. But in the dark the New Zealand player Doug Bruce sneaked up quickly on McGeechan's kick. The charged-down ball was then booted the length of the field by New Zealand players and a converted try resulted. The 18–9 final score to the All Blacks was somewhat flattering: Scottish supporters felt that Bruce was well over the offside line, and that the darkness preventing the referee seeing.

McGeechan was also a Lion, touring to South Africa in 1974 and to New Zealand in 1977. On both tours he played all four test matches, acquitting himself outstandingly in two tough rugby climates.

After retirement his sound ideas on the game soon saw him appointed Scotland's assistant coach, a position he held for the inaugural Rugby World Cup in 1987. With the retirement of Derek Grant he took over as Scottish coach in 1988, and acquitted himself so well in that role that he secured the British Isles coaching job for the Aus-

Ian McGeechan

Top: A selection of caps awarded to players at Rugby School between 1867 and 1893. Adrian Stephenson
Below: Some of the spoils of a compulsive programme-collector! Herb Grant

*Rugby is not always played on a hard
and fast track – but the players* . . .

. . . *and their loyal and stoical fans still
turn out in any weather.* Peter Bush

Alistair McHarg (second from left) with fellow Scottish lineout players Ian McLauchlan, Peter Brown and Roger Arneil.

tralian visit in 1989. That team won its series 2–1 over the Wallabies. Then followed the 1990 home season, where McGeechan guided Scotland to its fourth Grand Slam win. McGeechan by then was being acclaimed as one of rugby's greatest coaches, but such compliments rested lightly on the modest Scotsman's shoulders.

McHARG, ALISTAIR

West of Scotland, London Scottish and
    Scotland
44 internationals for Scotland 1968–79

An unorthodox lock who could leap at lineout time and push at scrum time with the best of them, Alistair McHarg could also turn up running like the wind in the most unusual places. As back moves swept upfield in international matches, the huge figure of McHarg would often join in – much to spectators' delight and opponents' confusion.

As a youngster McHarg had played in the backs, and enjoyed the experience hugely. But time saw him grow into a massive figure of a man at 6ft 5in (1.95m) and 15 stone (97kg) so a place was soon found for him in the forwards. McHarg was too loose a lock for the purists, but his mobile style of play, if unusual, was also successful.

An unusual record was set by McHarg in 1979 when, with 44 caps, he became the highest-capped player never to travel on a British Isles tour, breaking the 50-year-old 'record' of Irishman George Stephenson. Business comitments ruled him out for travelling on long tours. One feat that McHarg did achieve was to become Scotland's most capped lock. Indeed, when his international career ended in 1979, only Sandy Carmichael, the prop, had played more test matches for the dark blues.

McINTYRE, ANDY

Queensland and Australia
38 internationals for Australia 1982–89

A bulwark of Australian scrums in the 1980s, Andy McIntyre made his debut on the unheralded but reasonably successful tour by Mark Ella's team to New Zealand in 1982, playing all three tests after Stan Pilecki was unavailable. Pilecki kept him out of the test side at home in 1983, but McIntyre returned for the tests to France later

that year and went on to play 15 consecutive test matches before giving way to Mark Hartill in 1986.

But he returned for the World Cup, playing five of the six matches. He also played the Bledisloe Cup match against the All Blacks later that year, toured Argentina also in 1987, and played all six of Australia's internationals in 1988. But his career was finished when chosen only for the Bledisloe Cup match of 1989.

McLAUCHLAN, IAN

Jordanhill and Scotland
43 internationals for Scotland 1969–79
8 internationals for British Isles 1971–74

Originally John, but later Ian, McLauchlan was known throughout the rugby world as the 'Mighty Mouse', or – if you knew him well – just 'Mouse'. He became one of the best props in the game in his time. At only 5ft 9ins (1.75m), he was short for an international prop, but his scrummaging technique on the loosehead side was such that he disrupted and dominated the best scrummagers around.

McLauchlan played some outstanding games for Scotland, captaining it a record 19 times, but he perhaps saved his best rugby for the two tours he made with the British Isles.

The first was to New Zealand in 1971, when it was expected he would be the number two loosehead prop behind Ray McLoughlin of Ireland. Sadly, in a roughhouse tour game

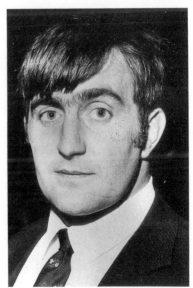

Ian McLauchlan

against Canterbury, both McLoughlin and Scotsman Sandy Carmichael were punched out of further action on the tour, so in stepped 'Mighty Mouse' McLauchlan and Irishman Sean Lynch to take over as first choice props. They performed admirably and played a vital part in the downfall of the New Zealand team. The man derisive New Zealanders called 'Mickey Mouse' returned home a hero.

In 1974 McLauchlan lived up to his reputation with the British Isles in South Africa. In game after game he met South African provincial and test opponents who were much bigger by far than he was, but his strength in the scrums belied his height and he was never bettered.

McLauchlan sometimes had his problems with the Scottish selectors: early in the 1977 home international series, after 32 internationals and four seasons as an excellent motivational captain, he was dropped. Without 'Mouse', Scotland's fortunes plummeted. He was eventually recalled, although not as captain, but by then the rot had set in for the team. Scotland played 13 internationals without a win and many said McLauchlan's inspirational leadership was one of the missing key factors.

Ian McLauchlan played his last international in 1979 at the age of 37. Appropriately it was against the All Blacks for, counting his tour for the Lions, it was the eighth time he had played a test against New Zealand. In a last gesture the captaincy was handed back to him but the Scots plunged to a 6–20 defeat. The 'Mighty Mouse' did not appear in top rugby again.

After his retirement he became a keen marathon runner, and also took up writing about the game.

McLEAN, DOUG (SNR)
Queensland and Australia
3 internationals for Australia 1904–05

McLEAN, DOUG (JNR)
Queensland and Australia
10 internationals for Australia 1933–36

McLEAN, BILL
Queensland and Australia
5 internationals for Australia 1946–47

McLEAN, JEFF
Queensland and Australia
13 internationals for Australia 1971–74

McLEAN, PAUL
Queensland and Australia
30 internationals for Australia 1974–82

McLEAN, PETER
Queensland and Australia
16 internationals for Australia 1978–82

A remarkable rugby-playing dynasty: six members of a Queensland family, who between them won 77 caps for Australia.

It all began with Douglas McLean, a pacy and strong wing who had his debut against Britain in 1904 and also toured New Zealand in 1905.

Doug had three sons who played for Australia. The first was Douglas (jnr), also a wing, who toured South Africa in 1933. Like his father, he later turned to rugby league.

William (Bill), the second son, was picked for the ill-fated team that arrived in England the week of the outbreak of World War II: it returned home without playing a game.

When rugby resumed after the war, in 1946, Bill was the Australian captain and his brother John (Jack) was also in the team which toured New Zealand. Bill played the tests, one as lock and one as flanker, but Jack, another wing, did not make the main XV.

The following year Bill was captain for one test against the All Blacks in Australia before being picked to lead a

Paul McLean

massive round-the-world trip in which 41 games were played. Sadly, in the sixth tour match he broke a leg and had to spend weeks in hospital. He did not play again, his great friend, Trevor Allan, taking over the leadership.

Bob McLean, a fourth son of Doug, did not reach any great heights as a player himself, but was actually the key to the family's rugby tradition. According to the family, Bob might have been the greatest of all the McLeans, but injuries cut his career short. Bob's two sons, Jeff and Paul, became Wallabies in the 1970s.

Jeff, who played on the wing for Australia, began his tests in 1971 in the protest-marred series against South Africa. He toured New Zealand in 1972 and Wales and England in 1973. He was a speedy player and a useful left-footed goal-kicker. The 1974 first test between New Zealand and Australia at Sydney was the only time that McLean brothers played together in the same test match. It also signalled the end of test football for Jeff (a broken leg ended further ambitions) but it was the start of the remarkable sequence by Paul McLean.

Paul played for his country for nine seasons, fashioning a worldwide reputation for deadly goal-kicking and astute, skilful play from either fullback or flyhalf. During that time he suffered leg, shoulder, arm and finger injuries that would have sidelined many other men. He was one of Australian rugby's truly great players.

His final total of 257 points was an Australian record, way ahead of Arthur McGill's next best total of 88 points. Paul McLean's records stood until his fellow Queenslander, Michael Lynagh, came through to set new figures in 1987.

Paul played 30 tests, emulating his Uncle Bill when he captained Australia on a tour to Fiji in 1980. He might have captained the team for a longer time but injuries disrupted the remainder of that season.

The seventh member of the McLeans to play for Australia was Peter McLean, son of Bill, who made the Wallabies in 1978. Peter was an industrious tight forward who gained 16 caps, including 11 in the company of his cousin, Paul.

Paul and Peter McLean played for Queensland in the years when rugby really took off in the sunshine state. The admiration Queensland's fans had

Peter McLean

for the McLean family was never better shown than in 1982, when a special match, attended by the Duke of Edinburgh, was put on to mark Paul's 100th appearance for the state. Queensland beat the Australian Barbarians and McLean scored two penalty goals which took him past 1000 points for Queensland.

MACLEAR, BASIL
Cork County, Monkstown, Blackheath, Bedford, Cork Constitution and Ireland
11 internationals for Ireland 1905–07

One of rugby's eccentrics, Basil Maclear was a Hampshire boy with an Irish father. When he was rejected by England as a potential international (an official said he was 'not good enough') he adopted Ireland in a bid to play top rugby.

This he did, making his debut for the Irish against England at the Mardyke in Cork in 1905. From all accounts Maclear played brilliantly and his try and assistance in two others was a firm reminder to England's selectors that they had let his talent slip through their fingers.

Maclear often played his rugby wearing distinctive white calfskin gloves. Once against Wales he added to his sartorial splendour by turning out in military puttees.

Maclear's colourful life in rugby lasted only three seasons. He had been

a soldier in the Boer War as a member of the Dublin Fusiliers, and he returned to that regiment when World War I broke out. He was one of eight Irish rugby internationals who lost their lives in the Great War.

McLEOD, HUGH
Hawick and Scotland
40 internationals for Scotland 1954–62
6 internationals for British Isles 1955–59

'Hughie' McLeod did not take up playing rugby until he was nearly 18 years old. At school he had no time for team games and it was only after taking on a working life of apprentice plastering that his strength and interest in rugby expanded. Within three years he was playing Scottish senior trials, and he eventually became a tough, hard prop.

McLeod made his debut against France in 1954, and once in the Scottish team he was never dropped. He began as a tighthead but finished as a loosehead and was equally adept in both positions. He retired at the surprisingly early age of 29, when many felt he could have played on for years.

He made two tours for the Lions, to South Africa in 1955 and to Australia and New Zealand in 1959, and he toured South Africa with Scotland in 1960.

McLeod gained a reputation as one of the hardest forwards of his time. His dedication was total and he demanded the same of his club and test team-mates. One writer described his attitude on the field as 'uncompromising – and brutally frank into the bargain!'

One Hawick story has it that once McLeod was faced with a brash young opponent in a club game who asked out loud, 'I wonder what lesson we'll learn from the great McLeod today?' In the next scrum the young fellow placed his hand on the ground for balance, whereupon McLeod promptly stood on it. As the scrum broke up and the young player was left holding his hand in excruciating pain, McLeod was heard to mutter in an audible voice, 'There endeth the first lesson, sonny boy'!

He was also an expert sevens player who could show surprising speed (for a prop!) in that game. In Scotland the colourful Hugh Ferns McLeod, a dedicated Hawick and South of Scotland man, is regarded as 'one of the greats'.

MacLEOD, KEN

Fettes College and Scotland
10 internationals for Scotland 1905–08

Remembered as the player who *could* have been a rugby international at the tender age of 15, Ken ('Grunt') MacLeod was invited to play for Scotland in 1903 while still a student at Fettes College in Edinburgh, but his headmaster refused him permission. Had he played he would have been even younger than Charles ('Hippo') Reid and Ninian Finlay, who had set the world's record for young international rugby players at 17 years and 36 days.

MacLeod was invited to play for Scotland on several other occasions before, finally, he was permitted. His debut, at 17 years and 9 months, was against New Zealand in 1905.

In all, MacLeod, a big centre or wing, played 10 internationals before he turned 21, but the death of his brother Lewis, also an international, during a game in 1907, led to his acceding to his father's request and quitting in 1908.

McLOUGHLIN, RAY

University College Dublin, Blackrock College, Gosforth and Ireland
40 internationals for Ireland 1962–75
3 internationals for British Isles 1966

Ray McLoughlin's rugby record alone speaks of a significant contribution on the field of play for Ireland and the British Isles. But in addition to the 43 internationals he played, McLoughlin had a profound influence in another sphere. He was a planner and schemer of the highest value for his various teams. He plotted and analysed forward play and tactical approaches and his greatest success came in improving communications between forwards and backs. Even for those in the depths of the scrum, he insisted that code words and signs be used for back play. That way, he said, everyone in the team, and not just insular units, would be informed.

It worked for McLoughlin when he was the captain of Ireland in 1965 and led his country in its best season for 13 years. After he had played well in 1966, there was surprise when he was relieved of the leadership, and according to his supporters, Ireland missed his high degree of motivation.

It is said that when McLoughlin was Ireland's captain no one was permit-

ted to smile for the pre-match photographs, lest the build-up atmosphere be broken!

After the 1966 British Isles tour of Australasia, in which McLoughlin appeared in three of the six test matches, he retired for a number of seasons. Business, studies and injuries prevented him from playing.

McLoughlin returned to play for Ireland in 1971 and for the Lions team on its next tour of New Zealand the same year. Sadly, injuries sustained in the controversial match against Canterbury meant he had to return home early. Even after he had gone, his remaining team-mates insisted that it was the McLoughlin influence in communication, motivation and technique that stayed with the team and played an important part in their series win over New Zealand.

MacNEILL, 'HUGO'

Blackrock College, London Irish and Ireland
37 internationals for Ireland 1981–88
3 internationals for British Isles 1983

His given name was Hugh, but everywhere in the rugby world this popular figure became known as 'Hugo'. He was a courageous fullback who came to his long international career via

rugby at Blackrock College and Oxford University. He made his international debut against France in 1981.

MacNeill played three times in the inter-varsities match, in 1982–83–84, and from then until the end of his career in 1988 he missed very few games for Ireland. He was a British Lion to New Zealand in 1983, where he played in two of the four tests and was a replacement in another.

MacNeill never flinched from any defensive situation; he could catch the high ball with aplomb and his tackling was always safe and tight.

MALAYSIA RFU

The first match in Malaya was recorded in 1892. In its early days, rugby in Malaya was played and substantially backed by expatriate Britons, but more recently the emphasis has switched to Malays, Chinese, Indians and Eurasians. The game is in good heart in Malaysia, with many competitions at various age groups and senior levels.

A key component of Malaysian rugby is the annual inter-state competition for the *HMS Malaya* Cup which was presented by the ship's crew in return for hospitality received on shore during a visit in 1922. The original cup was lost during the Japanese occupa-

Hugo MacNeill, playing for the Lions against New Zealand, 1983.

The 1926–27 New Zealand Maori team in Swansea.

tion, but was found in the jungle in 1961.

Malaysia's most consistent international rival is neighbouring Thailand. The two play a biennial match for the Vaijiralongkorn Cup, presented by the King of Thailand in 1955, and named after the Thai Crown Prince. Malaya scored a resounding 47–6 win in the first game, although competition has been much more even in the years since.

The 1978 Asian championships were hosted in Kuala Lumpur by the Malaysian Rugby Union. Malaysia has also competed a number of times in the Hong Kong Sevens tournament.

MANAWATU RFU

Based around New Zealand's North Island town of Palmerston North, the Manawatu Rugby Football Union was formed in 1886. For a time (1925–32) the province was amalgamated with the neighbouring coastal area of Horowhenua and during this period the combined union, named Manawhenua, won the Ranfurly Shield. Not for another 50 years was the symbol of New

Zealand provincial rugby strength back in the province. In 1976 Manawatu beat Auckland 12–10 to capture the shield and for the next 25 months it resisted 13 challenges. This is now remembered as the greatest era the province experienced.

The team had an immensely strong forward pack, one of the toughest ever seen in New Zealand provincial rugby, and included players such as the prominent All Blacks Gary Knight, Kevin Eveleigh, Mark Donaldson, Mark Shaw and Doug Rollerson.

North Auckland took the shield by 12–10 in 1978, but Manawatu's strength continued and in 1980 it won the national division one championship.

Manawatu plays its home games at the Showgrounds Oval in Palmerston North. The original grandstand was burned down in somewhat suspicious circumstances in the early 1980s, but a new stand was built in time for the province to host the Wales v Tonga game in the Rugby World Cup of 1987.

Manawatu does not have an impressive record against major touring

teams. In seven attempts, the combined Manawatu-Horowhenua team never beat a touring British team. Manawatu's first game on its own against the British Isles was in 1983, but again the home team lost, 18–25. Nor has Manawatu ever beaten a South African touring team. It has beaten Australia twice, in 1958 and 1978, but on many other tours Australia has beaten Manawatu.

Manawatu plays in green jerseys with narrow white bands.

MAORI RUGBY

An exciting part of the New Zealand rugby scene, where players with Maori blood play together in their own representative teams, working towards selection in the New Zealand Maori team (sometimes erroneously referred to as the 'Maori All Blacks'). To New Zealanders, the very expression 'Maori rugby' conjures up an image of fast, exciting football, played with adventure, dash and high emotion. The rugby writer T.P. McLean once said that Maori players deliver to the game 'the outstanding qualities of Maori war-

Sid Going receives a hero's welcome from coloured spectators, South Africa 1976.

riorhood: strength, pride, determination and skill'.

New Zealand rugby has been the richer for its Maori players. Men like George Nepia, Sid Going and Waka Nathan, the most famous of them, were leaders in uplifting the image of New Zealand rugby around the world. Other great players have been Davey Gage, Tom Ellison, Opai Asher, Tori Reid, the Smith brothers (Johnny and Peter), the other two Going brothers, Ken and Brian, Mac Herewini, Pat Walsh, Tane Norton, Hika Reid, Steven Pokere and Wayne Shelford. But these are only some of the scores of players of Maori descent who have played for the All Blacks.

Wayne Shelford first captained New Zealand in an international against Wales at Christchurch in 1988. Between then and 1990, when he was dropped from the team, he captained the All Blacks 14 times in tests – more than any other Maori player. Other Maoris who have captained the All Blacks in tests are Billy Stead (1905–08), Johnny Smith (1949) and Tane Norton (1977).

New Zealand Maori teams have often toured overseas. In 1888–89 a team, made up mainly of Maori players (but called the New Zealand Natives), toured the world in the forerunner for modern tours. They played 107 matches and were away from home for 14 months! (See NATIVES.) Other official Maori world tours were in 1926–27, 1982 and 1988, and there have also been numerous tours to Australia and to the Pacific Islands. For a time Australia awarded full international caps to its players chosen in games against the New Zealand Maoris.

Over the years New Zealand Maori teams have been involved in some epic encounters. Perhaps the most famous win was over France in 1961, when the Maoris won 5–3 in Napier. That town has featured strongly in Maori rugby history. In 1981 the New Zealand Maoris played a dramatic 12–12 draw with the South African touring team there. The game was played in front of hundreds of police in a ground surrounded by barbed-wire barriers aimed at keeping out anti-apartheid protesters. It was only a controversial dropped goal by Colin Beck that earned South Africa the draw.

In 1921 on the same ground, McLean Park, the Maoris had played a rough,

tough game against the first touring South African team. The Springboks won 9–8, but the struggle on the field was nothing compared with the furore that followed the game. A South African touring correspondent sent home an infamous cable which read:

'It's bad enough having to play a team officially designated New Zealand Natives (Maoris), but the spectacle of thousands of Europeans frantically cheering on a band of coloured men to defeat members of their own race was too much for the Springboks, who were frankly disgusted.'

A commotion followed and the South African government was forced to dissociate itself from the correspondent's remarks.

What the writer failed to grasp on his visit to New Zealand was the affection and pride New Zealanders had then, and still have today, for Maori rugby.

The only times Maori players have been unwanted in All Black teams have been when the New Zealand Rugby Union pandered to the demands of South Africa (in 1928, 1949 and 1960) and only white-skinned New Zealand players toured. Thankfully those days disappeared, for the New Zealand teams that travelled to the Republic in 1970 and 1976 were fully racially mixed and players such as Sid Going, Bryan Williams (part Samoan) and Billy Bush became rugby heroes to the coloured population in South Africa. It was a distinction that was denied earlier Maori stars like George Nepia, Waka Nathan and Johnny Smith.

Amidst the bitterness engendered in the continuing debate about sporting contact with South Africa and the politics of apartheid, the argument has been advanced that Maori rugby in itself is racist and should be abolished. Fortunately the commonsense view has prevailed: Maori rugby has always existed totally under the auspices of the New Zealand Rugby Union and is just one of a number of 'splinter' groups – such as Universities, Combined Services and New Zealand Marist (Catholic) teams – which also enjoy playing among themselves. To ban one might mean banning them all.

Every season the Northern Maoris of New Zealand play the Southern Maoris for the Prince of Wales Cup, a trophy presented for competition in

Maori rugby by the Prince of Wales in 1928. Every year the leading Maori player is awarded the Tom French Cup by the New Zealand Rugby Union. *See also* HAKA.

MARAIS, HANNES
Western Province, Eastern Province,
  North-East Cape and South Africa
35 internationals for Sth Africa 1963–74

A Springbok captain and tough prop who became one of his country's most accomplished players. His total of 35 test appearances was third in South Africa's all-time list, behind Jan Ellis and Frik du Preez.

A product of Stellenbosch University, Johannes Frederick Klopper ('Hannes') Marais came into the South African team for the first time in 1963, when he played one test against Australia. It was not until 1968 that he became a regular first choice prop. He was a mobile flanker earlier in his career, and he was equally at home on either side of the front row.

By 1971 he was appointed South Africa's captain for the protest-marred tour of Australia. His was the first Springbok team to complete an overseas tour without a single defeat. Marais was also captain in France in 1974 and for the dramatic series against the British Isles at home in 1974.

Altogether Marais captained his country 11 times, third on the all-time South African list. Counting all tour appearances he played 75 games in the Springbok colours.

MARIE, BERNARD
Bernard Marie, a leading French referee, was running as a touch judge in the France v Wales game at Stade Colombes in Paris in 1965. When the neutral referee for the day, R.W. Gilliland of Ireland, injured a leg and retired hurt after 32 minutes, Marie and his fellow touch-judge were faced with the choice of who should take over control of the game. So they tossed a coin. It is not recorded whether Bernard Marie won or lost the toss, but he did take up the whistle, thus becoming the first referee to replace another during a full international. France already had 22 points on the scoreboard but failed to score again, avoiding any charges of bias from a 'home' referee! (France won 22–13.)

MARKOTTER, A.F.
The dominant personality of South African rugby until the arrival on the scene of Dr Danie Craven. Markotter was a coach, administrator, selector and powerful rugby authority, but unlike Craven he rose to prominence without having been a leading Springbok player. Like Craven, Markotter had a strong association with the Stellenbosch rugby scene. His playing days were restricted (by a cricket injury) but nevertheless he achieved the feat of captaining the first South African provincial team to beat an overseas touring team when his Western Province Country XV beat the British team of 1903.

A South African selector and coach from 1921 to 1938, 'Oubaas Mark' or 'Mr Mark' was considered by many to be the finest judge of a footballer of his time. He created many Springboks with his early judgement of their talent – this was never shown better than in his early selection of Danie Craven himself. It is said that only Markotter wanted Craven in the Springboks of 1931–32: he managed to persuade his co-selectors and Craven's long career in international rugby began.

Markotter was widely influential in the South African rugby scene until his death in 1956.

MARLBOROUGH RFU
A New Zealand rugby province situated at the northern tip of the South Island. Marlborough RFU was formed in 1888 and is centred around the rural town of Blenheim. Marlborough plays its home games on Lansdowne Park in Blenheim, in cardinal (red) colours.

The Duke of Marlborough defeated the French in a famous battle in 1704 at a place called Blenheim and, in rugby terms, the Marlborough rugby team repeated that feat in 1968 when it scored one of its most sensational wins, beating the French tourists by 24–11. Marlborough later had a day of glory in 1973, when it won the Ranfurly Shield off a much-vaunted Canterbury team. The shield was retained in Blenheim for just over a year.

Marlborough's best known player was Alan Sutherland, the 1968–76 All Black. His brother Ray was captain of the province during the Ranfurly Shield era. Another star and later All Black was wing Brian Ford, whose runaway try on Lancaster Park sealed victory for the province when it lifted the Ranfurly Shield.

MARTIN, ALLAN
Aberavon and Wales
34 internationals for Wales 1973–81
1 international for the British Isles 1977

An outstanding lineout exponent from Wales, Allan ('Panther') Martin ended his career as Wales's most-capped international lock.

Martin was a loyal member of the Aberavon club, making more than 600 appearances and playing for the club for 21 years, his last game at the age of 38.

He made his debut for Wales against Australia in 1973. In 27 of his matches in the Welsh colours, he locked the scrum with Swansea's Geoff Wheel. He was also a more than useful goalkicker, something not seen very often in a forward.

On the 1973 tour of Canada he scored 28 points, which was then a Welsh record for an individual in one game. Martin's last game for Wales was against France in 1981.

He played for the British Isles on two tours, to New Zealand in 1977 and to South Africa in 1980, but on those tours he played only one international.

Allan Martin

MASO, JO

Perpignan, Narbonne and France
25 internationals for France 1966–73

Was there ever a more brilliant running back than Jo Maso of France? He had everything desired in a player: speed, elusiveness, nimbleness of hand and foot, inventiveness, a repertoire of amazing passes, flair, and the ability to kick. He epitomised the public image of French rugby players in the 1960s: he was handsome, open, sharp, attacking, with star quality in abundance.

Jo Maso had it all, yet he ended his career unwanted for his national team.

Maso first played for France against Italy in 1966 and came to the attention of British fans a season later. On the French tour of New Zealand in 1968 Maso displayed his unique talent on fast, dry fields and was quickly rated one of the best ever seen in that country.

While his talents were always appreciated by rugby fans, Maso soon found that they were not always admired by the selectors. It was his misfortune to play in 10 consecutive internationals which France could not win. No matter how brilliant he was as

an individual, he was associated with failure, so he was dropped.

Through 1970 and 1971 Maso languished out of the limelight. He had two appearances in 1972, and two more a season later, but by the age of 28 he was out of the national team for good.

Just why France treated his genius so casually has never really been explained – any other country in the world would have jumped at the chance of playing Maso regularly. He ended his career playing for the Narbonne club where, one would hope, he was appreciated more fully.

MEADS, COLIN

King Country and New Zealand
55 internationals for N. Zealand 1957–71

The most famous rugby forward in the world during his playing days, memories of Meads are soured by two incidents – one during his playing days and the other much later.

In 1967, Meads aimed to kick the ball as Scotland flyhalf David Chisholm was stooping to pick it up, and was ordered off by referee Kevin Kelleher. The decision was considered borderline at best, but it besmirched Meads's reputation.

Nineteen years later Meads again incurred unfavourable publicity when (then a New Zealand selector) he accompanied the Cavaliers on their tour to South Africa as coach. While the players incurred short suspensions, Meads was reprimanded – his 'suspension' came a few months later when he was dumped from the selection panel.

But these incidents should not colour the career of 'Pine Tree' Meads, who first played for a New Zealand side, the Colts, in 1955. A reserve with the All Blacks by the end of their gripping series with the 1956 Springboks, Meads became a full All Black in 1957.

In those days he was a loose forward, either a flanker or a No. 8, but he soon moved into the lock position and remained there for most of his career. Dropped once in 1959 and again in 1962, Meads then played 31 consecutive internationals before a broken arm kept him out of the opening of the 1970 series against South Africa.

Meads was vice-captain on that tour, and led New Zealand in the lost series against the Lions in 1971. That was his farewell to international rugby, though he remained available, and many felt he would have been of great value as a 'senior pro' on the troubled 1972–73 tour of Britain. He had long held that position unofficially anyway, and there are many stories of Meads sorting out boisterous young players and explaining to them the honour of playing for New Zealand and the standards of behaviour expected.

Never a great leaper in the lineouts, Meads nonetheless won his share of the ball and what he didn't win was usually untidy ball for the opposition.

He rucked, mauled and drove strongly, always with total commitment – often in the company of his brother Stan, also a test lock.

Meads played 361 first class matches, a record for a New Zealander, and his 55 test matches are also a record. He played 139 matches for King Country between 1955–72. A few years later, outsiders were astonished when the union turned down a nomination for life membership for Meads. Undeterred, he returned to serve the union as president, and also as coach.

Fergie McCormick said of Meads that he was 'a terrible man with the silver fern on. He regarded the All

The stylish Jo Maso, in action for France, 1968.

Colin Meads and Sid Going in typical All Black action.

Black jersey as pure gold. He could do so many things so much better than anyone else in a match, that he stood alone as the greatest player I have ever known.'

In any mythical All Black team of all time, Meads would always be chosen.

MELLISH, FRANK

Blackheath, Western Province, South
  Africa and England
6 internationals for England 1920–21
6 internationals for Sth Africa 1921–24

After serving in World War I for South Africa, Mellish's business interests took him to England where he played in the England trials and was named reserve for a match against Wales early in 1920. There were some high jinks on the train en route to Cardiff resulting in Wavell Wakefield being injured, so Mellish came into the side and stayed there for the rest of the season.

After two matches the next season, the South African selectors started taking notice of their expatriate. Bill Schreiner, the convener, told Mellish he wanted him back for the trials which would choose the first team to tour New Zealand. Mellish won selection and – sometimes a lock for England –

played flanker in the first and third tests, then all four tests against the touring 1924 British side.

After his retirement he represented South Africa on the (England) Rugby Football Union, and managed the highly successful 1951–52 Springboks.

MELROSE RFC

Founded in 1877, Melrose will forever be remembered for giving rugby the seven-a-side version of the game. Since 1883 it has played host annually to the Melrose Sevens, still one of the most prestigious sevens tournaments in the world. Ned Haig, a butcher concerned with increasing Melrose's shaky finances, is credited with 'inventing' the game. He was a member of the club team which won the inaugural tournament and received the cup from the ladies of Melrose.

Traditionally, the sevens tournament is part of a Melrose Sports day. In its first 100 years, the host club has won it nine times.

Great Scottish players who have worn Melrose's yellow and black colours include Keith Robertson, the veteran centre who was an international over 10 years and who became the club's most-capped player. Before

Robertson, the hooker Frank Laidlaw was capped 32 times. The grand running back, Charlie Drummond, was a Melrose player in the years either side of World War II and later became convenor of the Scottish selectors.

The famous halfback pairing of David Chisholm and Alex Hastie, Scottish internationals in the 1960s, played many seasons for Melrose. Their first 10 internationals together were in unbeaten Scottish teams. Chisholm's brother Robin, a fullback, was also an international over five seasons.

The Scottish captain and Lions coach Jim ('Creamy') Telfer, who won 25 caps, was a Melrose man, in the top XV at the age of 16.

The club's home ground is the Greenyards, which is situated in the town centre.

MEREDITH, BRYN

London Welsh, Newport and Wales
34 internationals for Wales 1954–62
8 internationals for British Isles 1955–62

Bryn Meredith is one of a long list of rugby players who, once picked for their country, maintained their form right through to the end of their careers and were always among the first choices of their selectors.

Bryn (Brinley) Meredith was a top class hooker who had nine seasons with Wales. He was famous as a quick striker of the ball in scrums, but was also a useful forward able to compete in the loose play.

He was a player in the mould of the modern hooker, capable of running fast and playing almost as a fourth loose forward. He was also an outstanding sevens player.

Along with England's Dickie Jeeps, Meredith created a record by travelling on three tours with the Lions. He quickly became the number one hooker in Britain, playing in all four test matches on the 1955 Lions tour of South Africa. He then had the misfortune to miss playing six test matches on the 1959 Lions tour of Australia and New Zealand: the other hooker, Ronnie Dawson of Ireland, was the tour party's captain, and Meredith acted as understudy for the whole tour. But he was back in the Lions in South Africa in 1962, playing in all the test matches.

'Beetle' Meredith was Wales's most-capped hooker when he halted his career at the end of 1962, having missed only two internationals – once when he stood down because of a family bereavement. His record of 34 international appearances as a hooker for Wales remains unbeaten.

MESNEL, FRANCK
Racing Club and France
36 internationals for France 1986–91

A dashing French flyhalf and midfield player, Mesnel's first match for France was in the test against New Zealand at Nantes in 1986. He went to New Zealand for the World Cup in 1987, where he played in five games, playing in the final as flyhalf. He was listed as weighing 90 kg for that game, which moved one writer to call him 'The Hulk'.

Mesnel was the wit behind much of the lighter side of rugby at his club, Racing, in Paris. He started a club within the club called 'Showbiz', and he encouraged members to play some of their games dressed in something other than normal rugby attire. Mesnel and his team-mates played in the French club final several times wearing bow ties; in other games they played in berets (well, the backs did anyway!) and huge baggy pants.

The pink tie became synonymous with Franck Mesnel. He started a boutique for sports leisure wear, calling his shop 'Eden Park', and the bow tie became the logo that was stitched on all the garments.

With the arrival on the scene of Didier Camberabero, Mesnel was

After some hard exchanges among the forwards, captains Philippe Dintrans (left) and Murray Mexted, are addressed by the referee. France v Wellington, 1984.

shifted to centre. At the end of 1991 he was still going strong in the French team with 36 caps to his credit.

MEXTED, MURRAY
Wellington and New Zealand
34 internationals for N. Zealand 1979–85

After playing two unofficial 'internationals' against Argentina in 1979, Mexted marked his full test debut at Murrayfield with a spectacular try against Scotland. That was the start of a remarkable 34 consecutive internationals, all at No. 8, and Mexted became a senior member of the All Blacks' pack.

He was an outstanding, athletic forward, among New Zealand's all-time greats in his specialist position.

There is little dispute that, with Andy Haden and Andy Dalton, he played a key part in organising the Cavaliers' tour to South Africa, which effectively marked the end of his career. Then under pressure for his position from Wayne Shelford, Mexted in quick succession married a former Miss Universe, Lorraine Downes, and had his autobiography published. Some cynics suggest the title, *Pieces of Eight*, was more a reference to the financial rewards the rebel players were rumoured to have secured in South Africa than to his playing position.

His father, Graham, also a No. 8, was also an All Black in 1950–51.

MIAS, LUCIEN
Mazamet and France
29 internationals for France 1951–59

A legendary figure in French rugby, Lucien Mias dedicated much of his sporting life to raising the standards of the game in France, particularly in the forwards. He had grown tired of the error-ridden game the French national team played in the early 1950s, and believed in a controlled game in which unity would replace traditional French individualism.

Mias had been an international lock for seven seasons when he was chosen for the tour of South Africa in 1958. He had taken part in many games where the French played attractive football but lost the game, and at one point he became so frustrated he retired from playing to concentrate on his medical studies.

On the 1958 tour Mias persuaded his other forwards to co-ordinate their individual qualities and blend them into one common purpose. It worked. The French team was transformed and South Africans were astonished when their mighty Springboks were held to a 3–3 draw in the first test at Cape Town. By this time Mias had assumed the captaincy because of injury to the original leader, Michel Celaya.

The second test was to be the last game of the tour. Mias, passionately committed to the team's new discipline and style, drove his team-mates to

Franck Mesnel

follow him. It is said that the night before the game he visited team members in their hotel rooms and offered each a drink of rum as a 'toast' to the next day. Mias ended the night roaring drunk, but next day he played the game of his life. France won by 9–5 and Mias's reputation was made for life. France had never before scored such a famous series win.

The newfound unity of purpose continued in the next Five Nations championship and for the first time France, led by Mias in three of the games, emerged as the overall winner. After that season he was happy to retire and let others carry on the good work.

French writer Georges Duthen likened Mias to the 'Four Musketeers in One: Porthos for size and appetite, d'Artagnan for enthusiasm and fighting spirit, Athos for inflexibility and Aramis for the liking of study.'

Former English international Peter Robbins, also a prominent writer, said that Mias 'enriched French rugby, showed them the way and can truly be said to be the most significant player in French rugby history.'

MID-CANTERBURY RFU
Mid-Canterbury RFU, founded in 1904, was known until 1952 as Ashburton County. It has never been a major force in New Zealand rugby, although in the 1980s there were signs of improvement. An ongoing difficulty for rugby in the region is the proximity of Christchurch – just an hour's drive away. Promising young players cannot be blamed for wanting to take advantage of the opportunities and challenges of a larger union. Doug Bruce and Craig Green are two who began their first–class rugby in Mid-Canterbury but made their marks on the rugby world as prominent All Blacks from Canterbury.

Mid-Canterbury has not yet produced a test player; its three All Blacks so far have only participated in tour games.

MIDDLESEX SEVENS
The largest and one of the most prestigious tournaments for the abbreviated version of rugby union. Established in 1926, the Middlesex Sevens tournament always signals the climax of the English rugby season.

On the first day all the teams play off against each other on eight club grounds. The 12 qualifying teams, plus two invited clubs (a feature since 1934), and the previous year's finalist and runners-up, all head for Twickenham, seven days later, for the final series.

The finals day is one of the most colourful days in world rugby. The ground is always full (gate-takings go towards charity) and noisy, exuberant crowds cheer for the underdogs in every match. Though lesser clubs have occasionally done well, it is a Middlesex tradition that one of the 'major' clubs will come through to win. In the first 64 years of play the most successful clubs at the Middlesex sevens were Harlequins (winners 13 times), Richmond (9), London Welsh (8) and London Scottish (6).

Twickenham has always been the venue on finals day, except for the six years of World War II when the Richmond Athletic Ground was the stand-in venue.

MIDLANDS RUGBY
The Midlands Division is currently made up of Leicestershire, Nottinghamshire, Lincolnshire, Derbyshire, Staffordshire, Warwickshire and the North and East Midlands. The strongest centres of the game are the cities of Leicester and Coventry. In the past there have been several different configurations of counties.

Perhaps the greatest day for Midlands rugby came in 1931–32, when the team, inspired by the great Irish forward George Beamish, inflicted the only defeat on the touring Springboks, winning 30–21. A Leicestershire and East Midlands team drew with South Africa in 1960–61, and in 1972 a Midlands Counties (West) team beat Ian Kirkpatrick's All Blacks at Moseley.

Midlands also beat the Wallabies on their tours of 1908–09, 1957–58, 1966–67, 1975–76, and 1981–82.

When the divisional rugby championship of England was founded in 1985, Midlands won the first Thorne-EMI trophy.

MILLAR, BILLY
Western Province and South Africa
6 internationals for Sth Africa 1906–13

This determined loose forward was the man who kept coming in the back door to South African teams. Millar was lucky to play international rugby at all, for as a patriotic 15-year-old, he was badly wounded in the Boer War. Tramping, mountaineering and boxing helped to restore his fitness, but he was an unlucky triallist for the 1906 tour to Britain.

Then Millar's luck changed: Eric Mosenthal was unable to tour and Millar took his place, scoring a try against England in his only international. Millar also played twice – as captain – in the 1910 home series against the British and was chosen in unusual circumstances for the 1912–13 second tour to Britain.

It is said that the selectors knew that if they chose Millar, the South African Rugby Board would appoint him captain. It seems they were divided on that possibility, and eventually, on a split vote, Millar was the last forward named. As surmised, he was appointed captain and a successful one at that, though he missed the England and Scotland internationals.

The rehabilitation therapy undertaken by Millar after the Boer War had successful spin-offs. He became the Cape Colony amateur heavyweight boxing champion, retiring with an unbeaten record, and a successful walker in track and field athletics.

Wounded again in the First World War, Millar again recovered fitness and refereed two of the 1924 tests against the touring British side.

MILLAR, SID
Ballymena and Ireland
37 internationals for Ireland 1958–70
9 internationals for British Isles 1959–68

A vigorous and powerfully built prop, who had a long career with Ireland, Sid Millar also went on five tours with British Isles teams: three times as a player, once as coach and once as manager.

He was a tighthead prop in his club days at Ballymena in County Antrim, and also a tighthead for Ireland, but as a Lion he was often required to switch to the loosehead side, which he did with no problem.

Millar played 23 times for Ireland between 1958 and 1964, but then was not picked at all for some years, not even for his home province of Ulster. He returned as a much fitter and wiser prop in 1968 and promptly made the Irish and British Isles teams again.

His last game for Ireland was in 1970. As early as 1972 he was coach of the same team, and in 1974 he gained fame as coach of the Lions team which travelled triumphantly around South Africa.

In all Millar made six tours to South Africa either as player, coach or manager for Ireland or the Lions, and he made several other private visits involving rugby. This made him a controversial figure to some, but Sid Millar defended his right to visit South Africa saying, 'One does more by communicating than by boycotting.'

MILLER, TONY
New South Wales and Australia
41 internationals for Australia 1952–67

It is doubtful whether any player in Australian rugby history was more admired than the veteran utility forward Tony Miller. The admiration stemmed from his lengthy service and his untiring efforts at every level of the game. Being a club or test player, coach, captain or supporter, made no difference to Miller: at all levels he gave rugby everything he had.

He was a late developer, but with a high degree of personal commitment he became a senior player in Sydney and then rose to be a respected and tough member of the Wallaby forward pack in the 1950s.

He first played for Australia in 1952, in two test matches against Fiji, and he remained an international until the 75th jubilee game with New Zealand at Wellington in 1967. In that year he was 38 – the oldest Australian test player. Miller's record total of 41 test caps for Australia could have been higher, but he was unavailable to tour for 10 years and gave away top football for several seasons while he built up his electrical business. He played first grade rugby for the Manly club for 23 years, ending in 1970 at the age of 42.

Miller was a utility forward, appearing twice in tests as a No. 8, 25 times as a lock, and 14 times as a prop. He was known universally as 'Slaggy', a name apparently stemming from an Australian tour of Wales. But the nickname could also have been attributed to his appearance: at the end of his life in rugby, Miller's face bore signs of the ruggedness of his long career. He was a player who loved the rough and tough of tight forward play and some of his admirers say he was the toughest player Australia ever had.

MILESTONES
in the development of rugby

1823	Running with the ball introduced at Rugby School, probably by William Webb Ellis.
1841	Running with the ball officially allowed in Rugby School rules, provided the ball was taken on the bounce. Passing still forbidden.
1846	Independent meetings held at Cambridge University and London to formulate a code to unite the various forms of football.
1863	The Blackheath club, formed five years earlier, broke away from the unofficial London football rules in a disagreement over 'hacking'. The clubs that stayed with the London football rules were, effectively, the first soccer clubs.
1871	The Rugby Football Union was formed. The first international played between England and Scotland. Teams were 20-a-side.
1873	Scottish Rugby Union formed
1874	First governing body for Australian rugby formed.
1875	The scoring of tries received major recognition in the laws. Matches were to be decided on a majority of tries if both teams had scored the same number of goals.
1877	Number of players on each side in an international match reduced from 20 to 15.
1879	Irish Rugby Union formed. First floodlit game of rugby played in Hawick.
1880	Welsh Rugby Union formed. Three three-quarters first used in an international game, by Scotland v Ireland.
1885	The authority for decisions in a game given to referees. Line umpires used for the first time. The first use of four three-quarters, by Cardiff Club.
1886	The International Rugby Board formed. The scoring system used at Cheltenham in the 1860s adopted by the Rugby Union. Numerical value was given for the first time to a try. Values varied until 1894.
1888	British team visits Australia and New Zealand – the first major tour abroad. New Zealand 'Natives' tour Britain.
1889	South African Rugby Board formed. Line umpires abolished in favour of touch judges.
1891	Points scoring applied to international championship matches so that scores now read as they do today.
1892	New Zealand Rugby Football Union formed.
1893	The referee was entrusted with the whole responsibility and discipline of running a game. The origination of the 'advantage' laws. A motion to allow payment of monies to players for lost time at work defeated at a meeting of the Rugby Union in London. Those who wanted to receive money for playing 'went North'. Thus the strict principles of amateurism were first associated with rugby union. The breakaway game was known as Northern Union until 1922 when it adopted the name rugby league.
1894	Variations in points values were consolidated. The try was worth three points, a conversion two points, a penalty three points, a dropped goal three points, a goal from a mark three points and a field goal three points.
1905	Present day scoring values adopted (though some have been altered since).
1905	Bouncing the ball into play from touch was outlawed, as was the free kick for goal, i.e. a field goal, fly-kicking a loose ball over the posts for a goal.
1920	Fédération Française de Rugby formed.

1925	Cyril Brownlie became the first player sent off the field in a test match, the New Zealand v England international at Twickenham.
1926	The laws of the game altered and redrafted, making the game look more like the way it is played today.
1930	The IRB formally took over the framing of all of rugby's laws.
1931	The four home unions broke off rugby relations with France because of alleged professionalism in the game in that country.
1932	The wing forward position was legislated out of the game, with much opposition from New Zealand.
1934	FIRA formed.
1938	The first rugby union international match to be broadcast live on television - the Calcutta Cup match between England and Scotland at Twickenham on March 19 1938.
1946	France resumed in the international championship and therefore was effectively back under the laws and guidelines of the IRB.
1948	Points value for the dropped goal reduced from four to three.
1954	A major revamp of rugby laws released.
1960	First anti-apartheid protests in New Zealand directed at rugby associations with South Africa.
1966	Standardised numbering of players decreed.
1967	New Zealand's tour of South Africa was postponed and replaced by a tour of Britain after the lack of an invitation from South Africa for a mixed-race All Black team to tour that country.
1968	Replacements were permitted in full international matches and the previous 'Australian' dispensation allowing players to kick into touch on the full only from behind their own 25-yard line was introduced to all rugby.
1969	South African tour of Britain disrupted by anti-apartheid demonstrations.
1970:	First racially-integrated team from New Zealand toured South Africa.
1971	South African tour of Australia disrupted by anti-apartheid demonstrations.
1971	The points value for a try increased from three to four in all games.
1973	South African tour of New Zealand cancelled by the New Zealand Prime Minister, Norman Kirk.
1976	27 nations (mostly black African) withdrew from the Montreal Olympic Games as a protest over the presence of a New Zealand national rugby team in South Africa.
1977	The public disclosure of plans to start a professional rugby union. The plans surfaced (mostly in New Zealand and Britain) then disappeared.
1981	South African tour of New Zealand disrupted by anti-apartheid demonstrations.
1981	Legislation introduced by the IRB to outlaw the 'pile-up' in rugby.
1983	Australian rugby entrepreneur David Lord travelled the world attempting to start a professional rugby troupe. The idea did not have the momentum to succeed.
1985	A High Court injunction by two New Zealand lawyers caused the proposed All Black tour of South Africa to be postponed only days before the team was due to depart. The IRB announced the first Rugby World Cup.
1986	The first 'rebel' rugby tour was staged. 31 top New Zealand players, all either current or past All Blacks, travelled to South Africa to play a 12-match tour without the permission of the NZRFU and despite strong protests by the IRB.
1987	Rugby's first World Cup played in Australia and New Zealand.
1990	IRB proposed sweeping changes to the amateur laws.
1991	One fully integrated rugby governing body proposed for South Africa. Second World Cup in Britain and France.

Iain Milne

MILNE, IAIN
Heriot's FP, Harlequins and Scotland
40 internationals for Scotland 1979–90

A rugged prop with expert scrummaging skills, Iain ('Bear') Milne was the strong man of the Scottish pack in the 1980s. Educated at George Heriot's School in Edinburgh, he made the Scottish national squad as a 20-year-old in 1978. His international debut came the following year, and in 1983 he toured New Zealand with the British Isles. One of his brothers, Kenneth, was also a Scottish international in the front row.

After missing an entire season, 1987–88, because of injury, Iain Milne returned to the Scottish team and looked well on his way to setting new marks as Scotland's and perhaps the world's most-capped prop.

MOBBS, EDGAR
Northampton and England
7 internationals for England 1909–10

One of England's rugby players who by dint of his sportsmanship, model behaviour and courage is remembered to this day. The annual Mobbs Memorial match is staged between the Barbarians club and East Midlands, two teams that Edgar Mobbs had captained, in memory of his bravery and loyalty during World War I.

Mobbs made the England team as a 27-year-old in 1909. He was a dashing wing, known for his very powerful fend or hand-off. His international career lasted only two seasons. In 1909 he scored four tries in his first five games and in his last game, in 1910, he captained England against France.

It was as a Barbarian and as a soldier that Mobbs became best known. His first match for the club was in 1912. With the advent of war, Mobbs became heavily involved in patriotic fund-raising rugby matches.

Mobbs was keen to serve himself, but was originally refused a commission because of his age (he was 32 in 1914). This did not deter him and he enlisted as a private instead. Then he set out to raise his own company of men.

Because he was so admired as a player and a leader, Mobbs recruited many rugby men and eventually 264 men went with him to serve in France. They became 'D' Company of the 7th Northants Regiment.

The corps' bravery under fire in the trenches became famous as a story of valour by rugby men. It is said that Mobbs himself led some of the charges by booting a rugby ball ahead and then urging his men to follow up!

Mobbs lost his life in 1917 at Passchaendale and there was tremendous loss of life too among his beloved 'D' Company. Only 85 men survived.

A memorial to Mobbs was unveiled in the Northampton market square in 1921, the same year the annual game was started in his memory.

MONCLA, FRANCOIS
Racing Club, Pau and France
31 internationals for France 1956–61

Moncla made his debut against an unusual rugby country, Czechoslovakia, in 1956, but went on to become one of France's most successful players in the 1950s. He was a fast, hawkish loose forward who had the difficult job of carrying on the French captaincy after the success of Lucien Mias.

When he took over in 1959 it was noted that, like Mias, he had a manner of shouting constantly at his players

on the field. But some hard-to-please reporters said that Moncla 'shouted like a corporal' whereas Mias 'shouted like a sergeant-major'.

Moncla led France in his last 18 internationals, including one outright and one shared Five Nations title. But in the end French fickleness was a problem for Moncla. Having weathered the comparisons with Mias and fashioned a superb reputation as a leader in his own right, Moncla was rightfully chosen to take France on its first tour to New Zealand in 1961. His team lost all three tests, the third by as high a margin as 3–32. It was said at the time that Moncla was to blame, though hindsight suggests that the All Blacks were very strong that year and Moncla was disadvantaged in not having a say in team selection on tour.

Despite that, Moncla is remembered as playing a vital part in the rise of French rugby. His record and ability cannot be denied.

MOON, BRENDAN
Queensland and Australia
35 internationals for Australia 1978–86

A flashing wing three-quarter, one of the fastest ever seen in the game, Brendan Moon played consistent and

often brilliant rugby for Queensland and Australia. He was Australia's highest-capped wing for a time, beating John Cole's previous total of 22, and held an Australian record of 12 test tries. Both marks were beaten by David Campese.

His debut for Australia was against the All Blacks in New Zealand in 1978, and in only his second test match he was part of the stunning 30–16 win over the All Blacks at Auckland.

In 1979 he scored twice in the second test against Argentina in Buenos Aires, as Australia scored its first win over the Pumas. He also scored twice against England at Twickenham in 1982.

Perhaps Moon's best try for Australia came on his home ground of Ballymore in Brisbane in 1980. Early in the second test against the All Blacks, he entered a back move at tremendous pace, sweeping through the New Zealand midfield defence to score under the posts. It was a move that left the All Blacks stunned, but the speed and expertise of Moon's run was typical of much of his play as a Wallaby.

A broken arm sustained on the 1984 tour of Britain meant Moon was not able to be part of the famous Grand

François Moncla, surrounded by admiring schoolboys, obliges with some autographs.

Brendan Moon

Slam tour. He returned home after playing in the England international, but he was back for four more test matches in 1986.

MORGAN, CLIFF
Cardiff, Bective Rangers and Wales
29 internationals for Wales 1951–58
4 internationals for British Isles 1955

One of Wales's most illustrious players and a gloriously gifted flyhalf, Cliff Morgan was one of rugby's most famous players of the 1950s. Later he became an executive of the BBC where he was a top rugby commentator and later a decision-maker in matters of broadcasting policy.

Morgan, a product of the Rhondda Valley, made his debut for Wales against Ireland in 1951, where he marked the other great flyhalf of the 1950s, Jackie Kyle. In that season, Morgan also faced the mighty Springboks during their march through Britain. The pressure he was put under by the loose forward trio of Basie van Wyk, Hennie Muller and Stephen Fry caused him to have only a modest game. Wales lost 3–6.

A lesser player might have had his confidence shaken by such an experience, but Cliff Morgan, a cheeky lad,

played through the season as though there had been no setbacks at all.

In 1952 the Grand Slam was won by Wales and Morgan was a vital man in the team. By then he had established a regular partnership with the very talented scrumhalf, Rex Willis.

One of Morgan's greatest years was 1953. He played brilliantly in the Cardiff team that beat Bob Stuart's New Zealand All Blacks, and a matter of weeks later he was a key man in the Welsh team that also toppled New Zealand.

By then Morgan was brimming with cockiness and confidence. He was a closely marked man but still had the brilliance to break and run swiftly. Strongly built, he was an excellent tackler and an adept and accurate kicker.

In 1955 he was a first choice and one of the stars of the British Isles team that toured South Africa. Morgan relished the hard grounds and fine weather and played his best rugby, showing the South Africans his inventive genius.

In the first test Morgan outstripped the South African loose men (van Wyk and Fry were still playing) to score one of the most brilliant tries ever seen in South Africa. That test, played in front of 95,000 at Ellis Park in Johannesburg, was called the 'greatest game of all' by several senior reporters present. The Lions won, 23–22.

Morgan was captain in the third test, which the Lions also won, making him the only Welshman to captain an international team to victory over the Springboks. (Wales has never beaten South Africa.) South Africa had wins in the second and fourth tests to square a dramatic series, 2–2.

He was captain of Wales when it won the championship in 1956 but surprisingly, in view of his enormous popularity on and off the field, he was never asked to lead the team again.

Morgan had three more seasons in international rugby before retiring at the age of 28. His 29 caps was a Welsh record for a flyhalf that still stood in 1990.

At the end of his career Cliff Morgan became a popular television reporter and commentator, who was also in demand as a writer and after-dinner speaker. All of these tasks were completed with a high degree of charm and charisma.

It was Morgan who commentated on the Barbarians club match against the All Blacks in Cardiff in 1973. His cry of 'what a score!', when Gareth Edwards dived over for his famous try, has been heard many times, for that try has been replayed more than any other in television history.

MORGAN, HAYDN
Abertillery and Wales
27 internationals for Wales 1958–66
4 internationals for British Isles 1959–62

A flanker who was an outstanding harasser of flyhalves, Morgan originally played as a centre. His nickname was the 'Red Devil', so called not only because he had red hair but also because he had served with the 'Red Devil' parachutist troupe while on national service.

First playing for Wales in 1958, Morgan showed such outstanding form he was included in the British Isles team to tour 'down under'. His form in New Zealand was excellent and he played in two of the test matches.

He also appeared in two internationals during the Lions tour of South Africa in 1962.

After his retirement from rugby Haydn Morgan left Wales and emigrated to South Africa.

MORGAN, TEDDY
Guy's Hospital, London Welsh and Wales
16 internationals for Wales 1902–08

Forever remembered as the Welshman who scored the try that brought about the only defeat for the first All Blacks in 1905.

The 3–0 score to Wales became a longstanding rugby controversy, when it was claimed that New Zealander Bob Deans scored later in the game, only to be pulled back by Welsh defenders before the referee could see accurately what happened.

Teddy Morgan played his own part in the controversy. In 1924, 19 years after the game, he was at a dinner for the second All Blacks. Morgan, wishing to send a message to his friend Billy Wallace of the 1905 New Zealand team, wrote on a dinner menu, 'To Billy Wallace from Teddy Morgan. Deans did score at Cardiff 1905.' The menu is preserved in New Zealand in a rugby museum and people still go to see it for themselves.

Teddy Morgan

Teddy Morgan was a speedy wing, very fast off the mark. He could also swerve and dummy with a high degree of skill. In 1904 he toured New Zealand with the British team.

He was a star player in Welsh teams in the first golden era of Welsh rugby, and together with Rhys Gabe, Gwyn Nicholls and Willie Llewellyn he formed a famous Welsh three-quarter quartet. These four are still often called the greatest combination Wales has ever fielded in those positions.

MORKEL FAMILY

Ten members of this family played in the Springbok jersey in official test matches and at one stage 22 of them were playing rugby in various places thoughout South Africa.

The most famous Morkels were Gerhard and 'Boy', who were two of the five family members who made the Springboks team which toured New Zealand in 1921. Gerhard, a fullback, was a huge kicker of the ball and his match-winning dropped goal against New Zealand at Auckland in 1921 was from half-way.

'Boy' was recalled to the Springboks for that tour after last having played for them eight years before. He was

captain in the three test matches, even though he had not been chosen as the tour leader. Earlier, he had forged the reputation as one of South Africa's great forwards.

The family spread its representation for South Africa over a period of 25 years. Gerhard's son Hannes was a fine player too, becoming Western Province's captain.

MOROCCO

Rugby was started in Morocco after World War I, but the national rugby federation was not formed until 1956.

There is a powerful French influence in the development of the game. In the African qualifying rounds for the 1991 Rugby World Cup, there were no fewer than 13 players fresh from playing in French first division club sides in the Morocco team. Morocco lost narrowly to Zimbabwe and Tunisia, but their presence indicated that qualifying in African rugby will be extremely difficult in future years.

Morocco's best-known player is Abdelatif Benazzi, who appeared as a vigorous forward for France in tests against Australia and New Zealand in 1990. In a decision that caused great upset in Rabat, he chose to continue his international footballing career in France rather in his homeland.

MORRIS, DAI
Neath and Wales
34 internationals for Wales 1967–74

They called him the 'Shadow' in Wales because he trailed so vigorously in support of his team-mates, halfbacks in particular.

Dai Morris, who was very popular with players and fans alike, had eight years on the side of the Welsh scrum, becoming Wales's most-capped flanker, though his first two caps in 1967 were as a No. 8. Later, with Mervyn Davies and John Taylor, he was one of a formidable Welsh loose forward trio during the highly successful years of the 1960s and 70s.

It was a major disappointment to Welsh fans that he missed the 1971 British Isles tour of New Zealand. Eleven of his national team-mates were chosen (plus three other reserves) but no place could be found for Morris. Earlier, in 1969, he had been one player of the well-beaten Welsh team who had impressed New Zealand fans.

MOSELEY FC

The leading rugby club of Birmingham, formed in 1873 as the offshoot of a cricket club. The club's home ground since its formation has been The Reddings. It has a strong tradition of open rugby and remains one of the more powerful and popular Midlands clubs.

In its first 100 years Moseley produced 40 English internationals, some of them highly significant in English rugby. Peter Cranmer was one of four English captains from the club, and he played in 16 consecutive England internationals, 1934–38. Later Cranmer was a radio commentator and newspaper writer on the game. After his retirement there was a gap of 21 years before a Moseley man again played for England. The newcomer in 1959 was Peter Robbins, who had been previously capped when studying at Oxford. Robbins too became a successful writer on the game.

Recent internationals from the club include John Finlan, Colin McFadyean (the 1966 Lion), Mike Coulman (1968 Lion), Sam Doble (a prolific points-

Phil Mostert

Top: The Barbarians' centenary was celebrated with special matches against England and Wales. Rob Andrew, of England, prepares to fend off Australian Michael Lynagh, playing for the Barbarians.
Below: Speedy winger Rory Underwood bursts through the defence. Fotopacific

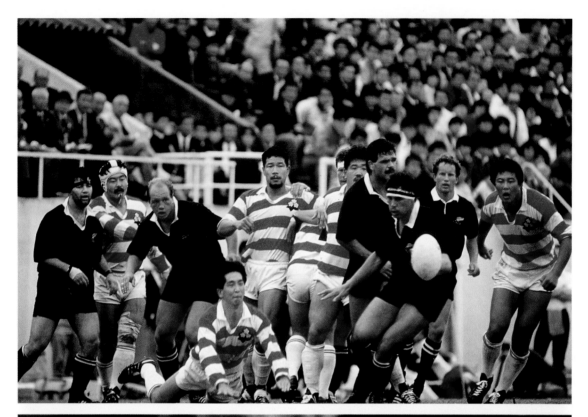

Top: All Japan v the All Blacks. Osaka 1987. Peter Bush
Below: A courageous tackle on big Steve Tuynman, Australia, from a much smaller Japanese player. Fotopacific

scoring fullback who died at a tragically young age), Jan Webster, Keith Fielding (later a rugby league player), Nick Jeavons (1983 British Isles) and tough lock Nigel Horton, who is the club's leading cap-winner (20), and who was also with the British Isles in New Zealand in 1977.

Moseley plays in red and black hooped jerseys.

MOSTERT, PHIL
Western Province and South Africa
14 internationals for Sth Africa 1921–32

Phil Mostert had that doyen of coaches, A.K. Markotter, to thank for his original Springbok selection. 'Oubaas Mark' knew he had little support for 21-year-old Mostert from his fellow Western Province selectors when it came to choosing the team for the 1920 Currie Cup competition, so he nominated Mostert as a reserve for every forward position. The majority of the selectors threw up their hands and let Markotter have his way.

From there, Mostert played his way into the team proper, then into the Springbok trials, and was chosen for the pioneering 1921 tour to New Zealand. Not only did he play all three tests, but the NZRFU awarded him a gold medal as 'best forward'.

From then until the end of the 1931–32 tour to Britain, Mostert was a first choice for South Africa, missing only the third test (because of influenza) against the touring 1924 British side.

He was captain in the 1928 home series against New Zealand, and such was his versatility that he hooked in the third test when Theuns Kruger withdrew; and he kicked a dropped goal from a mark in the second test. Mostert was surprisingly displaced by Bennie Osler as captain for the 1931–32 tour, but he was invariably pack-leader.

He was mostly a prop but could – and did – play anywhere in the pack. At 6ft (1.82m) and 15st (close to 100 kg), he was big enough to lock the scrum, or to be used as a third lock at No. 8, and in his younger days he often played as a flanker.

In such a long and fine career, stories grew around 'Mossie', a 'gentle giant' in the description of one prominent South African writer. One he denied was that he used to carry a black glove in his pocket, surreptitiously putting it on to assist the hooker to win scrum ball.

Phil Mostert was unquestionably South Africa's greatest forward of the 1920s.

MOURIE, GRAHAM
Taranaki and New Zealand
21 internationals for N. Zealand 1977–82

'Goss' Mourie was earmarked early as a potential New Zealand rugby leader. He captained most teams he was in, graduating to lead the second New Zealand touring side, when it visited Argentina in 1976.

The following year Mourie played the third and fourth test matches against the British Isles and, when test captain Tane Norton retired at the end of that season, Mourie was appointed captain for the tour of France, the first of the five full All Black teams he took to Europe. On those tours his test teams were beaten only once in 11 games.

Mourie, one of the most intelligent and inspiring of test captains, was blessed with more than leadership qualities. He was also an outstanding fast, constructive flanker, the star player of most of his games.

He was also a man of principle. He risked the wrath of the New Zealand rugby public by choosing not to play against the 1981 Springboks, but once that disastrous tour was over, the respect for him was such that he was welcomed back to the All Blacks for their next series, in France.

He captained the All Blacks in 19 tests, home and away. Many New Zealanders consider him their greatest captain.

His book, *Graham Mourie – Captain*, led to Mourie being suspended because he accepted the royalties, but it was an open secret he assisted John Hart to coach the Auckland side in the mid-1980s. Ironically, too, Mourie was employed to help market the first Rugby World Cup in 1987.

Graham Mourie meets Jean-Pierre Rives, captain of France, in 1979.

MULCAHY, BILL

UC Dublin, Bective Rangers, Bohemians
and Ireland
35 internationals for Ireland 1958–65
6 internationals for British Isles 1959–62

A strong and consistent Irish lock who, although not tall by modern standards, was a courageous performer at international level.

Mulcahy's first game for Ireland was against Australia in 1958, a game for which the Ireland selectors introduced six new caps. Four of those players became some of Ireland's all-time greats: Mulcahy, David Hewitt, Noel Murphy and Ronnie Dawson. He missed only two matches for his country after that and was captain on 11 occasions. In 17 matches he locked with Willie John McBride.

Mulcahy, a doctor, toured with the British Isles team twice: once to New Zealand and Australia in 1959, and the other to South Africa in 1962.

MULLEN, KARL

Old Belvedere and Ireland
25 internationals for Ireland 1947–52
3 internationals for British Isles 1950

A highly talented hooker and captain who led one of the most popular touring teams in rugby history, the 1950 Lions to New Zealand and Australia. He was also one of the key planners in

Ireland's most successful era in rugby when they dominated the Five Nations championship from 1948 until 1952.

A medical student, Karl Mullen came into the Irish team in 1947 for its first official international since the end of World War II, playing all his internationals thereafter in sequence.

Mullen was a much-debated choice for captain of his country in 1948. Ernie Strathdee had led Ireland to victory in the previous match, yet he was dropped and replaced by a 21-year-old hooker! However, under Mullen the performance of the Irish team rose considerably. The forwards became more efficient in both tight and loose play and the backs were encouraged to take only definite chances.

It was a winning formula, and one which projected Mullen into a high status as a tactical captain. He had the ability to analyse accurately the strengths and weaknesses of both teams in any match. His name will forever be associated with a great era in Irish rugby.

It was a tribute to Ireland's rugby successes of that time that Mullen was chosen to lead the 1950 British Isles team to New Zealand and Australia. Eight of his fellow-countrymen toured with him and Mullen's Lions were hugely popular all over the country.

Mullen encouraged the team to sing and enjoy themselves, which they did at every opportunity, soon endearing themselves to Kiwi rugby folk. They lost the test series, securing only a draw in the first test, but they are remembered as a highly entertaining team.

Mullen was considered the best hooker in the four home unions in the years immediately after the war and was also a very lively player in the loose.

His last international game was in 1952 against Wales in Dublin. After that he lost his place to the Rev. Robin Roe, who proved to be a worthy successor and who went on to hook for Ireland for as long as Karl Mullen had done.

MULLER, HENNIE

Transvaal, Western Province and South
Africa
13 internationals for Sth Africa 1949–53

Hennie Muller was the man South Africans themselves criticised for being 'too destructive' or 'too loose' as a loose forward, but whom they eventually came to respect because he was associated with significant wins for the Springboks.

Hendrik Scholtz Vosloo Muller was his full name but he became known simply as 'Hennie' or 'Windhond' ('the Greyhound'.) He had great speed (he was originally a wing) and developed a new style of loose forward's game, specialising in catching opposing flyhalves or centres when they received the ball from set play (remembering that in the years after World War II the last men in any lineout could stand out virtually in midfield).

Muller's style of chasing inside backs (from scrums as well) was a revolution for No. 8 forwards who were previously instructed to run behind their own backs (known widely as 'corner-flagging'). Certainly he was originally criticised for 'negative' and 'destructive' tactics, but years later almost every team world-wide employs one of its loosemen to do what he did first.

He played only 13 international matches, a modest total, but they were some of the most dramatic matches of the post-war era. In 1949, when the All Blacks lost all four test matches to the Springboks, Muller was a vital player, disrupting many of the New

Karl Mullen autographs a ball for a young admirer.

Zealander's backline attacks. His speed about the field was too much for the New Zealand team and they came to dread his presence on the field.

In 1951–52, after injury to the tour captain Basil Kenyon, Muller took over the leadership of the Springboks on the tour of Britain and Ireland. He was in dynamic form in match after match, and led his team to a superb tour record, winning all five internationals played, including the 44–0 whitewash of Scotland.

Muller was again Springbok captain in 1953 but, at 31, his form was not quite as formidable. At Cape Town, in the second international against the touring Australians, he suffered his only defeat as a test captain. The Springboks recovered to win the series 3–1 and at the end of the fourth test he was carried shoulder high off the field by team-mates and fans.

By 1965 Muller was so highly regarded as a coach – after earlier being Springboks manager – that he was given charge of the Springboks team that toured New Zealand and Australia. The test series in New Zealand was lost, and his appointment was not viewed as a great success.

He died suddenly of a heart attack in 1977, aged 55.

MULLIN, BRENDAN

Blackrock College, London Irish and
    Ireland
37 internationals for Ireland 1984–91
1 international for British Isles 1989

A noted Irish track and field sprinter, Brendan Mullin brought his athletic speed to top rugby in grand style. From the time he was first picked for his country as a centre, in 1985 against Australia, until he was sidelined briefly with injury five years later, he was never missing from any Irish international game. By the end of 1990–91, aged only 27, he had chalked up 37 internationals for his country. His total of tries was sitting on 15, one ahead of the record George Stephenson had set 60 years before.

Mullin was a Lion in 1986, against the Rest of the World in Cardiff and again on the 1989 tour of Australia, where he played in the first test.

In the 1987 Rugby World Cup he scored three tries v Tonga at Brisbane, to become the sixth Irishman to share that country's record for test tries.

The Munster pack that defeated the mighty All Blacks 12–0.

He won a number of Irish track titles in his career and early in the summer of 1986 he broke the 30-year-old Irish record for the 110 metres hurdles.

MUNSTER RFU

No doubt there were other days of glory in the history of the Munster branch of Irish rugby before October 31 1978, but it is hard to find any that approach the day at Thomond Park in Limerick, when Munster became the first Irish team of any description to beat the All Blacks. The score was Munster 12, New Zealand 0.

It was a performance that epitomised all the best in Munster rugby. The Munster men tackled with brutish determination, attacked with ferocity, and defended with passion. The New Zealanders had no answer and were bustled right out of the game.

The ground was packed to its maximum and at the end of a thrilling match the crowd charged on to the field and gave the Munster players a reception of which any pop group would be proud. In true show business style, the Munster players were called from their dressing rooms to take an encore.

Souvenirs of the day became collectors' items. The match programme, which had sold out an hour before kick-off, was reprinted again a day *after* the game! A commemorative tie

was struck showing the Munster emblem and the game's score, and locals even began singing the score in a catchy little jingle. The 1983 British Isles team in New Zealand also used to sing the same tune in tribute to the Munster team of five years before.

For the record, Munster's try-scorer that day was the flanker Christy Cantillon. The conversion and two dropped goals were added by one of Munster's most famous sons, Tony Ward.

The programme, sold out on match day, was reprinted in huge numbers.

The result that day was a just reward for Munster, for in earlier encounters against New Zealand it had gone very close to winning. The club's traditional fiery forward play gave it a 3–3 draw in 1973 and in both 1953 and 1963 New Zealand won by only 6–3.

Such results are typical of the spirit that has always prevailed in Munster rugby. The side won against Australia, for instance, in both 1967 and 1981–82. The 11–8 margin for Munster in 1967 was the first win by any Irish provincial side against a major touring team. Munster had also had a 3–3 draw with the 1957–58 Australian team.

The Springboks didn't play Munster until 1951, when they beat the home province 11–6 at Cork. In 1960–61 and again in 1969–70, South Africa won 9–3 and 25–9.

The leading clubs of Munster rugby, Cork Constitution, Garryowen, Shannon and University College Cork, compete each season, with other clubs, for the Munster Cup and league titles. The Munster Cup was first played for in 1886. After the first 100 years of competition Garryowen had scored most wins with 32, followed by Cork Constitution with 21 and University College Cork with 12.

MURPHY, NOEL

Cork Constitution and Ireland
41 internationals for Ireland 1958–69
8 internationals for British Isles 1959–66

Noel Murphy, a talented loose forward, played a leading role in British and Irish rugby over a period of 22 years. At a time when Ireland was blessed with outstanding leaders, he captained his club, his province and his country. After retirement he became a coach, guiding his club, Cork Constitution, to the Munster Cup in 1970 and coaching Munster in its 3–3 draw with New Zealand in 1973. He became an Irish selector and was appointed Irish coach in 1977, then the British Isles coach for the 1980 tour of South Africa.

Murphy was an openside flanker in his early days but changed to the more defensive blindside role later. He became known as a dynamic leader of forward packs, but many suspect it was his genial nature off the field that inspired others to play with confidence and to follow his aggressive lead when playing for club or country.

He was chosen for two Lions tours to New Zealand, in 1959 and 1966. His total of 41 caps was the Irish record for a flanker, which stood until Fergus Slattery broke it in 1980.

Murphy's last match for Ireland was against Wales in 1969, but it ended sadly for him when he was felled by a big punch from his old Lions teammate, Brian Price, the Welsh captain. The game was being played in Cardiff in front of the young Prince of Wales. It is not reported if His Royal Highness was impressed with the magnificence of the blow that knocked out one of Ireland's all-time rugby favourites!

Murphy's father, Noel snr, was also an Irish representative flanker, winning 11 caps between 1930–33. He was president of the Irish Rugby Union in 1960–61. Noel jnr's son, Kenny, became an Irish international, as a fullback, in 1990.

MURRAYFIELD

The headquarters ground of Scottish rugby. Beautifully turfed and maintained, Murrayfield presents one of the best playing surfaces anywhere in the world. The ground is nearly always in perfect playing condition, as it has rugby's first 'electric blanket' heating system under its surface.

In 1958–59 Edinburgh's winter weather was particularly severe, freezing rugby and soccer pitches all over the city. The ground staff at Murrayfield faced enormous problems ensuring major matches went ahead. Before the Wales v Scotland match, for instance, marquees were set up on the playing area with large oil heaters inside each. As the ground thawed out straw was laid across it and the marquees were moved to another frozen part further up the field.

Not previously known for its liberalism or forward thinking, the Scottish Rugby Union went into action during the summer season of 1959. A generous grant of £10,000 from a Glasgow businessman, Charles Hepburn, saw electric cables laid in the turf at a depth of six inches, and six inches apart, along the whole length of the field. Thus a unique and much envied undersoil heating and thawing system was brought into being. At first, costs to keep the ground playable were just £5 an hour!

The central heating system was the envy of all other winter sporting codes in the depths of the freezing winter of 1962. On the day of the Calcutta Cup match the whole of Britain was covered with frost and ice and hundreds of football games of all descriptions were postponed. But the England v Scotland rugby match proceeded without disruption on a flat, even and dry pitch and a British record crowd of 78,500 turned up to watch.

The first international at the ground (also a Calcutta Cup match) was played in 1925. It seems every rugby supporter in Edinburgh turned out and as a result of the tremendous crushes and confusion the kick-off had to be delayed while various entrance and crowd problems were sorted out. Thousands watched from in front of the crowd barriers on the field of play.

Scotland had to win the match to gain its first ever Grand Slam – and it just held England off 14–11. In the celebrations afterwards one Scottish newspaper said in an editorial that it would be 'the duty of Scottish sides in the coming years to confirm the Murrayfield precedent'. This was done in the early years as Scotland won or shared four Five Nations titles in five seasons.

Thereafter, though Murrayfield as often as not has been the venue for spirited Scottish play, it has seen only modest success, with no outright win for Scotland in the championship between 1939 and 1985. Murrayfield also had a gloomy day in 1951, when South Africa came to town and beat Scotland by the then world record score of 44–0.

In recent years the open embankment, which stretched along one side of the field, has been replaced. Although it afforded the ordinary man an excellent view for a modest ticket price, it was always exposed to the weather, so a second large grandstand on the eastern side was completed in the 1985 season, giving the ground a modern appearance.

It is a great sporting stadium, one of the best rugby venues in the world.

N

NAMIBIA

The 'newest' of Africa's rugby countries, but possibly the fastest to make its mark on the world scene. Formerly part of the structure of the South African Rugby Board, South-West Africa, as it was then known, joined the Currie Cup competition in 1954. A brilliant performance in 1988 resulted in a 9–12 loss to Transvaal in the semi-finals – a particularly meritorious result when it is considered that the country had only 1200 senior players.

South-West Africa also had a strong tradition of playing against major touring teams. Some of the hotshots of world rugby received a shock playing in Windhoek, the main town. The 1955 Lions won by only 9–0, the 1962 team won 14–6 and Willie John McBride's great Lions of 1974 could only score a 23–16 win. South-West Africa drew with the 1961 Australians 14–14 and also drew with the 1975 French 13–13.

South-West Africa played its last Currie Cup series in 1989 when it finished sixth. Independence under the new name Namibia followed, and the new SWAPO government insisted in breaking all sporting ties with South Africa.

Thus the South-West Africa Rugby Union was out on a limb with no one to play. There was already a Namibia Rugby Union, formed by mostly non-white players, and after negotiation the two formed a new, unified rugby governing body in 1990, and the South-West Union formally cut its ties to the South African board. The amalgamation was too late for Namibia to enter the 1991 Rugby World Cup qualifying series, but there is no doubt that Namibia will be a force in the future.

The new rugby body has a policy of engaging in as many international rugby games and tours as possible, in the hope this will prevent experienced players from departing for South Africa or other countries. Thus, in the first months of 1990 there was a test with Zimbabwe (which Namibia won 33–16), followed by an 86–9 win over Portugal, in which wing and captain Gerhard Mans scored six tries. Then followed tours to Namibia by Wales (Wales won 18–9 and 34–30, and caps were awarded to Welsh players), France B and West Germany. Namibia toured Europe late in 1990.

There is no doubt that already Namibia is an ambitious rugby power which cannot be underestimated. For African rugby, with the probable return of South Africa to join teams like Namibia, Zimbabwe, Tunisia and Morocco, the prospects are truly exciting, once, of course, all political differences and interferences are cleared aside.

NARBONNE

A rugby stronghold in southern France, Racing Club Narbonnais is known for its tradition of forward toughness and backline enterprise. Its greatest years were 1936 and 1979 when the club won the prestigious French championship. In 1936 Narbonne beat Montferrand 6–3, and 43 years later beat Bagnères in the 1979 final 10–0. In total the club scored 80 tries on its way to its second championship victory.

The 1979 game is remembered for the throwing of fireworks and bombs by spectators, with the result that the Narbonne club was suspended for two games.

The most famous rugby family of Narbonne is the Spanghero family. Walter Spanghero played 51 times for his country, while his brother Claude was capped 22 times.

The brilliant Jo Maso ended his career with the Narbonne club, which also fielded the talented backs Didier Codorniou and François Sangali, along with the front row forwards Joseph Choy and René Benesis.

NATAL RFU

The rugby union of Natal, formed in 1890, takes in the Indian Ocean coast of east South Africa and it is centred on King's Park in the city of Durban.

The earliest influences in Natal rugby came from the British regiments stationed near the town of Maritzberg and from old boys of some of the famous rugby-playing schools of England who had emigrated to South Africa to be schoolmasters. The British influence has remained strong in general life in

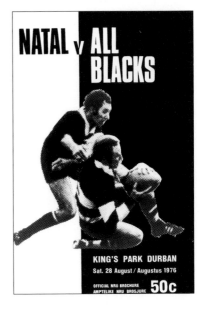

NATAL v ALL BLACKS

KING'S PARK DURBAN
Sat. 28 August / Augustus 1976

OFFICIAL NRU BROCHURE
AMPTELIKE NRU BROSJURE **50c**

the province. This is borne out by the many English names for prominent clubs in the province (Wanderers, Old Collegians, High School Old Boys) and even down to the English names of the players who represent Natal.

In the early days progress was slow. Natal conceded 24 points to Maclagan's British team in 1891, which under today's scoring system would have been a score of about 57! This was even after Natal laid on a large banquet which kept the touring team up late the night before the game.

Much closer matches in the next 20 years signalled a gradual improvement in Natal's playing standards and it was awarded its first hosting of the Currie Cup in 1914.

The first Natalians to play for South Africa were L.B. Siedle, Alfred Walker, W.H. Townsend, Walter Clarkson and Bill Zeller, all members of the 1921 Springboks in New Zealand. By then Natal's strength was considerable. The province played a draw with Cove-Smith's 1924 Great Britain team and was, for the first time, awarded a test match at Kingsmead in Durban which was, by then, the team's headquarters.

Natal's first win over a major touring team came in 1953, when it beat Australia by 15–14. It had a similar result (a 14–13 win) over the Wallabies of 1963 and a 19–14 win over the 1969 Australians. In 1960 it played a 6–6 draw with the touring All Blacks and only a missed late penalty attempt stopped Natal from scoring a famous win. In 1955, and again in 1962, the British Isles players stood back and applauded Natal's players off the field after close games (the scores: 11–8 and 13–3 to the Lions).

Kingsmead was the venue for several other test matches. In 1928, for instance, Natal fans witnessed the 17–0 demolition of Maurice Brownlie's All Blacks. The only home player in the team was Philip Nel, the famous Springbok who later toured Britain in Bennie Osler's team and to New Zealand in 1937, as captain. In 1949 New Zealand also lost at Kingsmead, 3–9. There were victories by the Springboks over Australia in 1953 and in 1969. Wales was thrashed 24–3 in Durban in 1964 and the 1967 French team was beaten 26–3.

In the late 1950s an ambitious building project resulted in Natal's rugby headquarters moving from Kingsmead to King's Park, about a mile away. The new ground was an all-seating stadium accommodating 33,000. The drawn match with the All Blacks in 1960 got the province away to a good start on its new ground. By 1986, after a second rebuilding, a record crowd of 48,000 turned out at the modernised ground to see the Springboks meet the New Zealand Cavaliers, the visitors scoring a thrilling 19–18 victory. A few days earlier, in a game in which rugby was sometimes forgotten and fighting took over, the Cavaliers beat Natal by 37–24.

Natal's highest-capped Springbok was probably its most famous player. Loose forward Tommy Bedford was a great Natal man and a South African captain who played 25 test matches and 119 matches for Natal. Close to him in reputation and popularity was the outstanding flyhalf Keith Oxlee, who was a vital man in Springbok and Natal teams between 1960 and 1965.

Other famous Natalians were Wynand Claassen, a Springbok captain in seven internationals in 1981–82; Ebbo Bastard, in the 1930s; Cecil Moss, who played all four tests against the 1949 All Blacks; Roy Dryburgh, the fullback and three-quarter who was also a South African captain; and Doug

Walton, the talented hooker of the 1960s.

Among a number of visitors who spent time in the province and who regularly wore the black and white of Natal were Australia's test players Dick Cocks, Gary Pearse, Tom Lawton and Mark Loane, and New Zealand's Murray Mexted.

There was genuine surprise and delight in the 1990 Currie Cup final. Natal, celebrating its centennial, won the cup for the first time, beating Northern Transvaal 18–12.

NATHAN, WAKA
Auckland and New Zealand
14 internationals for N. Zealand 1962–67

The 'Black Panther' was indeed a lucky omen for All Black sides of the 1960s: he was never in a losing side in a test match, though once his team had to share the honours in a draw. He also formed widely acclaimed loose forward combinations with Kel Tremain and John Graham or Brian Lochore.

Injuries restricted the international career of this dynamic flanker, a punch giving him a broken jaw on the 1963–64 tour of Britain, while leg injuries cut into his next two seasons. Another broken jaw brought his All Black career to an end in 1967.

Nathan was a popular choice to play a starring role in the opening ceremony of the first World Cup contest in 1976. Earlier, he had both coached and managed the New Zealand Maoris.

NATIVES, THE
When the 1888–89 New Zealand Native touring team set sail on the first major rugby tour from the southern hemisphere, it could not have realised that it would set the style for thousands of rugby tours and trips that followed. They were 26 New Zealanders (22 Maoris and four Pakehas, or Europeans), whose world tour was to last 14 months and take in the grand total of 107 games.

The tour was the brain child of an English businessman, Tom Eyton, who

Waka Nathan meets the Governor-General of New Zealand, Sir Bernard Fergusson, before the New Zealand v Australia NZRFU Jubilee Test in 1967.

The New Zealand Natives

lived in New Zealand. He had been home to England in 1887 and had wondered, when watching rugby there, what the reaction would be if he arranged for a team of New Zealanders to tour. The Rugby Football Union was sceptical at first, as it had no idea how New Zealanders played rugby, but Eyton persisted with his idea of forming an all-Maori touring team. He struck some problems due to insufficent Maori players being available, but again he was not perturbed – he simply invited four players who *looked* like Maoris to make up the numbers!

Eyton took £62 off each man for his fare and the team departed from New Zealand – but not before first touring the country, playing from north to south.

The Natives stopped first in Melbourne, where they adapted to playing under the Australian rules format. Then, the players taking turns to keep fit in the boiler room, they sailed for Britain.

Once there, the team's schedule picked up at a crazy pace and was maintained through a whirlwind tour of all four home countries, resulting in some incidents which have become some of rugby's classic tour stories.

When playing against Carlisle, the rain and sleet were so bad that in the second half the Natives backs played wearing raincoats.

Arthur Warbrick, tired of people repeatedly asking him to show his massive calf muscles, sometimes rolled up a trouser leg to facilitate an easier view for the curious.

Dick Taiaroa often used to wave to the crowds as he ran along. Once he blew a kiss to the opposition fullback as he ran through.

Before the game against Middlesex, which was played on a ground at Lord Sheffield's estate, the lunch was so sumptuous and the serving of drinks so liberal that several members of the team were incapable of playing. Lord Sheffield further impeded the Natives by sending out servants at half-time with more champagne!

The schedule of matches became so congested that at one point the popular Natives played six games in eight days, and at another stage eight games in 16 days. (Modern touring teams take note!) One of the team, Davey ('Iron Man') Gage, played many times more games than any other of the team. He appeared in 68 of the 74 games in Britain.

In the end the Natives headed homewards, having made many friends. But they kept active on the way home, dashing off a further 14 games in Australia, then staging another eight-game tour of New Zealand, retracing their steps from 14 months earlier.

It is reported that when the team finally reached Auckland, after the 107th game, the members did not want to break up and go their separate ways.

Considering the size of their itinerary, the Natives were very successful. Of their 107 games, 78 were wins, 23 were losses, and six games were drawn. The team beat a full Irish team 13–4

Tony Neary, airborne in a desperate, but unsuccessful, lunge for a Hawke's Bay player and the ball. With the Lions in New Zealand, 1977.

and lost close encounters to Wales (0–5) and England (0–7).

The Natives of 1888–89 are fondly remembered all over the rugby world, especially of course in New Zealand.

NEARY, TONY
Broughton Park and England
43 internationals for England 1971–80
1 international for the British Isles 1977

A flanker and former schoolboy basketball star, who capped his 10 seasons as an English representative by playing in its Grand Slam-winning team of 1980. His total of 43 caps – the most won in international rugby by an Englishman – was equalled by Rory Underwood in March 1991.

Neary made his debut in 1971 as one of eight new caps in the 6–22 loss to Wales in Cardiff. With consistent form as a fast-breaking flanker, with good hands and a keen sense of where the ball would be next, he survived the vagaries of the England selectors through the decade, to build up an impressive total of appearances.

Neary became captain of his country in 1975, leading the England team which toured Australia that northern summer, as well as in the full Five Nations series of 1975–76. Although he was rated an excellent leader, England's poor results saw him relieved of the position, but he was retained in the team for the rest of his career. In all, he was in a winning England team only 15 times in his 43 appearances.

Neary toured twice with the British Isles – to South Africa in 1974 and to New Zealand in 1977. He had good form in South Africa in 1974, but Ireland's Fergus Slattery was preferred. Neary's only test for the Lions was the fourth against the All Blacks in 1977 at Auckland.

NEATH RFC
Founded in 1871 and always one of Wales's leading teams, Neath was the first to reach its centenary.

There are several stories about how Neath came to be nicknamed either the 'All Blacks' or the 'Mourners'. One says that Neath adopted black as the club's colours after the death of a popular club member in a game in 1880. Another says that black was the colour of the South Wales Rugby Union in the early years and that Neath simply adopted those colours along with a distinctive Maltese Cross emblem that one player favoured.

The first captain of Neath was actually a Scotsman, Tom Whittington, who was also Neath's first international player, appearing for Scotland against England in 1873, seven years before Wales started playing internationals.

In its time Neath has produced many famous Welsh players, all of whom have been revered in the coal, steel and tin-plate town, so typical of South Wales in its devotion to rugby. The most-capped international in the club's first 100 years was the Wales and Lions forward Rees Stephens. He appeared 32 times for his country and twice for the Lions in internationals. His records stood until the popular Dai Morris broke them in 1974. Other prominent players include the lineout specialist, 'King' Roy John who played 19 consecutive internationals between 1950 and 1954, adding another six for the Lions in 1950.

The prop Courtney Meredith, also a Lion in the four tests in South Africa in 1955, won 14 caps for Wales 1953–57. Later, Brian Thomas, a tough and rugged forward, won 21 caps and became an equally determined manager/coach and personality of the club.

The names above would suggest that Neath's strength over the years has been in the forwards. While this is probably true, the club has nevertheless produced a number of highly talented backs, fullbacks in particular. In the early years of the twentieth century the Mourners' fullback, Joe Davies, was an international reserve on 17 occasions to the great Billy Bancroft. Grahame Hodgson won 15 caps in that position in the 1960s while Paul Thorburn, who set a new record for points in all internationals for Wales, rose to be his country's captain in 1989. The brilliantly talented Jonathan Davies, although a product

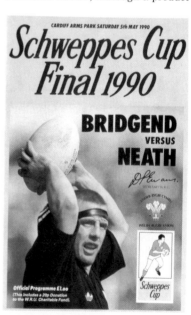

of Llanelli, was a Neath player when he first made the Welsh XV in 1985.

Albert Freethy, who was for years the world's highest 'capped' international referee, came from Neath. He was the first referee to send a player off the field in an international – New Zealand's Cyril Brownlie in a match against England. He refereed every England v France match staged in Paris between the two world wars, and also the Olympic Games final of 1924 between France and the United States.

When the Welsh Rugby Union launched its Challenge Cup in 1971–72, the knock-out series was won in its first year by Neath, a fitting way to cap the club's centenary season. In the first 20 years of the competition Neath won three times, confirming its modern strength by winning in 1989 and 1990.

Neath used to be combined with neighbouring Aberavon in matches with touring teams and they had several memorable games, although all ended in losses. The first game against an overseas team at Neath itself was with South Africa in 1912, a 3–8 loss. On its own, Neath scored a 21–21 draw with Japan in 1983. One of the biggest highlights of Neath's long history was the granting of a game against the 1989 All Blacks, but the undisputed top club in Wales lost by 15–26.

Neath is a club that runs only one playing XV. Its home ground is the Gnoll in Neath, where, on the adjoining cricket pitch, W.G. Grace once made a 'pair' of ducks at cricket.

NELSON BAYS RFU

A sunny city in the far north of the South Island of New Zealand, Nelson has a special place in New Zealand rugby history. While Christchurch is the oldest rugby club in the country, it played under a variety of rules. The first match to be played in New Zealand under the then rules of rugby is generally acknowledged to be the one that took place in May 1870 between Nelson College and Nelson Football Club.

It was instigated by a New Zealander, Charles Monro, whose father, Sir David Monro, was Speaker of the New Zealand House of Representatives from 1860 to 1870. Young Charles was sent to London to complete his education at Christ's College, Finchley, where he picked up the rules of the

George Nepia – an awkward but remarkably effective kicking style.

fledgling game. He brought them back to New Zealand, and from the early beginnings in Nelson the game spread quickly throughout the colony.

The Nelson union was formed in 1885, and amalgamated in 1969 with the tiny neighbouring Golden Bay-Motueka union (formed in 1920); together they are called Nelson Bays. The two unions, either separately or combined, cannot point to many major successes. Nelson Bays never aspired to winning the Ranfurly Shield, nor to contesting the first division championship, and individual national selections were few and far between. While unions like Canterbury and Auckland can point to 100 and more All Blacks, Nelson can claim only five. The most

significant were 'Fritz' Snow, a forward who toured South Africa in 1928, and Trevor Morris, who went to Britain as a fullback in 1972–73.

NEPIA, GEORGE

Hawke's Bay, East Coast and New
  Zealand
9 internationals for New Zealand 1924–30

A legendary figure in a legendary team, the 1924 'Invincibles'. Only 19 at the time, Nepia played all 38 matches during that gruelling tour of Australia, Britain, Ireland, France and Canada.

British sides were unstinting in their praise of Nepia, the rock on whom so many of their attacks foundered. His courage under the high ball and in repelling foot rushes, the crunching certainty of his tackling and the strength of his line kicking – all of these combined to restrict opposition teams to no more than 180 points against the All Blacks in those 38 games.

Nepia could also run with the ball. He had started his first-class career as a wing, then a five-eighth, before outstanding fullback displays in 1924 resulted in his being chosen as the only last line of defence. Early in the tour of Britain he made a sizzling run, but the dictatorial Mark Nicholls told him to leave the running to his five-eighths and three-quarters: his job was to defend. It was not until the 37th match of the tour, in Canada, that Nepia scored his first try!

A bogus telegram which advised the selectors of Nepia's 'unavailability' cost him a place with the New Zealand Maoris' trend-setting tour to Britain in 1927, and his All Black career finished after the 1930 home series against the British Isles. After a temporary retirement, Nepia returned to bid for a place with the 1935–36 All Blacks to tour Britain but was surprisingly not selected, though then playing as well as at any time of his career.

With his financial security in tatters at the end of the Depression, Nepia readily accepted the lure of rugby league money and played two seasons in England, and then for New Zealand. Reinstated to rugby in the war-time amnesty, Nepia played for East Coast in 1947, and in 1950 captained the Olympians club in a first-class fixture against Poverty Bay. George Nepia, father and son, were the fullbacks and captains on this historic day, George senior being 45 years old at the time.

He became an active referee and many spectators went to games just to watch Nepia referee, rather than see the two teams doing battle.

NETHERLANDS

Although rugby has been played in the Netherlands since 1879 and the rugby union was formed there in 1932, it was not until the 1970s that the game really took off in Holland. Previously rugby was played mainly around Amsterdam and The Hague, but generally it took very much a back seat to soccer, cycling and hockey in terms of public interest. Yet in the 1970s playing numbers increased six-fold.

The new look for rugby in Holland sprang from a five-year plan instigated in 1967 by a far-sighted administrator, Jus van Doorn. Having persuaded the FIRA, along with local television, to take an interest in Dutch rugby, he achieved a higher profile for the game which led to an increased number of players. Soon the Netherlands became respected by the other rugby-playing powers of Europe.

Indeed the Dutch had been represented at the launching of FIRA in 1934, but it was not until 1973 that they joined FIRA competitions, where they have generally been consistent performers in the second division. One of its more significant international wins was in 1980 when it beat Japan 15–13.

An impressive asset of Dutch rugby is the National Rugby Centre in Hilversum which regularly hosts international visitors.

A tour of South Africa by the national team was planned for 1973 but, as in other countries, the players were put under considerable political pressure not to tour and so the plans were abandoned.

The Netherlands has competed several times in the Hong Kong Sevens series. In 1988 one of its most promising players, Marcel Bierman, suffered a severe neck injury during a match in Hong Kong, leaving him confined to a wheelchair. Twelve months later, in a dramatic and moving gesture, the Dutch players, who had just won the Bowl championship final, wheeled him on to the pitch to take part in their victory celebrations. It was a moment that won many friends for Dutch rugby.

Several other Dutch players deserve special mention. One is John van Altena, who passed 100 games for the national team in more than 14 seasons. The others are the six brothers from the Marcker family, all of whom have played for their country. Up to four have taken the field for the Netherlands in the same match.

Leading clubs in Holland are RC Hilversum, RC Leyden, RC Castricum, Haagsche RC, LRC Diok and The Bassetts.

NEW SOUTH WALES COUNTRY

New South Wales Country first played against a touring team in 1950, losing 47–3 to the British Isles. In those days players from Canberra were included

in the Country teams, but in 1955 the new union was formed by enthusiasts in the country areas of New South Wales, with centres in Newcastle, Hunter Valley, Wagga Wagga, Riverina, Illawarra, and New England.

Teams have had regular contact with visiting teams and toured at an international level. The first was in 1954 when a NSW Country team visited New Zealand, losing only two of 11 matches on tour. Encouraged by its results and experiences, New South Wales Country became one of the first teams, outside of international sides, to tour regularly overseas.

Success against major teams did not come until 1973, when Tonga was beaten by 22–11. In 1975 the union had its most significant victory when it beat England by 14–13. There was a surprising scoreline of 97–20 when Country beat Japan the same year. Fiji was also beaten in 1976, Canada in 1985, and Italy in 1986.

The 1954 team was captained by Cyril Burke, a brilliant halfback and a man who is arguably Country's greatest rugby son. Burke played for Newcastle for years until his protégé, fellow halfback John Hipwell, came along. Hipwell continued as a highly effective player in that position for nearly 20 years. Other prominent players to have played for Country include Jim Lenehan, Beres Ellwood, Phil Hawthorne, Jon White, Geoff Shaw, Greg Cornelsen and Dick Cocks.

NEW SOUTH WALES RFU

Called the Southern Rugby Union until 1892, the rugby union of the Australian state of New South Wales was formed officially in 1874. The game was played in various forms as early as 1829.

New South Wales rugby has been the one constant factor on the Australian rugby scene. In other states the game's popularity waxed and waned, but it always maintained a strong hold in Sydney and the surrounding areas in the face of extremely strong outside pressures.

The rise of rugby league in the early twentieth century posed continuing problems, which have now been largely overcome, though some status was lost irrevocably in the early years. Rugby league is still the main game in the state, but union followers remain staunchly supportive of their game's

The first touring team from New South Wales, or the Southern Rugby Union, visited New Zealand in 1882.

standing. After some crippling financial problems in the late 1980s, there is plenty of confidence in growth in the future.

New South Wales has always had a strong association with New Zealand. The first contact between the two came in 1882, when New Zealand hosted a visit of the first touring New South Wales team. The tourists won four and lost three games against New Zealand provincial teams.

The first games against a full New Zealand team were in 1884. New Zealand won all three, but New South Wales has had some significant wins over the All Blacks. In 1907, for instance, New Zealand was beaten 14–0 by the home team, which included one of New South Wales's greatest union men, later to be a great rugby league pioneer, Herbert 'Dally' Messenger. In 1922 New South Wales beat New Zealand by two 'test' wins to one.

During the 1920s, New South Wales played nine series, either home or away, with the All Blacks. Officials on both sides of the Tasman viewed the repeated contact as vital for the survival of rugby in Australia.

New South Wales undertook a tour to Britain and France in 1927–28, suffering only five losses in 31 tour games (*see* WARATAHS). The strength maintained by New South Wales rugby was underlined when it thrashed the Great Britain team 28–3 in Sydney in 1930.

One of the greatest days in the state's sporting history came when the 1937 touring South Africans suffered a 17–6 loss on the Sydney Cricket Ground. The light blues scored five thrilling tries in a game played on a rain-sodden pitch.

By then rugby league was well established in the eastern states and rugby union teams had regular disappointments when their best players were lured with promises of big pay cheques to the 13-a-side game. This of course still happens, and is a continuing source of irritation to NSW rugby union officials – as well to neighbouring Queensland.

New South Wales was the sole outpost for the game in Australia after World War I, when Queensland rugby went into recession until 1929. Once Queensland resumed playing, New South Wales continued to dominate

proceedings, regularly winning the home and away inter-state clashes and repeatedly putting high percentages of players into Australian test or touring teams. Eighteen of the 1936 Wallabies team in New Zealand were from New South Wales, as were 19 of the 1946 team. The list goes on: 21 of the 1949 team to New Zealand; 22 to New Zealand in 1952; 25 of the 1957–58 team to Britain; 22 on the next tour there in 1966–67. In 1962 New South Wales beat the New Zealand touring team by 12–11 in Sydney; 13 and 14 players respectively then played for Australia in the two test matches that followed.

In recent years the rise and consolidation of Queensland rugby has meant that such high percentages are things of the past, and the formation of the rugby unions of Sydney and New South Wales Country has led to a more even spread of New South Wales's, and therefore Australia's, rugby talent.

Many of Australia's greatest players have turned out in the colours of New South Wales. Men like the Thornett brothers, the Ella brothers,

Ken Catchpole, Tony Miller, Aub Hodgson, Bill Cerutti, Cyril Towers, Trevor Allan, Jim Lenehan, Simon Poidevin, Peter Johnson, Greg Davis and David Campese have their names on a list that could go on and on. Hundreds of New South Wales players have played for their country and hundreds have held high the honour of rugby in one of the strongest, yet most pressurised environments in the rugby world.

NEW ZEALAND

Setting a date for the founding of rugby in New Zealand is no easy matter. The oldest rugby club in the country still in existence is the Christchurch Football Club, formed in 1863 but playing its own mixture of rules: basically soccer or Victorian (later Australian) rules, with a smattering of rugby.

A Christchurch school with strong English links and traditions, Christ's College, had its own set of rules in 1862 which included many rugby characteristics, for the majority of its staff was recruited from public schools in England.

These rules filtered through to the Christchurch club, whose president for 36 years was R.J.S. Harman, an old boy of Rugby School. But the club did not officially adopt rugby rules until 1876, so it was in Nelson that the first formal rugby match was played, on May 14 1870.

The Nelson Football Club (familiarly called the 'Town' club) was founded in 1868 by R.C. Tennant, but played soccer and Victorian rules for the first two years, until persuaded to try rugby rules by Charles Monro, a student returning from school in England.

The experiment was such a success the rules were adopted, so the next step was a proper match. Nelson College had played a match similar to the epic *Tom Brown's Schooldays* fixture early in the 1860s, but it followed the Town club in converting to rugby rules in 1870. The two met for the first time at the Botanical Reserve in Nelson, Town winning by two goals to nil. They played 18-a-side, and the next match was a fixture between 'sixteen Old College Members of the Club' and 'sixteen who were not Collegians'.

Before the end of the year was out, 'fourteen of Nelson' played 'thirteen of Wellington' in Wellington, the home side having trouble filling its side, and having to recruit the driver of its transport! Nelson scored two goals to one. The Wellington club itself was not formed until 1871, starting out under Victorian rules but changing to rugby.

The first match between representative sides of different areas was played on September 30 1871, between a Wellington team and combined Nelson clubs.

From these humble beginnings, rugby swiftly took root in New Zealand. An Auckland team toured the colony in 1875, and Canterbury made a tour the following year.

The first provincial union, Canterbury, was formed in 1879, Wellington a few months later, and as early as 1882 New Zealand played host to a visiting team for the first time, from New South Wales.

This was meant to be a tour in the other direction. The then Southern Rugby Union (it became New South Wales in 1892) invited a New Zealand team to tour, but the invitation through the Wellington union aroused little interest in the South Island unions, Canterbury and Otago. So the Southern Union picked up the idea to tour instead, and the party of 16 – managed by a player, Ted Raper, also the captain – had a programme of seven matches.

It played Auckland provincial clubs twice, Wellington twice, and had one match each against Canterbury, Otago and West Coast-North Island, a combination of players basically from the present Taranaki and Wanganui unions. New South Wales won four matches and lost three – a better record than many other touring sides have managed in New Zealand!

Two years later the first New Zealand team returned the visit, though this was not a properly chosen national team. Instead, the four major unions (Auckland, Wellington, Canterbury and Otago) were offered places in the team: Canterbury four, the others five, and they settled on their own representatives. The team wore dark blue with a gold fern leaf on the left breast.

New South Wales returned in 1886, and two years later New Zealand made proper contact with the outside rugby world when the 'Shaw and Shrewsbury' team of mainly English players (with a few Scots) toured both Australia and New Zealand.

In 1892 the New Zealand Rugby Football Union was formed, largely through the endeavours of 27-year-old Edward Hoben, who was prominent in the game in Tauranga and Hawke's Bay, and who had toured the country in 1891 promoting the idea of a national body. The inaugural meeting was held at Wellington's Club Hotel, seven unions being represented, with the significant absence of the oldest union, Canterbury.

Otago, Southland and Canterbury all refused to affiliate in the earliest days of the New Zealand Rugby Football Union, which meant that they had no representatives in the first full New Zealand side which went to New South Wales in 1893. That team was captained by Tom Ellison of the Poneke club, thought to be New Zealand's first Maori lawyer and the founder of the wing forward position.

It was Ellison who moved that the New Zealand playing uniform be 'Black Jersey with Silver Fernleaf, Black Cap with Silver Monogram, White Knickerbockers and Black Stockings'. Not a great deal has changed over the past 100 years, save the colour of the knickerbockers – and their style!

New Zealand first played as a team at home in Christchurch against the touring 1894 New South Wales team, setting the standard for a century of successes with an 8–6 victory. Its first full international was against Australia, on the Sydney Cricket Ground in 1903, and again New Zealand was victorious, winning 22–3.

The captain was a New Zealand rugby pioneer, James Duncan, and the fullback one of the all-time greats, Billy Wallace, who set a record which will never be broken by kicking two goals from a mark in this match.

The first New Zealand national team to visit Britain was the immensely successful 1905 'Originals' – original, too, in that they were the first team to be dubbed the 'All Blacks'. It is still not entirely clear whether this name came about because of the colour of their uniform or, more fancifully, because a journalist felt that this marvellously gifted all-round team played as if they were 'All Backs', with the cabling facilities of the day taking care of the rest.

The Originals barnstormed their way round Britain, annihilating much of the opposition, but tiring towards the end of a strenuous tour. After finishing strongly to edge out Scotland, it lost 0–3 to Wales in a match that has entered folk history due to the dispute over a try not awarded to the young All Black centre, Bob Deans.

But the Originals were not the first New Zealand team to tour Britain. As early as 1888, as the touring British side was still finishing its New Zealand tour, a New Zealand Natives team toured Britain. (see NATIVES). This team followed to some extent the principle of the Aboriginals' cricket tour of Britain, and would probably encounter opposition in these days of racial and cultural sensitivity if exploited in the same way.

New Zealand first met another giant of world rugby, South Africa, in 1921, though players from the two dominions had met in the King's Cup tournament which followed World War I, and during a New Zealand Army tour of South Africa.

The 1921 South African tour of New Zealand was a tense, tightly-fought contest finishing all square: New Zealand won the first test, South Africa the second, and the third was a scoreless draw.

New Zealand's first tour to South Africa, in 1928, also finished with honours even, two tests apiece, but since that time, no touring All Black or Springbok team has succeeded in so much as sharing a series on the other's soil, with one exception.

The 1937 Springboks were not a highly regarded side when they headed for Australasia, but they left New Zealand widely rated as the best ever to have played there. They scrummaged New Zealand into submission in the final test, and New Zealand pride was further dented in 1949 when a much vaunted touring side suffered from the accurate boot of prop 'Okey' Geffin, its own goal-kicking woes, and coaching problems, resulting in the loss of all four tests.

Retribution was demanded by the New Zealand public, and in the most amazing year of New Zealand rugby fervour, 1956, justice was seen to be done. In an almost religious atmosphere the All Blacks defeated a very useful Springbok team by three tests to one. In the eyes of the public the kicking colossus Don Clarke, the rampaging loose forward Peter Jones and the tough prop Kevin Skinner approached eligibility for canonisation.

Rugby fever, and spectators seize every available vantage point to watch the 1937 Springboks in action.

Playing the 1966 Lions at Christchurch. With the ball is Howard Norris and facing, from left, Brian Lochore,
Willie John McBride, Stan Meads, Colin Meads, Delme Thomas, Jack Hazlett and Alun Pask.

In the years and series that followed the home team has never been beaten in a series, though there have been some close calls. New Zealand failed to take advantage of an offer to have neutral referees in the 1976 tour of South Africa, and lived to bemoan the fact; while in the protest-ridden 1981 tour of New Zealand, the flamboyant referee Clive Norling ensured he would also be remembered when he awarded a last-minute penalty in the third and final test, which gave New Zealand victory.

New Zealand was next scheduled to tour South Africa in 1985, but the actions of two Auckland lawyers brought an injunction against the NZRFU which resulted in the cancellation of the tour. Aggrieved players then clandestinely organised their own tour, the self-styled Cavaliers, which

included 28 of the original 30 selections. But they had little chance when they toured the following year, having accepted an ill-conceived and heavily-loaded itinerary.

New Zealand's longest standing opponents are players from the British Isles and Ireland, if one puts aside the 'colonial connection' with New South Welshmen in 1882. Certainly conflicts with British Isles teams hold a place second only to those with the Springboks. The first British visit in 1888 was reciprocated in short order by the Natives. The 'Originals' tour has already been mentioned, and in the previous year 'Darkie' Bedell-Sivright's British team had felt humiliated when they lost to the New Zealanders in its only international, after a successful tour of Australia. When the British returned in 1908 with a

team consisting only of Welsh and English players, the All Blacks had hefty wins in the first and third tests and a surprise draw in the second.

The 1924 All Blacks not for nothing were dubbed the 'Invincibles', as they went one better than their 1905 predecessors. But their record was tarnished, if involuntarily, by Scotland's refusal to play them. The Scots were still annoyed by the RFU's decision to allow the 1905 team to be paid expenses of three shillings per man per day. Another source of irritation to the Scots was the fact that they had refused to pay the 1905 team a guarantee from their two games, instead allowing it to take the net gates. Alas, they had misread the potential appeal of the colonials, which cost the Scotland Rugby Union something like £1600 – a huge sum in those days.

The first strong and truly representative British team to tour New Zealand was the 1930 team, who wore the dark blue of Scotland, even if there was only one Scottish player in the side. These colours compelled the hosts to play in white jerseys for the only time, other than when they play the Scottish themselves. This series was the international swansong for some of the 1924 immortals, such as captain Cliff Porter, mercurial centre Bert Cooke, legendary fullback George Nepia, and the five-eighths Mark Nicholls. (But Cooke and Nepia did go on to play international rugby league.) A runaway try gave the first Lions the first test 6–3, but New Zealand had useful wins in the remaining three.

Perhaps the All Blacks' least successful tour to Britain was that led by Jack Manchester in 1935. Manchester himself was not a very distinguished player and was regarded by some New Zealanders as a colonial pretender to the English snobbery system. But he had something of a thankless task, for he led a team which was having major problems wrestling with a three-fronted scrum, having been forced to abandon its traditional 2-3-2 formation. The 1935–36 tourists lost only four games, but two of them were tests, one of which was won most convincingly by England, when Prince Alex Obolensky scored his historic two tries.

Irish hooker Karl Mullen led the next Lions tour to New Zealand in 1950, but we should mention briefly here a New Zealand tour of Britain which was international in all but name – the Second New Zealand Expeditionary Force team, more popularly known as the Kiwis, and it is doubtful if there has been a more popular international side. (See KIWIS).

Mullen's 1950 team had a similar record to that of Doug Prentice's team 20 years earlier, except it could only draw the first test. Indeed, British teams have often struggled down under. The 1959 side, also led by an Irish hooker, Ron Dawson (who never could convince the Welsh he deserved his test place ahead of their own Bryn Meredith), went close, but finished with a 1–3 series loss. That was a little unflattering, for the Lions scored four tries to six penalty goals while losing the first test to Don Clarke 17–18; and the same man scored a last-gulp try to

take his team to an 11–8 second test win. The Lions finally salvaged the pride they deserved in the final test.

The right captain has not always been selected for Lions teams. New Zealanders were certainly convinced that the wrong option was taken when Scottish army officer Mike Campbell-Lamerton's 1966 team lost all four internationals, but the record was markedly improved, and the right choices made, when Carwyn James, as coach, and John Dawes, as captain, led the 1971 Lions to an historic series win, 2–1 with one drawn. Having a manager like Doug Smith was another major factor.

Although Dawes the captain had proved to be a major success, Dawes the coach proved to be less so in 1977. Both he and captain Phil Bennett were visibly ill-suited for their respective roles. Dawes became antagonistic; Bennett retreated into himself, and there was the suggestion of a growing Welsh paranoia over its inability to come to terms with New Zealand teams.

Indeed, New Zealand touring sides to Britain from the 1960s on were powerful forces. The 1963–64 team, led by the renowned Wilson Whineray and coached by Neil McPhail, who had played for both the Kiwis and the Services teams after World War II, fell short of an historic 'Grand Slam' only through a scoreless draw with Scotland.

In 1967 Charlie Saxton managed a team, coached by Fred Allen and captained by Brian Lochore, which made a hastily-arranged tour of Britain after the New Zealand government had forced the cancellation of a tour to South Africa. A foot-and-mouth scare meant that this team had to forgo a planned visit to Ireland, and the only hiccup from this vastly talented side was a draw with East Wales.

The 1972–73 team, the last to make a very long tour, faced more than one crisis. The biggest was the tumultuous night after the international against Wales, when Keith Murdoch, a hero following his try in a tense and tight victory, became a villain after hitting a security guard, Peter Grant, in the Angel Hotel in Cardiff. Murdoch was sent home by manager Ernie Todd, seemingly at the insistence of the host administrators, but never actually making it, leaving the aircraft at

Singapore and cutting himself off from his homeland and rugby thereafter. Although the tourists lost five of their 33 matches, they were only a hairsbreadth – a 10–10 draw with Ireland – away from the first 'Grand Slam' against the four home unions.

The All Blacks made highly creditable tours to Ireland (1974) and Wales (1980) to help the two host unions to celebrate their centenaries.

Indeed, in 1974 the All Blacks had achieved something of a record by playing Ireland, a Welsh XV (the full Wales side in disguise) and the Barbarians (effectively the Lions) in the space of eight days, winning the first two matches and drawing with the Barbarians.

New Zealand also beat both England and Scotland in 1979, and although they had wins against each of the British nations in the space of those three tours, they also completed a long-held dream in 1978 by accounting for all four on the one tour. Graham Mourie's team went into the 'Grand Slam' series without an unbeaten record – it had lost to Munster. But that loss was one of only two – the other was to Northern Division at Otley in 1979 – between the 1972–73 tour and the tour to England and Scotland in 1983.

As a prelude to the latter tour, the All Blacks had hosted a British team which won only 12 of its 18 matches. The third Irish hooker to lead the Lions in New Zealand, Ciaran Fitzgerald, possibly held less claim to a test place than either of his predecessors, and it was a source of amazement to New Zealand observers that he was not displaced by Scotland's Colin Deans.

The tourists' problems were compounded by the inability of the manager, Willie John McBride, to accept his team's failings and he blamed all but the players themselves. A popular and successful tourist as a player, McBride's reputation suffered when he became an administrator. The coach of the Lions, Jim Telfer, toiled manfully in difficult circumstances and commanded respect on the tour, which was justified by his later successes with Scotland.

The 1983 New Zealand team which could only draw with Scotland – 25–25, the highest draw in an international – and lost to England, was very different from the team which only

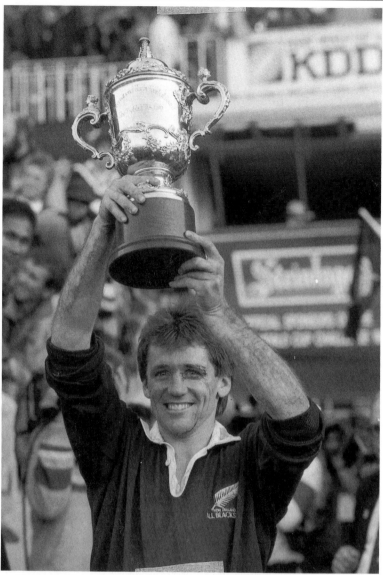

New Zealand: rugby world champions in 1987. David Kirk holds the Webb Ellis trophy after the World Cup final at Eden Park.

wonder its tours were two decades apart.

Scotland has been the most frequent visitor, first touring in 1975, and losing the 'water polo' test in dangerous aquatic conditions, 24–0. It visited again in 1981, when it lost both tests, as it did in 1989. But it went close in the first test, and even closer in the second, on that occasion.

Ireland has been more coy about touring, but visited in 1976, performing usefully in a sensible seven-match programme, losing only to the big guns – Auckland, Canterbury and New Zealand itself.

Situated as far as it is possible to be from the birthplace of rugby, New Zealand has nevertheless spread its wings widely, having either hosted or toured the Soviet Union, Romania, Italy, Spain, Namibia, Zimbabwe, Tonga, Fiji, Western Samoa, Japan, the United States, Canada, Sri Lanka, Malaysia, Singapore, Argentina and Uruguay. All these contacts have either been at full international level or through the myriad of 'national' teams fielded by New Zealand: juniors, colts, development or 'emerging' groups, Maoris, universities and services.

But New Zealand places great store on its opponents earning what it calls 'test' status against its very best team. Whereas Australia, especially, and some other countries tend to give caps for any match against another nation, the All Blacks take some time to admit other than their traditional opponents to full test status.

For instance New Zealand both toured and hosted Argentina before it agreed to full internationals with Hugo Porta's men in 1985. Fiji and New Zealand had a rugby association for a quarter of a century before they played their first full international during the World Cup – and it took that international tournament for outsiders such as Italy to join the select club of international opponents.

Not surprisingly New Zealand's most regular opponent is Australia, but as always its rugby administrators jealously guarded its international status, refusing to recognise as full internationals those matches of the 1920s when Queensland was in recess and New South Wales alone represented Australia. Australia now accords those matches full international status, whereas New Zealand does not.

months earlier had defeated the Lions so comprehensively at home. Retirements, injuries and unavailability had taken their toll, and while the first wing to lead New Zealand on a tour and in tests, Stu Wilson, was one of the most engaging characters of New Zealand rugby, the job sat uneasily with him and he was far removed from the action.

While New Zealand tours to the Northern Hemisphere amounted to overkill late in the 1970s, there has since been a tendency to spread them out, primarily because of the World Cup. In 1989 Ireland and Wales hosted the All Blacks, who barnstormed through both countries. Since then New Zealand has hosted individual British nations, rather than the composite group.

The first of the individual national teams to tour was England, in 1963. It lost four of the five matches (and both tests) in a tough itinerary. Wales took a drubbing in 1969, when it could rightly consider itself on top of the European pile. It lost both tests heavily, but not as disastrously as on its 1988 tour, when the world champions tended to score half centuries against the once-proud Welsh. No

The New Zealand team before the first test against France, Nantes, 1990. Below is a section of the boisterous crowd, with New Zealand supporters much in evidence. Peter Bush

Above: The All Black front row – Richard Loe, Sean Fitzpatrick and Steve McDowell.
Right: Grant Fox, New Zealand's finest goal-kicking exponent, in action for the All Blacks. Peter Bush

France provided another problem. New Zealand played matches there whenever it toured Britain and Ireland, but encountered grave difficulties in enticing France to reciprocate. In fact New Zealand was forced to tell France in no uncertain terms that if it did not tour in 1961, it would be shunned on subsequent All Black tours to Europe.

So France agreed to tour, losing all three tests and six of the total of 13 matches. It also failed to win series in 1968, 1984, and 1989, as well as losing the one-off test of 1986 and the World Cup final in 1987. But it was proud to share the 1979 series.

While the All Blacks are the showpiece of New Zealand rugby, the first-class programme, comparable only with South Africa, focuses squarely on provincial (as with state or county) matches. For a century, provincial unions played each other in what could be termed 'friendly' matches, but which were far from friendly in many cases.

The focus of these matches was the Ranfurly Shield challenge matches, but in 1976 a national championship was introduced, which has prompted a sternly contested programme of 10 matches for each of the top unions every season, with subsidiary second and third division competitions involving all 27 New Zealand unions.

This concept certainly benefited the top unions and players, but it became increasingly clear through the 1980s that the broad base of New Zealand rugby was shrinking, as promising and ambitious players left their home pastures for those where their potential could be more easily recognised, on the assumption that success in the national championship and the Ranfurly Shield, and winning national selection, was going to be beyond players who remained with the smaller and less successful unions. Gone are the days, perhaps, when New Zealand could produce test captains from 'minor' unions such as Wairarapa (Brian Lochore), King Country (Colin Meads) and Poverty Bay (Ian Kirkpatrick).

The focal point of New Zealand rugby is the club. Every club has a club-room, even if in some cases it is the local pub or a shed belonging to one of the members, housing a 50-litre keg of draught beer. The more affluent have magnificent facilities, some complete with gymnasium, squash courts, saunas and spas – even accommodation. A few clubs own their grounds, as distinct from unions being the property owners. It is traditional, even expected of teams, to return to their club-room (perhaps after briefly sampling opponents' hospitality) to share in the news of all the teams' performances.

The club structure does not bear comparison with that, say, in Britain or France. The larger cities such as Auckland, Christchurch and Wellington have at least 20 clubs each. Thus a better comparison with Cardiff or Toulouse would be the provincial team of Auckland, Canterbury or Wellington, which is chosen from the best players of those cities' clubs.

But clubs in New Zealand administer a wide gamut of players. They pick up children (including girls, in these enlightened days) from the age of five or even younger, and give them 'fun' games. Then there is 'new image' rugby, which can be played equally by all ages and both sexes; 10-a-side games, which have no technical aspects, such as lineouts or formalised scrums, and include on-field coaches organising their young charges. In addition there are the full 15-a-side games from the ages of 10 or so, the colts and serious 'senior' teams, and finally the 'president's' grades of more mature players who cannot bear to give the game away.

From these multifarious aspects of rugby emerged the 'golden oldies' competitions, with their unique rules, and touch football, which removes the more hazardous physical elements as well as enabling those not wishing to be encumbered by antiquated rules concerning 'professionalism' to play matches of 'rugby' against rugby league players, for example.

'Touch' was largely confined to Australia and New Zealand as the world moved into the 1990s, but history could well reflect on its potential to revolutionise world rugby, given its extraordinarily rapid growth in New Zealand, where it is already the fourth largest sport in terms of playing numbers, and the way it allows rugby union and rugby league players to compete together.

Rugby is New Zealand's greatest passion. During the 1950s, especially for the dramatic series against the 1956 Springboks, not to mention the highly popular Lions of 1959, the bigger grounds – Eden Park in Auckland, Lancaster Park in Christchurch and Athletic Park in Wellington – were crammed to capacity with between 50,000 and 60,000 spectators. People camped out on frosty nights with sleeping bags and thermos flasks of hot drinks at the gates; it was a case of first in, first served.

But with the advent of television the fanaticism waned, and tickets began to be presold. Hospitality boxes, leased in the main by corporations and businesses, plus the erection of stands in place of the standing-only embankments or terraces, have cut the capacities of Eden Park and Athletic to little more than 40,000 and of Lancaster Park to a little less than that.

Nor are there the huge crowds any longer to welcome visiting teams – far fewer than can be expected for a provincial team returning with the prized Ranfurly Shield!

New Zealand crowds are still loyal to their team, but whereas they accepted wins at any cost during the 1950s and 1960s, they now expect to be entertained. Having absorbed the fact that the game could be played both attractively and successfully, they would no longer readily settle for anything less. They have even been known to applaud fine play by visitors! But alas, they do not sing nearly as well as the Welsh – perhaps the New Zealand male's macho self-image inhibits him from finding expression in song.

All New Zealanders hold firm opinions on rugby, and both provincial sides and the All Blacks are debated as vigorously, but more often than politics and religion. But then rugby is said to be New Zealand's religion.

New Zealand rugby has known its rocky moments. It was challenged by the 13-a-side code in the first decade of the twentieth century, and some hold that rugby league was poised to become New Zealand's premier winter sport until, ironically, World War I gave rugby union time and space to retrench.

The banning of the two-fronted scrum, which deprived New Zealand of its traditional and much-vaunted 2-3-2 scrum and wing forward position, caused scrummaging problems in the 1930s which were not really rectified until the 1950s.

The visit by the 1981 Springboks caused severe social disruption and disaffection with rugby. This was fuelled by the Cavaliers' unsanctioned tour of 1986, and it was only the World Cup tournament and New Zealand's success which turned things around.

Perhaps New Zealand's rugby could be said to thrive on setbacks; it stumbles but grows stronger for the experience. Some would look at the record of New Zealand rugby and infer there have been precious few lean times.

NEWLANDS

The main rugby ground of Cape Town in the Western Province of South Africa. The ground is situated under Table Mountain, making it probably the world's most picturesque rugby arena. It is part of an historic two-sport complex, with a cricket ground just 800 metres away from the massive, modern rugby stadium. Both places are much loved by all South African sports enthusiasts. The first offices of the South African Rugby Board were situated there.

Newlands was in place in 1891 when the first overseas team toured the republic. The third test was played in Cape Town and the South African team included 11 players from Western Province. That, possibly, was because in the early days of rugby in South Africa the host province was permitted to choose the national playing XV!

The ground can present playing conditions that are considered 'foreign' even to South African teams. Playing at sea level is something that visiting teams are more used to than South Africans from the high veldt. And Newlands is the one test venue in the republic where it can rain as well as blow.

A scan of South Africa's results on Newlands, since major tours began in 1928, will show why the ground is considered unlucky for the Springboks. So many significant tests were lost there, South African fans and followers have become quite superstitious about it.

Losses were suffered by South Africa on Newlands to the All Blacks in 1928, in 1960 and 1970, to the British Isles in 1938 and 1974, and to Australia in 1953 and 1963. France played two drawn matches there, in 1958 and 1967.

One of the most dramatic tests on the ground was perhaps the fourth test in 1928, when New Zealand had to

Newport plays the 1925 All Blacks at Rodney Parade.

win the game to draw the series. This it did, by 13–5, in the most hideous playing conditions. Mud and water were the order of the day with the fans peering out from under umbrellas.

In 1949 South Africa gained some revenge by beating New Zealand, even if the manner of the victory created surprise around the rugby world. Aaron 'Okey' Geffin, the burly prop, kicked five penalties to enable the Springboks to win the first test by 15–11.

In 1962 a capacity crowd of 52,000 watched the third test between the Springboks and the Lions head for a 3–3 draw. But a late mistake by the brilliant Englishman Richard Sharp, who tried to pass a ball in a tight defensive position, enabled South Africa to break away and score a late try. That day Newlands also rocked to disturbances in the crowd. But the two deaths that occurred were attributed to the excitement of the game, rather than to battles with bottles and knives.

NEWPORT RFC

One of the strongest and most powerful clubs in Wales, Newport has produced many of Wales's most famous rugby sons as well as claiming a number of great moments against the best of the world's international touring teams.

Newport was founded in 1874. After an early period when club members debated about whether to embrace rugby or association football, Newport chose rugby and quickly developed into a powerful combination. The club did not suffer its first defeat until the 1879–80 season. Four years later it was again unbeaten, and the press by then was dubbing the club 'the invincibles'. It supplied nine players for the Welsh team which played Scotland in 1893.

The secret of the club's success could be put down to its enterprising style of play. Newport players were great passers of the ball and, led by the great Arthur 'Monkey' Gould, they were early influences on rugby's development into more than just a game of kicking and rucking.

Because of its location in the county of Monmouthshire, Newport was affiliated to both the English and Welsh Rugby Unions, joining with English rugby before the Wales RU was formed. A number of Newport players qualified and played successfully for England, and more than 100 Newport men played for Wales in the club's first 100 years.

In 1921 Newport fielded a team for a club match made up entirely of current international players: ten were Welshmen, three were English, with one Scotsman and an Irishman. There were three further Welsh internationals in the reserves! For the record, Newport beat Bristol that day by 17–0.

Obviously Newport was very strong in that era and in the following year, led by Jack Wetter, the club had another of its unbeaten seasons. In 1924 the club played a great game against the All Blacks (who later were also to be called 'invincibles') but New Zealand won by 13–10.

Newport was the club that inflicted the first defeat on the 1912–13 South African team, winning 9–3. The springbok head is still in the Newport club-house. In 1969 it again beat South Africa, this time by 11–6. The club beat Australia 11–0 in 1957, and in 1963, via a famous dropped goal by John Uzzell, Newport scored a 3–0 win over the New Zealand All Blacks. It is this victory that the club regards as its most significant: it was the only loss inflicted on that All Black team, one of New Zealand's finest. The game was a tough, dour struggle, and after Uzzell's drop-kick crossed for three points Newport put up a tenacious defence until the final victory was won. The scenes of jubilation in the crowd are remembered as some of Newport's sweetest moments.

Newport's highest-capped player in its first 100 years was the highly-acclaimed wing Ken Jones, who played in 44 internationals. Also from Newport was Tommy Vile, a Welsh scrumhalf international, who was later a referee of the highest class and a most able administrator.

Other men to appear in Newport's black and amber colours were Willie Llewellyn, Jerry Shea, 'Bunner' Travers, Malcolm Thomas, Bryn Meredith, David Watkins, Stuart Watkins and Brian Price, all of them great players at an international level.

Surprisingly, one of Newport's most fondly recalled sons was an international only once. Roy Burnett was kept out of Welsh teams by the brilliance of Cardiff's Cliff Morgan, but he was the 'king' at Rodney Parade and as a brilliant, attacking flyhalf he was one of

the main reasons why huge crowds came to watch the club team play in the late forties and early fifties.

Two other well-known Newport men were Richard Mullock, who was called the 'Father of Welsh Rugby'. He was the first secretary of the Welsh Rugby Union in 1881 and was also the selector of the first Welsh team to play England at Blackheath in 1881. Horace Lyne was president of the Welsh Rugby Union from 1906 to 1947.

NICHOLLS, MARK
Wellington, Auckland and New Zealand
10 internationals for N. Zealand 1921–30

Though never New Zealand captain, apart from in some tour matches in South Africa in 1928, Mark Nicholls had a profound influence on the direction of New Zealand rugby throughout the 1920s. Though he possessed considerable flair, Nicholls' forté was in controlling and dictating play, often with his educated boot or in making play for the dynamic Bert Cooke and other skilled attackers. He was an accurate goal-kicker and drop-kicker, who topped the scoring with 103 points on the 1924–25 tour. He was the backline leader, in fact if not in name, of the 1924 'Invincibles' but suffered strangely when vice-captain of the 1928 side.

Nicholls had played all New Zealand's internationals – three against South Africa, 1921, five on the 1924–

Mark Nicholls, 1926

25 tour – since his debut. But he played only 11 games in South Africa in 1928, and was not selected for the first three tests. With New Zealand down 1–2 in the series, Nicholls was restored to second five-eighths and played a critical part in the 13–5 victory, scoring 10 points with his boot. Bennie Osler rated Nicholls as the best player he marked – though it's worth noting Osler was a flyhalf and marked Lance Johnson in this game!

Bill Dalley, the test halfback in 1928, was to the point when asked for the reasoning behind Nicholls' frequent omissions on that tour: 'Wouldn't tackle.' But there have been suggestions of a clash of personalities between Nicholls and the equally strong-willed captain, Maurice Brownlie.

Mark Nicholls' career finished with two tests against the 1930 British side and he was a New Zealand selector in 1936–37.

Two Nicholls brothers, Harold ('Doc') and Harry ('Ginger') also played for New Zealand and a son, Mark, for Wellington. The latter recalled once how many rugby problems were solved on Sunday mornings at the Nicholls household by his father and Billy Wallace, with the boy Nicholls sometimes accorded the great privilege of being allowed to listen in – but never to speak!

NIL

That most noble of scores – nil! The end result of a game in which one or both of the teams taking part have given their total commitment – for absolutely no return. As is sometimes said in cricket, they have not bothered the scorer.

Perhaps the most famous game in international rugby when the scorers were not bothered by either side was the 0–0 draw played between New Zealand and South Africa in Wellington in 1921. The match was a classic both in its implication and application.

The first test had been won by the All Blacks, 13–5. The second test went to the Springboks, 9–5. South Africans and New Zealanders both regarded themselves as the best rugby players in the world, and the final test was seen as the match that would decide the series and establish the supremacy of one or other side once and for all.

Both teams played bravely in slithering, slippery conditions on Athletic Park, watched by a crowd peering out from under dripping umbrellas, as mud eventually took over from the surface water.

Excitement gradually built to fever pitch as the scores for both teams stayed on nil, and time ticked by. When the referee's whistle ended the contest it had been one of the most exciting ever seen at that time in New Zealand. Both the Springboks and the All Blacks were experts in attack, but they were equally as efficient in defence. Only miraculous saves stopped many tries, while the mud and slush prevented goals being kicked.

Was this game 'nil's' most glorious day?

The paradox of a nil score is that it can demonstrate either the total equality of two teams, where they cancel each other out – as in the game above – or the total dominance of one side over another. There are other notable games where no score was posted by one or both sides, representing both sides of this coin.

New Zealand 0, Wales 3. 1905
One of rugby's most talked-about days. Half a century later New Zealanders were still claiming their 'nil' score was

not deserved – that Bob Deans *did* score a try!

New Zealand 0, South Africa 17. 1928
Seven years after 1921, the next match between the two teams. Again there was great hope on both sides for a win but it was the All Blacks who were wiped aside.

Wales 0, England 0. 1936
This was the play-off of the two teams that had beaten that season's touring All Black team. After such excitement this was a major disappointment, the expectations of both teams being dashed in a lacklustre display.

Scotland 0, South Africa 44. 1951
This was then the biggest score ever seen in an international, a complete annihilation of Scotland by a superb Springbok team. It is after this game that the quote '. . . and they were lucky to get nil!' was first coined.

South Africa 0, Barbarians 6. 1961
Did the Barbarians change their traditional style from free-flowing to win-at-all-costs rugby to ensure that the unbeaten Springboks went home with at least one loss?

New Zealand 0, Scotland 0, 1964
The obduracy of the Scots prevented Wilson Whineray's team becoming the first All Blacks to do the Grand Slam in Britain (and it went on to beat France, too).

Australia 0, British Isles 31. 1966
A British team at the peak of its powers against a woeful Wallaby team.

New Zealand 0, Munster 12. 1978
Perhaps the most famous win by a provincial or club team over an international combination. Munster people certainly think so! Also a very rare nil score by the All Blacks, whose previous nil against a British club team had been the 0–3 loss against Newport in 1963.

Argentina 0, Australia 26. 1986
The end of a glorious six days for the Wallabies. The first test had been won 39–19 by Australia in Brisbane and Argentina were hopeful of doing better in the second.

Romania 0, Ireland 60. 1986
For the first time Ireland awarded full international caps for a game against a non-IRB country. The result was the

1951, another goal from Okey Geffin, and the crowds at Murrayfield are witness to Scottish rugby's most dismal day. South Africa won 44–0, then the highest score posted in an international.

biggest international score ever posted. Poor Romania, not only did it score nil in the game but the petrol gauge in its chartered jet plane read 'nil' as well. The Irish Rugby Union had to subsidise the cost of more fuel for the flight home.

NO. 8 FORWARDS

Whatever jersey numbering system is used, either with the fullback wearing No. 15 and a prop wearing No. 1, or the other way around, the last man of the scrum always wears the No. 8 – hence the name of the position.

The first requirements for this position in modern rugby are for a player who is tall, strong and fast, who must be equally at home in loose or tight play, on attack or in defence, and able to get quickly to the crunch areas of a game. He should have weight for solid scrummaging, and good jumping and lineout skills; he must be a deadly tackler; and a player who can 'read' in advance the flow of a game.

There have been many excellent players in this specialist position. Perhaps the first player to make maximum use of the No. 8's potential was South Africa's Hennie Muller, who broke away from what was previously a tight forward function to become a chaser of inside backs and a fierce tackler out in open field. True, Muller used the laws of the time to maximum effect for his style, but it was he who widened the role of the No. 8 forward.

Later, players like Mervyn Davies of Wales, Brian Lochore of New Zealand, Walter Spanghero of France and Morne du Plessis of South Africa emerged as the best of the new-look No. 8 players. A decade or so after them came Murray Mexted of New Zealand, who one of the fastest runners of all the world's No. 8s with, perhaps, more athletic skills than the others before him.

After Mexted, Wayne Shelford added tremendous leg-drive for moving mauls and surges forward. Shelford was also a successful captain, as were Davies, Lochore and du Plessis: No. 8 is a position from where the game can be viewed with a wide tactical vision.

Ireland gave the rugby world Willie Duggan, who enjoyed a very successful spell of scavenging for possession in the No. 8 jersey; England had Roger Uttley; South Africa, Tommy Bedford; France, Jean-Pierre Bastiat; Austra-

Peter Horton signals the number of tries scored by Wallaby No. 8 Greg Cornelsen, a record for a forward in a test match, against New Zealand, 1978.

lia, Mark Loane; Scotland, Peter Kininmonth. There are many many more who have distinguished this most athletic place on the rugby field.

NO SIDE

A somewhat archaic term, meaning the end of the match. It first came as a reply to the question asked at every scrum or lineout as to which side would have the ball to resume play. If the referee said 'no side!' he was really saying 'no side will put the ball in (because it is the end of the game)'.

NORLING, CLIVE

A native of Wales who became one of the game's most colourful and talented referees. Always firmly in control and efficient in his interpretation of law, Norling somehow was tagged by some as a controversial figure. Others saw him as an innovator who stamped his own style on the art of controlling a rugby game.

Clive Norling became a referee after suffering a back injury in a rugby game while a teenager. He rose quickly to first-class referee status while still a 20-year-old student at Hampshire Polytechnic in England.

He controlled his first international (Ireland v New Zealand at Dublin 1978) when he was 27. By then he was wearing the short shorts which were to become his trademark. He also had an

unusual habit of running backwards while following some play, but later in his career he virtually abandoned this practice.

Like any referee, Norling was not universally admired. This was especially so on the day in 1983 when he awarded a penalty try at the Sydney Cricket Ground against the touring Argentine team. The incident from which he interpreted that a try 'probably' would have been scored, occurred some 35 metres out from the goal-line.

The decision baffled most Australians and angered the Argentinians. Norling refused to discuss why he had made his decision and the Argentinian coach, Rodolfo O'Reilly, said the so-called try was an 'invention for the showman'.

Norling also became a member of that exclusive (but mythical) refereeing club, made up of those who have sent a player off for foul play in a full international match, when he dismissed the Frenchman Jean-Pierre Garuet for eye-gouging during the France v Ireland match in Paris in 1984.

He received acclaim for the manner in which he refereed the beleaguered third test of the 1981 series between New Zealand and South Africa at Auckland. (*See* PROTESTS.) In extraordinarily difficult circumstances, Norling controlled the game impeccably, even if he earned the ire of Springbok supporters by awarding a late penalty to the All Blacks – some said full-time should have been declared eight minutes earlier!

New Zealand's fullback Allan Hewson kicked the goal to allow the All Blacks a last-gasp 25–22 win and a 2–1 test series victory. The incident was a classic example of a referee being the sole judge of fact in a game. Only the implacable Clive Norling knew how much time had to be added on to make up for all the stoppages that he had had to deal with earlier.

By 1990 he shared a world record 23 international refereeing 'caps' with Kevin Kelleher and Gwynn Walters. Norling seemed likely to surpass that total in 1991.

NORSTER, ROBERT
Abertillery, Cardiff and Wales
34 internationals for Wales 1982–89
3 internationals for British Isles 1983–89

A tall, lean and excellent lock who, but for injury, might have played many more test matches for Wales than he did. Rob Norster was an expert lineout jumper and a bustling and vigorous forward around the field.

He was in the Welsh squad in 1977 as a 20-year-old – young for a lock. He played for Wales first in 1979, but the game against Romania was not awarded caps. So he had to wait until 1982 for his first recognised international, against Scotland at Cardiff.

Robert Norster

Clive Norling signals a goal attempt.

The following year Norster was in the British Isles team to New Zealand. Though the 1983 Lions lost all four tests there, Norster played some fine, aggressive football. He appeared in the first two tests but then had to withdraw with a back injury.

Injury dogged his 1987 World Cup aspirations in New Zealand too. He appeared in three games but then was forced out of any further play.

In 1989, when Wales toured New Zealand, Norster took over the captaincy when tour leader Bleddyn Bowen was hurt. But after the first test at Christchurch Norster himself injured a knee and did not play again.

Norster made his second Lions tour, out to Australia in 1989. He played in the first test, which the Lions lost 12–19, and after that Wade Dooley and Paul Ackford were preferred. Once home again, Norster had shoulder problems in 1989 and his career looked over when he was forced out of most football that season. His total of 34 caps for Wales was a lock's record, shared with Aberavon's Allan Martin.

NORTH AUCKLAND RFU
The most northerly of New Zealand's unions, North Auckland faces major geographical problems in assembling its representative side. Because of the great travelling distances involved, its competition is based on a sub-union or regional system.

First-class rugby in Whangarei, the only city in North Auckland, was first played at Rugby Park, then Okara Park. At both venues the North Aucklanders tried to ensure they had the country's and the world's tallest goal-posts. Estimated to be around 20 metres (65ft) tall, they were not difficult to find in North Auckland: it is the home of the mighty kauri trees and only some shaping and hewing off of branches was required to come up with the finished product!

Brothers Johnny and Peter Smith were outstanding centres immediately after World War II, and many consider 'J.B.' Smith the finest of all All Black centres. Dynamic halfback Sid Going also occupies a very special place in North Auckland rugby lore, and not only was brother Ken an All Black too, but brother Brian was not far away from those honours. Other Going family members played for North Auckland.

Peter Jones was a rampaging loose forward who occasionally played as a lock. 'Tiger' Jones once charged into Australian captain 'Chilla' Wilson with such ferocity that Wilson was moved to remark, 'I thought I'd been hit by a ruddy rhinoceros.'

North Auckland can never consistently challenge the major New Zealand unions, mainly because of its small population, but it has enjoyed its successes in the Ranfurly Shield, and has spent a fairly regular period in the first division championship.

NORTH HARBOUR RFU
Based on the northern area of greater Auckland, this is the 27th and most recently formed of the New Zealand unions. To most, the area north of the Auckland harbour bridge is known as the North Shore, but because a club of that name already existed, the union formed in 1985 was given the name North Harbour.

Based on a vibrant, mainly young population, blessed with many warm beaches and a social recreational lifestyle, North Harbour had a charmed run as it aspired to the upper reaches of New Zealand rugby. Placed initially in the third (and bottom) division, it won promotion to the second division after one year and all but reached the first division within another year.

That milestone was reached a year later, in 1988, by which time North Harbour could boast the All Black captain, Wayne 'Buck' Shelford, and another high profile All Black, Frano Botica.

The greatest moment in North Harbour's first five years of existence was its 1990 challenge against Auckland for the Ranfurly Shield. Led by the charismatic Shelford, North Harbour lost 18–9. Its courage and unusual tactics, including a 15-man 'monster maul', won the side considerable praise and ensured that future games between the two sides were not to be missed.

NORTH OF IRELAND FC
Formed in 1859, the North of Ireland Cricket and Football Club, with headquarters in Belfast, is the oldest club in Ulster and the second oldest in Ireland.

One of the north's leading rugby powers, NIFC can claim the envied record of supplying some of the world's most-capped rugby players. Foremost among these is Michael Gibson, the Irish and British Isles centre who, from 1964–79, had 81 full test appearances – a record 69 for Ireland and 12 for the British Isles.

Next must come Jack Kyle, who was also a North player for a time, with a career total of 52 caps, including six for the British Isles. The great centre, George Stephenson, won 42 caps. Like Kyle, Stephenson spent part of his playing career with Queen's. Noel Henderson was vastly experienced, winning 40 caps for Ireland, mostly as a centre. All of the above were also captains of Ireland.

More than 50 North players have been capped for Ireland: Jack Fulton, a fullback who had nine seasons in the Irish team at the turn of the century; Fred Gardiner, capped 22 times between 1900 and 1909 and who turned out for the club as either a back or forward; Des McKee, a wing, capped 12 times in the great Irish teams after World War II; and Frederick ('Fuzzy') Anderson who played 13 times for Ireland and who was picked to tour South Africa with the 1955 British Isles, only to withdraw because of ill-health.

Two colourful former club members were Dick Tooth, the Australian inter-

national of the 1950s, and the Maori player, Robert Kururangi. The latter first visited Ireland as a member of the 1978 All Blacks and later married a Belfast girl.

North has won a string of Ulster league and cup titles, enjoying a particularly strong period from 1892 to 1899, when it won both the league and the cup, each for seven seasons.

NORTH OTAGO RFU
One of New Zealand's smallest and least successful unions, North Otago is based on the town of Oamaru, which for years won more notoriety among New Zealanders for being 'dry' – that is, liquor could not be sold legally – than for the quality of its rugby players.

Formed in 1904, the union had to wait 59 years before producing an All Black, but Ian 'Spooky' Smith was a very tidy wing who played 24 matches, including nine internationals 1963–66. The next All Black from the union, Phil Gard, a centre, played seven times for New Zealand 1971–72.

North Otago is invariably amalgamated with neighbouring 'minor' unions – South and Mid-Canterbury – for matches with touring sides, but played alone the famous day in 1962 when it beat Australia 14–13.

Frequent suggestions of amalgamation with more powerful Otago have been mooted from time to time. Such a union would avoid the embarrassment of results such as the 0–88 defeat suffered in North Otago's Ranfurly Shield challenge against Canterbury in 1984 – then a record loss.

NORTH WALES RFU
The North Wales RFU was formed in 1931. Development was slow in the union's first years, and in fact it was not until 1965 that North Wales was given representation on the WRU. Although enthusiasm is high, the area suffers in comparison with rugby in the south and tends to lose players north to Merseyside clubs. Its main centres are Colwyn Bay, Llandudno, Rhyl, Bangor and Wrexham.

The prominent rugby schools of North Wales have produced some of the best players of the area. Wilfred Wooller went to school at Rydal; Dewi Bebb was a northerner from Friar's School in Bangor before he went south to make his name at Swansea; while

the former Welsh international player and Wales's 1987 World Cup coach, Tony Gray, went to the same school.

North Wales is occasionally granted games against overseas teams; in the first, in 1974, North Wales beat Tonga 12–3 at Rhyl. In 1980 an Overseas XV beat the home team at Colwyn Bay, 28–9, in a match to celebrate the Welsh RU's centenary. Western Samoa visited, and won, 24–12 in 1988.

NORTHAMPTON RFC
Founded in 1880 and with players nicknamed the 'Saints', this club has contributed significantly to English rugby. It was started by a curate of St James's Improvement Class in Northampton, to keep wayward schoolboys occupied, and developed from there into a powerful sporting club.

The club's first international player was Henry Weston, a forward for England against Scotland in 1901. Billy Weston, his son, later played 16 internationals for England in the years before World War II.

One of the other early heroes for Northampton was the England wing Edgar Mobbs. When he died in action in World War I, a memorial to him was erected in the Northampton market square. (See MOBBS.)

In its earlier years Northampton's strengths lay in its forwards. Arthur Blakiston, who won 17 England caps, was one of the great early forwards. He also played international rugby from Blackheath and Liverpool, but is most fondly remembered for his influence from the side of the scrum and as a lock at Northampton. Ray Longland is remembered too, as a powerful scrummaging forward who won 19 England caps.

Don White was a great Northampton stalwart and leader who won 16 England caps as a flanker between 1947 and 1953, and later became the club's senior coach and an England selector and coach.

After World War II it was mostly the backs from Northampton who made their mark in English teams. Lewis Cannell was a brilliant centre three-quarter who played with another club man, Jeff Butterfield, at international level. Cannell won 19 caps and Butterfield 28. Butterfield was Northampton's first England captain, and retired as England's most-capped back after the 1958–59 season.

Dickie Jeeps was always a staunch 'Saints' man and one of the brilliant men of English and British rugby.

Prop Ron Jacobs, who had 29 caps for England between 1956–64, was also later an England selector, like Jeeps and Butterfield. His total of caps was a Northampton record until Gary Pearce, another prop, passed it late in the 1980s.

Northampton has had an excellent record in providing players for Lions teams. Apart from the years when Butterfield and Jeeps travelled together, there were four Northampton players in the 1968 British team in South Africa (Peter Larter, Bob Taylor, Keith Savage and Bryan West).

Northampton has played its home games at Franklin's Gardens since 1891.

NORTHERN TRANSVAAL RFU

The powerful South African provincial rugby union which is centred on the city of Pretoria. The rugby team of Northern Transvaal (known as the 'Blue Bulls') is widely considered to be one of the strongest provincial teams in the world.

The earliest reports of the game in Pretoria date back to 1877. Loftus Versfeld founded the Pretoria Rugby Football Club in 1899, which gave the area its first impetus towards finding a rugby identity independent of the Johannesburg influence. The first moves for a northern breakaway from the Transvaal Rugby Union came in 1908, when the Pretoria sub-union was formed.

In 1937 the Northern Transvaal Rugby Union was formed, and the first official Springboks came from the province in the the first test match for South Africa against Sam Walker's 1938 British Isles team: Danie Craven (captain), Ferdie Bergh, Roger Sherriff, Benjamin du Toit and Lucas Strachan. Later in the tour the British team beat Northern Transvaal by 20 points to 12 in the new stadium named in honour of Loftus Versfeld.

From then, Northern Transvaal guaranteed one of the toughest games on any touring or provincial team's calendar. The first victory by Northern Transvaal against a major team was in 1953 when it beat the Wallabies by 27–11. It also beat the 1969 Australian team, the Lions in 1962, the Welsh in 1964, and France in 1967.

The province's match against New Zealand in 1976 was a classic which aroused some controversy. A 60,000 crowd saw Northern sneak home by 29–27 in a thriller, but there were allegations that the referee, Piet Robbertse, was spoken to in Afrikaans by Northern's captain, Thys Lourens, just before awarding a late penalty to Northern. The New Zealanders claimed Robbertse was alerted to the fact that the New Zealand team might be about to commit illegalities if Lourens pulled two men out of the next lineout. From the resultant offside, which Robbertse just happened to see, Joos le Roux kicked a penalty goal to give Northern Transvaal its first win over an All Black team.

In the domestic Currie Cup competitions, Northern has always had one of the strongest teams and has featured in many splendid cup contests over the years. One calls to mind the man who is perhaps the best known 'Blue Bull' of them all, Naas Botha, who helped Northern to win the cup final in 1987 when he scored all 24 points to beat rival Transvaal, 24–18. Botha, in a superb display of kicking, landed four penalties and four dropped goals.

If Botha was the most famous Northern Transvaal player of his time, there were many other stars as well. Frik du Preez was a giant of the 1970s, a real Loftus favourite; Hannes Brewis, unbeaten in the Springboks from 1949–53, was also a Northern man, as were men of the calibre of 'Fonnie' du Toit, Jaap Bekker, 'Salty' du Rand, Daan Retief, Piet Uys, Mof Myburgh, Louis Moolman, Ray Mordt and 'Moaner' van Heerden.

Frik du Preez, a famous 'Blue Bull' of the 1970s.

NORTON TANE

Canterbury and New Zealand
27 internationals for N. Zealand, 1971–77

First an international against the victorious Lions in 1971 at the age of 29, Tane (pronounced Tarnay) Norton was never dropped by the All Blacks until his retirement, and got his revenge against the British Isles when he captained New Zealand to a series win.

A smart hooker, who won his share of the ball and a bit more, Norton, especially in his younger days, was a very agile player in the loose, and an astute captain – befitting one christened Rangitane, the Maori name for a paramount chief or great leader.

O

OBOLENSKY, ALEXANDER
Rosslyn Park and England
4 internationals for England 1936

One of rugby's most colourful characters, Prince Alexander Obolensky was the son of Prince Alexis of Russia. The young prince was born in Leningrad in 1916 but was taken to England the following year, presumably to avoid the Russian revolution.

He was educated at Trent College and Brasenose College, Oxford. 'Obo', as he was known, was an elegant and speedy wing and his rugby prowess was quickly recognised. Late in 1935 he played for Oxford in the Universities match, the first of three appearances in that famous game.

As a 19-year-old, early in 1936, he played for England against New Zealand at Twickenham. England caused an upset by thrashing the All Blacks by 13–0. Obolensky scored two tries, one of which has become a classic. His diagonal run through the New Zealand defence, as he scored for the second time, can still be admired on newsreel film footage. That game thereafter became known by rugby writers as 'Obolensky's match'.

After he left Oxford University his form fluctuated and fell away. He won only four caps, all in the 1935–36 season, but his memory is ensured both because of his colourful family background and his extraordinary, if briefly flowering, rugby talent.

A world record in first-class rugby is still entered in the books under Obolensky's name. 'Obo' toured South America with a Rugby Football Union team in 1936, and in a game against Brazil he crossed for 17 tries, still a record for one game, though perhaps the first-class quality of the local XV might be called into question.

When World War II broke out, Obolensky joined the Royal Air Force. He died when the Hawker Hurricane he was piloting crashed on landing in East Anglia, the first of 111 rugby internationals from all countries to lose their lives in the conflict.

O'DRISCOLL, JOHN
London Irish, Manchester and Ireland
26 internationals for Ireland 1978–84
6 internationals for British Isles 1980–83

A modest and hard-working flanker for Ireland and the Lions over seven seasons. His debut was in 1978 v Scotland. He was part of the Irish team that won the Triple Crown in 1981–82 and again in 1982–83.

O'Driscoll made two tours with the British Isles. The first was in 1980 to South Africa, where his hard, tough play earned him a place in all four test matches. In New Zealand in 1983, he added two more tests for the Lions.

OFFSIDE
The rugby lawbook's definition for being offside is when 'a player is in a position in which he is out of the game and is liable to penalty'. The term is

THAT TWICKENHAM TRIUMPH.

NOT SINCE THE WAR HAVE WE SEEN 14 ENGLISHMEN AND ONE RUSSIAN PRINCE FLING THEMSELVES SO VALIANTLY INTO ANY FRAY.

THE RUSSIAN PRINCE WHO WAS BUILT BETTER THAN ANY FIVE YEAR PLAN ANSWERS TO THE NAME OF OBOLENSKY. A PRINCE OF A FELLOW

HE STARTED TO RUN LIKE LIGHTNING WHILE THE NEW ZEALANDERS WERE WAITING FOR THUNDER.

THE PRINCE GOT ENGLAND THE FIRST TWO RUSSIAN TRIES. HIS SECOND TRY WAS A TOUCH OF GENIUS. HE GOT THE NEW ZEALANDERS INTO SUCH A TANGLE AND

THEIR DEFENCE SO MUCH ON THE WRONG SIDE THAT —

— NOT EVEN EYES IN THE BACK OF THEIR HEAD WOULD HAVE HELPED THEM.

IN THAT SECOND TRY THE PRINCE TROTTED AWAY SO MUCH ON HIS OWN THAT HE EVENTUALLY HAD THE WORLD AT HIS FEET

BECAME A SPECK ON THE HORIZON AND —

— AFTER STOPPING TO TOUCH DOWN AT TWICKENHAM

HE POSSIBLY CONVERTED IT AT MOSCOW

As a doctor, O'Driscoll was an invaluable man in an emergency!
Here, he assists Ciaran Fitzgerald.

one of the most well-worn words in any player or referee's vocabulary – though, in interpretation of the law, none is so expert, dogmatic or vociferous as the member of the crowd who shouts at every game ever played, 'Offside, ref!'

The law occupies some 10 pages in the lawbook, in an attempt to define the many situations when a player could be said to be offside: offside in general play and offside at scrummage, ruck, maul or lineout. There is also accidental offside.

The punishment for the infringement is generally a penalty to the opposition except, on some rulings, when the non-offending team can choose a scrum instead.

OLD BELVEDERE RFC

Formed in 1930 for the old boys of Belvedere College in Dublin, the rugby club has played a significant role in Dublin rugby ever since. Its strength in its early years usually tied in with the strong periods of play from the school's first XV. In the 1970s the club went 'open' to allow membership from all players.

Old Belvedere took several years to find its way into the senior ranks of Leinster rugby, but by 1939 it had played its first cup final, losing to Blackrock College. Then followed a brilliant sequence for the club in which

it won the Leinster Senior Cup for seven seasons in a row. The sequence ended in 1947 when Belvedere reached the final but lost to the Wanderers club.

The Quinn family was a strong influence in the early years. Up to 1956 there had been a member of that family in every Old Belvedere cup side. Kevin Quinn was the best known, playing five internationals for Ireland after World War II.

Other well-known names from the club include the brilliant wing Tony O'Reilly, who was the most-capped player in the club's first 60 years, with 29 caps for Ireland and 10 for the British Isles. Karl Mullen follows closely with 25 caps for Ireland and three for the British Isles. Mullen captained Ireland to its consecutive Triple Crown wins in 1947–48 and 1948–49 while a member of Old Belvedere. Another club member who gained much fame for the club was Ollie Campbell, who had 22 caps for Ireland and seven for the British Isles.

'Belvo' plays in black and white hooped jerseys and has its club headquarters at Anglesea Road in the Dublin suburb of Ballsbridge.

OLD INTERNATIONALS

It is widely accepted that Ned Hughes is the oldest man to have played inter-

national rugby. The hardy front-row forward was 40 years 123 days old when he was recalled into the New Zealand team to play against the Springboks, having made his debut in 1907, and also having played rugby league for New Zealand in the years between. There had been a gap of 13 years, two months and one week between his test matches! Note, however, that Hughes's age record was under threat from Hugo Porta of Argentina, who returned to test rugby in late 1990 at the age of 39 years and one month.

The amazing career of Australian Tony 'Slaggy' Miller covered 16 seasons at international level (1952–67). Miller was 38 years, 112 days, when his career finished with New Zealand's jubilee test in 1967. He continued to play first grade rugby in Sydney until he was 42, and he was 56 when he stopped playing altogether.

No one else has played in a test involving IRB countries at the age of 38, though 'Charlie' Faulkner was just 10 days short of his 38th birthday when he last played for Wales in 1979. Some think that Faulkner had been playing jiggery-pokery with his date of birth and was, in fact, even older!

All these men played in the front row; Miller was also a lock for some time. Another long-lasting forward was Alfred Roques – the 'rock' at the heart of the French scrum from 1958 until 1963. Roques' international career didn't start until he was 33 and he was a month short of his 38th birthday when it finished.

The celebrated French lock, Francis Haget, overcame injuries to play his final game, in the first World Cup contest, four months short of his 38th birthday. Other 37-year-old test players were England's Reg Edwards, a principal in the Cyril Brownlie ordering-off during his last game in 1925, and Scotland's Ian McLauchlan, another prop.

Tommy Vile played halfback for the British Isles in 1904 when he was 20, but did not play for Wales until 1908, and played for the last time in 1921 when he was 37. Two years later, F.G. Gilbert had a couple of games for England at fullback when 37.

The oldest international back of all, though, and bidding belatedly to become the oldest test player, is the amazing Argentine wizard, Hugo Porta. The long-standing flyhalf, captain, goal-kicker and play-maker 're-tired' after the 1987 World Cup; but returned to lead Argentina on its ill-fated British tour late in 1990. He was 39 years, 60 days at the time of the Scotland international, and if he survived to play Argentina's final pool match at the 1991 Rugby World Cup, would be 40 years 30 days.

Another halfback of senior years was Welshman Dicky Owen, who kept Vile on the sidelines until he retired at 35.

Frank Sykes had two matches for England in 1955, toured South Africa with the Lions and was promptly thrown on the scrap heap at 27. He re-emerged in 1963, touring New Zealand with England and playing one test at 35.

Other internationals over the age of 35 include Stan Pilecki and Graham Cooke (Australia), Phil Orr (Ireland), Ernest Gardiner (England), 'Lofty' Nel (South Africa) and John Ashworth (New Zealand).

Not a recognised international, but an international captain nevertheless, is Canada's 'Buzz' Moore, who was 41 when he led his country on its second tour of Britain in 1962.

OLD TO DIE

The rigours of international rugby, 1899-style, seemed to have little effect on George Harman. The twice-capped Irish centre reached the grand age of 101 years 191 days before he died in 1975. William Milne was a hardy Scot; he was just seven months short of his century when he died in 1982.

Not too far behind these two was 'Jan' Stegmann, a Springbok of the early 1900s, who was well past his 97th birthday when he died in 1984. Thomas Baker-Jones, the scorer of Wales's first try in 1882, was 96 years 254 days when he died.

In 1989, Beethoven (named for his mother's favourite composer) Algar, a New Zealand representative in 1920–21 against New South Wales (effectively the Australian national team, but not a full international side) died aged 95 years and six months.

OLYMPIC GAMES RUGBY

The advent of the Rugby World Cup in 1987 seemed to silence the calls which had surfaced from time to time for the return of rugby union for the fifth time to the programme at the modern Olympic Games.

Three countries took part in the rugby competition at the Paris Games in 1900, France beating Germany, 27–17, in one match and Britain, 27–8, in the other. Most of the British team came from the Moseley club. Its loss to France may seem a surprising result, given the modest standard of French rugby at that time, but the British players had spent 24 hours travelling from London before match day and were reportedly exhausted.

France was awarded the gold medal, Germany the silver and Great Britain the bronze.

At the fourth Olympic Games in 1908 in London, only two nations took part: Australia, which was touring Britain at the time, and Britain itself. The English county champion side of that season, Cornwall, was chosen to represent Britain. Australia won 32–3 at White City Stadium in London.

At Antwerp in 1920, at the first Games after World War I, the under-dogs, the United States, won the gold medal, beating France in the final by 8–0. The French team had been the favourite to win, as five of the team had recently appeared in the Five Nations championship.

In both 1908 and 1920 only two teams had entered the games, but in 1924 in Paris a proper, if small, tournament took place. Most publications claim that France beat Romania 61–3 (although the French records say 59–3). The United States also beat Roma-

nia, by 37–0. In the final the United States met France.

The game was a classic, which the Americans won, 17–3. More than 30,000 French spectators watched in alarm as their team suffered such a humiliation at the hands of the Americans (many of whom had never played rugby before). As the end grew nearer and the result was inevitable, the Americans were jeered by the crowd and one visiting supporter was knocked out after being hit in the face with a walking stick.

At the medal ceremony, the playing of the United States' national anthem was drowned out by the booing and cat-calling of the crowd. Police protection was needed for the departure of the American team from the Stade Colombes.

Before the 1928 Games there was a vote by members of the International Olympic Committee over whether rugby should be included at Amsterdam. IOC members were inclined towards individual events rather than team sports, and there was also a demand for a greater opportunity for women to take part. There was a theory, too, that the British rugby-playing countries did not strongly endorse the sport's continuation at the Games.

The vote was lost, and rugby never regained favour at the Olympics (yet surprisingly soccer continued to be included).

The Romanian rugby team for the 1924 Olympics at Colombes Stadium.

There were strong attempts in 1980 (endorsed by the Soviet Union) and in 1988 (endorsed by Korea) to have rugby re-admitted, but nothing has worked so far to convince Olympic officials that rugby merits inclusion in the modern Games.

So the United States can rightly claim to be the current Olympic Games champion and rugby gold medallist!

There is one player in Olympic rugby history who deserves special mention. He is Daniel Carroll, the speedy wing from Sydney, Australia, who was a gold medallist with the Australian team at London in 1908, and later settled in America. He played for the United States in the Olympics of 1920 and won a rugby gold medal for that country, becoming the first and only player (probably for ever) to win two Olympic rugby gold medals. He was also coach of the 1924 United States team.

ONDARTS, PASCAL
Biarritz Olympique and France
36 internationals for France 1986–91

This tough prop chose an excellent game in which to make his international debut – against New Zealand in 1986 in the French win at Nantes. It had been a long wait for the Biarritz prop. He was over 31 when he played that day: indeed he had not even started to play rugby until after he had turned 21!

Ondarts built on his reputation as a tough scrummager, equally at home on either side of the front row. He toured to the 1987 Rugby World Cup where he played in five matches, including the final against New Zealand.

He played both tests in the 1990 series at home against New Zealand, switching sides from one side of the front row to the other. With an appearance as a hooker v Romania in 1988, Ondarts is one of the rare rugby figures to have played in all three positions in the front row.

'ONE CAP WONDERS'
A 'one cap wonder' is a player who has appeared only once (for one cap) in his international career. It is an expression used mainly in Britain, sometimes in a slightly derisory way ('He's playing so badly, he'll be a one cap wonder for sure'), but sometimes suggesting a measure of sympathy and perhaps af-fection for a good player who might, had there been different selectors, have played more than once.

Some one cap wonders had careers cut short through injury or the arrival of war; others were found to be woefully deficient of a decent standard of play, once they were exposed to the cauldron of international rugby. Still others were just plain unlucky.

Des van Jaarsveldt was a case of very confusing selection policies. He was made captain of the Springboks for their first international of the 1960s, against Scotland at Port Elizabeth. There was great delight in Rhodesia at his selection, for not only was it to be his test debut, but he also won the honour of becoming the first Rhodesian to captain South Africa at rugby. South Africans were less impressed. A Johannesburg paper expressed the view: 'It is an evil day for South African rugby when the country has had to seek its rugby captain from beyond its borders in the territory of a strange land.'

In 1960 South Africa's rugby bosses had decided that the test captain would also be the coach of the team, a change from the previous 11 years, when Danie Craven had been the boss. This was a tough introduction to test rugby. Van Jaarsveldt had to make his debut, captain the team, coach it as well, and follow in the massive footsteps of Danie Craven. Add to that the fact that there were nine other test newcomers in the team with him, and it can be seen that van Jaarsveldt's task to mould the new Springboks together in three days was well-nigh impossible.

Yet he did it! On Saturday May 1 1960, South Africa beat Scotland by 18–10. Van Jaarsveldt played well in the loose and sprinted 50 metres to score the final try. Yet afterwards there was little adulation and no reward. Van Jaarsveldt was dropped – along with five of the other new caps – and never appeared again.

In 1951, as one of a brilliant Newport team that had been unbeaten in 26 games, Roy Burnett was considered the favourite to be the next Welsh flyhalf. But in a crunch game against Cardiff, and in front of the Welsh selectors, Burnett missed several key chances to excel. This, it transpired, was because he played for much of the game with a broken collar-bone. The selectors went against public opinion (well, Newport opinion anyway) and chose Burnett's opposite player that day, the brilliant young Cliff Morgan.

Morgan went on to an illustrious career, but Burnett played only once in the Welsh colours (against England in 1953) when Morgan was absent.

Ten of the Ireland team that played Wales in 1884 were to be become 'one cap wonders' when the selectorial axe fell swiftly after their loss at Cardiff. Two Welshmen played for Ireland that day, after two of the selected Irish players failed to show up. One of the Welsh substitutes, Frank Purdon, had played four times before for Wales. But after playing for Ireland he was never chosen for an international, for either country, again. No doubt this qualifies him as an Irish 'one cap wonder'!

Basil Kenyon was brought into the Springbok team as captain in the fourth test against the 1949 All Blacks. He was adjudged an inspirational man and in 1951 he retained the captaincy for the important Springbok tour of Britain. Unfortunately he suffered an eye injury in the match against Pontypool early in the tour, and to avoid further damage to the eye he never played at any level again.

Wilfred Lowry of England was chosen to play against Wales in Swansea 1920. He appeared on the pitch before the game and had his picture taken with his 14 team-mates, but moments later, when the England team took the field to play, it was noticed that Lowry was absent. Apparently the English selectors had a late change of heart, questioning whether he had the right sort of form to play on a wintry day, and they substituted Harold Day instead! Lowry was allowed to keep his cap. There was happier news for him later that same season. He was selected, and did play, in the next game for England (against France). But that was the only time. He is an unusual 'one cap wonder' – he ended his career with two caps, one earned for playing, the other for not playing!

Other players who made only one international appearance include Mike Smith, later the England cricket captain, who played one international for England (v Wales) in 1956; and Marty Berry (New Zealand) made his one international showing as a replacement, for only a few seconds, against Australia in 1986.

Bloemfontein Stadium, home of rugby in Orange Free State, 1976.

Australia's Harold Tolhurst, who became the first international player from that country to referee an international later in his life, has been claimed by some Australians as a 'one cap wonder'. Official history books say this is not exactly so. Tolhurst was also 'capped' for his 1931 appearance against the New Zealand Maoris. (Australia awarded caps for games with the Maoris up until 1958.) *See also* ALCOCK, ANDURAN, JEFFREY (WALES).

ORANGE FREE STATE RFU

'Vrystaat!' ('Free State') they call from the grandstands in this strongly Afrikaans province bordering the Orange River on the high veldt of South Africa.

Rugby was introduced with the arrival of pioneer farmers from overseas, along with students returning from the Cape Province. The opening of the main railway line from Johannesburg in the early 1890s aided the rush of visitors to the capital of the Free State and rugby soon flourished. The Orange Free State Rugby Union was formed in 1895.

There was disappointment that a fixture against the 1896 British team was cancelled, and it was seven years before the 1903 British team became the first overseas side to visit. Free State played well but lost narrowly by 16–17.

Further encouragement was given to local rugby when Orange Free State was entered into the Currie Cup provincial championship for the first time in 1904, but it was not until 1976 that the cup rested in Bloemfontein for the first time.

Free State had its first success against touring teams in 1924, when it twice beat the Great Britain team. The province's record against All Black teams is impressive too. Orange Free State drew with the 1949 All Blacks, but beat the New Zealanders in 1960 and 1976. Another golden year was in 1953, when the locals twice beat the Wallabies by the impressive margins of 28–3 and 23–13.

Among the big names who have played for the province are Basie Viviers, the very popular Springbok fullback from 1951–56, who captained the Springboks on their epic tour to New Zealand in 1956; Nelie Smith, the Springbok scrumhalf and captain of the 1960s, who later coached South Africa; Boetie McHardy, who was the province's first Springbok; and also Piet Wessels, 'Popeye' Strydom, Piet Greyling, Joggie Jansen, and the brilliant speedsters of modern times, Gerrie Germishuys and Jaco Reinach.

Orange Free State scored what is believed to be a world record for a first-class match when it beat Eastern Free State by 132–3 in 1977. The goal-kicker, De Wet Ras, scored 48 points, also believed to be a world record for one player in a first-class match.

The province plays in pale cream jerseys with an orange collar. Its headquarters are at Free State Stadium in Bloemfontein.

ORDERED OFF

A player can be ordered off the field by the referee when he contravenes Law 26, which relates to foul play, defined as any action a player takes that is contrary to the letter of the law and the spirit of the game. The definition includes unfair play, dangerous play, misconduct, obstruction and unsporting behaviour. A player can also be ordered off for retaliating to foul play on himself or for repeated infringements of any law.

In the early years there were very few cases of players being sent from the field in disgrace, but in modern times more players have been sent off, perhaps reflecting a more rigorous approach by referees. In the 20 instances of ordering off during internationals, listed below, six of these occurred in 1990.

The first man to be sent off in an officially sanctioned test match was the New Zealand forward Cyril Brownlie, dismissed from the England v New Zealand match at Twickenham in 1925. The referee was the Welshman, Albert Freethy. It was alleged that Brownlie had kicked an Englishman, though this was vigorously denied by the New Zealanders. The Prince of Wales (later Edward VIII) was in the crowd and asked if it was possible that Brownlie could be returned to the field. This, it seems, was not possible.

When another New Zealander, Colin Meads, was sent off in 1967 during a Scotland v New Zealand match at Murrayfield, there was an immense storm created in the media over the reason for the dismissal. Meads lashed out with a boot as the ball bounced near a Scottish player. Referee Kevin Kelleher of Ireland stopped the game and immediately sent Meads on a lonely walk to the dressing room.

New Zealanders who watched the incident on television claimed it was not serious enough to warrant a sending-off. From Kelleher's point of view he had, earlier, issued a general and final warning to both teams about the amount of rough play in the game. He saw Meads's action as dangerous play and sent him off.

Off! The gesture is unmistakable, as referee Albert Freethy orders Cyril Brownlie off the field during the England v New Zealand match, 1924.

Under the letter of the law, Kelleher was correct. As the sole judge of fact in the game, he was also correct. What made the story sensational was the fact that, at the time, Meads was arguably the world's most famous player. That Kelleher was arguably the world's best referee at the time was largely lost on New Zealanders!

The headlines in New Zealand were banner-sized and even the New Zealand Prime Minister of the time, Keith Holyoake, was moved to send a sympathetic telegram to the team.

The following players have been ordered off the rugby field during rugby tests sanctioned by the International Rugby Board (to the end of 1990):

Cyril Brownlie (New Zealand), sent off by Albert Freethy (Wales) in the New Zealand v England game at Twickenham in 1925.

Colin Meads (New Zealand), sent off by Kevin Kelleher (Ireland) in the New Zealand v Scotland game at Murrayfield in 1967.

Mike Burton (England), sent off by Bob Burnett (Australia) in the Australia v England test at Ballymore in Brisbane in 1975.

Josateki Sovau (Fiji), sent off by Warwick Cooney (Australia) in the Australia v Fiji test in Sydney, 1976.

Willie Duggan (Ireland) and **Geoff Wheel** (Wales), both sent off by Norman Sanson (Scotland) in the Wales v Ireland match at Cardiff 1977.

Paul Ringer (Wales), sent off by Dave Burnett (Ireland) in the England v Wales match at Twickenham 1980.

Jean-Pierre Garuet (France), sent off by Clive Norling (Wales) in the France v Scotland match at Paris in 1984.

Huw Richards (Wales), sent off by Kerry Fitzgerald (Australia) in the Wales v New Zealand match in the World Cup match at Ballymore in Brisbane 1987.

David Codey (Australia), sent off by Fred Howard (England) in the Australia v Wales match in the Rugby World Cup match in New Zealand in 1987.

Mosese Taga (Fiji), sent off by Kerry Fitzgerald (Australia) in the Fiji v England match at Suva in 1988.

Alain Lorieux (France), sent off by Owen Doyle (Ireland) in the Argentina v France test in Buenos Aires in 1988.

Noa Nadruku and **Tevita Vonalagi** (Fiji), sent off by Brian Stirling (Ireland) in the Fiji v England match at Twickenham in 1989.

Kevin Moseley (Wales), sent off by Fred Howard (England) in the Wales v France match in Cardiff 1990.

Alain Carminati (France), sent off by Fred Howard (England) in the France v Scotland match in Edinburgh in 1990.

Abdelatif Benazzi (France), sent off by Tony Spreadbury (England) in the France v Australia test at Sydney in 1990.

André Stoop (Namibia), sent off by Fred Howard (England) in the Wales v Namibia test at Windhoek in 1990.

Philippe Gallart (France), sent off by Clive Norling (Wales) in the

France v Australia test at Sydney in 1990.

Federico Mendez (Argentina), sent off by Colin Hawke (New Zealand) in the England v Argentina match at Twickenham in 1990.

Although some of the instances listed above involved players from Fiji, Argentina and Namibia, which are not members of the IRB, the countries they were playing (England, France and Wales) were IRB members and awarded caps for those two games. No South African or Scottish player has ever been sent off in an international, or in any non-internationals played by those countries.

In other international matches there have been a number of instances of players being sent 'for an early shower'.

Two players, Rob Halstead, captain of Zimbabwe, and Gheorghe Caragea of Romania, were dismissed by English referee Roger Quittenton in the first test match between those two countries in 1982 in Bulawayo.

Four players were once sent off in the same major game. The referee was Alan Welsby of England and the match was Ireland 'B' v France 'B' in Dublin in 1975.

There are several instances of three players being sent off in the same game. In France in 1975 the game between Paloise Selection and Argentina had three players dismissed, and in 1977 at the European under-20 tournament at Hilversum in Holland, three Russian players were sent off in the Soviet Union v West Germany match. Two more Russians were sent off in their next game against France.

The earliest recorded sending-off in a match involving a full international team occurred in 1897. The New Zealander Will McKenzie was dismissed during the New Zealand v New South Wales match in Sydney. McKenzie was apparently a shrewd character (his nickname was 'Offside Mac'), and after receiving the referee's stern message to depart, McKenzie limped towards the sideline, feigning injury. The crowd applauded his departure from the field sympathetically!

O'REILLY, TONY

Old Belvedere and Ireland
29 internationals for Ireland 1955–70
10 internationals for British Isles 1955–59

An outstanding wing, whose dashing style made him one of the most popular players of his day. The red-haired flying Irishman became a cult figure for young followers of the game as a result of his tours for the Lions, to South Africa in 1955 and to Australasia in 1959. There, his individuality (right down to the unconfirmed story that he played with a comb tucked down his sock) made him a player who could draw crowds.

O'Reilly seemed destined for success. Shortly after his international rugby career seemed finished he became a highly succesful businessman. He was first a solicitor, then the chairman of the Irish Dairy Produce Marketing Board and later still the president of the huge Heinz Food Corporation and a successful newspaper owner. In later life he was one of the richest men in Ireland.

In 1970, after a gap of eight years and aged 33, he was recalled to the Irish team to play England. By then he was such a big name in business he was able to arrive at Twickenham for the game in a chauffeur-driven Rolls-Royce!

In his younger years Tony O'Reilly was well known for his wit and colour, on and off the field. In New Zealand in 1959, some of his comedy vocal duets with fellow-Irishman, Andy Mulligan, became popular requests on local ra-

Tony O'Reilly and fellow Irishman Andy Mulligan were a popular comedy duo, performing on radio and in public for their many fans, during the 1959 Lions tour to New Zealand. O'Reilly was by no means just a showman: he was also a fast and elusive wing.

dio shows. But being a funny man was not a front for inferior talent. O'Reilly was a great player. Tall and powerfully built, he was fast and elusive enough to score 16 tries in South Africa in 1955 and 22 tries in New Zealand and Australia four years later.

Having been chosen first for international rugby as an 18-year-old and finishing it 16 seasons later, his span of time at the top level was nearly the longest by any player in the game.

ORR, PHIL
Old Wesley and Ireland
58 internationals for Ireland 1976–87
1 international for British Isles 1977

When this tough Irishman retired after the Rugby World Cup of 1987, he had set all kinds of international records for a prop, as well as playing a significant role in Irish rugby for the previous 11 seasons.

Orr made his international debut in 1976, and thereafter played 49 consecutive games for Ireland, not missing an international until 1986. Nine more tests followed. After his last game for his country, against Australia in Sydney in the World Cupp quarterfinal, his total of caps was 58 in all, the world's best for a prop. He made four tours for Ireland, a record number

(more than his main 'opposition', Willie John McBride, Mike Gibson and Tom Kiernan). There were also two tours for the British Isles: to New Zealand in 1977 (when he played the first test in Wellington), and to South Africa in 1980.

In all his test appearances Orr never scored a try, but as a tireless prop he was hugely popular with Irish fans.

There is a delightful story told about Orr that epitomises Irish rugby humour. When he appeared for the Emerald Greens for the 50th time, he was given the honour of leading the team on to the field, which he did to a tumultuous reception from his loyal Lansdowne Road fans. Soon after the kick-off in the game (against Scotland in 1986) he had to leave the field to have stitches inserted into a cut under his eye. After several moments under the grandstand he returned to the field. Another huge cheer went up from the crowd. It is said that after the game his team-mates were sceptical about the injury. They claimed Orr had enjoyed the first ovation so much he had gone back to seek a second!

OSLER, BENNY
Western Province and South Africa
17 internationals for Sth Africa 1924–33

One of South Africa's top rugby stars of the 1920s and 30s, who was generally feared by his opponents for his ability to control the ebb and flow and outcome of matches. While Osler was a shrewd tactical flyhalf, who in his time won many an advantage for his teams, his playing methods often brought down on him the wrath of the critics.

Osler played first for his country against the Great Britain tourists of 1924 and remained a first choice until after the Wallabies toured in 1933.

He was a steady and diverse kicker who made life comfortable for the Springbok forwards of the time. Early in a match he would use his 'high skier' to unnerve fullbacks or wings in the deep. He was a master at the long kick for touch, or for the corners of the field. His backs might have grumbled at the lack of running ball but his forwards merely followed his tactical whim.

While South Africa was winning, no one dared criticise him (indeed Osler's dominance of the South African scene

Benny Osler

earned him the nickname 'Mr King of Rugby').

Possibly as a reaction to the repetitive style of his play, he was severely criticised when he captained the Springboks on their tour of Britain in 1931–32. Many Britons, perhaps smarting from the success of the team, asked whether the repetitve Osler kicking style was 'rugby as it should be played'. But the South Africans stuck to the style, Osler later claiming the cautious approach was simply 'playing to the strength' of his team. The record of his team on that tour (only one loss from 26 games) confirmed for South African followers that Osler was a great match-winner.

In 1933 there was intense pressure to lighten up the Springbok playing style for the home series against Australia, and perhaps this was why Osler was dropped as captain. Phil Nel took over, yet he did not change the tactics in the first test. The Springboks won handsomely, but boringly, said the newspapers and many of the

Phil Orr

fans. When Nel was injured, Osler was brought back as skipper for the second test. Perhaps he was soured by earlier having been dropped as leader, but he took the decision to fling caution to the wind and move the ball by hand. South Africa ran every ball it could through the backs, and the result was a win – to Australia! Osler was never asked to captain his country again. After appearing in all five tests that season, he retired with 17 international caps and 46 points.

He was an expert drop-kicker and his record of four dropped goals in tests stood until 1951. His total of 14 points in the first test against New Zealand in 1928 stood as the world record by an individual in a test match until 'Okey' Geffin beat it, also against New Zealand, in 1949.

Osler died in 1961. His steady flyhalf style has often been repeated in South African teams in the years since, by players such as Keith Oxlee, Gerald Bosch and Naas Botha.

Osler's brother, Stanley, played one test match, v New Zealand in 1928 and appeared for Oxford University against his brother's touring team in 1931.

OTAGO RFU

Many of Otago's early settlers were expatriate Scots, and its main city, Dunedin, is sometimes known as the 'Edinburgh of the south'. Just as Murrayfield once rang to the cry of 'feet, Scotland, feet', so Otago rugby has a reputation for producing tough unyielding players from its rural clubs and districts. But it is the university, which draws young men from all over New Zealand to its schools of medicine, dentistry, physical education and physiotherapy, which has provided most of Otago's All Blacks – nearly 40 from the University club, more than any other club in New Zealand.

Otago's population swelled in the mid to late 1800s with the discovery of gold in Central Otago and when a combination of Auckland clubs played the best of the Dunedin Union and Dunedin clubs on Wednesday 22 September 1875, Otago (or Dunedin clubs) won by $9\frac{1}{2}$ to $\frac{1}{2}$. The points system for that game was six for a goal, two for a touch-down and $\frac{1}{2}$ for a force-down!

This was the first year of rugby in Otago. Dunedin and Dunedin Union (originally North Dunedin) clubs were formed in 1872, but they played their own peculiar style of game – a mixture of Victorian (later Australian rules) and association football (soccer). By July in 1875 they played a strange compromise: 13-a-side, with the first half soccer and the second half rugby. The High School club (for old boys of Otago Boys' High School) was formed that year; later it was named Pirates.

The Otago Union was formed in 1881, the third (after Canterbury and Wellington, in 1879), but its members were independent thinkers. When the New Zealand Rugby Football Union was formed in 1892, Otago, Canterbury and Southland refused to affiliate. The latter two were admitted in 1894, but Otago held out for a year longer.

One of the independent thinkers was James Duncan, the inventor of the five-eighths system in New Zealand. Other great Otago players at the turn of the century were hooker Steve Casey, Alex McDonald, Ernest 'General' Booth (later to play and report the game in Australia), and in the 1920s, men like Jock Richardson (vice-captain but test captain of the 1924 'Invincibles'), Abe Munro, Dave Lindsay and Jack Hore. A dominant force in the 1930s was the match-winning flyhalf Dave Trevathan.

Otago reigned supreme in New Zealand rugby immediately after the Second World War. Its stars, and All Blacks, were hard forwards like Kevin Skinner, Ray Dalton (Andy's father), Charlie Willocks, Lester Harvey, Norm Wilson, all tight forwards; loose forwards Peter Johnstone and Jack McNab; and outstanding backs like Jim Kearney, Bill Meates, Ron Elvidge, and Jim and Laurie Haig. With 11 players away in South Africa with the All Blacks, Otago not only withstood six challenges for the Ranfurly Shield, but was able to provide four more internationals for the home season with Australia!

In the 1950s Otago had a splendid international prop in Mark Irwin, and a match-winning goal-kicker named 'Tuppy' Diack. But the first real star for many a year exploded into the All Black touring party of 1963. Chris Laidlaw had not long left school, but swiftly became an established All Black, and no halfback in the world could match his long, bullet-like pass from the base of the scrum. He established a fine partnership on the field with Earle Kirton, the pair becoming New Zealand's first choice halfback combination.

Otago never seems short of a very useful halfback; Laidlaw's successors include Lin Colling, David Kirk and Dean Kenny, though Kirk was in Auckland by the time he led the All Blacks to their victory in the first World Cup.

Duncan apart, the greatest influences on Otago rugby have been two great coaches. Vic Cavanagh and Charlie Saxton were also very good players, Saxton winning his 1938 All Black honours when in South Canterbury, and later leading the 'Kiwis' on their post-war tour of Britain, France and Germany.

Cavanagh was the great coach of the 1940s, a man who was a leader in sports psychology, but never invited to coach the All Blacks. It is widely recognised, and well documented, that a major blunder for the tour of South Africa in 1949 lay in appointing the gentlemanly Alex McDonald – an All Black as long ago as 1905 – as coach instead of Cavanagh.

Saxton was a youthful assistant and fellow selector with Cavanagh, and he espoused his theory of rugby in a priceless little book which promoted his 'three Ps' of rugby: pace, possession and position. This breezy little chap was also one of New Zealand's most successful managers, in 1967.

Otago had some low periods in the 1970s and 80s, but returned as a force when a former All Black fullback, Laurie Mains, then the biggest scorer in Otago rugby history, became coach. He appointed a 21-year-old, Mike Brewer, his captain, and Brewer quickly became a very good All Black loose forward.

The Otago record against overseas teams is certainly worth recording for, after a victory against the 1908 Anglo-Welsh team, it scored victories against successive Lions teams in 1950, 1959 and 1966. It has also beaten England and Scotland, Australia twice, and Fiji.

Otago plays in dark blue jerseys, shorts and socks.

OWEN, DICKY
Swansea and Wales
35 internationals for Wales 1901–12

A tough little Welsh scrumhalf who, given the small number of tours in the days when he was at his peak, accumulated a large tally of international caps. His tally of 35 international appearances stood as the Welsh record for over 40 years, until beaten by wing Ken Jones in 1955.

Owen built up several significant partnerships with scrumhalves (Billy Trew at his club Swansea, and Percy Bush for Wales) but he was known universally as the first scrumhalf to combine attacks with his loose forwards. Owen is also credited with inventing the reverse pass.

It was an unorthodox pass from Owen which helped Wales beat the 1905 All Blacks. Owen ran towards the open side of the field from a scrum, with the New Zealand backs following. Owen then flung a pass back across the scrum to change the direction of play dramatically – a most unconventional tactic in those days. Teddy Morgan went on to score the try which beat New Zealand 3–0.

Owen was not without some style and wit. Once, when he was playing for Wales against England, he was repeatedly penalised for incorrect feeding of the scrum. Finally, Owen invited his marker, one of the England halfbacks, to put the ball in to all scrums for the remainder of the match!

Owen played in the Welsh team in its first 'golden era'. He was in four Triple Crown successes, and two other championship wins.

OWEN-SMITH, 'TUPPY'

Cape Town University, St Mary's
  Hospital and England
10 internationals for England 1934–37

One of the most famous all-round sportsmen to be transported from South Africa, via a Rhodes Scholarship, to England, Owen-Smith was an international both for and against England.

When only 20, he toured England with the 1929 South African cricket team, demonstrating that he was a devastatingly aggressive batsman and a penetrating spin bowler – qualities he was to take to Oxford University and Middlesex.

But his international career was longer as a rugby player. Harold Geoffrey Owen Owen-Smith, always known as Tuppy, arrived in England on his scholarship in 1931, and eventually qualified as a doctor at St Mary's Hospital. England was not slow to call on

Members of the Oxford team are introduced to King George V, 1920.

his talents as fullback and only once – against Ireland in 1936 – was he on the losing side. He featured in the Triple Crown successes of 1934 and 1937 and captained England three times.

The best a Welsh team could do against an England team with Owen-Smith in it, was a draw in 1936. Both teams had beaten the touring All Blacks, and it sometimes seemed that Owen-Smith turned back the ferocious Welsh charges single-handed.

A man of extraordinary sporting prowess, he not only performed with distinction in cricket and rugby, but won Oxford Blues in athletics and boxing.

He returned to South Africa to serve with that country during World War II, and when he celebrated his 80th birthday in 1989 was in very active retirement. In a country often thought to produce dour individuals, Owen-Smith was one of the freest of spirits.

OXFORD UNIVERSITY RFC

The game of rugby had been seen at various colleges at the university for decades before the rugby club was

formed in 1869, and the university was a highly influential force in the development of rugby.

Some of the game's most successful innovations are associated with Oxford's early years. It was the first team to reduce the numbers in a playing team from 20 to 15, and it invented heeling the ball back from the horrific mauls and upright grappling which dominated rugby in those days, a development which allowed backs to come into the game far more than previously.

Former pupils of Rugby School itself exerted a strong influence in Oxford's early thinking. Fifteen of the team of 20 which played in the first match against Cambridge in 1872 were old boys of the school. This game began a tradition: the match between the two universities is the third oldest annual game (the others being the Merchiston v Edinburgh Academy game which dates from 1858, and the England v Scotland match which began in 1871).

One of Oxford's most famous early personalities was Harry Vassall, who was a great forward but who also made much more use of the backs than was usual at that time. The result was that

Oxford played a wide-ranging style of rugby which most other sides of the 1870s and 1880s could not counter. Oxford lost only two matches between 1880 and 1884.

Another of the key men in that 'golden era' was the halfback Alan Rotherham, a master in the distribution of the ball to the outer backs.

Next came Adrian Stoop, who had a philosophy on back play that was also ahead of its time. In the early years of the twentieth century Stoop inspired Oxford to four wins and a draw in five annual matches with Cambridge. A key member of that era was also named H.H. Vassall, a fast centre three-quarter who was a nephew of the original.

Hundreds of other famous names in rugby who played for Oxford University include: B.H. ('Jika') Travers, the Australian Rhodes Scholar who played for England; Scotsman John Bannerman, who was a double blue, then later a Life Peer; the three-quarter line of Smith, Wallace, Aitken and Macpherson, which was taken straight into the Scottish team in the 1920s; Alexander Obolensky, the Russian prince; 'Tuppy' Owen-Smith, the South African who captained England at rugby and played for South Africa at cricket; Onllwyn Brace, the free-thinking, tricky Welsh scrumhalf and captain, who was later a prominent BBC sports broadcaster, as was Nigel Starmer-Smith in the 1960s; Peter Robbins, a highly imaginative captain; All Black Chris Laidlaw, who led the university to its famous win against the Springboks in 1969; and David Kirk, captain of New Zealand's 1987 World Cup winning team.

Oxford has had regular matches with major touring teams. As well as its win over the Springboks, it beat New South Wales (the 'Waratahs') in 1927–28 and Australia in 1957–58.

OXLEE, KEITH
Natal and South Africa
19 internationals for Sth Africa 1960–65

A popular flyhalf who set a new record in 1963 for points by a South African in test rugby, when he passed the previous record of 55 points set by Gerry Brand in 1938.

Keith Oxlee was an attacking flyhalf who, observers claimed, was sometimes prevented from showing his true talents because of the South African tactics of the day. Nevertheless he was a vital member of Springboks teams through their tests with the All Blacks in 1960 and the Lions in 1962, and on the tours to Britain and France in 1961–62 and Australia and New Zealand in 1965.

That Oxlee played test rugby at all was a tribute to the courage he showed in fighting back from a severe ankle injury in 1958. Only two years later he was making his test debut against the 1960 All Blacks. He was a runner and a dashing player capable of mounting attacks from deep within his half. In the early years of his career, South African teams achieved a higher tries-to-matches ratio than they had under other famous players in the same position.

Oxlee did not take any kicks at goal until his fifth international, but in his first match as a test kicker he landed a penalty goal which beat Wales 3–0, on a flooded Cardiff Arms Park. Becoming the regular kicker only in his ninth test, he went on to score 14 points against Australia at Port Elizabeth in 1961, and then 16 points against the British Isles in the fourth test of the 1962 series (beating the old South African record of 15 points, set by 'Okey' Geffin v New Zealand in 1949). In that series he scored all the points for South Africa in the second and third tests, as well as contributing the 16 points in the final test.

After playing in the tests v Australia in 1963 and Wales in 1964, Oxlee toured New Zealand and Australia in 1965 where he played in two tests, but he was considered past his best by that stage.

In all he played 48 games for South Africa, including 19 internationals, and totalled 201 points in all games. His record of 88 test points was eventually beaten by Piet Visagie in 1971.

P

PACO, ALAIN
Béziers and France
35 internationals for France 1974–80

Alain Paco, who played first-class football as a hooker, flanker or flyhalf, was an excellent runner and a player of enormous strength. Eventually he specialised as a hooker in international play.

He came from the tough school of Béziers rugby, which in the 1970s had arguably the best club team in the world. As a 22-year-old, Paco toured Argentina with the 1974 French national team, where his start was highly promising. So when veteran René Benesis, of nearby Narbonne, retired in 1975, after 30 internationals, Paco became his natural successor.

Following early injuries, Paco steadily built on his reputation as a fit, and formidable member of France's front row. In combination with the tough props, Robert Paparemborde and Gérard Cholley, he took part in 21 internationals in the 1970s, a record which not even the famed Pontypool front row could match.

Paco's last international was in 1980 at Cardiff. After a shattering loss in which Wales scored four tries, the French selectors wielded a big axe. They made five changes, which included dropping Paco.

In a fit of Gallic pique, Paco refused to take a place on the replacements' bench, and so he retired from international rugby, fuming at the selectors. There was some consolation for him, in that his total of 35 caps was then a French record for a hooker.

In time he rose to become coach of Béziers.

PALMER, BRYAN
New South Wales and Australia
Australian representative 1931

Bryan Palmer was one of the most colourful characters in Australian rugby in the twentieth century. He committed his life to the game, serving it as a player, administrator and coach. He was so devoted to rugby, he even named his son Bryan Rugby Palmer!

Palmer was one of the youngest managers of a touring team. In 1931, when he toured New Zealand as a wing, he became ill and could not play. When the team's manager had to return to Australia for personal reasons, Palmer aged 32, took over. By all accounts he was very popular, and most successful.

He was also possibly the oldest coach of an international team, coaching the Australians in some of their matches in 1967 when he was 68 years old.

Towards the end of his life Bryan Palmer became a familiar figure and raconteur in Sydney rugby circles. He watched and enjoyed all levels of the game right up until his death at 91, in 1990.

PAPAREMBORDE, ROBERT
Pau and France
55 internationals for France 1975–83

The strong-man prop of the French XV for nine seasons, Paparemborde was an squat and enormously strong player with a powerful scrummaging technique. He was nicknamed 'Patou' and was first used by France on its tour to South Africa in 1975, where he broke all the rules for a front-rower by scoring a try in each of his first two internationals. Thereafter he became the cornerstone of the French scrum. Paparemborde was rarely disrupted from his strong scrummaging game and was also a useful ball-player in the loose.

He captained France three times and was so highly respected he was elected on to the FFR's committee while still an active international player. His final tally of 55 caps was a record for a French prop.

PAPUA NEW GUINEA
Papua New Guinea is a regular entrant in the Hong Kong Sevens tournament where it has an extremely popular team, cheered on by hundreds of noisy supporters. Though it is difficult to tell through the hubbub that accompanies the team's appearances in Hong Kong, it would seem either that the players representing Papua New Guinea are nicknamed the 'Wakwaks', or that somebody in Papua New

Robert Paparemborde (left) supported by Jean-Pierre Rives.

Guinea has invented the term as a noisy appreciation for PNG rugby!

In 15-a-side rugby PNG is a regular participant in the South Pacific Games competition.

Almost all PNG rugby is played in Port Moresby, the largest city, and by 1990 there were 16 clubs. Prominent clubs include University, Barbarians, Defence and Waliya. Increasing support for rugby union is found in Lae, the second largest city.

There has been a close association between Papua New Guinea's rugby people and Australia. The Ella brothers, Glen in particular, have regularly assisted in the preparation of the national squad for the Hong Kong Sevens. The sport is strongly supported by Australian businessmen and their companies. It has to be said, though, that the game is well behind rugby league in terms of public popularity. The rugby league national team, the 'Kumuls', are watched regularly by the biggest sports crowds in the country and they are given full test match status by rugby league's world governing body.

PARC DES PRINCES
The major multi-purpose sports ground of Paris and since the early 1970s the major home ground for French rugby.

The first full international game ever played by France (v New Zealand in 1906) was played on the Parc. It continued to be used for France's internationals at various times until 1920, when Colombes Stadium across the city became the venue. There was a gap of over 50 years before international rugby was played at the Parc again: after an £8 million face-lift it was used from 1972. The stadium, completely encircled by two-tiered grandstands, is now one of the most spectacular locations for the playing of rugby anywhere.

France has built up a strong record on the ground. Scotland, for instance, could not win there in the 20 years following its reconstruction.

The ground is the traditional location for the final of the club championship of France, when tens of thousands of out-of-town fans stream to the ground carrying flags, banners and even cockerels decorated in their club's colours. The Parc becomes a bubbling, boisterous place filled with the cheers, whistles and cat-calls of a huge parti-

san crowd. Rockets and fire-crackers add to the din.

It is also the venue for the home games of soccer played by the two first division clubs in Paris – Racing Club and Paris St Germain.

Unfortunately the Parc des Princes is now, as in the 1920s, becoming too small. From the 1970s the French federation has often held test matches elsewhere, as across the country there are at least five other grounds which are bigger.

PARTNERSHIPS
Rugby players who get to know each other's play well and who react instinctively to each other on the field add to any team's strength. There have been many famous combinations of players whose names are spoken of in one breath. A number of almanacs and annuals now list playing records for the 'best partnerships', some of which have been:

John Rutherford and Roy Laidlaw
Neither would qualify for any 'greatest individual' list but together they were a highly efficient and dangerous combination. Scotland made massive use of their talents in the 1970s and 80s and the two played 35 internationals together, more than any other recognised 'partnership'.

Cyril Kershaw and 'Dave' Davies
A brilliant pair of halfbacks who played for England in the four seasons after World War I. They appeared 14 times together for their country and were never on the losing side.

Cliff Morgan and Rex Willis
A dynamic duo at club and international level in the 1950s, continuing a strong tradition of Welsh pairs in the scrumhalf-flyhalf positions.

Gareth Edwards and Barry John
Together in 28 internationals for Wales and the Lions, they dazzled crowds in the 1960s and 70s and contributed greatly to one of Wales's winning eras. Edwards went on to play 24 times in partnership with Phil Bennett for Wales, another four for the Lions.

Guy and André Boniface
Brothers who were an intuitive and sparkling combination as centres, 18 times together for France in the 1960s.

Bobby Windsor, Charlie Faulkner and Graham Price
The famous Pontypool front row. They scrummaged hard and tough for their club and together played 19 times for Wales, then a record. The combination became so admired it was even popularised in song and verse.

John Rutherford and Roy Laidlaw – holders of the world record for international halfback appearances as a partnership.

Gary Knight, Andy Dalton and John Ashworth

A front row trio who played together for so long they eventually became known collectively as the 'Geriatrics'. Such a name belied their strength and vigour as a front row unit. They appeared together in 20 tests.

Other long-lasting partnerships included the New Zealand lock pairing, Gary Whetton and Murray Pierce, together 25 times; French halves Jaques Fouroux and Jean-Pierre Romeu played 24 times as a combination; their predecessors Pierre Lacroix and Pierre Albaladejo, 20 times.

Irish loose forwards Fergus Slattery, Willie Duggan and John O'Driscoll had 19 matches together; so – creditably, given their abbreviated programme – did Irish halves Mark Sugden and Eugene Davy in the 1920s and 1930s. South Africa had fewer games than most, but halves Dawie de Villiers and Piet Visagie played together 17 times, their successors, Divan Serfontein and Naas Botha, 15 times.

PASK, ALUN

Abertillery and Wales
26 internationals for Wales 1961–67
8 internationals for British Isles 1962–66

A superbly built flanker and No. 8 for Wales in the 1960s, Pask captained his country as well, leading it to the Five Nations championship in 1966. Once Pask had been identified as Wales's top No. 8, he was never dropped from the team until its 0–3 loss against Ireland in 1967.

There were many who thought Pask should have captained the British Isles on their tour of New Zealand and Australia in 1966. He played in five of the six internationals on that tour and was acclaimed as a highly diligent No. 8 by New Zealanders. Earlier, he had had a highly successful tour with the Lions to South Africa in 1962.

In his working career he was for a time involved in the production of rugby telecasts for BBC Wales.

PAXTON, IAIN

Selkirk and Scotland
36 internationals for Scotland 1981–88
4 internationals for British Isles 1983

A No. 8 or lock for Scotland and the British Isles in the 1980s whose total

---

WORLD RECORDS FOR PARTNERSHIPS

The *Rothman's Rugby Union Yearbook* has been listing world records for combinations for several years. At the beginning of 1991 its list was as follows:

Centre three-quarters
Brendan Mullin and Michael Kiernan (Ireland). 23 tests together.

Halfbacks
John Rutherford and Roy Laidlaw (Scotland). 35 tests together. This record was under threat from Australians Nick Farr-Jones and Michael Lynagh, who had played together 32 times. Given a busy World Cup year, they seemed likely to approach 40 tests together in 1991.

Front row forwards
Robert Paparemborde, Alain Paco and Gérard Cholley (France). 21 tests together. A record likely to fall at the outset of the 1991 southern hemisphere winter: the All Blacks Steve McDowell, Sean Fitzpatrick and Richard Loe had played together 20 times at the end of 1990.

Second row (locks)
Geoff Wheel and Allan Martin (Wales). 27 tests together.

Loose forwards
Jean Matheu, Guy Basquet and Jean Prat (France). 22 tests together.

---

of caps won as a No. 8 was a Scottish record. His skills as a basketball player in his youth assisted him to become a potent force at the end of the lineout.

Paxton was a member of Scotland's Grand Slam team of 1984. He toured New Zealand with the British Isles in 1983, playing all four test matches.

PEARCE, GARY

Northampton and England
35 internationals for England 1979–88

A strong prop who began his senior rugby at Aylesbury. After changing to Northampton, Pearce's fortunes took a turn for the better.

He was given an England trial at 22, a tender age for a prop, and a year later, in 1979, he made his international debut against Scotland. Thereafter he was in and out of England teams for a number of seasons, his record not helped by injuries.

His powerful technique won through in the end and in his last three seasons he racked up 18 internationals, including three for England at the 1987 Rugby World Cup in Australia. At the end of 1990 his total of 35 appearances was an English record for a prop.

PEDLOW, CECIL

CIYMS and Ireland
30 internationals for Ireland 1953–63
2 internationals for British Isles 1955

Having scored a try on his international debut against Wales in Swansea in 1953 while still only 19 years of age, Pedlow's early promise matured into a career spanning 10 years.

Cecil Pedlow was a tall wing or centre who, although hampered by poor eyesight, was always tough, determined and skilled. Experts at the time argued that if he had had more pace he would have been one of the all-time greats of Irish rugby. As it was he thoroughly deserved his 32 caps, including two in South Africa with the 1955 British Lions. On that tour he top-scored with 57 points.

He was an outstanding tennis player and represented Ireland at squash.

PENALTY KICK

A penalty kick is taken after the referee has punished the opposing team for an infringement. Any form of kick can be taken by any member of the team. Three points are scored if a penalty kick is kicked over the crossbar.

It is a regrettable fact that penalties play a major part in modern rugby, especially in the make-up of total points. They were not nearly so important in the early years of the twentieth century: in the Five Nations championship, for instance, there was a gap of 30 years (from 1895 until 1925) when Scotland did not score from a penalty in any match against England. Conversely at one point England did not score a penalty against Scotland for 41 years.

Such a gap is unthinkable in modern times. In the 1980s as many as 47 penalties were scored by the same two sides in only 10 games against each other. In 111 Five Nations matches from 1891, there were 31 penalties kicked; in a similar number of games from 1972 onwards, also in the Five Nations championship, 450 penalties were landed successfully.

Many rugby enthusiasts feel that the modern game, with its proliferation of penalties (as well as expert kickers such as Michael Lynagh, Grant Fox, Hugo Porta, Simon Hodgkinson, Dusty Hare and Naas Botha), is facing an increasing crisis, where the drive for success is forcing teams to opt repeatedly for penalty shots at goal, thus undermining the very fabric of the game. There have been numerous calls for the value of the penalty goal to be reduced from three to two points.

In modern rugby there have been many significant matches during which a side that has kicked penalties has defeated an opponent that has scored tries instead – a sorry situation, given that the principle of rugby union is to run with the ball and score tries. Some notable examples are given opposite.

Perhaps the most infamous day in the penalty goal's dominance came in 1977 when Argentina played France in the second test in Buenos Aires. The game ended in an 18–18 draw. All 36 points came from penalty goals – six from Jean-Michel Aguirre for France and six from Hugo Porta.

A newspaper headline at the time captured perfectly the mood of all concerned rugby purists – 'Aguirre 18, Porta 18, rugby nil!'

PENALTY TRY

'A penalty try shall be awarded between the posts if, but for foul play by the defending team, a try would probably have been scored.'

This lawbook definition gives the referee the responsibility for making a snap decision which is, more often than not, viewed as controversial, expecially by the team and supporters on the receiving end. The key word in the referee's mind must be 'probably'. If there is any doubt about an incident he should not award a penalty try.

There are few examples of penalty tries in internationals. The first to be awarded in a Five Nations championship was in 1981 (to Andy Irvine, in a Scotland v Wales match at Murrayfield). The earliest record of a penalty try in a major match was when Fred Roberts of New Zealand was awarded a penalty try by the referee of the All Blacks v Munster match in Limerick in 1905. Roberts was adjudged to have been tripped by the Munster fullback during a passing movement that threatened the Munster line.

The first penalty try involving New Zealand in an international was in 1947 when Harry Frazer, the All Black lock, was brought down in the Australian in-goal area at the Brisbane Exhibition Ground while chasing for a loose ball. The referee awarded Frazer a penalty try.

In 1963 South Africa's Tommy Bedford scored the first penalty try awarded in that country in the second test in Cape Town, against Australia.

By 1987 and the first Rugby World Cup, it was obvious that the party of international referees appointed for that series of games had decided not to tolerate collapsed scrums near the goal-line – long an area of contention for rugby's lawmakers. The result was increased vigilance in World Cup matches for deliberate collapsing of scrums in defensive situations.

There was also increased support from officialdom for the referees. Indeed the first try in World Cup history was a penalty try awarded to New Zealand after the Italian forwards were ruled to have deliberately collapsed their scrum near their own line. Four similar incidents occurred in other World Cup games. This effectively stopped teams deliberately taking scrums down.

The most sensational awarding of a penalty try in international rugby came in the second test match between Australia and New Zealand in Brisbane in 1968. Australia was leading 18–14 with only two minutes left in the game. When the All Black backs swung into a run at the Wallaby line, the New Zealand centre, Billy Davis, kicked ahead, but then was taken out of the game with a late tackle. Further out

---

FAMOUS GAMES WON BY PENALTIES

1949: South Africa v New Zealand at Cape Town.
South Africa won 15–11 when Aaron ('Okey') Geffin scored with five successful penalties. New Zealand had a try and also a dropped goal in its total. Geffin's five penalties were a world record for a test match.

1959: New Zealand v British Isles at Dunedin.
New Zealand won 18–17 with Don Clarke landing six penalties to beat Geffin's old mark, while a brilliant British team scored four tries.

Clarke's total was matched in IRB test matches many times, before it was finally bettered by England fullback, Simon Hodgkinson, against Wales in 1991.

1974: Argentina v France at Buenos Aires.
France won a high-scoring match, 31–27. Hugo Porta was responsible for 23 points for the hosts – a conversion to go with his world record seven penalties. Poor Porta: British sources tend to ignore feats by the Pumas generally.

1981: Scotland v Australia at Murrayfield.
Scotland won 24–15 but Australia scored three tries to one. At one point the game was locked at 15–15 with Australia having scored three tries and Scotland having scored five penalties by its fullback Andy Irvine.

An incident in the third test, British Isles v New Zealand in 1971. Gerald Davies tackled Bryan Williams before he had received the ball, and a penalty try was awarded to New Zealand.

the New Zealand wing Grahame Thorne appeared to be obstructed as he ran through for the ball. The referee, local man Kevin Crowe, had no hesitation in awarding a penalty try to New Zealand. The conversion from in front of the posts was a formality for Fergie McCormick and in an uproar the All Blacks were declared the match winners by 19–18. The victory also confirmed a test series win.

PENARTH RFC

This small town along the coast from Cardiff has played a significant role in Welsh and British rugby. From 1910 until 1971 the famous Barbarians club's Easter tours to Wales were always based at the Esplanade Hotel in Penarth.

In that time, and beyond, the Barbarians club repaid local hospitality by playing an annual match on Easter Friday with the Penarth club.

Penarth is a small place and a small club, and the match with the Barbar-ians was always akin to David against Goliath. Yet many memorable games were played in the annual match, which featured some of the greatest players of each era. Wins were rare, but treasured by Penarth. Many of the games were one-sided, in favour of the famous visitors – at one point Penarth waited 40 years for a win – but the club can proudly point to 11 wins in 74 games.

In the end the difficulties of continuing a four-match Easter tour proved too much, and in 1986 the annual match was dropped by the 'Baa-baas'.

Penarth Club was founded in 1880. Its most-capped Welsh player was Jack Bassett, who played 15 internationals in the 1920s and 30s and who toured New Zealand in 1930 with the Great Britain team.

PENGUINS RFC

Tony Mason and Alan Wright, vice-presidents of a junior English club, Sidcup RFC, formed this international invitation club in 1959. They did it,

they said, because they wanted to 'foster growth and camaraderie throughout the rugby world'. This they certainly have done. In 1984, when it celebrated its silver jubilee, the Penguins club had toured to 23 different countries and had travelled over 150,000 miles! All this from a club which obtains its players by invitation only and asks players to pay their own way – but one which is never short of those wanting to play. The Penguins have always had a penchant for touring but sometimes, for special celebrations or worthy charities, they appear in matches in Britain.

The Penguins motto is *'On court le ballon à la main'* ('They run with the ball in their hands') and by playing that way they have become an extremely popular touring party.

The quality of the players who turn out for the Penguins has always been high, but the club officials pride themselves in being able to spot future talent before international selectors do. In their first 25 years 30 young men appeared in the Penguin's colours before going on to play full internationals.

Tony Mason saw every match the Penguins played in its first 25 years, and his travel documents show the club appearing in such far-flung places as Bermuda (a regular and highly popular stop), Denmark, Zambia, Sri Lanka, Argentina and Tblisi (Georgia) where, in 1977 it won the Eastern European Nations tournament. Mason also played in a Penguins XV at Twickenham and one of his teammates was his son, Michael. This is believed to be the only time father and son have appeared in a match on the hallowed turf.

In 1987 the Penguins appeared at the Hong Kong Sevens with, in their ranks, another young player destined for international honours, the future rugby league star, Martin Offiah.

At the end of its first 25 years the club was committed to further touring and still had Messrs Mason and Wright as their two 'main men' on the club's committee.

PICKARD, JAN

Western Province and South Africa
4 internationals for Sth Africa 1953–58

A big bear of a man, Pickard was nick-named 'John Bull' at birth by an English midwife. He started rugby life as a back, before touring Britain in 1951–52 as a 23-year-old flanker. By the end of his international career, against France in 1958, Pickard was something of a man-mountain at 108 kg (17st) and 1.90 m (6ft 3in), and almost invariably played at lock, although his earlier test appearances were as a 'third lock' at No. 8.

Pickard was in a well-publicised fight with 'Salty' du Rand in the 1956 Springbok trials (which probably cost du Rand the captaincy), and controversy always surrounded the man.

On the high-profile tour of New Zealand that year, he developed a 'bad boy' image because he was such a distinctive figure – and he looked tough. Pickard was an enigma: sometimes an inspiration to his pack, at other times the laziest man on the field.

He immodestly claimed to leap higher than any other man in world rugby at the time, and it might well have been the case. But he achieved these heights with a running leap into the line, with team-mates blocking: he

was one of the few who thought that was legal.

Pickard captained the Springboks in two tour matches in New Zealand, though some felt he was too excitable and not enough of a tactician to do the job. He was also a part-time goal-kicker of some ability.

Pickard became a man of considerable influence in South Africa. Even as a young player he held company directorships, and he became a very wealthy viticulturalist. He took to entertaining touring teams and his old opponents – the stories of some of his parties are legend – and in rugby administration he became one of the most powerful men in South African rugby.

PIENAAR, 'SPORT'

He was christened Andries Jacobus, but the South African Rugby Board's longest serving president, before Danie Craven, was forever known as 'Sport'. Originally nicknamed the 'Sporting Parson' because he was the son of a moderator of the Dutch Reformed Church; the sobriquet was shortened

first to 'Sporting' and then to 'Sport'. Certainly sport was the abiding passion for this bachelor lawyer.

Pienaar actually achieved greater competitive honours in cricket than in rugby, playing for both Western Province and Eastern Province, but his contibution to rugby, on the administrative side, was enormous. On the death of Jack Heyneman in May 1927, he became president of the SARB until his death in October 1953. By then he was wracked with pain but he refused to leave the office he held so dear.

In 1947 he accomplished a unique feat in South African sport when he also became president of the South African Cricket Association, and this zealous disciple of amateurism became a year-round senior citizen of South African sport.

Often a brusque man, he held that 'rugby must not be turned into a bazaar'. He detested any moves towards commercialism and preferred to refer to 'an international game' rather than to a 'rugby test'.

'Sport' Pienaar would probably have found it hard to come to terms with World Cup contests, television commercials, increased allowances and book royalties for retired players, but in a different era he guided the game with wisdom and discretion.

PILLMAN, CHERRY
Blackheath and England
18 internationals for England 1910–14
2 internationals for Great Britain 1910

Nicknamed 'Cherry', Charles Henry Pillman was called one of the first 'true rugby geniuses' when he won his England caps in the years immediately before World War I. He is chiefly remembered as one of the most significant developers of the wing forward game in Britain.

Pillman was a roving loose forward who became a highly dangerous utility player, even appearing once as a flyhalf, in the second test in South Africa in 1910 when he toured with the Great Britain team.

It is hard to imagine any player getting better reviews than Pillman did for his play in that game. He moved from the forwards to flyhalf and was said to have 'beaten the Springboks single-handedly' as he roved about the field, appearing in all manner of places. One report said Pillman played a game

Jan Pickard, whose habit of taking a running leap into a lineout was not much appreciated by opposition teams – or referees.

'invented by himself'. The Springbok captain, Billy Millar, later commented, 'I confidently assert that if ever a man can have been said to have won an international match through his own unorthodox and lone-handed efforts, it can be said of the inspired, black-haired Pillman.'

Sadly, Pillman's career ended when he broke his leg in the England v Scotland game in 1914 and he never played rugby again.

His brother Robert was also an England international, actually taking his brother's place for the next England game, v France, in 1914.

'Cherry' Pillman was awarded the Military Cross after World War I.

POIDEVIN, SIMON
New South Wales and Australia
51 internationals for Australia 1980–89

When he 'retired' for the second time, at the end of the New Zealand tour to Australia in 1988, Simon Poidevin had become Australia's most-capped international and the first player from that country to reach 50 international appearances. The previous record was 42 internationals, set by hooker Peter Johnson.

Poidevin made his first retirement announcement earlier in 1988, after appearing for his country against an Overseas XV in Sydney. Later that year he was persuaded to turn out again for the Wallabies against the All Blacks, taking his total from 47 tests

Simon Poidevin

to 50. Then in 1989 Poidevin was persuaded to play for his country again, appearing in the Hong Kong Sevens tournament and in Auckland in the Bledisloe Cup match against the All Blacks. That was his 51st test match, a total that David Campese passed in 1990.

Poidevin was a tough loose forward with an uncompromising attitude and a very high work-rate. He was enormously respected by team-mates and opponents alike, especially the All Blacks against whom he appeared a record 18 times in test matches. He captained his country four times; twice against Argentina in Australia in 1986, once v Japan in the World Cup in 1987 and on the tour to Argentina in 1987. The next season he was replaced as captain by Nick Farr-Jones.

From his debut against Fiji in 1980, the flame-haired Poidevin played a key part in a very successful decade for Australian rugby, taking part in five test series wins and being a member of Australia's all-conquering Grand Slam-winning team in Britain in 1984.

He achieved ultimate world recognition by playing in the Overseas XV in the IRB's centenary matches in 1986.

POLAND
Although rugby had been played in Poland among military students since the 1920s, the game was knocked back by the Depression and the Second World War. It was not until 1956 that playing and club strengths had developed to the point where a Polish Rugby Union could be formed. The first international match was in 1958, when the German Democratic Republic was beaten 9–8 at Lodz.

Poland is a regular competitor in FIRA competition games, seeming to have settled for a regular place in the second division. The team's best year was in 1978–79, when it made it into the first division, having won the right to promotion by finishing ahead of sides like Italy and Czechoslovakia.

In 1989 Poland attempted to win a place in the final qualifying groups of the Rugby World Cup. In a round-robin tournament played in Madrid, Poland beat Belgium 25–23 but lost to Spain 9–23, and to the Netherlands 27–33.

Rugby is solidly based and centred around Warsaw, the Baltic Sea,

Gdansk, Sopot and the Silesian coal-fields.

PONTYPOOL RFC
This club was founded in 1901 and has its headquarters at Pontypool Park, surely the most picturesque rugby ground in Wales. Out of the beautiful tree-lined surroundings has emerged as tough and competitive a rugby club as can be found anywhere, with some of Welsh rugby's most vivid personalities.

The famous Pontypool front row, Bobby Windsor, Tony 'Charlie' Faulkner and Graham Price, notched up hundreds of appearances in the red, white and black hoops of the club, and went on to play 19 times together for Wales in the 1970s. Their work in the hard forward slog of so many internationals won them enormous popularity, even folk hero status. Songs and rhymes were written about them, and at Pontypool Park they were gods.

The main reason why those men became such great players was the presence at Pontypool of their famous coach, Ray Prosser. A fine player himself, reaching Welsh and British Lions status in the 1950s, 'Pross' drove Pontypool in an inimitable style to its finest era when he took over as senior coach in 1970. Pontypool became respected in all of Britain as a top club combination, especially for its hard forward pack. Prosser's captain through many of those seasons was Terry Cobner, who also captained Wales and toured with the British Isles to New Zealand.

Perhaps the club's richest prize came in 1983, when it won the Schweppes Cup final. That year five members of the club – Price, Eddie Butler, Staff Jones, John Perkins and Jeff Squire – made the Welsh forward pack in a team which went on to humble Ireland on Cardiff Arms Park. Three of the five became Welsh captains (Butler, Squire and Perkins) while four were British Lions (Butler, Squire, Jones, and Price). The Prosser years lasted from 1970 to 1988.

In the early days Pontypool was best known for the three Jones brothers – P.P. ('Ponty'), Jack and Tuan. All three were Welsh internationals with Jack winning 14 caps, and Ponty going on two British tours.

The club had several good years in the 1920s and in 1927 'Pooler' beat the

New Zealand Maoris, as well as the Waratahs of New South Wales. At that point no other club had beaten two touring teams in the same year.

For years Pontypool played matches against overseas teams in combination with its neighbour Cross Keys. When it did finally break away and merit individual games, its start was not auspicious. In its first match against the Wallabies in 1981 it lost 6–37, and in 1989, against the All Blacks, it was downed 6–47. The scores were not indicative of Pontypool's historical standing as one of the toughest clubs to beat in Wales.

POPPIES RFC

The northern Californian equivalent of the Barbarians club; a social rugby club where players are invited to participate and tours are arranged privately. The Poppies toured Britain in 1975 with a team which included some Canadian players.

PORTA, HUGO

Banco Nacion and Argentina
49 internationals for Argentina 1971–90
8 internationals for Sth America 1980–84

Hugo Porta was, for nearly 20 years, the most famous and powerful rugby personality in Argentina and the first from that country to make his mark on the wider rugby world. He was a deceptive, brilliant flyhalf, among the best anywhere, and his goal-kicking feats made him for a time the highest scorer in internationals in the game's history.

Like most boys in Argentina in the 1960s, Porta was a soccer player until his teenage years. (The arrival of Porta himself might have changed this tradition among later generations!) His soccer background, added to his natural talent, gave him outstanding ball skills. Indeed he could do things with a rugby ball that no other player could: he could punt, drop-kick and kick tactically with either foot. In practice he would bounce a rugby ball from boot to boot, like soccer players do with their round ball, and sometimes during a game, he would head the ball, soccer-style, across the touchline.

With talent like his, it was no wonder one of the top Argentine football clubs, Boca Juniors, tried to sign him as a youngster. Ironically, Porta later became one of the first non-soccer

Hugo Porta

sportsmen to receive recognition from the wider community of Argentina.

Porta's physical bearing did not give an immediate impression of nimbleness or fleetness of foot. He was slightly bigger and heavier in the hips than many would say was ideal for a flyhalf, yet he was an electrifying runner. He had extremely sharp speed off a standing start and he was capable of shifts of pace and direction that dazzled many an opponent.

He was originally a scrumhalf, but after a series of injuries to the prominent flyhalves of the time Porta was invited by Angel Guastella, who was the coach of Argentina B, to adopt that position and join Guastella's team to play in the 1971 South American championship. Porta was 19.

Porta didn't leave the Pumas from then until almost the onset of his mid-

dle-age. In his business life, he was a successful architect; in his time with Pumas rugby he built them up to be able to beat almost any team in the world.

From the start Porta took lovingly to the position of flyhalf. Under the tutelage of Guastella who, he says, taught him everything about the game, Porta was the vital man in Argentinian rugby planning in the 1970s and 80s, guiding the country's game through various styles.

First there was the free-running approach of men like Guastella; later there was a change to hard scrummaging and kicking for the forwards. Porta was adept at both, and though he won a reputation as a formidable kicker, the running game was his first love.

Porta captained Argentina at the 1987 Rugby World Cup, where the team put up some disappointing performances, losing to Fiji and New Zealand and winning only narrowly over Italy. Porta, 36 years old and slowing, was still recognised by most as a class act. But such was his greatness that he was criticised in some quarters for having forced Argentine teams to be over-dependent on him as captain, points-scorer and star player.

It was thought his last internationals would be against Spain and against Australia in a two-test series in 1987. In those matches the team scored 86 points; the familiar figure in the No. 10 jersey scored 54 of them.

Porta then retired from international play, but he remained in demand as a player for invitation teams all over the world. In 1990 he made a comeback, aged nearly 39, leading his club Banco Nacion to a shock victory over the England tourists. A change of Pumas coach saw Luis Gradin take over to prepare Argentina for its British tour, and he called Porta back to the Pumas and made him captain. Having passed 39, it was a remarkable comeback for Porta.

But the fairy tale did not quite work out. On tour his team lost all three internationals and the veteran player suffered injury. However, he showed enough skill and interest to suggest he might hang on to be involved in Argentina's World Cup effort in 1991.

Porta's contribution to Puma rugby was so enormous, that a list of his greatest achievements might seem selective. In his prime he was awesome, yet several games stand out as classics, by his own very high standards. One was against France in Buenos Aires in 1977 when he kicked all 18 points and forced an 18–18 draw. The other was for South America against South Africa in Bloemfontein in the second 'test' of 1982. Porta's 21 points enabled South America to beat the Springboks, in a massive upset, by 21–12. He also scored all 21 points when Argentina had its best result against the All Blacks, in the second test of 1985. Porta landed four penalties and three dropped goals and again the result was a draw.

His best total in a test match was 23 points v France in Buenos Aires in 1974 (a world record seven penalties and a conversion); and v Australia in the second test in Buenos Aires in 1987.

The 1986 tour to Australia underscored Porta's pivotal role in the Argentina rugby team. It remained unbeaten after several promising outings, but in the match with New South Wales Porta suffered a painful groin injury. That game was lost 18–30 and the next one (without Porta playing) was a 9–59 hiding by Queensland. Only half fit, he struggled back for the first test, which the Pumas lost 19–39. When he cried off the rest of the tour, the second and final test became a disaster. The Pumas crashed to a 0–26 embarrassment – they were nothing without their beloved Porta.

Establishing a definitive total of international points for Porta is something of a problem, for records of Argentine rugby tests are not readily available and British-based historians tend not to recognise matches against 'minor' international opponents. It is recorded that he played 49 times for Argentina and eight times for South America (in its 1980–84 matches with South Africa). In these matches Porta scored 514 points for Argentina and 50 for South America – a grand total of 564 points, and a world record, held jointly with Michael Lynagh.

PORTER, CLIFF
Wellington, Horowhenua and New
   Zealand
7 internationals for New Zealand 1924–30

Scots-born and New Zealand-raised, Cliff Porter began to lose his hair early in his 20s. That made little difference to his ability as a wing forward, a 'roving' position that existed only in New Zealand for any length of time, but it made him as distinctive as a triallist who wears coloured headgear to catch the selectors' eyes.

Originally a three-quarter or five-eighth, Porter became a wing forward in 1923. He was only 5ft 8in (1.75m) in height.

Dave Gallaher, who led the 1905 All Blacks, had attracted much criticism in Britain for his 'unfair' tactics; Porter, more destructive than constructive, endured similar criticisms when he led the 1924 side. (He also took over

Cliff Porter (right) meets Doug Prentice, captain of the 1930 British team in New Zealand

the New Zealand captaincy in controversial circumstances. *See* BADELEY.)

Illness forced him to miss the first international on that tour, against Ireland, and the outstanding display of his replacement, Jim Parker, meant he lost his place in the test team.

But personal ambition may have also played a part. It is said that in the selection deliberations for the next test, against Wales, two of the panel – 'Son' White and Maurice Brownlie, both players, opted for Parker. Porter, naturally, and team manager Stan Dean went for Porter. Porter looked to his lieutenant, vice-captain Jock Richardson. Perhaps eager for the top job, perhaps not, Richardson said,'You don't change a winning team' (though they did in some other positions).

Porter was to play only in the international with France near the tour's end, and although he was New Zealand's captain in Australia in 1926 he was only a reserve for the 1928 tour to South Africa. He returned to captain New Zealand in its series win against the 1930 British side.

PORTUGAL

The Portuguese Rugby Union was formed in 1957, but the game had been played there since the early years of the twentieth century.

As in many countries, students arriving back from France and Britain brought with them tales, then demonstrations, of a new game. Rugby took a firm hold, first in Lisbon then in the southern provinces.

Portugal was represented at the inaugural meeting of FIRA in 1934 and the national team began playing in FIRA competition games in 1979. Its best year season was in 1984–85 when it won Group B1 and was promoted to the prestigious first division. But competition in the higher level proved difficult and Portugal has played at a level just below the best of FIRA's top countries.

Its biggest win in its first 30 years was a 39–0 defeat of Switzerland in 1980. Conversely it had suffered a 14–56 loss to a French XV in 1957.

The country entered the 1991 Rugby World Cup series and beat Czechoslovakia by 15–13.

Reports of the match, played in 1989, stated that Portugal's back play was of a very high standard. Hopes of going further were dashed when Nether-

---

POSITIONS (ON THE FIELD)

Fullbacks and hookers are instantly recognised around the world because the name of their position is the same. Yet for other positions on the field there is considerable variation of names from country to country. The following shows some of the variations and similarities:

Fullback	Used everywhere
Wing	Sometimes winger or wing three-quarter, with either 'left' or 'right' added.
Outside centre	Centre three-quarter (NZ)
Inside centre	Second five-eighths (NZ)
Flyhalf	GB, SA. Also outside half. First five-eighths (NZ). Sometimes stand-off (GB, Aust.)
Halfback	Scrum half (GB)
No. 8	Sometimes lock (Aust.) or back-rower (GB), once eighth man (SA)
Flanker	Breakaway (Aust.), sometimes side-row. Wing forward (GB), not often heard these days.
Loose forwards	Sometimes loosies (NZ), also back row (GB)
Locks	Sometimes second row (GB, Aust.)
Props	Sometimes front row (Aust.)
Hooker	Used everywhere.
Reserves	Emergencies (NZ), sometimes replacements.
Referee	Used everywhere, usually shortened to 'ref' or even 'sir'!

---

lands beat Portugal 32–3 in the next round. The Portuguese captain was the No. 8, Bernardo Pinto.

Portuguese domestic rugby is soundly based on two divisions of club play involving about 1700 players. Further development of the game is hindered by a lack of coaches, playing fields, referees and of course finance, but it has a solid programme of exchange visits for club teams. Portugal is also used for training camps by countries in their off-seasons, England being one regular visitor.

POULTON PALMER, RONALD

Harlequins, Liverpool and England
17 internationals for England 1909–14

A number of the writers and historians have judged Ronnie Poulton to be the most outstanding English player of the era immediately before World War I.

A 'deceptively elusive' wing or centre, who scored eight tries for England in his 17 internationals, Poulton was enormously popular as a player, possessing an 'entirely unassumed modesty and complete unselfishness'. Other writers refer to him as a 'genius', the 'greatest figure who ever played' and 'a man apart'.

He set a record by scoring five tries in the Oxford v Cambridge match in 1909 and scored four tries against France in 1914, then a record for an international.

Poulton came into a large inheritance after the death of a wealthy relative – on condition that he assumed the name of his relative, Palmer. Thereafter you may see his name referred to as Poulton Palmer; sometimes he is listed with a hyphen between the two names.

Sadly he was cut down by a sniper's bullet in 1915, when aged 25. Such was his popularity among his fellow soldiers that a letter of condolence to his family from an officer who had witnessed his funeral said, 'When I went round his old company, as they stood to, at dawn, almost every man was crying.'

POVERTY BAY RFU

When Captain James Cook first discovered the easternmost point of the North Island of New Zealand he judged it to be poor country and named it Poverty Bay. He should have looked more closely, for the area was, in fact, rich in vegetation.

But the district has not been as rich in rugby players, for it has struggled along with a small population and many suggest it should have merged once again with the even smaller and far-flung East Coast union to the north.

Poverty Bay might not have the numbers, but it did produce two of the greatest forwards in New Zealand's rugby history. Richard 'Tiny' White, later elected mayor of Gisborne, the main town, became an All Black in 1949. When he retired after the final test against the 1956 Springboks – off the field, as he had been kicked in the base of the spine – White had played 23 consecutive tests, then a New Zealand record. White was a great lock and lineout leaper.

Ian Kirkpatrick was just as big, but became instead a magnificent loose forward for the All Blacks. Played occasionally as a No. 8, and once in a trial as a lock, Kirkpatrick's true position was as a blindside flanker and for several years astonishingly held New Zealand's test try-scoring record with 16 touchdowns.

Kirkpatrick was succeeded as an All Black by Lawrie Knight, also a Poverty Bay man, but the union's other All Blacks were all midfield backs: Brian Fitzpatrick (whose son Sean became an All Black hooker), John Collins and Mike Parkinson.

Poverty Bay, which was formed in 1895, plays in scarlet jerseys and white shorts.

This little union does not often get to play visiting international sides, and when it does it is usually combined with neighbouring unions. But it has beaten New South Wales Country twice, Western Samoa, Irish Universities and Victoria.

PRAT, JEAN
Lourdes and France
51 internationals for France 1945–55

He came from Lourdes and may well have been a miracle himself, such was his dominance and influence over French rugby in the years immediately after World War II.

Jean Prat was a powerfully built flanker who eventually totalled 51 international appearances for his country, a record until it was passed by Michel Crauste. He was also a point-scoring machine, totalling 145 points which, 35 years after Prat's retirement, is almost certainly the world's best total by a forward in international games. Prat was so versatile he dropped goals in international matches on five occasions, marking him as a true rugby rarity. Forwards have seldom achieved even one dropped goal in major matches.

Prat became one of France's great captains and led his country to its first wins in Wales (in 1948) and in England (in 1951). He also captained France and scored the winning try in its first win over New Zealand in Paris in 1954. The same year he led France to its first ever share of Five Nations championship honours. He captained Lourdes to six French championship final victories. No wonder he was called 'L'extraordinaire' or 'Monsieur Rugby'.

His brother, Maurice, was also a splendid French international player who played 31 times as a centre between 1951 and 1958, making it 82 appearances for the two brothers in France's colours.

PRICE, BRIAN
Newport and Wales
32 internationals for Wales 1961–69
4 internationals for British Isles 1966

An imposing figure on world rugby fields in the 1960s, Brian Price was a lock with fine lineout jumping skills. His international debut was against Ireland in 1961.

Brian Price

He toured to Australasia with the Lions of 1966 and captained Wales on their ill-fated journey to New Zealand in 1969. He was also captain of Wales in 1968 when, in front of the Prince of Wales, he lowered Ireland's captain Noel Murphy with a punch. The incident was one of the first of its nature to be vividly captured on television. Such an act was not looked upon kindly by some in British rugby, but it failed to overshadow a fine career as a hard-working lock.

Perhaps Price's finest moment in rugby came when he captained Newport to its historic 3–0 victory over the 1963 All Blacks.

In later years he became a very articulate commentator on the game for Welsh radio and TV.

PRICE, GRAHAM
Pontypool and Wales
41 internationals for Wales 1975–83
12 internationals for British Isles 1977–83

When he retired from international play, in 1983, after eight brilliantly successful years as a prop and tight play specialist, Graham Price (inevitably known as 'Pricey') had forged a record as a hard scrummager that was second to none. His tally of 41 appearances for the Welsh team was the most ever by a Welsh prop and his 12 tests for the Lions were spread over three tough tours.

He began his senior rugby with Pontypool, where, after being a schoolboy international, he soon joined his front row partners, 'Charlie' Faulkner and Bobby Windsor, to form the 'Pontypool front row'.

Price burst onto the test arena with a 70-metre dash for a try against France at Parc des Princes in 1975. A prop sprinting 70 metres to score? It was unheard of, but Price, for all the qualities he showed in tight play, could also foot it with the best in the loose.

With his two mates in the 'PFR' he appeared 19 times in full internationals. They played together through four Five Nations series, two Grand Slams and three Triple Crowns.

Graham Price toured to South Africa, and to New Zealand twice, with the Lions, and on those tours he never missed a test match. He was part of a powerful Lions scrum that completely outplayed its All Black counterpart during the test series there in 1977.

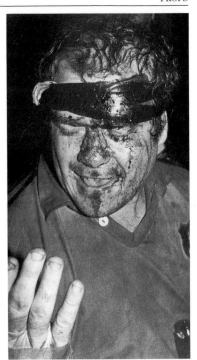

Quite an armful – Graham Price wrapped up by Murray Mexted.

Props! Chris Handy of Australia.

When his test days ended in 1983, the quietly spoken Price played on at club level. He was still good enough to play a solid game for Pontypool, to which he was always loyal, against the New Zealand All Blacks in 1989.

By then he was 38 years old and had played 558 games for his club! Surely there could be no finer example of a player giving back his wisdom to his club after he had enjoyed the fruits of a top international touring life.

In every way Graham Price was a champion, on and off the field, for Pontypool, Wales and world rugby.

PROPS

They come in all shapes and sizes, and for some inexplicable reason they are often the 'characters' of any rugby team. A prop can be a stout and roly-poly fellow so vital in scrummaging or he can have a long back and be quite tall, to be useful about the field and at lineouts. Modern international props have ranged in size from the 133 kilograms (21 stone) bulk of 'Flippie' van der Merwe of South Africa down to the 90 kg (14 stone) of the Welshman Brian Williams.

The essential requirement for props is strength. They are the pillars of the scrums (a French front row prop is *un*

pilier) and no scrum is successful unless there is a solid foundation on which everyone else pushes and from which the ball is won.

There are two props, one either side of the hooker in every front row. The loosehead prop packs down on the side nearest his own halfback at the put-in. His task is to hold up the opposing prop, so that his hooker can get the first, and best, view of the ball coming into the scrum; the tighthead prop on the opposite side works to hold the scrum steady and secure for that put-in.

Recent injuries involving collapsed scrums and resulting neck problems have meant that in some junior levels of the game the scrummage has been 'de-powered'. Yet at international level strong props are still sought by selectors.

Props can play a vital role in other aspects of the game. The tall types can operate at the front of the lineouts and gain very useful possession from short, flat throw-ins – a specialty in New Zealand rugby – but in Europe the tendency has been for the props not to be involved in lineout ball-winning tactics.

With their strong shoulders and forearms, props are invariably good

maulers of the ball. When they emerge from their duties in a scrum, they have to set out after the ball which, by then, could be spinning furiously through the backline as a result of their previous work.

Often the last ones to arrive at rucks or mauls, they may be on hand to take a short pass as the ball comes clear, or rip the ball away and pass it to the halfback for distribution.

In the modern game props have also become ball-carriers and try-scorers, which has revolutionised their attitudes to the game. This is exemplified in players like Steve McDowell of New Zealand who, at his best, was a powerful and respected scrummager, yet in open play was capable of storming runs. Graham Price of Wales took part in a 70-metre dash to score a try against France in 1975, possibly the most spectacular try ever scored by a prop.

Every rugby country has produced many great props, some of whom are listed below.

England had Fran Cotton, Ron Jacobs and Gary Pearce; Wales had Graham Price and 'Charlie' Faulkner, also Denzil Williams; Ireland had Phil Orr, Sid Millar and Ray McLoughlin; Scotland had Sandy Carmichael, Ian ('Mighty Mouse') McLauchlan, Hugh

McLeod and David Rollo; France had Robert Paparemborde, Alfred Roques, Amédée Domenech and Jean-Pierre Garuet; South Africa had 'Boy' Louw, Phil Mostert, Chris Koch and Hannes Marais; New Zealand, Kevin Skinner, Wilson Whineray, Ken Gray, Gary Knight and Steve McDowell; and Australia, John Thornett, Tony Miller, Nick Shehadie and Andy McIntyre.

PROSSER, RAY
Pontypool and Wales
22 internationals for Wales 1956–61
1 international for British Isles 1959

Ray Prosser was a fine prop by any standards, good enough to enjoy six seasons with Wales and one tour with the British Isles to New Zealand and Australia in 1959. But his fame and, one suspects, his ability as a player, was surpassed by his enormous talent as a coach. Another of the extraordinary lineup of players totally loyal to the Pontypool club in Gwent, Wales, Prosser finished his playing days with the club and then carved his niche in the rugby world all over again, as a coach.

He often claimed that his coaching views were shaped by what he learnt from his Lions tour to New Zealand, where he admired the ferocious attitude of some of the Kiwi forward packs. He guided and inspired Pontypool towards a similar hardened approach, between 1970 and 1988, totally winning over the hearts of the local people with his colourful use of language, his formidable planning and his drive for perfection, especially of course, in his beloved forward pack.

From teams coached by Prosser came such forwards as Bobby Windsor, Graham Price, 'Charlie' Faulkner, Terry Cobner, Eddie Butler, John Perkins, Staff Jones and Jeff Squire. It is perhaps not a coincidence that in the same era the Pontypool backs, with the exception of David Bishop, were not noted for their contribution.

As befitting a bulldozer driver, which he was for much of his working life, Ray Prosser was a coach who savoured the ethos of driving forward play. In his time as coach of the club – it won seven Whitbread Merit Table championships and the Welsh Cup final, which it took in 1983, beating Swansea 18–6.

PROTESTS, ANTI-APARTHEID
The issue of coloured players proving unacceptable to South African hosts dates back to the tour undertaken by the New Zealand Services team to South Africa in 1919, after the King's Cup tournament. A prominent New Zealand player, Nathaniel 'Ranji' Wilson, an All Black 1908–14, was not chosen because his English/West Indian parentage meant he was classified as 'coloured'.

The racial issue flared again in 1921 when the Springboks beat New Zealand Maoris by a single point in an ill-tempered match. A South African journalist despatched a cable to South Africa, the gist of which was 'the sight of Europeans cheering on a band of natives to defeat members of their own race was too much for the Springboks . . .'

The leaking of this cable drew an official enquiry, some heads rolled, and the matter of coloured rugby players meeting the Springboks or touring South Africa became an issue. However, there was less sensitivity to racial issues in those days, and the NZRFU blithely accepted South African dictates that it should not select Maoris.

Thus George Nepia never toured South Africa, and New Zealand teams in 1928 and 1949 had to go without their best halfbacks – Jimmy Mill, and Manahi ('Doc') Paewai and Vince Bevan on the latter tour – and the great centre, Johnny Smith. The 'problems' in 1921 also meant no match against the Maoris for the 1937 Springboks.

Very muted protests were uttered when the 1956 Springboks came to New Zealand – the country as a whole was more concerned with beating the tourists.

But active protest started in 1960. An organisation with the acronym CARE (Citizen's Association for Racial Equality) distributed pamphlets, made public comment and petitioned politicians to prevent the tour on the grounds that some New Zealanders were facing discrimination.

Banner-bearing protesters 'farewelled' a team that officially included no Maoris, though it is rumoured some of the players had Maori blood.

The protest movement had grown by 1965 when the Springboks next toured, and the groundswell of opinion prompted then Prime Minister Keith Holyoake to cancel the projected All Blacks tour of South Africa in 1967, because South Africa would not accept a New Zealand team chosen solely on merit.

Shocked South Africans, deprived of their favourite opponent, promptly made the appropriate moves to accept whatever team New Zealand chose, and that which toured in 1970 included Sid Going, 'Buff' Milner, Blair Furlong and Bryan Williams, who was part-Samoan.

But another Prime Minister, Norman Kirk, strong-armed the New Zealand union into calling off the invitation for a visit of the Springboks scheduled for 1973, as it would assuredly have

A last line of defence? Police presence during the 1981 Springbok tour of New Zealand.

Haka! Below, Wayne Shelford, flanked by Grant Fox and Richard Loe, issues the All Black challenge to Scotland.
Peter Bush

Above: The Scottish team, captained by Colin Deans, at the 1987 World Cup.
Right: Jean Condom, France, John Jeffrey, Scotland, and Laurent Rodriguez, France, wating for lineout ball. Scotland and France drew their World Cup match 20–20. Peter Bush

meant the collapse of the Commonwealth Games to be held at Christchurch the following year.

CARE, by then, had been displaced by another acronym, HART – for Halt All Racist Tours, a very active and vocal lobby group which took its cue from the anti-apartheid movement led by Peter Hain in Britain.

A South African himself, Hain led the bitter opposition to the tour of the 1969–70 Springboks, the issue of apartheid having been highlighted by the refusal of the South African government to accept a former Cape Coloured, Basil D'Oliveira, as a member of the touring MCC cricket team in 1969.

The protest group's activities meant Oxford University had to play – and beat – South Africa on the secure Twickenham ground, rather than on its more open field. Ironically, Oxford's captain, Chris Laidlaw, an All Black tourist in South Africa the following year, became a critic of the republic. He was later High Commissioner to Zimbabwe, before becoming New Zealand's Race Relations Conciliator.

The Springboks' matches in Britain were played before a huge police presence, grounds barbed-wired, and attendances restricted, yet still the protesters invaded the pitches, stopping play, sometimes scattering tacks on the field or throwing smoke flares. It brought a new and ugly dimension to rugby.

Many rugby folk, themselves critical of the apartheid policy, took part in the protests. John Taylor, the London Welsh and Wales flanker, and later a member of the Lions in New Zealand, refused to play against the tourists.

Little more than a year later the Springboks were in the firing line again, this time in Australia. Queensland's right wing premier, Joh Bjelke-Peterson, declared a state of emergency – though cynics reckoned he ruled the state in that manner all the time – and because the national air carriers refused to fly the Springboks, they often travelled in little two- and four-seater aircraft, owned and flown by rugby enthusiasts.

With one exception, this marked the end of major tours by South Africa. It visited France in 1974 for two internationals; and in 1980 visited the unlikely rugby venues, Paraguay, Uruguay and Chile. The 'South American'

sides it played, like that which toured South Africa the same year, were effectively the Argentine team with a few ring-ins. Argentina's 'protest' was muted and hypocritical.

In 1976, 27 nations (mostly black African) withdrew from the Montreal Olympic Games as a protest over another visit by the All Blacks to South Africa.

The tour which really finished the Springboks as an acceptable visitor was in 1981 to New Zealand (and the United States briefly afterwards).

In the interests of winning the general election that year, Prime Minister Robert Muldoon refused to cancel the tour, and relatively peaceful New Zealand knew the nearest thing to a civil war since the land wars of the 1860s. Neighbours fell out with each other, families were divided and rugby clubs argued, as the Springboks made their clandestine way around the country.

The second match, against Waikato, was cancelled when protesters stormed the field before the start; another, in Timaru, was also cancelled because security arrangements were inadequate; and the original itinerary was abbreviated.

Supportive clubs set up dormitories in their club-rooms for the hounded Springboks, and New Zealanders winced at their police, traditionally unarmed, clubbing down fellow citizens with long batons. The *piece de resistance* was a protester 'strafing' Eden Park during the third and final test, throwing flour bombs on the field. One struck All Black Gary Knight, and Welsh referee Clive Norling introduced a rare humorous note when he warned the medical attendant to go easy on the 'miracle water' in case Knight turned to paste.

While any idea of nations hosting the Springboks then went on the backburner, teams still looked at touring there. South America went again in 1982, England and yet again South America in 1984, and the All Blacks were scheduled to tour in 1985. But when the government of David Lange could not persuade the NZRFU to cancel the tour, two Auckland lawyers successfully sought a High Court injunction which delayed the team's departure until the tour became impossible. The NZRFU changed its rules to ensure a repeat of such legal action would not succeed again.

Plane buzzing Eden Park during the third test, South Africa v New Zealand, Eden Park 1981.

The disgruntled All Blacks then organised their own tour, 28 of the original party of 30 visiting South Africa as the 'Cavaliers'. The IRB was meeting in Britain at the same time, but SARB president, Danie Craven, insisted he knew nothing of the tour arrangements. Nevertheless, he welcomed the team fulsomely on his return.

The Cavaliers were little more than rebuked by their union when they returned – a two-test stand-down – but the organiser of the South Seas Barbarians (mainly Fijians) who toured the next year, former All Black and Fiji administrator Arthur Jennings, got a life suspension.

PUBLIC SCHOOL WANDERERS

Although the idea of providing rugby for public schoolboys had begun before World War II, this splendid club was officially founded in 1940 by Charles Burton, a highly successful Fleet St sportswriter.

So successful was his plan that soon the club expanded to provide rugby and cricket matches for members from the various armed services, hospitals and universities, all of which had problems arranging teams and fixtures during the difficult war years.

The first president of the club was Sir Henry Leveson-Gower, who had captained England at cricket. The status of the club rose quickly, so much so that by 1943 the club hosted the New Zealand Combined Services team, captained by Charles Saxton.

When the war ended the hectic days of providing teams every day of the week subsided. An accurate record of all the club's fixtures was impossible to keep, but it is estimated 1200 games were played by the club during the war, involving more than 5000 players.

One of the wartime players was a Natal representative, Lieutenant Edwin Swales (South African Air Force), who was awarded a posthumous Victoria Cross and was the highest decorated serviceman to have played for the Public School Wanderers.

After the war the traditional clubs of England resumed their normal fixtures and for a time interest waned in the PSW teams. In 1948, however, a tour of the West Country took place and thus began a fine tradition. Dr Doug Keller, who played for his native Australia as well as captaining Scotland, was on that first touring team.

These days there are usually several tours each season and a host of midweek social fixtures. The Public School Wanderers have played the Middlesex Sevens a number of times and have also appeared at the prestigious Hong Kong Sevens. It continues to be a social club and its aims are always to play bright open rugby.

Members say their proudest moment on the field came in 1980 when, with only a few days notice, they assembled a top team to play against the Zimbabwe XV. The Wanderers were captained by the famous Irishman, Fergus Slattery.

PULLIN, JOHN

Bristol and England
42 internationals for England 1966–76
7 internationals for British Isles 1968–71

John Pullin was for a time, along with Ireland's Ken Kennedy, the world's most-capped hooker, as well as being England's most-capped player in any position. He was also a quiet, thorough and dedicated captain of England on 13 occasions. Highly significant were his wins as captain over South Africa, New Zealand and Australia, all within the space of 12 months.

In 1971–72 England had had a dreadful home season, losing all four games in the Five Nations championship. There seemed little enthusiasm for the upcoming tour to South Africa, a feeling endorsed when seven international players signalled their unavailability to tour. Yet under John Pullin's quiet leadership, those who did travel banded together into a highly successful unit. England was unbeaten on that tour, winning the test against South Africa by 18–9, and stunning the locals.

Much the same thing happened in 1973, when England toured to New Zealand. The scenario was slightly different. Suffering from jet-lag, the team was confronted with a tough itinerary which started within a few days. Consequently it lost all the lead-up games against Taranaki, Wellington and Canterbury. In one-eyed New Zealand there was hardly a soul who gave England a chance against the mighty All Blacks. Yet in his unobtrusive way, Pullin had inspired and plotted a success for his men. New Zealand was toppled by 16–10 – as big a shock defeat as had ever been inflicted on the All Blacks.

Pullin completed his treble of significant victories when, on Twickenham two months later, he led England to a 20–3 win over the touring Australians. Analysts of the game, struggling to put a label on the achievement, eventually decided that Pullin was the first international captain to score victories over the three 'Dominion' countries.

John Pullin should also be remembered as a vital member of two Lions teams. He played three tests in South Africa in 1968 and was a member of

John Pullin

the Carwyn James-coached Lions team of 1971, which also defeated New Zealand at home.

As if Kiwis hadn't had enough of Pullin's presence, he hooked for the Barbarians club against the All Blacks in 1973, taking part in the fabulous try scored by Gareth Edwards. Pullin, the hooker, features twice in the oft-seen video of that famous score, and once again he was a part of a team which tipped over the All Blacks!

PUMAS, THE

The nickname given to the international rugby team of Argentina, following the first major overseas tour by Argentina, to South Africa in 1965.

When the team offered a press conference on its arrival in Rhodesia, one of the local reporters asked the name of the animal depicted on their team colours and blazers. When told it was a representation of the Yaguarete (a jaguar-like member of the cat family found in South America) the reporter nevertheless filed it to his office as a 'puma'. When published, the term stuck as the name for Argentina's national team. However, a keen student of natural history will tell you that, in the wild, pumas are found almost exclusively in North America!

Q

QUAGGAS RFC

Formed in 1956 in Transvaal, as one of a number of South African invitation club sides with similar attitudes and ambitions to the Barbarians club of Britain. In its early years, the club took top rugby to the smaller clubs and unions of the high veldt of South Africa. Its status rose to the point where it earned the right to be included on the itinerary for the British Isles tour in 1974. That game was one of the most dramatic and exciting of the era and resulted in the Lions sneaking home by 20–16. There were chaotic scenes at Ellis Park at the end of the game when the referee, Ian Gourlay, was attacked by some members of the crowd, no doubt disappointed at the result.

By 1976 the Quaggas had combined with the South African Barbarians club (which had been formed in 1960 in Natal) and the Quagga-Barbarians were given a game against New Zealand. It was a thriller. At one point the Quagga-Barbarians led by 24–9 but, inspired by their captain Andy Leslie, the All Blacks stormed back, to win 32–31.

The emblem of the club is a quagga, an extinct striped member of the horse family.

QUEENSLAND RFU

Known originally as the Northern Union, the Queensland RFU was founded in 1883. For a long time it languished behind New South Wales in influence on the Australian rugby scene, and the game even faded into recession for 12 years after the end of World War I. Only the dedication of a small band of Brisbane enthusiasts saw rugby restart in Queensland in 1929. From then on Queensland's record has swung on an upward curve to outstanding success. It might even be argued (and certainly argued vigorously by Queenslanders), that the state is now the centre of the game in Australia.

The history of Queensland rugby reflects a familiar story in Australian rugby: a continuous battle against the effects of the more powerful rugby league, which has regularly creamed off the top playing talent with lucrative professional offers. It is to the credit of the Queensland RFU's organisation that in the 1970s and 80s very few leading players were lured across to rugby league.

Another reason for that is the sheer attractiveness of playing rugby in Queensland. The weather is consistent and mild in winter, so the game there is invariably an open, fast one played in good conditions. The main clubs have modern facilities for the social activities that Australians enjoy so much and Ballymore, the headquarters of the union, in the tree-lined suburbs of Brisbane, is one of the best grounds anywhere in which to watch and enjoy a game.

Queensland's rugby history is packed with the names of men who have made their mark at the international level as well. On a number of occasions state teams from Queensland, 'Maroons' (or 'Reds' as they have become known lately), have played with up to four Australian test captains in the same team. Players such as Tommy Lawton (snr), Bill McLean, Nev Cottrell, Arch Winning, Des Connor, Tony Shaw, Mark Loane, Paul Mclean, and Andrew Slack were all Wallaby captains, and all were winners with Queensland as well.

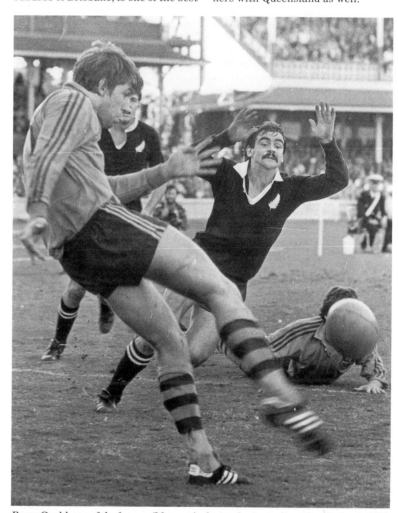

Roger Gould, one of the famous 'Maroons', playing for Australia v New Zealand, 1980.

Tommy Lawton is one of the true heroes of Queensland rugby. He was devoted to the game in the years after World War I, but had to transfer temporarily to Sydney in order to continue playing. He made the famous 1927 New South Wales Waratahs team, in essence the Australian team, and eventually returned to Brisbane, determined to see the restoration of the game there. This was achieved in 1929 and Lawton, perhaps as a tribute, assumed the Australian captaincy that year.

Of course there had been rugby in the state before World War I. Queensland was powerful in the pre-war years, beating New South Wales teams regularly. The annual interstate clash with the 'Blues' of Sydney dates back to 1882. That the Queensland RU was not formed until 1883 did not bother the state when it came to celebrating its centenary, which it did, with much fanfare, in 1982 – 100 years after the staging of the first game against New South Wales.

By the 1930s Queensland rugby was quickly back to top strength: 11 members of the Australian team which toured to South Africa in 1933 were Queenslanders. Nine players, including the captain Vay Wilson, made the ill-fated Australian touring team of 1939: the tour was abandoned because of the outbreak of World War II.

But it is the 1970s that Queensland historians look to for their best era in winning rugby. Throughout those years any visiting team could expect a match with a team that was arguably the best provincial or state team anywhere in the world.

Queensland beat Scotland in 1970, the British Isles in 1971 (its only loss in 26 tour games, 24 of them in New Zealand), Tonga in 1973, Japan in 1975, Fiji in 1976, and New Zealand in 1980.

The 'Maroons' were also world travellers in those days and they repaid the support of their home officials by staying with the game and building even better performances on the field. In modern times Queensland has visited New Zealand every year, a far cry from the gap of 67 years between its first trip across the Tasman (in 1896) to its second (in 1963).

Players such as Brendan Moon, Jeff McLean, Roger Gould, Stan Pilecki, Chris Handy, Stuart Gregory, Peter McLean, Duncan Hall, and literally dozens of others, emerged to assist the great captains Jules Guerassimoff, Dick Cocks, Tony Shaw and Mark Loane.

Standing apart from them, in terms of brilliance in play, points scoring and leadership, was the remarkable Paul McLean, the latest member of a Queensland family that carved a unique record in rugby service to the state. McLean passed 1000 points for the state in 1982, and only with the emergence of Michael Lynagh, a modern Queensland hero who many would say was the greatest goal-kicker the game has ever seen, have McLean's Queensland records come under threat.

Queensland's success in the 1970s was due in great measure to the influence, skill and popularity of Bob Templeton, the team's coach. Templeton built a reputation as a winning coach who continually strove for higher standards. That he was still involved as a national selector in the 1990s, after having started as state coach more than 20 years before, is a tribute to his talent and popularity.

The Queensland RU has staged internationals on a number of different grounds around Brisbane: the Brisbane Exhibition Ground, the Brisbane Cricket Ground, Lang Park and Ballymore. Queensland rugby was also headquartered for a time in the 1950s at the Brisbane Grammar School's ground at Normanby.

QUINNELL, DEREK
Llanelli and Wales
23 internationals for Wales 1972–80
5 internationals for British Isles 1971–80

One of the big names of Welsh rugby through the 1970s, Quinnell was a rugged and durable forward who could, and did, play in various positions in international matches.

He hit the headlines when he was named for the 1971 British Isles tour to New Zealand as the only uncapped player in the side. While on tour he made his international debut against the All Blacks at Wellington. His first

Derek Quinnell

game for Wales was as a replacement against France in Cardiff in 1972.

In his long career, which included three tours for the British Isles, he played in four teams that beat various All Black sides, which could be a record for a British player – twice in tests for the British Isles, once for the Barbarians and once for his club Llanelli, in its famous game in 1972.

When his playing days were over Quinnell was quickly promoted, first to being a Welsh selector and then as assistant coach of the Welsh team for the Rugby World Cup in 1987.

QUINTUPLE TIE
A quintuple tie in the Five Nations championship has happened only once in the 80 years since France joined the championship in 1910.

In 1972–73 each of the five countries won twice at home and lost twice in away games, so each took four points in the unofficial championship. While some historians record this as a tie between all five countries, others 'give' the title to Scotland on the basis that it scored more match points than any other team.

R

RACING CLUB DE FRANCE

One of the colourful rugby clubs in France. Original club members were cross-country runners through the Bois de Boulogne in Paris. Some of the more eccentric ones used to dress as jockeys and even whip themselves along as they ran! When the formation of a sports club was suggested, the name Racing Club seemed appropriate. So the famous sports club was formed, one that would in time reach a membership of 20,000.

This was in 1890, and within two years the rugby branch of the Racing club had won the French championship – admittedly before the event attracted the national spread of entries which it has had in recent years. In its first 100 years Racing won the national title in 1892, 1900, 1902, and in 1959, under the famous François Moncla.

Racing Club purchased Colombes Stadium in Paris to use for its home matches; France's home internationals were also played there up to 1973.

In the 1920s a number of the club's members were leading players and highly influential in the administration of French rugby: men such as René Crabos, who later became the French rugby president, Adolphe Jaureguy, later a French vice-president, and the legendary Yves du Manoir, of whom there is a statue outside the stadium's main gates. The Racing club organises the annual du Manoir tournament in his memory.

Gérard Dufau, France's most-capped scrumhalf, and Michel Crauste, who was France's most-capped international for a time, also spent some seasons at Racing.

Other notable members were Jean-François Gourdon, a brilliantly wing; the great flanker and captain Jean-Pierre Rives; the 1987 World Cup player, Franck Mesnel; and the modern utility back Jean-Baptiste Lafond.

RAEBURN PLACE

On March 27 1871 the first international rugby match was played at Raeburn Place in Edinburgh, the home ground of the Edinburgh Academical Cricket Club. The decision to have a rugby match on the ground was not one that found unanimous favour with club members and approval was given only after a vote had been taken.

The pitch was only 55 yards wide, which apparently suited Scotland which did not like moving the ball anyway! A crowd of 4000 watched as Scotland won by one try and a goal to one try.

The ground hosted internationals up until 1895, and today is the headquarters of the Edinburgh Academicals Club.

RAMSAY, WILLIAM

The first and, so far the only, man knighted exclusively for services to the game of rugby.

Ramsay served the game in an administrative capacity from the 1920s until his death in 1973. He was present when the first Middlesex Sevens organising committee was formed in 1926 and lived to see that event turned into one of the most spectacular and popular of every English rugby season.

By 1946 he was Middlesex's representative on the RFU and in 1950 he became treasurer, a post he held for 20 years. He became the president in 1954–55, continuing his treasurer's role at the same time. In 1970 he was returned for an unprecedented second term as president, for a period which covered the centenary of the RFU.

Ramsay was known as a brilliant financial administrator and was one of the first to make maximum use of the media for publicity which, it is said, he always welcomed.

He served on the International Rugby Board from 1957 to 1960.

RANFURLY SHIELD

The Ranfurly Shield is a challenge trophy, decided on only one match between New Zealand unions and with the odds stacked heavily in favour of the holder, who has the home ground advantage, is able to arrange a programme at its own convenience, and knows that only an outright win will take the shield. Yet, for all its seeming inequalities, the Ranfurly Shield has evolved an aura, mystique and passion which, to an outsider, may seem slightly unreal.

In 1901 the Governor of New Zealand, Lord Ranfurly, offered a trophy to the New Zealand Rugby Union. The offer was accepted and the trophy commissioned from England. It arrived as a shield – complete with a centre-piece depicting soccer goal-posts and a round football!

With the necessary changes made, the trophy was awarded first to Auckland for its outstanding record in the 1902 season and it did not become subject to a challenge until 1904, when Wellington won the match 6–3. The shield saga was under way.

Before World War I, shield games had to be played at home – and most unions were happy to reap the benefits of good gates – but Wellington successfully sought a change to the system and in 1919 took the shield down to Canterbury, for the afternoon only. Bold Wellington went even better the next year. Not only did it accept a record 12 challenges (the usual is somewhere between seven and nine) but scheduled the games against Taranaki, Auckland, South Canterbury, Otago, Southland and Canterbury to be played away. The battle-weary side finally succumbed to Southland.

Southland eventually returned the favour and duly lost to Wellington. Hawke's Bay then secured the shield and played twice away from home, beating Wellington and Canterbury. But the latter match was won only narrowly, by 17–15, and subsequent holders were persuaded it was safer staying at home!

That remained policy for more than 60 years until the dominance first of Canterbury, and then Auckland, persuaded the administrators to accept overtures from those unions to allow the shield to travel again. It was an instant success: Canterbury lost the shield before it was able to implement the policy, but Auckland won many friends (and matches) away from Eden Park.

Retention of the shield (everyone in New Zealand knows this is the

The Auckland team during the highly successful 1985–90 Ranfurly Shield era.

Ranfurly Shield) generates great enthusiasm and loyalty – and revenue – for the holder. It also provokes considerable discussion about the 'greatest era' and comparisons between the heroes of one generation and another.

The first of the great eras belonged to Auckland, which won 'the Log of Wood' back from Wellington in 1905, then withstood 23 challenges before losing to Taranaki in 1913. After the First World War Hawke's Bay started a great run, taking the trophy from Wellington in the first match of the 1922 season.

Though there were one or two narrow squeaks, the Bay remained invincible, hardly surprisingly as the team contained such great players as George Nepia, Jimmy Mill, Bert Cooke, Maurice and Cyril Brownlie and Lui Paewai. New Zealand representatives sometimes sat on the reserves benches. Under the brilliant coaching of Norman McKenzie (who filled the post from 1916 until 1946) Hawke's Bay rebuffed 24 challenges.

Otago finally won the shield in 1935, and that began a 15-year period in which the trophy stayed in the deep south. Southland, the holder at the outbreak of World War II in 1939, did not lose the shield until 1947 (no games were played in the war years), thus enjoying the 'longest' reign of all.

Otago, which regained 'the Log', defended it 18 times – another great era. Perhaps its finest performance was to turn back six challenges in 1949 with 11 Otago players away with the All Blacks in South Africa.

Canterbury's thumping of Wellington, 24–3, at the end of the 1953 season, marked the beginning of another great run. Including a couple of draws, Canterbury withstood 23 challenges, one short of the Hawke's Bay record. Canterbury fielded virtually a team of internationals, with a hard uncompromising pack, swift outsides and dependable inside backs.

When Auckland lost, and then retrieved the shield in 1960, another great reign was on its way – a record

one, in fact, for Fred Allen guided his team to 25 defences through to 1963. Yet the record run could well have ended in its first season. Canterbury led 18–14 on the stroke of time, but Waka Nathan scored a breathtaking try under the crossbar which was converted to snatch a 19–18 win.

Though Hawke's Bay went some way towards returning to its palmy days of the 1920s, when it held off 20 challenges 1967–69, the next really memorable tenure as Ranfurly Shield champion was enjoyed by Canterbury. After some patchy seasons, Canterbury turned to its old captain and All Black, Alex Wyllie, as coach in 1982. 'Grizz' Wyllie obtained instant results, his team winning the shield from Wellington and embarking on some decisive defences, including a then record thrashing of little North Otago 88–0.

At Wyllie's insistence, Canterbury accepted a challenge from Auckland in 1985 which, if successfully rebuffed, would have set a record of 26 successive defences. Before a record crowd of

52,000 – more than Lancaster Park could really hold – Auckland went to a stunning 24–0 half-time lead, before winning by only 28–23.

Thus began another great reign which, in 1988, beat the record jointly held by Auckland (1960–63) and Canterbury (1982–85) of 25 defences. Appropriately the record-setting match was against Canterbury. By the end of 1990 the Auckland reign, with a team containing such greats as John Kirwan, Grant Fox, Michael Jones, the Whetton brothers, Sean Fitzpatrick, Steve McDowell, Joe Stanley, Zinzan Brooke and Terry Wright, had extended to 40 defences, The team's coach, Maurice Trapp, said he hoped to reach 50!

In the final match of 1990, Canterbury had its hooker ordered off and used a New Zealand domestic rule to decline scrums on safety grounds. The result was a match played at a frenetic pace, with similarities to rugby league and touch. A disorganised Auckland team escaped with a 33–30 victory.

RAVENHILL

The headquarters of Ulster rugby in Belfast, constructed in just 62 days in 1924. One report of the ground's early development suggests it was 'born in haste after a long, slow pregnancy'.

Since the 1890s the Ulster branch members had been urging the Irish Rugby Union to secure such a venue. Early international matches had been played in the Northern Ireland province at Ormeau and at the Royal Ulster Agricultural Society's Balmoral grounds. The Irish union meantime had ambitions to develop Lansdowne Road in Dublin, and there were not the finances to build up first-class grounds in both cities. So Belfast took a back seat.

When the first improvements were completed at Lansdowne Road, encouragement was given to the Ulster plans and nine acres at Ravenhill were levelled with pick and shovel. It was intended that Dublin and Belfast would share home internationals, so a grandstand was built in time for the opening international at Ravenhill, between Ireland and England in 1924. Playing conditions were good, but other facilities were very basic and the players changed in marquees behind the stand. England won 14–3 in what was to be its only appearance in Ulster.

Ireland scored its first win on Ravenhill in 1925 when it beat Wales 19–3. This was the start of reasonably regular games for Ireland on the ground, always against either Wales or France.

A splendid day at the ground came in March 1948 when Ireland, captained by Karl Mullen, edged out Wales by 6–3, to give Ireland the Triple Crown and Grand Slam for the first time in the twentieth century. The scene of jubilation as the Ravenhill crowd lifted their Irish heroes shoulder-high to carry them triumphantly off the field remains one of Ulster rugby's great memories.

The last international was played there in 1954, when Ireland beat Scotland 6–0. After that, dwindling attendances in Belfast and the IRU's preference for the development of Dublin's Lansdowne Road, saw Ravenhill used only for Ulster home games against touring teams and in the Irish provincial championship.

Another special day came in 1972 when the All Blacks ignored political tensions and journeyed north to play Ulster. The Ravenhill welcome to the touring team was warm and appreciative – as it always has been, despite its many disappointments.

REFEREES

In the lawbooks the referee is sole charge of fact. It has not, however, always been that way. In rugby's early days, in the 1870s, the opposing captains would decide the laws before their match, so there was no need for referees at all. Games stopped only when there were breaches of what had previously been agreed by the captains. This led to disagreements and heated arguments so two umpires were introduced (one from each side) to roam the field watching the ebb and flow of the game and to arbitrate when one of the captains protested an infringement had occurred.

This led to further problems, as the question of the umpires' impartiality was often raised. So a third arbitrator was called in to assist and make decisions when the umpires could not agree after one of the captains had protested! Confused? You should be, and so too were the law-makers of the time.

A whistle was introduced for the referee to blow if he approved of a particular protest. Umpires would

raise a stick if they saw an infringement. If the other umpire did not raise his stick the referee would be left to decide the issue. A blast on the whistle would indicate that the referee upheld the protest. It was not until 1893 that the referee could blow his whistle for what he himself judged to be an infringement, regardless of what the umpires thought. With the whistle allowed and the referee having powers of independent decision-making, the role of the two umpires diminished. The referee had effectively risen above their authority.

The role of the solo referee evolved until 1906 when it came to resemble, more or less, what it is today. The umpires were retired to the sidelines, where they remain today for most club, first-class or international fixtures. For years there was always one line umpire from each of the two teams assigned to a match. (Later they were called flagmen or touch judges). Even in the 1960s international touring teams provided a reserve player to fulfill that function. Today line umpires carry on the tradition of holding a stick or small flag to signify the ball being out of play or rough play noted.

Modern referees are an extension of that orginal whistle-blower of 1893, although their task is vastly more intricate and exacting than before. To-

Respected French referee, Francis Palmade.

day the referee is generally a fit athlete who dresses in a smart uniform which is intended to give the impression of confidence and authority.

The poor referee has always been subjected to scorn and ridicule from fans on the sideline or in the grandstands. Now, via television, referees of international games are under the scrutiny of millions of armchair judges as well, many of whom claim to know every one of the 28 laws in a fat rugby lawbook. With so much prestige and honour riding on the outcome of modern games, at club, national or international level, referees' gestures and decisions can upset or anger. The standardisation of refereeing hand signals, so that language difficulties are lessened, has helped immensely. For television, the use of a microphone hidden in the referees' clothing for the purpose of informing commentators has also been a useful tool in easing the difficulties of law interpretations.

Referees form a part of rugby society which, sadly, is not always embraced or included by the players. In most countries the referees form a separate society or association and their social life, so much part of the game, is often divided from officials and players. Yet referees remain a cheerful lot who seem to relish the test of trying to control 30 vigorous players in sometimes boisterous pursuit of victory. The satisfaction for referees is to do the job well and enjoy their role, and of course not to over-penalise the home team!

There have been many personalities among the top referees of rugby.

John Dallas (Scotland) made the decision not to award a try to New Zealand's Bob Deans at Cardiff in 1905, and a controversy raged thereafter between the two countries. Many said that Mr Dallas was too old to keep up with the play as it swept downfield in that particular international, but in fact he was only 27 years old. He wore street clothes with flat shoes which might have impeded his progress on a slippery field.

Albert Freethy (Wales) was courageous enough to send Cyril Brownlie off in the England v New Zealand match at Twickenham for rough play – the first such dismissal in rugby's

history. The then Prince of Wales, who was at Twickenham that day, tried to intervene to have the New Zealander returned to the field of play but this was not permitted. Freethy also refereed the Olympic Games final in Paris in 1924 between the United States and France, along with 16 other international games.

Cyril Gadney (England) had the rare distinction of refereeing before and after World War II. He controlled 13 internationals and no fewer than six Oxford v Cambridge University matches. He also controlled the first match played by the Barbarians club, v Australia in 1948.

Gwynne Walters (Wales) was the man who set a new mark in achievement for top referees. He controlled 23 internationals between 1959 and 1966, beating the old 'record' of 21 tests controlled by **Ray Williams** (Ireland) between 1957–64.

Kevin Kelleher (Ireland) equalled that mark in 1971 after refereeing internationals for 11 years. Kelleher's name will forever be associated in New Zealand minds with the sending off of Colin Meads in the New Zealand v Scotland game in 1967.

Kerry Fitzgerald (Australia) gained distinction for being honoured with the whistle in the first Rugby World Cup final between New Zealand and Australia in 1987 in Auckland.

Clive Norling (Wales) equalled the record of 23 internationals, shared by Kelleher and Walters, in 1990. Norling started with the Ireland v New Zealand match in 1978 and was still going strong 13 years later.

REFEREES, NEUTRAL

In countries outside Britain, neutral rugby referees are a relatively new phenomenon. It was not until the late 1970s that New Zealand, Australia and South Africa had 'neutrals' control all test matches. Previously internationals in those countries (with a few exceptions) were the domain of 'home' referees. This led to some outcries of protest when 'home' teams won the games controlled by fellow countrymen.

New Zealanders grumbled about South African referees every time they toured South Africa; South Africans did the same when they went to New Zealand. The Welsh complained bitterly about New Zealand referees on their first tour 'down under' in 1969; so did the French in 1961. New Zealanders did not like Australian referees . . . The list could go on. The problem of charge and counter-charge was largely eliminated by the time a panel of neutral referees controlled the first Rugby World Cup in 1987.

The first neutral referee was H.L. Robinson, an Irishman who was invited to control the Calcutta Cup match between England and Scotland at Manchester in 1882. The previous year's game had been controlled in Edinburgh by the Scottish RU's president, D.H. Watson. There was a controversial try to Scotland late in the game, when the English players thought an offside should have been awarded. That try forced a draw in the game and England's players and officials became the first to cast aspersions in public about a 'biased' referee. Since then most internationals played in the Five Nations championship have been whistled by a disinterested neutral, though this move was a long time coming in other places in the rugby world, probably due to isolation and travel difficulties.

The first neutral referee of an international rugby match outside Britain was W.G. 'Gun' Garrard. Garrard, London-born but living in New Zealand, was attending a referees' course in Sydney when he was invited to control the match between Australia and the touring Great Britain team in June 1899. Australia won the match, 13–3. Even as a neutral, Garrard was not spared criticism: the British captain, the Rev. Matthew Mullineux, strongly disagreed with the call on the first of the Australian tries.

RENWICK, JIM
Hawick and Scotland
52 internationals for Scotland 1972–84
1 international for British Isles 1980

His hairline receded until he was practically bald, and sometimes he might have looked anything but a rugby player, but Jim Renwick was a brilliant, dashing centre who was a regular and popular member of the Scottish team in the 1970s and 1980s.

Borders stalwart, Jim Renwick

When he ended his career he had become Scotland's most-capped player and the world's most-capped centre. He won 52 caps for Scotland and one for the British Isles while on tour to South Africa in 1980.

Surprisingly he was in the winning team in only 18 of his Scottish internationals, such was the state of Scottish rugby at the time. The poor ratio of successes had little to do with Renwick; he was, as always, a delight to watch with his speed and flair.

Renwick scored a try for Scotland on his international debut, against France at Murrayfield in 1972, and scored eight test tries in all. He was also Scotland's part time goal-kicker, and something of a snap-shot dropped goal specialist.

REPLACEMENTS

Replacements coming onto the field to take the place of injured players are accepted at all levels today. But things were not always that way.

It is not recorded why replacements were not originally allowed for injured players – perhaps it had to do with nineteenth century concepts of 'manliness' and 'toughness' – but it was only in 1968 that the laws were changed to allow a replacement to come onto the field in an international match.

In previous years, many an international match became hopelessly lop-sided when injuries caused one side to outnumber the other. Perhaps the worst example was in 1950, when injuries reduced the New Zealand forward pack to just six players in the third test against the British Isles. One of the New Zealanders, Johnny Simpson, had badly smashed a knee and did not play again. He left the field and, by law, was unable to be replaced. Then a second player, All Black captain Ron Elvidge, became hurt. Elvidge felt he could not leave his side even though he had a seriously injured collar-bone, so he stayed on the field, possibly endangering his health (and he was a doctor). He wandered about in midfield while six forwards battled eight in the opposition pack. (A New Zealand loose forward had gone to the wing to keep the number of backs even.) Although the situation was turned into an All Black folk story when the injured Elvidge went over for a try to narrowly win the game, the risk factor convinced New Zealand administrators that substitutes (as they were called then) should be allowed at all levels in the game.

New Zealand had earlier had a private arrangement for replacements in some of their post-war test matches with Australia; one game in 1946 had seen three replacements come onto the field, one from New Zealand and two from Australia.

Further fuel was added to New Zealand's case in 1965, when a highly talented New Zealand Universities team played South Africa in a tour match in Auckland. No fewer than three Universities players retired hurt, thus leaving them with 12 men to play 15. The result was a 55–11 thrashing of the 12-a-side team!

Thankfully commonsense prevailed in 1968, much to the delight of the New Zealand delegates to the International Rugby Board. On June 8 1968, Mike Gibson of Ireland, playing for the British Isles, came on in the first test against South Africa in Pretoria, replacing the injured Barry John. This added yet another 'record' to Mike Gibson's list – it was the first time a replacement had been permitted in a full international.

A week later, an equally famous rugby name, All Black Ian Kirkpatrick, came on to replace his captain Brian Lochore in the first test against Australia. Kirkpatrick underlined the value of having a fresh man on the field by scoring three tries, still a record for a replacement player in a test.

Following the alteration of the law, two players were permitted to come onto the field from either side in any test match. A sideline doctor had to authorise that the player going off was 'sufficiently hurt'. The number of replacements in internationals was extended to three per side in 1989.

RHODESIA

The Rhodesia Rugby Football Union was formed in 1895 as part of the South African Rugby Board. The new body struggled through its early years against a background of the Matabele and Mashona rebellions, and the Anglo-Boer War, 1899–1902. But after those conflicts Rhodesia's progress as a strong and sometimes powerful rugby province was only disrupted by the two world wars.

In the early days life was hard for those who wanted to play rugby in Rhodesia. Indeed, the first games were played by the pioneers in their great marches from the Cape Colony. Later there were reports of 600-mile treks in mule-drawn carts for travelling teams!

In 1898 the first Rhodesian team was chosen to tour to South Africa. Intermittent entries were also made in the South African Currie Cup competition between 1898 and 1914.

An annual interprovincial match sprang up between Mashonaland and Matabeleland, which was later developed into a four way interprovincial tournament, along with teams from Midlands and Manicaland. Each of the provinces had its time as the 'top dog' in Rhodesian rugby.

In 1911 there was a political division into Northern and South Rhodesia and players of the south were thereafter called 'Rhodesian' players. The two provinces remained separate unions until 1946, when they merged again.

Rhodesia's first match against an overseas touring team was in 1910, when the British Isles won at Bulawayo by 24–11. Great Britain also won, 16–3, in 1924. Then came the first appearances against New Zealand and Australia. In 1928 the All Blacks beat Rhodesia 44–8 and in 1933 Australia won 24–5. The British won again by 45–11 in 1938.

It was not until 1949 that success over a touring team came for the colony. Rhodesia played two games against Fred Allen's All Blacks. In the first, at Bulawayo, Rhodesia scored a thrilling 10–8 win and in the return game in Salisbury a 3–3 draw was played. Rhodesians claimed a moral victory as their only score, a dropped goal, had always had a value of four points, and was only changed back to three points during 1948!

The team that beat New Zealand is still called 'Rhodesia's greatest.' Even in New Zealand history books the two matches are recorded as being classics for their inventiveness and excitement. The crowds in Salisbury were the largest to have ever gathered in the city.

Because Rhodesia was affiliated to the SARB, Rhodesian players could play for the Springboks. Two to do so featured in the games against New Zealand: Ryk van Schoor, a very hard tackling centre who played 12 tests, and Jacobus 'Salty' du Rand, who was eventually to total 21 internationals between 1949 and 1956. He captained South Africa in the first test in New Zealand in 1956.

The 1949 Rhodesian fullback was Joe Pretorius, whose matches against New Zealand were the first he had played in first-class rugby. He was courageous and safe, performing some famous feats. The captain, John Morkel, was another outstanding forward.

In 1953 three matches were played against the Australian touring team for two losses and an 8–8 drawn match. In 1955 there were two narrow losses to the British Isles. The 1960 All Blacks reversed the results of 1949, winning twice in the colony.

In 1965 Rhodesia won again against a major touring team when it beat Argentina's first touring side in Southern Africa, by 17–12. Other wins of significance were against Italy (42–4) in 1973 and the United States Cougars (32–15) in 1978.

The last match Rhodesia played under that name was against Orange Free State in a Currie Cup match in 1979. Later that season, political changes meant a name change as well, and Zimbabwe Rhodesia came into being. That name lasted until 1980 when 'Rhodesia' was finally dropped for good.

In all, Rhodesia contributed eight full Springbok test players: 'Salty' du Rand, 21 tests 1949–56; Ryk van Schoor, 12 tests 1949–53; Ron Hill, seven tests 1960–63; Ray Mordt, six tests 1980; Ian Robertson, five tests 1974–76; Andy McDonald, five tests 1965; David Smith, four tests 1980; Des van Jaarsveldt, one test 1960. Mordt eventually moved to South Africa and totalled 18 internationals for that country up until 1984.

See also ZIMBABWE.

RIBERE, EUGENE
Perpignan, Quillan and France
34 internationals for France 1924–33

A speedy French loose forward who had to wait three years for his first win in the national colours. His debut was against Ireland in 1924 and he was the French captain from 1929 to 1933. His final total of caps became the French record for the years between the two world wars. His record total stood until 1954, when it was passed by the great Jean Prat.

He had the distinction of captaining France in 1931 in its last match in the Five Nations series for 16 years. After that the French were banned from the championship until 1947 because of accusations that the affairs of the FFR were not being run in a truly amateur way.

Ribère played for two more seasons for France, being further capped in their matches against Germany in

1932 and 1933. Altogether he led his country 12 times for eight wins.

RICHMOND RFC
A club which played a significant role in rugby's development, Richmond was formed in 1861, 10 years before the Rugby Football Union was established. Richmond joined with Blackheath in 1866 to abolish the hacking rule, thus contributing to the game's resemblance its modern appearance.

Richmond provided the first president, secretary and treasurer when the RFU was formed in 1871. The president was Algernon Rutter, who was only 29 at the time, and served in the role for three seasons.

The first secretary of the RFU was Edwin H. Ash, who was one of Richmond's founders and who won appreciation for the way in which he commandeered the Richmond Green ground for the playing of rugby. He simply went to the ground and erected rugby goal-posts there, every Saturday for 10 years!

In the first 110 years of the Richmond club more than 100 members played international rugby, and not just for England. Peter Kininmonth was the most capped, with 21 caps for Scotland as a loose forward from 1949 to 1954. In 1975 Chris Ralston won his 22nd cap as a lock for England, to become Richmond's most senior international in the club's first 130 years.

Other famous players to wear the distinctive old gold, red and black hooped jerseys include 'Nim' Hall, Peter Cranmer, Alan Rotherham, Christopher Tanner, Arthur ('Monkey') Gould, and Tommy Bedford, the South African.

The club's headquarters are at the Richmond Athletic Ground in Surrey.

RINGLAND, TREVOR
Ballymena and Ireland
34 internationals for Ireland 1981–88
1 international for British Isles 1983

A hard-working player who in 1988 set a new record for most caps won by an Irishman playing in the wing position. The previous mark, 25 caps, was shared by Alan Duggan and Tom Grace. Trevor Ringland made his international debut in 1981 against Australia and, apart from one game when he was injured, he never missed an appearance for Ireland until the

Irish wing, Trevor Ringland

Jean-Pierre Rives, his appearance testimony to the total commitment with which he played.

end of his career. He toured to New Zealand with the British Isles in 1983 but was only required to play in the first international.

He was one of the Irish players invited to play in the IRB centenary in 1986, appearing for the British Isles against the Rest of the World, then for the Five Nations against the Overseas XV.

Ringland appeared in all Ireland's games in the first World Cup tournament in Australia and New Zealand in 1987.

RIVES, JEAN-PIERRE
Toulouse, Racing Club and France
59 internationals for France 1975–84

Not only was Rives one of the world's great flankers in the 1970s and 80s, but he was also a charismatic leader of French teams. He completed his career by setting a world record for the most appearances as a captain in international matches, 34 in all. Jean-Pierre Rives was also one of the most easily

distinguishable players in world rugby with his shock of long, blond hair.

He was a superb openside flanker with dashing style and speed, with courage at the tackle and excellent tactical vision. It was often easy to pick out Rives at the end of any international match, for more often than not he would be the French player with his face covered in blood, testimony to the many times he would throw his body fearlessly in the direction of the ball or its carrier.

His spirit belied his size – he was slightly built for a forward, at 1.78 metres tall (5ft 10in) and weighing 83 kilos (13 stone).

Rives made his debut in international play in 1975 when he played against England as part of a brilliant French team which scored its biggest total on Twickenham that day, winning 27–20. Rives was such a success that his future was secure. Eleven of his first 13 internationals were victories for France. In that time he had his share of injuries, missing the 1975

tour of South Africa and the 1977 home tests against New Zealand.

In his early days he was part of a formidable trio of loose forwards, the others being Jean-Pierre Bastiat and Jean-Claude Skrela. The three played together in 18 internationals.

Rives succeeded Bastiat as the French captain early in the 1978–79 season and captained France until he retired from the game in 1984.

His most satisfying season would no doubt have been 1981, when France, under his leadership, won the Grand Slam. He also played brilliantly in France's win over the All Blacks, in the 'Bastille Day' test in Auckland in 1979.

Rives became France's most-capped flanker, beating the previous record held by Michel Crauste.

After his retirement Rives remained a headliner in French society. Several books were written about him and he starred in several films. He was also a sculptor in metal, his works being exhibited widely.

ROBERTSON, BRUCE
Counties and New Zealand
34 internationals for N. Zealand 1972–81

New Zealand's most-capped centre when he retired before the New Zealand v South Africa test series in 1981, a series Robertson refused to play on principle.

Though dogged by injuries, he was chosen for the All Blacks whenever available, until surprisingly omitted from the 1980 tour to Australia. But the Counties stalwart still made the trip when called on as a replacement, and he immediately made the test side. Had injury not kept Robertson out of the sole 1975 test against Scotland, he would have played internationals in 10 consecutive years, a rare feat for a midfield back.

Some doubt whether New Zealand has ever fielded a finer centre, and comparisons are only made in terms of great players such as Bert Cooke, Johnny Smith or Joe Stanley. Beautiful hands, the ability either to glide or to explode through a gap, and fine service to his wings, were Robertson trademarks.

Robertson scored 34 tries for New Zealand and kicked two dropped goals.

He played 102 matches for the All Blacks, his tour selectors juggling his programme so that Robertson's century came up when he led the side on to the National Stadium for the Wales centenary test.

ROBERTSON, KEITH
Melrose and Scotland
44 internationals for Scotland 1978–89

A sharp and stylish Scottish three-quarter who eventually had 11 seasons in international rugby, winning 20 caps as a centre and 24 as a wing.

Robertson came into the Scottish team for its match against Graham Mourie's Grand Slam All Black team in 1978, a game played in what must have been the worst lighting conditions for an international ever. It was so dark, even Robertson could have played badly and no one would have noticed!

Robertson was part of Scotland's Grand Slam winning team of 1984 and one of his five tours for Scotland was to the inaugural Rugby World Cup in New Zealand in 1987.

Bruce Robertson, in Counties colours.

He scored eight tries in internationals and continued to represent his country until he was 34, a considerable age for a back to be still at the top. He was a loyal member of the Melrose club in the Scottish Borders area.

RODRIGUEZ, ENRIQUE
Cordoba and Argentina; New South
   Wales and Australia
15 internationals for Argentina 1977–83
8 internationals for Sth America 1980–84
26 internationals for Australia 1984–87

At home in Argentina the rugby public called him 'Topo' and he was a hugely popular rugby figure, playing 15 tests for the Pumas. Later in his career, after emigrating to live in Australia, he won the same status as a favourite there.

A superb scrummaging loosehead prop, Rodriguez toured for the Pumas to New Zealand, England, France, and Australia between 1977 and 1983. He also went to South Africa with the South American teams of the early 1980s.

Australian rugby officials were delighted when he chose to emigrate to Australia after touring there in 1983. He was the first American, North or South, to play for Australia.

By 1984 he was included in the Wallaby touring party to Fiji. Later in the same year he became a cornerstone of Australia's scrummage in all four internationals with the Grand Slam-winning Wallaby team in Britain. Rodriguez also played for Australia in New Zealand in 1986 when the Bledisloe Cup was lifted by two test victories to one. New Zealanders also considered him a scrummage expert.

'Topo' hung on through 1987 and the Rugby World Cup series, and to his great joy he was chosen to return to Argentina with the touring team of his new country.

He played an invaluable role for Australia on that tour, both on the field and off it, as unoffical interpreter. His final two international matches were in fact against his old team-mates, the Pumas, in Buenos Aires.

RODRIGUEZ, LAURENT
Mont-de-Marsan, Montferrand, Dax and
   France
56 internationals for France 1981–90

Laurent Rodriguez was one of the most versatile forwards in French history, and a powerful hard-driving player who appeared in four different positions in the various French test packs of the 1980s. His driving, bullocking runs off the back of scrums, rucks and mauls became a familiar pattern for French teams in that time.

His first international was in 1981 against Australia in Sydney, when he appeared as a flanker. He won 20 caps as a flanker in all, three as a lock and 33 as a No. 8. He also played part of a test as a prop, in the 1984 match with Ireland, after his confrère Jean-Pierre Garuet had been sent off. Rodriguez captained France six times.

In the early days of his career he struggled somewhat to hold down his position in the top French team, but the famous win by the French over the All Blacks at Nantes in 1986 sealed his place. Rodriguez was a member of the French team in the Rugby World Cup final of 1987, scoring four tries in the tournament.

He was one of a number of modern footballers who loathed air travel. There is a story of how he once drove his car from Montferrand to Bordeaux to fly to Paris for a match. At the airport he was apparently struck with a bad case of flying nerves, so instead of flying he then drove a further 600 kilometres to Paris!

ROGERS, 'BUDGE'
Bedford and England
34 internationals for England 1961–69
2 internationals for British Isles 1962

His given names were Derek Prior, but throughout the rugby world he was known as 'Budge'.

Rogers was a flanker who one writer described as 'one of the greatest harrying forwards the game has ever known'. His career total of 34 caps for England beat the old mark which had stood for 42 years (held by Wavell Wakefield) and set a new one which stood until John Pullin made a new total in 1974.

Rogers made his international debut in 1961. He captained England seven times and also toured South Africa with the Lions in 1962, playing in two tests.

He played through a time when the laws of the game were changed to give less scope to a destructive type of side row play. Rogers had perfected just such a game, known these days as 'open-sided' play. In fact there were some who said the rules were changed precisely to curb him – perhaps the game's lawmakers had seen too much of him destroying opposition backlines in English club competition! Whatever the changes, they were no problem to 'Budge' Rogers. He was always a strong and powerful force in the England forward game of the 1960s.

After his retirement Rogers continued to contribute to rugby. He was England's coach and selector for years and later was awarded an OBE for his services to the game.

ROLLO, DAVID
Howe of Fife and Scotland
40 internationals for Scotland 1959–68

A tough Fifeshire farmer who played 40 internationals for his country in the front row. He was a strong and durable type, a key man in the scrum as a tighthead prop. In the lean years of the sixties he was a consistent force in the Scottish forwards.

He played for nine seasons for the Scottish team and only injury in 1962 and again in 1967 prevented his 40 internationals from being played consecutively. When he retired, his total equalled Hugh McLeod's record for a Scottish player in any position. He and McLeod were together in Scotland's front row for four seasons.

Rollo toured twice to South Africa, once with Scotland in 1960 and once with the British Isles in 1962. He was the first player from the Howe of Fife club to play international rugby.

ROMANIA
Although rugby originated in England, Romania owes much of its beginnings in the game to the French. Students travelling home to Romania after sojourns to Paris in the early twentieth century took back knowledge of the game to their friends.

The Romanian federation was formed in 1914, but could make little progress while Europe was fighting the Great War. But in the early years after the war Romania stepped up its rugby activity. There are records which show it as a national team playing France in 1919, losing by 5–48. However, there is no record of the French treating this game as a full international. On the contrary, they claim it as a match between two army sides.

Romania entered a team in the 1924 Olympics, where the losing margin was worse (either 3–59 or 3–61 – depending on which book you read), and the Romanians finished third out of the three teams taking part at the games.

After World War II, real progress was made. Before 1957 Romania's internationals were restricted to countries like Czechoslovakia, Yugoslavia and East Germany, but in 1957 France came to play the national team in Bucharest for the first time since 1938. That there was a 'B' soccer international to follow may have had something to do with the 95,000 fans that turned out.

In front of the huge crowd Romania gave a brave account of itself, and was narrowly beaten in a tight one-try game by 15–18.

Romania gave France many tough games about this time – and remember that France was probably at its most powerful in the late 1950s. Romania had a great day in Bucharest in 1960, when it scored a huge upset over France, beating it for the first time, 11–5. It was the start of an annual match between the two countries. The 1960 win also marked the first in a sequence of four games when France could not beat the Romanians (two were drawn games) up to 1964.

Domestically, the Romanians put great emphasis on the league and club system. At the peak of their rugby in the the 1970s, there were over 200 teams playing throughout the league with two clubs, Steaua (the army) and Dinamo (the Ministry of the Interior) dominant.

Further expansion came in the 1970s when Romania made its first ventures outside Europe. It went to Argentina in 1973, to New Zealand in 1975 and to Wales in 1979, and made an excellent impression in all those countries, giving several reputations a fright. It drew with the New Zealand juniors 10–10 and lost narrowly to a Welsh XV by 12–13.

But the 1980s had many twists and turns brought about by political and financial upheavals at home. In the early years of the decade Romania had some moments of great honour. It drew with Ireland 13–13 in Dublin in 1980, then beat France later in the same year in Bucharest by 15–0 and again in 1982 by 13–9. It next beat Wales in a full international in Bucharest by 24–6 in 1983, and shocked the Grand Slam-winning Scotland team by winning 28–22 in 1984. But from then on there was an alarming slip-back in form, a slide which coincided with difficult days at home.

The national federation was run by specially placed government-appointed officials, instead of rugby club members. The country's economic woes hit rugby hard, as the game was entirely state funded, and when budgets were cut there was a real threat to the continuation of the international fixture list.

There was even one story of a Romanian team flying in a chartered jet plane to Dublin to play an international – without enough money to buy fuel for the flight home. There was also not enough money for a decent length of stay before the game or for reasonable room rates. It is no wonder that Ireland won the game 60–0.

In the inaugural World Cup in 1987, Romania took a team rebuilt after the Dublin farce. In New Zealand the team scored a 21–20 win over Zimbabwe, but then took two thrashings (12–55 against France, and 28–55 against Scotland) which did nothing for its dwindling confidence.

Gheorghe Dumitru wins the ball against Wales, 1983. Romania won the game 24–6, one of its finest victories.

The fall of the Ceaucescu regime in 1989 resulted in a rugby silence from Romania for a time. Then came the news that in the street battles that had taken place all over the country, several significant rugby personalities had died. The most notable on the world scene was Florica Murariu, who had played in the World Cup (and scored two tries against Scotland in Dunedin) and had captained his country to an historic away win in Cardiff over Wales in December 1988. He died in a roadblock incident while returning to his army unit. Another former Romanian captain, Raducu Durbac, was another who perished.

Since then stories have emerged of the years of neglect the game had suffered at the hands of the previous rulers. Funding had slipped to the point where boots and balls could not be bought because hard currency could not be spent. Grounds and training facilities had slipped into neglect. It was even said that the players lacked the drive to play 80 minutes of rugby because they had not been regularly eating a true athlete's diet.

Major changes are occurring to Romanian sports since the fall of the communist government. Budgets for sports federations have been increased to allow them to rebuild the domestic club scene. A priority has been to restore Romania's pride on the international scene. This was to take more time. Romania cancelled its 1990 tours to New Zealand and Japan and rescheduled them for 1991 – World Cup year.

Then in May 1990 came a surprise stimulation for the game. At Auch (Jacques Fouroux's old club), Romania beat a full strength French team by 12–6 – its first win on French soil. Further encouragement came in October 1990, when the team qualified to play in France's section of the 1991 World Cup.

Those wins in 1990 were a surprise, given that only months before the whole country had been on its knees, at the point almost of self-destruction. But this proud and honourable country has shown before that it can come back. In rugby, the wins over France and World Cup qualification proved that the recovery had started already.

Men from the past who have given their guts for the game – Arthur Vogel, Viorel Moraru, Valeriu Trimescu, Mircea Paraschiv, Mihai Bucos, Gheorghe Dumitru, Theodor Radulescu and his son Alexandru, and many others – would all have approved of the way the climb back from the floor had begun.

ROMEU, JEAN-PIERRE
Montferrand and France
34 internationals for France 1972–77

Jean-Pierre Romeu made his debut for his country in 1972 for the match against Romania, landing four successful goals. He was not required again by the top French team until the next season, but thereafter he became a regular choice as flyhalf or fullback and a regular points-gatherer for the French team until 1977. He was a sturdy and reliable performer, especially as a tactical kicker.

By the time he retired he was France's top points scorer in internationals. His best totals were 20 points against Argentina in 1975 and 25 points v USA in 1976. His final total was 265, nearly 100 points better than the previous record (175 points set by Michel Vannier 1953–61).

Romeu was later a French selector.

ROOS, PAUL
Western Province and South Africa
4 internationals for South Africa 1903–06

Though he enjoyed a relatively brief career, and does not enjoy a reputation as one of South Africa's finest flankers, Paul Roos has a secure place in that nation's rugby history.

He was chosen for the vital final test against Mark Morrison's touring 1903 British side, not a selection universally welcomed and credited by the cynical to the captain 'Fairy' Heatlie promoting fellow Western Province players.

Roos became captain of Western Province. He had a chequered playing record at the time: a schoolteacher, he was based for a while in the bundu and cycled every Saturday the 113 km (70 miles) from Rustenberg to Pretoria for a game!

He was deeply religious and refused to play on Sundays, turning down Western Province representation at one point because the match involved Sunday travel.

He did not even attend the 1906 South African trials, but was chosen for the first side to tour Britain, the players electing him captain on a unanimous vote. He coined the name 'Springboks' or 'De Springbokken' for the benefit of the British media on that tour, and the name has stuck, Roos missed the (lost) Scottish international and retired soon afterwards.

His brother, Gideon, became a Springbok in 1910.

But Paul Roos remained an influential figure in South African rugby, rising to the vice-presidency of the South African Rugby Board. He was the manager of the first Junior Springboks, who toured Argentina in 1932, and in 1937 sent a famous cable

to captain Philip Nel on the eve of the third and final test against the All Blacks. It simply exhorted Nel to 'scrum, scrum, scrum,' and Nel – having a choice in those days of scrummaging instead of having a lineout – did just that to score a famous victory.

Roos became a respected politician in the ruling Nationalist party, and died in 1948, succeeded in Parliament by an old team-mate, Bob Loubser. He remains one of South Africa's most revered figures.

ROQUES, ALFRED
Cahors and France
30 internationals for France 1958–63

Alfred Roques was on the losing team in an international only three times in 30 appearances. He was an immensely powerful prop who didn't begin playing tests until he was 33, having been a local club soccer player until he was 26!

Nicknamed 'The Rock', Roques was one of the first of France's hard-nosed props. Before him there were few who

Two of the grand early characters of South African rugby: Paul Roos, right, and Theo Pienaar, captain of the first Springboks to tour New Zealand in 1921.

relished working hard at the physical parts of the forward game. His most significant contributions were in the French tests against South Africa in 1958, and in the Five Nations championship wins in 1959, 1961 and 1962.

When he made his last appearance for France, against Scotland in 1963, he was one month short of his 38th birthday.

ROSSLYN PARK RFC

Formed in 1879, Rosslyn Park has risen to be one of the more glamorous and social clubs of English rugby, building a reputation for fielding many teams and giving any willing player a game, especially during the two world wars.

From its beginnings at a ground near the Hampstead Heath station, the club moved in 1894 to the Old Deer Park in Richmond. After 1957 it was headquartered at Roehampton for a time, and is now based at Priory Lane in Upper Richmond Road.

There are several references in history books to Rosslyn Park being a 'missionary' rugby club. In 1892 it was the first English rugby club to play in France, and in 1911 it took the game into Austria and Hungary, where it had never been seen before. Exhibition matches were played in Prague, Budapest and Vienna and the team travelled 3000 miles in 10 days! Later, Rosslyn Park was the first English club to play in the United States.

Surprisingly, for a club that soon won status for being superbly run by its early officials (only 15 secretaries in its first 100 years), and for having the largest playing membership of any club in the world (in the 1930s), it was not until 1937 that the first international player was contributed to English ranks. Wing Ernest Unwin won four caps and later travelled to South Africa with the British Isles team.

By the early 1950s Rosslyn Park's team could boast an all-international three-quarter line: John V. Smith, Brian Boobbyer, and Christopher Winn (all of England) with George Phipps (Ireland). Smith was president of the RFU in 1985.

Many consider the 10 years after World War II to have been the best in the club's history.

Other prominent rugby men who played in the red and white hoops of Rosslyn Park include the Russian prince, Alexander Obolensky, Bruce Neale, Peter Warfield and John Ranson, all England internationals, and Ted Hunt and John Burges, the Irish internationals and club stalwarts.

At the end of the club's first 110 years, its most-capped player, with 24 internationals for England, was the dapper and unconventional loose forward Andy Ripley, who also toured South Africa with the 1974 British Lions.

The club marked its centenary in 1979 with an international schoolboys seven-a-side tournament – appropriate as fostering the interests of young players has always been a high priority for the club.

'The club,' wrote the famous England player, W.J.A. (Dave) Davies, in a foreword to the club's history of its first 50 years, 'will always occupy a unique place in the history of the English game because of its annual dinner – the outstanding social event in the rugby football calendar.'

ROUX, 'MANNETJIES'

Western Province, Northern Transvaal and South Africa
27 internationals for Sth Africa 1960–70

His given names were Francois du Toit, but throughout his rugby life he was known as 'Mannetjies' or 'Mannie'. Blessed with aggression and speed, he was a fast, exciting wing and centre three-quarter. He was as tough as teak, a ferocious tackler and an uncompromising midfield man, becoming one of South Africa's most admired players through the 1960s.

His international debut was against Wales on the South African tour to Britain in 1960–61. He soon developed a reputation there as a tough tackler and one of rugby's hard men. In 1962, one tackle he made on Lion Richard Sharp, broke Sharp's jaw. Not everybody in the British camp agreed that the tackle was fair – not the only time in his career that strong words were levelled at Roux's manner on the field.

ROWLANDS, CLIVE

Pontypool, Swansea and Wales
14 internationals for Wales 1963–65

A real character of Welsh rugby who has given a lifetime to the game and has achieved honour from it in various spheres.

Rowlands played for his country 14 times, on each occasion as captain. He was a lively scrumhalf with the ability to motivate players – some close to him said he did this chiefly by appealing to the players' Welsh nationalism. He had strong views on tactics, not always promoting attractive rugby, but always dedicated totally to a desire for glory for Wales.

Within three years of retiring from playing the game, Rowlands was the Welsh international team's coach, a position he held with great success from 1968–74. Then followed five years as a selector, with another three-year term from 1982.

He also was an accomplished international team manager, taking Wales to Australia in 1978 and to the World Cup in New Zealand in 1987. 'Top Cat' Rowlands also managed the highly successful Lions team to Australia in 1989. The latest accolade came in 1990 when Rowlands was appointed chairman of the Welsh Rugby Union.

Immediately on taking that office Rowlands was embroiled in a controversy over Welsh players heading for a World XV tour of South Africa. He resigned for a time in protest at the actions of some Welsh players and officials, but when the wrangle died down, he was back in charge, once again a central figure in Welsh rugby, as he had been since the early 1960s.

RUCK, THE

A fast, sure and ruthless way of winning possession of a loose or tackled ball.

Rucks were born in New Zealand, particularly in Otago in the South Island. The technique was taken into the All Blacks by the Otago forwards of the late 1940s, and soon rucking became known as a feature of the New Zealand style of play. For years the rest of the rugby world could only watch and marvel. Only much later did teams from outside New Zealand take to rucking as a way to win the ball.

The basic requirements of rucking are to approach the ball at speed with body bent low at the waist and with shoulders hunched in a dynamic drive over the ball, while gripping one or more team-mates and staying on one's feet. Such a forceful attack drives the opposition backwards and lets the ball be walked over or heeled back to the halfback.

Top: Scotland v France, Rugby World Cup, 1987. Below left: The Scottish front row: Iain Milne, Colin Deans and David Sole. Right: Scotland playing against Zimbabwe at the World Cup; Alan Tait scoring. Peter Bush

Top: Scotland v New Zealand, second test 1990. The Grand Slam-winning Scots put on an impressive display in their two-test series with New Zealand, but though they ran the All Blacks close, they still had to concede two losses. Fotopacific Below, left: Skipper of Scotland's famous 1990–91 team, David Sole. Right: Roy Laidlaw: 47 caps for Scotland. Peter Bush

'Football at Rugby', 1870.

Rucks have often been misunderstood, critics seeing them as dirty play. Far from it – a ruck executed well by three or four forwards, all with feet flying, while certainly no place to stay around in, is a thing of beauty! (So say New Zealanders anyway.)

Vic Cavanagh, an Otago coach of the 1940s, is regarded as the father of the ruck who put into practice techniques his father, Vic senior, had taught him. Rucking became synonymous with Cavanagh's name and Otago's game.

RUGBY SCHOOL

It is widely accepted, but never confirmed as a proven fact, that William Webb Ellis, a student at Rugby School in Warwickshire, England, started the game named after the school, by picking up the ball and running with it towards the opposing team.

Certainly, at that time, 'football' rules were constantly evolving and changing. Some time between 1830–40, running forward with the ball in a player's hands 'obtained a customary status' under the laws of the school football game.

Past students of Rugby School took the idea of the game to other public schools and then to Oxford and Cambridge where the game developed, always with old Rugbeians to guide it along. Indeed, when the Rugby Football Union was formed in 1871, three old boys of the school, E.C. Holmes, L.J. Maton and A.E. Rutter were among the founder members.

In 1923 a centenary match was played at Rugby to celebrate 100 years since Webb Ellis's act.

Playing in that game were such famous rugby men of the day as Davies and Kershaw, the scrum-flyhalf combination of England; Wavell Wakefield and Tom Voyce of England; Ernie Crawford and George Stephenson of Ireland; Rowe Harding of Wales; and the rugged Scottish forward John Bannerman and fellow Scot Leslie Gracie.

The celebratory game at Rugby, watched by only 2000 people (all that could be fitted around the field), has been described as one of the greatest days in the game's history. Guests of the headmaster and the RFU included survivors of the first international matc played in 1871, representatives of any club over 50 years old and visitors from countries where rugby was known to be played. The remainder of the crowd were pupils of the famous school.

For the record, a combined England and Wales team beat Scotland and Ireland by 21–16.

In 1873 a rugby football club was formed in the town of Rugby and it is still going strong at its ground with an address that is entirely appropriate – Webb Ellis Road.

The club's most-capped player in its first 120 years was Geoffrey Conway, who played 18 games for England (some while representing Manchester) between 1920 and 1927. He was a master at Rugby School for a time.

RUTHERFORD, JOHN

Selkirk and Scotland
42 internationals for Scotland 1979–87
1 international for British Isles 1983

John Rutherford is widely considered to be the best flyhalf ever to have played for Scotland. Certainly he was his country's most-capped player in that position. His 42 caps could have increased, but for injuries which affected his last playing years.

Rutherford was a loyal Selkirk player who first played in an international in 1979 against Wales. He was tall (6ft, 1.83m) but slim (12 st, 76kg), and for a time there were questions whether he had the physical qualifications for the rigours of top class football. However, with every game he played, confidence grew, and he became an elegant flyhalf, with admirable running, kicking and tactical skills.

When scrumhalf Roy Laidlaw came into international play in 1980, the two struck an immediate accord. Their 35 internationals together was to become a world record as a halfback partnership.

Laidlaw and Rutherford had their greatest moments for Scotland in 1984, when their smooth well-oiled combination was a vital part of Scotland's team which won the Grand Slam.

Rutherford performed many other fine exploits for Scotland, including a darting run for a try in the Calcutta Cup match against England in 1986.

He was never dropped by his country, but he had an injury-plagued last few years in rugby. On a short social tour to Bermuda early in 1987 he twisted a knee so badly he only just made selection to travel to New Zealand for the first Rugby World Cup. In New Zealand, however, the leg failed him during the first match against France in Christchurch and Rutherford was invalided out of the series. The injury was seen as a major blow to Scotland's chances of winning the cup.

Rutherford is congratulated by his Selkirk and Lions team-mate Iain Paxton, after scoring a try in the third test against New Zealand in 1983.

He was a Lion in 1983 in New Zealand, but was not a first pick as flyhalf for any of the tests. In what must have been a tough decision, Ollie Campbell of Ireland was preferred. But Rutherford's ability as a runner was recognised when he was chosen as a centre in the third test in Dunedin. His try there did a lot to boost the Lions' sagging fortunes. An injury prevented him playing in the final test in Auckland.

In his career Rutherford kicked 12 dropped goals in internationals, another Scottish record.

S

SALE FC

This Cheshire rugby stronghold, founded in 1861, had, for a time, a run in providing international rugby captains – and not just for England. The famous Welsh international players of the 1930s, Claude Davey and Wilfred Wooller, were both Sale players who went on to captain their country. Kenneth Fyfe was a Scottish captain in 1934 who joined Sale later, as did Fran Cotton, who had captained England from Coventry before joining Sale in 1976.

Three players from the club's top XV in the years after World War II, Eric Evans, Joe Mycock and Steve Smith, were all England skippers. Evans, the hooker, was an international for 10 years from 1948–58. Steve Smith, the halfback, played for England from Sale for 10 years, 1973–83.

Like a number of other prominent English clubs, Sale was originally a cricket club. Life was tough in the early days, as games were hard to organise for clubs in the north-west. Yet soon Sale was a real force on the club scene.

Its first international player for England was Patrick Davies, a loose forward, who played against Ireland in one international in 1927. Davies, a

Sale's Steve Smith

staunch Sale man, was the club's chairman in its centenary year, 1961.

Playing numbers strengthened in the 1930s, when Hal Sever was capped 10 times for England and Duncan Shaw six times for Scotland. In his international debut, Sever scored one of the tries that led to England's demolition of the 1935–36 All Blacks. Along with Wooller, Davey, Mycock and Fyfe, Shaw and Sever provided the backbone for some glorious years for Sale in the 1930s.

Since World War II, prominent Sale players have included the speedy wing Jim Roberts (18 caps for England over five seasons in the 1960s); Bill Patterson (an England centre and a British Lion in New Zealand in 1959); Keith McMillan, a South African-born flanker (four caps for Scotland 1953); and Vic Harding, (six caps as a lock for England). Sale player Peter Stagg played 28 times for Scotland as a lock from 1965–70 (plus three further caps for the British Isles in South Africa in 1968).

As a scrumhalf for Old Milhillians, Johnnie Williams totted up eight international appearances from 1954–56, including touring South Africa with the 1955 British Isles team. Then, as a 24-year-old, he was discarded by the England selectors. When he next appeared as an international for his country, nine years had passed! A fortnight short of turning 33, Williams, by then with the Sale club, was recalled into the England team which lost to Wales in 1965.

This was believed by some historians to have been a record 'gap' for a player between caps, but the New Zealander Ned Hughes went 14 years without a rugby union international, between 1907 and 1921, and Australian Graham Cooke had a similar break, 1937–46.

SAXTON, CHARLIE
Otago, South Canterbury, Southland,
    Canterbury and New Zealand
3 internationals for New Zealand 1938

A successful All Black manager, coach and theoriser of the game, who wrote

Charles Saxton

a useful coaching manual, and a fine halfback whose career was cut short by World War II.

But Charlie Saxton's greater claim to fame was as captain of one of the most respected New Zealand rugby sides. Post-war blues were lifted throughout the British Isles and Europe by the sparkling play of the 'Kiwis' – a side chosen from New Zealand servicemen.

Captain of the side, and then 32, Saxton lost nothing by comparison with the talented young men joining him, 16 of them going on to become All Blacks. The side won 32 of its 38 matches in a five-month tour, the Saxton dive pass setting off his backs on many a thrilling movement.

He was an outstanding All Blacks manager in 1967 and a life member of the NZRFU.

SCHREINER, BILL
W.F.R. Schreiner never achieved great heights as a rugby player, though he appeared three times in the Western Province front row of 1911 and captained SACS (now the University of Cape Town) and Villagers club sides. But he had an extraordinarily long administrative career and an unprecedented term as a national selector.

Schreiner, then only 23, was on a train between Bloemfontein and Johannesburg, touring with the 1909 SACS team he captained, when his game of bridge was interrupted by the appearance of the Border union secretary, who asked him if he would represent Border on the South African Rugby Board.

Schreiner reluctantly agreed to do the job temporarily – and retired in 1952, 43 years later, by which time he was vice-president.

In 1912 Schreiner was missing from a board meeting which appointed him as one of five Springbok selectors; only 26, he was chosen to help deliberate over men some years his senior.

It was an interesting start, for the last man chosen was Billy Millar, who had also toured Britain and Ireland in 1906 only because of the withdrawal of Eric Mosenthal. The Springbok selectors nominated another man as captain, but the SARB overturned the recommendation and appointed Millar – an inspired choice as it happened.

Schreiner was to have few other defeats as a selector. Appointed convener of the panel in 1921, he was reluctant to continue in 1949 when South Africa was to host the All Blacks in its first international series since 1938. Then 63, Schreiner was arthritic and walked with a stick, but his old friend, SARB president 'Sport' Pienaar, who had legal offices across the corridor from Schreiner, refused to accept his retirement, and the veteran selector had the satisfaction of seeing his teams whitewash the All Blacks for the first and only time.

Two years later only one man was nominated as a selector by all 13 of the South African unions: Bill Schreiner, who thus completed a record 40 years in office.

He was rated an exceptionally gifted convener, capable of containing and controlling even the dogmatic A.F. Markotter, with whom he shared the vice-presidency of the Western Province union.

Schreiner developed the policy of selectors having the freedom to go outside nominated lists for Springbok trials, with some spectacular results. He also disagreed with critics of the trial system, claiming they allowed unrecognised players to emerge, provided a test of temperament, and allowed selectors to experiment.

Bill Schreiner was an expert angler in his youth, but as South African journalist A.C ('Ace') Parker wrote, his reputation was more for 'successful fishing expeditions after rugby Springboks'.

SCOTLAND

One of the first two nations to play international rugby and the first winner of an international match.

A game of what might loosely be called football, with carrying and passing, was played in Scotland in the eighteenth century, and the Border towns were especially prominent in playing ball (or ba') games.

Edinburgh was the home of rugby in Scotland, as it is today. The High School was playing a form of football in 1810, and other schools to emerge were Edinburgh Academy, Loretto and Merchiston in the 1820s and early 1830s. Merchiston first played Edinburgh Academy in 1858, which is held to be the longest existing fixture of all.

The schoolboys needed somewhere to play rugby when they left school, so senior clubs started springing up: Edinburgh Academicals in 1857, West of Scotland eight years later, then in successive years, Glasgow Academicals and Royal High, with Kilmarnock and Edinburgh Wanderers both in 1868.

In March 1870 Scotland played England for the first time, but this match was organised by the Football Association in England and the entire Scotland team was chosen from the London area – London Scottish it would be today. A second match, eight months later, included only one northerner. So a Glaswegian wrote to *The Scotsman* and suggested 10 players from Scottish rugby clubs should join with 10 Londoners and play England at rugby.

The northern Scots certainly felt rugby was more their national game, but entreaties for such a fixture were ignored by Football Association secretary C.W. Alcock. But when five senior Scottish club captains wrote to *The Scotsman* and *Bell's Life in London*, suggesting such a match, London clubs took up the challenge. So the first international came about, at the Academical ground in Edinburgh's Raeburn Place. It was played on a Monday, March 27 1871, and the stronger and fitter Scots dealt out a lesson to the English, winning by two tries and a

conversion to a try. All the points came in the second half, and the first try of all was scored by Angus Buchanan from a pushover scrum, which is not, after all, such a new feature.

It should be mentioned that the 'pushover' try was illegal according to England laws, but its protests were to no avail. Buchanan was an appropriate man to lead off international scoring: as well as later playing cricket for Scotland, he umpired and refereed rugby internationals and became Scotland RU president.

England won the next five internationals, but when the game first became 15-a-side at this level, in 1877, Scotland won by a dropped goal to nil. The same season Scotland started playing Ireland with a hiss and a roar: six tries (four of them converted) and two dropped goals to nil – that would be 38–0 in modern scoring values.

England was a law unto itself in those days and in 1884, when Scotland forward Charles Berry 'fisted' the ball in a lineout – knocking back as it was then called – England appealed for an infringement and the honest Scots stopped play to await the outcome. The not-so-chivalrous English went on to score; the dispute which followed became known as 'The Dispute' and Scotland temporarily refused to play England. The eventual result was the formation of the International Rugby Board.

The Scotland Rugby Union itself was formed in 1873, and the Border clubs rushed to affiliate, among them such famous names as Langholm (1872), Hawick (1873), Gala (1875), Kelso (1876), Melrose (1877) and Jedforest a little later. Gala and Melrose were actually a combined club, playing at Gala, until the day the Gala men arrived to find the merry men of Melrose

had shifted the posts to their own ground, the Greenyards.

Wales joined Scotland as an international opponent in 1883, the Scots winning by three converted tries to one. Two years earlier, Scotland had made history by being the first nation to field three men in the three-quarter line. The usual formation (but not the only one) was to have a fullback, two three-quarters, two halves, and the other 10 men in the forwards. One of the Scotland three-quarters was William Maclagan, who was to captain the pioneering British team in South Africa in 1891, after finishing for Scotland the year before with a record 25 caps.

That three-quarter line served Scotland well – in 31 matches it won 21 and drew four – so its proponents scoffed at the four-man three-quarter line introduced by Wales. But in 1893 Scotland had to eat humble pie, as Wales scored three tries without reply, and by the next season Scotland too had four three-quarters. It struggled, but the next year won the Triple Crown, only its second such success (the first was in 1891).

But maybe the Welsh initiative rankled with the Scots, for when Arthur Gould was presented with the deeds to a house to mark his retirement, the Scots claimed it an act of professionalism and refused to play Wales in either 1897 or 1898.

So England and Wales had both felt the wrath – and the boycotts – of the Scottish rugby men. France was next. The French crowd at the Parc des Princes in 1913 reacted bitterly and vigorously to the refereeing of Englishman James Baxter (the same 'Bim' Baxter who was to so antagonise New Zealanders with his criticisms of their beloved wing forward position when he was manager of the 1930 British Isles team). So enraged were the Scots by the crowd behaviour, they refused to play the match in 1914, and the war meant the series did not resume until 1920.

Next in the boycott stakes was New Zealand. The Scots were unhappy enough with the upshot of the tour by the 1905 'Originals': canny about the All Blacks' drawing power, the Scots refused guarantees of £200 a match and instead offered the net gates of two games. The powerful New Zealanders were unbeaten when they

The all-Oxford Scottish three-quarter line of the 1920s: Johnny Wallace, George Aitken, Phil Macpherson and Ian Smith.

reached Scotland and the big crowds meant they walked away with about £1600.

That in itself upset the Scottish, who demanded a set of accounts from the tour. When they received them, they were affronted to learn the Rugby Football Union had approved expenses of three shillings a day being paid to the touring players. Accordingly, Scotland refused to be part of the British tour to New Zealand in 1908 and would not play against the 1924 'Invincibles'. That was a pity, for their meeting would have been for a mythical 'world championship', such was the strength of the Scotland team of the mid-1920s.

Scotland had marvellous teams then. At the outset, there were dazzling three-quarters like Leslie Gracie and Eric Liddell. Dan Drysdale, a notable fullback, was also a stalwart. But the real impact came when centre three-quarter Phil Macpherson was joined in the three-quarters by three colonials: George Aitken of New Zealand, who had captained the All Blacks in 1921; A.C. 'Johnny' Wallace, who was

to captain the touring New South Wales 'Waratahs' in 1927–28, and later coached the Wallabies; and brilliant Melbourne-born wing Ian Smith.

The great Scotland side did the Grand Slam of the other nations in 1925, but was surprisingly tripped up in both the next two years by Ireland. When that team broke up, Scotland had a couple of bad seasons, but won the Triple Crown in 1933 and again in 1938. It's worth noting that in 1931 a Scotland prop, John Allan, kicked five conversions against England. But after World War II Scotland had some lean years, changing captains constantly. In 1951, when it used three, it lost all five internationals – to South Africa humiliatingly by 0–44 – and conceded 99 points in those games, scoring only 22.

Given that Scotland had lost its last two matches of the 1951 championship, it went on to lose 17 in succession, the horrendous pattern ending against Wales (the last team it had beaten) in 1955. Thus encouraged, it failed by only a 6–9 loss to England to secure the Triple Crown.

The Scots finally managed a share of the Five Nations championship again in 1964, and held the strong touring All Blacks to a scoreless draw; but Scotland was the wooden-spooner in three successive seasons late in the 1970s.

Long overdue successes came in 1984. Scotland opened the season with a 25–25 draw with New Zealand, then had a Grand Slam in the Five Nations championship. Rather oddly, it then lost to Romania at the end of the season. Topsy-turvey Scotland: wooden-spooner the following season, co-winner the next, and as rugby entered the 1990s, again on top of the pile in Europe with another Grand Slam in 1990.

Scotland was very cautious in the matter of touring overseas, other than to Ireland or France. Its first tour was not until 1960, to South Africa, where it lost the only test 10–18. The next tour was no more successful: only three of the six matches in Australia in 1970 were won and the tourists lost the only international, 3–23.

Much the same happened on the first tour to New Zealand in 1975.

Scotland lost to both Auckland and Canterbury in the six lead-up games and was literally swamped by the All Blacks in what became known as the 'water polo test', 24–0. The next tour was also to New Zealand, in 1981, and although New Zealand was preoccupied with the tumultuous upcoming tour by the Springboks, it beat the Scots 11–4 and 40–15, the tourists also losing to Wellington.

Andy Irvine, that great artist at fullback and wing, captained the side, but one of the pities of Irvine's glittering career was that he was rarely seen at his best on those demanding short tours. He was also captain in Australia the next year, and while the Scottish tourists lost to Queensland and Sydney at the opening of the tour, they accomplished a feat unmatched by any of their predecessors by winning the first international, 12–7, at Ballymore, Brisbane.

The forwards did a fine job in that match, but the Wallabies had the beating of them at the Sydney Cricket Ground, and Irvine's career finished with a 9–33 hiding.

After some semi-regular one-off trips to Bucharest to play Romania, and the first World Cup, Scotland's only other tour was a third visit to New Zealand. David Sole's side arrived in 1990 as the northern hemisphere's undisputed champion, and while it ran the All Blacks close in both matches, it still had to concede two losses, 16–31 and 18–21.

Scotland's first touring captain was Gordon Waddell, son of the famed Herbert Waddell, both an international and a prominent administrator. Some said that Waddell snr's influence brought early representative honours to Waddell jnr, who was a rather ponderous flyhalf. A kicker rather than a runner, he was actively disliked by large sections of Murrayfield crowds.

Hooker Frank Laidlaw was captain to Australia in 1970: he had just succeeded Jim Telfer, who had led Scotland in 10 straight internationals. The heavy defeat at the SCG cost Laidlaw his leadership role to Peter Brown, and seven players their places.

Another front row man, the 'Mighty Mouse' Ian McLauchlan, was captain

Scott Hastings, Gary Armstrong and Ivan Tukalo prevent Simon Hodgkinson and Rory Underwood from scoring during the climactic Grand Slam encounter of 1990. Scotland triumphed over England 13–7.

in New Zealand in 1975 and went on to lead Scotland in 18 consecutive games, before losing his place, then returning just before his 35th birthday to play a further 11 matches, the last of them again as captain. His 19 games as captain was the Scottish record.

Scotland, conservatively, long held out against the idea of a coach, but succumbed in 1971 when it appointed Bill Dickinson. He made a huge impact, especially in developing fine forward packs, and that work was extended by men like Jim Telfer – who became an unashamed disciple of the New Zealand style and attitude, and sought to emulate it – and Ian McGeechan. Significantly, Telfer and McGeechan were the most recent coaches of Lions teams.

By the end of the 1990–91 season, Scotland had won 39 games, lost 51 and drawn 17 against England, its oldest opponent. It had played Ireland 102 times, for 52 wins, 45 losses, only four draws and one match abandoned. And Scotland trails Wales: 41 wins, 52 losses and two draws.

It couldn't be closer against France: in their games there have been 29 wins, 30 losses and three draws.

Scotland has never beaten New Zealand; its best results a 0–0 draw in 1964 and a 25–25 draw in 1983. The record is better against South Africa, though Scotland lost the only match away, in 1960. South Africa won in 1912, 1932 (by only 6–3), 1951 (that walloping) and 1961, but Scotland's 8–5 win in 1965 and 6–3 win in 1969 give it an outstanding record against such a strong nation.

Against Australia, Scotland has won seven times and lost five; while it has three times beaten Romania and once lost in the 1980s. Another new opponent, in the first World Cup, was Zimbabwe, which Scotland beat 60–21, with Gavin Hastings kicking eight conversions.

SCOTLAND, KEN

Heriot's FP, Leicester, and Scotland
27 internationals for Scotland 1957–65
5 internationals for British Isles 1959

A brilliant runner and tactical wizard of Scottish rugby, Kenneth Scotland became much more than the man who played for the country of his name. He was a player who was years, decades even, ahead of his time. As a rugby

country, New Zealand in particular could not believe his style of play when he toured there with the British Isles in 1959. Only with the advantage of hindsight was Ken Scotland recognised as being a rugby genius.

Scotland eventually equalled the Scottish record for caps won by a fullback (25 caps, along with Dan Drysdale), but he could cope in any position in the backline. He was a scrumhalf too, (playing two important games in that position in New Zealand for the Lions in 1959). He was also flyhalf (two caps when captaining Scotland in 1963) and a centre (two games for the Lions in 1959, including the fourth test won at Auckland).

Only slightly built, he was a running fullback years before Andy Irvine, Serge Blanco, David Campese and others revolutionised that previously 'steady' position. Ken Scotland set new standards as a counter-attacker and back line intruder, and did it superbly.

New Zealanders in particular marvelled at his running brilliance. In the first match of the Lions tour he showed Kiwi fans what he'd been showing British crowds for a couple of years. Scotland ran in three successive tries from fullback against Hawkes Bay in the tour opener and scored 10 tries in all on tour.

Scotland was also an innovative goal-kicker. Though he could kick straight-on using the toe, he also experimented successfully with the round-the-corner style and was one of the first players anywhere to perfect the method. He was also expert at drop-kicking for goal.

He was educated at George Heriot's School in Edinburgh, one of a series of international fullbacks to emerge from that school (including Dan Drysdale and Andy Irvine). Scotland made his international debut against France in Paris in 1957, scoring all the points for his side as it won 6–0. It was the first time in 19 years that a Scot had achieved such a feat.

He suffered a loss of form in 1958 but by 1959 was back in favour and in the Lions team on tour 'down under'. From then he was a first choice for his country until 1963. His last international was against France in 1965.

Ken Scotland was the second player to play for the country of his name. John Ireland (of Ireland!) was the first in 1876.

Bob Scott demonstrating his ability to kick goals from half-way, in his bare feet.

SCOTT, BOB

Auckland and New Zealand
17 internationals for N. Zealand 1946–54

After first making his mark on international rugby during the 'Kiwis' tour of Britain and Europe 1945–46, Scott soon became the regular All Black fullback, playing 12 consecutive internationals 1946–50.

Not available to tour Australia in 1951, he then retired, but was persuaded to demonstrate his class to British crowds on the tour of 1953–54. Turning 33 during that tour, Scott showed he had lost none of his exceptional ability: a fullback who could defend admirably, with his positional sense a great asset, and with a fine eye for the right moment to join an attack.

Broadcaster Winston McCarthy, who witnessed all Scott's major games, referred to him as a genius, the greatest footballer he had seen. 'He had the greatest balance, the greatest poise that I've seen in any man.'

Scott regularly entertained crowds by practising his goal-kicking in bare feet. He sometimes removed his boots and kicked goals from half-way in charity matches.

But even with his boots on, Scott had a terrible time goal-kicking in South Africa in 1949. His general form was sublime, and Hennie Muller reckoned he was 'altogether the greatest player I've ever played against in any position'. But the goals wouldn't go over, and the All Blacks plummeted to a 0–4 series loss, thanks primarily to the Springboks' greater goal-kicking skills.

After his second retirement, Scott continued to play club and charity rugby in Wellington. He was asked – but declined – to be available to play against the 1956 Springboks. He was then 35.

Scott scored 242 points in his 52 matches for New Zealand. If only more of them could have been scored in South Africa!

SCOTT, JOHN

Rosslyn Park, Cardiff and England
34 internationals for England 1978–84

When he retired from international play, John Scott was England's high-est capped No. 8, with 31 caps. He also appeared three times as a lock.

He was a hard-working and popular player who at 17, in 1971, was England's youngest ever triallist. He first played against France in 1978, as a No. 8. Early in his second season he was tried at lock against New Zealand, but the experiment was not a success. Thereafter he was a No. 8 until two late tests in his career, again as a lock, against South Africa in 1984.

John Scott was a product of Exeter who played his early club rugby for Rosslyn Park. Later he transferred to Cardiff, where he captained the club from 1980–84. He became England's captain for four tests, two in 1983 and two on tour to South Africa in 1984. Sadly, for this hard-driving player, all of those tests were losses.

SCRUM

Officially a 'scrummage', this is the formation of forward players designed to restart the game after a minor infringement. Scrummaging was first introduced into the game as a organised alternative to the puffing, heaving masses, sometimes of 20 players, wrestling together for the ball for several minutes at a time. The scrummage was a formalised way of retaining that character of the game, while allowing the ball freer and much quicker access from the forwards to the backs.

A modern scrum is formed by eight players from each team, in three rows. The two three-player front rows close in against each other to allow the halfback to place the ball in the passage between the opposing front rows. A team wins the ball by hooking it back through its scrum to a second row of four players. It then passes on through the feet of the 'last man down', the No. 8, to the halfback.

The usual description for the modern scrum formation is '3-4-1', indicating the numbers of players in each line. In earlier times the scrum was designated as '3-2-3', especially popular in Britain, or '2-3-2' with a roving wing forward, as developed in New Zealand. It was the 2-3-2 scrum which

Scrum: an organised formation of forwards from opposing teams . . . ?

was used by the great New Zealand teams in Britain in 1905 and 1924, which between them lost only one game out of 67.

Meanwhile, in the 1920s, that crafty South African rugby thinker, A.F. Markotter, was leading the way towards the 3-4-1 formation. His three-man front row was eventually deemed to allow a stronger pushing base, though many old-timers in the game from New Zealand will argue vigorously for the two-fronted scrum of their days. They claim one less man in the front row made for a faster hook, and it can be argued that if a seven-man scrum using a 2-3-2 formation pushed against a 3-4-1 scrum there were 12 shoulders available for pushing in each pack.

The problem of the three different types of scrum ended in the early 1930s, when the International Rugby Board changed the laws relating to scrummaging.

The manager of the 1930 Great Britain team in New Zealand, 'Bim' Baxter, developed a distaste for the New Zealand way of playing the game. His scorn was not so much for the 2-3-2 scrummage but for the eighth man who was not needed at scrum-time, the extra roving wing forward, who hung off waiting to attack opposition inside backs.

As a member of the IRB, on which New Zealand was not then represented, Baxter argued for a change to the scrum laws. As a result, a law was passed in 1932 stipulating that the ball could not be hooked until it had passed three feet in the front row. This effectively ruined the New Zealand style and the two-fronted scrum was abandoned. New Zealanders claim that it took 20 years for them to adapt to the three-man front row. In modern scrums a minimum of five players must take part in each scrum, always with three in the front row.

In many levels of the modern game the power of the scrum has been reduced so that heavy pushing no longer occurs. Such a change was introduced to avoid the number of serious neck injuries that occurred, particularly in the early 1980s. However, at international level teams are still allowed to push heavily, and possessing big powerful forwards with the strength to shove back the opposition is still a vital component of the game.

Philippe Sella

SELLA, PHILIPPE
Agen and France
72 internationals for France 1982–91

A brilliant French runner and try-scorer who set new appearance records for his country as a centre three-quarter. His debut in international play was against Romania in 1982 and he was a regular selection for France in every other year of the 1980s.

In six of his first seven internationals he was played as a wing, thereafter he was a centre in 38 consecutive tests and eventually passed Roland Bertranne's French record as a centre (52 internationals) in the second test against New Zealand in 1989. He also had one appearance as a fullback, against Australia at Lille in 1989.

Sella was a thrusting and evasive runner, but he was equally strong in defence. He delighted crowds all over the rugby world, and many critics rated him the world's best centre of his day.

By the end of 1990–91 he had scored 23 tries in his test matches. In 1985–86 he became only the fourth player to score a try in all four matches of a Five Nations series. (The others were Carston Catchside of England in 1924, 'Johnny' Wallace of Scotland in 1925 and Patrick Estève of France in 1983.)

Sella came from the Agen club, the power base of modern French rugby, and four times he played for the club in the final of the French club championship. He was on the winning team twice (in 1982 and 1988).

SERVICES RUGBY
The influence of British servicemen in the development of rugby has never really been recognised, but it was they who took the game to parts of the globe where it had never been seen before.

In Britain the first Army v Navy match took place as early as 1878, and the first official inter-services tournament was held in 1907. After the First World War, the Royal Air Force was introduced to make a three-way inter-services competition which has been played annually at Twickenham ever since (with the exception of the years of World War II, when the players presumably had other things on their minds!) In the first 70 years of the tournament, from 1920–90, the Army won 28 times, the Royal Navy 16 times, and the Royal Air Force 11 times.

In other countries teams from the services are also involved in their own internal annual tournaments. Services rugby is still powerful in South Africa, perhaps reflecting the compulsory national call-up, but elsewhere peace has meant a general drop in standards in services rugby.

Major touring teams to Britain used to play regularly against combined service sides. A team called 'Officers of the Army and Navy' played the Australian Wallabies of 1908–09, Australia winning 9–6. The 1912–13 South African side met a similarly-named team. The narrow loss, 16–18, against the Springboks at Portsmouth indicated the strength of British services rugby at that time. The first time the All Blacks played Combined Services

(as they were known by then, because of the addition of the Royal Air Force) was in 1924. New Zealand won comfortably 25–3.

In South Africa there was great excitement in 1960, when the All Blacks suffered a 3–8 loss to the South Africa's Combined Services team. It was the first game for the servicemen of that country against a major touring team. They also beat Australia in 1969.

In New Zealand, although there has been a regular services tournament since 1947, the teams have not enjoyed sufficient status to play major touring sides. As in South Africa, policemen are considered for selection in such New Zealand teams.

When a representative team of British servicemen tours overseas, there is a slight distinction in the team's title when the police are included. Such touring teams are known as the 'British Combined Services and Police'.

In Australia for a time there was a special services amnesty towards rugby league players. They were permitted, while doing service, to make the switch to rugby union without any difficulty or prejudice. Thus Bobby Fulton, the great Australian rugby league star of the 1960s (and coach in the 90s), played in the Australian Combined Services team which met the All Blacks of 1968.

See also 'KIWIS'

SEVENS RUGBY

This is the more compact version of rugby union, with teams made up of three forwards and four backs. From modest beginnings, sevens rugby is now universally popular and enjoys a high international profile. A Rugby Sevens World Cup has been introduced by the International Board, which will be first played in Scotland in 1993.

Sevens rugby, sometimes called 'seven-a-side' or 'the short game' was invented in the Borders area of Scotland in the 1880s by a butcher from Melrose, Adam 'Ned' Haig. He was said to have been bitterly disappointed when his club did not have the numbers to field a full 15-a-side team so, in 1883, he came up with the idea of playing a sports day involving a fund-raising tournament of teams with only seven players per side.

To this day the Melrose Sevens annual tournament remains one of the showpieces for the short game any-

where in the world. It is held at the Greenyards ground in Melrose and attracts a full house each finals day.

Sevens rugby seems to have been confined to the Borders of Scotland until 1926 when the concept headed south into Sassenach territory. The Middlesex Sevens started that year and the annual tournament is now a huge charity event involving hundreds of teams and held over several weekends. Its finals, on the last Saturday of the season, are held at Twickenham. Finals day is a raucous fun-filled six hours, usually watched by 50,000 spectators.

In many other parts of Britain and Ireland, usually to signal the end of the season, there are regular sevens tournaments. The Snelling Sevens in Wales is another big annual day for the short game.

The sevens game did not spread abroad in major tournament form until after World War II. In 1976 the Hong Kong Sevens started, and that tournament has become the most consistent and best international showcase for the game. Each year tens of thousands of visitors flock to enjoy the delights of Hong Kong and to watch 24 invited sides, international selections mixed with prominent club sides, battling for two exciting days to win the prestigious cup title.

The first totally international sevens tournament was held as part of

Ned Haig of Melrose, founder of the seven-a-side game.

Centenary Season
April 7th
1973
Murrayfield

International Seven-a-side Tournament

NON · SINE · GLORIA

1873 – 1973

Price 10p

the Scottish Rugby Union's centenary celebations in Edinburgh in 1973, when seven countries sent teams and England beat Ireland 22–18 in the final.

The New South Wales Sevens, which began in 1986, was the first serious attempt at a regular, fully international sevens event. Sixteen countries accepted to play in Sydney and a very succesful start to a global sevens event was made. However, money problems of the host union saw the tournament falter after only three stagings.

Most countries of the rugby world now have a number of showcase sevens events each season.

The attraction of the game is the openness of its play. Quite simply, with fewer players on the field there is more room in which to run, so most games are fast and exciting, with quick passing and maintenance of possession a priority. In major tournaments all matches are of seven minutes each way in duration, with one minute for half-time. Finals matches stretch to 10 minutes each way.

It is difficult to assess where the world strength in sevens lies as, somewhat surprisingly, the four home unions have rarely fielded their national teams in Hong Kong. The announcement of the Sevens World Cup encouraged more countries to seek invitations to Hong Kong's event.

Nevertheless, Hong Kong is perhaps the best yardstick to gauge world strengths. In recent years Australia, Fiji and New Zealand have dominated, and games between those countries are always fast and exciting. Perhaps the ebullient Fijians would win number one ranking, certainly in terms of crowd popularity, as the game really suits the fast, strong and long-legged Fijian physical types. It is expected that those three countries will be among the top seeds when sevens gets its first World Cup in 1993.

SHARP, RICHARD
Wasps, Bristol, Cornwall and England
14 internationals for England 1960–67
2 internationals for British Isles 1962

The pale-complexioned, blond-haired flyhalf who was seen as England's and the Lions' ready-made replacement when Bev Risman 'went north'.

Sharp actually broke into the England team in 1960, before Lions star Risman had followed his father to rugby league, and took full advantage of the established player's injury. He struck a swift accord with Dicky Jeeps and was considered the key to England's Triple Crown success, kicking a critical dropped goal against Ireland, and another against Scotland.

The following season, indecisive England selectors couldn't choose between the two talented men available, so played both, Risman at inside centre until he turned professional.

That gave Sharp an unchallenged position, for all that 1959 Lion Phil Horrocks-Taylor was still playing, but his international career was effectively to end within little more than a year. A smashing tackle early in the 1962 Lions tour of South Africa put Sharp out of action until midway through the tour, though he recovered to lead England to a championship win in 1963.

That was his international career, save for a brief return – also as captain – when England went down heavily to Australia in 1967. Sharp was not called on again.

He later became a journalist, covering rugby for the *Sunday Telegraph*, and was awarded the OBE in 1986.

SHAW, GEOFF
New South Wales and Australia
27 internationals for Australia 1969–79

A 20-year-old at his debut against Wales, the burly Shaw went on to become Australia's most-capped centre with a reputation for creating space for his wings.

He played only one test (as a replacement) on the 1969 tour to South Africa, but was a regular choice by the time the Springboks returned the visit in 1971, and in France later the same year. But then he found himself on the outer, kept out by combinations of David Burnet, David Rathie, David L'Estrange – he should have changed his name to David! – and Trevor Stegman, before returning on a regular basis in 1973.

Shaw played 18 of Australia's next 19 internationals, succeeding to the captaincy against Japan (when he scored his only two test tries) and again on the 1975–76 British tour when captain John Hipwell was injured. Also captain in the 1976 tests against Fiji and in France, Shaw made only one further appearance, in the Bledisloe Cup triumph against the 1979 All Blacks.

SHAW, MARK
Manawatu, Hawkes Bay and New
  Zealand
30 internationals for N. Zealand 1980–86

A tough, hard man of New Zealand rugby in the 1980s, 'Cowboy' Shaw was an aggressive and pugnacious flanker.

Mark Shaw

His debut was in the series with Australia in 1980 and he played tests over the next six years. He was also a member of the rebel Cavaliers team to South Africa in 1986. He returned to the All Blacks for one more test match, v Australia at Auckland in 1986, and finished his time as an All Black on the tour to France later in the same year.

SHAW, TONY
Queensland and Australia
36 internationals for Australia 1973–82

A rugged and uncompromising loose forward, who also played at lock during his final three seasons, Shaw became a regular test player in 1975 and played in 34 of Australia's next 36 internationals.

After two tours to Britain, one to France and home series against New Zealand, England, Japan and Fiji, he succeeded the unrelated Geoff Shaw as test captain in 1978. He led the Wallabies in a whitewash of Wales in a two-match series, and in the 1–2 series loss in New Zealand – the win being the match forever known as Greg Cornelsen's match after the flanker scored four tries.

After Australia lost its home series with Ireland in 1979, Shaw was replaced as captain by Mark Loane. But he was back in charge as a successful captain when the Wallabies beat the All Blacks 2–1 in the home series in 1980. There was further success with a series win against France in 1981, then Shaw completed his touring days with a disappointing 1981–82 tour to Britain, the Wallabies beating only Ireland.

Yielding the captaincy to Mark Loane in 1979, and to Paul McLean against Fiji in 1980, cost him the chance of equalling or bettering the records of John Thornett and Greg Davis, both of whom were captains of Australian test teams 16 times.

SHEHADIE, NICK
New South Wales and Australia
30 internationals for Australia 1947–58

'Drop your tweeds at Nick's,' said the sign in a Sydney street in the 1950s, but it wasn't a lewd parlour in King's Cross. The colourful Lebanese-descended Wallaby lock and prop Nick Shehadie was advertising, in his inimitable way, his drycleaning business.

Nick Shehadie

Shehadie's story has a whiff of Dick Whittington about it, except the son of new Australians went on to become Lord Mayor of Sydney town, not London town. He further showed how a local boy could make good by becoming president of the Australian Rugby Union and receiving a knighthood.

Shehadie never seemed to miss a trick. He first played international rugby against New Zealand in 1947, and on his first tour, later that year, became the first overseas player to be invited to turn out for the Barbarians, against his own team. His first test was as a lock, the next two at prop, then he played six in a row at lock. He filled either position with ease until settling down regularly into the front row in South Africa in 1953.

Three times, when John Solomon was injured, he captained Australia. But Shehadie's physical presence was the key to his value to Australia in what were some lean years. Of 31 successive internationals played by the Wallabies, Shehadie appeared in 29 of them, the last on the unsuccessful 1957–58 tour of Britain.

His total 30 internationals was comfortably an Australian record until broken four years later by Tony 'Slaggy' Miller, but Shehadie had far from finished with international rugby when he discarded his boots. He became an administrator and managed the 1981–82 Wallabies on their British tour. He also managed Australian teams to the Hong Kong Sevens.

SHELFORD, WAYNE ('BUCK')
Auckland, North Harbour, Northampton and New Zealand
22 internationals for N. Zealand 1986–90

Wayne Shelford was New Zealand's 'people's captain' for three years until he was unceremoniously dropped in 1990, when many considered he was still at the peak of his powers.

Shelford's aggressive loose forward play was always popular with the New Zealand fans. When he played at North Harbour and was a commanding figure in game after game at a representative level, the locals called him 'God'.

As a young man in the navy, Shelford worked his way around the world on duty before turning to concentrate on his rugby quite late in life.

He was chosen for the All Black team to tour South Africa in 1985, but like the others he did not go because the tour was cancelled for political reasons, so he went instead with the New Zealand team to Argentina.

The next year he joined the rebel Cavaliers tour of South Africa which meant he had to leave the New Zealand Navy and was banned for two internationals when he returned home. That further delayed his test debut until the All Blacks toured France late in 1986.

From then on Shelford became a first-pick All Black. He played in the World Cup final of 1987 and his form in the whole tournament had many writers rating him as the best No. 8 forward in the world. His hard drives off the back of the scrums and his willingness to commit his body were totally impressive.

A short tour of Japan followed, for which Shelford was named New Zealand captain. He was such a success that it was natural for him to continue as leader for the tests of 1988.

He gained enormous popularity with New Zealand fans. Everything he did, including the way he ferociously led the team's haka before every game, marked him as a player towards whom the public could relate.

Win after win followed Shelford's team. Wales was dispatched 52–3 and 54–9 in 1988, and Australia by 32–7 and 30–9 (a 19–19 draw was the only hiccup to the winning sequence). Then came the 1989 tests: France was turned back 25–17 and 34–20, followed by Argentina 60–9 and 49–12, and Aus-

tralia 24–12. Later there was the tour to Britain: Wales was thumped 34–9 and Ireland 23–6. Came 1990 and next victim was Scotland, 31–15 and 21–18.

An aura of impregnability was raised around Wayne Shelford by his public, fuelled by popular newspapers and other media. But what they had omitted to see was a slight decline in his playing performance, game by game. Shelford still looked like the archetypal Maori warrior, he still did the haka like no one else, and still spoke to the ordinary man with the simplicity of his public utterances. But the New Zealand selectors had perceived some shortcomings.

Shelford was dropped before the first test against Australia in 1990. A national outcry broke out which continued unabated by his supporters for months afterwards. That the All Blacks lost three games several months later under the new captain Gary Whetton only recharged the call for 'Buck' Shelford's return.

His 14 test matches without a defeat did constitute an amazing tally, a best for a New Zealand captain.

Shelford carried on playing at representative level and spent the 1990–91 season with the Northampton club in England. At the end of the season he returned to New Zealand and was still publicly enquiring whether the All Black selectors might want to choose him again.

SINGAPORE
There is evidence that British servicemen were playing rugby in Singapore before the turn of the century. Rugby was formalised there in 1922, when the Royal Navy's *HMS Malaya* donated a rugby cup to be competed for in Malaya, and later Singapore.

In the first half of the century, rugby in Singapore was essentially a game for expatriates. Only after independence in 1959 and the withdrawal of British troops did the locals take up the game and develop national teams. The annual Singapore Sevens tournament is probably the biggest event in domestic rugby.

Singapore has always competed strongly in the Asian championship, its best performance being a third placing in 1978. It also attends the Hong Kong Sevens regularly, where the team's speed and dexterity make it extremely popular with the crowds.

Singapore calls itself the 'strongest rugby power in South-East Asia' and the game there is well-based and well organised, headquartered at the excellent Singapore Cricket Club ground.

SKINNER, KEVIN
Otago, Counties and New Zealand
20 internationals for N. Zealand 1949–56

The legendary strong-arm tactics of Kevin Skinner in the final two internationals of the 1956 series with South Africa tend to overshadow the outstanding ability of this great prop.

Skinner was selected for New Zealand at the unusually early age of 20, and at 21 made his debut on the 1949 tour of South Africa. His form was so compelling that he displaced the tour vice-captain, Ray Dalton, and propped in all four tests with Has Catley and Johnny Simpson.

Skinner went on to play 18 consecutive tests, including captaining New Zealand in 1952, until he retired soon after the 1953–54 tour of Britain.

But he was persuaded to make a comeback for the 'Battle for the Rugby Crown' against the Springboks in 1956, and after New Zealand had experienced all sorts of front row problems in the first two tests, Skinner returned for the last two.

Given the job of subduing the tough Springboks, Chris Koch and Jaap Bekker, Skinner succeeded admirably. The so-called punch-ups have become vivid chapters in the histories of New Zealand and South African rugby, but Skinner in later years insisted he threw only two punches: the first when Koch was stepping off-side in the lineouts without being penalised; the second to slow down Bekker, who was (illegally) trying to disrupt the New Zealand scrum.

Those incidents apart, Skinner should be remembered as a strong resilient prop, usually on the loosehead, a fierce rucker and a very valuable winner of lineout ball near the front. He refused to be intimidated – as the Springboks discovered!

SKRELA, JEAN-CLAUDE
Toulouse and France
46 internationals for France 1971–78

A brilliant French flanker who formed part of a dynamic loose trio in the mid-1970s. Skrela teamed with Jean-Pierre Rives and Jean-Pierre Bastiat for 18 internationals. In that time the speedster Rives, the jumper Bastiat and the stylish aggressor Skrela were superb as a unit. Their tight rein on opponents helped France win the Grand Slam in 1976–77.

Skrela, always a stalwart of the Toulouse club, came into the French team for its second test on the tour to South Africa in 1971, a test described by some as the roughest ever seen. Skrela survived, and went on to be a regular for eight seasons in all.

SLACK, ANDREW
Queensland and Australia
39 internationals for Australia 1978–87

One of the Australian record-holders for appearances as a captain, Slack led the Wallabies in internationals 19 times before retiring after the first World Cup, in which his team finished fourth.

Steady rather than scintillating, similar in mould to his predecessor as captain and centre, Geoff Shaw, Slack made his debut against Wales; but he soon had to give way to injury and the combined talents of Michael O'Connor and Michael Hawker. He played all four tests on the 1981–82 British tour, was dropped again, then returned late in 1982.

He was dropped again the next year against France, but with Alan Jones installed as coach and unable to establish a rapport with captain Mark Ella, Slack returned to the test side and as captain in 1984.

Captain in all eight internationals that year, including the Grand Slam of the home unions, he was again out in 1985. He returned for the World Cup build-up matches and the cup itself, scoring five of his nine international tries in 1987.

Australia was warmly favoured to contest the cup final with New Zealand, but its demise, and the end of Slack's career, was signalled when it lost to both France and Wales in the latter stages. He hastened his end by becoming involved in fruitless efforts at organising a rebel tour to South Africa.

By the end of that season, too, Slack was 32, his representative career having started for Australian Combined Services in 1975 and for Queensland the following year.

SLATTERY, FERGUS
University College, Leinster and Ireland
61 internationals for Ireland 1970–84
4 internationals for British Isles 1971–74

The 1970 international between the touring Springboks and Ireland was a strange occasion for Lansdowne Road. Barbed wire ringed the ground and no spectators were allowed behind the goal-posts. For these Springboks were tracked down by protesters as surely as hounds pursue the hapless fox in the hunt. This was the introduction to international rugby for Fergus Slattery and his team secured a famous draw. Fourteen years later, Slattery was shown the door, the price for a hefty loss to France – one of the first casualties from the 'Dad's Army' pack which had played eight times together.

In the intervening years, Slattery became the most-capped loose forward of all, and earned affection and respect throughout the rugby world. He toured New Zealand with the champion 1971 Lions as a new-boy flanker, unable to break into the brilliant test side; but he won a place in the full series in South Africa in 1974, the team and tour which broke records during its humiliation of South African rugby.

Only injury cost Slattery a place in the Ireland side in 1976, after he had played his first 28 internationals without interruption. When he returned, he played a further 33 internationals for Ireland, also in succes-

Fergus Slattery

sion. In 17 of those matches he was the Ireland captain, including leading the team which toured Australia in 1979. He spanned the careers of Sid Millar and Michael Kiernan, and played alongside giants such as Mike Gibson, Willie John McBride and Tom Kiernan.

Not the greatest loose forward the world has seen, Slattery nevertheless was a tireless, unflinching, dedicated servant of Irish rugby.

SLEMEN, MIKE
Liverpool and England
31 internationals for England 1976–84
1 international for British Isles 1980

A polished player of the mid-1970s who set a new mark as England's most-capped test wing. A product of the Liverpool rugby scene, Slemen played first for his country in 1976 against Ireland. He was a regular player for the next five seasons, establishing himself as a smart and elusive runner. He had three good games in particular against the 1978 All Blacks, playing for England, North of England and the Barbarians, for whom he scored two tries.

Perhaps Slemen's best season was in 1980. He was part of England's Grand Slam season in the Five Nations championship, scoring tries against Ireland and Scotland. He then won selection for the 1980 British Lions' visit to South Africa.

He was top try-scorer after the first test match with the Springboks. For family reasons he had to return home soon after, but his tally of tries scored stayed as the team's best for that trip!

Slemen missed several tours because of unavailability (he was a schoolmaster and therefore not always free to travel) but when he was included in England's teams he always added danger, authority and thrust to the team's wing attacks. His record tally of 31 tests remained England's best for a wing until passed by Rory Underwood in 1989.

SMITH, ARTHUR
Gosforth, Ebbw Vale, Edinburgh
　Wanderers and Scotland
33 internationals for Scotland 1955–62
3 internationals for British Isles 1962

A graceful and speedy wing whose excellent qualities as a man made him a prominent international captain.

Arthur Smith was a brilliant mathematics scholar, a Cambridge blue and a Scottish long jump champion, who had played only three internationals when he was chosen for the 1955 British Isles tour of South Africa. There he broke his hand in the first match at Potchefstroom and did not play again for two months. He spent the enforced break positively by practising goal-kicking, and was to kick seven goals in international rugby. He returned in time to play the late mid-week games on tour and had a sweet day at Nairobi on the way home when he scored five tries against the East Africa XV – a team which included Idi Amin in its reserves!

Smith returned to South Africa on two other occasions, with the Barbarians in 1958 and as captain of the 1962 Lions.

From that rare rugby place of leadership, the wing, he was also captain of Scotland 15 times and became its most-capped wing with 33. His record was still standing nearly 30 years later. In 1962 he skippered Scotland to a victory over Wales at Cardiff – its first win on Welsh soil for 35 years.

Nearing the end of his career in 1962, Smith led the Lions out to South Africa. He played in the first three tests which were very close calls indeed (3–3, 3–0 and 8–3) but when he was unavailable for the last test, the Lions were thrashed 34–14.

Arthur Smith was a very dignified and popular figure in British rugby. There was great sadness when he died, aged only 42, in 1975.

SMITH, GEORGE
Auckland and New Zealand
2 internationals for New Zealand 1905

This great all-round athlete had to wait until the age of 31 to play his first international. But it was a memorable one: Smith scored two tries for the All Blacks in their 12–7 win against Scotland in 1905, the second of those coming only four minutes from time, when Scotland led 7–6. A week later, Smith also played against Ireland, but an injury prevented his playing more matches and he was not chosen for New Zealand again.

Between 1897 and 1901 Smith was an outstanding athlete. He won 15 New Zealand titles, at sprint distances and over hurdles, two Australasian

hurdles titles, and a British AAA hurdles title in 1902. He set a world 440yd hurdles record in 1904.

He had also been a jockey, riding the winner of the prestigious New Zealand Cup in 1894.

When his services as a rugby international were no longer required, Smith turned to rugby league and was a member of the pioneering All Golds Australasian (but mainly New Zealand) team in 1907. He returned to play for Oldham until the age of 42, and never set foot again in his native New Zealand.

SMITH, IAN
Oxford University, Edinburgh University and Scotland
32 internationals for Scotland 1924–33
2 internationals for Great Britain 1924

An Australian-born wing who became the world's highest test try-scorer and Scotland's most capped wing. Ian Smith's record of tries in tests (24) stood until David Campese of Australia broke the record at the World Cup in 1987.

Included in Smith's impressive record were consecutive games in which he scored four tries (v France and v Wales in 1925). No other player has ever approached this achievement in full internationals. Smith had scored three tries against Wales in the previous season, making seven against the Welsh in just two appearances. It is one of rugby's curiosities, if not a record, that he actually scored six tries in a row for Scotland (three in the second half of the 1925 game against France and the first three tries of Scotland's next international against Wales).

Smith toured to South Africa in the British team of 1924.

His final total of caps won on the wing stood until his namesake Arthur Smith beat the mark in 1962.

Ian Smith was a superb runner and finisher but he always spoke highly of his fellow Oxford international three-quarters, Johnny Wallace, George Aitken and Phil Macpherson. The four were an outstanding combination of their time.

Smith captained Scotland in his last season, 1933. After having lost all their matches the previous season, Scotland under Smith won all three in 1933 and the 'Flying Scotsman', as he was by then being called, led the Scots to their first Triple Crown in eight years.

SMITH, JOHNNY ('J.B.')
North Auckland and New Zealand
4 internationals for New Zealand 1946–49

Those who dwell on the feats of the 'Kiwis', New Zealand's army team which toured Britain and Europe after World War II, would find it hard to believe Johnny Smith played only four times in test matches for the All Blacks.

But everything seemed to conspire against him. Injuries severely hampered his appearances against Australian teams in 1946–47, and he was not considered for the tour to South Africa in 1949, because of that country's racial policies. Instead, that same season he captained another New Zealand team, chosen from the stay-at-homes, to back-to-back losses against Australia in full internationals.

Then the selectors of the day did not want the talents of Smith in the 1950 series against the British Isles, and he retired two years later.

It was a shocking waste of talent in a man with a great footballing brain and intuitive skills. He had a lightning break and tactical ability, a powerful fend, and ranks as one of New Zealand's best three or four centres.

SOLE, DAVID
Bath, Edinburgh Academicals and
   Scotland
32 internationals for Scotland 1986–91
3 internationals for British Isles 1989

Being captain of Scotland in its Grand Slam win in the Five Nations championship of 1989–90 capped a fine rise in form for this ex-Bath club player. Front-rower Sole, who had been a Scottish international for four previous seasons, was offered the leadership for the 1990 home season when the previous leader, Finlay Calder, was injured. When Calder returned to fitness there were many who called for him to be restored to Scotland's leadership, but the Scottish selectors held firm and said they preferred David Sole's style.

The gamble worked. Not only did Sole lead Scotland superbly in 1990, but he and his Scottish team clinched the Five Nations title in a famous game with the 'auld enemy', England,

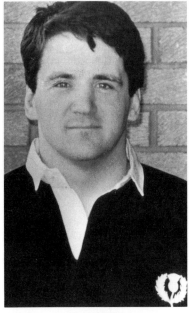

David Sole

on its home turf at Murrayfield. That win placed David Sole along with Phil Macpherson (1924–25) and Jim Aitken (1983–84) as a member of Scotland's exclusive club of Grand Slam skippers.

Sole also led Scotland on its 1990 tour of New Zealand where the test results, although close losses, confirmed that his team was one of the fastest rising in form heading into the 1990s.

Sole was the right kind of leader for Scotland's teams. His modesty and commonsense seemed to fit with the team's style. As a prop he was shortish in stature, a bit like the famous Ian 'Mighty Mouse' McLauchlan of 20 years before, but Sole had strength in abundance and a richness of technique that made him a handful as a scrummager for anyone in the world.

SOUTH AFRICA
Though political forces and the opponents of the apartheid system combined to isolate South Africa in the 1980s, the former British dominion has been one of the most commanding forces in world rugby.

The sport goes back a long way. Only 39 years after William Webb Ellis committed his memorable sin, the first rugby match was played in South Africa. Military played the Civilians on August 23 1862, at the Green Point Common in Cape Town. Unfortunately, one of the Civilians was ab-

sent, so his team played with only 14 men. The goals were 135m (150yd) apart and the game concluded (with no score) an hour and three-quarters later – called off because the wind changed and the Military did not want to take an unfair advantage. One Adriaan van der Byl kicked off for the Civilians, inspiring an anonymous poet to record:

> *Van der Byl started the football,*
> *Mauliana!*
> *His crest shone first amongst us all.*

The *Cape Argus* told of the fair play in the game: '. . . no ungenerous hurt was received and no advantage beyond that of superior weight was taken.'

The poet was not so sure:

> *They stomped upon me where I lay,*
> *How could I rise and kick away?*
> *Methought, 'This is but grewsome*
>   *play!'*
> *A dozen fellows on me lay,*
> *They almost crushed me into clay.*
> *Mauliana!*

The same year, Diocesan College (Bishops) started a form of rugby – appropriately, as its old boys' jerseys later became the Springbok jerseys (*see* SPRINGBOK).

The Swellendam club is assuredly the oldest club still existing in South Africa. It dates from some time prior to 1865, in that year losing all its records in the Great Fire. The oldest authenticated club, Hamilton, was formed in 1875.

The Cape Colony, or Western Province, was unquestionably the stronghold of rugby in South Africa in the nineteenth century. The Western Province union was formed in 1883, and the first inter-

town tournament was played at Cape Town in 1884.

A team from Kimberley, in what became the Griqualand West union, toured to Cape Town in 1888 and suffered from the bane of many touring teams: a lack of uniformity in rule interpretation. Their experience prompted a move to establish a central body, not only to standardise rules but also to organise and finance tours.

The planning for the South African Rugby Board was initiated by Percy Ross Frames, of Kimberley, and William Bissett, from Cape Town, and as Kimberley was the next centre to stage a tournament, Ross Frames was chosen as the first SARB president, in 1889.

One of the great pities of history is that the SARB's first records have been lost, believed to have disappeared – probably dumped – when the Central Diamond Company (which housed the records) merged with De Beers company.

Players were not slow to make an impact on the new board. From the first board for which there are records, in 1892, delegates included Robert Sneddon and Alf Richards, both of them South African captains in 1891, and Bissett and Ben Duff, who also played in that series. The unions represented in those early meetings were Western Province, Griqualand West, Transvaal, Natal, Border and Eastern Province.

International rugby was not slow to come to South Africa. In 1891 a British team captained by the experienced Scottish wing, William Maclagan, toured the colonies.

While the British found it difficult to assemble a team, the tour was regarded with even more trepidation in South Africa. There were fears the fledgling SARB would be sent broke, but Cecil Rhodes undertook to foot any losses, and the spiritual leader of southern Africa, old Paul Kruger, promised to host the visitors royally.

The visitors must have enjoyed themselves, for they were unbeaten and conceded only one try, to Hasie Versfeld for Cape Town clubs. England centre Randolph Aston scored 30 tries in his 19 matches, and scrumhalf Arthur Rotherham, then uncapped by England, kicked goals from all over the field.

South Africa's international pioneers were versatile men. The first captain,

Herbert Castens, was dropped for the second test, but was back at the third – as referee! He also captained South Africa on its first cricket tour of England, in 1894. Alf Richards, captain in the third test, also played for South Africa at cricket.

A British side toured again in 1896, captained by Johnny Hammond, who had been vice-captain on the first tour, but the Boer War precluded any further international contact until 1903, when the third British side toured under the captaincy of Mark Morrison. In 1896 South Africa won its first test; in 1903 its first series.

There was some rugby during the war, however. Field General S.G. Maritz of the Transvaal Scouting Corps, at Concordia, wrote on April 28 1902:

'The Hon. Major Edwards, O'Kiep – Dear Sir: I wish to inform you that I have agreed to a rugby match taking place between you and us. I from my side will agree to order a cease-fire tomorrow afternoon from 12 o'clock until sunset, the time and venue of the match to be arranged by you in consultation with Messrs Roberts and Van Rooyen who I am sending in to you.'

Whether Major Edwards could respond is lost in the sands of time, for the invitation was written in Afrikaans.

New horizons opened for South African rugby in 1906, when Paul Roos captained the first team to tour Britain, Ireland and France. That team fashioned a splendid record, losing only twice (to Scotland and Cardiff) and drawing once in 29 matches.

This team was labelled the Springboks – or more strictly, De Springbokken – by captain Roos, and the South African name was then well-established.

Tom Smyth's fourth British team of 1910 lost the series 1–2; and Billy Millar's 1912–13 Springboks toured Britain, winning an historic Grand Slam, before another war intervened.

The end of World War I brought a new opponent to South Africa. A New Zealand Army side, captained by a pre-war All Black, Charles Brown, made a 14-match tour in 1919, having already won an inter-service tournament in England, the King's Cup.

For the 1921 tour to Australia and New Zealand, national trials were held

for the first time at Newlands. Of the 29 players named to tour, Theo Pienaar was appointed captain, though he could not win a test place and one of the five Morkels, W.H. ('Boy') was the test captain. As with South Africa's first tour to Britain, this was an outstanding success. Five games – virtually always against New South Welshmen – were won in Australia, and in 24 matches in New Zealand the Springboks lost only twice, to Canterbury and the first test All Blacks. They drew with Taranaki and the third test All Blacks.

For the third series in succession, South Africa beat a touring British side. The 1924 team led by Ronnie Cove-Smith managed one draw in the four matches.

More fresh ground was broken in 1928 when the first All Blacks toured South Africa. The great Maurice Brownlie was the captain, and a tough tour and tight test series concluded with honours even. But it was only in the fourth test that the two great tactical flyhalves, Bennie Osler of South Africa, and New Zealand's Mark Nicholls opposed each other. Osler became South Africa's captain in name as well as in fact when South Africa toured Britain again in 1931–32 – a successful but dour tour in a miserable winter.

Then came another new venture for South Africa: hosting the first Australian team to visit. A second new venture, in fact, and unique in international rugby: a five-match series, won by the Springboks 3–2.

Philip Nel's 1937 Springbok team was often said to be 'not the greatest side to leave South Africa, but assuredly the best to return'. This team played 11 matches in Australia and 17 in New Zealand, and it broke the deadlock between the All Blacks and Springboks.

In a much-recalled third and final test, the Springbok scrum demolished the All Blacks and completed a 2–1 series win.

The Springboks won the 1938 series by the same margin against Sam Walker's British side, and a long period of South African world supremacy continued in 1949, when South African international rugby resumed after the Second World War. South Africa whitewashed the touring All Blacks, 4–0, but there was some disquiet – especially in New Zealand – that the

Top: Springbok Louis Moolman is wrapped up by Andy Haden. New Zealand v South Africa, first test, 1981. Peter Bush
Below, left: Referee Clive Norling takes opposing captains Wynand Claassen and Andy Dalton aside for a discussion. 1981.
Right: The 'Geriatrics' – New Zealand's long-serving front row trio, Gary Knight, Andy Dalton and John Ashworth –
playing against the Springboks, 1981. Fotopacific

Top: Halfback Divan Serfontein passes from a scrum, and below, wing Gerrie Germishuys chases a loose ball. South Africa v Auckland 1981, during the Springboks' most recent tour to New Zealand. Peter Bush

A cartoonist's impression of the 1937 Springboks.

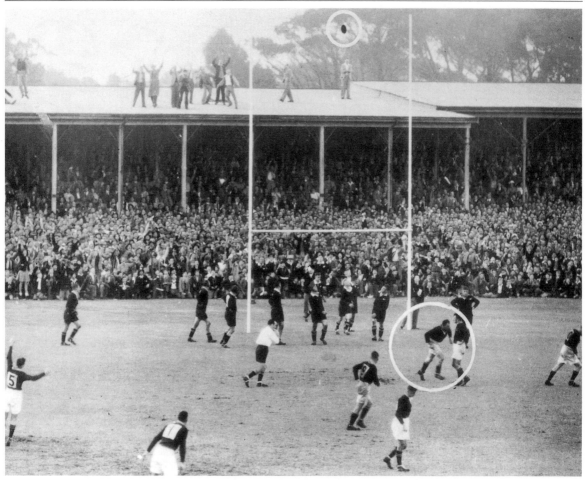

Okey Geffin (circled) turns away after kicking one of the five penalty goals which gave South Africa the first test against New Zealand at Newlands .

Felix du Plessis is carried off the field in triumph after the first test victory over the 1949 All Blacks.

first and third tests were won entirely on penalty goals.

The 1951–52 side which toured Britain is a strong challenger to the 1937 team as South Africa's finest. It lost only to London Counties and the international victories included a 44–0 demolition of Scotland, which erased long memories of the 1906 loss, then the only test defeat suffered by the Springboks in Britain. The team was initially led by a loose forward, Basil Kenyon, but he suffered a serious eye injury very early in the tour and was succeeded by Hennie Muller.

But chinks started appearing in the apparently invincible armour of the mighty 'Boks. An entertaining but flighty and vulnerable Australian team was disposed of in 1953, but the Wallabies shocked their hosts by snatching one of the four test matches.

Then Robin Thompson's Lions of 1955 shared the series, forcing the Springboks to come from behind in the fourth test. Nevertheless, South Africans convinced themselves that they had had to tame a side replete with brilliant backs such as Cliff Morgan, Jeff Butterfield and Tony O'Reilly, and held high hopes for the tour to Australia and New Zealand in 1956.

It's appropriate to mention here that 1956 was also the year Danie Craven became the seventh president of the South African Rugby Board. After Ross Frames (1889–93) had come William Simkins (1893–1913), then William Schreiner (1913–14) – not the famous selector of the same name, Jack Heyneman (1915–27), 'Sport' Pienaar (1927–53), and Edgar Tudehope (1954–56). Craven was to beat Pienaar's record length of service easily.

Craven had become the South African coach after the war, but for the 1956 tour he was the supremo – manager and coach. He had a deputy, Dan de Villiers, but found it hard to give him a job, and de Villiers spent much of his tour addressing – and criticising – New Zealand referees.

The Springboks went through Australia unbeaten, but lost their first match in New Zealand, against Waikato, and found themselves confronted by a nation bent on revenge. There has probably been no more dramatic tour (save those disrupted by anti-apartheid protests) than this, as New Zealanders sought retribution for what they saw as the injustices of 1949.

In a straight repeat of 1921, South Africa lost the first test, then lost to Canterbury and drew with Taranaki, but it also lost the third and fourth tests. The bad news continued two years later. A French team captained originally by Michel Celaya, then by Lucien Mias, had a draw and a win in the two-test series to inflict on South Africa its first home series loss in the twentieth century.

Since that time, South Africa has not enjoyed its former dominance. One of its blackest years was 1965. The Springboks made a brief tour to Scotland and Ireland and returned without a solitary win; they lost the test series in Australia 0–2; and to the All Blacks, 1–3 – and were lucky to win the one test. And salt was rubbed into the wounds when a rookie Argentina side surprised by upsetting the Junior Springboks.

South Africa continued to be a difficult opponent at home, however, winning its home series against New Zealand in 1960, 1970 and 1976, though South African referees came in for considerable criticism. But it struck its bleakest time in the 1974 series against the touring Lions, only a drawn final test preventing the Springboks being on the receiving end of a 0–4 loss.

Tours by South African teams have become increasingly difficult. The Springboks toured Britain in 1960–61 and New Zealand in 1965 without major disturbances, and with success in Britain. Avril Malan's effective but lacklustre side was only deprived of a clean sweep of the internationals by a draw with France, in a torrid encounter, and a loss to the Barbarians.

But the anti-apartheid movement created considerable disruption to the Springboks' tour of Britain in 1969–70 and that tempestuous tour – which started badly, with All Black Chris Laidlaw's Oxford University side winning the opener at Twickenham – spelt the beginning of the end for Springbok tours.

The tour to Australia in 1971 was beset by problems with demonstrators, and subsequent (political) administrations vetoed further tours.

New Zealand Prime Minister Norman Kirk prevented the planned visit to New Zealand in 1973 and the 1981 tour to New Zealand split the country and actually resulted in an adverse

reaction to rugby – only briefly, certainly, but rare and unexpected by that country's administrators.

In the 1980s, South Africa became increasingly isolated from international rugby, as the British unions and Australia, partly under political pressure, declined tours; and while France and New Zealand had a greater willingness to tour, political forces usually succeeded where the anti-apartheid movement had failed.

Argentina – in both 1980 and 1984 hiding under the banner of South America – gave South Africa some international competition, and in one extraordinary reversal of form in 1982 came from a first test drubbing to win the second match.

South Africa, however, continued to be a member of the inner circle of the sport's administration as a full member of the International Rugby Board, and attempted to keep its international status alive on two fronts. One was by inviting 'international' XVs to various anniversaries through the 1980s, though not all nations would pass on invitations to their players. New Zealand, the World Cup holder, was not officially represented at the South African Rugby Board's 1989 centennial celebrations.

The other tactic was the clandestine organising of 'rebel' tours. SARB president Danie Craven was embarrassed – or was he? – when the Cavaliers arrived in South Africa while he was away at an IRB meeting.

South Africa generously backed out of possible World Cup competition in 1987 (see WORLD CUP) but its spies were at the event anyway, and the upshot was another 'rebel' tour – something Craven had said would not recur. This was by the South Seas Barbarians, a mixture of Fijian, Tongan and Western Samoan players.

South African rugby has had a glittering history and there has been considerable frustration in many quarters that its team has been unable to measure up against the rest of the world in free and open competition for the past 25 years. However, in 1991, South Africa took major steps towards returning to the fold.

During the years of protest against apartheid and Springbok tours, the case for South African rugby had not been helped by the republic having four separate and racial rugby bodies.

The South African Rugby Board was composed of white players only during the first 80 years of the twentieth century. The South African Rugby Federation was composed of coloured players, and there were two bodies which catered for black players only: the South African Rugby Association and the South African Rugby Union.

Progress was made towards unification when in the 1980s two of the above bodies, SARF and SARA, joined the powerful SARB. This meant that coloured players were chosen to play for South Africa. The first of these was the utility back Errol Tobias, who played against Ireland at home in 1981, then toured New Zealand and the United States in the same year, before playing against England in 1984. To the end of 1990 the only other coloured player to play for the Springboks was wing Avril Williams, who also appeared against England in 1984.

Thus resistance to accepting South Africa back as an equal partner in world rugby was only held up by the separation of SARU from the main governing body, still named the South African Rugby Board.

The loosening of the tight bonds of apartheid in 1990–91 led to meetings taking place, and agreement was eventually reached that SARU and SARB would form a new, unified, multiracial body, to be known as the South African Rugby Football Union. This new organisation was scheduled to come into being in October 1991, with the expectation that this would open the way to South Africa's acceptance back into the mainstream of world rugby.

As Danie Craven said, 'We deserve it. After the long drought we've had in rugby, the steps taken by our government should warrant our being back in the world. Nothing stands in the way any more.'

SOUTH AMERICAN RUGBY CONFEDERATION

This body, founded in 1981, was set up to look after the combined interests of rugby on the South American continent. The founding nations were Brazil, Chile, Paraguay and Uruguay. The most powerful country in the region, Argentina, stayed out of the original formation. The main function of the body is to organise the South American senior and junior championships.

SOUTH AUSTRALIA RFU

Rugby is not one of the major sports in and around the city of Adelaide and the strong sports of the region, Australian rules football and soccer, dominate public interest. However, enthusiasm for rugby is keen among those who are committed. The union was founded officially in 1932, and after 60 years of official existence there are a dozen clubs in the area. A number of these are strictly social – in fact in descriptions about rugby in South Australia the world 'social' appears a number of times! Club games are not usually noted for their fierce competition.

Sadly, in rugby terms the area is best known for the huge scores touring New Zealand sides have notched up while enjoying South Australian hospitality. Among the 13 highest scores the New Zealanders have ever registered anywhere in the world, four have been against South Australia: 117–6 in 1974, 99–0 in 1984, 77–0 in 1962, and 75–3 in 1980! *See* ADELAIDE.

However, balanced against that was a famous win scored by South Australia over Fiji in 1976, when the southerners triumphed by 10–7, their only win over a major country in their first 60 years in existence.

Two players from South Australia have represented Australia. The first was Malcolm van Gelder, who came to prominence while studying at the Royal Military College in Duntroon near Canberra. Returning to Adelaide, van Gelder, a loose forward, was chosen to tour New Zealand in 1958. He appeared only twice and did not play a test match. Then halfback Rod Hauser, a former Queenslander, made the 1973 Australian touring team for the British tour while studying in the south. After returning to Queensland in 1974 he went on to win 17 caps for his country.

SOUTH CANTERBURY RFU

The southerners were originally members of the Canterbury RFU. The South Canterbury and Temuka clubs were formed in 1875, and they played a 'Town v Country' match before choosing the side to play the Christchurch club in Canterbury's first inter-club match that year.

One of the instigators of South Canterbury rugby was an old boy of the Marlborough Nomads club, Alfred Hamersley. An England forward in the first international of all, against Scotland in 1871, he went on to play the next three matches as well and was captain in 1873.

The Waimate club was formed in 1876, and by 1888 South Canterbury clubs had seceded from Canterbury and formed their own union, based in Timaru.

South Canterbury rugby cannot be said to have flourished, but in 1949, it provided brothers Jack and Maurie Goddard and Lachie 'Goldie' Grant to the All Black team in South Africa. Two 1938 All Blacks, Tom Morrison and Charlie Saxton (better known as an Otago man), lost their best years to the Second World War but became distinguished coaches and administrators.

Perhaps the finest of South Canterbury's All Blacks was Ron Stewart, a youngster with the 1924 'Invincibles' and a stalwart of the 1928 All Blacks in South Africa, where he played 18 of the 22 matches.

South Canterbury does not boast a glittering record against overseas teams, but did beat France in 1961, California in 1972 and Romania in 1975; while it held the Ranfurly Shield for one match in 1950 and for a slightly longer period in 1974. Ah, those were the days.

Until 1977, South Canterbury wore green and black hooped jerseys and black shorts. But hooped jerseys cost a bit much to produce these days and South Canterbury jerseys are now just green with some black trim.

SOUTH PACIFIC CHAMPIONSHIP

Though bearing a fairly grand title, in truth this series, contested 1986–90, was a regional invitation tournament conducted by the New South Wales Rugby Union and featuring the top Australian state sides, New South Wales and Queensland, the national side of Fiji, and New Zealand's pre-eminent provinces – Auckland, Canterbury and Wellington.

Staged in April and May each year, a pipe-opener to the full representative season, it gave the Australian sides relief from having to play each other to get hard competition; it gave Fiji additional tough competition which undoubtedly aided its development; and the All Black selectors generally welcomed the matches. While it made for a very long season for the leading players, it gave the majority of the All Blacks very useful and hard early season play, which was important with most overseas tours to New Zealand starting in May or June.

The series was played as a round-robin, each team having two or three games at home, the balance away, and the reverse the following year. Canterbury was the first winner, though losing to New South Wales – in fact Canterbury lost to NSW all five times. Canterbury also won the second year, beating Auckland in the decider when both teams were depleted by World Cup calls on the All Blacks. The following three tournaments were won by Auckland, though after losing to NSW in 1989, the Auckland team had to count on Queensland beating its southern rival in the final round – which it did.

Other strong New Zealand unions resented the privileged status of Auckland, Canterbury and Wellington, and the NZRFU attempted to influence places going to the top three teams in the national championship, but the NSW union pointed out (rightly) that this was its own invitation tournament. The three unions chosen were also the only three in New Zealand with international airports. So the Otago union started its own 'CANZ' tournament – the initials standing for Canada, Argentina and New Zealand.

The South Pacific championship was suspended by the impoverished NSW union after the 1990 series.

SOUTHLAND RFU

The most southern rugby union in the world, Southland is also renowned for the local delicacy, Bluff oysters, a never-ending supply of which are fed to touring teams, especially before a game. Is it any wonder then, that eight Australian sides and the Lions of 1950 and 1966, the 1957 Fijians and the 1979 and 1989 French should all have succumbed to Southland?

The Southland union was formed in 1887, originally as part of the Otago union. Rugby was first played in the area in 1876. One game between Invercargill and Otautau lasted three hours, with large stones on the farmer's paddock 'greatly obstructing play', according to one contemporary report.

Southland was the first South Island union to win the Ranfurly Shield, in 1920. From 1937 to 1950 the shield was the constant property of the southern neighbours, Otago and Southland, but since then Southland has only once, briefly in 1959, held the 'Log of Wood'.

Billy Stead, vice-captain of the 1905 All Blacks, was the first great player to emerge from the union. Jock Richardson was vice-captain of the next team to tour Britain, 19 years later, and he achieved the distinction of captaining the test side with tour captain Cliff Porter unable to win a place. 'Son' White was another fine forward in that team.

Ned Hughes, the oldest of all internationals, was a Southland All Black; and a fiery international forward was Bill Hazlett, whose nephew, Jack, propped with distinction for the All Blacks in the 1960s.

Southland had 49 All Blacks in its first 100 years, and none had a better temperament for the big time than Brian McKechnie. Nicknamed 'Colt', McKechnie was called up to take a critical kick against Wales in 1978, the All Blacks trailing 10–12 and with time all but up. The kick was taken in nerve-wracking conditions, the crowd baying its disapproval following the infamous 'dive' from a lineout by Andy Haden (although the penalty was actually awarded for Geoff Wheel levering himself off the shoulder of Frank Oliver, another Southland All Black).

Ice-cool McKechnie never looked like missing. A New Zealand representative cricketer as well, McKechnie was also the recipient of the infamous underarm ball bowled by Trevor Chappell at the end of a one-day international in Melbourne.

Southland has always worn maroon jerseys, with black shorts until 1950. It then changed to white shorts – perhaps better to highlight the mud which is often on the pitch at Rugby Park, Invercargill.

SPAIN

The game in Spain made slow but steady progress through the first half of the twentieth century before experiencing a boom in the 1960s and 70s. By 1980 there were more than 10,000 registered players, mostly around Madrid and Barcelona, and two national leagues are now in operaton. By 1990, and Spain's first appearance in the Rugby World Cup, there were more than 12,000 players and more than 100 clubs.

The Spanish playing style mirrors that of their neighbours, the French, who have been a strong influence. Backline play in Spain is slick and fluent while forward play can be hard, though too often inexperience shows at an international level.

The Spanish province of Catalonia was a foundation member of FIRA in 1934 and Spain has been a regular in

Bernard Dutin (right), of the 1968 French team, samples Southland's famous oysters. French rugby writer, Denis Lalanne (in cap), and Jo Maso look on.

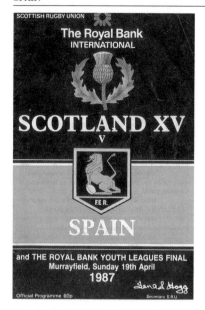

FIRA's leagues since they were formed in 1973–74. Over the years Spain has been in and out of division one.

Spanish rugby really hit the headlines in 1986, when the national sevens team travelled to Australia for the inaugural New South Wales International Sevens tournament. Stories were published in the local newspapers of several of the Spanish players asking for videotapes so they could see how sevens was played!

Imagine the sensation when, on the first day of the tournament, the Spanish whipped England by 24–6! A win followed against the Netherlands and Spain only bowed out of the series after a 6–12 loss to Argentina in the quarter-finals. Invitations to compete at other prestigious sevens tournaments, like Hong Kong, followed.

Spain entered the 1991 Rugby World Cup qualifying series and hosted one of the European qualifying tournaments. The Madrid series was one of the great moments for Spanish rugby and was extremely well organised. Spain won through to the final European qualifying stage by beating the other three teams, Netherlands, Poland and Belgium.

A year later Spain played off in Italy for a place in the final 16 teams for the cup. It won one game and lost two, finishing third in the group and just missing out. It was an encouraging effort for the Spaniards, who had earlier been relegated out of FIRA's first division.

Rugby in Spain has some tremendous difficulties to overcome. Lack of grounds is one major problem, as is a shortage of referees. The distance to travel is another enormous hurdle. Yet the game has a strong core of interest, and in some of the regional areas the followers of bull-fighting and soccer (the main national pastimes) have had to become more aware of rugby in recent times.

A powerful personality in the development of Spanish rugby has been the Basque coach, Gérard Murillo. A Frenchman from St Jean de Luz, he has been regularly involved with the coaching and preparation of the Spanish national XV.

An early Spanish player to break through internationally was the centre Alfonso Garoia, who was invited to tour South Africa in 1977 with the World XV. By the 1991 World Cup series, the experience of some Spanish players was starting to come through. The stylish fullback Francisco Puertas had appeared in 44 full internationals, the speedy centre Jon Azkargorta in 49, the captain and prop, Julio Alvarez, in 46, while the veteran centre Salvador Torres had appeared 57 times for his country.

SPANGHERO, WALTER
Narbonne and France
51 internationals for France 1964–73

The most prominent of a family of fine rugby-playing brothers from the town of Narbonne in southern France. Walter Spanghero was powerful and aggressive, playing for his country in three forward positions during a brilliant and sometimes turbulent career which spanned 10 seasons.

His younger brother, Claude, was also a top performer and had 22 caps as a loose forward. Two other brothers, Jean-Marie and Laurent, were also prominent in local rugby. Jean-Marie joined his two international brothers in the Narbonne team which narrowly lost the French club championship final to Béziers in Paris in 1974. Laurent, the oldest, led the way into the Narbonne pack, and at times all four played together in what was then called 'half a ton of Spangheros!'

Walter was a late inclusion in the 1964 French team which toured South Africa and he won his first cap in the only international ever played at

Springs. France won in a big upset by 8–6. South African writers were lavish in their praise of the new discovery, calling him 'the fastest 15-stone forward in the world'.

From then until 1970 he was a regular choice in the French pack, though he changed from lock to loose forward during his second tour to South Africa in 1967. He forged a huge reputation as a tough and talented ball player. His most noticable physical attribute was a pair of huge hands; some even said he had the biggest hands ever seen in rugby.

In 1970 Spanghero published a book in which he made several cracks at selections in the French team, including one at his old team-mate, Benoit Dauga. The remarks put him offside with the selectors and he announced his retirement at the end of that year – just ahead, it was said, of the selectors dropping him.

Yet only two months into 1971, Walter was back in the national side to play England. He locked the scrum with his brother, Claude, the first time two French brothers had achieved this distinction.

It was at this time that France began a losing sequence of 10 consecutive internationals. The run of misfortune only ended when the selectors turned to Walter Spanghero to became an inspirational captain. In the match which bade farewell to Colombes Stadium, the French team thrashed England by 37–12.

By now Spanghero was being called 'Walter the Magnificent'. He continued as captain for a further 10 matches until his retirement in 1973.

He is recalled as one of France's all-time greats.

SPRINGBOK
South African rugby teams have been known, perhaps incorrectly, as the 'Springboks' since 1906, the name distorted from the original 'springbuck'.

Until 1906 South Africa wore jerseys organised by the host union, which was also usually charged with selecting the side. When 'Fairy' Heatlie captained South Africa in the final of the 1896 series against Britain, he used the green jerseys of his club, Old Diocesan. The club was in recess by 1903, but Heatlie still had a set of jerseys and resurrected them for the final test that year.

In 1906 the South African Rugby Board took a conscious decision to set the colours, as revealed by its minutes of September 12: 'The Board's colours . . . shall be a green jersey having Springbuck badge on left breast and white collar, black knickers, dark blue stockings with two white stripes at the top, green cap with gold trimmings, having Springbuck head as badge.'

However, the 'springbuck' head was already used on the 1903 Springbok cap and the cap and badge became official wear in 1904.

J. Cecil Carden, manager of the 1906 team in England, recalled that 'No uniforms or blazers had been provided, and we were a motley turn-out at practice at Richmond. That evening I spoke to [Paul] Roos and [Paddy] Carolin and pointed out that the witty London press would invent some funny name for us if we did not invent one ourselves. We thereupon agreed to call ourselves Springboks, and to tell pressmen we desired so to be named. I remember this distinctly, for Paul reminded us that 'Springbokken' was the correct plural. The *Daily Mail*, after our first practice, called us the Springboks and the name stuck.'

Caps disappeared in 1933 and in 1960 were abolished formally. The diagonal old gold stripes on the green Springbok ties were replaced in 1937 with the springbok emblem – the same year as the team adopted white shorts.

The other springbok is the stuffed and mounted head taken by each touring side and given to the first host team to beat it.

That practice began in 1912 with Billy Millar's side.

SQUIRE, JEFF
Newport, Pontypool and Wales
29 internationals for Wales 1977–83
6 internationals for British Isles 1977–83

A fine energetic and industrious Welsh loose forward who made three British Isles tours in all, Jeff Squire had only played two internationals for his country when he made his first Lions tour, to New Zealand in 1977, as a replacement for Roger Uttley. He had the difficult job of taking over from the great and much-lamented Mervyn Davies, who had been injured and retired from rugby.

In New Zealand Squire displayed expert control of ball from the back of

Jeff Squire in action for the British Isles.

the scrum, and perhaps he deserved to play in more than just one test match.

In 1980 he cemented his place with the Lions in South Africa, enjoying an excellent tour and playing in all four tests. He was back for his third Lions tour, to New Zealand, in 1983. He appeared in the first test but then was sidelined with a shoulder injury.

All the while Squire was adding to an impressive record with his home club Pontypool and with Wales. In his first three seasons he was part of Welsh teams which won the Triple Crown three times and added a Grand Slam in the second season.

In 1980 Squire's experience earned him promotion to captain of Wales, and he was the leader at Twickenham that year when Paul Ringer was sent off and accusations flew concerning Welsh players' attitudes to rough play on the field. Squire scored one of Wales's tries that day.

Jeff Squire captained Wales six times, for three wins.

SQUIRES, PETER
Harrogate and England
29 internationals for England 1973–79
1 international for British Isles 1977

A former flyhalf and fullback, before he became a wing who rose to the top

in British rugby in the 1970s. After he had played two internationals against France and Scotland, he scored a try on Eden Park in Auckland in 1973, which helped England beat New Zealand in one of the big surprises of that decade.

Such form meant Squires was a candidate for the 1974 Lions tour of South Africa, but he was also a good Yorkshire cricketer and the events clashed. Squires chose to play cricket for his county instead, which he did for five seasons.

Squires's chance with the Lions came in 1977 when he toured New Zealand. He played in only the first test before being inexplicably left out of the second test – one of a number of mystifying decisions made on that tour. An injury then denied him the chance to press his claims later in the tour.

His last game for England was in 1979 against Wales. In all he scored six tries for his country.

SRI LANKA
The Ceylon Rugby Union was formed as early as 1878. In early days the game was played mostly by British servicemen and sailors, but since independence the locals have continued rugby traditions in fine style. Nowadays the game has a good hold, especially among police and soldiers – perhaps a continuation of the traditions set by the British services. Rugby is very popular in the capital city of Colombo and in the hill capital of Kandy. Crowds of up to 15,000 have watched top club games.

The British Isles stopped in Colombo for a game on the way home from their tour of New Zealand and Australia in 1950 and England played two matches in the same city in 1971. In 1954 and 1955 Australian and New Zealand Colts teams had toured.

Physically, Sri Lankans are lightly framed, but they have height, and their forwards can be very competitive on the Asian rugby scene. They have competed regularly in the Hong Kong Sevens since its inception in 1976 and had a major breakthrough when its national team toured Wales in 1987.

In 1990 Sri Lanka had a fine series at the Asian championship which was held on home soil at Colombo. Coached by a former All Black, Jeff Matheson, the team beat Taiwan 9–6, lost narrowly to Hong Kong (13–21) and to the eventual winner, Korea (13–26). The interest raised was such that 30,000 fans turned out to watch the final when Korea beat Japan. Local rugby followers were delighted with the new public profile.

Sri Lanka plays in white jerseys with a prominent symbol of an elephant, its national rugby crest.

ST HELEN'S GROUND

The rugby ground in Swansea which hosted Wales's first home match, v England in 1882, and which has since grown to be one of the most prominent sports fields, summer and winter, in Wales. St Helen's is owned by the municipality of Swansea and is the headquarters of the Swansea rugby team as well as a regular venue for the Glamorgan County Cricket Club. Rugby league tests have also been played there.

St Helen's is also remembered for one of the more remarkable cricket feats. The great West Indian cricketer Garfield Sobers once hit a Glamorgan

bowler, Malcolm Nash, for six sixes in one over on the ground.

In that first rugby international against England the Welsh team conceded six tries. On other occasions there were happier results for Welsh and Swansea teams. Between 1899 and 1954 internationals in Wales were shared fairly evenly between Swansea and Cardiff, but after 1954 the bigger capacity at Cardiff Arms Park meant all internationals shifted to the east.

The St Helen's Ground could never be called one of the most modern rugby stadiums in the world. In 1982, the great All Black fullback George Nepia went back to Wales for his first trip there since he had been a member of the victorious 1924–25 New Zealand team. He was taken to watch a game in Cardiff but said he 'could not recognise the ground in any way at all'. But when he was taken across Wales to Swansea and went to a game at St Helen's (where his All Black team had played Wales) he said 'It's exactly the same as when I played here.'

St Helen's in the 1920s, with every available space taken!

STAGG, PETER
Sale and Scotland
28 internationals for Scotland 1965–70
3 internationals for British Isles 1968

A strong and sturdy lock who gave grand service for Scotland for five years from the mid-1960s. He was best known, perhaps, as the tallest of all international players. Stagg stood at 2.08 metres (6ft 10in) and weighed more than 115 kilograms (18 stone).

He made his debut for Scotland in 1965 v France when one reporter said the sight of him caused 'consternation' among the French team and crowd at Colombes Stadium. Earlier, in 1961–62, he had twice played for Oxford University in the annual game with Cambridge. In 1968 he toured South Africa with Tom Kiernan's Lions. He played in three of the four test matches in that series.

STEPHENS, REES
Neath and Wales
32 internationals for Wales 1947–57
2 internationals for British Isles 1950

Glyn Stephens was a notable figure in rugby, being a former Welsh international, a WRU president and a delegate to the IRB. His son, Rees, became a highly acclaimed Welsh forward in the years after World War II.

A Neath man through and through, Rees Stephens was born in the town and played for it all his rugby life. The intrusion of the war years meant that he did not make his international debut until he was nearly 25. Although he did not win continual first team selection, Stephens was a fine lock or No. 8 who played for Wales for 11 seasons and was still in the team, as captain, one month short of his 35th birthday, his total of 32 caps becoming a new test record for a Welsh forward.

Stephens toured New Zealand and Australia with the 1950 British Isles team. A shoulder injury restricted his appearances in New Zealand to eight games, but he played both test matches in Australia on the way home.

STEPHENSON, GEORGE
Queen's University, Belfast, London Hospital and Ireland
42 internationals for Ireland 1920–30

A brilliant Irish centre whose final tally of 42 internationals stood for 26 years as the world record for caps won by any one player from any country.

Stephenson made his debut in April 1920, aged only 18 years and 5 months. Over the next 10 years he missed only two internationals, and those only because of injury. He scored 14 tries in tests, which was not beaten as the Irish record until 60 years later. He captained his country in his last 13 test outings, spread over three seasons.

He is remembered in Ireland as a brilliant runner who only knew the straight and hard way through the opposition. He was also an excellent tackler and a top goal-kicker.

Stephenson played much of his rugby in England while studying medicine, and in 1929 he was in the Middlesex team that won the English county championship.

His brother Henry was a wing for Ireland on 14 occasions.

STEWART'S-MELVILLE FP

When two Edinburgh Schools, Daniel Stewart's and Melville College, amalgamated, it was logical that the rugby clubs of both schools' former pupils would follow suit. This was achieved in 1973 and as both clubs were well established it took only a few seasons for the combined club to grow into one of the most respected in Scotland.

Stewart's-Melville has been led in the years since its formation by some of Scotland's most accomplished players. Its highest-capped players have been the Calder twins, Jim and Finlay.

Jim was the first to wear the Scottish and Lions colours, eventually playing 27 caps for his country. Finlay followed him into the flanker's position, playing 28 times and captaining the Lions on the series-winning tour of Australia in 1989. He also captained Scotland the previous season.

For much of the 1980s there were four Calder brothers in the Stewart's-Melville forward pack. Television commentator Bill McLaren used to relish telling the story of when he broadcast their games. 'When there was a pushover try happening for Stewart's and it was difficult to see who'd got it, I'd just say "try to Calder!" That way I'd know I'd have a 50–50 chance of getting it right!'

Other Stewart's-Melville men include another former Scottish captain, Douglas Morgan, a 21-cap veteran at scrumhalf; Douglas Wyllie, the flyhalf for four games in the 1987 Rugby World Cup, and Alex Brewster, who became a long-serving Scottish international as either a flanker or a prop.

The most-capped player from either of the two original clubs was Stewart's College FP's Thomas Weatherstone, who had 12 internationals as wing, 1952–59.

SULLIVAN, JACK
Taranaki and New Zealand
6 internationals for New Zealand 1937–38

World War II, then a leg injury, cost Jack Sullivan the best footballing years of his life, but his form against the 1937 Springboks was sufficient to stamp him as a centre of high quality. The All Black selectors' mentality was apparently not of the same quality, for after he had scored two tries from centre in the second test, he was banished to the left wing!

Sullivan furnished a record of unusually broad service to rugby in New Zealand. He coached Taranaki for six years, and also coached the North Island, New Zealand Juniors and the All Blacks.

Then he turned to administration and succeeded to the chairmanship of the New Zealand Rugby Union council (which carried with it a seat on the IRB). He became notorious for media statements which usually amounted to 'no comment'.

SULLIVAN, PETER
New South Wales and Australia
13 internationals for Australia 1971–73

A disappointingly brief international career came to an abrupt end when Sullivan, who was Australian captain at the time, turned to rugby league in 1974.

Sullivan took over the captaincy when veteran leader Greg Davis was injured just after half-time in the second test against New Zealand in 1972. His inspiring performance in those 36 minutes suggested a long career in succession to Davis. But after home tests against Tonga and leading the Wallabies on their tour to Wales and England, Sullivan had gone.

The mobile flanker made his debut in the three-test series when Australia was whitewashed by the 1971 Spring-

boks. He played against France, both away and at home in 1971 and 1972.

Sullivan missed only one test in his short career – the third international in New Zealand in 1972 – and then only because of injury.

SWANSEA FC
Correctly named, this powerful and influential west Wales club is actually the Swansea Cricket and Football Club. It was formed in 1874 and has always been one of the foremost Welsh clubs – one of the 'big four' (the others being Cardiff, Llanelli and Newport). Many of the greatest of Welsh players have worn the famous all-white uniform of Swansea.

The club has its headquarters at St Helen's along the seafront of the wide Swansea Bay. Many a great contest was hosted by Swansea, including the first home match played by Wales in 1883, and the All Blacks' visit in 1924.

The club itself has had its moments with touring teams. Swansea toppled the Australians in 1908 by 6–0; it beat the Springboks 3–0 on Boxing Day 1912; and in 1935, on what was arguably Swansea's greatest day, it became the first Welsh club side to beat an All Black team, by 11–3. The great Welsh centre Claude Davey ran in two tries.

That was the day Haydn Tanner and Willie Davies, two schoolboys from nearby Gowerton Grammar School, were chosen to play for Swansea. The two lads were cousins and were only 18 and 19 years old, but they were not in awe of the mighty All Blacks. The win to Swansea brought forth one of the more famous quotes from All Black skipper Jack Manchester, who said to a press man after the game, 'You can say what you like about this result, but just don't tell New Zealand we were beaten by a couple of schoolboys!'

Swansea also drew with the All Blacks in 1953 and beat Australia in 1966.

In its first 115 years Swansea's most-capped international player, and one of its all-time greats, was the No. 8 Mervyn Davies, who was a 38-cap player until a severe head injury cut his career short.

There are many others from Swansea who have graced the world rugby stage. 'Dicky' Owen had 35 caps for Wales – a Welsh record until Ken Jones of Newport beat it a generation later.

The brilliant wing of the 1960s, Dewi Bebb, had 34 caps, while in the nineteenth century, Billy Bancroft had 33 caps in a row, then a world record for any international from any country. Billy's brother, Jack, a great goalkicker, was also a Swansea man, winning 18 caps.

Robert Jones, the modern halfback, made his debut in 1986 and raced to 32 caps before he was dropped by the Welsh selectors. He did, however, give promise that in the 1990s he would come back and win many more. Billy Trew, a Welsh international over 14 seasons, also the Welsh captain and an international player in three positions, won 29 caps.

Swansea was the first British club to play behind the iron curtain, touring to Romania in 1954. The Welsh and Lions flanker Clem Thomas was captain of that team. Thomas had 26 caps for his country. Later he established several big businesses in Swansea as well as becoming a prolific and respected writer on the game.

SWEDEN

Swedish rugby began officially in 1931 when the SRF (Svenska Rugby Forbundet) was formed. The status of the game was such that by 1934 Sweden was one of the founder members of FIRA, but only two months later it withdrew in favour of Belgium, for reasons which are obscure. The records show it was reaffirmed in FIRA in 1958.

As in any Swedish sport, rivalries with other Scandinavian countries are strong. Denmark provided the first international opposition in 1949 and along with Finland is a regular opponent. The Scandinavian Cup is at stake in regular competition between these nations.

Sweden made a significant step forward in its rugby when it entered the qualifying stages of the 1991 Rugby World Cup. The team travelled to Tours in France for a European qualifying tournament and wins over Israel, Denmark and Switzerland saw Sweden through to the fourth round. There it

lost 3–24 to the Netherlands. Playing in the tournament nearly bankrupted the SRF but the whole project was considered a big step forward for rugby in that country.

In 1990 there were 3000 adult rugby players in Sweden, playing in one national league and two regional leagues, with 60 clubs involved. Most of the clubs are centred around Stockholm and Gothenburg; it is too cold in the north to play rugby during the winter.

SWITZERLAND

The Swiss Rugby Federation was not formed until 1971, although the game was played there as far back as 1869. One publication's assertion that Switzerland is 'one of the oldest rugby-playing nations in the world' might come as a surprise to many, but it is true. Two of the top football clubs, Grasshoppers Zurich and Servette Geneva, actually began as sporting clubs which specialised in rugby. It was only later that they changed to playing soccer.

Rugby faded away in Switzerland during World War I, largely as a result of British and French residents returning home from their temporary Swiss lifestyles. After a brief revival in the 1930s, World War II sent the game reeling into oblivion again. It was not until 1967 that the game restarted and the national federation was formed four years later.

For a time the Swiss played 'with the big boys' in the FIRA competitions, having been accepted in 1973. But in 1985 they withdrew to concentrate on developing their junior rugby and forging a better international standard.

At international level Swiss progress was slow. In 1979 the national squad toured Portugal and Morocco, where it not only lost both internationals, but failed to score a solitary point! (The scores were 43–0 and 31–0.)

At the time of the Swiss bid in the qualifying rounds of the 1991 Rugby World Cup there were 1000 registered club players spread over 23 clubs. In the World Cup Switzerland opened a

four-team qualifying series in Tours, France with a win over Israel. Then followed losses to Denmark and Sweden. The venture was considered a success, considering the previous modest history and the fact that international experience was severely lacking in a young team with an average age of only 22.

SYDNEY CRICKET GROUND

Although its name tells you its primary sport, the Sydney Cricket Ground had a long and illustrious record as a ground for rugby test matches. Many top players regarded it as one of the finest surfaces on which to play the game.

The association of rugby and the Sydney Cricket Ground goes back to August 1882, when New South Wales played Queensland in the first interstate game.

The first international game followed two years later when New Zealand arrived to play a 'Combined Suburbs XVII'. New Zealand won by 23–5.

The first test match on the ground – the first ever undertaken by an Australian team – was in 1899, when Australia beat Great Britain by 13–3.

The SCG continued to be used for major games until just before the Rugby World Cup in 1987. By then the New South Wales and Australian Rugby Unions had made a commitment to develop their own rugby stadium. So major games shifted to Concord Oval and World Cup games were played there in 1987.

In recent years, politicking in Sydney has seen the venue for major rugby union games shift again, to the new Sydney Football Stadium. It seems now that the cricket ground will be essentially lost to rugby union: major games will be played on to the next door SFS, while club and representative games will stay at Concord.

In all 71 test matches were played at the SCG, with Australia winning 32 and drawing four. Over the last 10 years the Wallabies were pretty formidable there, winning 17 of 20 test matches.

TAIWAN

As Formosa, Taiwan was under Japanese rule for half a century, so it is logical that rugby came to Taiwan out of Japan. According to one story, a Chinese student, Chen Chin-chung, returned to his homeland carrying a rugby ball in his baggage. He started teaching other boys to play and so the game slowly developed.

When Japanese rule ended after World War II, the army decided that such a virile and vigorous game would be useful as a training exercise for the troops. Thus rugby gained a serious foothold and, along with students, soldiers are still the main source of players today.

Taiwan has always keenly contested the Asian Rugby championship, hosting the event in 1980. Since 1984, the Kwang Hua-Taipei provincial team has been invited to play in the Hong Kong Sevens.

TANNER, HAYDN

Swansea, Cardiff and Wales
25 internationals for Wales 1935–49
1 international for British Isles 1938

One of Wales's greatest players, and certainly its longest serving (his international career lasted 15 seasons and spanned World War II). Haydn Tanner was a sharp and innovative scrumhalf whose forté was his strength and superb ball-handling ability. Playing in an era when the grounds were not the well-drained, even-grassed lawns of today, Tanner won a reputation for being able to clear his pass, no matter how heavy the ball or the footing. He was a strong, incisive runner too, in a distinctive hunched manner, though he never scored a try for Wales. There are many old-time rugby watchers who claim Tanner was the greatest of scrumhalves.

Tanner was an 18-year-old sixth former at Gowerton Grammar School in 1935 when he and his cousin, Willie Davies, were selected for Swansea to play the All Blacks. The two combined in a sensational display of halfback play which paved the way for a famous 11–3 win.

Kwang-Hua Taipei plays Fiji at the Hong Kong Sevens tournament.

As a result, the teenaged Tanner was rushed into the Welsh team to play New Zealand. That side also won (13–12) and Tanner had the enviable record of two wins over the All Blacks from two outings – and he never played them again!

Tanner was never dropped as Welsh scrumhalf and it was a tribute to his strength and stamina that he continued just as strongly after the eight-year gap in international rugby during World War II. The only other Welshman to play both before and after the war was the Llanelli fullback Howard Davies.

Tanner also played in eight services international matches and the four 'Victory' internationals of 1946. He was given the honour of leading the Barbarians club to a 9–6 win in its first match against an overseas touring side, the Wallabies of 1948–49 at Cardiff.

As a member of the 1938 British Isles team in South Africa Tanner added one extra cap to his total, playing the second test at Port Elizabeth.

TARANAKI RFU

On the west coast of New Zealand's North Island, within sight of the mag-
nificent Mt Egmont, is the city of New Plymouth, home of the Taranaki Rugby Union. Over the years, on their home ground of Rugby Park, the amber and black hooped jerseys of Taranaki have provided stern opposition to all visiting sides.

Taranaki is essentially a rural union, and its rugby players are traditionally strong men of the land. Some of their finest moments came when they were holders of the prized Ranfurly Shield in two eras, 1957–59 and 1963–65. In those seasons, week after week, the top teams of New Zealand came to New Plymouth only to be turned back by a tight home team. Ross Brown, Peter Burke, Kevin Briscoe, Roger Urbahn, Terry O'Sullivan, Neil Wolfe, John McCullough and John Major all became All Blacks.

The Taranaki team did not play what you might call 'bright' rugby. Instead it was tough stuff up-front, designed to win the ball back to first five-eighths Ross Brown for a drop-kick; but it was winning rugby and the years with the Ranfurly Shield are remembered as Taranaki's best.

In recent years, two of New Zealand's greatest players came from Taranaki. Graham Mourie and David Loveridge were both farmers from small towns around the base of Mt Egmont. From their modest backgrounds they rose to stand alongside the very best in the world in their respective playing positions: Mourie as a fast-breaking flanker and All Black captain; and Loveridge, also a captain of his country, as a superb test halfback.

Another little Taranaki hamlet, Kaponga, gave the province two leading players. The 1972–73 All Black lock, Ian Eliason, who set the provincial record for appearances, played 222 games for the colours over 17 years.

The ever-reliable All Black fullback, Kieran Crowley, was also from Kaponga. He was not always first choice as All Black fullback, but in the 1980s and 1990s, when in doubt, the selectors always went back to him for steadiness and security in the No. 15 jersey.

Although it has played regular games against major touring teams,

Taranaki has not had great success. It beat Australia, 11–10 in 1931 and England, 6–3 in 1963; drew twice with South Africa (0–0 and 3–3) in 1921 and 1956, and twice with Wales (9–9 and 13–13) in 1969 and 1988.

TASMANIA RFU

The first rugby played in Tasmania was an exhibition match played between the sailors of two New Zealand ships in 1926. The game was first organised locally in 1932, in the south. Travelling distances to the north created problems for many years, and in 1961 the Northern Tasmanian Union was formed to cater for interest there.

Rugby has been keenly pursued by a minority of sports followers in the years since. Australian rules football is the biggest sport on the island, but rugby union has held its own, defeating the challenge of rugby league in the 1950s.

Major touring teams to Australia travel on a regular basis to Tasmania. The first of these was the All Black team of 1968 which beat 'Tazzy' by 74–0. Tasmania has never beaten a major side and in its first 60 years no Tasmanian player made the Australian team.

TAYLOR, JOHN

London Welsh and Wales
26 internationals for Wales 1967–73
4 internationals for British Isles 1971

Called 'Basil Brush' because of his distinctive long hair and beard, John Taylor was a lightweight flanker who played a vital role in the hugely successful Welsh teams of the late 1960s and early 1970s.

The Lions liked his style too. He toured with them to South Africa in 1968 and to New Zealand in 1971, where he was particularly impressive, appearing in all four tests on that highly successful trip. He was also in New Zealand with Wales in 1969.

Taylor made his debut for the Welsh team in 1967 against Scotland at Murrayfield – the season Wales suffered four successive defeats. However, by 1969 Taylor and the rest of the Welsh team were really firing up. They won the Triple Crown and the championship that year; they shared the Five Nations title with France in 1970, followed by another outright win in 1971 when the Grand Slam was also secured.

In the latter season it was John Taylor who secured one of Wales's most dramatic wins. The Scotland team led 18–14 near the end of the game, when Gerald Davies crossed for a try in the corner for Wales. The conversion was all important. Taylor, a left-footed kicker, was invited to attempt the goal from the right touchline. Though he had kicked two conversions in the previous game against England, he was only a part-timer as an international goal-kicker. But his superb kick sailed straight between the posts and Wales won 19–18.

Taylor never kicked another conversion in a test match, but for Welsh fans that one was enough!

After his retirement Taylor became a skilled sports journalist and television commentator.

TELFER, JIM

Melrose and Scotland
25 internationals for Scotland 1964–70
8 internationals for British Isles 1966–68

A tough and hard Scottish loose forward who later became an accomplished coach, Telfer set a new Scottish record for most internationals as a No. 8. His 22 caps stood until equalled by John Beattie and then beaten by Iain Paxton in 1988. He also captained his country 12 times.

Jim 'Creamy' Telfer came out of the tough school of Scottish Borders rugby. He played his rugby in an uncompromising manner and expected all his team-mates to do the same. He always

Jim Telfer

claimed to have learnt much from an early tour of New Zealand with the Lions in 1966, when All Black forward play impressed him to such an extent that he, later as a coach, did his best to pass the New Zealand style on to Scottish teams.

It was the ultimate dream for Jim Telfer to win in New Zealand. This he never managed to do, either as a player or coach, over three tours, but New Zealanders respected him for the honesty and courage he put into all his attempts.

In the second test match of 1981, for instance, the All Blacks led at Eden Park in Auckland by 22–15 late in the game. The Scottish wing Steve Munro broke away on an intercept which could have made the score 22–21. Miraculously he was caught and the Scots failed to capitalise. They had played so hard they were then exhausted and allowed New Zealand to regroup and run in three last-gasp tries. The final score, 40–15, looks like a thrashing, but New Zealanders who were there remember how close Jim Telfer's team came to causing an upset.

Telfer was back in New Zealand in 1983 as coach of the British Isles but again disappointment came his way. His team went the same way as the 1966 Lions had gone, when Telfer was a player: the All Blacks blitzed the series 4–0.

TEMPLETON, BOB

Coaches come and coaches go, but 'Tempo' seemed to hang in and hang around for ever. He started coaching Queensland in 1961, after a career as a hard-bitten prop with the Grammar Public School's club side. He succeeded Des Connor as Australian coach in 1971, becoming a national selector as well – the start of a reign probably only exceeded by that of South African Bill Shreiner.

They were rocky days for Templeton and the Wallabies, both failing to win a series, and he was replaced for the tour to Britain in 1975–76 by Dave Brockhoff. Templeton returned, but briefly, before Bob Dwyer had his first term as Wallabies coach, and when Dwyer took over again from Alan Jones in 1988, he took Templeton on board as his assistant.

Templeton had most to do with Queensland emerging from the 'easybeat' category to become a world class team at provincial (or state) level. Under his guidance it achieved a run of 20 straight victories in the 1970s before being forced (by Canterbury, New Zealand) to choke on the special celebration cake it had had baked to celebrate its 21st win!

In times of adversity, Templeton never lost his composure or his voice: he was quick to praise a victorious opponent and was generous in victory.

Those who lent him their telephone also found to their cost that he could talk rugby at great length with anyone, anywhere in the world! Not for nothing did 'Tempo' get the MBE for his services to rugby.

THAILAND

The game was introduced to the country by expatriate British businessmen in the 1920s, but was not firmly rooted with the native Thai population until after the coup d'etat in 1932, when many who had been studying or working in England returned home. The union was established in 1938 and by 1952 it was sufficiently well-founded and organised for a team of Thai nationals to tour back to Britain. In 1959 a combined Oxford-Cambridge team toured through the east, with Thailand on its itinerary.

Some of the major countries visit Thailand for tours, but not as many as the locals would like. Scotland played Thailand in 1977 and won 82–3, the first national team from the British Isles to play in Bangkok.

The game is mostly played by university students, the police and armed forces, with some expatriate clubs still operating. The game is well-based and popular within the schools system.

Thailand was a founding member of the Asian Rugby Football Union in 1968. It regularly attends the biennial Asian championship and the Hong Kong Sevens. In 1978 Thailand lost narrowly to its rival Singapore (15–16) in the play-off for third place. It also finished fourth at the Asian championship in Colombo in 1990, and along the way beat Singapore by 49–3. Those two efforts were Thailand's best performances in the first 20 years of the Asian championship. Bangkok has hosted the tournament twice.

THAMES VALLEY RFU

Though this union was not formed until 1922, it is one of the original areas of rugby in New Zealand, the Thames club having played Auckland club sides in 1873 and 1874. These games were only 10-a-side, but the players from the rich gold-mining area must have been rich in fitness as well: after an hour and a half of the second game, according to a contemporary account, 'Mr Reed, the photographer, took a picture of the two teams, which gave them a short respite.'

A mere 112 years later, Thames Valley would have been glad of a respite against Auckland, when it yielded 97 points – without reply – in its Ranfurly Shield match, establishing a new record high score in shield games.

The 'Swamp Foxes' have been struggling for years and their largest ground has a capacity of only 5000. They have long helped to prop up the bottom divisions of New Zealand's rugby competitions, but in 1988 won a famous promotion to the second division. They could never aspire to anything higher.

But they have beaten sundry Pacific tourists: Fiji, Tonga and the Cook Islands. They also, on a famous day in 1962, beat the touring Australians who, not for nothing, were known as the 'Awful Aussies'.

Thames Valley seems fated to a long wait to add to its short list of All Blacks: flanker Bob O'Dea, who played only five times for the 1953 All Blacks because of a knee injury; and Kevin Barry, who could play just about anywhere in the pack and nearly did so in his 23 games for New Zealand in the period 1962–64. None of those games was an international.

The 'Swamp Foxes' have appeared in a variety of garb. Until 1951 the jerseys were light blue with a gold band; then gold with a scarlet band; and currently they are plain gold with red trim, worn with black shorts.

THOMAS, CLEM
Swansea and Wales
26 internationals for Wales 1949–59
2 internationals for British Isles 1955

One of the finest loose forwards Wales produced in the post World War II era, who later became one of the best writers on the game. His full name is Richard Clement Charles Thomas, but from his earliest days the shortened 'Clem' was a welcome diminutive.

A tough flanker, he was a 'Swansea Jack' through and through, who first made the Welsh team for its end-of-season international against France in Paris in 1949. France won narrowly by 5–3, in what was a battle to avoid last place in the championship. Thomas paid the price for what some in Wales saw as a premature selection (he was only 20 years old) and he was not asked to play internationally again for two seasons.

He was recalled in 1952 as part of the Grand Slam-winning Welsh team and continued to represent Wales until 1959. He toured South Africa as part of the 1955 Lions team, but appendicitis restricted him to two of the four test matches.

Thomas was Welsh captain in his last two seasons, 1957–58 and 1958–59, and was tipped as a possible captain of the British Lions to New Zealand in 1959. Perhaps it was Wales's modest record in the 1958–59 season which held him back from winning that honour.

When Thomas retired, the butcher became a successful businessman, as well as writing for the *Guardian* and the *Observer* with much distinction.

When discussions about Clem Thomas arise in Welsh rugby he is invariably remembered as the player who put in the famous cross-kick against New Zealand in Cardiff in 1953. Thomas was close to the touchline on one side of the field, and, seeing his way ahead blocked by All Blacks, he kicked the ball on an angle towards the goal-posts. The two rival wings, arguably the fastest two men in world rugby at that time, Ron Jarden of New Zealand and Ken Jones of Wales, were both standing clear of any other players. When Thomas's kick landed, it bounced perfectly into the hands of Jones and he sprinted in for a winning try.

As the kicker of the ball Thomas was acclaimed as a hero for Wales, but in the years since, he has often reflected how his life might have changed had the ball bounced the other way into the hands of Jarden, the flying All Black!

THOMAS, DELME
Llanelli, Wales and British Isles
25 internationals for Wales 1966–74
6 internationals for British Isles 1966–71

British Isles teams occasionally, just occasionally, take an uncapped player

Delme Thomas

on tour. They're not often successful, but William Delme Thomas, a lanky Llanelli lad when he went on the ill-fated Lions tour of Australia and New Zealand in 1966, was an exception.

Thomas was very much the fourth lock: rated ahead of him were the captain, Mike Campbell-Lamerton, an emerging Irishman named Willie John McBride, and a craggy Welshman named Brian Price. Perceptive New Zealanders had a look at them all, and in the whitewash by the All Blacks they were pretty certain the best of them was this chap the Welsh hadn't even capped.

The British hierarchy listened long enough to drop Campbell-Lamerton for the second international and to play this gifted lineout leaper. He did well, so they kept him. But they also shuddered at the thought of leaving their leader out again, so they shifted Thomas into the front row, where he'd never played before, and left it to coach John Robins (who had been entrusted with nothing else thus far on the tour) to teach him some of the propping skills he'd learnt as a Welsh international.

As it happened, Thomas did tolerably well, but he was injured and not considered for the fourth test. Where would he have played there?

Thomas went on to play extremely well for Wales, without perhaps ever being accorded the respect his first

admirers in New Zealand considered his due. He did not play in a full Five Nations series until 1970, but toured twice more with the Lions: to South Africa in 1968 and back to New Zealand in 1971, on both occasions again playing only two test matches. All told he played 44 matches for the Lions, a record for a Welshman.

THOMAS, MALCOLM

Newport and Wales
27 internationals for Wales 1949–59
4 internationals for British Isles 1950–59

A stylish centre and wing for Wales who played over 11 seasons, Malcolm Thomas was the first Lions player to make two tours of New Zealand.

As a 19-year-old, he made his international debut in 1949 in Paris, for Wales against France, at the same time as his namesake Clem Thomas played his first game. It was also the farewell match for the great Haydn Tanner.

The following year the young naval lieutenant crashed across for a try at Ravenhill in Belfast, clinching for Wales its first Triple Crown for 39 years. His 1950 form was so good he was selected to tour New Zealand with the British Isles, where he scored 21 points in the first match, a Lions record.

Thomas was a regular in Welsh teams throughout the 1950s, apart from a time when he was sidelined with a broken leg.

When the 1959 Lions tour to New Zealand was on the programme, Thomas was again in contention. Never before had a player gone on two tours to New Zealand, but Thomas's form could not be denied and he toured again as part of a brilliant Lions back line.

He was very much a utility on the tour, playing in every backline position except scrumhalf. He beat his own record for points in one match, this time scoring 25 points, ironically against the same opponents he had scored so heavily against nine years earlier – the combined side of Nelson, Marlborough and Golden Bay–Motueka.

It was often said that Lions selectors would not choose a player who had reached the landmark age of 30, but tthey slipped up with Thomas. His form killed the policy and paved the way for other oldtimers.

THOMPSON, ROBIN

Instonians and Ireland
11 internationals for Ireland 1951–56
3 internationals for British Isles 1955

Robin Thompson was a Belfast-born lock and No. 8 whose record might not look as impressive as some others. But he made his mark in rugby as captain of the 1955 British Isles team in South Africa.

The Springboks and the Lions won two tests each, and the quality of the rugby played and the public interest was such that the tour is widely regarded as the most thrilling ever undertaken.

Thompson, a Belfast graduate food chemist, was a fine forward and an excellent leader. He had only captained Ireland twice (both for losses) when he was invited to captain the Lions of 1955. He followed Sam Walker (1938) and Karl Mullen (1950) as Irish captains of the Lions on an overseas tour.

While in South Africa Thompson worked hard with the team and played a brilliant game in the first test which the Lions won by 23–22. Later he missed the third test because of a knee injury, and his play was affected by the injury when he returned in the fourth test. Still, Thompson's contribution and place in rugby history was assured by the performance of his team.

Sadly, he was lost to rugby union soon after. After recovering from his knee problems he played only once more for Ireland before switching codes and playing professionally for the Warrington rugby league club.

THORBURN, PAUL

Neath and Wales
36 internationals for Wales 1985–91

A solid and high-scoring Welsh fullback who was also controversial at times. By the end of the 1990–91 season, Thorburn was the elder statesman in the Welsh team and had set new points records for his country along the way.

Thorburn's first cap was against France in Paris in 1984. In the next season his goal-kicking came into its own: he landed 16 penalties in the Five Nations championship season, a new record for any player. Included in that total was a stunning kick at Cardiff against Scotland, which measured 64.2 metres (70 yards 8 and a half inches) and was reckoned to be the longest goal ever landed at Cardiff. His total of points in the Five Nations season, 52, was also a Welsh record. Unfortunately he was injured the following season with a broken collar bone and was unable to emulate or better that feat.

In 1987 Thorburn travelled to the Rugby World Cup in New Zealand. In the battle for third place with Australia at Rotorua, Thorburn landed the second of the more remarkable kicks of his career. His sideline conversion in the last minute of the game was a superb effort and Wales won the game 22–21. In the following year he landed yet another amazing kick. This time it was a last-gasp penalty goal, kicked against Ireland, which gave Wales a 12–9 win and the Triple Crown.

Thorburn became the Welsh captain in 1989, but made some injudicious and angry gestures towards the Cardiff Arms Park press boxes after Wales had saved its season from complete disaster by beating England. It was an action that brought great wrath down on Thorburn. Although he later captained his country on the 'B' tour of Canada, he was passed over for the British Isles tour of Australia, many said for disciplinary reasons. By then Thorburn had apologised, but he was not invited to be Welsh captain in the Five Nations series the next season.

He scored a further 28 points in five tests in 1989–90. Then followed the 1990 tour of Namibia and the restoration of the captaincy to him for the game against the Barbarians, for which Wales awarded caps, and the 1990–91 season.

Thorburn played well in all of those games and also scored well. His total of points at the end of 1990–91 was 301, making him easily Wales's top test scorer of all time.

THORNE, GRAHAME
Auckland, Northern Transvaal, Natal
  and New Zealand
10 internationals for N. Zealand 1968–70

A centre by inclination and choice, but usually chosen as a wing, Thorne had a disappointingly brief career for New Zealand. Two tries in an All Black trial, before he had played for Auckland, brought him selection for the 1967 tour of Britain at the age of 21.

Thorne played a full part in New Zealand's series wins against Australia and France in 1968, against Wales in 1969, and in South Africa in 1970, where New Zealand narrowly lost the series.

Thorne made a great impact on the crowds there, scoring 17 tries, a total unmatched by a tourist in the twentieth century, and displaying goal-kicking proficiency as well.

At 24 Thorne turned his back on All Black rugby and returned to South Africa. His three years there brought him Springbok trials and he was on the verge of selection when he returned to New Zealand, playing only three more matches of any significance in 1973–74.

He then became a comments man for television before moving into other areas of television production, and from there into a career in local and national politics.

THORNETT, JOHN
New South Wales and Australia
37 internationals for Australia 1955–67

One of a trio of top footballing brothers. John and Dick played rugby union for Australia, and when Dick switched to rugby league he joined the third brother, Ken, as a rugby league international.

John Thornett was usually a hard flanker and lock, but later he switched to prop, with considerable success. He played in Australian teams for 13 seasons, going on eight tours for his country, four of them as captain. He played in 16 test matches in all, becoming the second Australian player, after Nick Shehadie, to play 100 games for his country, reaching the mark in Hawick against South of Scotland in 1966.

His main attribute in any team was his inspiring leadership. He led Australia back from some dark years to some startling wins in the mid-1960s, including four tests over South Africa, in 1963 and 1965, and also over England and New Zealand.

His brother Dick had 11 tests in rugby union and 10 in league. Together as locking partners on the Wallaby tour of New Zealand in 1962, they tested their New Zealand opponents, Colin Meads and Nev McEwan, in the first two tests. In the third test, Stan Meads was brought in to lock with

John Thornett is carried off the field after an Australian test win against South Africa in 1965. From left, Dave Shepherd, Jon White and Jules Guerassimoff.

Colin, thus making a rugby rarity of brothers locking against brothers.

TINDILL, ERIC
Wellington and New Zealand
1 international for New Zealand in 1936

Usually a halfback but turned into a five-eighths, 'Snowy' Tindill played only one test on the All Blacks' tour of Britain – the match that is chiefly remembered for Prince Obolensky's two tries.

The greater significance of the sporting career of Tindill, a sharp drop-kicker, incidentally, was that he was a 'double All Black' which means he played for New Zealand at both cricket and rugby. Of the six men to achieve this feat, only Tindill played internationals in both sports.

The Tindill record went further. In 1950 he refereed test rugby (between New Zealand and the British Isles) and eight years later he umpired test cricket. Even further, he was also a New Zealand cricket selector.

Somebody should have made him a rugby selector, just to round his career off nicely!

TOBIAS, ERROL
Boland and South Africa
6 internationals for Sth Africa 1981–84

Errol Tobias set the rugby standard for other South Africans of his race when he became the first non-white to play for the Springboks.

Under South Africa's racial system Tobias was classed as a coloured player and therefore belonged to the South African Rugby Federation (the Proteas). He toured with that team to Britain in 1971 and went back to Britain as a Barbarian in 1979.

He first played for South Africa in 1980 on its tour of South America. In 1981 he played two tests against Ireland in South Africa, before becoming a central part of the controversial Springbok tour of New Zealand. Tobias was seen by those who condemned the tour as a token selection. It is true that he did not often play to top international standard on the tour, but he did turn out in five tour games, none of them tests.

The South African selectors then ignored him as a Springbok until 1984, when he turned out twice each in tests against England and South America.

By then Tobias was 34 years old and he retired soon after that season.

TOMES, ALAN
Hawick and Scotland
48 internationals for Scotland 1976–87

Scotland's most-capped lock, a powerful scrummager and worker in the tight, who had 12 seasons in the national team. He ended his career with strong showings in an excellent Scottish pack at the 1987 Rugby World Cup in New Zealand. Earlier he played in all four internationals for his country as it won the Grand Slam in 1984.

A borderer from the famous Hawick club, Tomes made six tours with Scotland and two others to South Africa, with the Barbarians in 1976 and with the 1980 British Isles team. On that tour he played midweek games only.

TONGA
The early growth of rugby in the friendly islands of Tonga was directly related to the development of a schools system based on the teachings and disciplines of the Methodist Church.

Rugby was introduced into Tonga through the Tupou and Tonga Colleges at the beginning of the twentieth century when both of those schools favoured non-Tongan teachers, many

Errol Tobias

TONGA

from Australia. These men arranged the first games on the islands and were soon copied in a casual fashion by visiting traders and civil servants from England, Australia and New Zealand.

When advanced Tongan students returned from Australia (especially Newington College) and New Zealand, with copies of the laws of the game, more organised rugby took place, leading to the formation of the Tongan Rugby Union in 1923.

An Australian, Mr H. Selwood, who was then sportsmaster at Tonga College, was a powerful early coaching influence. In 1924 Fiji visited Tonga for the first series of test matches, all three of which were played in Nuku'alofa. Tonga won the first test, 9–6, Fiji the second, 14–3 and the third was drawn, 0–0.

Tonga replied with a tour of Fiji in 1926, when Fiji won two tests to one, and thereafter there were exchanges between the countries until 1934. After that the years of depression and World War II set back the regularity of tours.

Australia underlined its close association with Tonga when it was the first major country to tour, with an invitation team, in 1954.

In 1969 the Tongans made their first venture to a major rugby country, touring New Zealand, with their 'tests' being against the New Zealand Maori teams. But in 1973, to celebrate 50 years of rugby, it was appropriate that Tonga should tour Australia to play its first full tests against a country other than its near Pacific neighbours.

Australia won the first test by 30–12 in Sydney, but there was a huge celebration back home when Tonga

A linesman's view of Twickenham Peter Bush

1987 Rugby World Cup action: Romania v France, and below, Wales v Tonga, with Wales playing in the alternate green strip. Peter Bush

won the second test in Brisbane by 16–11. That result was surely one of the biggest upsets in rugby history.

The first Tongan tour to Britain took place in 1974. The Tongans won the first match of the tour against East Wales at Cardiff, but then struck difficulties, losing the next nine games, including an 8–44 loss to Scotland and a 7–26 loss to Wales.

The Tongan manager said afterwards the tour had been 'a learning experience' and that they were 'quite happy' with the way the tour had gone. Such quotes serve to emphasise the typical Tongan approach: quiet, modest and dignified.

After winning the Triangular South Pacific championship in 1986, beating Western Samoa and Fiji, Tonga was invited to the first World Cup in New Zealand in 1987. There it made a splendid impression. It might have lost its three pool matches, 4–37 to Canada, 16–29 to Wales and 9–32 to Ireland (in Brisbane), but the Tongans' demeanour and vigour, particularly against Wales in Palmerston North, made them worthy cup entrants.

The best Tongan players were the halfback Talai Fifita, flanker Fakahau Valu (in his 15th year playing for his country!) and the quick wing Kutusi Fielea. Valu and Polutele Tuihalamaka

were both veterans of the win over Australia in 1973.

A particular difficulty for the Tongans had been the decision made to play Canada on a Sunday. The sabbath, in highly devout Tonga, is a day of prayer when all sport is banned. Even swimming in the sea is not permitted. But for the World Cup the government and the churches gave full blessing to the Tongans playing on Sunday.

The church-rugby combination is still a powerful bond in Tonga. There is a local saying that wherever you find a group of Tongans you will find a church and a rugby union club.

It was sad that Tonga failed to qualify for the second World Cup in 1991. It played in a qualifying pool in Tokyo where its Pacific rivals, Western Samoa, took its place as Pacific representatives.

By tradition Tongan rugby players are big and fast, and though they may lack some basic footballing skills they are always exciting to watch. Like Fijians and Samoans, they are very dangerous in sevens rugby, and have produced many fine showings at the annual Hong Kong Sevens.

Tonga has produced some exciting players in recent years, none more so than the brilliant Tali Kavapalu, a speedy centre who excited crowds in

Britain in 1974 and New Zealand in 1975. Also in that team was Sione Mafi, a big robust No. 8 and captain, whom the authoritative annual *New Zealand Rugby Almanack* voted as one of its 'Five Players of the Year' in 1975.

TRANSVAAL RFU

It has been argued that Transvaal is the true home of South African rugby, but your opinion on that probably depends on which part of South Africa you might favour or live in. What cannot be debated is the enormous influence this province has had over the history of South African rugby.

A number of the names of Transvaal's early rugby clubs reflected the type of work being done in the Transvaal region: there were the Diggers, the Villagers, Main Reef club, and the Mines club, among many others. It is said that in the early days, rugby hopefuls from Transvaal were hampered by the nature of the work they did. Generally the men were hard-working types who were underground daily in the mines and unable to practise their football on a consistent basis.

The union was formed in Johannesburg in 1889, and the first winner of Transvaal's Grand Challenge Cup was the Pretoria club. (In those days, and

Tongan halfback, Talai Fifita, on the way to brilliant try, confronts Robert Jones of Wales. World Cup, 1987.

Welsh player Kevin Hopkins is thoroughly wrapped up by the Tongan defence. World Cup, 1987.

until 1937 when the Northern Transvaal union was formed, players from Pretoria played for Transvaal.)

The first Transvaal representative team in 1889 travelled to the South African Rugby Board Cup series in Kimberley. The province hosted its first overseas tourists in 1891. William Maclagan's British team which played three matches in Johannesburg, winning them all without conceding a single point.

Still, standards climbed in the region. In 1896 John Hammond's British team toured, and seven Transvaal men played in the tests for South Africa, a forerunner of future days when a good percentage of many Springbok test or touring teams would be from the province.

By 1903, after the Boer War, Transvaal scored two fine wins (12–3 and 14–4) over Mark Morrison's British team, its first wins over a major touring team. Again seven Transvaalers played in the tests, with the test in Johannesburg, played at Wanderers, drawn 10–10.

When the South African team was chosen for the 1906–07 tour of Britain, once again seven players from Transvaal made the tour party. Three of them were named Morkel, the first of 10 Springboks to come from branches of that family.

By 1924 Transvaal was such a force that in four matches inside the province, Ronald Cove-Smith's British team could not win a single game. (Transvaal drew 10–10, Witwatersrand won 10–6, South Africa won the test match at Wanderers Ground by 17–0 and Pretoria Combined beat them 6–0.)

A great year for Transvaal was 1928: Ellis Park was opened in the suburb of Doornfontein in Johannesburg, and the All Blacks, coming to Johannesburg for the first time, were honoured by being the first overseas team to play on the new ground. Fittingly, the first honours went to the home team as Transvaal won by 6–0, but the All Blacks took revenge a week later, winning 5–0. The two games are remembered as classic, very tough encounters.

When New Zealand played South Africa in the second test of that 1928 series, it was the first test match on Ellis Park. About 38,000 fans turned out – then a record for a rugby match

in South Africa – to see the New Zealanders win 7–6.

The next major team Transvaal beat was Australia in 1933, while the Lions fell in 1938 in the first season after Pretoria-based players broke away to form Northern Transvaal.

After World War II Transvaal, along with Western Province, and later Northern Transvaal, emerged as one of the three super forces of South African rugby. Transvaal secured victories over the 1953 Australian team, the 1968 British Lions (their only loss to a provincial team on that tour), the 1969 Australians and the 1975 French team. The All Blacks stayed unbeaten against Transvaal after their sole loss in 1928. And all the time Transvaal's administrators amassed a tremendous wealth, Transvaal becoming one of the richest rugby unions in the world.

In the late 1970s, plans emerged for the construction of a new ground at Ellis Park. Despite being able to hold huge crowds (a world record 95,000 for one test in 1955), the old ground had become a collection of outmoded grandstands and flimsy scaffolds. So it was torn down and while the new ground was being built, nearby Wanderers was used again. The new ground was opened in 1982 when a Five Nations XV, captained by Fergus Slattery of Ireland, met a South African Board President's XV, captained appropriately by a Transvaal man, Okkie Oosthuizen. The Board XV won 35–19.

The new stadium at Ellis Park was, at the time of its construction, the most advanced ground in any sport in

the world, but its cost ran the Transvaal Rugby Union into enormous money problems. It plummeted into debt over the new ground, by sums of more than 20 million rand. The union was racked with controversy and the long-time boss, Jannie le Roux, was ousted and replaced by millionaire Louis Luyt. For a time the Transvaal Rugby Union's finances were never off the front pages of the newspapers, but slowly they have battled back into the black.

Transvaal won the Currie Cup for the first time in 1922. Its best era in the competition was from 1950, when a four-year sequence of wins began. In recent years, when Western Province and Northern Transvaal have dominated, Transvaal was runner-up in 1987 and 88.

The most-capped player from Transvaal in its first 100 years was the tough but brilliant centre Syd Nomis, who had 25 caps for his country between 1967 and 1972. He is perhaps best recalled for his brief but fiery clashes with All Black Fergie McCormick during the 1970 test series in South Africa.

Also from Transvaal were Gerald Bosch, the big-kicking flyhalf of the 1970s, and Kevin de Klerk, the big-leaping lock of the same era. In the 1950s and 60s there were 'Fanie' Kuhn, the hard-working prop; Avril Malan, a Springbok captain and lock; 'Lofty' Nel, also a No. 8 and lock (who at 36 years and 1 month was the oldest test Springbok ever); Johnny Buchler, the stylish fullback; Clive Ulyate, the flyhalf of the two important series, against the Lions in 1955 and New Zealand in 1956; Martin Pelser, the one-eyed flanker who was so good against New Zealand in 1960 and on the British tour which followed; 'Hennie' van Zyl, a flying wing who scored two tries on his test debut; and the balding flanker 'Basie' van Wyk, who was also part of this great era.

More recently, Waal Bartmann the flanker for all four 'tests' against the New Zealand Cavaliers in 1986, was a Transvaal man. Another veteran from that series went on to become the Springbok captain in the two matches celebrating the centenaries of both the South African and Transvaal unions in 1989; he was Jannie Breedt, the Transvaal No. 8.

TREMAIN, KEL
Southland, Manawatu, Canterbury, Auckland, Hawke's Bay and New Zealand
38 internationals for N. Zealand 1959–68

One of the greatest try-scoring forwards rugby has seen, Tremain totalled 136 in his 268 first-class matches. Only Ron Jarden and Bernie Fraser, both wings, could beat that record in New Zealand.

'Bunny' Tremain was a real match-winner – a rare beast for a forward. Not only was he one of the world's finest loose forwards, usually as a flanker, but occasionally at No. 8, but he had a nose for a try, and a fierce will to cross the line. Colin Meads reckoned he was 'the hardest man in the world to stop within the last 10 metres'.

One such match-winning try came in the 'hurricane test' at Wellington's Athletic Park in 1961, when Tremain snatched the ball from the toe of French fullback, Claude Lacaze, as he tried to clear from behind his own line.

Sometimes a lock in his younger days, Tremain established superb loose forward combinations with Waka Nathan and John Graham, and later Brian Lochore.

He played for New Zealand first in the 1959 series with the British Isles, and had tours to South Africa, Australia twice, Britain twice, and home series against Australia (three times), England, the Lions, the Springboks and France. He even played prop once or twice for New Zealand and led the All Blacks once in a test.

TREW, BILLY
Swansea and Wales
29 internationals for Wales 1900–13

One of the earliest of Wales's backline heroes, Billy Trew made his test debut six days into the twentieth century when he scored a try against England in Gloucester. His time in the Welsh jersey did not end until 1913 against France in Paris.

By then Trew had become a big star, as a graceful runner and accurate kicker. He was a true all-rounder, winning six caps on the wing, fourteen as a centre and nine as a flyhalf, which was his preferred place. In all he contributed to three Grand Slams, five Triple Crowns and six championship wins. (Wales also won the Triple Crown in 1902 when Trew did not play.)

Trew captained Wales 14 times. He was a staunch Swansea man, once choosing to go on a club tour, rather than play for Wales against France.

The rugby critic of the *South Wales Echo*, who went under the name 'Dromio', once said this about Billy Trew: 'Name whom you will for knowledge of the game, individual skill, the ability to inspire or fit into a scheme of combination; praise whom you may for the power to give the best and educe the best – and there is no one to place above Trew for unobtrusive skill and unfailing judgment.'

TRIES
While there are those who say the most important thing to achieve in any game of rugby is winning the game, the main object for any team, at any level, is to carry the ball forward with the intention of scoring tries.

The advent of television and video has brought the game to a world-wide audience of millions. Brilliant tries can be witnessed 'live' – and watched and analysed over and over with replays and slow-motion study; famous

Kel Tremain joins the Meads brothers, Stan and Colin, in a scrum.

tries from the early days are part of rugby lore and cannot be judged by the same means. So opinions on the 'greatest' tries will always prompt a vigorous debate.

The try scored by Gareth Edwards for the Barbarians club against New Zealand in Cardiff in 1973 is widely regarded as the greatest try of all time. It was a superb team effort sweeping 90 metres, beginning with two brilliant Phil Bennett sidesteps to bring the ball out of defence, followed by interpassing between forwards and backs until Gareth Edwards sprinted on to a pass to dive over. That is listed opposite, as number 1. After that are other famous tries and notable try-scoring feats.

TRIPLE CROWN

An honour, in name only, for one of the four British teams in the Five Nations championship which beats each of the other three, in the same season. The Triple Crown can never be won by France. It was a term in common usage among rugby followers before the end of the nineteenth century.

The first Triple Crown winner was England in 1883. Scotland won its first in 1891, Wales in 1893 and Ireland in 1894.

By the end of the 1990–91 season, Wales had won 17 Triple Crowns, England 16, Scotland 10 and Ireland six.

There was a 49-year gap between Ireland wins (1899–1948) and a 46-year gap between Scottish wins (1938–84). Wales's biggest gap was 39 years (1911–50), while for England the longest time between Triple Crown wins was 20 years (1960–80).

TUCKER, SAM

Bristol and England
27 internationals for England 1922–31

A tough hooker who was wounded in the Battle of the Somme in World War I and who was first picked for England in 1922. He was replaced after that game and did not reappear until the 1925 fixture against New Zealand. Thereafter Sam Tucker became a regular in England's teams of the late 1920s and early 30s, captaining them three times.

Though he was a fine, hard forward, Tucker is perhaps best remembered for a dash he made on match day across the Bristol Channel to Cardiff in 1930.

Tucker had not originally been picked to play for England against Wales and was at his office in Bristol on match day, tidying his desk before going home, when he received a phone call from the secretary of the Rugby Football Union, Sydney Cooper. Henry Rew, the front rower, had fallen off a motorcycle on the eve of the game and on match day he was ruled unfit to play. Tucker was asked to try to get to Cardiff for the game. As the last train had gone and the road journey would take too long, an aeroplane was sought to get him there in time. Remember this was 1930, when planes were not yet common, and there was no airstrip in Bristol.

But there was an airstrip at nearby Filton, so Tucker rang there and arranged for a small two-seater biplane to take him. First he had to assemble his playing gear and by the time he arrived at the airstrip it was 1.45 pm, only 75 minutes before kick-off.

The plane arrived over Cardiff at 2 pm. For Tucker, who had never flown before, it must have been quite an experience, flying in an open cockpit, circling over Cardiff, with the pilot looking for a break in the cloud cover so that a landing could be made!

Eventually a field was spotted and the pilot touched down on the bumpy surface. Tucker jumped out and had to run across the fields to find a road – and find out where he was!

Tucker then did the obvious, he hitchhiked towards Cardiff Arms Park, securing a ride with a man driving a truckload of coal, who took him right to the gates.

By this time there was half an hour to go until kick-off, but Tucker still had problems to overcome. The throng of people crowding the gates made it impossible for him to get in. Then he recognised a former Welsh international, who happened to be a police inspector, and after some persuasion he believed Tucker's story and ushered him through a side entrance.

So Tucker arrived in the ground, but on the wrong side of the field. He ran around the grandstands and made it to the England dressing room with about five minutes to spare. Everyone was pleased to see him, with the exception, perhaps, of Norman Matthews of Bath, who had been in Cardiff and was also changed ready to go on in case Tucker did not arrive.

Tucker changed quickly, and ran on to the field, at the end of perhaps the most dramatic call-up to a rugby international.

The postscript to this story is that England played superbly and won the match by 11–3. Tucker performed so well he held his place for the next match against Ireland and before the end of that season he had been made captain.

As for poor Norman Matthews, the standby man who had probably hoped Tucker would not make it to the ground, he was never asked to play for England again.

TUNISIA

Another of the fast emerging and improving African rugby nations. Tunisia's rugby federation was formed in 1972. Seven years later the team considered its game was strong enough to enter the Mediterranean Games in Split, Yugoslavia. Its first opponents, France, thrashed the newcomer by 104–3!

Tunisian rugby followers were undaunted by this apparent setback. They entered FIRA's European competition and have steadily progressed since then. In 1985, when in the first division, they scored a famous 17–15 win over Romania. That remains its greatest day, although playing against New Zealand in the Hong Kong Sevens in the 1989 competition rated highly as well. New Zealand won 38–0, but Tunisia's courage and skill were well in evidence.

At the African qualification series for the 1991 Rugby World Cup, Tunisia scored two good wins (beating Morocco 16–12 and Ivory Coast 12–7) and in the series final it led the favourites Zimbabwe 13–12 at half-time, only to lose 13–24 in the end.

Like Morocco and Namibia, Tunisia has ambitions to test Zimbabwe and South Africa in future Rugby World Cup qualification matches. The prospect of its continued improvement means an exciting rugby future for all of African rugby.

TURNER, FREDDIE

Eastern Province and South Africa
11 internationals for Sth Africa, 1933–38

This wonderfully-gifted all-rounder was playing junior rugby when he was plucked into the Eastern Province

GREAT TRIES

- Gareth Edwards for Barbarians v New Zealand, Cardiff, 1973.
- Teddy Morgan for Wales v New Zealand, Cardiff, 1905.
- A.L. Gracie for Scotland v Wales, Cardiff, 1923.
- Prince Alexander Obolensky's second for England v New Zealand, London, 1936.
- Jim Sherratt for the 'Kiwis' v Wales, Cardiff, 1946.
- Col Windon for Australia v England, London, 1948.
- Ken Jones for British Isles v New Zealand, Auckland, 1950.
- Jack Kyle for Ireland v Wales, Cardiff, 1951.
- Garth Jones for Australia v South Africa, Cape Town, 1953.
- Cliff Morgan for Wales v Ireland, Cardiff, 1955.
- Cliff Morgan for British Isles v South Africa, Johannesburg, 1955.
- Arthur Smith for Scotland v Wales, Edinburgh, 1955.
- Tom van Vollenhoven for South Africa v British Isles, Cape Town, 1955.
- Wilf Rosenberg for South Africa v New Zealand, Christchurch, 1956.
- Peter Jones for New Zealand v South Africa, Auckland, 1956.
- Peter Jackson for England v Australia, London, 1958.
- Jean Dupuy for France v New Zealand, Wellington, 1961.
- Richard Sharp for England v Scotland, London, 1963.
- Wilson Whineray for New Zealand v Barbarians, Cardiff, 1964.
- Andy Hancock for England v Scotland, London, 1965.
- John Gainsford for South Africa v New Zealand, Christchurch, 1965.
- Stuart Watkins for Wales v Scotland, Cardiff, 1966.
- Ian Kirkpatrick for New Zealand v British Isles, Christchurch, 1971.
- Phil Bennett for Wales v Scotland, Edinburgh, 1977.
- Andy Irvine for Scotland v Wales, Edinburgh, 1979.
- Hika Reid for New Zealand v Australia, Brisbane, 1980.
- Graham Mourie for New Zealand v Wales, Cardiff, 1980.
- David Campese for Australia v New Zealand, Wellington, 1982.
- John Kirwan for New Zealand v Italy, Auckland, 1987.
- Noel Mannion for Ireland v Wales, Cardiff, 1988.
- Serge Blanco for France v Australia, Sydney, 1987.
- Serge Blanco for France v Australia, Brisbane, 1990.

Most tries in a test or international match: 5
- George Lindsay for Scotland v Wales, Edinburgh, 1887.
- Daniel Lambert for England v France, Richmond, 1907.
- Rory Underwood for England v Fiji, Twickenham, 1989.

Most tries in a test or international match by a forward: 4
- Greg Cornelsen for Australia v New Zealand, Auckland 1978

Most tries in test rugby (until the end of March 1991):
- 37 David Campese, Australia, 1982–90.
- 33 Serge Blanco, France, 1980–91.
- 28 John Kirwan, New Zealand, 1984–90.
- 27 Rory Underwood, England, 1984–91.
- 24 Ian Smith, Scotland, 1923–33.
- 23 Christian Darrouy, France, 1956–67.
- 23 Philippe Sella, France, 1982–91.
- 23 Gerald Davies, Wales and British Isles, 1966–67.

Most tries scored by a forward in all tests: 16
- Ian Kirkpatrick, New Zealand, 1967–77.

Other try-scoring feats
- Ian Smith (Scotland) scored four tries in two consecutive internationals: v France, then v Wales in 1925.
- John Kirwan (New Zealand) scored tries in eight consecutive tests in 1987–88, 14 tries in total.
- Patrice Lagisquet scored seven tries for France against Paraguay in 1988.

team, and was just three months past his 19th birthday when called into the Springboks against Australia in 1933. Leon Barnard was invalided out of what was to be his debut match, and Turner became the first Springbok to fly to a test venue. Poor Barnard never played for South Africa.

A wing in his first game, Turner went to centre for the second test, then back to the wing again. His third test position was fullback, when he replaced an injured Gerry Brand for the first international against New Zealand in 1937.

Turner could sidestep and swerve and had a delicate change of pace which made him a most elusive man to mark. Some held the view that Turner would have been better placed at centre, but the excellent 1937 Springbok team relied heavily on Turner and D.O. Williams as its wings, and was otherwise well served for centres.

In his 19 matches on the full tour of Australia and New Zealand, Turner scored 122 points, despite being second-choice place-kicker to Gerry Brand. He had 16 tries and, in all matches for South Africa, 145 points.

TUYNMAN, STEVE
New South Wales and Australia
34 internationals for Australia 1983–90

Nicknamed 'Big Bird' after the Sesame Street television character, Tuynman was still at school (and an Australian Schoolboys' representative) when chosen for Australia's 1982 tour of New Zealand. He was carefully nurtured into the Australian test team, first achieving international status in France in 1983. The strapping No. 8, and sometimes flanker, failed to win a test place in Fiji or at home against New Zealand in 1984, but he played all the four Grand Slam tests in Britain later that year. From then, a run of 21 consecutive tests was only halted in the 1987 World Cup semi-finals by injury.

Tuynman then became a less regular choice for the Wallabies, unavailability sometimes playing a part, as he played only two of Australia's six matches in 1988, missing the French tour late in 1989, and playing only once at international level in 1990.

TWICKENHAM
In the early twentieth century the Rugby Football Union was growing increasingly agitated about its team, England, playing its 'home' internationals at different venues. There had been games at places like The Oval, Blackheath, Dewsbury and Bristol, and while each of those places was fine in itself, it was felt there was a need for a real home for English rugby.

A keen referee and RFU committee member, Billy Williams, took on the task of finding a permanent place of residence. After searching long and hard for a year, he recommended that a 10-acre market garden site in the suburb of Twickenham be purchased. Originally there was opposition to the site: it was 12 miles from the centre of London, and close to the River Crane, with the risk of flooding.

However, after persuasion, the RFU brought the land for a little more than £5,500 in 1907. By October 1909 the grounds, nicknamed by some 'Billy Williams' cabbage patch', had been developed to a point where the first club match could be staged. Harlequins beat Richmond. Just three months later, on January 15 1910, the first international was played there, England v Wales. About 18,000 fans saw England make a brilliant beginning on its new ground – it scored a try within two minutes of the kick-off and went on to win by 11–6, its first over Wales for 12 years, and one that sent it on the way to its first Five Nations championship for 18 years.

After only five years of rugby and the onset of World War I, Twickenham was returned to a more mundane role. Horses and sheep needed for the war effort grazed on its already luxurious turf. The war over, the Twickenham crowd enjoyed the thrilling play of England in the 1920s, when it won six championships in a decade. All this success meant the ground could be developed further, so between 1925 and 1932 the North Stand was built at one end of the pitch, an upper deck was added to the East Stand, which runs down one side of the playing field, and a double-decker West Stand was constructed.

Those were the only alterations for nearly 50 years, until 1981 when the South Stand was closed in and covered in a most futuristic design. The other major change before the hosting of the 1991 Rugby World Cup final was the complete demolition and rebuilding of the North Stand.

Despite the changes, Twickenham still retains much of its original dignity. It has tradition oozing from its rafters and many a rugby follower goes there just to breathe in the atmosphere of actually being at a game at rugby's 'headquarters'. Before a game the sight of luncheon parties taking place out of the backs of cars is commonplace – all part of the 'Twickers' experience.

Only the players and ground staff are allowed to walk on the playing surface, a tradition that many a rugby

Steve Tuynman

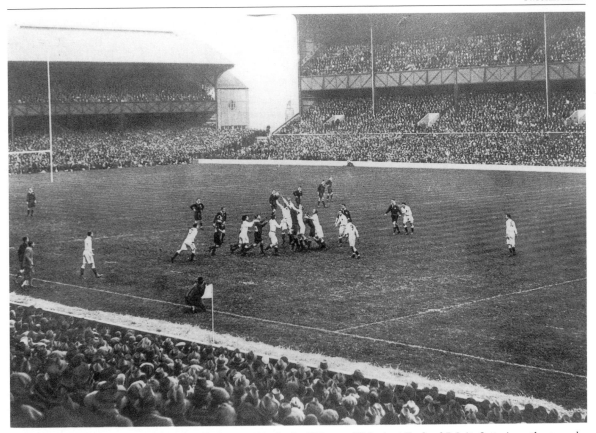

Sixty thousand people turned out at Twickenham on this day in 1933 to see Wales beat England 7–3, its first win on the ground.

follower has seen (and heard) enforced by an irate groundsman or official for merely putting a toe over the sidelines. On a big match day the grass is mowed and swept into the straightest of lines. People say this is for television purposes, but it has been done that way for decades.

Under the stands, the dressing rooms have become part of the mystique that is Twickenham. Only the players and very few others are allowed into the rooms where the players change. No photography is allowed there and certainly no women. There are large baths in each room which are run to an exact temperature and depth at an exact time each match day. The clocks on the walls of the Twickenham dressing rooms are set, also by tradition, to run three minutes fast.

Another Twickenham treat is the excellence of the view. The grandstands are close to the pitch and the upper decks are steeply inclined to give an intimate feeling when one is watching a game.

There are many glorious moments stored away in the Twickenham memory bank. Some of the tries scored have been among rugby's finest, like Prince Alexander Obolensky's two tries in 1936 against New Zealand; or Andy Hancock's 95-yard dash to glory (and the saving of the match!) against Scotland in 1965; Peter Jackson's try against Australia in 1958; or Richard Sharp's match-winner against Scotland in 1963. There have been many others of course, too many to recall, but there have been tense moments as well. All Black Cyril Brownlie was sent off the field in front of the Prince of Wales in 1925; Paul Ringer of Wales was sent off in 1980, and two Fijians, Noa Nadruku and Tevita Vonalagi, were sent off in the same game against England in 1989.

Over the years the dignity of Twickenham has sometimes been severely tested. In 1974 a male streaker dashed on to the playing surface and caused commotion. There is a famous photograph showing a policeman's helmet in an unusual position as the man was led away. Even greater commotion was caused in early 1982 when topless Erica Roe made her sensational run. She chose half-time during an England v Australia match as the moment when she ran into page three of many of Fleet Street's dailies. On a dull day and during a dull match, many publications described her run as 'the highlight of the day'.

Twickenham has a strict regimen of games played each season. The Harlequins club is permitted to use the ground for some fixtures, but only up to the start of the international series. The annual Oxford v Cambridge match is played there, as are the inter-services championship (three matches), the finals of the Middlesex Sevens, the final of the county championships, the final of the RFU club championship, and occasional matches for London Counties and the Barbarians.

Playing on Twickenham, for most players, is a once-in-a-lifetime event.

U

ULSTER RFU

Rugby was first played in Ulster following the return home to Belfast of students who had been studying in England. In January 1870 the newly formed North of Ireland Football Club played its first game, a three-weekend affair against Queen's College.

Rugby had modest beginnings in Ulster, with very few early clubs, so no delegation was sent south to Dublin in 1874 to see the formation of the Irish Rugby Football Union, even though the northerners had been invited to attend. But the realisation of a national body motivated Ulster to form its own governing organisation. Thus the Northern Football Union of Ireland was formed in 1875.

It seemed that in its early days the NFU existed merely to make sure Ulstermen were included in a fair proportion in the first nationally chosen Irish teams. The emphasis seemed to work: there were eight Belfast players and 12 from Dublin in the 'first 20' team chosen to play England in 1875.

The two unions, the Irish Union and the Northern Union, came together in 1879 to form one national body. The name Irish Rugby Football Union was retained, its headquarters were established in Dublin, and those from the north were called the northern 'branch' (a unique rugby term still used today to describe the Irish provincial unions).

There was always a healthy rivalry in Ulster between the game of rugby and soccer and Gaelic football. In fact it is stated in several Ulster histories that the popularity of Gaelic football in the country areas inhibited the development of rugby outside of the city of Belfast.

The first international game in Belfast was Ireland's contest with Scotland in 1891, which attracted 3000 to Ballynafeigh. The Scots won by 14–0. There was one character in the home team. From the original Belfast club of Northern Ireland FC, the fullback for Ireland was a chap called Dolway Walkington. He marked himself as a unique type by playing his football wearing a monocle!

One of the earliest questions for rugby in Ulster was the difficulty and expense of rail travel. Teams from rural areas had difficulty getting around. In 1892 a rival organisation to those already based in Belfast and Dublin sprang up when smaller centres formed their own Irish Provincial Towns Rugby Football Union. It existed primarily to protest the domination of Dublin and Belfast which, the new body claimed, organised games and competitions with only the big cities in mind. It seems to have been successful, although it only lasted 20 years, for Ulster has always seemed to have taken great care to involve all clubs, city and rural, in its various levels of club competition.

The first overseas team to play Ireland in Belfast was the 1906–07 South Africans. They beat Ireland by 15–12 at Balmoral, but only after the locals were thrilled by a spectacular try by Munster's hard-running wing, Basil Maclear. Not to be outdone by Dolway Walkington, Maclear often used to play wearing white kid gloves!

Rugby was suspended in Ulster during the years of World War I, apart from schools rugby which carried on and became very popular. After the war there was a boom in Ulster rugby, brought about by shorter working hours and more leisure time for young men. The arrival of bus services did much to aid the ability of teams and fans to move about in support of the code. This boom led to increased finances, so that soon the Ulster branch began to discuss the need for a permanent headquarters for its rugby.

By then in Irish society there were political differences which had seen the Anglo-Irish treaty signed in 1922 and the country partitioned into Northern Ireland and the Irish Free State. But political differences did not interfere with rugby's united body, the IRFU, which carried on as before. Indeed, in the years after partition, co-operation seemed to be greater than ever. As a gesture, the northern branch agreed to give Dublin both home internationals in 1922–23 in return for the IRFU agreeing to start and maintain a ground of international quality in Belfast.

So the Irish Union purchased the ground at Ravenhill in Belfast for development. The northern branch had the responsibility of preparing and laying out the pitch, as well as building a grandstand, and the Northern Ireland government even helped by

Willie-John McBride (centre) in action for Ulster, v New Zealand, 1972.

paying the labour costs. The first international match was played at Ravenhill in 1924. England beat Ireland by 14–3, the only appearance the English have ever made on the ground.

With the advantage of hindsight it was lucky for Ulster rugby that Ravenhill was developed when it was, as soon times became tough for ordinary people and gate-takings dwindled. An entertainment tax was levied on all sports events in the north, so that often an extra £450–£500 had to be paid into the government coffers. The generosity of spirit between the two unions was exemplified by the north agreeing that the 1927 international game between Ireland and Wales, scheduled for Belfast, be instead played at Dublin. That way the entertainment tax was avoided.

The rugby spirit of Ulster soon rallied and there were international matches at Ravenhill right through until 1954, when the greater crowd capacity at Lansdowne Road saw the decision made to play all Ireland fixtures there.

Some of Britain's best players have been Ulstermen – Willie John McBride and Mike Gibson for a start. McBride was from the Ballymena club and from there won his 63 caps for Ireland (plus 17 for the British Isles). Michael Gibson was from the North of Ireland club, and played 69 times in the emerald green of Ireland (and 12 times for the British Isles). Until 1990 these two were the highest-capped rugby players in the world.

Also from Ulster were the top Irish rugby stars, George Stephenson and Jack Kyle, who also both held the world record for caps for a time, Stephenson with 42 and Kyle with 46. From the post-war period Noel Henderson won 40 caps while more recently the hooker, Ken Kennedy, notched up 45 caps and wing Trevor Ringland, 34 caps.

Ulster teams have had their moments against major touring countries. Strangely, it is drawn matches that feature most in their history. They had tight tough drawn matches with two New Zealand teams: 3–3 in 1935–36 and 5–5 in 1953–54. They drew 6–6 with the Wallabies of 1966–67. The 1965 Springboks drew with Irish Provinces, 8–8, when they played in Belfast.

Ulster achieved its proudest moment against a major touring team when it beat the 1984 Australians. Ironically it was a Dublin-based fullback, Philip Rainey, who was the star. He kicked four penalties and a dropped goal in a 15–13 win. That result was against the Wallaby team which went on to win the Grand Slam of victories over the four home nations. Ulster scored its biggest win over a touring team from any country when it beat Western Samoa 47–15 in 1988.

In the last six years of the 1980s, Ulster won the Irish inter-provincial championship, underlining the steady increase in the playing standards of its teams.

UNDERWOOD, RORY
Leicester and England
43 internationals for England 1984–91
3 internationals for British Isles 1990

A dashing wing, as befitted his occupation as a flight lieutenant in the Royal Air Force. Rory Underwood, to the end of the 1990–91 season, had played 43 internationals, equalling Tony Neary's English record. Underwood was also England's highest test try-scorer, his five tries in 1990–91 boosting his total to 27. This placed him fourth on the all-time test try-scoring record, behind David Campese, Serge Blanco and John Kirwan.

Born in Middlesbrough, he is of part-Chinese origins, a rugby rarity in itself, and he spent some of his childhood in Malaysia. His first cap was against Ireland in 1984. Most of his caps have been won on the left wing, but he can play more than competently on the right side (his world record-equalling total of five tries against Fiji at Twickenham in 1989 came when he was playing on the right wing side).

His Air Force commitments have meant he has missed several England tours, but this popular and dynamic England star was a member of the England team which contested the first Rugby World Cup in New Zealand in 1987, and the team which won the Five Nations title in 1991. He also toured with the British Isles to Australia in 1989.

UNITED STATES
There is a long and colourful history of rugby football in the United States, and there are records of the game being played Yale, Harvard and Princeton Universities as far back as 1840. Mind you, the records also show that the game was prohibited at Harvard and Yale by 1862. It was apparently thought the game was too rough and tough for the decent men of those ivy league institutions.

In the early 20th century a resurgence of the game took place in California. The 1906 All Blacks passed through on their way home, and had such a great time that in seven years (a short gap in those days) they were invited back again. But if there was damage done to the rugby game in America it might have been done by that second All Black team of 1913. It played 16 tour games and averaged nearly 38 points per victory! There was a test against 'All America' and the All Blacks won 51–3. Effectively the game in California was demoralised to such an extent by the New Zealanders, and the Australians who had toured the year before, that the widespread popularity rugby people had hoped for was cut back to a few still-keen universities and colleges.

One claim to fame the Americans do have is their success at the Olympic Games. They are the reigning champions, having beaten France 8–0 in Antwerp in 1920 and retaining their title with a 17–3 win over France in Paris in 1924. See OLYMPIC GAMES.

A few colourful personalities were associated with US rugby at various stages of the century. Horror movie star Boris Karloff founded the Southern California Rugby Union in 1935. Later still the British actors David Niven and Richard Harris were both active in rugby in California.

Even though American teams regularly hosted Australian and New Zealand touring teams on the way home from British tours, American rugby stayed in the schools and a few clubs

The 1924 USA Olympic rugby team (in white) defeated Devonport Services 25–3, in a game at Plymouth.

for nigh on 40 years until the mid-1970s. The USA Rugby Football Union was formed in 1975 and a year later Australia played the first post-World War II international in the United States, beating the home team by 24–12 at Anaheim, Los Angeles.

The annual clash with Canada (*see* CAN-AM SERIES) began in 1977 and has continued since, a valuable measuring point for current swings and trends of rugby in North America. The first national club championship was played in 1979.

The USARFU plucked up enough courage to ask the touring All Blacks to stop on their way to Wales in 1980, for a rematch of the 1913 game. This time the All Blacks won 53–6 in San Diego, but the ever-optimistic Americans regarded that as an improvement over the 1913 result. As one reporter said, 'The margin was one point better than 67 years ago. At this rate the USA can expect to draw a game with New Zealand in the year 5129!'

The United States played in the first Rugby World Cup in Australia in 1987. They were more than satisfied when they secured a victory over Japan by 21–18 and were also reasonably happy

in going down to Australia by 12–47 and to England by 6–34.

In 1990 the Americans went back to Australia, but this time their test hopes were dashed by 67–9 by the Wallabies. Nor could they beat either Canada or Argentina and so they qualified for the 1991 World Cup in the toughest group of all, meeting England and New Zealand.

It is true that the United States rugby scene is fraught with problems. There is no heritage of the game for young players to look to. There is comparatively little or no play in schools, so attracting keen young players is not easy. Most take to rugby after having had a crack at American football, basketball or even soccer, so there is no instinctive rugby reaction on the field. But are the American rugby officials discouraged? As they themselves might say – 'Hell no!'

There is no doubt the United States has an important role to play in the world game. At a rugby congress in Hong Kong in 1990, one of the more enlightening addresses concerning the IRB's attitude to the future of the game came from the USARFU chairman Bob Watkins.

And it is worth recalling the words of the New Zealand coach Jack Gleeson, who said when he was in the States in the mid-1970s, 'American rugby is like a great slumbering giant flexing its muscles, contemplating which direction to take next.' Amen to that.

UNIVERSITY MATCH

The first match between the university sides of Oxford and Cambridge took place in 1872. Since then Oxford University, in its dark blue colours, and Cambridge, in the light blues, meet early in every season at Twickenham. The day has grown to become a glittering social occasion; anyone who deems himself to be anyone, likes to be seen among the big crowds who attend. A recent report on the Oxford v Cambridge day at Twickenham described it as 'one of the occasions of the privileged.'

The game was not always played at Twickenham. The first venue was at the University Parks in Oxford; the next year it was at Parker's Piece in Cambridge. A neutral venue was pushed for, and Kennington Oval was the first one chosen. The Blackheath club grounds and the Queen's club in

London were also used for a time. Twickenham became the venue in 1921 and the two rivals have met there since, with the exception of the World War II years, on the second Tuesday in December. During the war the two sometimes played each other more than once a season, at venues were chosen on a home and away basis.

The 100th playing of the University Match was in December 1982. Twickenham was covered in three inches of snow, but the game (and the various celebration dinners) went ahead. The centenary match, cause for celebration in itself, had an added dimension, for the teams' records were nicely poised After 99 games both universities had won 43 times and there had been 13 draws. Cambridge won the 100th game, by 9–6.

The match has its own set of records and traditions. Up to 1990 the biggest scores posted by each team were 35 points scored by Oxford in 1909 (in a 35–3 win) and 34 by Cambridge in 1975 (in a 34–12 win).

In the first 100 years the most appearances any one player had made in the match was five. Peter Enevoldson, Oxford's captain in the 100th match, was making his fifth consecutive appearance. H.G. Fuller (Cambridge 1878–82) and J.E. Greenwood (Cambridge 1910–13 and 1919) were the others with five appearances.

Many famous players studied at either Oxford or Cambridge, and the annual match was often the first sig-

nificant adult rugby the undergraduates played. Names which spring to mind are: Harry Vassall, the great early innovator of Oxford's back play; Adrian Stoop, the superb handler and passer of the early years of the 20th century, who played for Oxford in 1902–03–04; Ronald Poulton Palmer, the scorer of five tries for Oxford in 1909 and three others in the next two years; Wavell Wakefield, the brilliant Cambridge forward and match-planner of 1921–22; the famous Oxford three-quarter line of the 1920s ('Johnny' Wallace, George Aitken, Phil Macpherson and Ian Smith); Alexander Obolensky, the unique Oxford wing of 1935 and 1937.

In the years after World War II, there were men like Onllwyn Brace, Richard Sharp, Michael Gibson, Tommy Bedford, Chris Laidlaw, Gerald Davies, Stewart Wilson, John Robbie, and David Kirk. Hundreds of others have graced this game to give it a status as one of the more eagerly awaited rugby days of every season.

Of course cynics abound. While the game, in its early days, was the showcase for some of the most inventive displays in the rugby world, the standard of the play in the modern Oxbridge series has often been questioned by critics, who say the quality of the rugby these days is sometimes only second class. Nevertheless it is a fact that the first 100 matches between these two prestigious universities featured over 500 young players who went on to play international rugby. And not just for England, but for almost every major-rugby playing nation in the world.

Teams are always chosen by the captains who are themselves elected from last year's team. Ten weeks of preparation culminate in the great day at Twickenham, a day that still best exemplifies some of the old world charm of rugby: amateur players giving their best, young men striving for victory for their schools, simply for the love of playing the game.

URUGUAY

Founded in 1951. The game largely originated with expatriate British citizens who were members of the Montevideo Cricket Club, or the British school in the same city. The sport has struggled through the twentieth century, but has regularly fielded an

international side in the South American championships.

Uruguay was a founder member of the South American Rugby Union in 1981. Its most regular opponents are, of course, its nearest neighbours, Argentina, Chile, Brazil and Paraguay. The record of the Uruguay team reflects the variation of standards of play on the South American continent. Uruguay beat Brazil in 1981 by 77–0, but itself suffered a 0–70 loss against Argentina in 1977.

In 1980 a Uruguayan wing, Roberto Canessa, made the tour of South Africa with the South American touring team.

USSR

It was a Scotsman named Harper who introduced the sport of rugby to the Soviet Union in 1884. Almost immediately it was banned by the Czarist authorities: they saw the game as rowdy, violent and ungentlemanly.

It reappeared 40 years later after encouragement from a French journalist with the famous sporting paper *L'Equipe*, Jean Nau. In 1936 the national club leagues were started, although expansion was slow. The game obtained wide exposure in 1957 at the World Student Games held in Moscow, where there was a grim final between Llanelli and the Romanian club, Grivita Rosie.

Soviet rugby finally emerged from the shadows in 1976, when the Soviets decided that their national team was good enough to join the FIRA competitions. Their first efforts in the second division were so successful that soon they were promoted to division one where they have been a force ever since. By the end of the 1980s the Soviets had defeated French 'A' teams no fewer than three times, Italy once and Romania several times. They have also defeated the USA and a Welsh XV.

Rugby is growing steadily in popularity within the Soviet Union. There are two divisions of 12 clubs each, based around the cities of Moscow, Leningrad, Kiev and Tbilisi, with 20,000 players and 500 full-time coaches. Up to 20,000 people watch the games when the national team is in action.

The Soviet's most experienced player is the utility back Igor Mironov. He has been the outstanding player of the decade and has captained and kicked goals for the national team on many occasions. By the end of 1990 he had appeared over 60 times for his country in internationals.

With the advent of glasnost and perestroika, outside interest in Russian rugby has also built tremendously and invitations for the Soviet Bears to tour have been received from all over the world. The Soviets have jumped at the chance. In 1989 they toured to England; in 1990 they went to Australia, as well as the Hong Kong Sevens; and in 1991 they were scheduled to tour New Zealand.

One question many ask is why is there no Soviet Union involvement in the Rugby World Cup? No one seems to know for sure. In 1987 it was said the Soviets missed out because they said they would not compete if South Africa was invited. The IRB felt some sort of affront at this so did not invite them. In 1991 it was thought to be merely a communication breakdown – it was said that nobody at the Soviet rugby headquarters replied to the cables and faxes!

UTTLEY, ROGER
Gosforth, Wasps and England
23 internationals for England 1973–80
4 internationals for British Isles 1974

A tough, rugged English loose forward and lock who played a vital role in the British Isles series win in South Af-rica in 1974. He was later to become a prominent and successful coach for both England and the Lions.

Uttley first played for England on its tour of the Far East in 1971, but he did not make his international debut until the match against Ireland in 1973. Later that year he toured New Zealand with John Pullin's England team – the side that scored an upset win over the All Blacks on Eden Park, after having lost all of its other tour matches. In South Africa in 1974 Uttley played superb rugby on the side of the scrum in Willie John McBride's Lions team. He was also chosen for the 1977 Lions tour of New Zealand but a back injury saw him miss the trip.

Uttley was big and tall and had good handling skills. He was also blessed with a strong-willed temperament. In many ways he was an ideal international forward. He played as a lock in the first part of his career, eventually winning 11 caps there. Later he changed to No. 8, winning seven caps and finally he became a flanker for five caps. But for injuries, including missing whole seasons at times, his total of caps would have been much higher. He captained England in 1977.

After his playing days were over Uttley carved out an impressive record as a coach, including coaching England and travelling to Australia as assistant to Scotland's Ian McGeechan in the winning British Isles touring team

Roger Uttley

of 1989. In 1991 Uttley achieved a unique distinction. He coached England in its Five Nations championship-wining season, and became the first Englishman to have played in and coached a Grand Slam-winning team.

V

VAN VOLLENHOVEN, TOM
Northern Transvaal and South Africa
7 internationals for Sth Africa 1955–56

Acclaimed as a man who might have become South Africa's finest wing, van Vollenhoven indeed fashioned a reputation as a great try-scoring wing – but it was for St Helen's at rugby league.

His international rugby career was cruelly brief. After his debut as a centre against the 1955 Lions, van Vollenhoven moved to the wing and promptly became the first player to score three tries in a test in South Africa. In the second test in Australia the next year, he kicked a dropped goal – it was only the second time he had ever attempted one – but his form fell away in New Zealand and while he played eight of the first nine matches, he played only the third test.

The crew-cutted van Vollenhoven was reckoned to be inconsistent, but there was nothing unreliable about him in the matter of scoring tries. In his 19 matches on that long tour, van Vollenhoven scored 16 tries, but was such a natural and instinctive player that selectors found him difficult to fit into a team pattern.

He certainly proved them wrong, or misguided, with St Helen's.

VANNIER, MICHEL
Racing Club de France, Chalon and
France
43 internationals for France 1953–61

A stylish French fullback who became that country's most-capped last line of defence, Michel Vannier was a gifted runner who was also blessed with a calm assurance. He played in three French teams which won the Five Nations Championship and was a member of the great French team which went to South Africa in 1958 and won the test series.

Vannier first came into the French international side in 1953 against Wales, in Paris. He had an unhappy day but held his place for the internationals of the next season. He steadily built up his tally of caps over the next five seasons. He was an excellent goal-kicker and had a sure touch with a drop-kick. In the end he totalled 175 points in international matches.

Vannier was most unfortunate that a serious knee injury forced him to miss the tests in South Africa in 1958. He missed all of 1959's international matches but was back in 1960, a comeback that was highly acclaimed and popular with the rugby followers of France.

His last international was in Australia at the end of the French tour there and to New Zealand in 1961. His form on tour had not been as impressive as before, but his total of caps won had reached 43. The mark stood as a French record until the great Serge Blanco passed it in 1987.

VEITCH, DENNY
A unique figure in Canadian rugby, Denny Veitch represented British Columbia as a flanker. He toured Japan in 1959 with BC and later that season played against Ronnie Dawson's British Lions team, which was on its way home from a tour of Australia and New Zealand.

Denny Veitch is unique to rugby because he had lost an arm in a childhood accident. A lesser man might have called this a huge physical disability, but Veitch never saw it that way. As a flanker he was considered a tough hard player and a good tackler. This courageous player was a big hit in Japan in 1959, featuring prominently in the newspapers and on television. Denny Veitch always made light of his physical difference from other players and was still playing rugby in Vancouver when he was over 40 years old.

He continued to contribute to rugby after his playing days were over and was manager of the Canadian team in the Rugby World Cup in New Zealand in 1987.

VICTORIA RFU
In the home of Australian rules football, Victorian rugby faces severe competition from the state's favourite game.

The 1888 British team, touring Australia at the time, found little serious opposition in rugby in Victoria, so some Australian rules games were hastily organised. The New Zealand Natives also passed through on their way to Britain. They at least played rugby, and had several tough games against the locals. Thus encouraged, a Melbourne Rugby Union was formed in that same year (1888).

The next year a team played in Sydney for the first time. There were no Victorian-born players in the side: it consisted of 10 New Zealanders and some Britons and South Africans. This is a trend which has continued to a certain extent. Although Victoria has had a number of highly talented native-born players, even today many of the big names of Victorian rugby have come from outside the state. In the early days this was no wonder; some businesses used to sack young sportsmen who did not play Australian rules!

The first Melbourne premiership was staged in 1909, but the Melbourne Rugby Union faded out before World War I.

Rugby league started in the city after the war, but it slumped when the 1926 All Blacks were rumoured to be coming to play in the state. Players and officials wanted to play the famous rugby union stars so they got together, changed codes, and the Victoria Rugby Union was formed.

A crowd of 13,000 turned up at the Carlton Australian Rules club for the game. New Zealand scored 14 tries and won 58–15, but the Victorians scored four tries and the game gave rugby union a great boost in the state.

Rugby was strong in the 1930s and Victoria gave tough opposition to all touring teams, but after World War II it began to struggle against the massive popularity of Australian rules, against which it has made little headway since.

Victoria has only once beaten a major touring team. In 1973 it toppled Tonga by 13–10 – and Tonga went on to beat Australia in the second test only weeks later. That win followed what had been a great year by Victorian standards. In 1972 the team was led by the former Lion, John O'Shea, who had settled in Melbourne. It pushed the New Zealand Juniors, losing only 15–6, and went on to beat both Sydney and Queensland.

In 1973, capitalising on the win over Tonga and the good results from the year before, Victoria made its first overseas tour, appropriately to New Zealand. For seven members of the tour party it was a trip 'home'.

Victoria has gone close with several other major teams, most notably a 14–24 loss to the British Isles team of 1966, a 6–11 loss to France in 1981, and an 8–13 defeat by USA in 1983.

The first Australian test player from the state was Gordon Sturtridge, who was chosen to play New Zealand in 1929. He was a Queenslander by birth, so Ernest ('Weary') Dunlop, who played against New Zealand in 1932 and 1934,was the first Victorian-born player to play tests.

Two Victorians toured New Zealand with the Wallabies in 1931 and three went to South Africa in 1933. They included Owen Bridle, a loose forward who eventually went on three tours, and Dave Cowper, a centre. Cowper's son, Bob, was a Victorian rugby rep who also played 27 cricket tests for

Australia in the 1960s. Three Victorian players also toured to New Zealand in 1936 and three went on the ill-fated Australian tour to Britain in 1939.

After Eric Davis was in the Australian teams in Britain in 1947–48 and in New Zealand in 1949, there was no Victorian test player until Robert Kay in 1958. In the 1960s there were seven players who were to become internationals: Art Turnbull, Jim Douglas, Dick Webb, Paul Gibbs, Russ Tulloch, David Shepherd and Geoff Vaughan.

In the 1970s the courageous prop John Meadows, though English-born (like Turnbull, Gibbs, Shepherd and Webb of the 60s), was a powerful figure in Victorian rugby who played 22 tests over 10 seasons. He and New Zealand-born Doug Osborne were the state's only internationals in that time.

VILE, TOMMY
Newport and Wales
8 internationals for Wales 1908–21
3 internationals for Great Britain 1904

A remarkable example of longevity at the top in rugby. Tommy Vile's record as a test player extended for 17 years, and he was one of the few players to play internationals for Wales on ei-

ther side of World War I. After his playing days were over he was almost immediately elevated to being a top referee. By 1923 he was in charge of his first international, and he eventually presided over 13 internationals until he hung up his whistle in 1931.

Vile's record of service to rugby did not end there. As an administrator he also showed admirable skill and in 1946 he became a Welsh representative on the International Rugby Board. He served seven years there, as well as two years as Welsh Rugby Union president, 1955–56.

Tommy Vile, a lively scrumhalf, toured New Zealand and Australia with the 1904 British team, as an uncapped player. His first game for Wales came in 1908 against England at Bristol. In a high-scoring game played in fog Wales won 28–18. He made seven international appearances before the war, and he would have played many more games but for the presence of the great 'Dicky' Owen in the same position in Welsh rugby at the time. Vile captained his country in its match with South Africa at Cardiff in 1912. The 0–3 loss was Wales's first defeat at home since 1899.

After the war, the 37-year-old Vile resumed his rugby career. He was re-

Basie Viviers and his troupe: the 1956 Springbok team touring New Zealand turns on an impromptu concert.
From left: Viviers (at back), Ian Kirkpatrick, Harry Walker, Daan Retief, Tom von Vollenhoven, Brian Pfaff and 'Butch' Lochner.

called for one match, to captain Wales against Scotland at Swansea. This was the infamous game where the crowd of 50,000 spilled onto the playing area several times and the game was under threat of being called off. Scotland won 14–8 and Vile ended his international career as a player.

Less than two years later he was refereeing an international, the Scotland v France game of 1923. Vile's understanding of the game quickly won him a reputation as a sound and sensible referee, and in that season he controlled four games in the Five Nations championship. Many of the players he whistled for had been opponents only two seasons before.

When he retired as a referee in 1931 Tommy Vile was 47 years old and had been involved on the rugby field, either as a player or referee, for nearly 35 years.

VILLEPREUX, PIERRE
Toulouse and France
34 internationals for France 1967–72

One of France's most brilliant fullbacks, a superb runner, an intuitive attacker, and long-range goal-kicker who later became a top coach for his club, Toulouse.

The physical education instructor began his international career with a game against Italy in Toulon in 1967. That day the French ran the ball and scored 11 tries. The intrusions of Villepreux from fullback assisted in a number of those.

Yet it was not all plain sailing for Villepreux. His early rival for the fullback berth was the great Claude Lacaze, and the two more or less shared test matches for France for the next several seasons and tours. Villepreux had a good tour to New Zealand in

1968 (earlier in 1967 he had had one test in South Africa while Lacaze had three). In the second test in Wellington Villepreux kicked what was then the longest goal ever seen on Athletic Park. Helped by a moderate wind, the ball soared nearly 70 metres before flying between the posts.

That sort of play was typical of Villepreux. In everything he attempted during his career he had a touch of brilliance, and he could surprise at any time. He was fast and elusive, and had an array of trick passes and handling skills that few in rugby have ever matched.

After his playing days were over, Villepreux passed on his rugby philosophy to young hopefuls around the world, in places like Italy and Tahiti. For a time English coaches were very interested in his methods.

Once Villepreuex had returned to coach his own club, Toulouse, speculation built up that he would someday overtake Jacques Fouroux as coach of France. But though Toulouse grew to be a fine example of what Villepreux could do with a team, he was never invited to make the final step up. There were rumours of difficulties between Villepreux and the establishment of French rugby that apparently could not be overcome. Thus, by the early 1990s, the Villepreux method of playing had never been tested as a philosophy for the top modern French players.

VIVIERS, 'BASIE'
Orange Free State and South Africa
5 internationals for South Africa 1956

Stephanus Sebastian Viviers led South Africa on perhaps its most dramatic tour and in one of the most pulsating series against the 1956 All Blacks. It

was by strange chance that this man, only warmly favoured even to win touring selection, should become captain. 'Salty' du Rand, a lock and flanker who had played for South Africa since 1949, was expected to be captain, but got into a fight with Jan Pickard during the trials. Such unseemly behaviour meant his rejection, though he remained vice-captain.

Viviers had toured Britain in 1951–52, playing mostly at fullback but occasionally also in the three-quarters. The brilliance of Johnny Buchler kept Viviers out of the test side, but he scored 58 points in other games. Buchler's form late in the Australian section of the 1956 tour suggested Viviers might be lucky to win a test position, but an injury to Buchler opened the way for him.

A big man of 1.82m (6ft) and about 95kg (15st), Viviers actually played flyhalf in the second test against Australia, because of a lack of confidence in the only fit specialist, 'Peewee' Howe. Viviers himself missed the first test in New Zealand because of an injury, but he played the other three.

The best goal-kicker in that team, he scored 107 points on the full tour, but he was generally a solid player rather than one given to brilliance.

His captaincy suffered on two fronts: the fullback is rather remote from the action, and he did not have the full confidence of his team. They felt he had failings as a player and therefore could not hope to be a first class captain. But Viviers won many plaudits on the tour for his gracious acceptance of defeat – and his singing. He had had a stammer as a child, but overcame the affliction with singing; as well as singing magnificently in his own voice, he could do a superb imitation of Gracie Fields – and the sound of a trumpet.

W

WAIKATO RFU

No union in New Zealand has gone through greater trauma in becoming established than Waikato. Once a South Auckland sub-union of the Auckland RFU, the first Waikato union was formed at a meeting of the Cambridge, Huntly and Hamilton clubs in 1887, joined the next year by the Te Awamutu and Ohaupo clubs.

But that was as far as the union got before going into recess. It was 'founded', so to speak, again in 1892, with five clubs. Another nine in the district weren't much interested in joining the new group. Effort No. 2 lasted until 1901.

Effort No 3 came in 1903, but things continued to muddle along, with various groups joining and leaving, until the whole disparate mess was tidied up with the affiliation of today's Waikato union in 1921.

Waikato was accorded poor relation status when it came to playing overseas teams. One of the best efforts by a combined side from the area came in 1937, when a few men from Thames Valley and King Country joined Waikato in holding Philip Nel's fearsome Springboks to a 6–3 win.

One of Waikato's early stars from that game, who had his final match in 1956 when he was 41, was Has Catley. By that time Waikato had produced another great All Black hooker, Ron Hemi, a very mobile young man, and in the same season, Don Clarke played his first match for the All Blacks. A great match-winner, Clarke amassed a record 737 points for Waikato between 1951 and 64. An older brother and prop, Ian Clarke, was an All Black 1953–64. Other All Blacks from Waikato were tiny halfback 'Ponty' Reid, and New Zealand's record-breaking captain, Wilson Whineray.

Catley and the Clarkes were not the only long-serving Waikato players. Another All Black, little-known prop Jack Leeson, had his first game for Waikato in 1929, his last in 1945, and played his last first-class match, at nearly 45, in 1954.

Waikato really came of age after the Second World War, and the high point

for the union is still its defeat of the 1956 Springboks in the tour opener. It also had brief Ranfurly Shield reigns 1951–53, 1966 and 1980.

A colourful combination of red, yellow and black hoops forms the Waikato jersey – an improvement on the original colours of white jersey with a black band.

WAIRARAPA-BUSH RFU

This low-population union is based on the south-east coast of the North Island of New Zealand, with half of its population of about 40,000 in the town of Masterton.

The Wairarapa-Bush union came about in 1971, the result of the amalgamation of the Wairarapa and Bush unions, but the history of rugby in this scattered region goes back more than a century.

The first club in the Wairarapa region was established in 1876, and in 1886 Wairarapa became the second union outside the main centres to be formed in New Zealand.

The Bush RFU – its original title planned to be the Seventy Mile Bush RFU – was formed in 1890. While Bush remained a minnow among New Zealand unions, providing only Athol Mahoney (1929–36) as an All Black, the Wairarapa union flourished in the 1920s, partly because of the great competition provided to the north by the powerful Hawke's Bay union, which was replete with All Blacks.

A record-breaking Ranfurly Shield reign by Hawke's Bay was ended in 1927 by Wairarapa, which itself lost the shield soon afterwards back to Hawke's Bay. Wairarapa regained it in 1928 and held it through to the end of the following season. It has otherwise held New Zealand's most prestigious trophy only in 1950, for just one match.

Wairarapa's most famous early player was William 'Offside Mac' McKenzie, so nicknamed because of the style of his wing forward play. (See ORDERED OFF.)

Great forwards in the 1920s were Quentin and Jim Donald, the latter an All Black captain, while Quentin Don-

ald was joined in the 'Invincible' 1924 All Blacks by Ian Harvey. A later great Wairarapa captain was Alan 'Kiwi' Blake, who had an impressive career spanning from 1941 to 1960 for Wairarapa, by which time the area's other great leader, Brian Lochore, had come along.

Lochore was also to coach Wairarapa-Bush when it won promotion, for the first time, to New Zealand's first division championship in 1981, reaching the heady heights of fourth in the 11-team competition. But with such a thin population base, it found the battle to remain in the top division too tough, and slipped back to the second division in 1987.

The old Bush union played variously in all white, or maroon jerseys with blue bands. Wairarapa played in green jerseys with white shorts, and since amalgamation, the union has played in grass green jerseys with red collar and cuffs, red shorts and green socks with a red top.

WAKEFIELD, WAVELL
Leicester, Harlequins and England
31 internationals for England 1920–27

William Wavell Wakefield was a highly successful player, thinker, innovator and captain. He became one of the world game's best administrators, becoming an England committee man before rising to be president of the Rugby Football Union in 1950. He served as a delegate on the International Rugby Board for the seven years up until 1961 and wrote extensively about the game, in his later years becoming a symbol of wise counsel for rugby and its future.

The young Wavell Wakefield was a supremely fit rugby player, winning his 31 international caps as a flanker, lock or No. 8. He first played for England in 1920, when he and 10 other new caps were thrashed by a strong Welsh side. The selectors persevered with many of the new players, and out of their rising confidence came one of England's best eras.

The England team, with Wakefield, the brilliant halfbacks 'Dave' Davies

Above:Welsh captain Paul Thorburn (centre) offers encouragement to his team. Fotopacific
Left: The Welsh team lines up for a World Cup game. Peter Bush

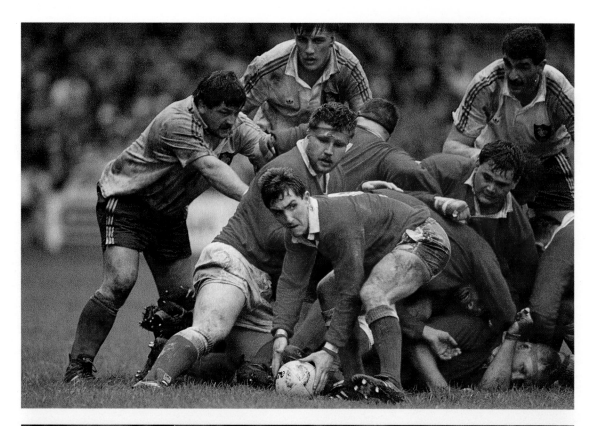

Top: Welsh scrumhalf Robert Jones clears from the scrum. France won the 1990 Five Nations match, 29–19. Fotopacific
Below: Paul Dean of Ireland escapes the attentions of Jonathan Davies (left) and Mark Ring. Wales v Ireland, World Cup, 1987. Peter Bush

Wavell Wakefield

and Cyril Kershaw, Cyril Lowe the wing, and forwards Tom Voyce and Ronald Cove-Smith, combined to win the Five Nations crown three times in the first four years of the 1920s.

Wakefield played his first 21 internationals consecutively, winning 17 times with one draw. By 1927, when he was hampered by injuries, the highly popular and respected 'Wakers' had reached 31 caps – an England record for any position and one that stood until 1969, when it was passed by D.P. 'Budge' Rogers.

Wakefield is often remembered as England's best captain and tactical planner. As captain of Cambridge University and England, he insisted on each member of the forward pack undertaking set roles, rather than plodding together from set piece to set piece, as had been the style.

Under his leadership, England's back row combinations became the first in the world to work together as a 'team', which is commonplace in modern times.

Certainly he was highly successful. In his seven seasons in the England team he took part in three championship wins, three Triple Crowns and three Grand Slams. It is a tribute to him that those years came to be known in English rugby as the 'Wakefield Era'.

After his active rugby days he was a Member of Parliament and then became the first Baron Wakefield of Kendal. He died in 1983.

WALES

The real passion in British rugby comes from the Welsh. It always has. The Welsh love the game with an intensity that outstrips that of the English, the Irish or the Scots.

For Welshmen, especially those from along the strip of the south coast and up in the Rhondda Valley area, rugby is revered with a devotion that consumes all other interests. The interest in the game in Wales crosses all the social boundaries and it is admired and played by men from university colleges, coal mines and steel works.

This passion is never better expressed than on international day at the famous shrine of Welsh rugby, Cardiff Arms Park. There, slowly, the rumblings of the crowd's animated pre-match conversation changes on some invisible cue to the harmonious melodies of traditional rugby songs. Before every international in Cardiff 50,000 voices are raised in celebration of being there. The power of the voices, rising and falling in perfect harmony, can make the strongest and toughest of opposing team members tremble with foreboding. They say that the singing of the crowds brings a sense of togetherness to the Welsh that is worth 10 points in every test they have played at home.

Yet the game in Wales headed into the 1990s in a state of anxiety. Social conditions for the working class lads who have populated so many club and national teams have deteriorated to the point where many top players, out of work during the week, have been lured 'north' to the big-money game of rugby league. The remaining players in the national team exposed a rare uncertainty about the game.

In recent years Wales has taken some fearful thumpings in top games: New Zealand beat it 49–6, 52–3, 54–9 and 34–6 within the space of three years in 1987–90; the New Zealand under-19 team beat Welsh under-19 54–9 in 1987; and Australian Schools beat Welsh Schools 44–0 in 1990. Such results were unheard of in the previous 100 years: Wales had always put on to the 'fields of glory' teams and individuals capable of matching the best in the world.

The Welsh Rugby Union was formed after a meeting of clubs at the Castle Hotel in Neath in March 1881. International matches against England, Ireland and Scotland followed shortly afterwards.

Even in those early days the Welsh rugby players were thinkers and innovators. Right from the start they wanted to move the ball wide on the field by hand. Frank Hancock is credited with bringing to the Cardiff club the idea of playing a four three-quarters formation with three other backs to facilitate real authority in the midfield. Most other teams preferred nine forwards and only six backs. The exciting new Welsh idea was used first by the national team in its game with Scotland in 1886. That the idea did not work in that match (Scotland won using nine forwards) did not deter men like Hancock. It was tried again and was successful. Wales embarked permanently on four three-quarters, seven backs in all, supported by eight forwards. Their idea gradually influenced the other countries and by 1894 the other three countries in the international championship had all adopted the Welsh way and were playing two wings and two centres, in the modern manner.

The turn of the century saw Welsh rugby further expand. Passionate fans watched the national XV regularly

Wales v England at Blackheath, 1892.

Gwyn Nicholls, an early Welsh star.

knock aside all comers. Those years were called the first 'golden era' of Welsh rugby. Between 1900 and 1911 Wales won six Triple Crowns and three Grand Slams and it also beat the 1905–06 All Blacks 3–0.

There was total adoration of the top Welsh players by the public in that era. It is said that the first hero of Welsh rugby was Arthur 'Monkey' Gould, who had 27 caps up until 1897. Men like Gwyn Nicholls, Percy Bush, Rhys Gabe, Dicky Owen, Jack and Billy Bancroft, Billy Trew and Teddy Morgan followed.

Between the two world wars Welsh rugby went into a decline which was said to be brought about by lowering living standards in the Depression and the need for young men to work hard to stay alive. As in the 1980s and 90s the professional rugby league game dragged away a number of leading players. Still Wales did score outright wins in the international championship in 1922, 1931 and 1936.

The 1936 Welsh team was unbeaten and included a 13–12 win over Jack Manchester's New Zealand side. In the Welsh team at that time were

great men like Cliff Jones, Wilfred Wooller, Vivian Jenkins, Haydn Tanner and Idwal Rees.

After World War II there were two early successes in the Triple Crown in 1950 and 1952 as Wales consolidated. It beat the All Blacks of 1953–54 with the aid of players like Bleddyn Williams, Ken Jones, Cliff Morgan, Rex Willis, Rees Stephens and Clem Thomas. That was the last time Wales has beaten New Zealand.

The second 'golden era' came in the mid-1960s and extended through to 1979. In that time Wales won the championship eight times, including three Grand Slams and seven Triple Crowns. A list of players who took part speaks of the wealth of individual talent that Wales had on offer in those years: men such as Gareth Edwards, Barry John, John Dawes, Clive Rowlands (as a player, then as a coach), David Watkins, Brian Price, Alun Pask, Haydn Morgan, Mervyn Davies, Keith Jarrett, Dewi Bebb, Gerald Davies, J.P.R. Williams, Delme Thomas, John Taylor, Derek Quinnell, Bobby Windsor, Graham Price, Phil Bennett, Ray Gravell, Allan Martin,

Geoff Wheel, J.J.Williams, Steve Fenwick and Gareth Davies are all reviewed individually. They were the rugby superstars of the day. One book title described the 1970s as 'The Decade of the Dragon'. Welsh rugby boomed, and no one would have believed that in a decade's time the scores totalled against various Welsh teams would be huge and horrifying for the public to contemplate.

Wales celebrated 100 years in the 1980–81 season. By then Cliff Jones, one of the greats of the 1930s, was the president of the Welsh Rugby Union. He told the New Zealand RFU that to celebrate the first 100 years of rugby in Wales no other opponent would be contemplated. 'We want only to play against the All Blacks.'

So Graham Mourie arrived with an All Black team and, sad to say, the New Zealanders somewhat spoilt the Welsh party. Well, they won the test 23–3 with a superb display, and in many respects that day in 1980, which had promised so much for Wales, turned out instead to be the start of the downslide in its game. In the 1980s the Men of Harlech could not win another Five Nations championship outright, though they shared one with France in 1988.

The Rugby World Cup loomed in 1987. Beforehand there was public optimism but private worries. The Welsh squad was young and keen, but had some painfully obvious shortcomings. Its scrum was considered short of a decent international standard, and that was how it proved.

In the World Cup preliminary games Wales reversed a defeat by Ireland from its most recent Five Nations clash. But the crowd at Wellington was unimpressed. Wales then struggled with Tonga and then had its best game of the first round against Canada. Still, they were all wins, as was a dull game with England in the quarter-finals.

It was at the semi-final that Wales was so badly exposed. New Zealand came on strong and won by 49–6, scoring eight tries. Even though Wales won the match for third place against Australia (22–21), the shock of the All Black match could not be shaken off. When New Zealand scored 18 tries in two tests on the next tour in 1988, the loyalty of the fans back home was sorely tested. In the first 'golden era' of Welsh rugby it had taken opposition

teams 13 games to register a similar number of tries!

Perhaps such scorelines created a malady within the team. By 1990 the biggest noise in Welsh rugby was the sound of rugby boots thundering northwards to the lure of money in rugby league. Prominent players such as Adrian Hadley, Paul Moriarty, John Devereux, Stuart Evans, David Young, Jonathan Griffiths, Mark Jones and others were all gone from rugby union before planning for the next Rugby World Cup could be started. The one bright star for Wales, Jonathan Davies, a brilliant flyhalf in the mould of Cliff Morgan and Barry John, also crossed the barriers in 1989 and went to play his future football for pay. In 1989–90, for the first time ever, Wales failed to win a single game in the Five Nations championship.

There is great heart and passion still in Welsh rugby, but the events of recent years has dimmed the pounding hearts and the loud voices somewhat.

Brave players like Robert Jones and Paul Thorburn have stayed loyal to the cause when things have not always gone their way. With them at the helm, Welsh fans still held eternal hope for the 1991 Rugby World Cup.

One thing is certain, when the crowds in Cardiff sense that the national XV is coming out of its slump (and they no doubt hope it can be on their home grounds during the World Cup) then their roars and cheers and voices lifted in song will once again be heard world-wide.

WALLACE, BILLY
Wellington, Otago and New Zealand
11 internationals for N. Zealand 1903–08

A participant in New Zealand's first test match, Billy Wallace's place in history was firmly established on the 1905 tour of Britain. He started indelibly, with 28 points in the tour-opener against Devonshire. His reputation was secure by the second match, when

Wales v New Zealand, 1969. Players clearly visible are Welshmen Brian Price, Brian Thomas and Jeff Young, and All Blacks Tom Lister, Brian Muller, Alan Smith and Colin Meads.

Billy Wallace, a 1905 'Original'.

he scored a try against Cornwall while wearing a sun-hat; by the third game, he had passed 50 points.

The century came in eight matches, and by the end of the tour, Wallace had scored 246 points in 26 matches (only three players had more games), with 74 conversions, and his 27 tries were bettered only by Jimmy Hunter. Wallace played in every backline position, except halfback, for the All Blacks.

'Carbine' Wallace, nicknamed after a great racehorse of the day, retired after the visit to New Zealand by the Anglo-Welsh side of 1908. He later became an administrator, serving on the New Zealand RFU council and executive, managing the 1932 All Blacks and the 1935 New Zealand Maoris side.

Wallace, as much a three-quarter as he was a fullback, died in 1972, a little short of his 94th birthday.

His total of 379 points for New Zealand remained a record for 52 years.

WALTERS, GWYNNE

A Welsh referee who controlled 23 full internationals, becoming, in 1965, the world's most 'capped' referee.

In the first half of the twentieth century, it took time for referees to come through a hierarchical system of appointments, and they tended to be older men – preferred, perhaps, as well, for the air of authority they could bestow upon a game.

Gwynne Walters changed all that. He was only 30 years old when he controlled his first international, France v Scotland in Paris in 1959. He looked a gentle person from afar, often smiling as he called players into check. But players soon came to respect his quiet determination that the game should be fair, and his understanding of the laws and his willingness to let play flow enhanced the games he controlled.

Walters had been a promising player at Gowerton Grammar School in West Wales, where players such as Haydn Tanner, Willie Davies, and Onllwyn Brace had been educated as well. But a shoulder injury sustained in a car accident ended his playing days, so as a 17-year-old he took up the whistle instead.

In 1950, when only 21, he controlled a secondary schools international between Wales and France at Cardiff Arms Park. It was said he looked younger than some of the teenaged hulks who were playing! Indeed those boyish looks never left Walters.

He won his way on to the Welsh international panel in 1956–57 season, joining those two other fine Welsh whistlers, Ivor David and Gwilym Treharne. By 1957 he was being appointed to top games, like the Oxford v Cambridge Universities match at Twickenham.

Once his international career started, Walters had the usual referee's problem of controlling some tough matches. In 1961 the match between France and South Africa at Colombes Stadium opened with prolonged bouts of fisticuffs. Walters called the two captains, Avril Malan and François Moncla, together and gently reminded them of the futility of the game carrying on in a rough manner. The two players returned to their teams and conveyed Mr Walters' attitude. There was no more trouble in the game. The incident was seen as a triumph of the Walters style.

He passed the Irishman Ray Williams's previous record number of refereeing appointments at the Scotland v South Africa match in 1965. His final tally of 23 was equalled by Kevin Kelleher of Ireland in 1971, and by fellow Welshman, Clive Norling, in 1990.

WANDERERS RFC

Founded in 1870, after University College, Dublin and North of Ireland, but before the formation of the Irish Rugby Union, Wanderers club sprang out of the University College club when the second team players broke away to form their own club.

After a brief spell in modest surroundings (a mud cabin at a suburban ground was their first club-house), Wanderers acquired a site for a club at Lansdowne Road. It was never to be entirely their own ground and was shared with the Lansdowne club. The two club-houses are still at Lansdowne Road, but they are separated (and in fact hidden from each other) by the new, towering stands of the stadium.

Wanderers club has provided more than 75 Irish internationals, including three players in the first Irish team chosen in 1875. Since then its ranks have included some of the best known Irish players in history: the legendary 'Jammie' Clinch and his father 'Coo', Ronnie Dawson, Ronnie Kavanagh, Andy Mulligan, Mark Sugden, Paul Murray, Gerry Culliton, Kevin Flynn, Tony Ensor, Robbie McGrath, 'Freddie' McLennan, Phil Matthews, Michael Fitzpatrick and many others. In at least two seasons six players from Wanderers have been included in the Irish team.

Two Wanderers players, Tommy Crean and Bob Johnston, won the Victoria Cross for gallantry in the Boer War, and in World War I Frank Harvey, another Wanderers man, won the same award.

The club has been a regular winner of the major Leinster trophies, the cup and the league, and went into the 1990s with real confidence. In the season which started the decade, Wanderers won both trophies.

WANGANUI RFU

Though the Wanganui union was not formed until 1888, the area in the south-west of New Zealand's North Island is one of the oldest seats of rugby in that country.

As early as 1872, rugby was played in Wanganui, spurred by the arrival in the area of one A. Drew, who had captained Nelson in New Zealand's first inter-district match, against Wellington. He organised a Town v Country match, which had to be delayed a fortnight until a suitable ball could be found!

They really had problems with that first match: it lasted two hours and as no goals were kicked it had to be continued a week later. That was no better, for different reasons. A contemporary report reveals that one of the Country players 'forgot he was playing with gentlemen, and descended into the more congenial atmosphere of Billingsgate. The Town captain left the field, followed by his subordinates, the game being effectually stopped.'

It is also worth noting that the Country side included a player named Wirihana, the first Maori to play an organised game of rugby.

The first club was formed that year and by 1879 Wanganui clubs and Wanganui district were playing quasi-representative matches.

Wanganui has as its near neighbours sometimes strong unions Taranaki and Manawatu, and others like King Country, Wairarapa-Bush and Wellington, so it has no problems getting regular competition and has produced 16 All Blacks, a creditable tally for a 'minor' union.

One of the first was 'Mona' Thomson, of the 1905 'Originals', a small but swift wing. Peter 'Sammy' Henderson, of the 1949–50 All Blacks, was even faster and shorter, and spent seven years scoring 214 tries for the Huddersfield rugby league club in England. He was also an Empire Games track sprinter.

Wanganui's most famous forward was 'Moke' Bellis, a regular All Black choice as a wing forward or loose forward in the period 1920–23. He captained the 1922 All Blacks on their tour of Australia.

In more recent years, Wanganui's best player was Bill Osborne, who first played for the All Blacks in 1975 and was a regular choice at second five-eighths or centre until 'retiring' early in 1981. He returned to play again for the All Blacks in 1982, and came out of yet another 'retirement' to be chosen for the All Blacks in 1985.

Wanganui has never beaten a major touring team, though it had wins against Fiji in both 1951 and 1980; nor has it won the Ranfurly Shield.

Wanganui's colours for some years were varieties of blue and black hoops; but since 1980 has played in royal blue jerseys and shorts.

WARATAHS

Rugby teams from New South Wales wear the waratah flower as their monogram, but the term is best known as the nickname given to the touring New South Wales team of 1927–28, which made a major tour of Britain and France, winning against the full test sides of Wales, Ireland and France. At the time New South Wales was the only affiliated state playing rugby in Australia, but the Waratahs were not allowed to be called Australian representatives (though in 1986 the Australian Rugby Union awarded full caps retrospectively to those who had played international teams for New South Wales in the 1920s).

The team was one of the most accomplished sides ever to emerge from Australia. Its line-up contained such names as Syd Malcolm (from Newcastle, the only non-Sydney player in the team), Tommy Lawton (a Queenslander then playing in Sydney), J.W. ('Brecker') Breckenridge and Cyril Towers. The captain 'Johnny' Wallace was Sydney-born, but represented Scotland in nine internationals as part of a brilliant Oxford University backline.

Eric Ford was top try-scorer on tour with 17, and Tommy Lawton was top points-scorer with 124.

Touring teams from New South Wales are commonplace now, especially in New Zealand, but there was no tour from a Waratahs team between 1928 and 1970, a surprising gap of 42 years.

WASPS RFC

Another of the great clubs of England. A representative of the club was asked to attend the meeting in London in 1871 that resulted in the formation of the Rugby Football Union. Unfortunately the Wasps delegate went to the wrong meeting place; the pub seemed a convivial place and he saw no good reason to interrupt his pleasant sojourn to attend a committee meeting. As a result Wasps cannot claim to have been at the formation of the parent body of English rugby!

The Wasps club was formed in 1867 by some young medical students at University College Hospital. Their choice of name was in keeping with the times, for nearby were teams like the Flamingoes, the Arabs and the Gipsies. A Wasp emblem was a feature of the playing colours from 1873 onwards.

The first international player from the club was the forward John Biggs, who was capped in 1878 – and he was to be the last until after World War II. The most famous Wasps players were Richard Sharp, the outstanding England flyhalf of 1960–67; Ted Woodward, the big bustling wing of the 1950s; and Peter Yarranton, Ron Syrett and Bob Stirling, who were all hard forwards of the same era.

Modern player Roger Uttley was with the club for a time, as were Nigel Melville, Simon Smith, and the two big front-rowers, Paul Rendall and Jeff Probyn. The club's most-capped player in its first 125 years was the England flyhalf of the 1980s, Rob Andrew.

Wasps can also boast that three Australians – Garrick Fay, Russ Tulloch and Geoff Richards – were all Wasps before they became internationals at home. The New Zealander Mark Taylor was also an influential figure as a player, captain, and later a coach to the club's top XV.

The club's headquarters are at Sudbury, near Wembley in London. One of the more colourful stories from the club's history comes from 1940, when a bomb exploded on the ground. At the next game on the field, an interim law was introduced – if the ball bounced into the large crater in the corner of the field then the teams had to scrum back!

WATKINS, DAVID
Newport and Wales
21 internationals for Wales 1963–67
6 internationals for British Isles 1966

There was genuine sadness throughout the rugby world when David Watkins went over to rugby league in 1967, for in his four years as a rugby international he had quickly forged a reputation as one of the most exciting and talented backs in the game.

As a 20-year-old he made his debut for Wales in its 1963 loss to England – a match which many claimed should not have been played, because the ground was frozen so hard. But Watkins kept his place as flyhalf and his first 18 test matches were played consecutively. Only the arrival of Barry John on the scene in 1966 broke the sequence.

In 1964 Watkins was a vital member of the Newport team that beat Wilson Whineray's New Zealanders by 3–0. He also toured South Africa with Wales that year.

In 1966 he was in the British Isles team which toured Australia and New Zealand, captaining the team in tests at Christchurch and Auckland. After returning home he was initially dropped in favour of Barry John, but after two losses he was restored to the team as captain. He led the team for three more matches, with Wales eventually breaking a four-game losing streak with a brilliant 34–21 win over England at Cardiff.

That was to be Watkins's last game of rugby union for Wales. In October 1967, at the beginning of the new season, he shocked rugby followers by signing with the Salford rugby league club for a record £16,000 fee.

He was successful in his new game as well, winning over many who doubted that such a small man could play such a tough game. He played internationals for both Great Britain and Wales, and coached both teams as well. At one stage he scored points in 92 consecutive league matches.

WATKINS, STUART
Newport and Wales
26 internationals for Wales 1964–70
3 internationals for British Isles 1966

A tall, solid wing from Newport who first came to prominence as a member of the Newport team which beat the 1963 All Blacks. His powerful running style soon took him on to the first of his 26 caps for Wales, in the game against Scotland in Cardiff in 1964. In his first seven games for his country he scored six tries.

In 1966 Watkins thrilled Welsh fans with a 75-metre runaway try against France, which sealed the match and the championship for Wales. Such form took him into the British Isles team which toured Australia and New Zealand. There he played 14 games and scored five tries, although he was often hindered by hamstring injuries on the tour. He also toured New Zealand in 1969 with the Welsh team.

Watkins once gave up rugby to play soccer, because all his friends did. It was to rugby's benefit that he returned to the running, passing game, and he is remembered as one of the most exciting runners and wings of his time.

WEBB ELLIS, WILLIAM
The man who started it all. Or did he? It is said that in 1823 William Webb

Ellis, while playing in a football game on Bigside field at Rugby School in England, caught a football and ran forward with it, thus forming the first idea for a ball game that could incorporate running and handling as well as footwork.

A plaque set in the wall at the school says: 'This stone commemorates the exploit of William Webb Ellis who, with a fine disregard for the rules of football as played in his time, first took the ball in his arms and ran with it, thus originating the distinctive feature of the Rugby game. A.D. 1823.'

Some historians have questioned whether Ellis actually started what is now known as rugby or whether the game had, in fact, existed in some form for years. There is a belief that a 'primitive' game involving handling had been played at Rugby in the early years of the nineteenth century. Certainly the rules of the Rugby School football games were constantly being revised by the students there.

Catching of the ball had been allowed there some years before 1823, although the player was required to retire, then kick the ball forward towards goal. It was the running forward that was the 'fine disregard' for what were then the school's rules. The handling of the ball probably evolved more gradually than from just 'one run by one boy on one day' leading to a whole new game.

It is not recorded what happened to young Ellis for his act of defiance, or why he alone was chosen to be singled out as the game's originator. Nor is it known whether he showed any further interest in the game that he might have started with his now famous run.

In the years after 1823 the expansion of football with Rugby's rules was achieved mainly by other former pupils of the school, but it is recorded that Ellis's son was part of the founding of the game in public schools in Natal, South Africa.

Ellis later became a minister of the Church of England at St Clement's Dane, in The Strand, London. He travelled to France to convalesce from an illness and died there in 1872. His grave, only discovered in 1969, is regularly tended at its site in Menton on the Côte D'Azur. In 1972, on the 100th anniversary of his death, Rugby School presented a replica of the school plaque to be placed on his modest gravesite.

In 1987 Ellis's name was further honoured when the first Rugby World Cup in New Zealand and Australia was played for a fine gold trophy named the Webb Ellis Cup.

WELLINGTON RFU
Wellington RFU was founded in 1879. Nine years earlier the first local club, the Wellington Football Club, had played Nelson in what was the first inter-club rugby fixture in New Zealand.

Wellington, with its headquarters in New Zealand's capital city and its main ground at Athletic Park, is a strong and typical New Zealand rugby centre. More than 20 clubs fight out three divisions of senior play and the provincial team has always been one of the best in New Zealand.

Wellington won the first Ranfurly Shield match, beating Auckland in 1904 by 6–3. Since then, its longest tenure with the shield has been through 15 defences in 1919 and 1920. It won the national championship three times in its first 15 seasons, in 1978, 1981 and 1986.

Wellington has provided New Zealand rugby with some of its finest players: men like the great Billy Wallace, the All Black of 1903–08; Mark Nicholls, the gifted five-eighths and New Zealand representative of the 1920s; Freddy Roberts, of the same era; Artie Lambourn, Jack Griffiths and Joey Sadler of the 1930s; Ron Jarden, Bill Clark and Nev MacEwan of the 1950s; and Mick Williment, Andy Leslie, Graham Williams, Ken Gray, Grant Batty, Allan Hewson, Murray Mexted, Stu Wilson, Bernie Fraser, Murray Pierce and John Gallagher.

Wellington's first win over a major touring team came in 1886 when it beat New South Wales 7–0. The province also beat Great Britain in 1930, Australia in 1931, South Africa in 1965, British Isles in 1966, England in 1973, Wales in 1988, France in 1989 and Fiji in 1990. Its best win was in 1896 when it defeated Queensland by 49–7.

On the reverse side of the coin, the 1971 British Isles team beat Wellington 47–9, a result which forced the side to reassess its attitudes and tactics. Influenced by the lessons it learned from watching the brilliant running of men such as Mike Gibson, Barry John, John Bevan, David Duckham and J.P.R. Williams, the Wellington team became impersonators of the Lions' style and the next few seasons were some of the best Wellington ever enjoyed.

WELSH CHALLENGE CUP

The first Welsh club knock-out series, begun in 1878, for the South Wales Cup, was discontinued due to controversy and crowd disturbances. It was revived in 1971. Later a soft-drink company contributed substantial sponsorship, and the name Schweppes Cup was introduced.

This is Welsh rugby's equivalent of English soccer's F.A. Cup. The knock-out format is simple, and all clubs that are members of the Welsh Rugby Union may enter. Excitement runs high as the junior clubs battle bravely against the big ones, and there are inevitable upset results.

Each succeeding round brings increased competitiveness, until the last two clubs head for Cardiff Arms Park and the grand finale. This is the domestic rugby highlight in Wales, and is always played in a highly electric atmosphere in front of a packed house.

In the first 20 years of competition, Llanelli and Cardiff were the most successful clubs. Llanelli played in the first five finals and included wins for four years in a row (1973–76).

Cardiff did not win the cup until 1981, but eventually won five times in that decade.

WEST AUSTRALIA RFU

Rugby has had a long struggle in the west of Australia, and only comparatively recently has it been safe to say that the sport is there to stay.

British soldiers were reported to have played the game there in 1868. In 1881 the first set of rugby rules arrived, brought to Perth by Tom Beuttler, a teacher. A competition of sorts was started between clubs, but this lasted only four years until the players switched en masse to Australian rules football.

The first West Australian Rugby Union was formed in 1893 and survived until World War I when, as in all the Australian states but New South Wales, the game went into recession. In 1928 there was a resurgence of interest, but again it dwindled when the next war arrived. The main problem in those years was Perth's isolation from the other main Australian rugby centres, and this was not overcome until the arrival of the jet age in the 1960s.

The first overseas team to play in Perth was the 1930 Great Britain team, which stopped for an afternoon on its way home to Southampton, and beat the locals 71–3. New Zealand did not play in the west until 1949, when the All Blacks turned up for a practice during their voyage to South Africa. The New Zealanders changed all 15 players at half-time, an indication of how light-heartedly they regarded the westerners, and won 31–3, scoring nine tries but only attempting two conversions!

Once the 1962 Empire and Commonwealth Games had been held, an international airport opened in Perth and teams could more easily fly in. Perth became, for a time, the location for opening tour games in Australia. The 1965 Springboks, on their way to the eastern states and New Zealand, breezed in and played twice in Perth on the same day. The famous 'WACA' (West Australian Cricket Association) ground was the venue, and South Africa beat West Australia by 60–0 and the second XV by 102–0.

In 1970 the All Blacks, again en route to South Africa, also played twice in Perth in one day, winning the games by 50–3 and 52–3. A local player from the University of West Australia, 19-year-old Jamie Hendry, played for New Zealand in one of the matches.

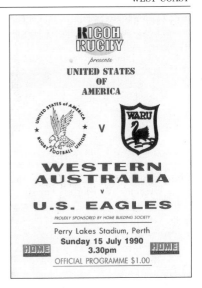

Western Australia has only twice beaten major touring teams – Canada by 16–6 in 1985, and the United States by 33–23 in 1990. It came close in 1975, when it lost 10–14 to Japan, and in 1983 when it lost 18–25 to the United States.

In 1984 the WARFU made its first overseas tour (to New Zealand) and it also secured a long-term lease on Perry Lakes Stadium, which is now considered the game's permanent home in the state.

In recent years rugby has been much stronger in West Australia, helped by the influx of New Zealanders who have come to live in the area – to such an extent that there is concern that not enough native Australians are playing the game there. However, at the beginning of the 1990s, it seems that at least the challenge of rugby league has been beaten off.

WEST COAST RFU

There are many legends and fables about the West Coast of New Zealand's South Island. In the years when New Zealand had ridiculously early closing times for pubs, and no drinking at all on Sundays, the West Coasters operated their own Rafferty's rules.

The hardy Coast miners found they had another common factor with their north of England cousins – a considerable devotion to rugby league. And in such a sparse and scattered population – the population of 34,000 at the beginning of the 1980s was steadily dropping – maintaining a top-class rugby team as well as being one of the powers of New Zealand rugby league was a difficult matter.

The Greymouth club was formed in 1875, and the two main towns on the West Coast, Greymouth and Hokitika, first met in rugby in 1882. By 1890, when the West Coast union was formed, there were 13 clubs in the area.

Only seven All Blacks have come from the West Coast, one of them, John Corbett, touring Britain with the 1905 'Original' All Blacks. The most famous player from the district was Jack 'Frosty' Steel, a bumping, barging wing with a good turn of speed, one of many stars of the 1924 'Invincibles'.

The next New Zealand team to visit Britain, that of 1935, also had West Coast representation: sole fullback Mike Gilbert, who later played rugby league in Britain, and lock Ron King, New Zealand's captain against the 1937 Springboks. After a long career with the West Coast, spanning his school days in 1928 until 1945, King became a New Zealand selector.

West Coast rarely gets to play visiting international sides – though it can boast wins over New South Wales Country, twice – and usually combines with neighbouring Buller. Their biggest days were when they beat the Australians in 1949 and 1972.

West Coast plays in red and white jerseys and with a great deal of spirit – a necessary ingredient for the battlers who always concede weight and talent.

WESTERN PROVINCE RFU

Founded in 1883 with headquarters at Newlands in Cape Town, Western Province is one of the richest and most powerful unions in South Africa, and therefore in the rugby world.

The history of South African rugby is inextricably linked with Western Province, which has almost always had the country's top two or three teams every season, and a list of its top players reads like the Who's Who of South African rugby.

Rugby was introduced to the Cape peninsula in 1858 by the Rev. G. Ogilvie ('Gog'), who brought his knowledge of football from Buenos Aires. Early forms of the game in the Cape were a combination of the rules of Winchester School, Rugby School, and association football. One historian

Morne du Plessis, a famous Western Province player.

described the game as 'offering a splendid outlet for lusty youth. It has certainly done that, and more, in the years since.

Hamilton club was formed in 1875, Western Province club early the next year, and Villagers still later in 1876 (some histories say Villagers was formed in 1875). Disputes over which rules to play provided early controversy. So many players left Western Province club, which favoured Rugby's rules, that it became defunct. The remaining clubs played Winchester rules.

All this changed when the former England player, William Henry Milton, arrived from Britain to settle in the

Cape. Milton, later private secretary to Cecil Rhodes, persuaded clubs that Rugby's rules were better and so gradually the Winchester style disappeared. By 1883, when the formation of the Western Province union was mooted, there were five clubs in the region, two of them secondary schools. Among them was the Stellenbosch club, which was to contribute enormously in playing strength and influence over the years.

After the formation of the South African Rugby Board in 1889 at Kimberley, Western Province won the country's first interprovincial tournament, and in 1899 it won the first Currie Cup tournament.

Sixteen of the 29 players in the 1906–07 Springbok team to Britain were current or former wearers of the Western Province colours, a trend which has continued in every touring team since.

Western Province's first wins over touring teams came with defeats of the British teams of 1903 and 1910. The 1938 tourists suffered the same fate. The 1928 All Blacks lost 10–13 to Western Province, and the New Zealand team of 1976 went down by 11–12. Australia lost twice in the Cape, in 1933 and 1963. The biggest win Western ever had over a major touring team was in 1964, when it beat France, 29–11.

Danie Craven, 'Mr Rugby' himself, was a Stellenbosch and a Western Province man, and so too was the great flyhalf, Benny Osler.

The big prop Hannes Marais was the most-capped test player in the first 110 years of the union. He bagged 35 caps for South Africa, while the two brilliant three-quarters, John Gainsford and Jannie Engelbrecht, won 33 each. Lionel Wilson, the steady and dependable fullback, had 27 caps, as did 'Mannie' Roux, one of the Springboks' greatest centres. Dawie de Villiers and Divan Serfontein were two grand halfbacks from the union, and the South African captain of the 1970s, Morne du Plessis, had 10 seasons with Springbok teams – one of the finest players ever to grace the blue and white narrow hoops of Western Province.

Men such as Dawie Ackermann, Roy Dryburgh, Stephen Fry, Doug Hopwood, 'Tjol' Lategan, 'Butch' Lochner, 'Boy' Louw, Rob Louw, Abe Malan, Gert Muller, 'Tiny' Naude, Jan Pickard and Hennie and Hugo van Zyl were all outstanding players, part of a list of Springboks that almost doubles the next best tally for one South African province.

With such strength it is not surprising that Western Province's record in the Currie Cup has been outstanding. In the first 19 tournaments, spread over 37 years from 1899 to 1936, Western Province was the winner 16 times. It also held the cup from 1959–66 and was the winner for a record five times in a row in the 1980s.

WESTERN SAMOA

The Western Samoa RFU was founded in 1927 as the Apia RFU, and was originally affiliated to the New Zealand union.

Samoa's first test match was against Fiji in 1924. The venue was a fine field in Samoa's capital, Apia – its most distinctive feature a large and shady tree situated prominently on the field of play!

Western Samoan rugby suffered from isolation in the early days, with most games played against the minor nations of the area such as the Cook Islands and the Solomon Islands. Fiji did not play there again until 1955, and in 1956 Samoa toured to Fiji.

The New Zealand Maoris first toured in 1960, returning in 1973 and 1979, and Samoa made its first sortie to New Zealand in 1976. It was one of the original competitors at the South Pacific Games, taking the bronze medal in 1963. By the fourth games, in 1971, the medal was gold.

Western Samoa was first invited to the Hong Kong Sevens in 1978 and made superb progress to reach the final with Australia just one year later. In 1982, when the first triangular Pacific tournament was staged, Western Samoa won again, and repeated the win in 1985.

On its first tour to Britain in 1988, it played two full internationals. Results were encouraging only, but the experience was to prove vital. There were four wins out of ten games, but Samoa lost to Ireland 22–49 and to Wales 6–24. In 1989 there was a further tour of Europe, where two lesser rugby powers, West Germany and Belgium, were comfortably beaten.

The population of Western Samoa is still under 200,000, so it was a remarkable effort to qualify for the 1991 Rugby World Cup. Competing in the four-way Asian qualifying group in Tokyo, Samoa beat Korea 74–7, Tonga 12–3 and Japan 37–11, to win its way into the same World Cup pool as Wales, Australia and Argentina.

Samoan rugby's steady progress has been greatly assisted by the experience of players living in New Zealand, who have the choice of playing international rugby for New Zealand or Samoa, and there is now a system set up for the Samoan selectors to monitor the form of New Zealand resident players.

Two of the most famous Samoan rugby players are Bryan Williams and Michael Jones, both among the very best of their time. Both chose to play for New Zealand, though Jones played first for Western Samoa against Wales in Apia in 1986. Other modern Samoan All Blacks are John Schuster and Va'aiga Tuigamala.

Others chose to play for Western Samoa. Experienced and battle-hardened men such as Timo Tagaloa, the big wing who played for both Auckland and Wellington, and burly prop Peter Fatialofa, of Auckland's highly successful Ranfurly Shield squad, were cornerstones of the Samoan success in the World Cup qualifying rounds. Before them, Lolani Koko was a strong performer in New Zealand, Britain and also South Africa, where he played as part of the South Pacific Barbarians team in 1988.

The game is extremely popular in Samoa, and there was a crowd of 25,000 to watch the international with Wales in 1986. Players who live and play in the islands still provide about half of the national team squad and interest is climbing as success at an international level continues to soar.

WESTON, MIKE
Durham City and England
29 internationals for England 1960–68
6 internationals for British Isles 1962–66

A stylish English centre three-quarter and flyhalf whose first international for his country was against Wales at Twickenham in 1960. Mike Weston captained England on the short tour of New Zealand and Australia in 1963, the first home nation to tour 'down under'. But after all the tests were

Irish Rugby Football Union (Ulster Branch)

ULSTER
v.
WESTERN SAMOA
at Ravenhill Park, Belfast.

on
Wednesday
2nd November
1988
at
7.30 pm

PROGRAMME
30p

lost, he lost the captaincy on the team's return.

He toured twice with the Lions, to South Africa in 1962 and again to New Zealand and Australia, in 1966. Injury in New Zealand kept him out of the test line-ups.

Mike Weston retired after his last match for his country, as captain again, against Scotland at Murrayfield in 1968. He is remembered as a very capable kicker, a steady backline player and a loyal Durham City club man.

Within a few years he was back in the limelight when he was elected to England's selection committee, and in 1985–86 he was chairman of the selection panel.

WHEEL, GEOFF

Swansea and Wales
32 internationals for Wales 1974–82

A colourful and controversial player who was admired in Wales as a hard-working, hard-mauling lock. Geoff Wheel had several brushes with the rugby authorities, which made him very popular with the ordinary fans of Welsh rugby.

His international debut was in 1974, in a drawn match with Ireland. In that game he partnered Allan Martin of Aberavon and the two went on to make 27 appearances together in Welsh test scrums, a world record for a locking pair.

Wheel was involved in the first sending-off of an international player at Cardiff Arms Park, when he and Irishman Willie Duggan were dismissed by the Scottish referee, Norman Sanson, in 1977. Officialdom was not pleased with Wheel, but his popularity with the fans soared.

Chosen for the 1977 British Isles tour of New Zealand, Wheel was later ruled unfit because of a heart condition. It was a decision Wheel was not at all happy with, and despite the doctor's recommendation he continued to play his honest forward's role right up until 1982.

WHEELER, PETER

Leicester and England
41 internationals for England 1975–84
7 internationals for British Isles 1977–80

A hard-working hooker who captained his country, took part in a Grand Slam

winning season, and made two tours with the British Isles.

Peter Wheeler was a product of Midlands rugby, where he was an essential component of the Leicester 'Tigers' throughout his career. He captained Leicester to three John Player Cup wins from 1979–81.

His first international was against France in 1975, and thereafter he became first choice as the wearer of England's No. 2 jersey. He played well in New Zealand with the Lions in 1977 as part of a powerful British scrum, one which the New Zealanders could not contain in that series.

In 1980 he was part of the England team that won the Grand Slam, and the same year he travelled again with the Lions, this time to South Africa, where he appeared in all four tests.

Wheeler was a lively and aggressive player and a very good lineout thrower. He was also rather an outspoken character and this was said by some to have cost him the English captaincy. However, in 1983, one week short of his 35th birthday, he was finally awarded the leadership against the All Blacks. England promptly won the game, scoring its first win over New Zealand at Twickenham since 1935.

WHETTON, GARY

Auckland and New Zealand
48 internationals for N. Zealand 1981–90

WHETTON, ALAN

Auckland and New Zealand
29 internationals for N. Zealand 1984–90

Tall, strong and athletic forwards, the Whettons were the first twins to play for the All Blacks.

Gary was a lock, blessed with superb ball skills and a surprising turn of speed in the open. Alan was mainly a blindside flanker, also a good ball handler, and both were excellent in lineouts.

Gary Whetton made his test debut under a deluge of flour bombs in the third test v South Africa in Auckland in 1981. In his early years he was dogged with injury, but from 1984 became an automatic test selection. His brother Alan joined him in the All Blacks that season, though his first four test appearances were all as replacements. From 1987 until the end of the decade the two brothers played almost every test together.

Peter Wheeler

At the end of 1990 Gary Whetton had played 48 test matches, a total second only to Colin Meads's 55 in New Zealand rugby history. Alan had played 29. Both played in the 1987 World Cup, where Alan scored tries in five consecutive tests, believed to be a world's best try-scoring sequence for a forward.

In 1990 Gary Whetton was chosen as the New Zealand captain, replacing Wayne Shelford, whose rejection by the selectors became one of the greatest All Black controversies of the decade. He had qualified success, defending the Bledisloe Cup against Australia and beating France in France, but the All Blacks also had three (rare) losses in a short space of time.

WHINERAY, WILSON

Wairarapa, Mid-Canterbury, Manawatu, Canterbury, Waikato, Auckland
and New Zealand
32 internationals for N. Zealand 1957–65

Few would question that Wilson Whineray was one of the finest rugby captains the world has seen, and the respect in which he was held was well illustrated at the Cardiff Arms Park in 1964. After Whineray scored the final try in a 36–3 thrashing of the Barbarians – by selling an outrageous dummy rarely seen from a prop – the crowd rose, chanting his name, and sang 'For he's a jolly good fellow'.

Strong-running forward Gary Whetton is supported by Murray Mexted as he outsprints Lions Ollie Campbell and John Rutherford.

A thoughtful Wilson Whineray at half-time; Brian Lochore in the background.

Whineray first played senior club rugby at the age of 16 (in Southland), and he was playing representative rugby at 17. But then Whineray was young at most things rugby – he was only 23 when appointed New Zealand captain in 1958, the youngest since Herb Lilburne 29 years earlier.

Whineray made his New Zealand debut in Australia in 1957, where he also played both tests. He then played a further 26 consecutive internationals as New Zealand captain, before dropping out of top rugby for 1964. But he returned to captain the All Blacks in their 3–1 series win against the 1965 Springboks, before retiring.

Whineray led New Zealand on tours of South Africa, Australia and Britain and France, and in home series against Australia (twice), the British Isles, France and South Africa.

Usually a loosehead prop, he was not noted as a particularly powerful scrummager, and had his problems with Piet du Toit in South Africa, but team-mate Colin Meads insisted the New Zealand scrum rarely suffered because of any weakness in the front row.

He was an unusually gifted player in the loose, often playing at No. 8, and developing a peeling-off movement from the lineouts, named 'Willie Away' in recognition of the man who brought the move to perfection.

A New Zealand Universities heavyweight boxing champion in his younger days, Whineray received the OBE at the conclusion of his playing days, before becoming a leader of New Zealand industry.

WHITE, JIMMY
Border and South Africa
10 internationals for Sth Africa, 1931–37

The ferocity of Jimmy White's tackling earned him the nickname of 'Killer', and he was an essential part of Springbok international sides throughout the 1930s. White was one of the long line of players 'spotted' by A.F. Markotter: on holiday, 'Uncle Mark' saw White playing at fullback, and promptly invited him to the 1931 Springbok trials as a centre.

White won a place in the side to tour Britain in 1931–32, playing in the Wales international. He played all five tests against the 1933 Australians, but must have wondered about his best position: centre for the first three games, he was moved to the wing for the fourth test and to fullback for the last.

However, he was back to centre for the 1937 tour to Australia and New Zealand, and his solidity complemented the craft of Louis Babrow in the internationals. White's unyielding defence paved the way to South African's first test win against Australia, after the tourists had lost to New South Wales.

He missed the final test against New Zealand because of injury, and his test career was over.

WHITE, 'TINY'
Poverty Bay and New Zealand
23 internationals for N. Zealand 1949–56

The year 1949 was a disaster for New Zealand rugby: it lost all four tests in South Africa and two more besides, played by another selection against Australia. But those two home tests made Richard White Poverty Bay's first All Black.

From that inauspicious beginning, White went on to play 23 consecutive tests for New Zealand and became the world's pre-eminent lock. On a tour to Britain, France and North America in 1953–54 (he had also toured Australia in 1951), White played 30 of the 36 matches and never showed any sign of wilting. His career was cruelly ended when he was kicked at the base of the spine, while lying on the ground, by a Springbok prop. But White's reputation was then well established as a strong scrummaging lock who was dynamic in the loose, and the finest lineout forward in the world.

White's technique was to soar high, catch the ball in both hands, and almost immediately flick it on to his halfback. The All Black coach of the early 1950s, Arthur Marslin, far preferred the 'Otago style' where the catcher took the ball down and the pack started a drive, but White's peerless technique won through.

WILLIAMS, BLEDDYN
Cardiff and Wales
22 internationals for Wales 1947–55
5 internationals for British Isles 1950

Bleddyn Williams was just on 24 when he turned out for Wales as a flyhalf against England in 1947. There were 13 new caps in the Welsh team and it lost 6–9, but Williams, in partnership with the great Haydn Tanner, held his place in the next match, although moving to centre.

He was already an accomplished and experienced player, having built up a strong reputation in services teams and the 'victory' internationals which followed the war.

Williams was a powerful runner with the ability to make a clean backline break and to deliver the ball to his wings with impeccable timing. These attributes were exploited fully by Welsh teams and Wiliams became a huge name in the game in Wales.

He toured New Zealand with the British Isles, where his reputation was enhanced. In partnership with his fellow countryman, Jack Matthews, in the centres, he guaranteed good service to the team's fast wings. Leg injuries bothered Williams on that tour, as they were to do at other times of his career.

New Zealand won the test series, but Williams had the last word over the All Blacks when he led Cardiff and Wales to victory over Bob Stuart's 1953 team.

Bleddyn Williams came from a proud Cardiff rugby family – all eight boys in the family played for the club. His brother Lloyd went on to play for Wales for five seasons (1957–62) and won 13 caps, including one as captain.

The father of the Williams boys was once asked the main ingredient in the production of all his famous rugby-playing sons. He replied, 'Plenty of beef stew and rugby conversation every day!'

Bleddyn Williams later became an accomplished rugby writer.

WILLIAMS, BRYAN
Auckland and New Zealand
38 internationals for N. Zealand 1970–78

New Zealand's most-capped wing when he retired in 1978, with 36 of his test appearances in that position, 'BG' ranks as one of the most devastating three-quarters in New Zealand's history.

First playing for Auckland at the age of 17, Williams was just 19 when chosen to tour South Africa in 1970. He was an instant sensation, scoring a try on his debut and running in 14 altogether in 13 matches on the tour.

Apart from being left out of an internal 'tour by the All Blacks in 1972, Williams missed only one of the following 31 test matches, because of injury. His long sequence ended when he dislocated a hip on the 1977 tour of France, but he returned to play full series against the 1978 Australians and in Britain.

A strapping man of Samoan descent, Williams had rare speed and balance, determination and a powerful fend. In his 113 matches for New Zealand – he was preceded only by Colin Meads and Ian Kirkpatrick to the century – Williams scored 401 points, including a record 66 tries. His total was boosted by useful goal-kicking: occasionally the first-choice kicker in days of drought for New Zealand, he landed 53 goals by way of conversions, penalties and a dropped goal.

Williams remained involved with rugby after his retirement, in 1987 becoming assistant coach to the Auckland side he had graced so successfully and for so long. In 1991 he played a coaching role in the preparation of the Western Samoan team for the World Cup.

WILLIAMS, DENZIL
Ebbw Vales and Wales
36 internationals for Wales 1963–71
5 internationals for British Isles 1966

A hard-working prop who had nine seasons in the Welsh pack, becoming the pack-leader in his last season, 1971. Denzil Williams became Ebbw Vale's highest-capped player and Wales's most-capped front rower and most-capped forward for a time. His record total of caps for Ebbw Vale was still standing 20 years later, although the other Welsh marks were passed by Graham Price.

Denzil Williams went on the 1966 British Isles tour of New Zealand, where his steelworker's strength enabled him to play 20 times, including both successful tests with Australia and three of the four in New

Bleddyn Williams (right) with Lions team-mate Karl Mullen.

'B.G.' Williams scores.

Zealand. He also toured South Africa with Wales in 1964 and to New Zealand with Wales in 1969.

Williams played for a time in France, appearing for the Vichy club.

WILLIAMS, D.O.
Western Province and South Africa
8 internationals for Sth Africa 1937–38

With a name like David Owen Williams – and answering equally to Dai and Owen – he sounds like a fully-fledged Welsh wing. Indeed, D.O. Williams's father was a product of Tallyn, but his son played his rugby for South Africa.

D.O. Williams was the outstanding Springbok wing between the wars, and holds a special place in South African rugby. His idol, Jock van Niekerk, injured a knee trying to prevent a practice ball going over the side of the *Windsor Castle* en route to Britain in 1931. The injury was aggravated in his first game, and van Niekerk was never to play again. Only four months past his 18th birthday, Williams was summoned to Britain, South Africa's youngest representative.

Not that he had much of a tour. Williams's short studs had him slipping all over the place on his debut against Cardiff, but he scored a try against Llanelli. His next game, against Lancashire and Cheshire, was the last of the tour for 'D.O' – he broke his collarbone.

One would have thought that to be a minor hiccup in his career, but the South African selectors made some

curious choices in the five-match series against the 1933 Wallabies, such as choosing seven different wings – including fullback Gerry Brand and centres Jimmy White and Frank Waring – but there was no place for Williams.

His reputation was made, however, on the 1937 tour to Australia and New Zealand, and embellished at home against the Lions the next year. By then this big man of 1.86m (6ft 1½in) weighed in at more than 90kg (14 stone)

'J.J.' Williams

and with his great speed – 10 seconds for the 100 yds as a youth – and strength, he was a fearsome opponent.

There were few refinements about Williams as a runner. He barely needed them, apart from a finely-balanced swerve which confounded many prospective tacklers, and he possessed a centering kick of pinpoint accuracy. He was also a tiger for work, and was not afraid to leave his flank to seek the loose ball. Williams scored three tries in the two tests in Australia, then played nine of the 17 matches in New Zealand, scoring 12 tries in all, three of them in tests.

In the first of the three tests against Sam Walker's Lions in 1938, Williams scored two tries. But then came the Second World War, a particularly harrowing time for Williams in the Western Desert, and when he again wore the Villagers club jersey, he was 33 and his capacity for and interest in rugby had faded.

WILLIAMS, JOHN ('J.J.')
Bridgend, Llanelli and Wales
30 internationals for Wales 1973–79
7 internationals for British Isles 1974–77

A speedy wing whose speciality was scoring tries after chasing and beating defenders. He was widely known as 'J.J.' to avoid confusion with the other John Williams of Bridgend and Wales, 'J.P.R.'

The first time J.J. Williams made international sports news was as a sprinter for Wales at the 1970 Commonwealth games at Edinburgh. His basic speed became his greatest asset on the rugby field.

Originally a Bridgend player, he later switched to Llanelli. He made his debut for Wales against France as a replacement in Paris in 1973. In the next season he cemented his place in the team and from then on a steady flow of test tries followed.

His form took him into the British team that toured South Africa in 1974. The hard grounds suited him ideally and he appeared 12 times, including in all four tests. He scored six tries v South-West Districts at Mossell Bay, which equalled the Lions' record for one player in a match. He averaged a try per game on tour, including four superbly taken test tries.

In New Zealand in 1977 he was again one of the Lions' stars. He played in the first three tests, including scoring a brilliant try at Christchurch in the second test. But he was injured so severely in the third, he did not play again on tour.

He may have appeared light of frame, but J.J. Williams was a vital part of Wales's scoring machine in its highly successful era in the 1970s.

WILLIAMS, JOHN ('J.P.R.')
Bridgend and Wales
55 internationals for Wales 1969–81
8 internationals for British Isles 1971–74

Courageous and sturdy, brilliant at times, and always totally reliable, John Williams was a young tennis star who became a rugby fullback, and who rose to be one of the symbols of the success of Welsh and British rugby in the 1970s.

Williams had an outstanding career as a young tennis player, winning the Wimbledon junior singles event in 1966. He made his rugby debut as a 19-year-old, playing for Wales in the 1968 tour of Argentina. Called 'J.P.R.' to distinguish him from the other John Williams in the Welsh team at the time ('J.J.'), he had an excellent tour and moved up to test rugby the following season. He swiftly proved to be the powerful attacking force from fullback that Wales had been looking for. The team won the Five Nations championship in his first season, as well as the Triple Crown.

A tour to New Zealand with Wales followed in 1969, and two more domestic seasons, before Williams went back to New Zealand as part of John Dawes' Lions team. J.P.R. was an automatic test selection, even though England's Bob Hiller was also an excellent fullback. His dropped goal in the fourth test at Eden Park, his only one in 63 internationals, was a vital kick which helped the Lions earn a draw and take the test series.

By then he was a famous figure in world rugby and one of the first fullbacks to exploit the change in the laws which meant one could no longer kick out on the full from any part of the field. Williams saw this as an opportunity to attack by bringing the ball up by hand, and became known for powerful running and bursting into the backline as an extra man.

There was further success for Williams with the Lions. He travelled to

All aggression, 'J.P.R.' Williams leaves the defence sprawling in his wake.

South Africa with Willie John McBride's team in 1974, again being first choice at fullback, even against Scotland's Andy Irvine. There he was tough and fearless, attacking brilliantly, while his consistency and determination on defence kept out many opposition attacks.

When the British won the series and the team was hailed as one of the best of all time, J.P.R was counted among the team's special heroes, and named by South Africans as the world's best fullback.

He continued to be a force in Welsh backlines throughout the 1970s, gradually accumulating a total of tests that was to make him the world's most-capped fullback. He also proved himself to be highly versatile, playing a test in 1978 in Sydney as a flanker – one of the few test players to appear as a forward and a back.

During his career, Wales won or shared eight championships. Williams captained Wales throughout the 1978–79 season, the team won the championship, and Williams retired.

He was persuaded to return in 1980 for the Welsh centenary match with New Zealand, where he showed that he had lost nothing of his bravery and resolution. His last test match was against Scotland at Murrayfield in February 1981.

WILLIAMS, RHYS
Llanelli and Wales
23 internationals for Wales 1954–60
10 internationals for British Isles 1955–59

Rhys Williams was one of the best forwards in the world in the 1950s. While he had many fine games for his country, spread over seven seasons, perhaps his best football was played while on two tours for the British Isles. Williams had only six Welsh caps, but had played superbly in the lineouts before touring South Africa in 1955.

There he was outstanding, appearing in all four tests, and imposing his will on the best the Springboks could offer – including men like Johan Claassen and 'Salty' du Rand. He did the same thing in Australia and New Zealand in 1959, appearing in all six tests, and dominating many players who had built fine reputations 'down under', including the great Colin Meads, who always listed Williams among his 'best ever' opponents. On his two Lions tours, he appeared in all 10 test matches in three countries.

Williams played his 23rd and last international in 1960, when he appeared as captain in a losing Welsh team at Twickenham.

After retirement the ever-cheerful, ever-modest Rhys Williams stayed in touch with the game and in the mid-1980s became chairman of the Welsh national team selectors.

WILSON, LIONEL
Western Province and South Africa
27 internationals for Sth Africa 1960–65

A rock-steady South African fullback who, because of his fitness and consistency, stayed in senior rugby for 17 years. Lionel Wilson was a senior club player in Cape Town as a 17-year-old, but it wasn't until he was 27 that he was called on by the South African selectors.

Wilson was steadiness personified, a player who could always be relied on under the high ball and in the face of charging opponents. His nickname was 'Speedy', surely an irony, for he had no great reputation as an attacker, although it should be remembered that he played in the era when a fullback's primary role was defensive.

Wilson made his test debut against New Zealand in Bloemfontein in the dramatic drawn third test of 1960. He was also there at fullback when the fourth test was won by the Springboks to clinch the series.

He was first choice for his country for the next five years, touring Britain and France in 1960–61, Ireland and Scotland in 1965, and Australia and New Zealand the same year. His final tally of 27 caps was the South African record for a fullback.

WILSON, STU
Wellington and New Zealand
34 internationals for N. Zealand 1977–83

The illustrious career of Stu Wilson finished on two disappointing notes: he captained New Zealand to one of its worst international records on a short tour – a draw with Scotland and a loss to England – before he was suspended from the sport for accepting royalties from *Ebony and Ivory*, a biographical story of Wilson and long-time wing partner, Bernie Fraser.

But those hiccups do little to dull the memory of an explosive wing and some-time centre who began international rugby when he toured Argentina with New Zealand's pioneering, if under-strength, team in 1976.

The next year Wilson became a test player, invariably on the right wing, and the only interruptions to his career came on the 1980 tour of Australia, when he broke a finger.

During the 1983 series against the Lions, Wilson extended his total of test tries to 19, breaking Ian Kirkpatrick's record of 16, but his succession to the captaincy, with Andy Dalton unavailable, was not the highlight it should have been.

Wilson did not enjoy the experience, not just because the wing is not an ideal captaincy position, but also because the humorous extrovert found himself bowed down by the responsibilities. He was always what New Zealanders would call 'one of the boys'.

This particular boy scored 50 tries in all matches for New Zealand. Only two men, Kirkpatrick again and Bryan Williams, had beaten him to that tally, and it was Williams he succeeded on the right wing. Wilson himself was succeeded by another star in John Kirwan: riches indeed for New Zealand, and Wilson lost nothing by comparison with those other two great players.

WINDSOR, BOBBY
Cardiff, Pontypool and Wales
28 internationals for Wales 1973–79
5 internationals for British Isles 1974–77

The hooker at the centre of the famous Pontypool front row of the 1970s who, along with his props Graham Price and Tony ('Charlie') Faulkner, became one of the best known faces of Welsh

Stu Wilson in action against the Barbarians, 1983.

Bobby Windsor

rugby. A tough, hard player, an excellent mauler and a throw-in expert, he was seldom bettered by any opponent in his long career.

Windsor first played for Wales against Australia in 1973. Being on the winning team became a familiar place for him, for only eight times in his 33 internationals was he not part of a team celebration at the end of a test match.

In 1974 he toured South Africa with Willie John McBride's Lions, playing in all four tests. His second Lions tour, to New Zealand in 1977, was less successful for him and he played only the first test before being replaced by Peter Wheeler. His international career came to an end when he suffered back injuries in 1979.

Bobby ('The Duke') Windsor continued to play socially. In 1985 it was reported in *Rugby World and Post* magazine that he played a game on his 42nd birthday – the day he became a father for the second time and a grandfather for the first time! Welsh hookers really are amazing people!

WING FORWARD

The wing forward position existed from the 1890s until 1932, when it was outlawed. Teams which used wing forwards had seven players in each scrum. The eighth forward stood several paces off the scrum with a 'roving commission' to assist attacks by his own team and to resist those by the opposition. In Britain he was called a 'rover'.

The position is accepted as having been invented by the 1893 New Zealand captain, Tom Ellison, a Maori pioneer in both rugby and the law.

New Zealand, with its 2-3-2 scrum formation, was the first country to utilise wing forwards, and the 1905–06 All Blacks in Britain took the idea beyond New Zealand.

The captain of that famous team was Dave Gallaher, a wing forward who became a thorn in the side of opposing teams. Some British rugby watchers claimed the wing forward was clearly trying to be obstructive and destructive. Rugby, they argued, should be on a much higher plane of 'decency' than to have players exist to do just that. Some labelled Gallaher a 'cheat'.

The noted E.H.D.Sewell said, 'I believe he [Gallaher] is a fair player, but we do not like the position and it will never be part of the game in the four home unions.'

Yet the British did embrace the wing forward role, albeit in a different way from the New Zealanders. Charles ('Cherry') Pillman of England and Ivor Morgan of Wales were fine loosemen who were both rovers, although they concentrated on attack rather than obstruction. Pillman in particular built a fine reputation and took the art of roving play out to South Africa with the British team in 1910. Players like Samuel M.J. Woods, an Australian, who was also a prominent cricketer, played for Cambridge University and

The 1905 All Blacks, playing Middlesex, use their 2-3-2 scrum to good effect. Dave Gallaher, right, is standing well off the scrum in the wing forward position.

Top: Rugby: the international game. One representative from each country at the 1990 Hong Kong Sevens.
Below: Glasnost in Hong Kong. The USA and USSR teams after their match, 1990.   Peter Bush

Fans . . . and future champions.
Peter Bush

England before the turn of the century; George Boots of Newport did the same roving job for Wales.

The New Zealanders of 1924–25 used wing forwards on their unbeaten tour of Britain and so did the 1928 All Blacks, but by 1930, when Great Britain toured New Zealand, the writing seemed to be on the wall for the position. The manager of that team, James ('Bim') Baxter, was a member of the International Rugby Board and favoured a universal law for forward positions in the scrum. Within two years the law was changed and all scrums were required to have three front-rowers.

The last test match to have a wing forward was New Zealand v Australia in 1931. The last wing forward in world rugby was the All Black that day, Frank Solomon.

WINGS

Wings, wingers, or wing three-quarters – call them what you like, these are usually the fastest men in the team. The wearer of the No. 11 or No. 14 jersey is expected to have passing and ball skills, kicking ability, sound defence, width of vision, and creativity. Above all, his function is to finish off all attacking moves and score tries.

So who are the great wings? New Zealanders of modern vintage would argue for John Kirwan or Stu Wilson, while those slightly older might suggest Bryan Williams, Grant Batty or Ron Jarden. Welshmen would swear by Gerald Davies or J.J. Williams, perhaps Dewi Bebb or Stuart Watkins. If they were older they would say Ken Jones. Irishmen would be outraged if Tony O'Reilly were not included in any list of superstar wings; South Africans would claim Jannie Engelbrecht as one of the best, and Tom van Vollenhoven (until he went to league?). Gerrie Germishuys and Jaco Reinach would also make their list. Australians would trumpet the case for David Campese, and also Brendan Moon, Eddie Stapleton or John Cole; Scots would go misty-eyed over their Smiths, Arthur and Ian; while the French would enthuse over Patrice Lagisquet, Jean Dupuy and Christian Darrouy.

But it is the English who have produced the world's greatest wings. Who could say which were the best from the following list: Alexander Obolensky, Cyril Lowe or Ronnie Poulton Palmer from the first half of the twentieth century; or modern players such as Peter Jackson, David Duckham, Mike Slemen or Rory Underwood?

To the end of 1990 the highest-capped international wing was Ken Jones with 44 appearances for Wales and three for the Lions. That total was under threat from the current international, Rory Underwood of England, with 43 caps won. At only 27 years of age he seemed likely to become the first player to pass 50 caps as a wing.

WINTERBOTTOM, PETER
Headingley, Harlequins and England
42 internationals for England 1982–91
4 internationals for British Isles 1983

His talent, energy, toughness and strength made Peter Winterbottom a regular in England's pack for most of the 1980s. His test debut was against Australia in 1982 and within a year he was off to New Zealand with Ciaran Fitzgerald's Lions team. Winterbottom had had experience of New Zealand conditions before, having had a season with Hawke's Bay in 1982. He relished the chance to play there again, appearing in all four test matches.

He also toured South Africa in 1984, playing in both tests. He enjoyed it so much he returned there to live for a time in 1988. Returning home in 1989 he regained his place in the England team and was soon their most-capped player.

Peter Winterbottom

Winterbottom was known as an excellent chaser, hassler and tackler. In 1990 he was still playing as well as ever after nine years of international rugby. He toured Argentina with England during the year. Two tests there, and five in the next home season, three months later, brought his tally of caps for England to 42, just one short of Tony Neary's record of 43 caps, the best by an English test flanker.

WOLFHOUNDS RFC
Ireland's equivalent of the Barbarians, the Wolfhounds club was formed in 1956 with the aim both of playing attacking rugby, and taking teams to the country districts of Ireland to give young Irishmen an opportunity to play against top players.

Almost every leading British player has at some time played in the green and white hoops of the Wolfhounds. One of the early hard workers behind the club, and its first honorary secretary, was the British and Irish captain, Karl Mullen.

The first committee included names such as Jack Kyle, Tony O'Reilly and Des O'Brien. Later Mullen became president, and committee members were added from England, Wales and Scotland. There is also a strong connection with France. Jean Prat captained the club's first opponents; France is represented on the committee and has received tours from Wolfhounds teams.

Whereas in the early days there was hesitation in some quarters in welcoming the Wolfhounds, those days are now long gone. The club tours regularly and plays many centenary matches, charity games and regular fixtures. The teams are invariably cosmopolitan in make-up and the club has spread and popularised the game in many places.

The club's emblem is, obviously, an Irish wolfhound. Once I was privileged to be presented with a Wolfhounds tie on which the dog was depicted in a sitting position. Several years later, I noticed an Irish friend wearing a tie on which the wolfhound was standing upright. When I asked why the emblem had been changed so soon after the club was established, the Wolfhound club member replied, 'Tony O'Reilly got the tie changed because the club is now on its feet!'

WOMEN'S RUGBY

Only a few decades ago the idea of women playing rugby seemed unlikely. As recently as the early 1970s, rugby was considered too 'tough' a game for females to play. But through the 1980s there was an upsurge in interest by women in playing the game.

In Britain a number of clubs resisted early efforts to have women's teams, so the women simply formed their own clubs; but as the quality of preparation and play improved, more and more men's clubs admitted them as playing members.

In some areas women's rugby has been coached and encouraged by enlightened males, but going into the 1990s women were showing increasing confidence in making their rugby a game that had its own touches of style. International matches have been played, world tournaments have been staged and a Women's World Cup was played in Britain in 1991. It could be said that the development of women's rugby has come about more quickly than the administration of the game has been able to cope with.

The United States was the first to make progress as a women's rugby nation. By the 1980s there were 300 clubs in action, and the Americans might still be the best women's players in the world. France and the Netherlands were two others to show early interest. In Britain in 1983 the Women's Rugby Football Union (like the men they did not use the word 'England' in their title) was formed, and other countries, such as Italy, New Zealand, the Soviet Union and Canada, followed with their administrative bodies late in the decade.

The first full international match for women was played in 1982, when France beat the Netherlands in Hilversum by 4–0. The first international played by a British women's team was at Richmond in April 1986, when a side called Great Britain lost 8–14 to France. A year later England beat Wales 22–4 at Pontypool Park.

The standard in those two games impressed watchers. There is no doubt that the arrival of New Image rugby, with its integrated teams, had helped young girls to assimilate the basics of the game.

The next major step in women's rugby was the formation at a meeting in Paris in 1988 of the International Federation of Women's Rugby. Six nations attended – Britain, France, Italy, the Netherlands, Spain and Belgium. It is believed that women's rugby could become more of an international experience than the tightly-controlled world of the men's game, because it shows no signs of being hemmed in by the élite group of countries that are members of the IRB or FIRA.

WOOD, GORDON

Garryowen and Ireland
29 internationals for Ireland 1954–61
2 internationals for British Isles 1959

From Limerick in the Munster province of Ireland, Gordon Wood was a solid prop who had eight seasons as a test player. His debut was against England in 1956 at Twickenham.

He built a reputation as a pugnacious forward and won his way into the British Isles tour of New Zealand and Australia in 1959. He played in two of the six tests of that tour, but missed most of the Australian section of the tour with a broken finger.

Wood died in 1982, aged only 51.

WOOLLER, WILF

Cardiff, London Welsh and Wales
18 internationals for Wales 1933–39

'Attractive and gifted' was how one Welsh rugby writer described this Cardiff centre three-quarter.

Wilf Wooller took part in two very famous Welsh rugby victories. In his debut match in 1933, one of seven new caps, Wales scored its first victory on Twickenham. Four years later, he was part of an inspirational Welsh back line which tipped over the 1935–36 All Blacks by 13–12. The tall and elegant Wooller was on the wing that day in a backline with the great Cliff Jones, Haydn Tanner, Vivian Jenkins and Claude Davey.

By 1939 Wooller had become captain of Wales, but after three games the war intervened. Wooller was only 26 years old and it seems that but for the war he would have gone on to a long and even more successful career

During the war, Wooller was a Japanese prisoner-of-war and after returning to Wales in poor physical condition he had to give up rugby. Instead, he commanded enormous respect as a cricketer, captaining Gla- morgan for 13 years, scoring more than 12,000 runs and capturing 892 wickets. He also put in long service as secretary of the Glamorgan Cricket Club (1946–78), as an England cricket selector (1952–58), and as a rugby and cricket writer and commentator (from the post-war years right through to the 1990s).

WORLD CUP

It is a measure of rugby's conservatism, or at least reluctance in some areas to progress, that it was the last major sport in the world to embrace a world championship. Certainly, rugby had featured three times at the Olympic Games, but the rugby powers paid scant regard to those competitions, only Australia, France, Romania and the United States fielding 'national' teams.

Yet rugby-playing nations were enamoured with the idea of being world champion, especially those who fancied themselves at the top of the pile at the time! In the 1980s, the balance of power was in New Zealand, though sometimes most sorely tested by Australia, as South Africa became increasingly isolated. And at this time, the hints and suggestions from the South Pacific for a world championship became more powerful arguments.

There was most resistance at IRB level. British unions had a long history of regarding organised competition as anathema, and the first steps to professionalism. Perhaps they also saw no need for a 'world cup' as they already had their own self-styled 'international championship'.

A private sports promoter, Neil Durden-Smith, had proposed a World Cup in 1982, 24 years after the IRB had passed a resolution specifically forbidding member nations getting together in such a tournament!

By then, however, the major objection seemed to be to such a tournament not being under the wing of the IRB, rather than towards the tournament as such. By 1984, both Australia and New Zealand had presented proposals for a World Cup, and the IRB approved a feasibility study that was accepted at the IRB's Paris meeting in 1985.

The organisers had two frantic years to make it work. The next year, 1986, was the preferred timing, but was too soon; 1988 was an Olympic Games year so, almost by default, 1987 was chosen. New Zealand and Australia were to stage the competition jointly, New Zealand the senior partner, but Australia having a slice of the action because of its unfailing support.

That was one mistake – not the support, but spreading the tournament between two countries. Another, perhaps, was in appointing John Kendall-Carpenter, an England international forward of the 1950s, as chairman of the organising committee. The argument was not with the individual, but with the nonsense of having a man living 20,000km away attempting to direct operations.

As it happened, herculean efforts by locally-based officials and administrators made the first World Cup a resounding success. Unlike World Cup competitions in other sports, however, there was no qualification for attending: the choice of 16 nations was made at IRB level. For strictly political reasons, and with that country's agreement, South Africa was excluded, and for commonsense reasons, the field included established rugby-playing powers: New Zealand, France, Australia, England, Wales, Scotland and Ireland.

Argentina was an automatic choice after the growing stature of its performances against strong nations, and the other choices were made geographically. Canada and the United States represented North America; Japan was there for Asia; Fiji and Tonga were the Pacific representatives; Zimbabwe from Africa; Italy and Romania from mainland Europe.

Countries which considered themselves hard-done by included the Spain, South Korea, Western Samoa and Malaysia – and, of course, more than a few South Africans.

It was perhaps no coincidence that the IRB broadened its vision and its membership in the lead-up to the tournament, admitting associate members for the first time. At the time of the 1987 World Cup, only Fiji, Romania and Tonga did not have membership.

The tournament opened in damp conditions at Auckland's Eden Park on May 22 1987. New Zealand marked the occasion by defeating Italy by a record score, 70–6. A penalty try was the first score, and new All Black, flanker Michael Jones, was the first to cross the line. But the match feature

was an astonishing 70m try by wing John Kirwan.

The World Cup was alight, and for the next month matches were played at 11 different New Zealand venues, while the pool containing Australia, England, United States and Japan played its matches at Sydney and Brisbane. Those teams finished in that order, Australia then beating Ireland, but England losing to Wales (a dreadful match) in the quarter-finals.

On the other half of the draw, New Zealand successively demolished Italy, Fiji and Argentina, the latter surprisingly failing to finish in its seeded second position, thanks to a shock loss to Fiji and a struggling win against Italy, while Italy beat Fiji.

The fourth pool was by far the toughest and Scotland, the best of the British entrants, drew with France but finished second on a countback and had to play New Zealand in the quarter-finals, losing 3–30. France beat Fiji in a spirited match.

The semi-finals matched France and Australia, and the old rivals, New Zealand and Wales. The former was a magnificent match, snatched from defeat at the death by France through a

Serge Blanco scores the winning try in France's World Cup semi-final match against Australia.

315

try to French fullback Serge Blanco, but there was no such drama in the other game. New Zealand inflicted a 49–6 defeat on Wales, at that time the biggest in a game between the two proud nations.

Before the grand final, Australia and Wales met for third place at Rotorua, and just as Wales had had a player ordered off against the All Blacks at Brisbane (Huw Richards), so Australia lost David Codey early in this match. Worse, Australia seemed uninterested in the minor placing, having expected to be in the final, and went down 21–22. Australia, in fact, never bothered to collect its fourth place trophy, a Maori carving, and this is now in the hands of a Christchurch collector!

While New Zealand had been rampant in all its five matches to the final, France had had its problems and the host nation confidently expected – and demanded – victory. It came, 29–9, but less easily than expected, for France was a very competitive side.

New Zealand was ecstatic that its claims for world supremacy were now justified, though there were rumblings about 'they've got to beat South Africa before . . .' Some of the British media were also uncharitable, describing the All Blacks and the final as boring. They were also upset that a British referee was not allocated the final – it was controlled by outstanding Australian, Kerry Fitzgerald.

But these were muted murmurings as the crowds clamoured for more, and a cycle of four-yearly competition was quickly established, with the second World Cup in 1991 scheduled for Britain and France, and with hopes rekindled that South Africa might participate, or even stage, the 1995 event.

For 1991, there was a system of direct entry (dependent on world seedings) and also qualification. One would expect that ultimately, as with soccer and other sports, all nations bar the title-holder and the host will have to undergo some form of qualification. Then it will truly be a World Cup.

WORLD RECORDS

There has never really been a true set of world rugby records. The history of the game has been well recorded by IRB countries, but language problems probably contribute to a lack of knowledge and appreciation of events from other rugby-playing countries.

There has also been the dilemma for statisticians that some countries are unwilling to reward lesser known rugby countries with 'official' test match status. For instance, French record books give Grant Fox a share of the world record for most points scored in a test, with his 30 points scored for New Zealand against Japan in Tokyo in 1987, but New Zealand does not recognise that score because it does not recognise Japan as a test match opponent.

The difficulty is highlighted in the case of Hugo Porta of Argentina, who would have rewritten the record books had he played for an IRB country. For instance, Simon Hodgkinson's seven penalties for England v Wales in 1991 were hailed in Britain as a world record – yet Hugo Porta achieved the feat 17 years earlier in a match against France. France awarded caps for this game, and had a Frenchman kicked the penalties, this would have been noted as a world record. Because Argentina is not a full IRB member, the total was not recognised by some statisticians.

The records opposite are from matches where one member country of the IRB awarded full international caps, even if the other country playing did not! Hugo Porta's achievements, which in some cases are greater than the 'records', are noted below.

WYLLIE, ALEX
Canterbury and New Zealand
11 internationals for N. Zealand 1970–73

'Grizz' Wyllie got his nickname when he was leaving the field after playing in a game against a long-time teammate, Lyn Davis. A halfback, Davis had been hounded all match by loose forward Wyllie, and commented: 'All you've done today is grizzle, grizzle, grizzle.' So Wyllie became 'Grizzly', usually abbreviated to just 'Grizz'.

He was more than just a grizzler, however. Wyllie was an uncommonly fine loose forward: a fast and aggressive flanker when younger, and a

---

1987 WORLD CUP RECORD

Pool One

Australia 19	England 6		
United States 21	Japan 18		
England 60	Japan 7		
Australia 47	United States 12		
England 34	United States 6		
Australia 42	Japan 23		

Pool Two

Canada 37	Tonga 4
Wales 13	Ireland 6
Wales 29	Tonga 16
Ireland 46	Canada 19
Wales 40	Canada 9
Ireland 32	Tonga 9

Pool Three

New Zealand 70	Italy 6
Fiji 28	Argentina 9
New Zealand 74	Fiji 13
Argentina 25	Italy 16
Italy 18	Fiji 15
New Zealand 46	Argentina 15

Pool Four

Romania 21	Zimbabwe 20
France 20	Scotland 20
France 55	Romania 12
Scotland 60	Zimbabwe 21
Scotland 55	Romania 28
France 70	Zimbabwe 12

Quarter-finals

New Zealand 30	Scotland 3	Australia 33	Ireland 15
France 31	Fiji 16	Wales 16	England 3

Semi-finals

France 30	Australia 24		
New Zealand 49	Wales 6		

Finals

New Zealand 29	France 9
Wales 22	Australia 21

First: New Zealand   **Third:** Wales
Second: France   **Fourth:** Australia

New Zealand was captained by David Kirk and France by Daniel Dubroca.

WORLD RECORDS

TEAM RECORDS

Highest score in a test match: 74
New Zealand v Fiji 1987, Christchurch. (74–13)

Biggest winning margin in a test match: 64
New Zealand v Italy, 1987, Auckland. (70–6)

Most tries in a test match: 13
England v Wales, 1881, Blackheath; New Zealand v USA, 1913, Berkeley; France v Romania, 1924, Paris; France v Zimbabwe, 1987, Auckland.

Most conversions in a test match: 10
New Zealand v Fjij, 1987, Christchurch.

Most penalty goals in an international: 7
Argentina v France, 1974, Buenos Aires; South Africa v France, 1975, Pretoria; England v Wales, 1991, Twickenham.

Most consecutive test victories: 17
New Zealand, 1965–69.

Most consecutive internationals undefeated: 23
New Zealand, 1987–90.

Highest score in a drawn test: 25–25
Scotland v New Zealand, Edinburgh, 1983.

INDIVIDUAL RECORDS

Most test matches: 85
Serge Blanco, France, 1980–91.

Most test matches as fullback: 73
Serge Blanco, France, 1980–91.

Most test matches as wing: 47
Ken Jones, Wales and British Isles, 1947–57.

Most test matches as centre: 65[1]
Philippe Sella, France, 1982–91.

Most test matches as flyhalf (or first five-eighths): 52[2]
Jack Kyle, Ireland and British Isles, 1947–58.

Most test matches as scrumhalf (or halfback): 63
Gareth Edwards, Wales and British Isles, 1967–78.

Most test matches as No. 8: 46
Mervyn Davies, Wales and British Isles, 1969–76.

Most test matches as flanker: 65
Fergus Slattery, Ireland and British Isles, 1970–84.

Most test matches as lock: 80
Willie John McBride, Ireland and British Isles, 1962–75.

Most test matches as prop: 59
Phil Orr, Ireland and British Isles, 1976–87.

Most test matches as hooker: 52
Colin Deans, Scotland, 1978–87.

Most consecutive test matches: 53
Gareth Edwards, Wales, 1967–78.

Most test matches as captain: 34
Jean-Pierre Rives, France, 1979–84.

INDIVIDUAL SCORING RECORDS

Most points in all test matches: 564[3]
Michael Lynagh, Australia, 1984–90 (in 43 tests).

Most points in one test match: 30
Didier Camberabero, France v Zimbabwe, Auckland, 1987.

Most points in a test match by a player on debut: 21
Robbie Blair, South Africa v World XV, Pretoria, 1977; David Knox, Australia v Fiji, Brisbane, 1985.

Most tries in all test matches: 37
David Campese, Australia, 1982–90.

Most tries in one test match: 5
George Lindsay, Scotland v Wales, Edinburgh. 1887; Daniel Lambert, England v France, Richmond, 1907; Rory Underwood, England v Fiji, Twickenham, 1989.

Most tries in a test match by a player on debut: 5
Daniel Lambert, England v France, Richmond, 1907.

Most conversions in one test match: 10[4]
Grant Fox, New Zealand v Fiji, Christchurch, 1987.

Most penalties kicked in one test match: 7
Hugo Porta, Argentina v France, Buenos Aires, 1974; Simon Hodgkinson, England v Wales, Twickenham, 1991.

Most dropped goals kicked in one test match: 3
Pierre Albaladejo, France v Ireland, Paris, 1960; Phil Hawthorne, Australia v England, Twickenham, 1967; Hugo Porta, Argentina v Australia, Buenos Aires, 1979; Naas Botha, South Africa v South America, Durban, 1980; Naas Botha, South Africa v Ireland, Durban, 1981; Jean-Patrick Lescarboura, France v England, Twickenham, 1985; Hugo Porta, Argentina v New Zealand, Buenos Aires, 1985; Jean-Patrick Lescarboura, France v New Zealand, Christchurch, 1986; Didier Camberabero, France v Australia, Sydney, 1990.

Longest time span as a test player: 18 seasons[5]
Tommy Vile, Great Britain and Wales, 1904–21

Longest gap between test matches: 13 years, 2 mths
Ned Hughes, New Zealand, 1908–21.

Oldest test match player: 40 years, 123 days
Ned Hughes, New Zealand, 1921.

Youngest test match player: 17 years, 36 days
Ninian Finlay, Scotland, 1875; Charles Reid, Scotland, 1881.

---

[1]Inside or outside centre, including the position called second five-eighths.

[2]A list from Argentina shows Hugo Porta played 57 internationals as a flyhalf between 1971–90, but eight of those were for South America v South Africa. While South Africa awarded caps for those games, the 'South American' teams, while being mostly Argentine players, did not appear with the sanction of the Argentine Rugby Union.

[3]Hugo Porta (1972–90) equalled this record late in 1990 (57 tests).

[4]Fox kicked 15 conversions v Japan in Tokyo in 1987 but New Zealand did not award caps.

[5]Hugo Porta's reappearance for Argentina in October 1990 meant that he had a span of 19 years in international play for that country.

(With thanks to the *Rothmans Rugby Yearbook*; *New Zealand Rugby Almanack*, the *South African Rugby Annual*, *The International Rugby Championship 1883-1983*, *The Complete Who's Who of International Rugby*, *The Guinness Book of Rugby Facts and Feats*, *Guinness Rugby – The Records*, *The Phoenix Book of International Rugby Records*.)

Alex Wyllie

tough, hard-driving and even dictatorial No. 8 when he became a first-choice captain.

Much of Wyllie's teams' play revolved round this man, who made a speciality of driving with the ball from the back of the scrum, and committing so many of the opposition's players before releasing the ball for his strength-in-numbers backs.

Dropped by New Zealand too soon, Wyllie retired early in 1980 after captaining Canterbury in more than 100 first-class matches, only the second man to achieve such a feat in New Zealand rugby.

But by 1982, he was the Canterbury coach, and guided it to and through an historic era in Ranfurly Shield rugby. In 1986, he was appointed an All Black selector, assisting in the preparation of the New Zealand team for the first World Cup, and within a year of becoming a selector, he was the convener and thus the coach.

That caused some distress among supporters of John Hart, a co-selector who had had charge of one All Black side, but Wyllie justified his selection when he guided the All Blacks to half-century thrashings of Wales and retention of the Bledisloe Cup against Australia in his first season.

Wyllie coached the All Blacks on their tour of Canada, Wales and Ireland in 1989, where they went unbeaten. In 1990 his teams retained the Bledisloe Cup against Australia and then scored comprehensive victories over France. Those successes meant he retained his position of coach, for the 1991 Rugby World Cup.

A rough, tough and sometimes abusive fellow as a player, he mellowed when he became a coach – but only a little bit!

X, Y, Z

XV

Roman numerals for 15, the number of players in a modern rugby team. The term has become synonymous for 'team' – thus the first XV, the top XV, the Barbarians XV etc.

YOUNG INTERNATIONALS

A physical contact sport such as rugby could be considered a mature man's game, and most selectors shy away from picking youngsters. But the age 17 years and 36 days has an unusual significance in recording the youngest international players.

A Scottish back, Ninian Finlay was this tender age when first selected to play against England, in 1875. He was only 23 when his nine-match career finished in 1881. His second to last game, against Ireland, was the first for a forward, Charles 'Hippo' Reid, and he too was 17 years 36 days. But Finlay is given the nod as the youngest international player because he had only four leap years to the time of his debut; Reid had five!

By coincidence, New Zealand five-eighth Lui Paewai was also 17 years 36 days when he first played for his country. The opposition in 1923 was New South Wales, effectively the Australian national side, as Queensland was then in recess, but it does not count as a full international. Paewai never played a test match, though he toured Britain with the 1924 'Invincibles'.

Others to have played internationals before their 18th birthdays include Frank Hewitt, a member of the famed Irish family, who was five months and five days past his 17th birthday when he first played in 1924. Hewitt retired at 21 for religious reasons.

Merchiston Castle School in Scotland must have taught the Neilson boys more than their spelling and sums too. Both Walter and William made their debuts at the ages of 17 years 5 months in the 1890s. Their brothers George and Robert also played for Scotland, but not until they were 19 and 20.

Charles Rooke, a forward in the 1890s, and John Quirke, a halfback in 1962, were other 17-year-old Irish internationals – the same age as Scotland's all round sportsman 'Grunt' MacLeod.

MacLeod's debut was against New Zealand in 1905, and his career finished three years later on the death of his brother, but he would have been the youngest of all had he not had an overly protective headmaster at Fettes College. Chosen to play for Scotland in 1903, at 15, MacLeod was refused permission by the head, who reckoned him too young!

The other under-18 was Robert 'Bulldog' Irvine, also a Scot, who was a month off his 18th birthday when he played in the first international against England in 1871.

Other nations have not capped their players at such tender ages. England's record holder is Henri Laird, 134 days past his 18th birthday on his debut in 1927.

South Africa, for years considered 'Bob' Loubser (19 years 1 month) its youngest international, but David Cope, killed in a rail accident at the age of 20, was also 19 – exact age unknown – when he played against the 1896 British touring team.

Paewai apart, New Zealand's youngest international was Edgar Wrigley, 19 years 79 days in his first test, against Australia in 1905. Craig Wickes was actually just 18 years 196 days when he played against Fiji as a replacement wing in 1980, but New Zealand has always been very coy about international status and refused to recognise that match as a full international.

The youngest Wallaby is a wing, Brian Ford, who played for Australia in 1957, when 18 years 4 months old.

The youngest Welsh international, Norman Biggs, was just 18 years 49 days when he played against the New Zealand Natives in 1888, while France's youngest cap, Claude Dourthe, was only a week past his 18th birthday.

The youngest international captain was the first, Frederick Stokes of England, who was aged 19 years and 3 months. Clive Rowlands, captain in all his matches for Wales, was also coaching the Red Dragons at the age of 30; while Stanley Wickham was managing Australia at the age of 29, just two years after captaining the team.

YOUNG, ROGER

Queen's University, Belfast and Ireland
26 internationals for Ireland 1965–71
4 internationals for British Isles 1966–68

A popular Irishman who earned the affection and respect of players and fans during his seven seasons as an Irish and British Isles scrumhalf. In the drawn Ireland v France match in Dublin in 1965, Ireland fielded an inexperienced team but played superbly, none more so than Roger Young, then a 21-year-old dental student. His play in combination with Mike Gibson gave Ireland real strength close to the scrums that season. That form set Young on a run of nine consecutive internationals and helped him win selection in the 1966 Lions team which went to Australia and New Zealand.

Down under, Young also played well, impressing locals with his excellent

Roger Young

passing. He played both test matches in Australia, which the Lions won but only in one test in New Zealand. He also toured South Africa with the Lions in 1968, enjoying it so much he emigrated there shortly after his last game for Ireland in 1971.

YOUNG TO DIE

Sad to say, there was a young fellow named Richard Stafford who propped for England in all its four internationals in 1912, yet did not live to see his 20th birthday. Only 18 on his debut, Stafford died of spinal cancer, four months after his nineteenth birthday.

He is the youngest international rugby player to die, while David Cope (see above) was only 20. Jasper Brett, a teenaged wing for Ireland, died of illness during World War I at the age of $21^{1}/_{2}$. Others to die before reaching their 22nd birthdays include Douglas Monypenny of Scotland, from wounds suffered in the Boer War, and William Holmes.

A strange case, the latter. Born in Argentina, Holmes was England fullback four times in 1949, then returned to play twice for Argentina against the touring French team the same year. Two months later, and only married a week, poor Holmes died of typhoid fever.

ZAGO, F (France)
ZELLER, W.C. (South Africa)
ZIMMERMAN, M. (South Africa)

These three players are the only ones under 'Z' to have played test matches for an IRB rugby country.

Fernand Zago was a prop from the Montauban club who played for the French XV against England and Ireland in 1963 when he was just 20 years old.

Bill Zeller was a Springbok wing who toured New Zealand in 1921, appearing in two internationals. He later became a South African selector.

Maurice Zimmerman made the South African team for its tour of Britain in 1931–32. 'Zimmie' was also a wing and he played in all four internationals, scoring 14 tries on the tour. He too became a Springbok selector.

ZAMBUCK

A friendly and familiar nickname used, particularly in South Africa and New Zealand, for the officers of St John who attend rugby matches as ambulance or medical attendants.

The word 'zambuck' is of South African derivation. It was the name of a well-known embrocation used by medical attendants in the early years of this century and in the two world wars. Eventually those who brought it to sick soldiers (and injured army footballers!) were themselves dubbed 'zambucks'.

ZIMBABWE

When Southern Rhodesia became Zimbabwe in 1980, its former association with South Africa in the Currie Cup rugby competition came to an end.

Earlier the rugby relationship between the two countries had always been strong. Up to 1980 Rhodesia had provided eight Springbok test players: 'Salty' de Rand (1949–56), Ryk van Schoor (1949–53), Ron Hill (1960–63), Ray Mordt (1980), Ian Robertson (1974–76), Andy Macdonald (1965), David Smith (1980), and Des van Jaarsveldt (1960).

The last game played by Zimbabwe in South Africa was in 1980 against Natal at King's Park, Durban. After that the new Zimbabwe government decreed that from then on it would stand on its own as a rugby force.

As many white Rhodesians emigrated to South Africa or elsewhere following independence, the game's progress was slow in the early years, with the loss of experienced players. In 1980–81 Zimbabwe embarked on a tour of Britain, where its team played mostly sides of county strength, winning three games out of the seven played.

Two of its players were sent off in one game on the tour, and generally only a fair impression was made.

In 1982 Romania toured Zimbabwe, playing some vigorous games that resulted in two players, Rob Halstead of Zimbabwe and Gheorghe Caragea of Romania, being sent off in the first test. Halstead was captain of Zimba-

bwe at the time. Romania won the two tests by 25–23 and 25–24.

Zimbabwe gained its first major international recognition when it was included in the 1987 World Cup final draw of 16 nations. Although the team had by far the smallest number of players from whom to pick a team, it performed heroically, its best performance being a 20–21 loss to Romania at Eden Park in Auckland.

But it was after the 1987 World Cup that a transformation came over rugby in Zimbabwe. Sensing that progress was slowing down, a far-sighted programme to encourage black players was adopted. Within a year rugby became the fastest growing game in secondary schools, some headmasters reporting that where only a short time ago they had had no more than a couple of black players in their first XVs, this situation had almost been totally reversed.

So Zimbabwe was feeling much happier about its rugby when the time came to qualify for the 1991 World Cup. When the African zone finals were held in Harare, Zimbabwe won through by beating Côte d'Ivoire, Morocco and Tunisia in the quadrangular series.

The probable return of South Africa to the World Cup scene will provide Zimbabwe with formidable problems for future qualification, as will the presence of the highly promising Namibia. But with the progress that has been made, and the optimisim that exists once more, Zimbabwe will be a leading force in African rugby in the twenty-first century. *See also* RHODESIA

BIBLIOGRAPHY

The author gratefully acknowledges the authors and publishers of the following books:

1950 – The Year of the Lions, D.J. Williams, D.J. & J.A. Williams, Hamilton, 1988.

All Blacks in Wales, John Billot, Ron Jones Publications, Cardiff, 1972.

Australian Rugby Union. The Game and the Players, Jack Pollard, Angus & Robertson, Sydney, 1984.

Barbarians, The, Nigel Starmer-Smith, Macdonald & Jane, London, 1977.

Between the Posts, Ron Palenski (Ed.), Hodder & Stoughton, Auckland, 1989.

Book of Rugby Lists, The, Norman Giller (Ed.), Sidgwick & Jackson, London 1984.

Centenary History of the Rugby Football Union, Uel Titley & Ross McWhirter, The Rugby Football Union, 1970.

Centenary: 100 years of All Black Rugby, R.H. Chester & N.A.C. McMillan, Moa Publications, Auckland, 1984.

Complete Who's Who of International Rugby, The, Terry Godwin, Blandford Press, Poole, 1987.

Encyclopaedia of Rugby Football, J.R. Jones, Sportsman's Book Club, London, 1960.

Encyclopedia of New Zealand Rugby, The, R.H. Chester, N.A.C. McMillan & R.A. Palenski, Moa Publications, Auckland, 1987.

Encyclopédie Française, Pierre Lafond & Jean-Pierre Bodis, Editions Dehedin, Paris, 1989

Famous Flankers, Joseph Romanos, Rugby Press, Auckland, 1990.

Famous Fullbacks, Joseph Romanos, Rugby Press, Auckland, 1989.

Gareth Edwards' 100 Great Rugby Players, Gareth Edwards, Queen Anne Press, London, 1987.

Great Fight of the French Fifteen, The, Denis Lalanne, A.H. & A.W, Reed, Wellington, 1960.

Guinness Book of Rugby Facts and Feats, The, Terry Godwin & Chris Rhys, Guinness Superlatives Ltd, London, 1981.

Guinness Rugby – the Records, Chris Rhys, Guinness, London, 1987.

Haka – The Maori Rugby Story, Winston McCarthy & Bob Howitt, Rugby Press, Auckland, 1983.

History of New Zealand Rugby Football, A.C. Swan, A.H. & A.W. Reed, Wellington, 1948.

History of New Zealand Rugby Football, Vol. II, A.C. Swan, New Zealand Rugby Football Union, Wellington, 1958.

History of South African Rugby Football, Ivor Difford, Speciality Press, Cape Town, 1933.

History of Welsh International Rugby, John Billot, Welsh Rugby Union, Cardiff, 1970.

Hong Kong Sevens, The, Kevin Sinclair, Arden, Hong Kong, 1985.

100 Years of Irish Rugby, Edmund van Esbeck, Gill & MacMillan, Dublin, 1974.

International Rugby Championship 1893–1983, The, Terry Godwin, Collins Willow, London, 1984.

Joy of Rugby, The, David Irvine, Melbourne, 1978.

La Mélée Fantastique, Denis Lalanne, A.H & A.W. Reed, Wellington, 1962.

Lions, The , Wallace Reyburn, A.H. & A.W. Reed, London, 1954.

Love of Rugby, The, Peter Walker (Ed.), Octopus, London 1980.

Men in Black, H. Chester & N.A.C. McMillan, Moa Publications, Auckland, 1978.

Men in Green, The, Sean Diffley, Stanley Paul, Dublin, 1974.

Naas, Edward Griffiths, Leo Publishers, Pretoria, 1989.

Oxford Companion to Sports and Games, The, John Arlott, Paladin, 1977.

Phoenix Book of International Rugby Records, The, John Griffiths, Phoenix House, London, 1987.

Portrait of Scottish Rugby, A, Allan Massie, Polygon, undated.

Ranfurly Shield Rugby, A.H. Carman, Wright & Carman, Wellington, 1967.

Rhodesia Rugby, Jonty Winch, Zimbabwe Rhodesia Rugby Union, Salisbury, 1979.

Rise of French Rugby, The, Alex Potter & Georges Duthen, A.H. & A.W. Reed, Wellington, 1961.

Rugby, John Hopkins, Cassell, London, 1979.

Rugby: a History of Rugby Union Football, Chris Rea, Hamlyn, London, 1977.

Rugby –A Way Of Life: An Illustrated History of Rugby, Nigel Starmer-Smith (Ed.), Stanley Paul, London, 1986.

Rugby Clubs of Wales, The, David Parry-Jones, Stanley Paul, London, 1989.

Rugby Companion, The, Wallace Reyburn, Hutchinson, Auckland, 1969.

Rugby Football Today, E.H.D. Sewell, John Murray, London, 1931.

Rugby Remembered, David Parry-Jones, Partridge Press, London, 1988.

Rugby – the Great Ones, Cliff Morgan (Ed.), Pelham Books, London, 1970.

Rugby Union Football Book, The, Jack Cox (Ed.), Purnell, London, 1965.

Shield Fever: The Complete Ranfurly Shield Story, Lindsay Knight, Rugby Press, 1986.

Springbok Annals: International Tours to and from South Africa, 1891–1958, compiled by D.H. Craven, Mimosa, Johannesburg, 1959.

Springbok Saga, The, Chris Greyvenstein, Don Nelson and Toyota (South Africa) Ltd, Cape Town, 1981.

Springboks 1891–1970, The, A.C. Parker, Cassell, London, 1970.

Visitors: the History of International Rugby teams in New Zealand, The. R.H. Chester & N.A.C. McMillan, Moa, Auckland, 1990.

World of Rugby, The, Jack Cox (Ed.), Purnell, London, 1970.

World of Rugby, The, Wallace Reyburn, Elek Books, London, 1967.

World of Rugby: a History of Rugby Union Football, The, John Reason & Carwyn James, BBC, 1979.

All the books of Terry McLean, published by A.H. & A.W. Reed, Wellington; Hutchinson, Auckland; and Hodder & Stoughton, Auckland, between 1954 and 1990.

All the books of J.B.G. Thomas, published by Pelham, London; and Stanley Paul, London, between 1954 and 1985.

Annual editions of the following publications: *New Zealand Rugby Almanac,* 1935–91; *New Zealand Rugby Annual,* 1971–90; and *Rothmans Rugby UnionYearbook,* 1972–90.

The following periodicals: *Rugby News,* New Zealand; *Rugby News,* Great Britain, *Rugby World and Post,* Great Britain; *The Game,* Great Britain, and *Sports Digest,* New Zealand.

The author also wishes to acknowledge the many newspapers and international match programmes he drew on for information.

ACKNOWLEDGMENTS

The author acknowledges the following sources of illustrations:

African Press Features: 266.

Peter Bush: 8, 12, 15, 16, 17, 19, 24, 26, 27, 30a, 32, 33, 34a, 35, 36, 37b, 43, 49a, 53, 55, 59, 60, 63, 64, 66b, 69, 73, 75, 76a, 79, 82, 83, 89, 91, 92b, 97, 101b, 104, 106, 107, 109, 112, 115, 116a, 124, 125, 132, 137, 138, 139b, 140b, 145a, 153b, 154b, 156, 160, 161, 162b, 165, 167, 168, 169a, 170, 171, 174, 175, 177, 178a, 183, 185, 187, 190, 192, 198, 205, 206, 210, 216a, 220, 224, 226, 227, 230, 231b, 232, 235, 236, 238, 243b, 244, 251, 263, 275, 280, 281a, 286, 288, 292, 299, 304, 306, 307b, 309, 311, 312, 315, 318.

P.J. Carr: 51.

The Hulton-Deutsch Collection: 184b, 204, 216b, 290, 297.

Illustrated London News Picture Library: 7, 50, 65, 72, 87b, 98, 130, 136, 147, 193, 218, 249, 287, 298a.

Moa collection: 209.

New Zealand Herald: 14, 20, 22, 28, 29, 30b, 34b, 41, 46, 48b, 57, 62, 66a, 68, 70, 71, 76b, 78, 86, 92a, 94, 96, 101a, 108, 113, 119, 121, 122, 133, 139a, 140a, 142, 143, 144, 145b, 153a, 154a, 159, 162a, 169b, 176, 178b, 186, 197, 200, 203, 208, 215, 225, 228, 233, 234, 247, 253, 255, 257, 260, 261, 265, 269, 276, 278, 279, 281b, 294, 308, 310, 319.

New Zealand Rugby Museum: 10, 18, 40, 44, 74, 74a, 87a 105, 116b, 150, 173, 184a, 191, 195, 202, 214, 272, 298b, 300, 312.

Outram Picture Archives, Glasgow: 254.

Ross Setford: 47a, 48a, 117, 123, 158, 172, 181, 231a, 239, 243a, 250, 251a, 256, 259, 271, 307a, 313.

Southland Times: 84.

Adrian Stephenson: 126.

Sydney Morning Herald: 37a, 182.

Chris Thau: 31, 211, 246.

Tweeddale Press Group: 111, 221, 241.

Where more than one photograph appears on the page, 'a' indicates photo on the left or nearest the top of the page, and 'b' indicates photo on the right or bottom of the page. Sources of colour photographs are acknowledged in the captions.

INDEX OF NAMES

Note: Numbers in **bold** indicate individual entries; numbers in *italic* indicate caption references.

Aarvold, Carl **7**, *7*, 32, 47
Ackermann, Dawie **8**, 305
Ackford, Paul **77**
Ackford, Wade 206
Aguirre, Jean-Michel *8*, **9**, 14, 31, 102, 223
Aikman Smith, J. 128
Aitken, George **9**, 54, 88, *253*, 253, 262, 291
Aitken, Jim **9**, 53, 104, 263
Albaladejo, Pierre **9**, 222, 317
Albertyn, P.K. **9**, 54
Alcock, Arnold **10**
Alcock, C. W. 252
Algar, Beethoven 211
Allan, John 254
Allan, Trevor **11**, *11*, 19, 52, 54, 171, 196
Allen, 'Ellie' **11**, 43, 159
Allen, Fred **11**, *11*, 17, 54, 60, 61, 150, 161, 199, 242
Allen, Glyn 43
Allen, Jorge *14*
Allen, Nicky 64
Allen, Peter 13
Alvarez, Julio 270
Amin, Idi 262
Anderson, Eric 27
Anderson, Frederick 207
Anderson, Harry 62
Anderson, Willie 157
Andrew, Rob **12**, 73, 96, *111*, 301
Anduran, Joe **12**
Argus, Wallie 150
Arigho, Jack 156
Armit, 'Barney' **15**
Armstrong, Gary *254*
Arneil, Rodger 83, 95
Ash, Edwin H. 242
Asher, Opai 174
Ashworth, John **15**, *15*, 69, 100, 150, 168, 211, 222
Aston, Randolph 40, 264
Astre, Richard 32, 53, 96
Azarete, Jean-Louis 29, 129
Azkargorta, Jon 270

Badeley, Ces **21**
Bagot, John 130
Bainbridge, Steve 110
Baird, Roger **21**, *92*
Baker, 'Snowy' **22**
Baker, Harald 22
Baker-Jones, Thomas 211
Bancroft, Billy **23**, 102, 103, 192, 274, 298
Bancroft, Jack 23, 138, 274, 298
Bannerman, John **23**, 163, 219, 249
Barnard, Leon 286
Barnes, Stuart 26
Barrière, Raoul, 31
Barrow, Graeme 100
Barry, Kevin 277
Bartmann, Waal 282
Basquet, Guy *8*, **25**, 60, 222
Bassett, Arthur 7
Bassett, Jack 224
Bastard, Ebbo 190
Bastiat, Jean-Pierre **25**, 205, 243, 261
Batigne, Marcel 93

Batty, Grant **26**, 302, 313
Baxter, James 'Bim' 13, 17, **26**, *41*, 52, 253, 257, 312
Bayly, Alf 15
Beamish, Charles 43
Beamish, George 43, 157, 179
Beattie, Jock 119
Beattie, John 276
Beaumont, Bill **27**, *27*, *53*, 61, 87, 112, 135, 163
Bebb, Dewi **28**, 207, 274, 298, 313
Bedell-Sivright, 'Darkie' **28**, 47, 88, 198
Bedford, Tommy **28**, 112, 190, 205, 242, 291
Beese, Mike 159
Behoteguy, André **29**
Behoteguy, Henri 29
Bekker, Corrie 29
Bekker, Daan 29
Bekker, Dolf 29
Bekker, H.P.J. (Jaap) 29, 208, 261
Bekker, Martiens 29
Bell, Sir Ewart 129
Bellandi, Stefano 134
Bellis 'Moke' 301
Benazzi, Abdelatif 184, 214
Benesis, René *8*, **29**, 189, 220
Benetton, Treviso 8, 31
Bennett, Phil *24*, 26, **30**, *30*, 42, 52, 71, 96, 138, 160, 284, 285, 298
Berbizier, Pierre *8*, 13, **30**, *30*, 97, 117
Bergh, Ferdie 208
Bergiers, Roy 160
Berry, Charles 252
Berry, Marty 52, 212
Berry, Tom 157
Bertranne, Roland 13, **31**, 257
Besomo, Keith 110
Bettarello, Ottarino 31
Bettarello, Romano 31
Bettarello, Stefano **31**, *31*, 133
Beuttler, Tom 303
Bevan, John 7, 302
Bevan, Vince 232
Biermann, Marcel 194
Biggs, John 301
Biggs, Norman 319
Birkett, John 118
Birtwhistle, Bill 78
Bish, Roy 134
Bishop, David 232
Bishop, Ian 120
Bissett, William 264
Bjelke-Peterson, Joh 233
Blaikie, Colin 121
Blair, Robbie, 317
Blake, Alan 296
Blakeway, Phil 108
Blakiston, Arthur 207
Blanco, Serge 13, 25, **32**, *32*, 52, 58, 99, 101, 102, 149, 153, 253, 285, 289, 293, *315*, 316, 317
Blazey, Ces **33**, *33*, 128
Bledisloe, Lord 33
Bolawaqatabu, Epi 93
Bollesan, Marco 133
Bona, Ambrosia 134
Boniface, André **34**, 221

Boniface, Guy **34**, *34*, 221
Boobyer, Brian 248
Booth, Ernest 'General' 217
Boots, George 312
Bosch, Gerald **35**, *35*, 217
Botha, Naas **35**, *36*, 37, 52, 96, 135, 208, 217, 222, 223, 317
Botica, Frano 21, 104, 168, 207
Bouquet, Jacques **36**
Bourgarel, Roger **36**
Bourrier, Jean-Claude 93
Bowen, Bleddyn 54, 71, 206
Boyce, Jim 43
Boyce, Max 100, 160
Boyce, Stuart 43
Brace, Onllwyn 160, 219, 291, 300
Bracewell, Barry 64
Brand, Gerry **36**, *37*, 102, 219, 286, 309
Breckenridge, J.W. 301
Brewer, Mike 211, 217
Brewis, Hannes 208
Brewster, Alex 273
Bridle, Owen 294
Briscoe, Kevin 154, 275
Brockhoff, Dave, 34, **42**, 60, 276
Brooke, Zinzan 239
Brophy, Niall 32
Brophy, Thomas 159
Brown, Charles 264
Brown, Gordon 14, **42**, *43*
Brown, Jock 43
Brown, Leonard 32
Brown, Peter **42**, 255
Brown, Ross 275
Brownlie, Cyril **44**, 181, 119, 193, 210, 213, 214, *214*, 238, 240, 287
Brownlie, Laurie **44**, 119
Brownlie, Maurice **44**, *44*, 119, 190, 203, 229, 238, 264
Bruce, Doug 168, 179
Bruce, Norman 125
Buchan, John 52
Buchanan, Angus 252
Buchanan, J.C.R. 88
Buchler, Johnny 102, 295
Bucos, Mihai 246
Budge, Grahame 39
Bulpitt, Mike 32
Burges, John 60, 248
Burke, Cyril 89, 117, 122, 194
Burke, Peter 275
Burnet, David 259
Burnett, Bob 214
Burnett, Dave 214
Burnett, Roy 203, 212
Burton, Charles 234
Burton, Mike 108, 214
Bush, Billy 174
Bush, Percy 55, 298
Bush, Ron 25, 33
Butler, Eddie 226, 232
Butterfield, Jeff **45**, 87, 207, 267
Byers-Barr, R.A. 63

Cabrol, Henri 31
Cail, W. 128
Cakabau, George **46** *46*
Calder, Finlay 42, **46**, *47*, 53, 263, 273

Calder, Jim **46**, 95, 273
Calder, John 47
Callender, Gary 125
Camberabero, Didier **47**, 96, 119, 178 , 317
Camberabero, Guy 33, **47**, *47*
Camberabero, Lilian **47**, *47*
Campbell, Ollie **47**, *48*, 94, 131, 147, 210, 250, *307*
Campbell-Lamerton, Jeremy 49
Campbell-Lamerton, Mike, 39, 41, **48**, *48*, 199, 278
Campese, David 13, 19, 20, **49**, *49*, 85, 102, 133, 149, 182, 196, 255, 262, 285, 289, 313, 317
Canessa, Roberto 291
Cannell, Lewis 207
Cantillon, Christy 187
Cantoni, Jack 32
Caragea, Gheorghe 215, 320
Carden, J. Cecil 271
Carelse, Gabriel 81
Carleton, John **55**
Carling, Will 52, 118
Carmichael 'Sandy' 13, **55**, *55*, 169, 170, 231
Carminati, Alain 214
Carolin, Paddy 151, 271
Carpmael, 'Tottie', 23, 25
Carrère, Christian *99*
Carroll, Daniel 212
Casey, Steve 217
Cassayet, Aimé **56**
Castens, Herbert 54, 264
Catchpole, Ken 19, 53, 54, **56**, *56*, 89, 117, 120, 122, 196
Catchside, Carston 257
Catley, Has **56**, 296
Cavanagh, Vic **57**, 61, 217, 249
Celaya, Michel 13, **57**, *57*, 60, 99, 178, 267
Cerutti, Bill 19, 196
Cester, Elie **58**, *99*
Chambers, Mike 50
Champ, Eric **58**
Chang-Kyu Sin 16
Chen Chin-Chung 275
Chilcott, Gareth 26
Chisholm, David 43, 145, 176, 177
Chisholm, Robin 43, 117
Cholley, Gérard **58**, 150, 220, 222
Choy, Joseph 189
Claassen, Johan 53, **58**, *59*, 60, 103, 163, 311
Claassen, Wynand 54, *59*, 190
Clark, Bill 302
Clark, Robert 125
Clarke, Brian 59
Clarke, Don 16, **59**, *59*, 97, *101*, 102, 168, 197, 199, 223, 296
Clarke, Doug 59
Clarke, Graeme 59
Clarke, Ian 24, **59**, 296
Clarke, Peter 51
Clarkson, Walter 189
Clinch, 'Coo' 300
Clinch, 'Jammie' 12, **59**, 78, 145, 300
Cobner, Terry 226, 232
Cocks, Dick 42, 190, 194, 236
Codey, David 214, 316

Codorniou, Didier *32*, **61**, 189
Coffey, John **61**
Colclough, Maurice **61**
Cole, John 182, 313
Colling, Lin 217
Collins, John 230
Collopy, Dick 43
Collopy, William 43
Communeau, Marcel 98
Condom, Jean 13, 58, **62**, *62*, *116*
Connor, Des 17, 42, 60, **62**, *63*, 89, 117, 158, 235, 276
Conway, Geoffrey 146, 249
Cooke, Bert **63**, 120, 151, 199, 203, 238, 244
Cooke, Graham 211, 251
Cooney, Warwick 214
Cooper, Sydney 284
Cope, David 67, 319
Corbett, John 304
Corbett, Len 38
Cornelson, Greg, *205*, 259
Cotton, David 64
Cotton, Fran **63**, *64*, 231, 251
Cottrell, Nev 235
Couderc, Roger 9
Coulman, Mike 184
Cove-Smith, Ronald 47, **64**, *65*, 111, 164, 189, 264, 297
Cowper, Bob 294
Cowper, Dave 294
Crabos, René 54, **65**, 138, 237
Cranmer, Peter 184, 242
Cranston, Alistair 119
Crauste, Michel 13, 53, **65**, 70, 95, 230, 237, 243
Craven, Danie 14, 51, 53, 60, **65**, *66*, 75, 78, 117, 128, 164, 175, 208, 212, 225, 267, 268, 305
Crawford, Ernie 12, **66**, *66*, 102, 156, 249
Crean, Tommy 300
Crossan, Keith **67**
Crowe, Kevin 23, 224
Crowe, Morgan 156
Crowe, Phil *34*
Crowley, Kieran 119, 168, 275
Cucchiella, Giancarlo *133*
Cullen, Ross **67**
Culliton, Gerry 300
Culpepper, Clarence 64
Cunningham, Rob 104
Cuppaidge, John 130
Curley, Terry **67**, 102
Currie, Donald 67, 113
Currie, John 38, 118
Cusworth, Les 157
Cutler, Steve **68**, 163
Cuttita, Marcello 133

Dallas, John 74, 128, 240
Dalley, Bill 52, 203
Dalton, Andy 15, 27, 54, 57, 64, **69**, *69*, *94*, 95, 100, 125, 148, 150, 155, 178, 222
Dalton, Ray 69, 217, 261
Dancer, G.T. 'Beef', 28
Danos, Pierre **69**
D'Arcy, Tony 42
Darrouy, Christian 52, **70**, 153, 285, 312
Dauga, Benoit 13, 65, **70**, *70*, 163, 270
Davey, Claude 88, 251, 273, 314
David, Ivor 300
Davies, Gareth **70**, 71, 96, 299
Davies, Gerald 13, *41*, 55, **70**, 83, 88, *224*, 276, 285, 291, 298, 313
Davies, Howard 275
Davies, Huw 64
Davies, Joe 192

Davies, Jonathan 54, **71**, 96, 144, 160, 192
Davies, Mervyn 53, **71**, *71*, 88, 184, 205, 271, 273, 298, 317
Davies, Patrick 251
Davies, Phil 45
Davies, Terry 102, 160
Davies, W.J.A. 'Dave' 12, **71**, *72*, 87, 112, 146, *147*, 221, 248, 296
Davies, Willie 273, 275, 300
Davis, Bill 120, 139
Davis, Eric 294
Davis, Greg 53, 57, *63*, **72**, *72*, 95, *108*, 196, 259, 273
Davis, Lyn 52, 316
Davis, Mike 118
Davy, Eugene **72**, 156, 222
Dawai, Orisi *92*, 93
Dawes, John 26, 41, *41*, 52, 60, *60*, **73**, *73*, 88, 108, 199, 298
Dawson, Ronnie 39, 54, **73**, 100, 125, 131, 141, 177, 186, 199, 293, 300
Day, Harold 157, 212
de Bruyn, Johan 110
de Gaulle, President 70
de Goede, Hans 51
de Gregorio, J. 29
de Plooy, Amos 81
de Villiers, 'Boy' 151, 163
de Villiers, Dan 267
de Villiers, Dawie 29, 34, 53, **75**, *75*, 117, 222, 305
de Villiers, Pierre 117
Dean, Paul 12, **73**
Dean, Stan 229
Deans, Bob 52, **73**, *74*, 160, 183, 240
Deans, Bruce 43, 52, 74
Deans, Colin 13, **74**, *74*, 94, 100, 119, 125, 146, 199, 317
Deans, Max 74
Deans, Robbie 8, 43, 52, 74, 122
Deering, Seamus, jnr 105
Deering, Seamus, snr 105
Delahay, Bobby, 38
Delport, Willem 81
Devereux, John 299
Devine, Dauncey 65, **75**
Diack, 'Tuppy' 217
Dickinson, Bill 60, 255
Dintrans, Philippe 8, 13, 54, **75**, *76*, 79, 97, 100, *178*
Dixon, George, 38
Dixon, Maurie, 52
Dixon, Peter 110
Dobbin, Fred 'Uncle' 113, 151
Doble, Sam 184
Dobson, Denys **76**
Dodge, Paul **76**,157
D'Oliviera, Basil 233
Domenech, Amédée 13, 29, **76**, *76*, 232
Don Wauchope, Andrew **77**
Don Wauchope, Patrick 77
Donald, Andy 148
Donald, Jim 296
Donald, Quentin 296
Donaldson, Mark *117*, 117, 173
Dooley,Wade **77**, 206
Doubell, Thys, 34
Douglas, J.W.H.T. 22
Douglas, Jim 294
Dourthe, Claude 54, **77**, 165, 319
Downes, Lorraine 178
Doyle, Mick 32, 105
Doyle, Owen 214
Drummond, Charlie 177
Dryburgh, Roy 52, 190, 305
Drysdale, Dan 9, 102, 121, 252, 254, 255

du Manoir, Yves 61, **77**, *77*, 237
du Plessis, Felix 54, 78, 106, *266*
du Plessis, Morne 53, **78**, 205, *304*, 305
du Preez, Frik 36, **78**, *79*, 85, 158, 167, 175, 208, *208*
du Rand, 'Salty' 164, 208, 225, 242, 295, 311, 320
du Toit, Benjamin 208
du Toit, 'Fonnie' 208
du Toit, Piet 307
Dubroca, Daniel 8, 30, 54, 75, 76, **78**, *79*, 97, 99, 100, 316
Duckham, David 64, **79**, *79*, 87, 303, 313
Dufau, Gérard 'Zeze' **79**, 117, 237
Duff, Bob, 52, 53, 58, 264
Duggan, Alan 156
Duggan, Willie 32, **79**, 205, 214, 222, 306
Dumitru, Gheorghe 246, *246*
Duncan, James 53, 54, 55, **80**, 95, 197, 217
Dunlop, Ernest 294
Dupuy, Jean 70, 77, **80**, 285, 313
Durbac, Raducu 246
Durden-Smith, Neil 314
Duthen, Georges 99, 179
Dutin, Bernard *269*
Dwyer, Bob *20*, 60, 85, 276
Dwyer, Larry 52

Eagles, Harry 52
Earl, Andy 21
Edwards, Alun 7
Edwards, Gareth 13, 24, 30, 52, 53, 55, 71, **83**, *83*, 109, 117,123, 140, 144, 155, 183, 221, 234, 284, 285, 298, 317
Edwards, Major 264
Edwards, Reg 210
Elder, Bob 51
Eliason, Ian 275
Elissalde, Jean-Pierre 30
Ella, Gary **84**, *85*, 109, 195, 221
Ella, Glen **84**, *85*, 109, 195, 221
Ella, Mark 19, *19*, 52, **84**, *85*, 89, 166, 169, 261
Elliot, Douglas 83
Elliot, Tom 104
Ellis, Jan 28 **85**, 95, 112
Ellison, Tom 174, 196, 312
Ellwood, Beres 194
Elvidge, Ron 52, 217, 241
Enevoldson, Peter 291
Engelbrecht, Jan *75*, **86**, *86*, 305, 313
English, Mickey 156
Ensor, Tony 300
Erbani, Dominique 8, **88**
Estève, Alain 32
Estève, Patrick 257
Evans, David 43
Evans, Eric 54, 88, 125, 251
Evans, Geoff 88
Evans, Gwyn 134
Evans, John 54
Evans, Roddy 38
Evans, Stuart 299
Evanson, Arthur, 43
Evanson, Wyndham 43
Eveleigh, Kevin 27, 173
Eyton, Tom 190

Fairfax, Russell 144
Farr-Jones, Nick *20*, 25, 53, **89**, *89*, 117, 144, 155, 222, 226
Farrell, James **89**
Fatialofa, Peter 305
Faulkner, 'Charlie' 100, 210, 221, 226, 230, 231, 232, 311
Fay, Garrick 301

Fenwick, Steve 38, **89**, *89*, 108, 299
Ferguson, Craig **90**
Fergusson, Sir Bernard *190*
Ferrasse, Albert 8, **90**
Fielding, Keith 185
Fielea, Kutusu 281
Fifita, Talai 281, *281*
Finlan, John 184
Finlay, Ninian 172, 317, 319
Fitzgerald, Ciaran 42, 54, 75, **94**, *94*, 100, 125, 131, 199, *210*, 313
Fitzgerald, Kerry 90, **94**, 214, 240, 316
Fitzpatrick, Brian 95, 230
Fitzpatrick, Sean 21, 69, **95**, 101, 125, 148, 222, 239
Fitzpatrick, Michael 300
Flynn, Kevin 300
Ford, Brian 175, 319
Fordham, Bob 94
Forrest, A.J. 130
Forsyth, Bob 110
Foster, Ron 131
Fouroux, Jacques 30, 53, 60, 79, **96**, *97*, 99, 222, 246, 295
Fox, Grant 17, 59, 96, *96*, **97**, 147, 165, 223, 239, 312, 317
Frames, Percy Ross 264, 267
Francescato, Bruno 43, *133*
Francescato, Ivan 43
Francescato, Nello 43, 133
Francescato, Rino 43, 133
Francis, Bob 15
Fraser, Bernie 302, 311
Fraser, Malcolm 142
Freethy, Albert 44, 193, 213, 214, 240
Freyberg, Sir Bernard 149
Fry, Charles **101**
Fry, Stephen 183
Fuller, H.G. 291
Fulton, Bobby 258
Fulton, Jack 207
Furlong, Blair 232
Fyfe, Kenneth 251

Gabe, Rhys 55, 88, **103**, 151, 160, 298
Gachassin, Jean **103**
Gadney, Bernard 13, 103, 157
Gadney, Cyril **103**, 240
Gaffney, Brother Henry 61
Gage, Davey **103**
Gainsford, John 86, **103**, *104*, 285, 305
Gale, Norman 125
Gallagher, John 102, **104**, 302
Gallaher, Dave 17, 53, 80, **104**, *105*, 228, 312, *312*
Gallart, Philippe 214
Gallion, Jérôme 96, 117
Ganilau, Penaia 46
Gard, Phil 207
Gardiner, Ernie 211
Gardiner, Fred 207
Garnett, Harry **105**
Garoia, Alfonso 270
Garrar, W.G. 240
Garrigues, André 60
Garuet, Jean-Pierre **105**, 205, 214, 232, 244
Geffin, Aaron **106**, 202, *204*, 217, 219, 223, *266*
Geldenhuys, Burger, 57
Gent, Dai 108
Gerber, Danie 81, 104, **106**, *106*
Germishuys, Gerrie 107, 213, 313
Ghizzoni, Serafino 133
Gibbs, Paul 294

Gibson, Michael 13, *24*, 47, 58, **107**, *107*, 130, 167, 207, 216, 241, 262, 289, 291, 302, 319
Gilbert, F.G. 210
Gilbert, Mike 304
Gilliland, R.W. 175
Glasgow, Ossie 131
Gleeson, Jack 14, 60, 115, 189
Goddard, Jack 43, 268
Goddard, Maurie 43, 268
Godwin, Terry 127
Going, Brian 109, 206
Going, Ken 109, 174
Going, Sid *83*, **108**, *108*, 117, 154, 174, *174*, *177*, 206, 232
Gordon, Thomas **110**
Gould, Arthur 102, **110**, 202, 242, 253, 298
Gould, Bert 110
Gould, Bob 110
Gould, Roger 85, 102, **110**, 133, *235*, 236
Gourdon, François 237
Gourlay, Ian 58, 235
Grace, Tom 52
Grace, W.G. 193
Gracie, Leslie 118, 249, 253, 285
Gradin, Luis 14, 228
Graham, John 190, 283
Grant, 'Lachie' 268
Grant, Derek 119, 168
Gravell, Ray **112**, *112*, 160, 298
Gray, Ken *11*, **112**, *113*, 232, 302
Gray, Tommy 121
Gray, Tony 207
Green, Craig 104, 133, 179
Greenwood, J.E. 291
Gregory, Stuart 236
Grenside, Bert 120
Greyling, Piet 95, **112**, *113*, 213
Griffiths, Jack 302
Griffiths, Jonathan 299
Guastella, Angel 227
Guerassimoff, Jules 72, 236, *279*
Guiral, Marius 8
Gurdon, E. Temple 128

Haden, Andy 14, 17, 57, 58, **115**, *115*, 133, 145, 163, 177, 269
Hadley, Adrian 299
Haget, Francis **115**, *116*, 210, 218
Haig, Jim 217
Haig, Laurie 217
Haig, Ned 177, 258, *258*
Hain, Peter 319
Hall, 'Nim' 242
Hall, Duncan 236
Hall, John 26
Halstead, Rob 215, 320
Hamersley, Alfred 268
Hamlet, George **117**, 145, 163
Hammond, Johnny 264
Hancock, Andy 285, 287
Hancock, Frank 54, 297
Handy, Chris *34*, 42, *231*, 236
Hanekom, Melt, 34
Harding, Rowe 249
Harding, Vic 251
Hare, 'Dusty' 102, **117**, *117*, 157, 223
Harman, George 211
Harman, R.J.S. 196
Harris, Richard 189
Harris, Stanley **118**
Hart, John 185
Hartill, Mark 169
Harvey, Ian 296
Hastie, Alex 177
Hastings, Gavin 12, 88, 102, **118**, *119*, 147, 255
Hastings, Scott *111*, **118**, *254*
Hauser, Rod 268

Hawke, Colin 215
Hawker, Michael 261
Hawthorne, Phil 56, **120**, *120*, 194, 317
Hayashi, Toshi 137
Hazlett, Bill 269
Hazlett, Jack *198*, 269
Hearn, Danny 28, **120**
Heatlie, 'Fairy' 13, **121**, 247, 270
Hemera, Bruce 95
Hemi, Ron 296
Heming, Rod 163
Henderson, 'Buddy' 51
Henderson, Michael 108
Henderson, Noel **121**, 207, 289
Henderson, Peter 143, 301
Hendry, Jamie 303
Hepburn, Charles 188
Herewini, Mac 17, 174
Hervey, Lester 217
Heunis, Johan 102
Hewitt, David 43, 186
Hewitt, Frank 43, 319
Hewitt, Tom 43
Hewitt, Victor 43
Hewson, Alan **121**, *121*, 206, 302
Heyneman, Jack 225, 267
Higgins, Reg 159
Hignell, Alistair 38
Hill, Andy 160
Hill, Richard 26, *111*
Hill, Ron 242, 320
Hill, Stan 'Tiny' 52
Hiller, Bob 102, 118, 310
Hindson, Ro 51
Hipwell, John 89, 117, **122**, *122*, 194, 259
Hirao, Seiji 137
Hirsch, J.G. 81
Hobbs, Jock 57, 58, 148
Hoben, Edward 196
Hobson, Tommy 151
Hodgkinson, Simon 223, *254*, 316, 317
Hodgson, Aub 19, **122**, 196
Hodgson, Grahame 192
Hogan, G.P.S. 128
Holmes, E.C. 249
Holmes, Terry 70, **122**, *123*
Holyoake, Keith 214, 232
Hoogenhout, F.P. 163
Hopkins, Kevin *281*
Hopwood, Doug **125**, 305
Hore, Jack 217
Horrocks-Taylor, Phil 157, 259
Horton, John, 26
Horton, Nigel 185
Horton, Peter *34*, *205*
Howard, Fred 214
Howe, Bennett 'Peewee' 35
Howitt, Bob 109
Hughes, Ned 210, 251, 269, 317
Hullin, Billy 140
Hunt, Ted 248
Hunter, Gordon 154
Hunter, Jimmy **126**, 300

Iachetti, Alejandro 43
Iachetti, Marcos 43
Innocenti, Marzio 133
Iraçabal, Jean 29, **129**
Ireland, John 255
Irvine, Andy 13, 101, *101*, 102, 119, 121, **131**, *132*, 147, 168, 223, 255, 285, 310
Irvine, Robert 319
Irwin, Mark 217
Ito, Tadayuki 137

Jackson Peter 64, 87, **135**, 285, 287, 313
Jacob, Hohepa 125

Jacobs, Ron 63, 208, 231
James, Billy 54
James, Carwyn 31, 41, 60, 61, 71, 108, 133, **135**, 141, 160, 199, 234
James, Evan 43
James, Kevin 7
Jansen, Eben 43
Jansen, Joggie 43, 213
Jarden, Ron **137**, *137*, 143, 277, 283, 302, 313
Jarrett, Keith **138**, *138*, 298
Jaureguy, Adolphe 70, **138**, 237
Jaureguy, Pierre 138
Jeavons, Nick 185
Jeeps, Dickie 87, **138**, *139*, 177, 208, 259
Jefferd, Andy 81
Jeffrey John (Scotland) **139**, *139*
Jeffrey, John (Wales) **139**
Jenkins, Albert 160
Jenkins, Ned 7
Jenkins, Vivian 38, 41, 88, 102, 298, 314
Jennings, Arthur 233
Jennings, Cecil 34
Jennings, Mike 34
John, Barry 30, 55, 71, 84, 96, **139**, *140*, 142, 160, 221, 241, 298, 299, 301, 302
John, Roy 192
Johnson, Lance 120, 203
Johnson, Peter 72, 125, **141**, 146, 196
Johnson, Tom 109
Johnston, Bob 300
Johnston, Pat *51*
Johnstone, Peter 217
Joinel, Jean-Luc 13, *140*, **141**
Jones, Alan 60, *60*, 85, **141**, 261, 276
Jones, Cliff 47, 55, **142**, 98, 299, 314
Jones, Garth 285
Jones, Ivor **142**, *142*, 160
Jones, Jack 43, 226
Jones, Ken 54, **142**, 203, 218, 273, 277, 285, 298, 313, 317
Jones, Lewis 160
Jones, Mark 299
Jones, Michael 17, 95, **143**, 239, 305, 315
Jones, P.P. 'Ponty' 43, 226
Jones, Peter **143**, *143*, 197, 206, 285
Jones, Robert 54, 117, **143**, *144*, 274, *281*, 299,
Jones, Staff 226, 232
Jones, Tuan 43, 226
Judd, Phil 64
Judd, Sid 55

Karam, Joe 8, 125, 160
Karloff, Boris 189
Kavanagh, Paddy 145
Kavanagh, Ronnie **145**, 300
Kavapalu, Tali *281*
Kay, Robert 294
Keane, Moss 13, 73, **145**, *145*, 156, 163
Kearney, Jim 217
Kelleher, Kevin **145**, 176, 206, 213, 214, 300
Keller, Doug 234
Kelly, Jimmy 105
Kendall-Carpenter, John 26, 315
Kennedy, Ken 88, 125, **146**, 234
Kenny, Dean 217
Kenyon, Basil 35, 54, 187, 212, 267
Kerr, David 121
Kerr, James 121

Kershaw, Cyril 'K' 72, 87, **146** *147*, 221, 297
Ketels, Rod 64
Kewney, 'Kicking Ginger' 157
Kiernan, Michael **147**, 156, 222, 262
Kiernan, Tom 13, 14, 41, 52, 63, 101, 131, **146**, 216, 262, 272
King, Ron 304
Kingsburgh, Lord 128
Kininmonth, Peter 205, 242
Kipling, Herbert 113
Kirk, David 21, 53, 117, **148**, *200*, 217, 219, 291, 316
Kirk, Norman 181, 232, 267
Kirkpatrick, A *294*
Kirkpatrick, Ian 57, 58, 95, 112, **148**, *149*, 179, 201, 230, 241, 285, 308, 311
Kirton, Earle 217
Kirwan, John 17, 21, 133, 148, **149**, *149*, 239, 285, 289, 313, 315
Knight, Gary 15, 69, 100, **150**, 168, 173, 222, 232, 233
Knight, Laurie 230
Knox, David 317
Koch, Chris 34, 232, 261
Koko, Lolani 305
Konno, Shigero 136, **150**
Koroduadua, Severo 93
Krige, Japie **151**, 163
Krige, Willie 151
Kruger, Paul 264
Kruger, Theuns 185
Kururangi, Robert 207
Kyle, Jack 13, 52, 96, 121, **151**, 183, 207, 285, 289, 313, 317
Kyle, William 119

Lacans, Pierre 32
Lacaze, Claude 102, **153**, *153*, 283, 295
Lacroix, Pierre 222
Lafond, Jean-Baptiste 237
Lagisquet, Patrice **153**, *153*, 285, 313
Laidlaw, Chris 17, 54, 108, *113*, 117, **153**, *154*, 217, 219, 233, 267, 291
Laidlaw, Frank 125, **154**, 177, 255
Laidlaw, Roy 13, 89, 17, *117*, **154**, 221, *221*, 222, 250
Laird, Henri 319
Lalanne, Denis *269*
Lambert, Daniel 285, 317
Lambert, Douglas 118
Lambourn, Artie 302
Lane, Michael 147
Lange, David 233
Lanza, Juan *14*, 43
Lanza, Pedro 43
Larter, Peter 208
Lategan, 'Tjol' 305
Laughland Iain 88, **156**
Laulau, Senivalati *92*, 93
Lawrie, Ken 104
Lawton, Robbie 156
Lawton, Tommy (jnr) *156*, **157**, 190
Lawton, Tommy (snr) 19, 52, **156**, 235, 301
le Roux, Jannie 85
le Roux, Joos 208
le Roux, Pietie 151
Leeson, Jack 296
Lenehan, Jim 102, 194, 196
Lenihan, Donal 63, **157**, *158*
Lescarboura, Jean-Patrick 317
Lesieur, Emile 98
Leslie, Andy 25, 54, 302

Leslie, David 104, **158**
L'Estrange, David 42, 259
Leveson-Gower, Sir Henry 234
Levula, Joe *92*, 93
Lewis, Allan 7, 140
Liddell, Eric **158**, 253
Lightfoot, Ned 156
Lilburne, Herb 54, 307
Lindsay, Dave 217
Lindsay, George 285, 317
Lineen, Sean 64
Lister, Tom *299*
Llewellyn, Willie 88, **160**, 203
Lloyd, Dick 78
Lloyd, John 38
Lloyd, Richard 159
Lloyd, Trevor 138
Loane, Mark 19, 53, **160**, *161*, 190, 205, 235, 236, 259
Lochner, 'Butch' *294*, 305
Lochore, Brian 53, 54, 60, 112, 133, 154, **161**, *162*, 190, *198*, 199, 201, 241, 283, 296, *307*
Lockyear, Dick 113
Loe, Richard 101, 222
Longland, Ray 207
Lord, David 181
Lorieux, Alain 15, **163**, 214
Lotz, Jan **163**
Loubser, 'Bob' 151, **163**, 319
Lourens, Thys 208
Louw, 'Boy' **164**, 232, 305
Louw, Fanie 164
Louw, Japie 164
Louw, Rob 133
Loveridge, Dave *47*, 117, *123*, **164**, *165*, 275
Lowe, Cyril 32, 111, **164**, 292, 313
Lowry, Wilfred 212
Luke, Mike 51
Lupini, Emilio *133*
Luscombe, Francis 43
Luscombe, John 43
Lux, Jean-Pierre **165**
Luyt, Fred 43
Luyt, John 43, 81
Luyt, Richard 43
Lynagh, Michael 89, *96*, 96, 97, 147, 155, *156*, **165**, *165*, 171, 222, 223, 228, 236, 317
Lyne, H.S. 128

McBain, Mark 42
McBride, Willie John 13, 35, 42, 53, 78, 107, 121, 130, 131, 157, *162*, 163, **167**, *167*, 186, 189, *198*, 199, 216, 262, 278, *288*, 289, 292, 310, 312, 317
McCarthy, Winston 255
McCormick, Fergie 52, 102, 141, 155, **167**, 176, 224
McCullough, John 275
MacDonald, Andy *113*, 242, 320
McDonald, Alex 57, 217
McDowell, Steve 101, **168**, 222, 231, 232, 239
MacEwan, Nev 279, 302
McFadyean, Colin 184
McGeechan, Ian 60, 108, **168**, *168*, 255, 292
McGill, Arthur 171
McGrath, Robbie 300
McGregor, Duncan 52
McHardy, Boetie 213
McHarg, Alistair 88, 156, 163, **169**, *169*
McIntyre, Andy **169**, 232
McKay, Don 62
McKechnie, Brian 115, 269
McKee, Des 207
McKenzie, Norman 60, 238

McKenzie, William 215, 296
McKibbon, Alistair 43
McKibbon, Christopher 43
McKibbon, Des 43
McKibbon, Harry 43
Maclagan, William 67, 83, 88, 113, 189, 253, 264
McLaren, Bill 26, 273
McLauchlan, Ian 13, 53, **169**, *169*, 210, 231, 255, 263
McLaughlin, Bill 67
McLean Hugh 25
McLean, Bill 11, 19, **170**, 235
McLean, Bob 171
McLean, Doug (jnr) **170**
McLean, Doug (snr) **170**
McLean, Jack 170
McLean, Jeff 42, **170**, 236
McLean, Paul 19, 42, *112*, **170**, *170*, 235, 259
McLean, Peter **170**, *171*, 236
McLean, Terry 138, 173
Maclear, Basil **171**, 288
McLennan, 'Freddie' 300
MacLeod, Ken **172**, 319
MacLeod, Lewis 172
McLeod, Bruce 64, 112, *113*
McLeod, Hugh 23, 119, **171**, 232, 245
McLoughlin, Ray 32, 110, 169, **172**, 231
McMillan, Keith 251
MacMyn, David 13
McNab, Jack 217
MacNeill, 'Hugo' 32, **172**, *172*
McPhail, Neil 199
Macpherson, Phil *253*, 253, 262, 263, 291
MacRae, Ian 120
Madsen, Duncan 110, 125
Mafi, Sione 281
Mahoney, Athol 296
Mains, Laurie 217
Maitland, George 43
Maitland, Richard 43
Major, John 275
Malan, Abe *113*, 125, 305
Malan, Avril 53, 125, 267, 300
Malcolm Syd 117, 301
Manchester, Jack 199, 273, 298
Mannion, Noel 285
Mans, Gerhard 189
Marais, F.P. 34
Marais, Hannes 53, 81, **175**, 232, 305
Marcker family 194
Marcker, André, 43
Marcker, Hans 43
Marcker, Mats 43
Marcker, Peter 43
Mariani, Piero 132
Marie, Bernard **175**
Marindin, F.A. 128
Maritz, S.G. 264
Markotter, A.F. 9, 60, **175**, 185, 252, 257, 307
Marques, David 118
Marsburg, Arthur 43, 113
Marsburg, Peter 43, 113
Marslin, Arthur 308
Martin, Allan 7, 67, **175**, *175*, 206, 222, 306
Martin, Harry 122
Martinez, Gérard 30
Maso, Jo **176**, *176*, 189, *269*
Mason, Michael 224
Mason, Tony 224
Masters, Read 52
Matheson, Jeff *108*, 271
Matheu, Jean 222
Maton, L.J. 249
Matthew, Phil 157, 300

Matthews, Jack 55, 308
Matthews, Norman 284
Matthews, Stanley 135
Mauriat, Paul 98
Meadows, John 294
Meadows, Ron 141
Meads, Colin *11*, 13, 53, 57, *76*, 78, 82, *104*, 112, *120*, 145, 147, 161, *162*, 167, **176**, *177*, *198*, 201, 213, 214, 279, 283, *283*, 299, 306, 307, 308, 311
Meads, Stan 112, 147, *198*, 279, *283*
Meates, Bill 217
Meikle, Graham 43
Mellish, Frank **177**
Melrose, RFC **177**
Melville, Nigel 301
Mendez Federico 215
Meredith, Byrn 73, 100, 124, **177**, 199, 203
Meredith, Courtney 192
Mesnel, Franck **178**, *178*, 237
Messenger, Herbert 'Dally' 195
Mexted, Graham 178
Mexted, Murray *123*, **178**, *178*, 190, 205, *231*, 302, *307*
Mias, Lucien, 53, 65, 99, **178**, 181, 267
Mill, Jimmy 120, 231, 238
Millar, Billy **179**, 226, 252, 264, 271
Millar, Sid 60, 131, **179**, 231, 262
Miller, Jeff 95
Miller, Tony 'Slaggy' **180**, 196, 210, 232, 260
Milliken, Dick 108
Mills, Stephen 108
Milne, Iain 43, 121, **181**, *181*
Milne, Kenneth 181
Milne, William 211
Milner, 'Buff' 232
Milton, William 304
Mironov, Igor 291
Mitchell, Terry 25
Mitchie, Kim 54
Mobbs, Edgar 24, **181**, 207
Moloney, John 117
Moncla François 53, 77, 99, **182**, *182*, 237, 300
Monro, Charles 193, 196
Monro, Sir David 193
Moolman, Louis 208
Moon Yung Chan 16
Moon, Brendan 42, **182**, *183*, 236, 313
Moore, D.L. 'Buzz' 39, 50, 51, 211
Moraru, Viorel 246
Mordt, Ray 208, 242, 320
Morgan, Cliff 41, 51, 71, 96, 136, **183**, 203, 212, 221, 267, 285, 298, 299
Morgan, Douglas 273
Morgan, Haydn 7, **183**, 298
Morgan, Ivor 312
Morgan, Teddy 88, 103, 114, **183**, *184*, 218, 285, 298
Moriarty, Paul 299
Moriarty, Richard 43, 44
Morkel family **184**
Morkel, 'Boy' 184, 264
Morkel, Gerhard 102, 184
Morkel, Hannes 184
Morkel, John 242
Morley, Alan, 38
Morris, Dai 95, **184**, 192
Morris, Trevor 193
Morrison, Mark 43, 42, 21, 151, 163, 247, 264
Morrison, Tom 168, 268
Moseley, Kevin 214
Mosenthal, Eric 179, 252

Moss, Cecil 190
Mostert, Phil 85, 163, *184*, **185**, 232
Mourie, Graham 14, 30, 31, 38, *53*, 54, 69, 95, 115, 144, 149, **185**, *185*, 199, 275, 285, 299
Mulcahy, Bill **86**
Muldoon, Robert 233
Mullen Karl 41, 54, 100, 125, 130, 131, 151, **186**, *186*, 199, 210, 239, 278, *308*, 313
Muller, Brian *299*
Muller, Gert 305
Muller, Hennie 53, 60, 125, 183, **186**, 205
Mulligan, Andy 88, 215, *215*, 300
Mullin, Brendan **187**, 222
Mullineux, Matthew 240
Mullock, Richard 203
Munro, Abe 217
Munro, Steve 276
Murariu, Florica 246
Murdoch, Keith 199
Murillo, Gérard 270
Murphy, Kenny 188
Murphy, Noel 60, 63, 95, 105, 131, 147, 186, **188**, 230
Murphy, Noel (snr) 63, 147, 188
Murray, George 63
Murray, Paul 300
Myburgh, Mof 208
Mycock, Joe 251

Nadruku, Noa 214, 287
Nahr, Orlando 45
Namoro, Rusiate *14*
Nau, Jean 291
Naude, 'Tiny' *104*, 305
Neale, Bruce 248
Neary, Tony 13, 95, **192**, *192*, 289, 313
Neethling, J.H. 163
Neilson, George 43, 118, 319
Neilson, Robert 319
Neilson, Walter 319
Neilson, William 43, 118, 319
Nel, Philip 53, 163, 190, 211, 216, 217, 247, 264, 296
Nepia, George 66, 81, 102, *116*, 120, 174, **193**, *193*, 199, 232, 238, 272
Nicholls, Gwyn 11, 55, 151, 298, *298*
Nicholls, Harold 'Doc' 203
Nicholls, Harry 'Ginger' 203
Nicholls, Mark 21, 194, 199, **203**, *203*, 302
Nicholson, George 17
Niven, David 189
Nomis, Syd 168
Norling, Clive *69*, 106, 145, 198, **205**, *206*, 214, 233, 240
Norman, Bruce **44**
Norris, Howard *198*
Norster, Robert 54, 71, 157, **206**, *206*
Norton, Tane 125, 174, 185, **208**
Nykamp, Joe 13

Obolensky, Alexander 13, 87, 199, **209**, *209*, 219, 248, 280, 285, 287, 291, 312
O'Brien, Des 88, 131, 313
O'Callaghan, Ron 131
O'Connor, Michael 261
O'Connor, Tony 7
O'Dea, Bob 277
O'Driscoll, John 88, **209**, *210*, 222
Offiah, Martin 224
Ogasawara, Hiroshi 137
Ogden, Peter, 38

Ogilvie, G. 'Gog' 304
O'Gorman, John *86*
Ohnishi, Tetsunosuke 137
O'Leary, Mike, 52
Oliver, Charlie, 52
Oliver, Frank 269
Oliver, Greig 155
Omaido, Jackson 146
Ondarts, Pascal **212**
O'Reilly, Rodolpho 205
O'Reilly, Tony 88, 135, 157, 210, **215**, *215*, 267, 313, 314
Orr, C.E. 43
Orr, J.E. 43
Orr, Phil 13, 211, **216**, *216*, 231, 317
Osborne, Bill 301
Osborne, Doug 294
O'Shea, John 294
Osler, Bennie 52, 185, 190, 203, 264, **216**, *217*, 305
O'Sullivan, Terry 275
Owen, R.M. 'Dicky' 117, 142, 211, **217**, 273, 294, 298
Owen-Smith, 'Tuppy' 102, **218**, 219
Oxlee, Keith 190, 217, **219**
Oyago, Atsushi 137

Paco, Alain 32, 220, 222
Paewai, Lui 120, 238, 319
Paewai, Manahi 'Doc' 232
Palmade, Francis *239*
Palmer, Bryan **220**
Palmer, John 26
Palmie, Michel 32
Paparemborde, Robert 13, **220**, *220*, 222, 232
Paraschiv, Mircea 246
Park, James Cecil 78
Parker, A.C. 252
Parker, Jim 229
Parkinson, Mike 230
Pask, Alun 7, *198*, **222**, 298
Paterson, Duncan 104
Patterson, Bill 251
Paxton, Iain *123*, **222**, *250*, 276
Pearce, Gary 190, 208, **222**, 231
Pedlow, Cecil **222**
Pell, Arthur 47
Pelser, Martin 110, 282
Perkins, John 226, 232
Peter, Jeff *51*
Peter, Richard 129
Pfaff, Brian *294*
Phillips, Alan 67
Phillips, Bill 147
Phillips, Kevin 54
Phipps, George 248
Pickard, Jan **224**, *225*, 295, 305
Pickering, David 54
Pienaar, 'Sport' **225**, 252, 267
Pienaar, Theo 10, *247*, 264
Pierce, Murray *68*, 222, 302
Pilecki, Stan 169, 211, 236
Pillman, C.H. 'Cherry' 32, 40, 312, **225**
Pillman, Robert 226
Pique, Jean 60
Plantefol, Alain 8
Poggi, Enardo 13
Poidevin, Simon 13, 49 95, 141, 196, **226**, *226*
Pokere, Steven 174
Porta, Hugo 9, 14, *15*, 52, 96, 97, 135, 147, 165, 210, 223, **227**, *227*, 316, 317
Porter, Cliff 21, 53. 54, 199, **228**, *228*, 269
Potter, Alex 99
Poulton Palmer Ronald 118, 159, **229**, 291, 313

Powell, Jackie 151
Pradie, Michel 8
Prat, Jean 13, 53, 65, 222, **230**, 242, 313
Prat, Maurice 230
Preedy, Malcolm 108
Prentice, Doug 7, 157, 199, *228*
Pretorius, Joe 242
Price, Brian 188, 203, **230**, *230*, 278, 298, *299*
Price, Graham 13, 67, 100, 158, 221, 226, 231, 232, **230**, *231*, 298, 311
Probyn, Jeff 301
Prosser, Ray 226, **232**
Prothero, Gary 38
Puertas, Francisco 270
Pullin, John 38, 54, 100, 125, 146, **234**, *234*, 245, 292
Purdon, Frank 212

Quaglio, Isadoro 134
Quinn family 210
Quinn, Kevin 210
Quinn, Mick *145*
Quinnell, Derek *27*, 160, **236**, *236*, 298
Quirke, John 319
Quittenton, Roger 115, 215

Rafter, Mike 38
Rainey, Philip 289
Ralston, Chris 242
Ramsay, Sir William **237**
Ranfurly, Lord 237
Ranson, John 248
Raper, Ted 196
Raphael, John 13
Ras, De Wet 213
Rathy, David 259
Reason, John 136
Rees, Clive 88
Rees, Elgan 67
Regan, Martin 159
Reid, 'Ponty' 296
Reid, Charles 172, 317, 319
Reid, Hika 17, 95, 174, 285
Reid, Paddy 105
Reid, Tom 105
Reid, Tori 174
Reidy, Gerry 147
Reinach, Jaco 213, 313
Rendall, Paul 301
Renwick, Jim 13, 74, 119, **240**, *241*
Retief, Daan 208, *294*
Rew, Henry 284
Reyburn, Wallace 159
Rhodes, Cecil 264, 304
Rhys, Idwal 298
Ribère, Eugene **242**
Richards, Huw 214
Richards, Alf 54, 264
Richardson, Jock 217, 229, 269
Ridge, Matthew 104
Riley, Norman 82
Ring, John 7
Ringer, Paul 214, 271, 287
Ringland, Trevor **242**, *243*
Ripley, Andy 248
Risman, Bev 87, 259
Rives, Jean-Pierre 25, 53, 59, 95, *185*, *220*, 237, **243**, *243*, 261, 317
Robbertse, Piet 208
Robbins, Peter 179, 184
Roberts, Freddie 302
Roberts, Jim 135, 251
Roberts, Mike 88
Robertson, Bruce 64, **244**, *244*
Robertson, Ian 242, 320
Robertson, Keith 177, **244**

Robertson, Percy 52
Robilliard, Alan 21
Robins, John 278
Robins, Peter 219
Robinson, Geoff, 50
Robinson, H.L. 242
Rodriguez, Enrique **244**
Rodriguez, Laurent 88, **244**
Roe, Erica 287
Roe, Robin 156, 186
Rogers, 'Budge' 28, **245**, 297
Rollerson, Doug 173
Rollo, David 232, **245**
Romagnoli, Stefano *133*
Romeu, Jean-Pierre 222, **246**
Rooke, Charles 319
Roos, Gideon 247
Roos, Paul 9, 13, **247**, *247*, 264, 271
Rope, Bryce 164
Roques, Alfred 29, 210, 232, **247**
Rose, Marcus 64
Rosenberg, Wilf 285
Rotherham, Alan 64, 219, 242
Rotherham, Arthur 264
Roux 'Mannetjies' 248, 305
Rowell, Jack 26
Rowland Hill, Sir George 128
Rowlands, Clive 53, 60, **248**, 298, 319
Royds, Sir Percy 128
Rutherford, Don 60, 108
Rutherford, John 89, 117, 155, 221, *221*, 222, **250**, *250*, *307*
Rutledge, Lester 95
Rutter, Algernon 242
Ryan, Jim 50

Sadler, Joey 302
Saisset, Olivier 32
Sakata, 'Demi' 137
Salviac, Pierre 9
Sangali, François 189
Sanojo, Djakaria 134
Sanson, Norman 79, 214
Saunders Mike *51*
Saunders, Rob 88
Saurel, Claude 32
Saux, Jean-Pierre *76*
Savage, Keith 208
Sawson, Ronnie 156
Saxton, Charlie 12, 149, 161, 199, 217, 234, **251**, *251*, 268
Schreiner, Bill 177, **251**, 267
Schuster, John 104, 305
Scotland, Ken 27, 47, 102, 121, 157, **255**
Scott, Bob 17, 66, 102, 150, **255**, *255*
Scott, John **256**
Seddon, R.L. 40
Selfridge, Tom 81
Sella, Philippe 8, 13, 99, 153, **257**, *257*, 285, 317
Selwood, H. 280
Serevi, Waiseke 93
Serfontein, Divan 117, 222, 305
Sever, Hal 251
Sewell, E.H.D. 11, 312
Sharp, Richard 38, 87, 135, **159**, 202, 248, 285, 287, 291, 301
Shaw, Duncan 251
Shaw, Geoff 52, 194, **259**, 261
Shaw, Mark 173, **259**, *259*
Shaw, Tony 42, *161*, 235, **259**
Shea, Jerry 203
Sheehan, Paddy 91
Sheffield, Lord 24, 191
Shehadie, Nick 24, 57, 232, **259**, 260, 279
Shelford, 'Buck' 53, 174, 178, 205, 207, **260**

Shell, Clive 52
Shepherd, David *279*, 294
Sherratt, Jim 285
Sherriff, Roger 208
Sielde, L.B. 189
Siggins, Jack 131
Silva, Hector 60
Simkins, William 267
Simpson, Bobby 241
Simpson, Johnny 150
Skinner, Kevin 29, 64, 197, 217, 232, **261**
Skinner, Mickey *111*
Skrela, Jean-Claude 25, 243, **261**
Skym, Archie 160
Slack, Andrew 19, 52, 89, 235, **261**
Slattery, Fergus 13, 25, 32, 53, 95, 131, 188, 222, 234, **261**, *261*, 317
Slemen, Mike 159, **262**, 313
Slocock, L.A.N. 10
Smith, Alan 299
Smith, Arthur 41, 52, 75, **262**, 285, 313
Smith, David 242, 320
Smith, Doug *41*, 199
Smith, George **262**
Smith, Ian 49 121, 207, 253, *253*, **262**, 285, 291, 313
Smith, John V. 248
Smith, Johnny 'J.B.' 150, 174, 206, 232, 244, **263**
Smith, Mike 212
Smith, Nelie 213
Smith, Peter 174, 206
Smith, Simon 301
Smith, Steve 251, *251*
Smith, Wayne 133
Smyth, Tom 131, 264
Sneddon, Robert 54, 264
Snow, 'Fritz' 193
Snyman, Dawie 43
Snyman, Jackie 43
Sobers, Garfield 272
Sole, David 26, 53, 83, 255, **263**, *263*, 255
Solomon, Frank 312
Solomon, John 260
Sovau, Josateki 214
Spanghero, Claude 189, 270
Spanghero, Jean-Marie 270
Spanghero, Laurent 270
Spanghero, Walter 13, *99*, 189, **270**
Spence, Donn 39, 51
Spiers, John 64
Spreadbury, Tony 214
Squire, Jeff 226, 232, **271**, *271*
Squires, Peter **271**
Stack, George 129
Stagg, Peter 251, **272**
Stanger, Tony 22
Stanley, Joe 21, 239, 244
Stanley, R.V. 13
Stapleton, Eddie 313
Starmer-Smith Nigel 118, 219
Stead, Billy 53, 80, 174, 269
Steel, Jack 304
Stegman, Anton 163
Stegman, Trevor 259
Stegmann, 'Jan' 211
Stephens, Ian 67
Stephens, Rees 54, 192, **272**, 298
Stephenson, George 169, 187, 207, 249, **272**, 289
Stephenson, Henry 273
Stewart, J.J. 60
Stewart, Ken *35*, 95
Stewart, Ron 268
Stirling, Bob 301
Stirling, Brian 214

Stoddart, A.E. 40
Stofberg, Theus 133
Stokes, Frederick 32, 54, 319
Stoop, Adrian 43, 118, 219, 291
Stoop, André 214
Stoop, Frederick 43, 118
Strachan, Lucas 208
Strathdee, Ernie 186
Stringer, Nick 118
Strydom, 'Popeye' 213
Stuart, Bob 52, 53, 183
Stuart, Kevin 52
Sturtidge, Gordon 19, 294
Sugden, Mark 78, 117, 222, 300
Sullivan, Jack 33, **273**
Sullivan, Peter **273**
Sutherland, Alan 175
Sutherland, Ray 175
Swales, Edwin 234
Sykes, Frank 211
Syrett, Ron 301

Taga, Mosese 214
Tagaloa, Timo 305
Taiaroa, Dick 191
Tait, 'Boy' 67
Tanner, Christopher 242
Tanner, Haydn 53, 55, 88, **285**,
    278, 298, 300, 308 308, 314
Tauroa, Hiwi 64
Taylor, Arthur 43
Taylor, Bob 208
Taylor, Henry 43
Taylor, John 88, 95, 184, 233,
    276, 298
Taylor, Mark 301
Taylor, Peter 144
Telfer, Colin 119
Telfer, Jim 60, 154, 177, 199,
    255, **276**, *276*
Templeton, Bob 60, 161, 236,
    276
Tennant, R.C. 196
Thimbleby, Neil 120
Thomas, Brian 192, *299*
Thomas, Clem 41, 47, 143, 274,
    277, 298
Thomas, Delme 160, **277**, *278*,
    298
Thomas, J.B.G. 12
Thomas, Malcolm 27, 203, **278**
Thompson, Robin 41, 267, **278**
Thomson 'Mona' 301
Thomson, Ian 121
Thorburn, Paul 54, 138, 192,
    278, 299
Thorne, Grahame *11*, 224, **279**
Thornett brothers 195
Thornett, Dick 279
Thornett, John 19, 53, 57, 232,
    259, **279**, *279*
Thornett, Ken 279
Thrift, H. 128
Tikoisuva, Pio Bosco 93
Tindill, Eric **280**
Tobias, Errol 268, **280**, *280*
Todd, Ernie 199
Tolhurst, Harold 212
Tomes, Alan 119, **280**
Tooth, Dick 207
Torres, Salvador 270
Towers, Cyril 196, 301

Townsend, W.H. 189
Trapp, Maurice *17*
Travaglini, Alejandro 43
Travaglini, Gabriel 43
Travers, 'Bunner' 203
Travers, B.H. 'Jika' 219
Treharne, Gwilym 300
Tremain, Kel 54, 95, 112, 120,
    153, *153*, 190, **283**, *283*
Trevathen, Dave 217
Trew, Billy 274, **283**, 298
Trick, David 26
Trimescu, Valeriu 246
Tucker, J.S. 'Sam' 38, **284**
Tudehope, Edgar 267
Tuigamala, Va'aiga 305
Tuihalamaka, Polutele 281
Tukalo, Ivan *254*
Tulloch, Russ 294, 301
Turnbull, Art 294
Turner, Freddie 81, **284**
Turner, Frederic 159
Tuynman, Steve **286**, *286*
Tynan, Chris, *51*

Underwood, Rory 13, 43, 164,
    192, *254*, 262, 285, **289**, 313,
    317
Underwood, Tony 43
Unwin, Ernest 248
Urbahn, Roger 275
Uttley, Roger 110, 205, 271, **292**,
    292, 301
Uys, Piet 208
Uzzell, John 203

Valu, Fakahau 281
van Aswegen, Jannie 106
van der Byl, Adriaan 263
van der Merwe 'Flippie' 231
van der Merwe, Bertus 34
van der Schyff, Jack 106, 113
van Doorn, Jus 194
van Gelder, Malcolm 268
van Heerden, Izaak 13, 60
van Heerden, Moaner 163, 208
van Jaarsveldt, Des 54, 212, 242,
    320
van Niekirk, Jock 309
van Schoor, Ryk 242, 320
van Vollenhoven, Tom 285, **293**,
    294, 313
van Wyk, 'Basie' 183, 282
van Zyl, Burmann 61
van Zyl, Hennie 282, 305
van Zyl, Hugo 305
van Zyl, Sakkie *75*
Vannier, Michel 102, 247, **293**
Vaquerin, Armand 32
Vassall, H.H. 219
Vassall, Harry, 32, 218, 291
Vaughan, Geoff 294
Veitch, Danny 110, **293**
Versfeld, Hasie 264
Versfeld, Loftus 163
Vile, Tommy 203, 210, **294**
Villepreux, Pierre 9, 134, **295**
Vincent, Pat, 54
Visagie, Piet 113, 222
Viviers, Basie 213, *294*, **295**
Viviers, Dawie 52
Vogel, Arthur 246

Vonalagi, Tevita 214, 287
Vorege, Josaia 93
Voyce, Tom 108, 146, 249, 297

Waddell, Gordon 255
Waddell, Herbert 111, 255
Wakefield, Wavell 47, 53, 87, 88,
    118, 146, 157, 163, 177, 245,
    249, 291, **296**, *297*
Waldron, Ollie 67
Walker, Harry *294*
Walker, Alfred 189
Walker, Sam 41, 131, 208, 264,
    278
Walkington, Dolway 288
Walkington, R.B. 130
Wallace, A.C. 'Johnny' *253*, 253,
    257, 262, 291, 301
Wallace, Billy 102, 183, 203, **299**,
    300, 302
Walsh, H.D. 129
Walsh, Pat 64 174
Walters, Gwynne 146, 206, **300**
Walton, Doug 190
Warbrick, Arthur 191
Ward Tony 47, 48, 96, 105, 131,
    187
Warfield, Peter 248
Waring, Frank 309
Warren, R.G. 128
Watkins, Bob 189
Watkins, David 71, 96, 140, 203,
    298, **301**
Watkins, Harry 54
Watkins, Stuart 203, 285, **302**,
    313
Watson, D.H. 240
Weatherstone, Thomas 273
Webb Ellis, William 22, 86, 88,
    156, 180, 249, 263, **301**
Webb, Dick 294
Webb, John 7
Webster, Jan 185
Wells, Ray 27
Wemyss, Jock 63, 104, 213
West, Bryan 208
Weston, Billy 207
Weston, Henry 207
Weston, Mike **305**
Wetter, Jack 203
Wheel, Geoff 79, 115, 145, 175,
    214, 222, 269, 298, **306**
Wheeler Colin 54
Wheeler, Peter 76, 100, 125, *125*,
    157, **306**, *306*
Whetton brothers 239
Whetton, Alan **306**
Whetton, Gary 17, 163, 168, 222,
    306, *307*
Whinerary Wilson, 17, 24, 53, 54,
    112, 161, 199, 204, 232, 285,
    296, 301, **306**, *307*
White, 'Chalky' 157
White, 'Snow' 17
White, 'Son' 229, 269
White, Don 207
White, Jimmy 35, 309, **307**
White, Jon 194, *279*
White, Richard 'Tiny' 163, 230,
    307
Whittington, Tom 192
Wickes, Craig 319

Wickham, Stanley 319
Wilke, Ken 51
Williams, Abe *59*
Williams, Billy 286
Williams, Bleddyn 52, 54, 55,
    298, **308**, *308*
Williams, Brian 231
Williams, Bryan 17, 174, *224*,
    232, 305, **308**, *309*, 313
Williams, Brynmor 26, *27*, 123
Williams, Chris 67
Williams, Clive 7
Williams, Denzil 231, **308**
Williams, D.O. 286, **309**
Williams, Graham 95, 302
Williams, J.J. 79, 160, 299, **309**,
    309, 313
Williams, J.P.R. 13, 15, 37, *37*,
    52, 83, 102, 107, *112*, 132, 298,
    303, **310**, *310*
Williams, Johnnie 138, 251
Williams, Lloyd 308
Williams, Ray 60, 240, 300
Williams, Rhys 160, 163, **310**
Williams, Syd 7
Williment, Mick 168, 302
Willis, Rex 53, 54, 55, 117, 183,
    221, 298
Willocks, Charlie 217
Wilson, 'Chilla' 206
Wilson, Lionel 102, 305
Wilson, Nathaniel 'Ranji' 232
Wilson, Norm 217
Wilson, Stewart 291
Wilson, Stu 14, 49, 52, 149, 200,
    302, **311**, *311*, 313
Wilson, Vay 236
Windon, Col *11*, 285
Windsor, Bobby 100, 125, 221,
    226, 230, 232, 298, **311**, *312*
Winfield, Herbert 55, 102
Winn, Christopher 248
Winning, Arch 54, 235
Winterbottom, Peter *48*, 118,
    313, *313*
Wirihana 301
Wolfe, Neil 62, 275
Wood, Gordon 105, **314**
Woods, Samuel M.J. 312
Woodward, Clive 55, 157
Woodward, Ted 301
Wooller, Wilfred 47, 55, 88, 142,
    207, 251, 298, **314**
Wright, Alan 224
Wright, Terry 21, 239
Wrigley, Edgar 319
Wyllie, Alex 52, 60, 238, **316**, *318*
Wyllie, Douglas 273

Yarranton, Peter 301
Young, Arthur 32
Young, David 299
Young, Denis 52
Young, Jeff 125, *299*
Young, John 77, 118, 135
Young, Roger **319**, *319*

Zago, F **320**
Zeller, W.C 189, **320**
Zimmerman M. **320**